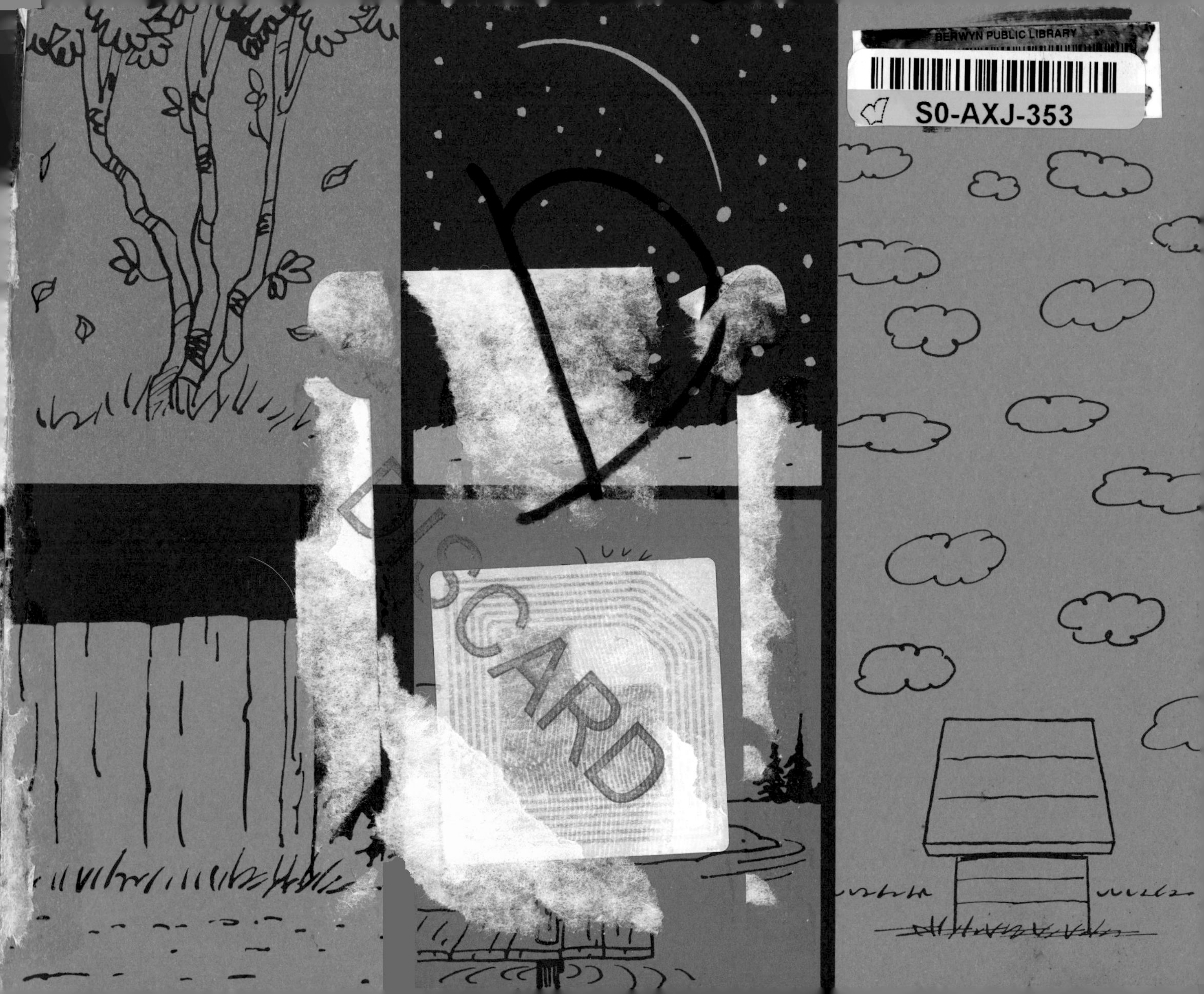

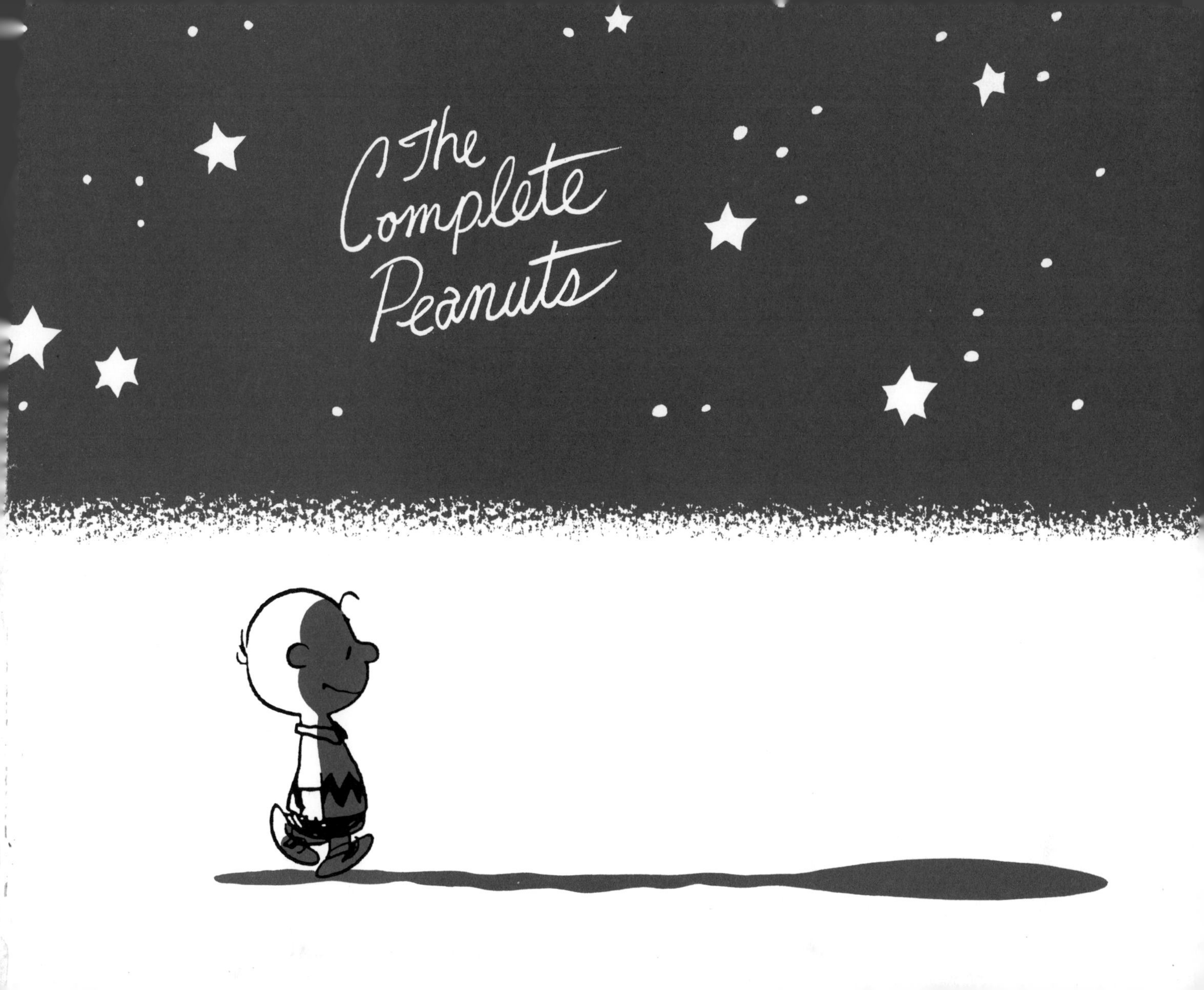
The Complete Peanuts

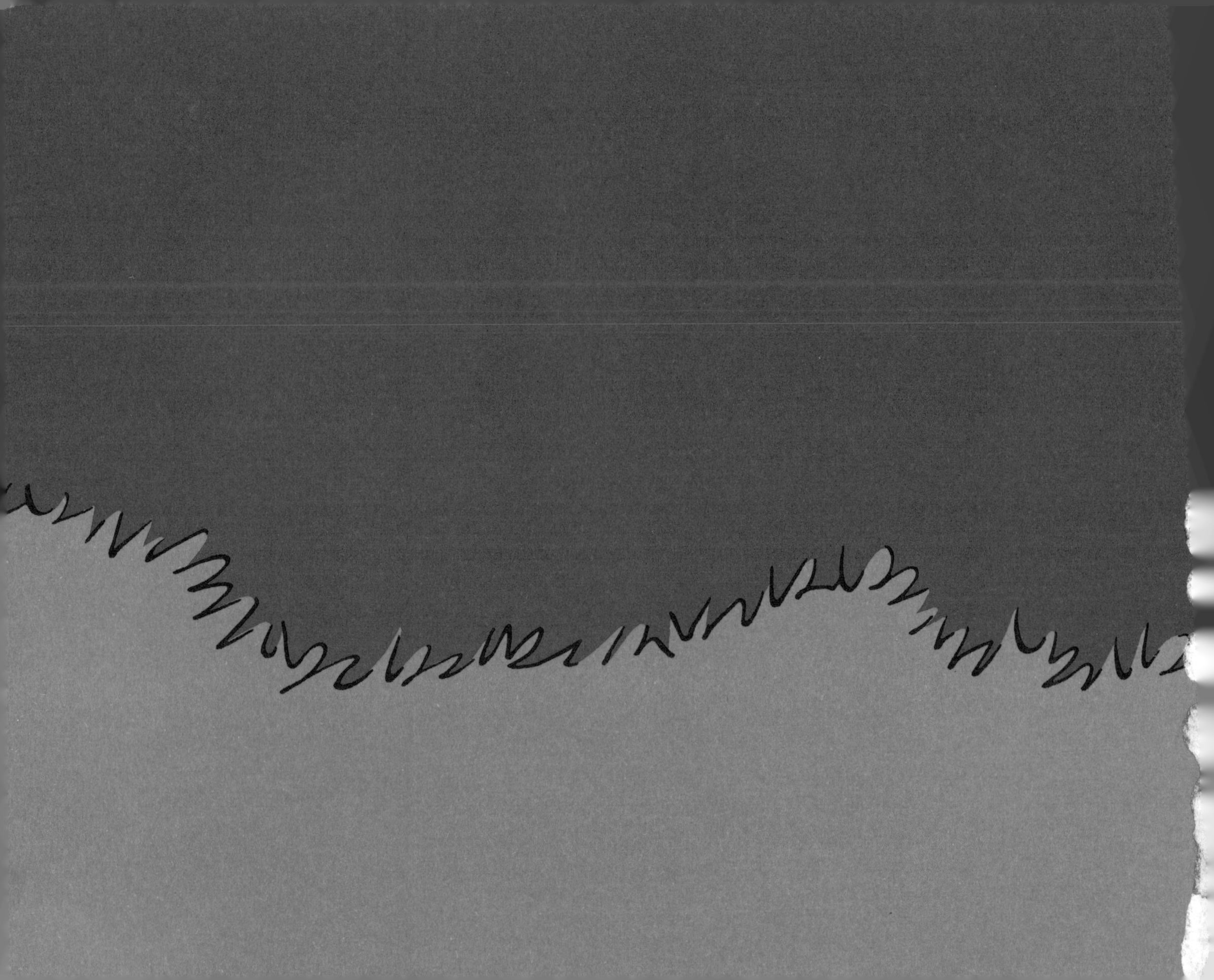

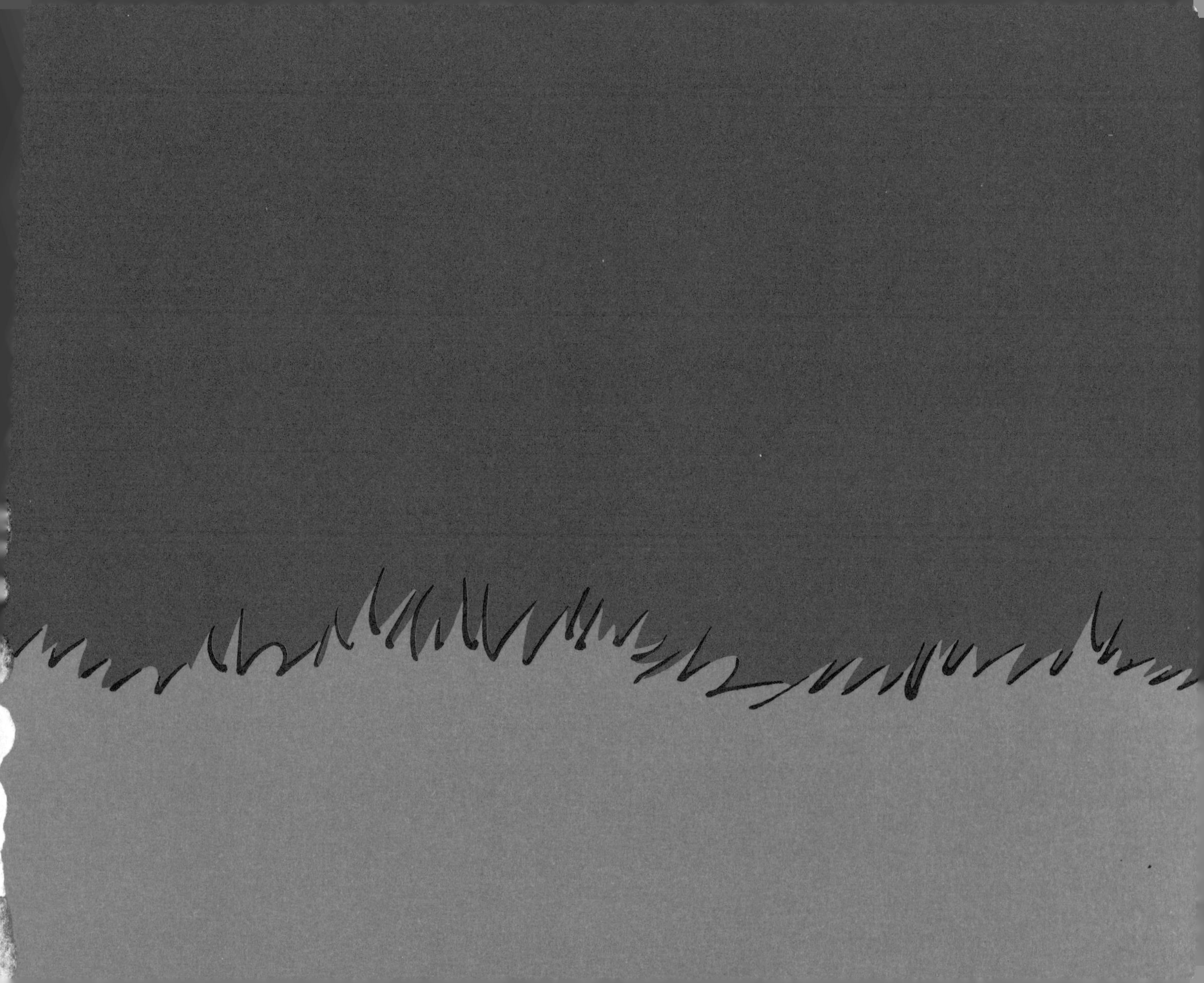

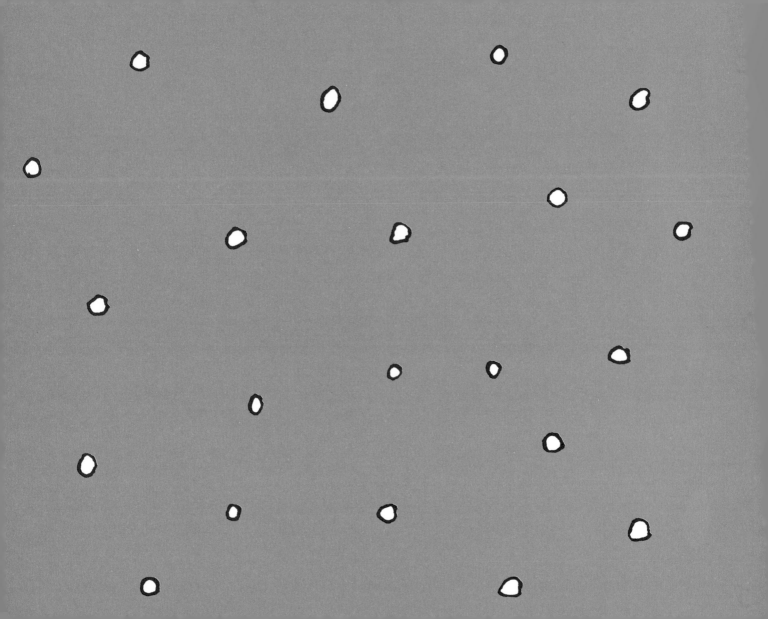

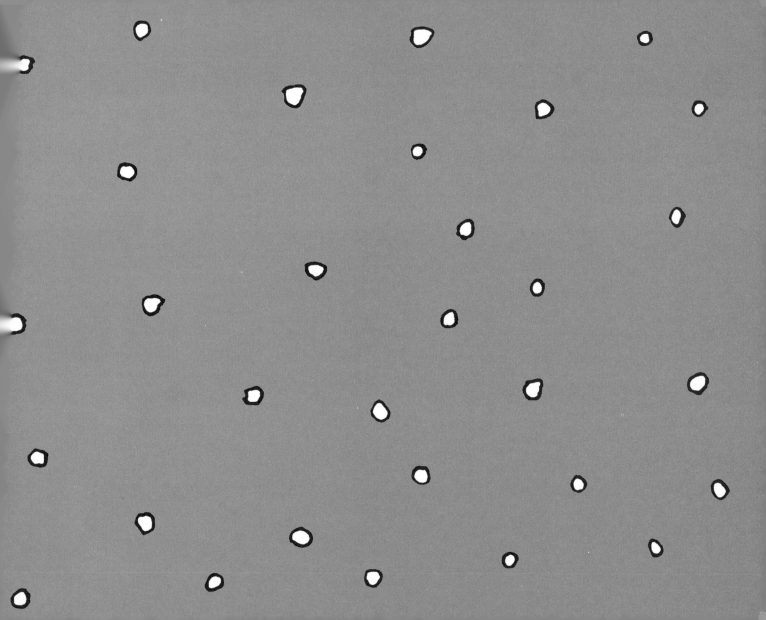

THE COMPLETE PEANUTS
by Charles M. Schulz
published by
Fantagraphics Books

Editor: Gary Groth
Designer: Seth
Production Manager: Kim Thompson
Production, assembly, and restoration: Paul Baresh
Archival and production assistance: Marcie Lee and Alexa Koenings
Index compiled by Ben Neusius
Promotion: Eric Reynolds
Publishers: Gary Groth & Kim Thompson

Special thanks to Jeannie Schulz, without whom
this project would not have come to fruition.
Thanks also to the
Charles M. Schulz Creative Associates,
especially Paige Braddock and Kim Towner.
Thanks for special support from United Media.

Fantagraphics Books, 7563 Lake City Way, Seattle, WA 98115, USA. For a free full-color catalogue of comics,
call 1-800-657-1100. Our books may be viewed on our website at www.fantagraphics.com.

Distributed to the book trade by:

USA: W.W. Norton and Company, Inc.
500 Fifth Avenue, New York, NY 10010
212-354-5500
Order Department: 800-233-4830

CANADA: Canadian Manda Group
165 Dufferin Street, Toronto, Ontario CANADA M6K 3H6
Order department: 416-516-0911

ISBN: 978-1-60699-286-9
First printing: August 2009   Printed in China

CHARLES M. SCHULZ

THE COMPLETE PEANUTS

1973 TO 1974

"LIFE SURE IS STRANGE...
AND THEY SAY WE ONLY
COME THIS WAY ONCE.."

▫ FANTAGRAPHICS BOOKS ▫

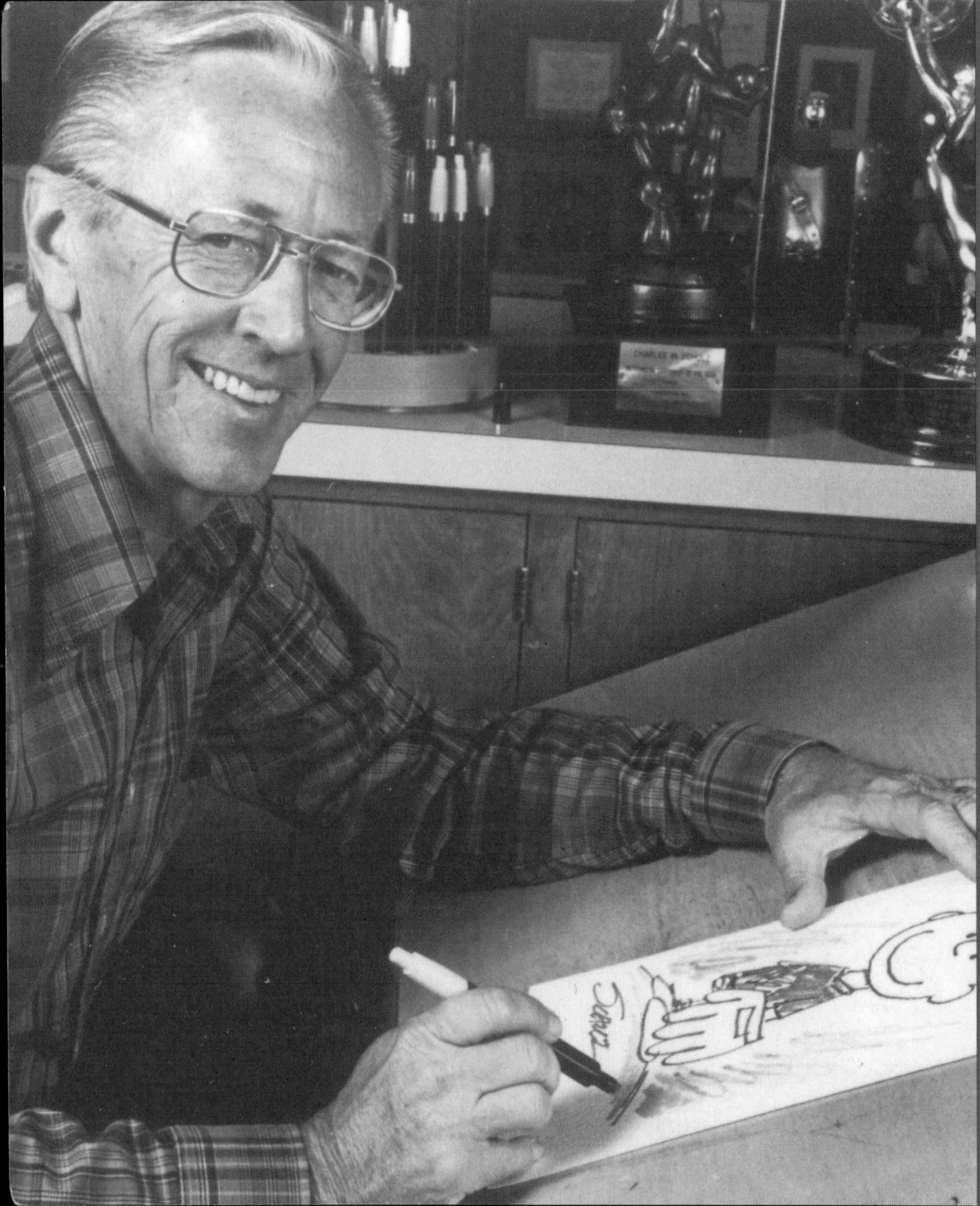

Charles M. Schulz at his drawing board at 1 Snoopy Place, circa 1975. Courtesy of the Schulz Family.

FOREWORD by BILLIE JEAN KING

The 1970s were one of the most formative decades in the history of our nation. It was a time where our society was coming of age — a new age for many of us — and issues like integrity, equality, humanity and acceptance were being debated in the streets, in corporate boardrooms and at dinner tables all across the country.

Yet in the midst of all of these life-changing moments stood at least one constant and stable voice of reason — the writings of Charles M. Schulz.

As a professional athlete I was blessed to travel the globe. During these years I had many won-

derful, eye-opening experiences. Regardless of where I was, I knew that any day I could read *Peanuts* first thing in the morning it was going to be a great day. Especially on those days when I was away from home there was a comfortable feeling, a special type of security that I enjoyed with Charlie, Lucy and the gang. My friend Charles "Sparky" Schulz gave that gift to me and to millions of other loyal readers all around the globe.

It was only fitting that our mutual support of Title IX, the groundbreaking legislation that in 1972 called for equal opportunities in the classroom and in sports for women and men at educational institutions around the country, brought Sparky and me together.

He was an ardent supporter of women's sports and the work being done by the Women's Sports Foundation and was one of the first trustees of the organization. Sparky frequently featured women athletes and referenced Title IX in *Peanuts*.

Shortly after I finished my days on the professional tennis tour, Rosie Casals, founder and owner of Sportswoman, promoted the Women's Tennis Classic and we competed for the Snoopy Cup. Sparky hosted the annual event, which was played at the Redwood Empire Ice Arena in his hometown of Santa Rosa, California. The tournament was a favorite of many of us because we were treated so well. It wasn't that we were pampered, it was that Sparky and everyone around him treated us as family — it was how he treated most everyone who was lucky enough to get to know him. While I have been fortunate enough to win some of the most prestigious titles in tennis, the trophy from the Snoopy Cup remains one of my most cherished mementos from my tennis career.

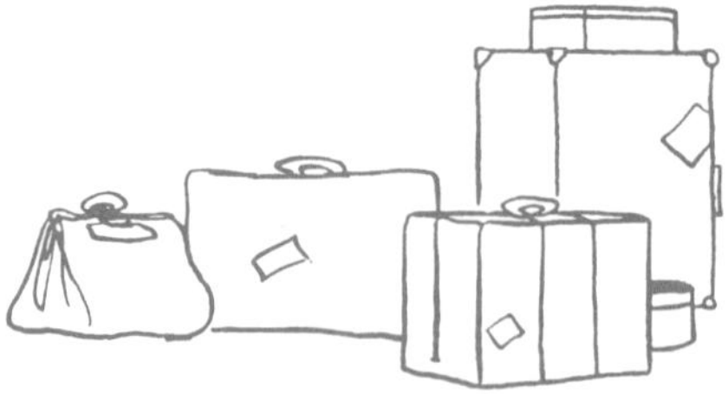

Sparky was a sound tennis player himself. He made very quality decisions on the court and was always looking for ways to improve his game. He also was an ardent fan of the sport and became one of the most loyal fans of Ilana Kloss and the Golden Gaters of World TeamTennis, the co-ed professional tennis league started in 1974.

While it may have been our mutual support of Title IX and our shared enjoyment of tennis that initially brought us together, it was a common love for life that kept us close through the years. Sparky taught me to be truthful and through his comic strip he shared his real life experiences with each of us on a daily basis.

Sparky was Charlie Brown. He was not a real talkative man, but was definitely a very deep thinker. It was when he put a pen in his hand and went to work on a *Peanuts* comic strip he became insightful and poetic, and truly exposed himself to the world.

I remember once he had listed President Dwight Eisenhower, golfer Sam Snead and me as his three favorite people. I was both honored and embarrassed. It blew me away that he thought so highly of me. The feeling was mutual. We shared quiet lunches of tuna salad sandwiches, root beers and chocolate chip cookies and solved the world's problems together. Then I would go back out on the road and he would go back to the drawing board to create his next *Peanuts* strip. Those were the special moments where we bared our souls to each other.

I wasn't the only athlete that was close to Sparky. He had a love for figure skating and he admired Olympic Gold Medalists Peggy Fleming and Scott Hamilton and ice dancer Judy Sladky, who often performed as Snoopy in various ice skating shows and was Alice Snuffelupagus on *Sesame Street*. He also included my friends, and fellow tennis players, Rosie Casals, Sharon Walsh, Tracy Austin, John McEnroe and John Newcombe in *Peanuts*. He had a deep impact on their lives just as he did on mine.

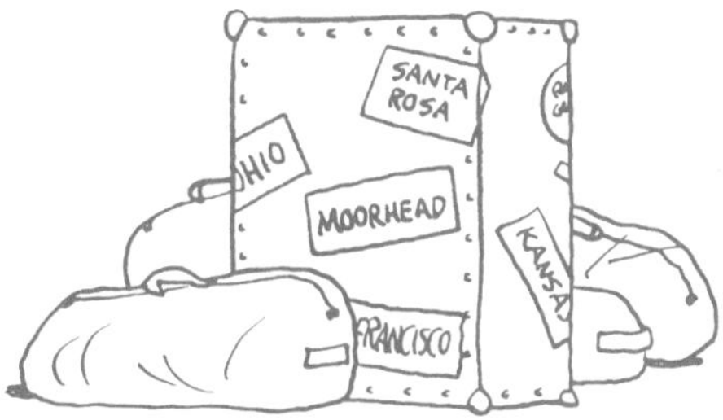
SANTA ROSA
MOORHEAD
FRANCISCO

From time to time, Sparky included me in *Peanuts*. A particular favorite of mine had Peppermint Patty telling Marcie, "Has anyone ever told you that when you're mad, you look just like Billie Jean King?" Trust me: my friends had a heyday with that one.

Sparky referenced me several times in *Peanuts* and it was his way of letting me know that we needed to talk or just catch up with one another. He rarely phoned me, but when he wanted to check in, he dropped a reference in *Peanuts* because we both knew I would read it every day I could. So I would call him and we would talk and then — you know what? — life was better. As we say today, it was all good. Like so many of Sparky's insightful characters, he gave me strength and often a healthy laugh when I needed it the most.

Jeannie Schulz, Sparky's wife, said, "He was not worried about his legacy, he was living it." Truer words were probably never spoken about Sparky. He lived in the "now" and he shared his insightful take on life with all of us through the whole *Peanuts* gang.

Sparky Schulz got it and still, today, I know that any day I can start by reading *Peanuts* is a great day.

I hope you enjoy the humor and the real life reflection in this collection of *Peanuts* strips and every day brings you joy.

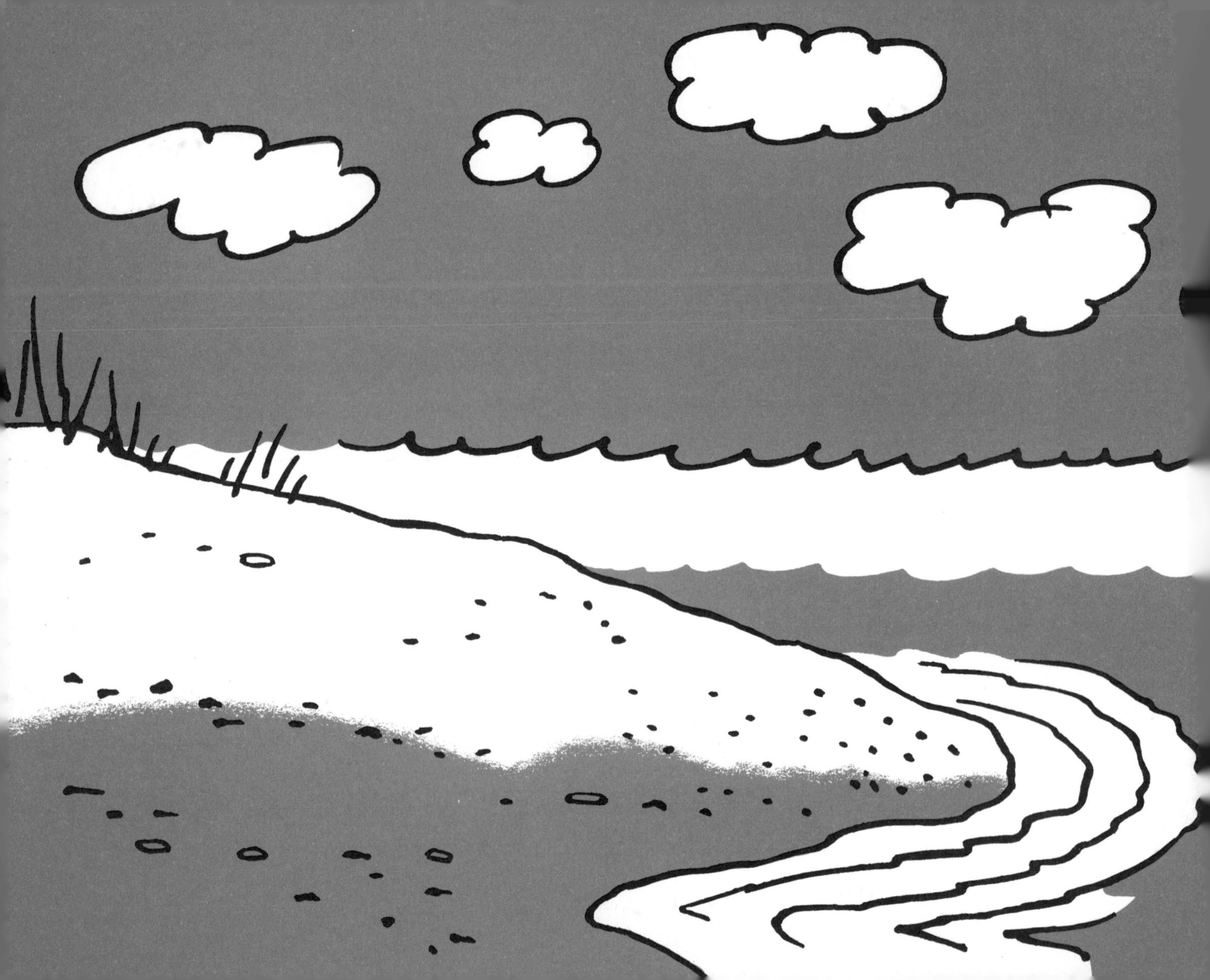

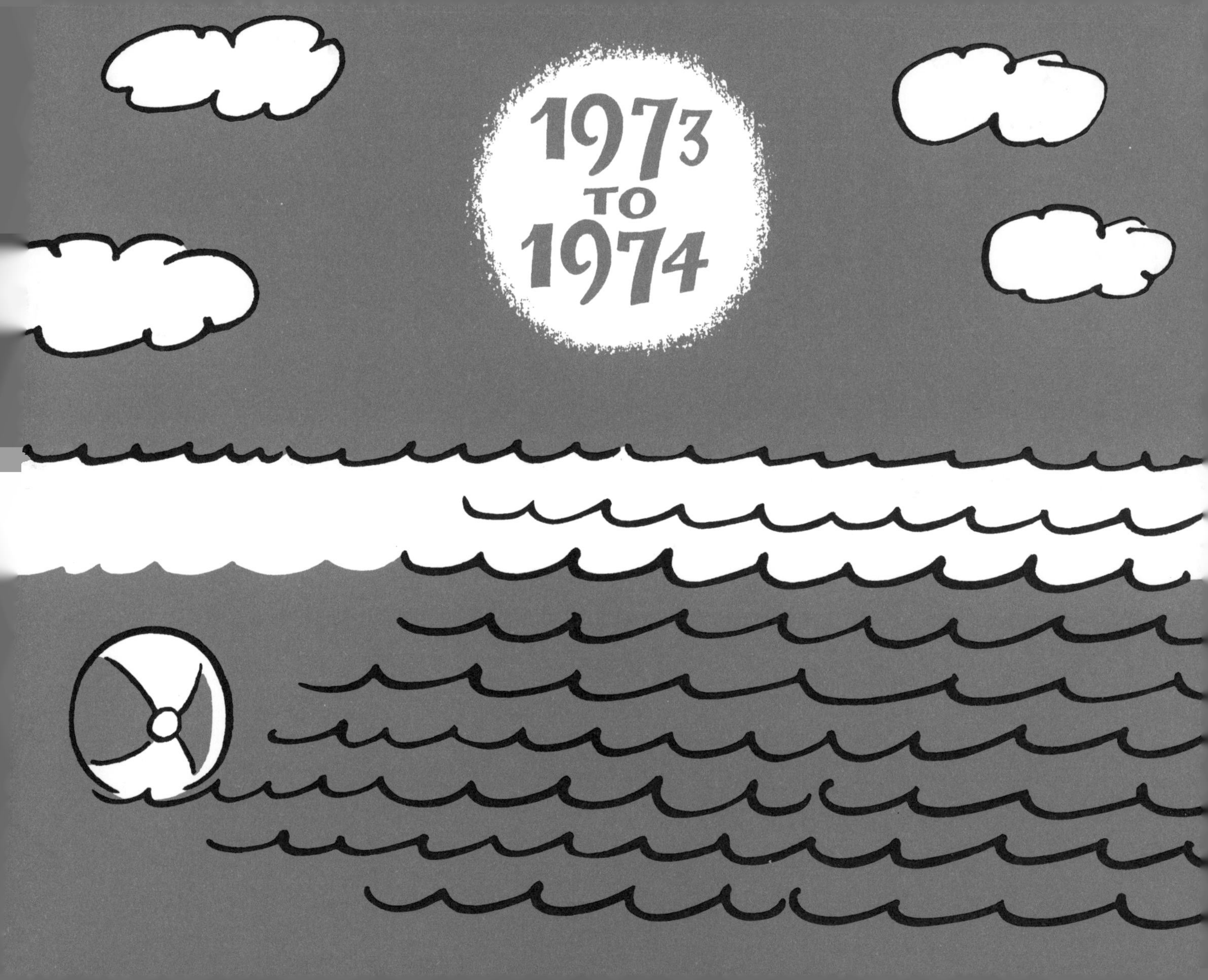
1973
TO
1974

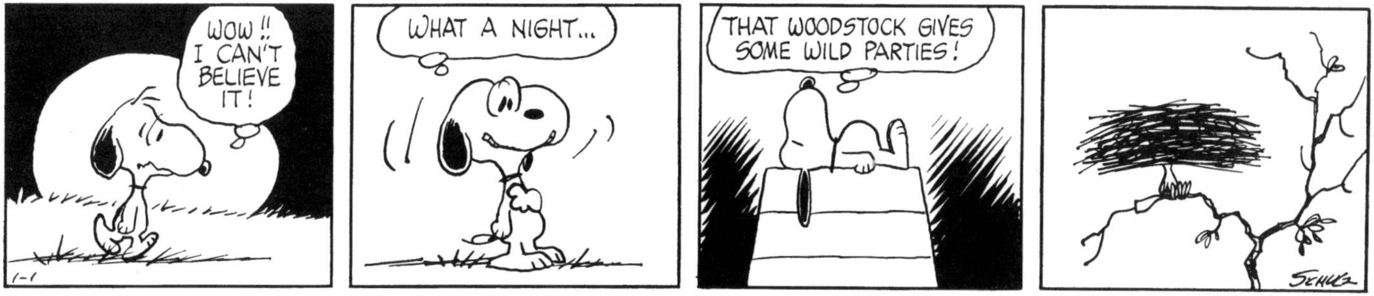
WOW!! I CAN'T BELIEVE IT!
WHAT A NIGHT...
THAT WOODSTOCK GIVES SOME WILD PARTIES!
1-1

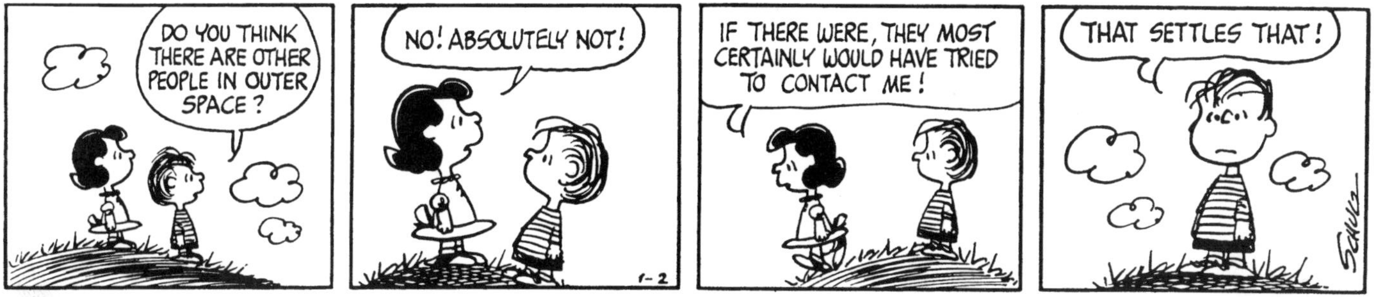
DO YOU THINK THERE ARE OTHER PEOPLE IN OUTER SPACE?
NO! ABSOLUTELY NOT!
IF THERE WERE, THEY MOST CERTAINLY WOULD HAVE TRIED TO CONTACT ME!
THAT SETTLES THAT!
1-2

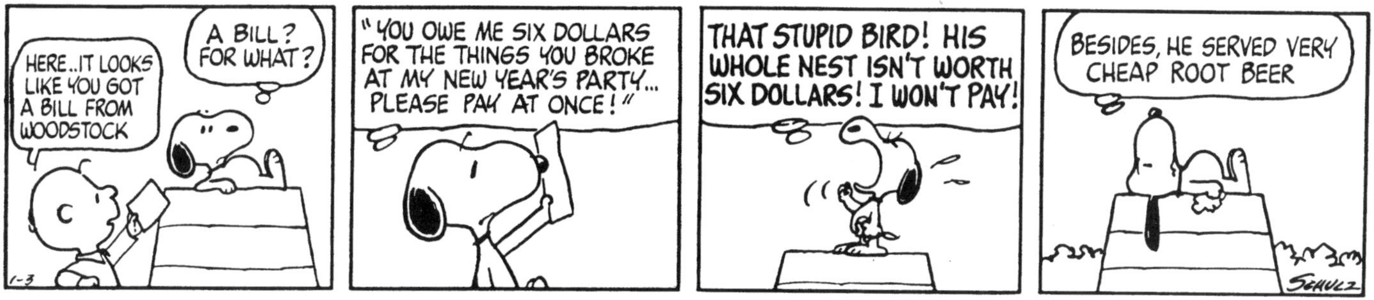
HERE..IT LOOKS LIKE YOU GOT A BILL FROM WOODSTOCK
A BILL? FOR WHAT?
"YOU OWE ME SIX DOLLARS FOR THE THINGS YOU BROKE AT MY NEW YEAR'S PARTY... PLEASE PAY AT ONCE!"
THAT STUPID BIRD! HIS WHOLE NEST ISN'T WORTH SIX DOLLARS! I WON'T PAY!
BESIDES, HE SERVED VERY CHEAP ROOT BEER
1-3

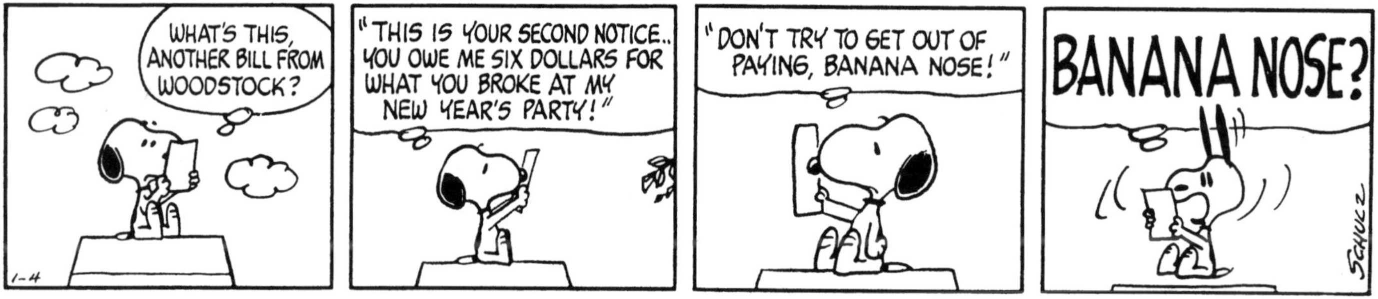
WHAT'S THIS, ANOTHER BILL FROM WOODSTOCK?
"THIS IS YOUR SECOND NOTICE.. YOU OWE ME SIX DOLLARS FOR WHAT YOU BROKE AT MY NEW YEAR'S PARTY!"
"DON'T TRY TO GET OUT OF PAYING, BANANA NOSE!"
BANANA NOSE?
1-4
SCHULZ

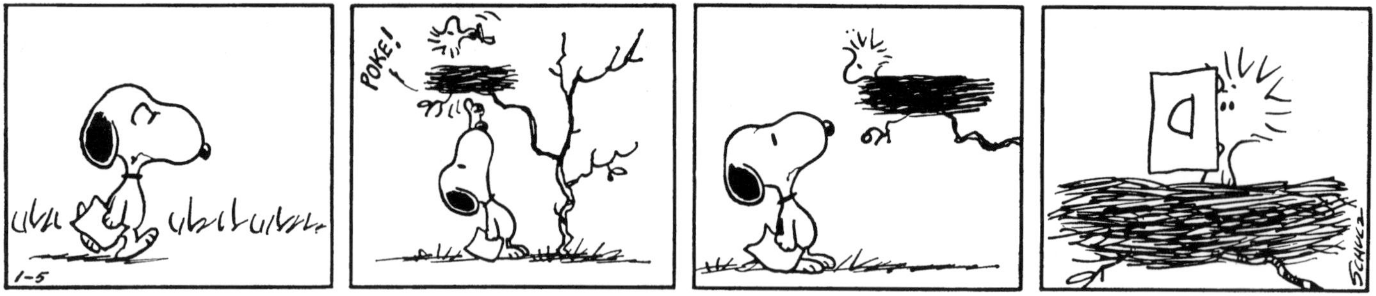
1-5
POKE!
SCHULZ

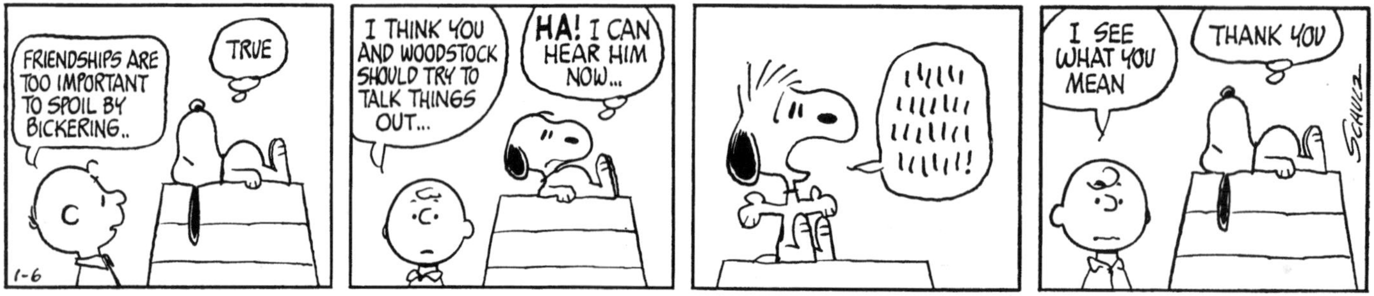
FRIENDSHIPS ARE TOO IMPORTANT TO SPOIL BY BICKERING..
TRUE
I THINK YOU AND WOODSTOCK SHOULD TRY TO TALK THINGS OUT...
HA! I CAN HEAR HIM NOW...
I SEE WHAT YOU MEAN
THANK YOU
1-6
SCHULZ

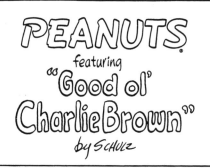

PEANUTS featuring "Good ol' CharlieBrown" by SCHULZ

WHY COULDN'T SHE JUST STAY AWAY?

WHY DID SHE HAVE TO COME BACK?

POOCHIE, IT'S GOOD TO SEE YOU AFTER ALL THESE YEARS..

WHERE'S SNOOPY?

YOU WERE THE ONE WHO FIRST STARTED TO CALL ME CHARLIE BROWN...

I WONDER IF SNOOPY WILL REMEMBER ME...

HE'S CHANGED A LITTLE SINCE YOU LIVED AROUND HERE...

HE'S PROBABLY OUT IN THE BACK YARD AND...

I'M REALLY ANXIOUS TO SEE HIM...I REMEMBER WHAT A CUTE LITTLE PUPPY HE WAS...

SNOOPY?

SNOOPY, WHERE ARE YOU? SNOOPY?

!

THOMAS WOLFE WAS RIGHT...YOU CAN'T GO HOME AGAIN!

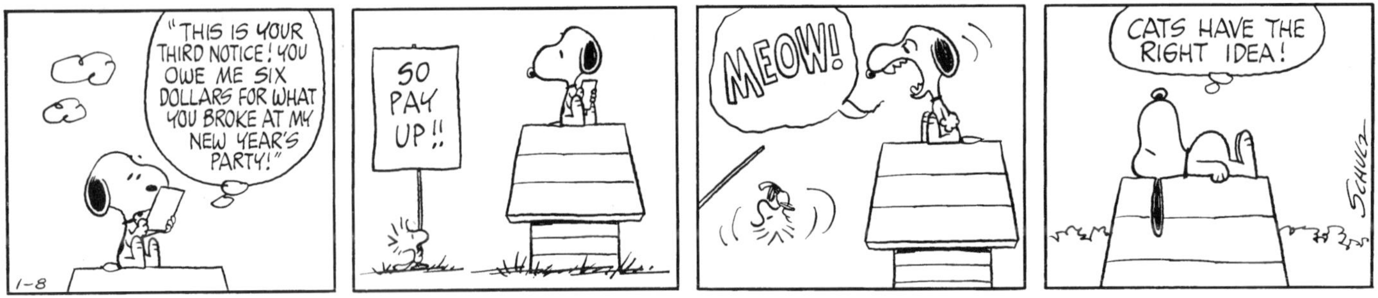
"THIS IS YOUR THIRD NOTICE! YOU OWE ME SIX DOLLARS FOR WHAT YOU BROKE AT MY NEW YEAR'S PARTY!"
SO PAY UP!!
MEOW!
CATS HAVE THE RIGHT IDEA!
SCHULZ
1-8

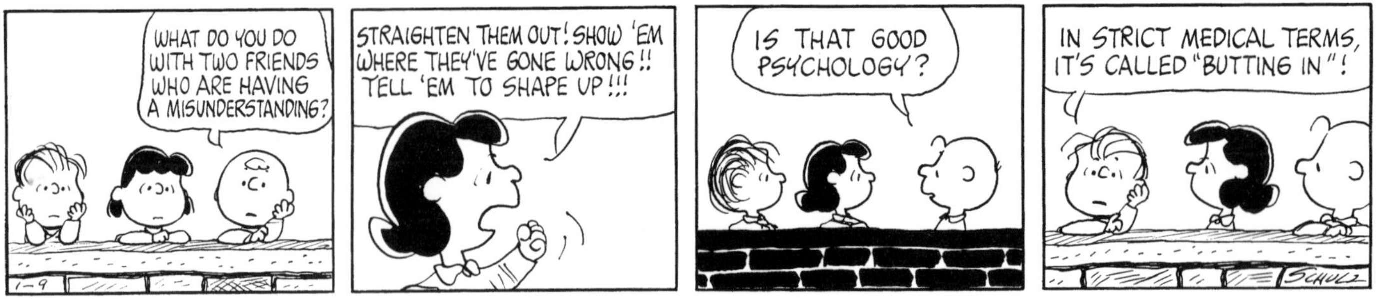
WHAT DO YOU DO WITH TWO FRIENDS WHO ARE HAVING A MISUNDERSTANDING?
STRAIGHTEN THEM OUT! SHOW 'EM WHERE THEY'VE GONE WRONG!! TELL 'EM TO SHAPE UP!!!
IS THAT GOOD PSYCHOLOGY?
IN STRICT MEDICAL TERMS, IT'S CALLED "BUTTING IN"!
SCHULZ
1-9

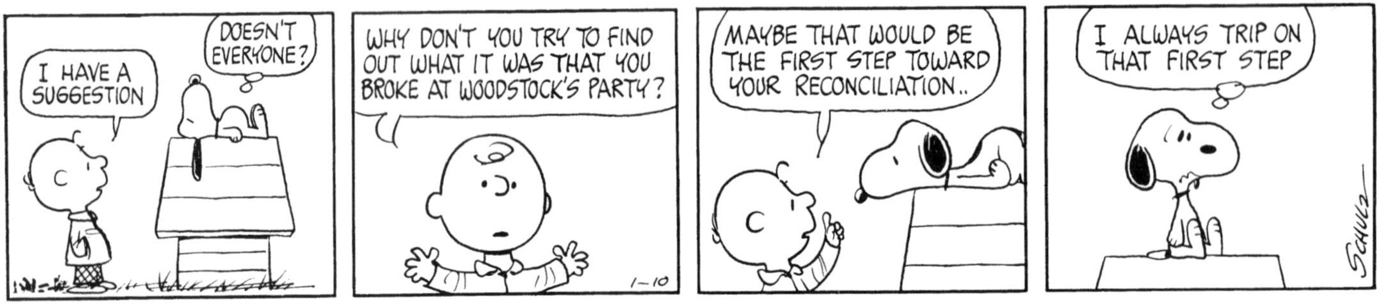
I HAVE A SUGGESTION
DOESN'T EVERYONE?
WHY DON'T YOU TRY TO FIND OUT WHAT IT WAS THAT YOU BROKE AT WOODSTOCK'S PARTY?
MAYBE THAT WOULD BE THE FIRST STEP TOWARD YOUR RECONCILIATION..
I ALWAYS TRIP ON THAT FIRST STEP
SCHULZ
1-10

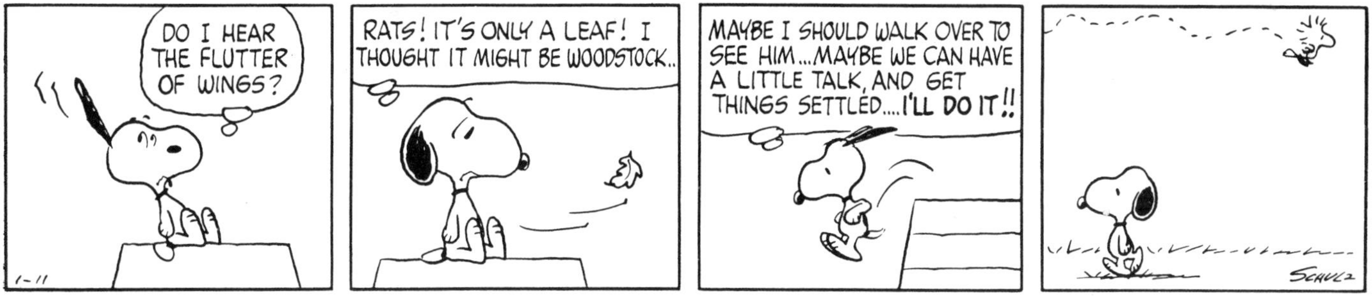
DO I HEAR THE FLUTTER OF WINGS?
RATS! IT'S ONLY A LEAF! I THOUGHT IT MIGHT BE WOODSTOCK..
MAYBE I SHOULD WALK OVER TO SEE HIM...MAYBE WE CAN HAVE A LITTLE TALK, AND GET THINGS SETTLED....I'LL DO IT!!

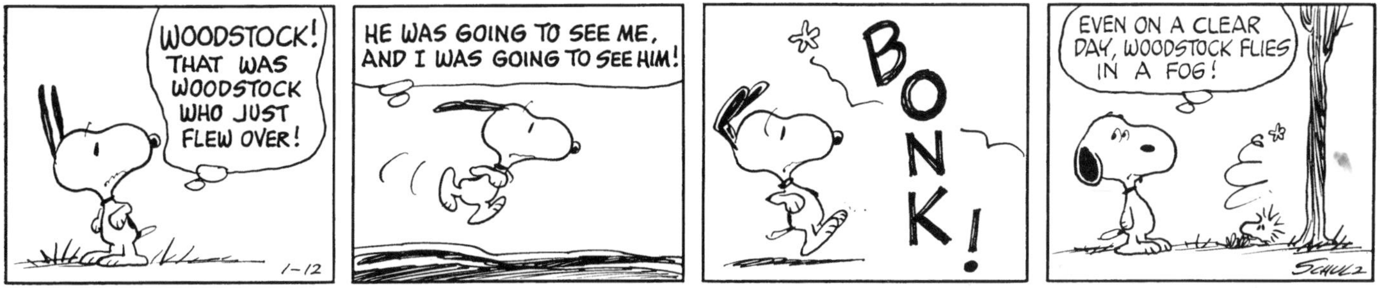
WOODSTOCK! THAT WAS WOODSTOCK WHO JUST FLEW OVER!
HE WAS GOING TO SEE ME, AND I WAS GOING TO SEE HIM!
BONK!
EVEN ON A CLEAR DAY, WOODSTOCK FLIES IN A FOG!

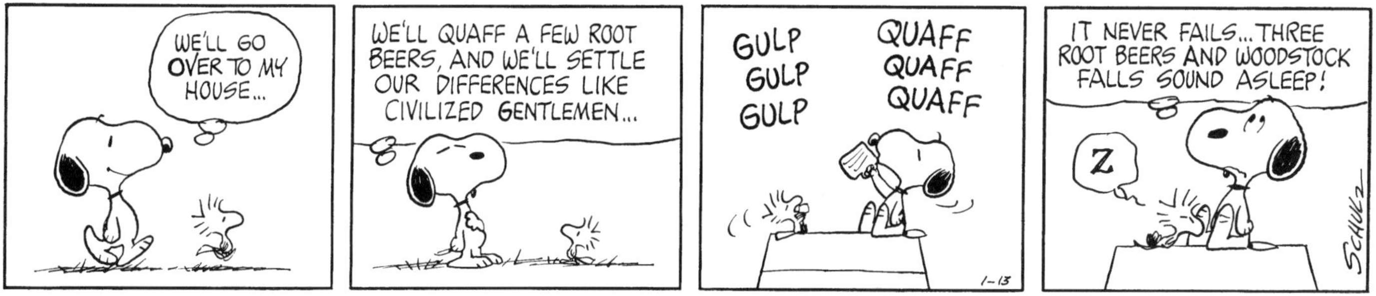
WE'LL GO OVER TO MY HOUSE...
WE'LL QUAFF A FEW ROOT BEERS, AND WE'LL SETTLE OUR DIFFERENCES LIKE CIVILIZED GENTLEMEN...
GULP GULP GULP
QUAFF QUAFF QUAFF
IT NEVER FAILS...THREE ROOT BEERS AND WOODSTOCK FALLS SOUND ASLEEP!
Z

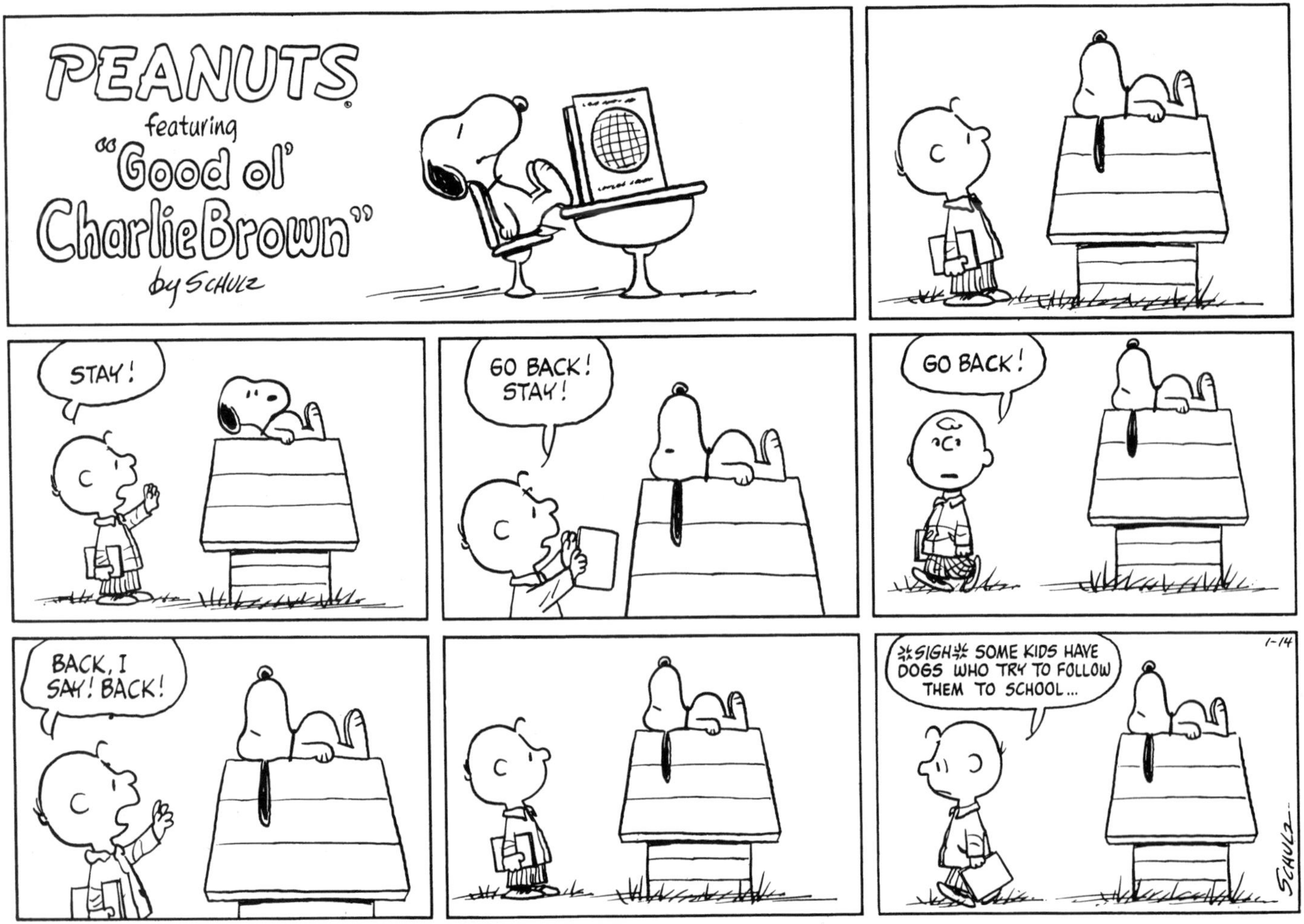
PEANUTS®
featuring
"Good ol' Charlie Brown"
by SCHULZ
STAY!
GO BACK! STAY!
GO BACK!
BACK, I SAY! BACK!
SIGH SOME KIDS HAVE DOGS WHO TRY TO FOLLOW THEM TO SCHOOL...
1-14
SCHULZ

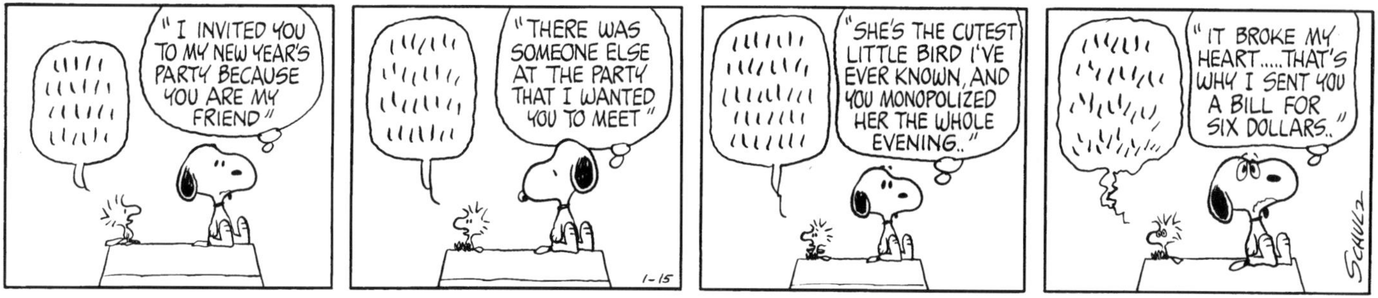
"I INVITED YOU TO MY NEW YEAR'S PARTY BECAUSE YOU ARE MY FRIEND"
"THERE WAS SOMEONE ELSE AT THE PARTY THAT I WANTED YOU TO MEET"
1-15
"SHE'S THE CUTEST LITTLE BIRD I'VE EVER KNOWN, AND YOU MONOPOLIZED HER THE WHOLE EVENING.."
"IT BROKE MY HEART.....THAT'S WHY I SENT YOU A BILL FOR SIX DOLLARS.."
SCHULZ

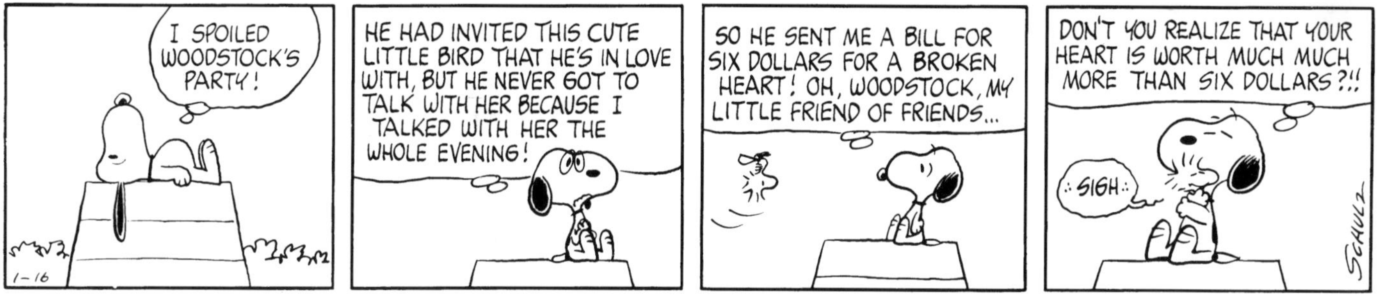
I SPOILED WOODSTOCK'S PARTY!
1-16
HE HAD INVITED THIS CUTE LITTLE BIRD THAT HE'S IN LOVE WITH, BUT HE NEVER GOT TO TALK WITH HER BECAUSE I TALKED WITH HER THE WHOLE EVENING!
SO HE SENT ME A BILL FOR SIX DOLLARS FOR A BROKEN HEART! OH, WOODSTOCK, MY LITTLE FRIEND OF FRIENDS...
DON'T YOU REALIZE THAT YOUR HEART IS WORTH MUCH MUCH MORE THAN SIX DOLLARS?!!
SIGH
SCHULZ

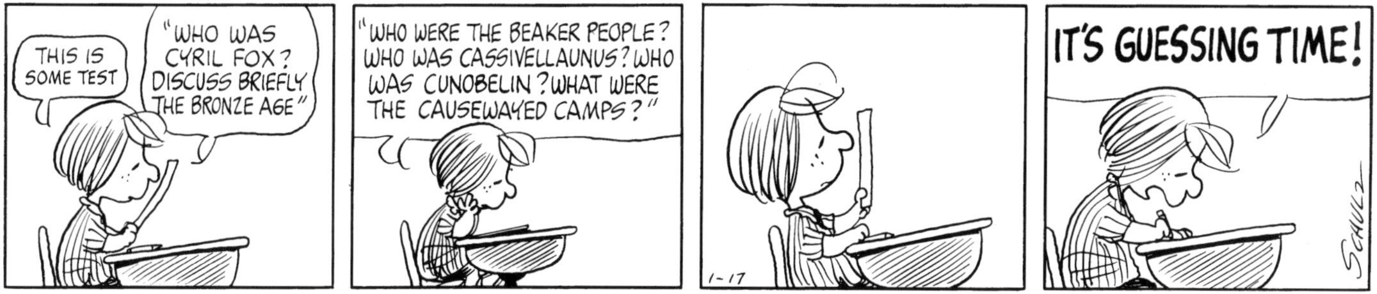
THIS IS SOME TEST
"WHO WAS CYRIL FOX? DISCUSS BRIEFLY THE BRONZE AGE"
"WHO WERE THE BEAKER PEOPLE? WHO WAS CASSIVELLAUNUS? WHO WAS CUNOBELIN? WHAT WERE THE CAUSEWAYED CAMPS?"
1-17
IT'S GUESSING TIME!
SCHULZ

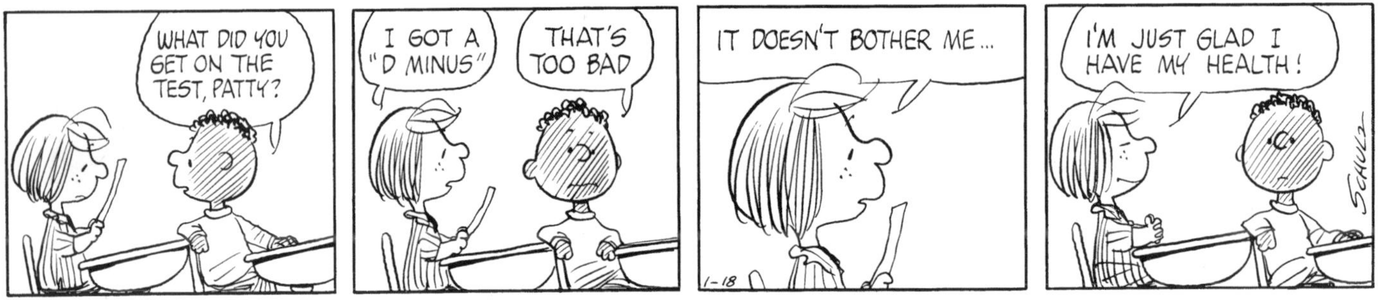
WHAT DID YOU GET ON THE TEST, PATTY?
I GOT A "D MINUS"
THAT'S TOO BAD
IT DOESN'T BOTHER ME...
1-18
I'M JUST GLAD I HAVE MY HEALTH!

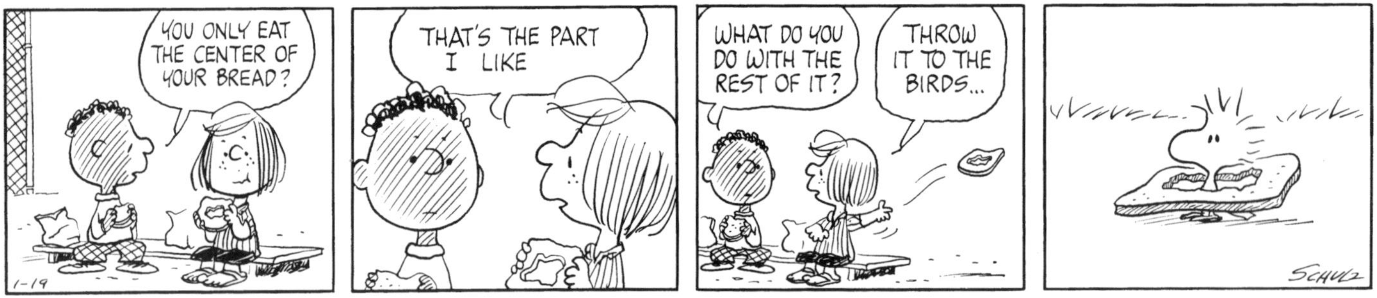
YOU ONLY EAT THE CENTER OF YOUR BREAD?
1-19
THAT'S THE PART I LIKE
WHAT DO YOU DO WITH THE REST OF IT?
THROW IT TO THE BIRDS...

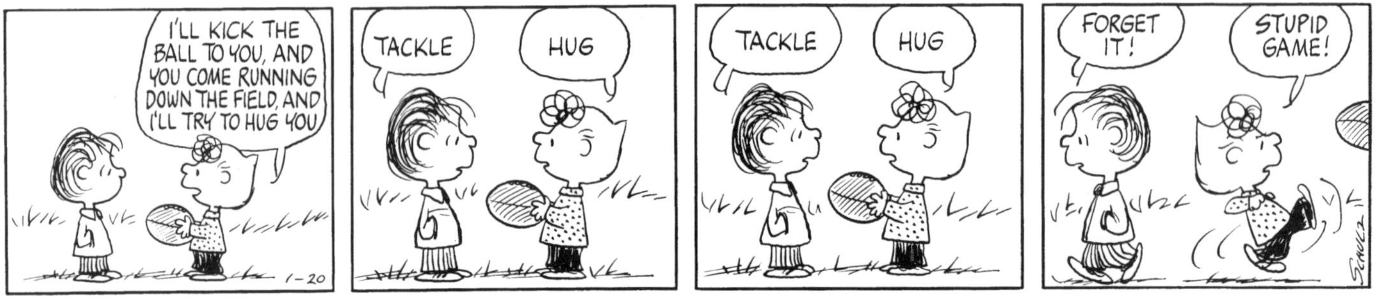
I'LL KICK THE BALL TO YOU, AND YOU COME RUNNING DOWN THE FIELD, AND I'LL TRY TO HUG YOU
1-20
TACKLE
HUG
TACKLE
HUG
FORGET IT!
STUPID GAME!

PEANUTS featuring "Good ol' Charlie Brown" by Schulz

DO YOU WANT TO TAKE ME TO THE SENIOR PROM?

1-21

THAT WON'T BE FOR ANOTHER TEN YEARS

I JUST WANTED TO GIVE YOU A BREAK....IN TEN YEARS I PLAN TO BE THE MOST SOUGHT-AFTER GIRL IN SCHOOL!

I HAVE NO INTENTION TO SEEK AFTER YOU..

 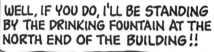

WELL, IF YOU DO, I'LL BE STANDING BY THE DRINKING FOUNTAIN AT THE NORTH END OF THE BUILDING!!

THERE'S NO SENSE TO BEING SOUGHT AFTER IF YOU CAN'T BE FOUND!

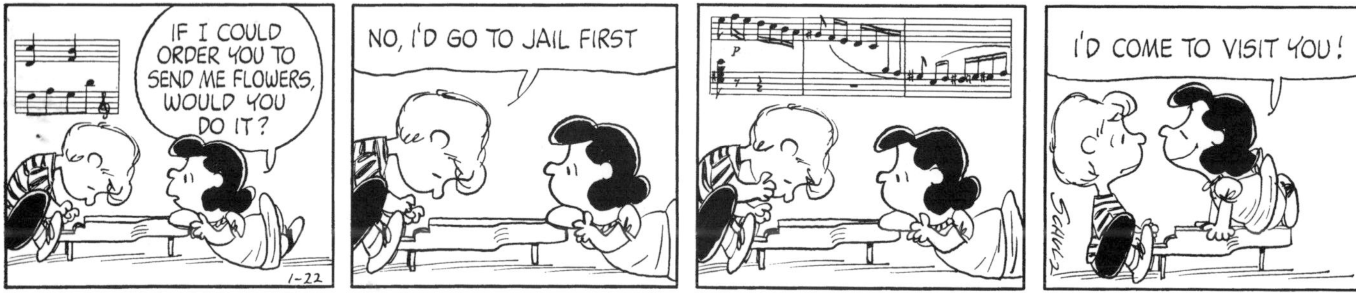
IF I COULD ORDER YOU TO SEND ME FLOWERS, WOULD YOU DO IT?
1-22
NO, I'D GO TO JAIL FIRST
I'D COME TO VISIT YOU!
SCHULZ

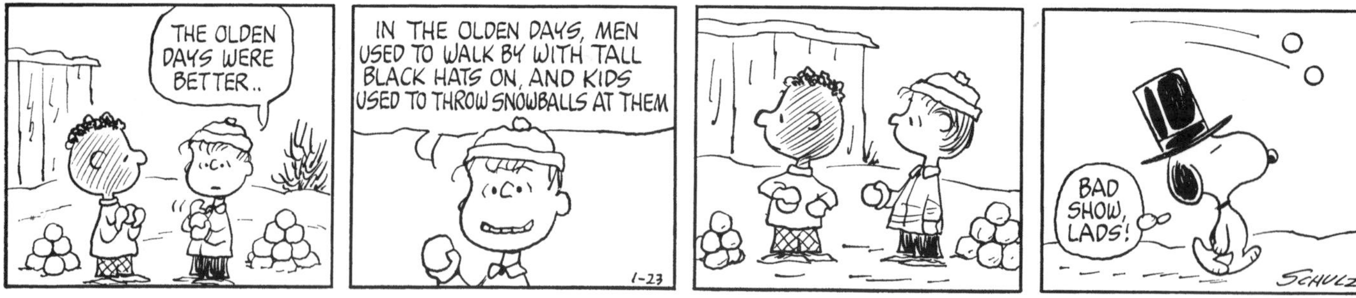
THE OLDEN DAYS WERE BETTER..
IN THE OLDEN DAYS, MEN USED TO WALK BY WITH TALL BLACK HATS ON, AND KIDS USED TO THROW SNOWBALLS AT THEM
1-23
BAD SHOW, LADS!
SCHULZ

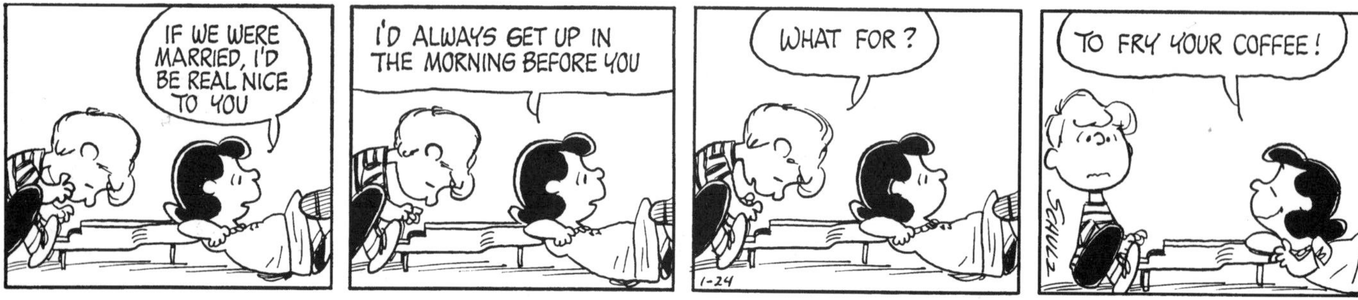
IF WE WERE MARRIED, I'D BE REAL NICE TO YOU
I'D ALWAYS GET UP IN THE MORNING BEFORE YOU
WHAT FOR?
1-24
TO FRY YOUR COFFEE!
SCHULZ

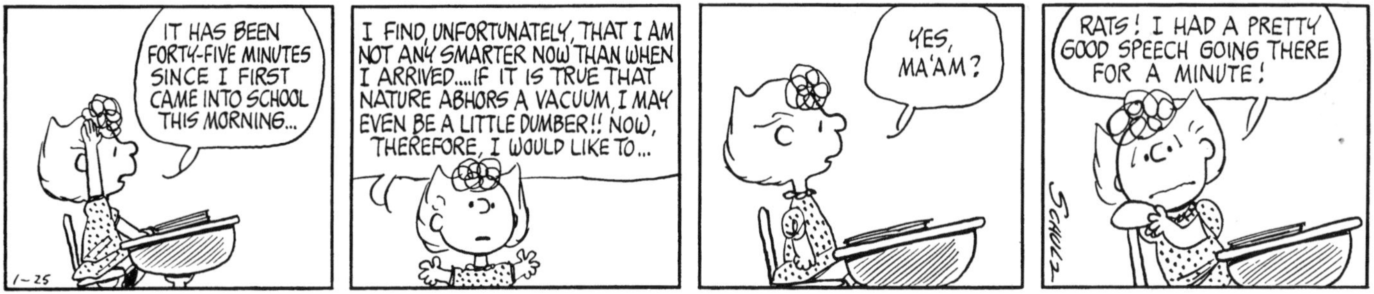
IT HAS BEEN FORTY-FIVE MINUTES SINCE I FIRST CAME INTO SCHOOL THIS MORNING...
I FIND, UNFORTUNATELY, THAT I AM NOT ANY SMARTER NOW THAN WHEN I ARRIVED....IF IT IS TRUE THAT NATURE ABHORS A VACUUM, I MAY EVEN BE A LITTLE DUMBER!! NOW, THEREFORE, I WOULD LIKE TO...
YES, MA'AM?
RATS! I HAD A PRETTY GOOD SPEECH GOING THERE FOR A MINUTE!

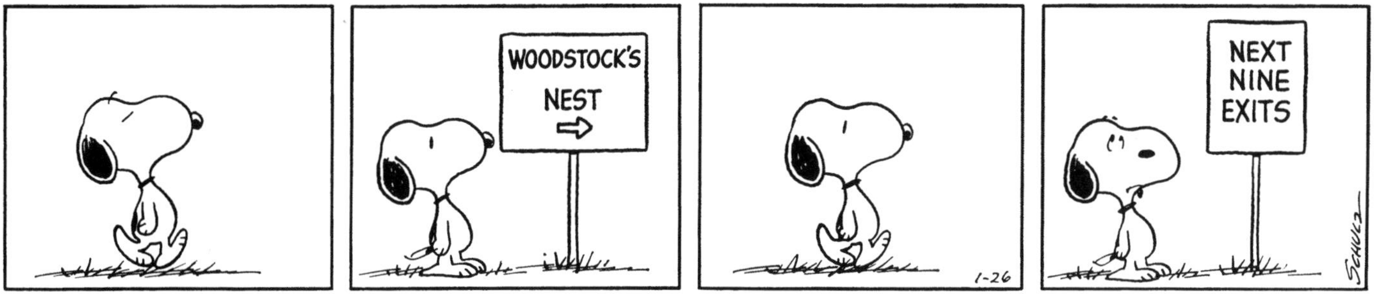
WOODSTOCK'S NEST
NEXT NINE EXITS

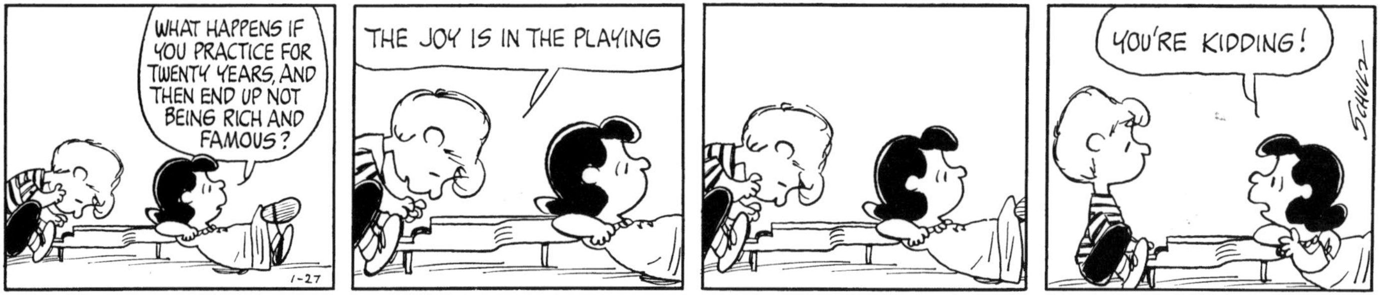
WHAT HAPPENS IF YOU PRACTICE FOR TWENTY YEARS, AND THEN END UP NOT BEING RICH AND FAMOUS?
THE JOY IS IN THE PLAYING
YOU'RE KIDDING!

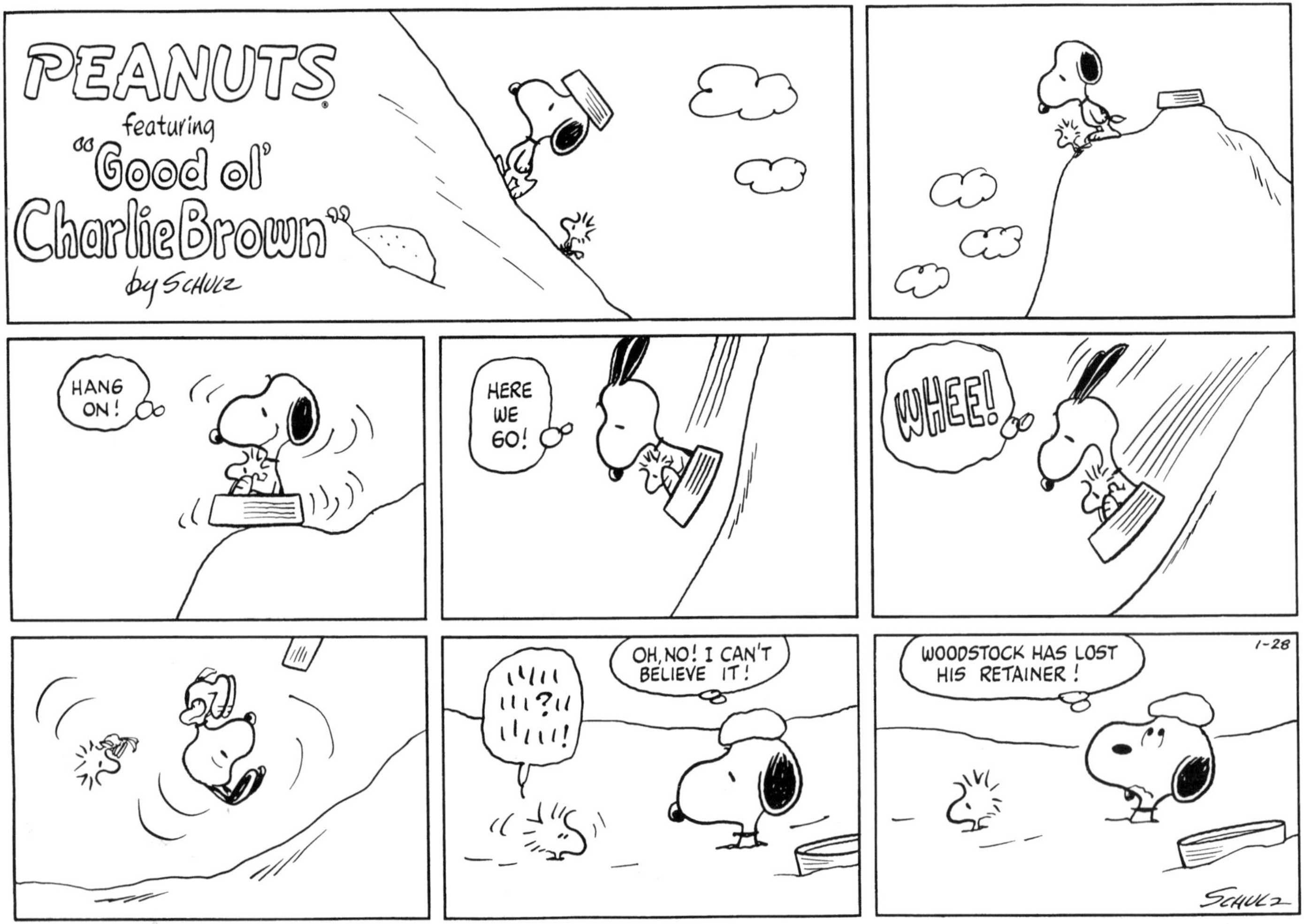
PEANUTS®
featuring "Good ol' CharlieBrown"
by SCHULZ
HANG ON!
HERE WE GO!
WHEE!
?
OH, NO! I CAN'T BELIEVE IT!
WOODSTOCK HAS LOST HIS RETAINER!
1-28
SCHULZ

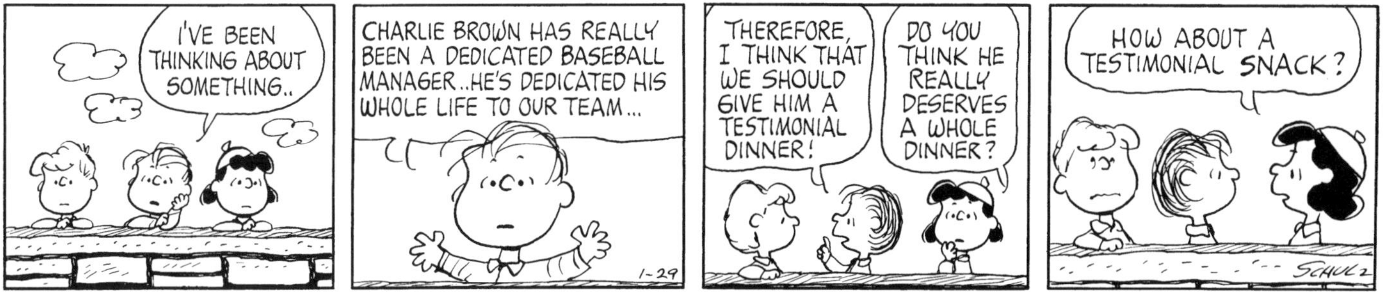
I'VE BEEN THINKING ABOUT SOMETHING..
CHARLIE BROWN HAS REALLY BEEN A DEDICATED BASEBALL MANAGER..HE'S DEDICATED HIS WHOLE LIFE TO OUR TEAM...
1-29
THEREFORE, I THINK THAT WE SHOULD GIVE HIM A TESTIMONIAL DINNER!
DO YOU THINK HE REALLY DESERVES A WHOLE DINNER?
HOW ABOUT A TESTIMONIAL SNACK?
SCHULZ

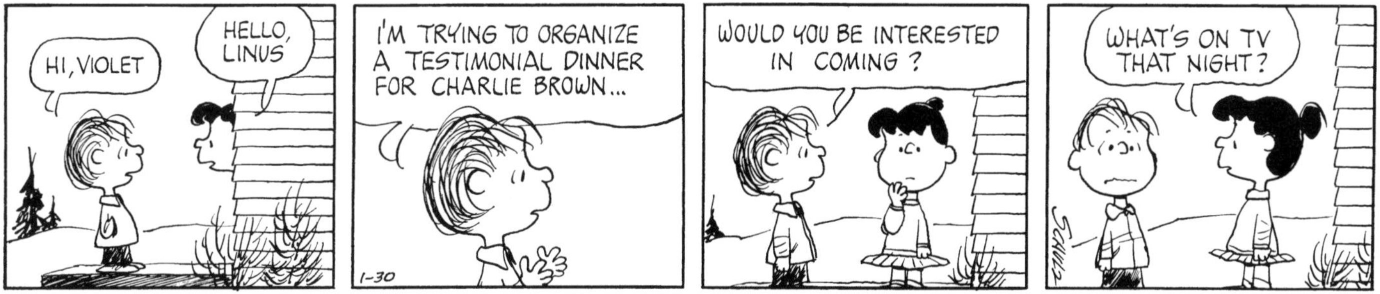
HI, VIOLET
HELLO, LINUS
I'M TRYING TO ORGANIZE A TESTIMONIAL DINNER FOR CHARLIE BROWN...
1-30
WOULD YOU BE INTERESTED IN COMING?
SCHULZ
WHAT'S ON TV THAT NIGHT?

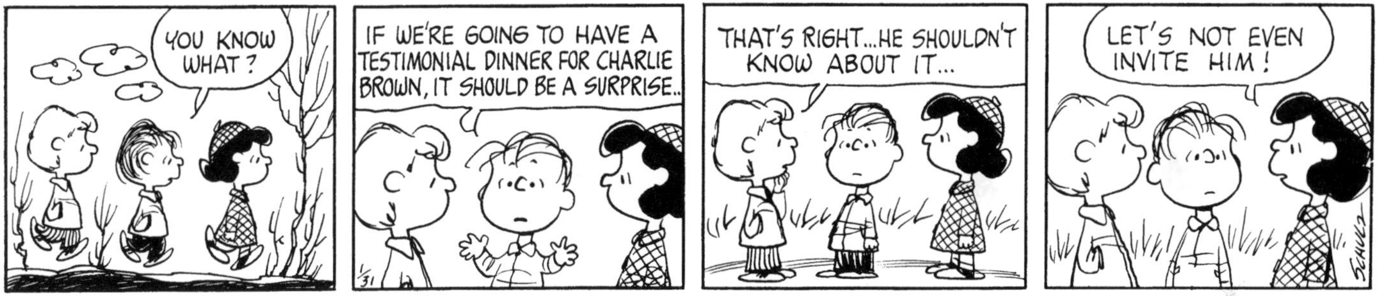
YOU KNOW WHAT?
IF WE'RE GOING TO HAVE A TESTIMONIAL DINNER FOR CHARLIE BROWN, IT SHOULD BE A SURPRISE..
1/31
THAT'S RIGHT...HE SHOULDN'T KNOW ABOUT IT...
LET'S NOT EVEN INVITE HIM!
SCHULZ

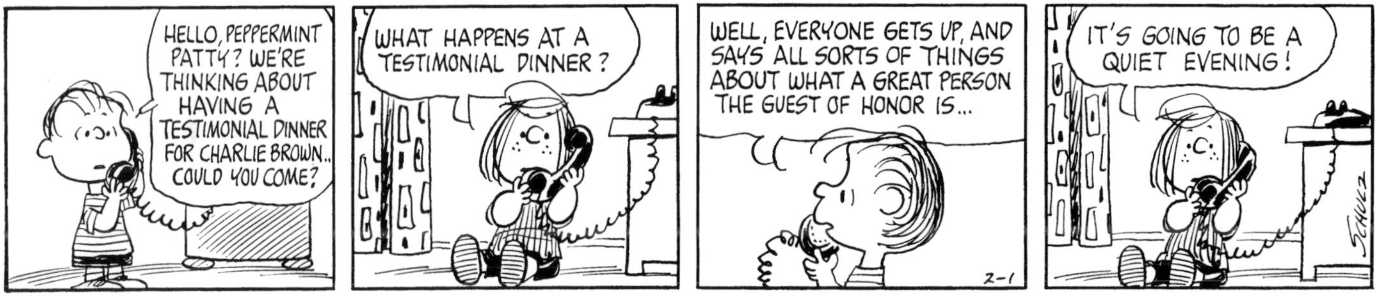
HELLO, PEPPERMINT PATTY? WE'RE THINKING ABOUT HAVING A TESTIMONIAL DINNER FOR CHARLIE BROWN.. COULD YOU COME?
WHAT HAPPENS AT A TESTIMONIAL DINNER?
WELL, EVERYONE GETS UP, AND SAYS ALL SORTS OF THINGS ABOUT WHAT A GREAT PERSON THE GUEST OF HONOR IS...
2-1
IT'S GOING TO BE A QUIET EVENING!
SCHULZ

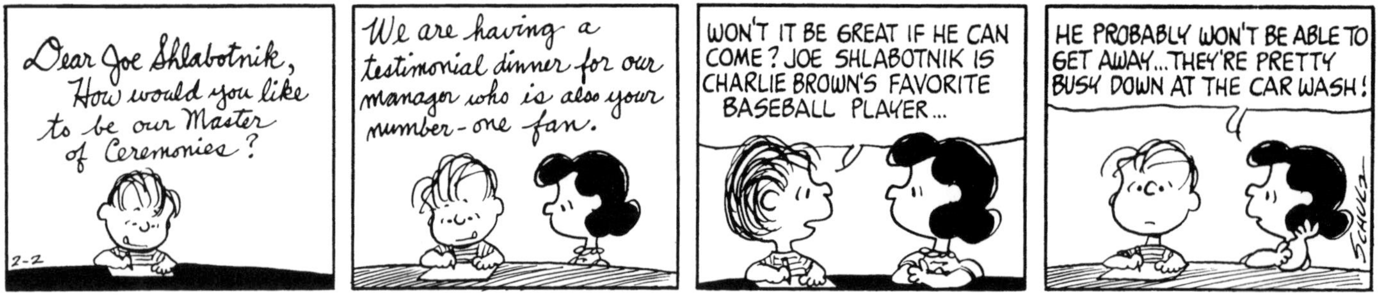
Dear Joe Shlabotnik, How would you like to be our Master of Ceremonies?
2-2
We are having a testimonial dinner for our manager who is also your number-one fan.
WON'T IT BE GREAT IF HE CAN COME? JOE SHLABOTNIK IS CHARLIE BROWN'S FAVORITE BASEBALL PLAYER...
HE PROBABLY WON'T BE ABLE TO GET AWAY...THEY'RE PRETTY BUSY DOWN AT THE CAR WASH!
SCHULZ

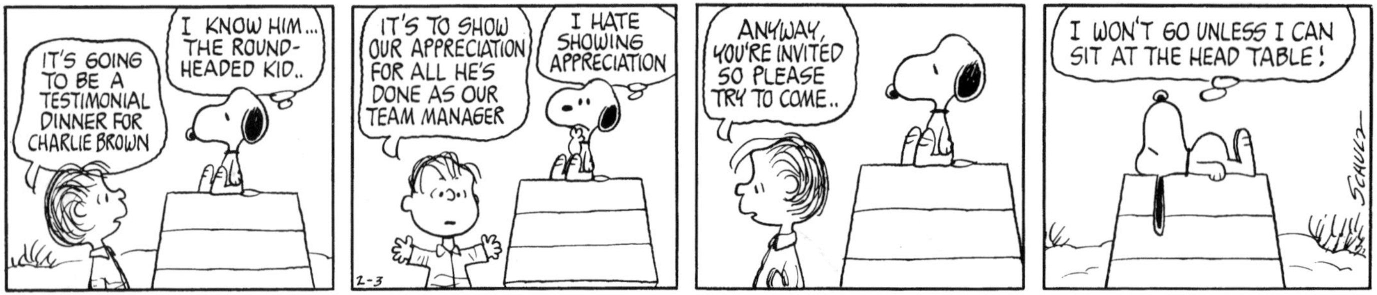
IT'S GOING TO BE A TESTIMONIAL DINNER FOR CHARLIE BROWN
I KNOW HIM... THE ROUND-HEADED KID..
IT'S TO SHOW OUR APPRECIATION FOR ALL HE'S DONE AS OUR TEAM MANAGER
I HATE SHOWING APPRECIATION
2-3
ANYWAY, YOU'RE INVITED SO PLEASE TRY TO COME..
I WON'T GO UNLESS I CAN SIT AT THE HEAD TABLE!
SCHULZ

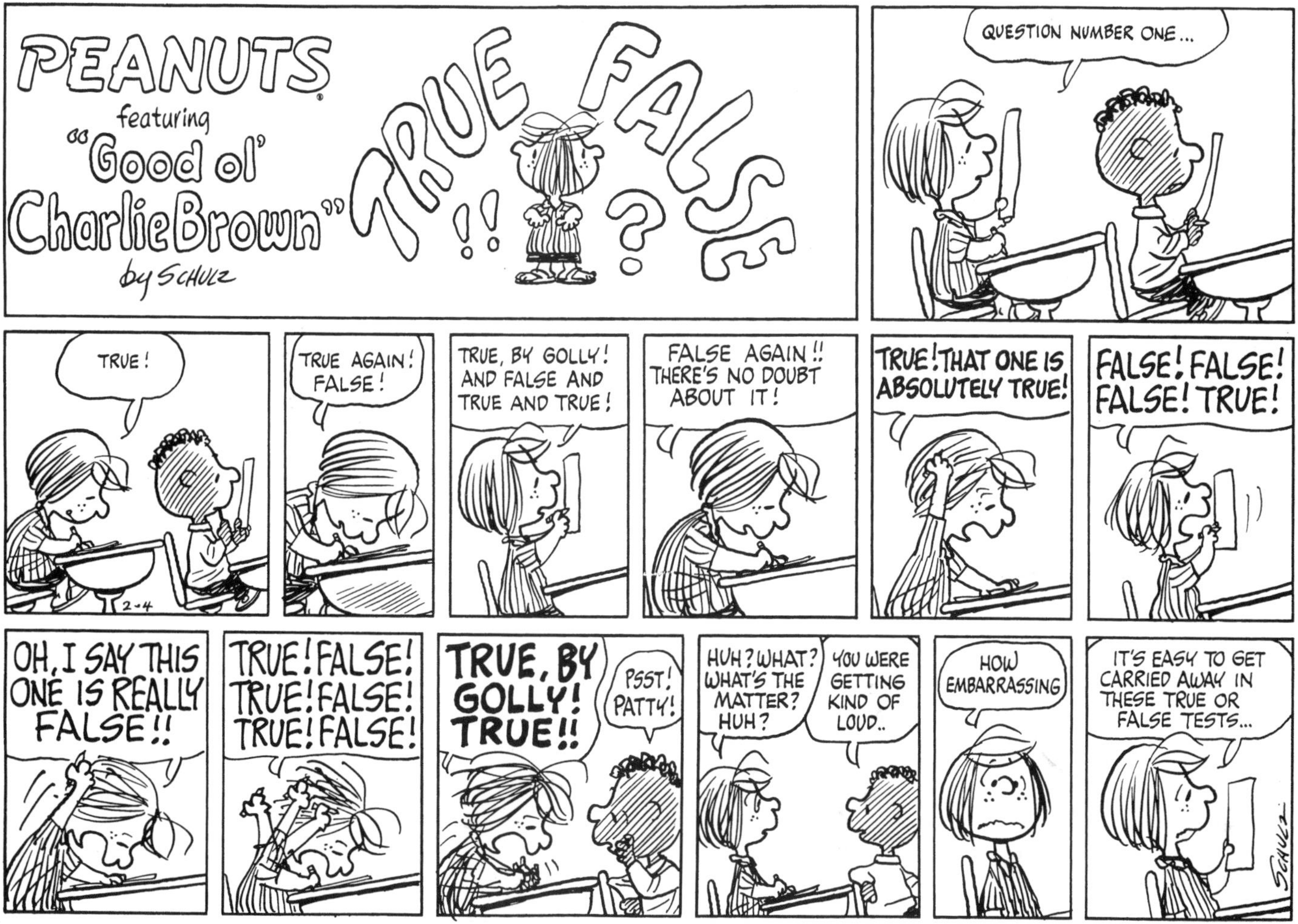
PEANUTS
featuring
"Good ol' CharlieBrown"
by SCHULZ
TRUE
FALSE
!!
?
QUESTION NUMBER ONE...
TRUE!
TRUE AGAIN! FALSE!
TRUE, BY GOLLY! AND FALSE AND TRUE AND TRUE!
FALSE AGAIN!! THERE'S NO DOUBT ABOUT IT!
TRUE! THAT ONE IS ABSOLUTELY TRUE!
FALSE! FALSE! FALSE! TRUE!
OH, I SAY THIS ONE IS REALLY FALSE!!
TRUE! FALSE! TRUE! FALSE! TRUE! FALSE!
TRUE, BY GOLLY! TRUE!!
PSST! PATTY!
HUH? WHAT? WHAT'S THE MATTER? HUH?
YOU WERE GETTING KIND OF LOUD..
HOW EMBARRASSING
IT'S EASY TO GET CARRIED AWAY IN THESE TRUE OR FALSE TESTS...
SCHULZ

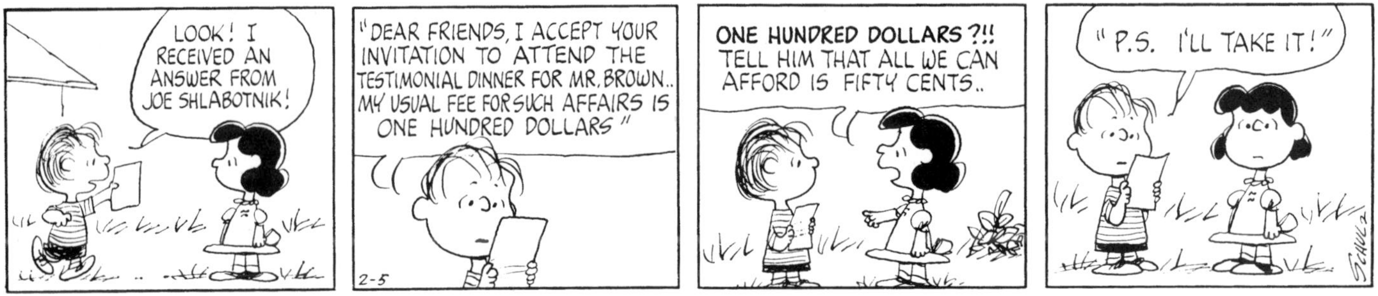
LOOK! I RECEIVED AN ANSWER FROM JOE SHLABOTNIK!
"DEAR FRIENDS, I ACCEPT YOUR INVITATION TO ATTEND THE TESTIMONIAL DINNER FOR MR. BROWN.. MY USUAL FEE FOR SUCH AFFAIRS IS ONE HUNDRED DOLLARS"
2-5
ONE HUNDRED DOLLARS ?!! TELL HIM THAT ALL WE CAN AFFORD IS FIFTY CENTS..
"P.S. I'LL TAKE IT!"
SCHULZ

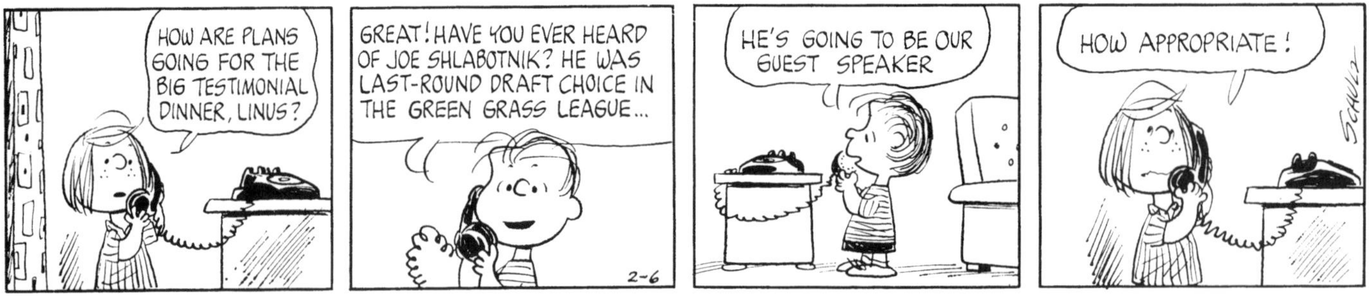
HOW ARE PLANS GOING FOR THE BIG TESTIMONIAL DINNER, LINUS?
GREAT! HAVE YOU EVER HEARD OF JOE SHLABOTNIK? HE WAS LAST-ROUND DRAFT CHOICE IN THE GREEN GRASS LEAGUE...
2-6
HE'S GOING TO BE OUR GUEST SPEAKER
HOW APPROPRIATE!
SCHULZ

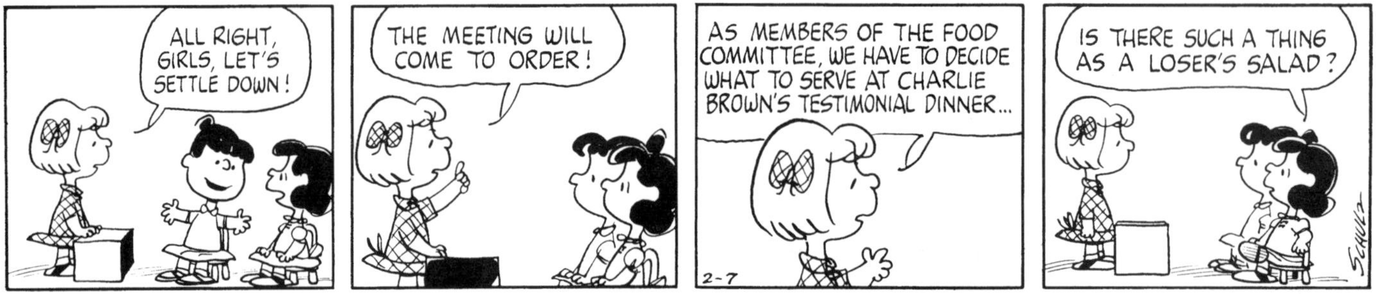
ALL RIGHT, GIRLS, LET'S SETTLE DOWN!
THE MEETING WILL COME TO ORDER!
AS MEMBERS OF THE FOOD COMMITTEE, WE HAVE TO DECIDE WHAT TO SERVE AT CHARLIE BROWN'S TESTIMONIAL DINNER...
2-7
IS THERE SUCH A THING AS A LOSER'S SALAD?
SCHULZ

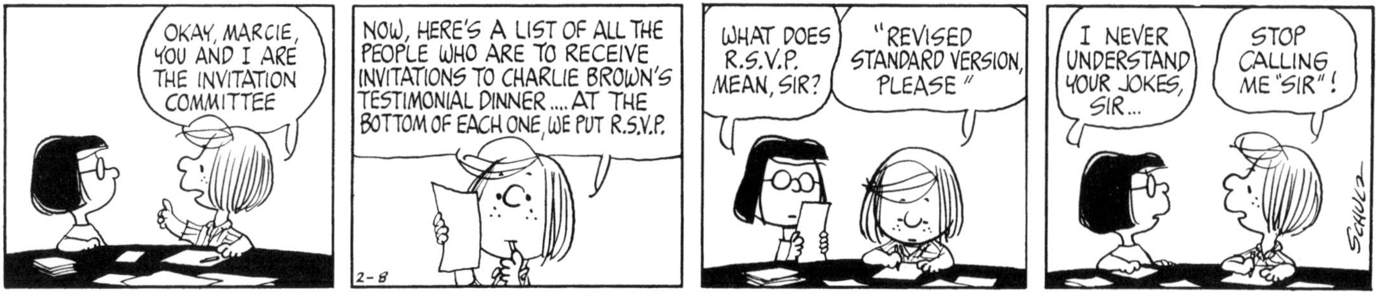
OKAY, MARCIE, YOU AND I ARE THE INVITATION COMMITTEE
NOW, HERE'S A LIST OF ALL THE PEOPLE WHO ARE TO RECEIVE INVITATIONS TO CHARLIE BROWN'S TESTIMONIAL DINNER.... AT THE BOTTOM OF EACH ONE, WE PUT R.S.V.P.
2-8
WHAT DOES R.S.V.P. MEAN, SIR?
"REVISED STANDARD VERSION, PLEASE"
I NEVER UNDERSTAND YOUR JOKES, SIR...
STOP CALLING ME "SIR"!
SCHULZ

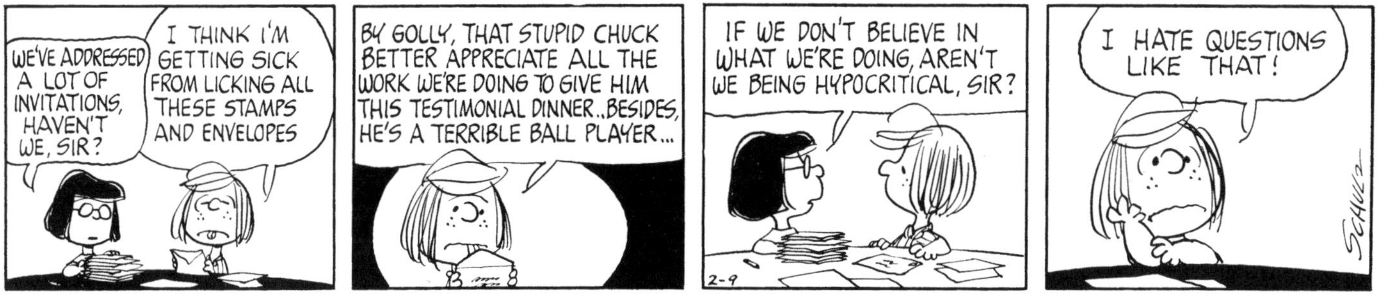
WE'VE ADDRESSED A LOT OF INVITATIONS, HAVEN'T WE, SIR?
I THINK I'M GETTING SICK FROM LICKING ALL THESE STAMPS AND ENVELOPES
BY GOLLY, THAT STUPID CHUCK BETTER APPRECIATE ALL THE WORK WE'RE DOING TO GIVE HIM THIS TESTIMONIAL DINNER..BESIDES, HE'S A TERRIBLE BALL PLAYER...
IF WE DON'T BELIEVE IN WHAT WE'RE DOING, AREN'T WE BEING HYPOCRITICAL, SIR?
2-9
I HATE QUESTIONS LIKE THAT!
SCHULZ

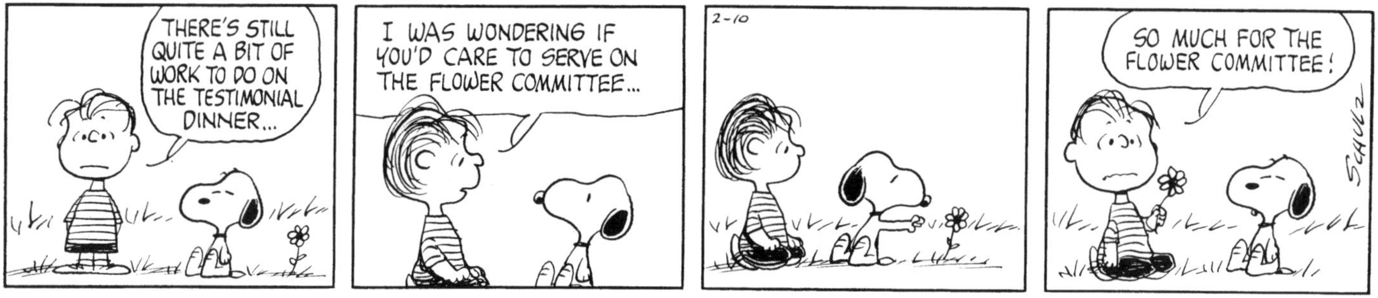
THERE'S STILL QUITE A BIT OF WORK TO DO ON THE TESTIMONIAL DINNER...
I WAS WONDERING IF YOU'D CARE TO SERVE ON THE FLOWER COMMITTEE...
2-10
SO MUCH FOR THE FLOWER COMMITTEE!
SCHULZ

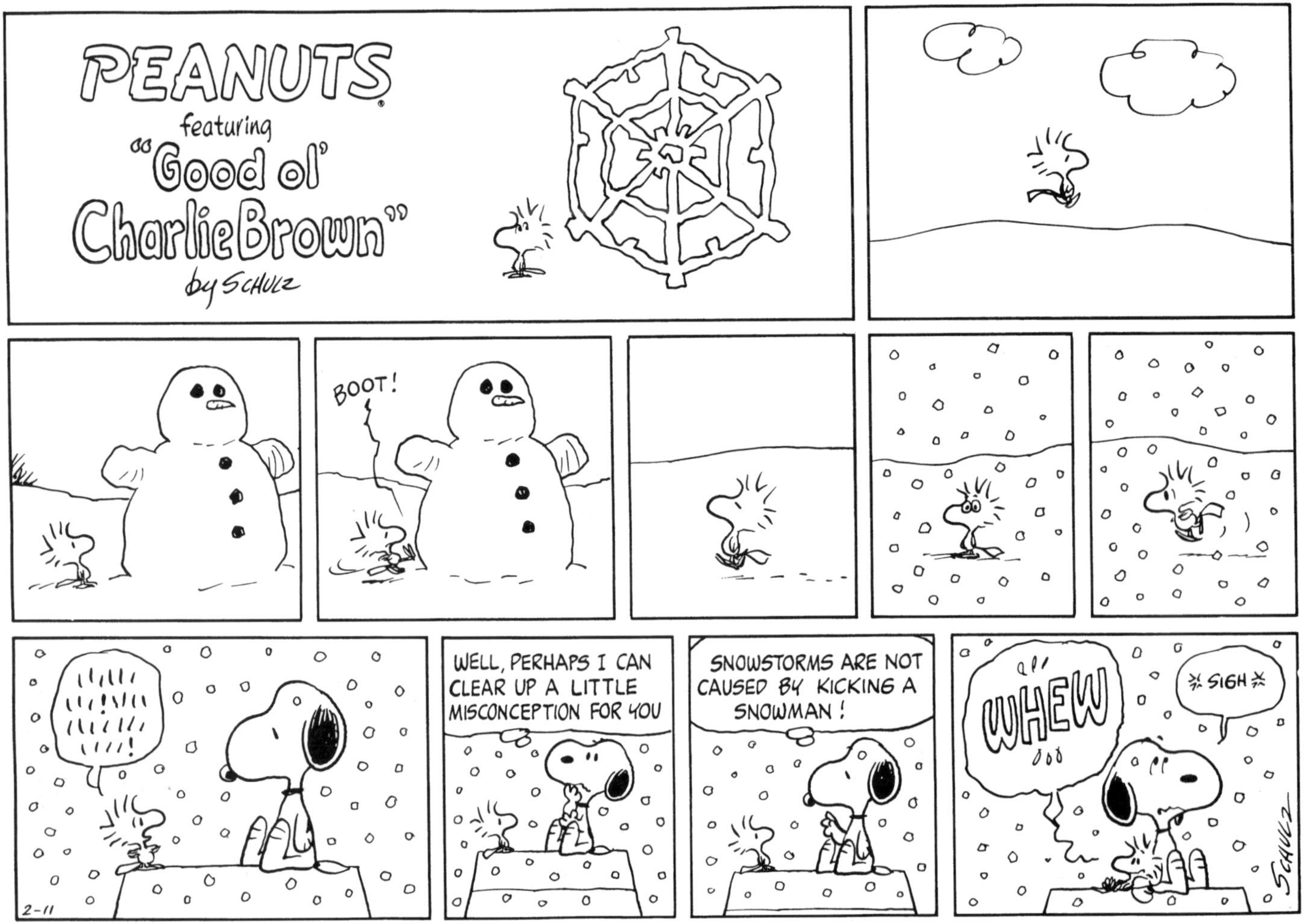
PEANUTS
featuring "Good ol' Charlie Brown"
by SCHULZ
BOOT!
WELL, PERHAPS I CAN CLEAR UP A LITTLE MISCONCEPTION FOR YOU
SNOWSTORMS ARE NOT CAUSED BY KICKING A SNOWMAN!
WHEW
SIGH
SCHULZ
2-11

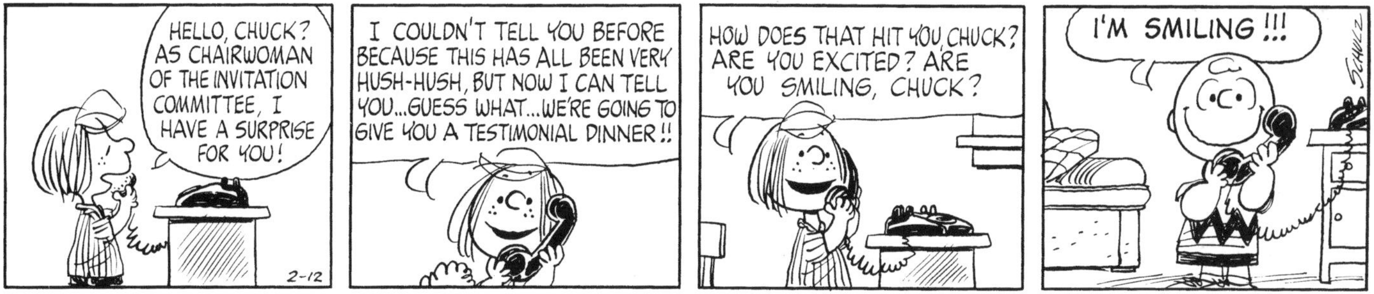
HELLO, CHUCK? AS CHAIRWOMAN OF THE INVITATION COMMITTEE, I HAVE A SURPRISE FOR YOU!
2-12
I COULDN'T TELL YOU BEFORE BECAUSE THIS HAS ALL BEEN VERY HUSH-HUSH, BUT NOW I CAN TELL YOU...GUESS WHAT...WE'RE GOING TO GIVE YOU A TESTIMONIAL DINNER!!
HOW DOES THAT HIT YOU, CHUCK? ARE YOU EXCITED? ARE YOU SMILING, CHUCK?
I'M SMILING!!!
SCHULZ

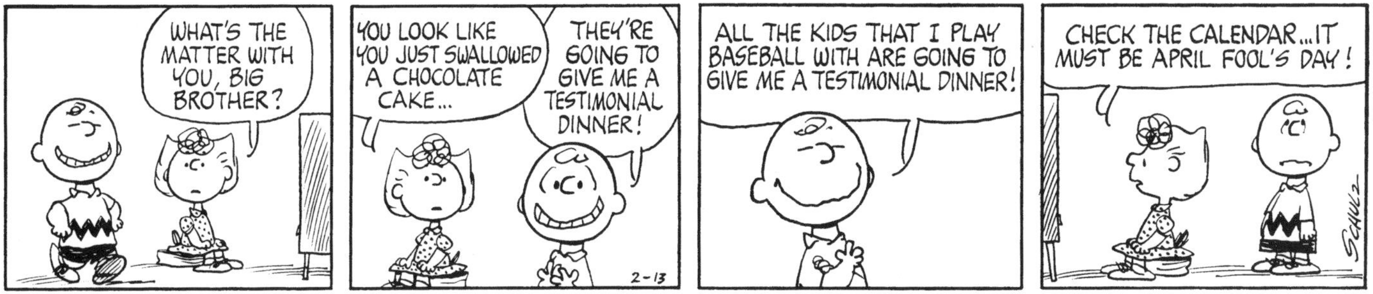
WHAT'S THE MATTER WITH YOU, BIG BROTHER?
YOU LOOK LIKE YOU JUST SWALLOWED A CHOCOLATE CAKE...
THEY'RE GOING TO GIVE ME A TESTIMONIAL DINNER!
2-13
ALL THE KIDS THAT I PLAY BASEBALL WITH ARE GOING TO GIVE ME A TESTIMONIAL DINNER!
CHECK THE CALENDAR...IT MUST BE APRIL FOOL'S DAY!
SCHULZ

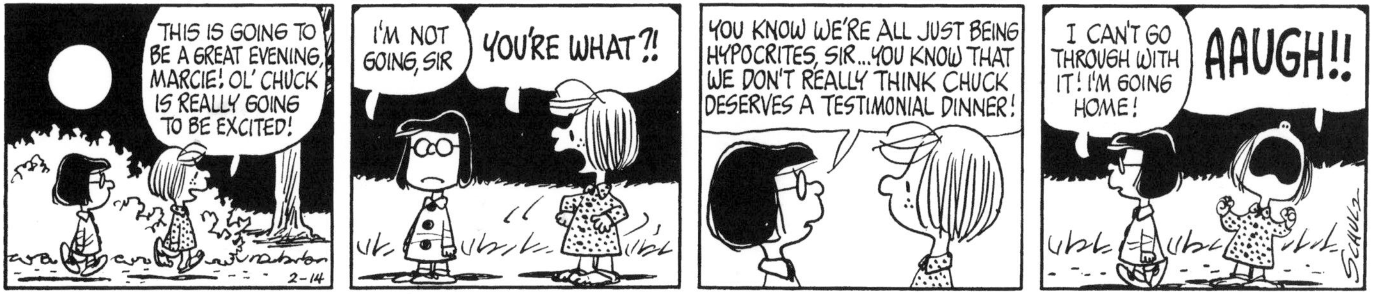
THIS IS GOING TO BE A GREAT EVENING, MARCIE! OL' CHUCK IS REALLY GOING TO BE EXCITED!
2-14
I'M NOT GOING, SIR
YOU'RE WHAT?!
YOU KNOW WE'RE ALL JUST BEING HYPOCRITES, SIR...YOU KNOW THAT WE DON'T REALLY THINK CHUCK DESERVES A TESTIMONIAL DINNER!
I CAN'T GO THROUGH WITH IT! I'M GOING HOME!
AAUGH!!
SCHULZ

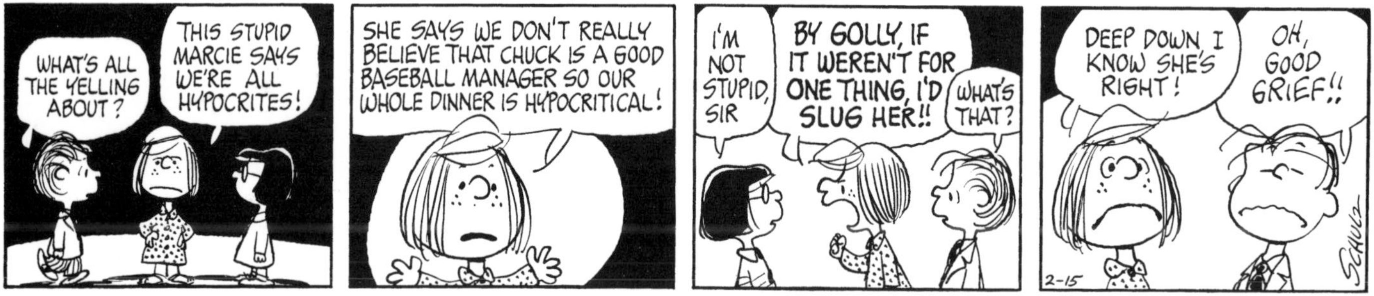
WHAT'S ALL THE YELLING ABOUT?
THIS STUPID MARCIE SAYS WE'RE ALL HYPOCRITES!
SHE SAYS WE DON'T REALLY BELIEVE THAT CHUCK IS A GOOD BASEBALL MANAGER SO OUR WHOLE DINNER IS HYPOCRITICAL!
I'M NOT STUPID, SIR
BY GOLLY, IF IT WEREN'T FOR ONE THING, I'D SLUG HER!!
WHAT'S THAT?
DEEP DOWN, I KNOW SHE'S RIGHT!
OH, GOOD GRIEF!!
2-15
SCHULZ

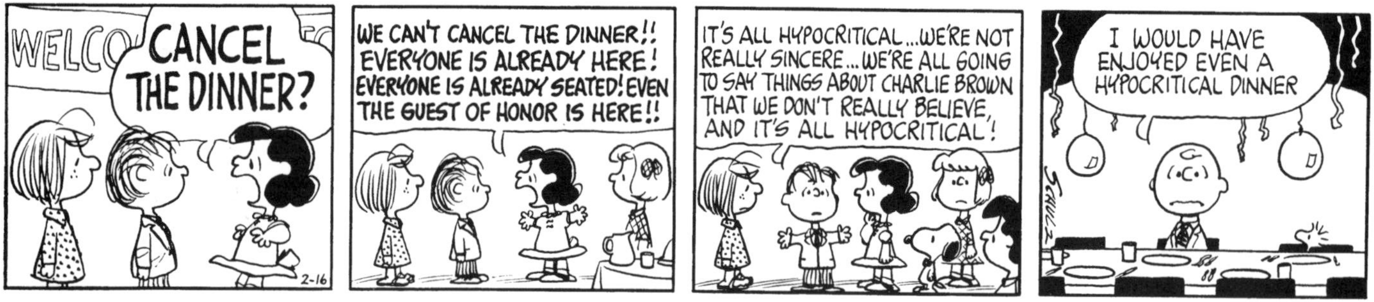
WELCO
CANCEL THE DINNER?
2-16
WE CAN'T CANCEL THE DINNER!! EVERYONE IS ALREADY HERE! EVERYONE IS ALREADY SEATED! EVEN THE GUEST OF HONOR IS HERE!!
IT'S ALL HYPOCRITICAL...WE'RE NOT REALLY SINCERE...WE'RE ALL GOING TO SAY THINGS ABOUT CHARLIE BROWN THAT WE DON'T REALLY BELIEVE, AND IT'S ALL HYPOCRITICAL!
I WOULD HAVE ENJOYED EVEN A HYPOCRITICAL DINNER
SCHULZ

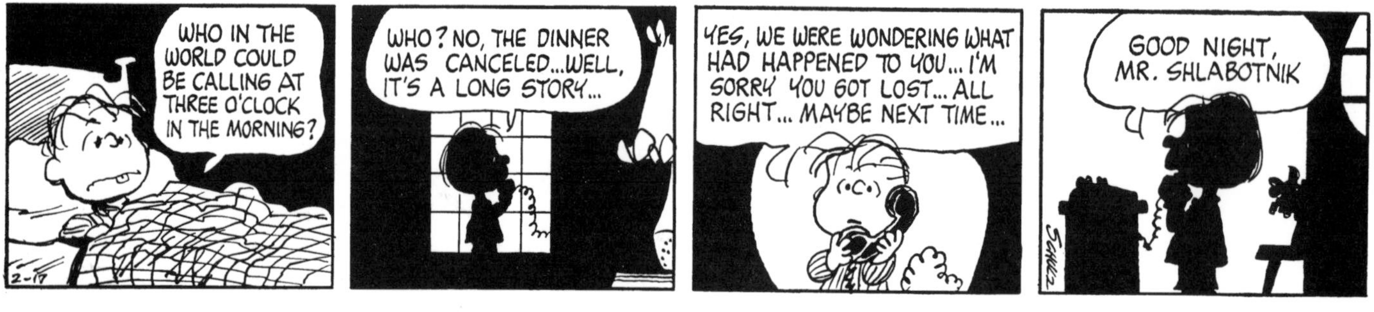
WHO IN THE WORLD COULD BE CALLING AT THREE O'CLOCK IN THE MORNING?
2-17
WHO? NO, THE DINNER WAS CANCELED...WELL, IT'S A LONG STORY...
YES, WE WERE WONDERING WHAT HAD HAPPENED TO YOU... I'M SORRY YOU GOT LOST... ALL RIGHT... MAYBE NEXT TIME...
GOOD NIGHT, MR. SHLABOTNIK
SCHULZ

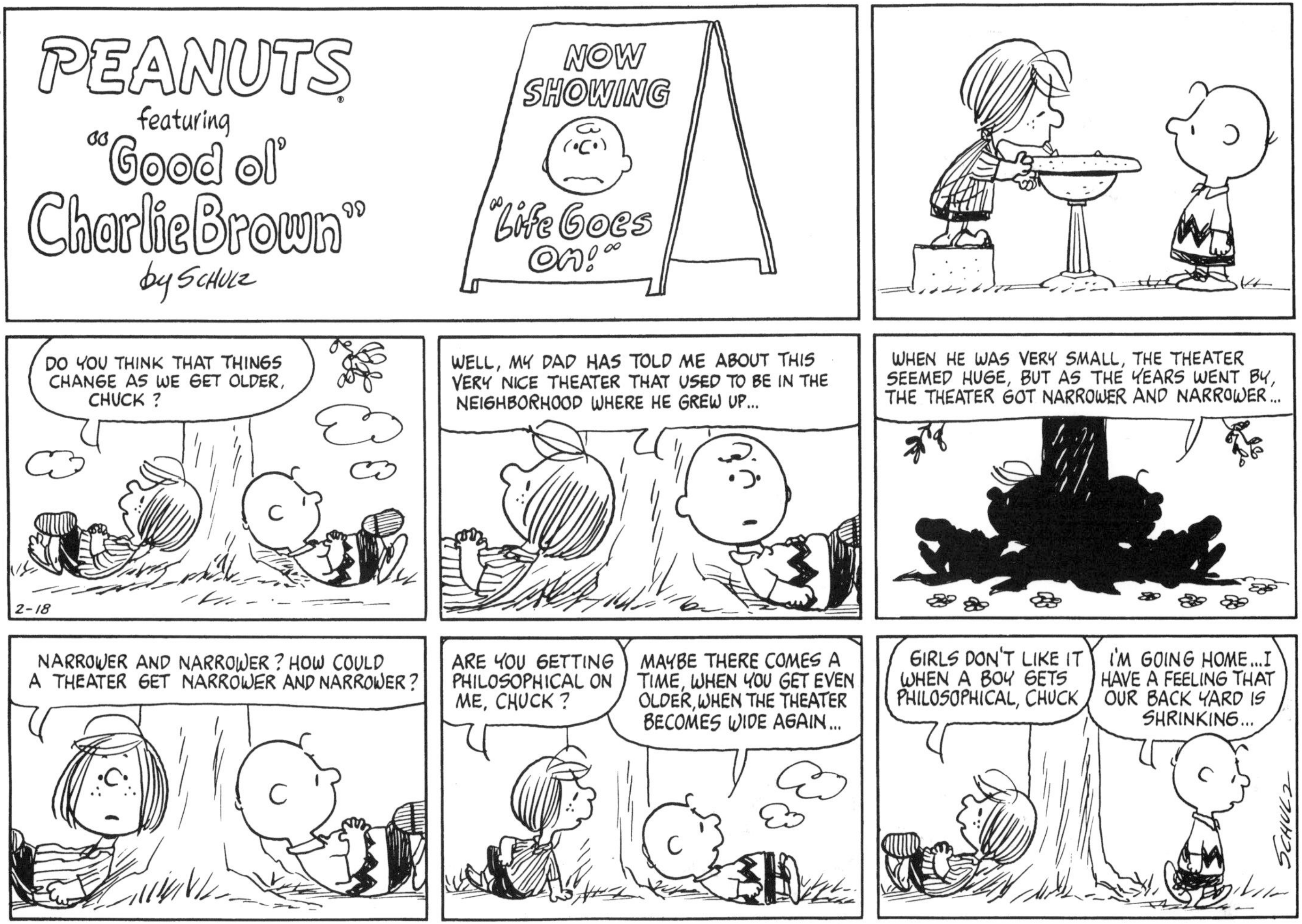

PEANUTS
featuring
"Good ol' Charlie Brown"
by SCHULZ
NOW SHOWING
"Life Goes On!"
DO YOU THINK THAT THINGS CHANGE AS WE GET OLDER, CHUCK ?
2-18
WELL, MY DAD HAS TOLD ME ABOUT THIS VERY NICE THEATER THAT USED TO BE IN THE NEIGHBORHOOD WHERE HE GREW UP...
WHEN HE WAS VERY SMALL, THE THEATER SEEMED HUGE, BUT AS THE YEARS WENT BY, THE THEATER GOT NARROWER AND NARROWER...
NARROWER AND NARROWER? HOW COULD A THEATER GET NARROWER AND NARROWER?
ARE YOU GETTING PHILOSOPHICAL ON ME, CHUCK ?
MAYBE THERE COMES A TIME, WHEN YOU GET EVEN OLDER, WHEN THE THEATER BECOMES WIDE AGAIN...
GIRLS DON'T LIKE IT WHEN A BOY GETS PHILOSOPHICAL, CHUCK
I'M GOING HOME...I HAVE A FEELING THAT OUR BACK YARD IS SHRINKING...
SCHULZ

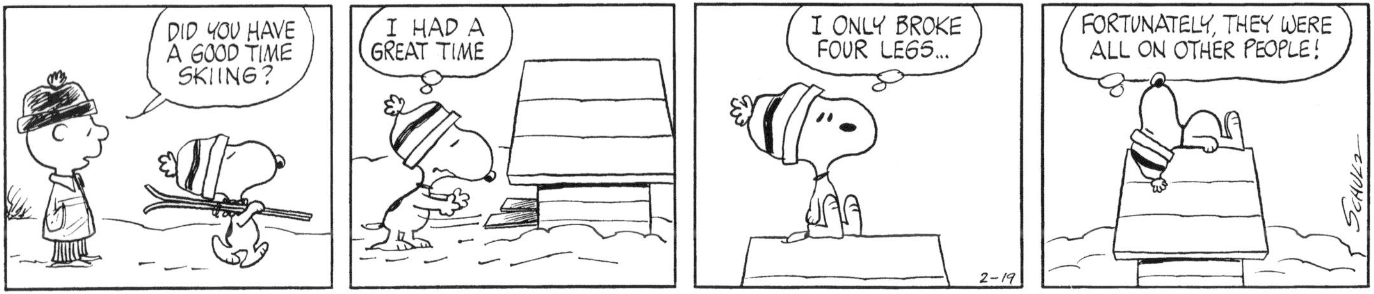
DID YOU HAVE A GOOD TIME SKIING?
I HAD A GREAT TIME
I ONLY BROKE FOUR LEGS...
2-19
FORTUNATELY, THEY WERE ALL ON OTHER PEOPLE!
SCHULZ

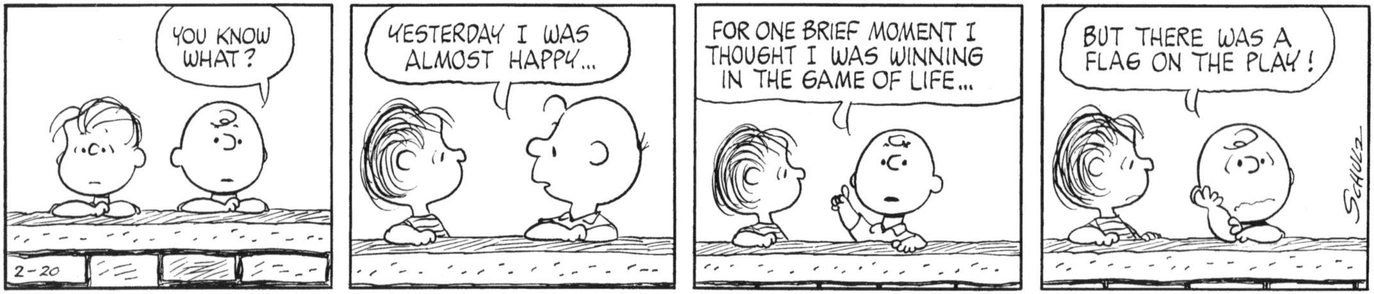
YOU KNOW WHAT?
2-20
YESTERDAY I WAS ALMOST HAPPY...
FOR ONE BRIEF MOMENT I THOUGHT I WAS WINNING IN THE GAME OF LIFE...
BUT THERE WAS A FLAG ON THE PLAY!
SCHULZ

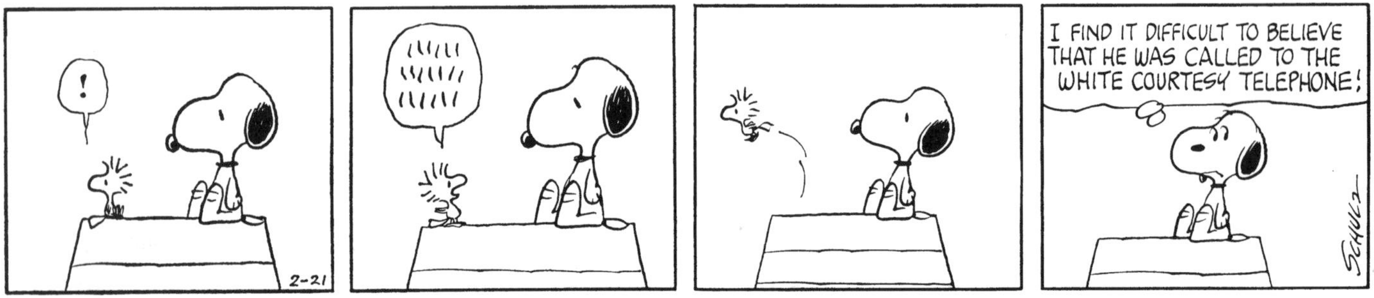
!
2-21
I FIND IT DIFFICULT TO BELIEVE THAT HE WAS CALLED TO THE WHITE COURTESY TELEPHONE!
SCHULZ

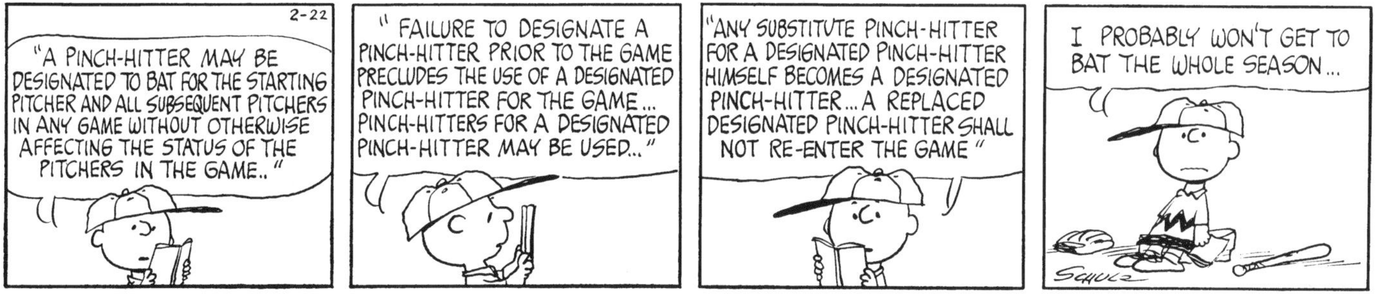
2-22
"A PINCH-HITTER MAY BE DESIGNATED TO BAT FOR THE STARTING PITCHER AND ALL SUBSEQUENT PITCHERS IN ANY GAME WITHOUT OTHERWISE AFFECTING THE STATUS OF THE PITCHERS IN THE GAME.."
" FAILURE TO DESIGNATE A PINCH-HITTER PRIOR TO THE GAME PRECLUDES THE USE OF A DESIGNATED PINCH-HITTER FOR THE GAME... PINCH-HITTERS FOR A DESIGNATED PINCH-HITTER MAY BE USED..."
"ANY SUBSTITUTE PINCH-HITTER FOR A DESIGNATED PINCH-HITTER HIMSELF BECOMES A DESIGNATED PINCH-HITTER... A REPLACED DESIGNATED PINCH-HITTER SHALL NOT RE-ENTER THE GAME"
I PROBABLY WON'T GET TO BAT THE WHOLE SEASON...
SCHULZ

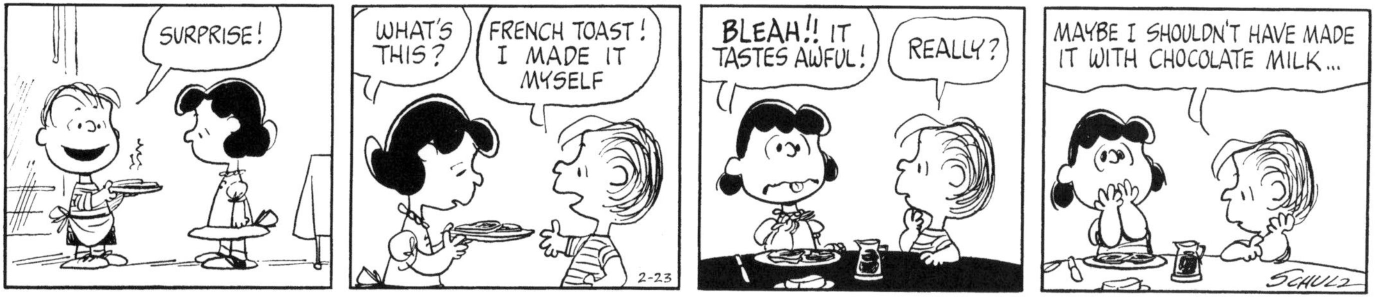
SURPRISE!
WHAT'S THIS?
FRENCH TOAST! I MADE IT MYSELF
2-23
BLEAH!! IT TASTES AWFUL!
REALLY?
MAYBE I SHOULDN'T HAVE MADE IT WITH CHOCOLATE MILK...
SCHULZ

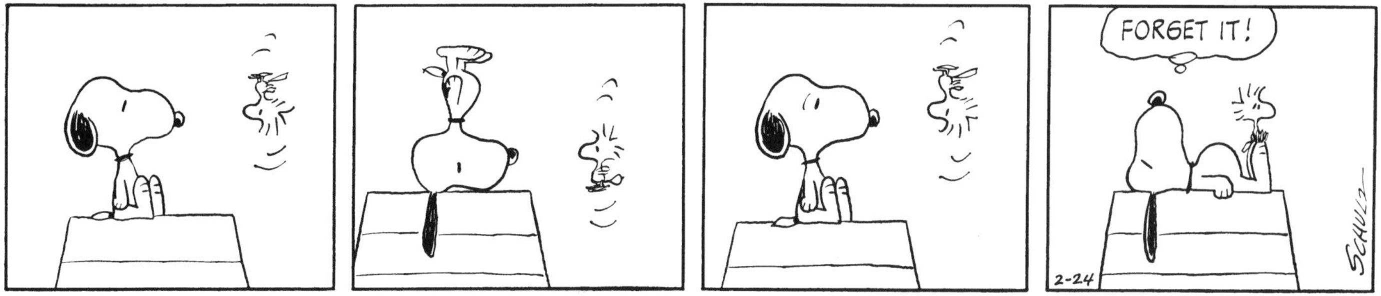
FORGET IT!
2-24
SCHULZ

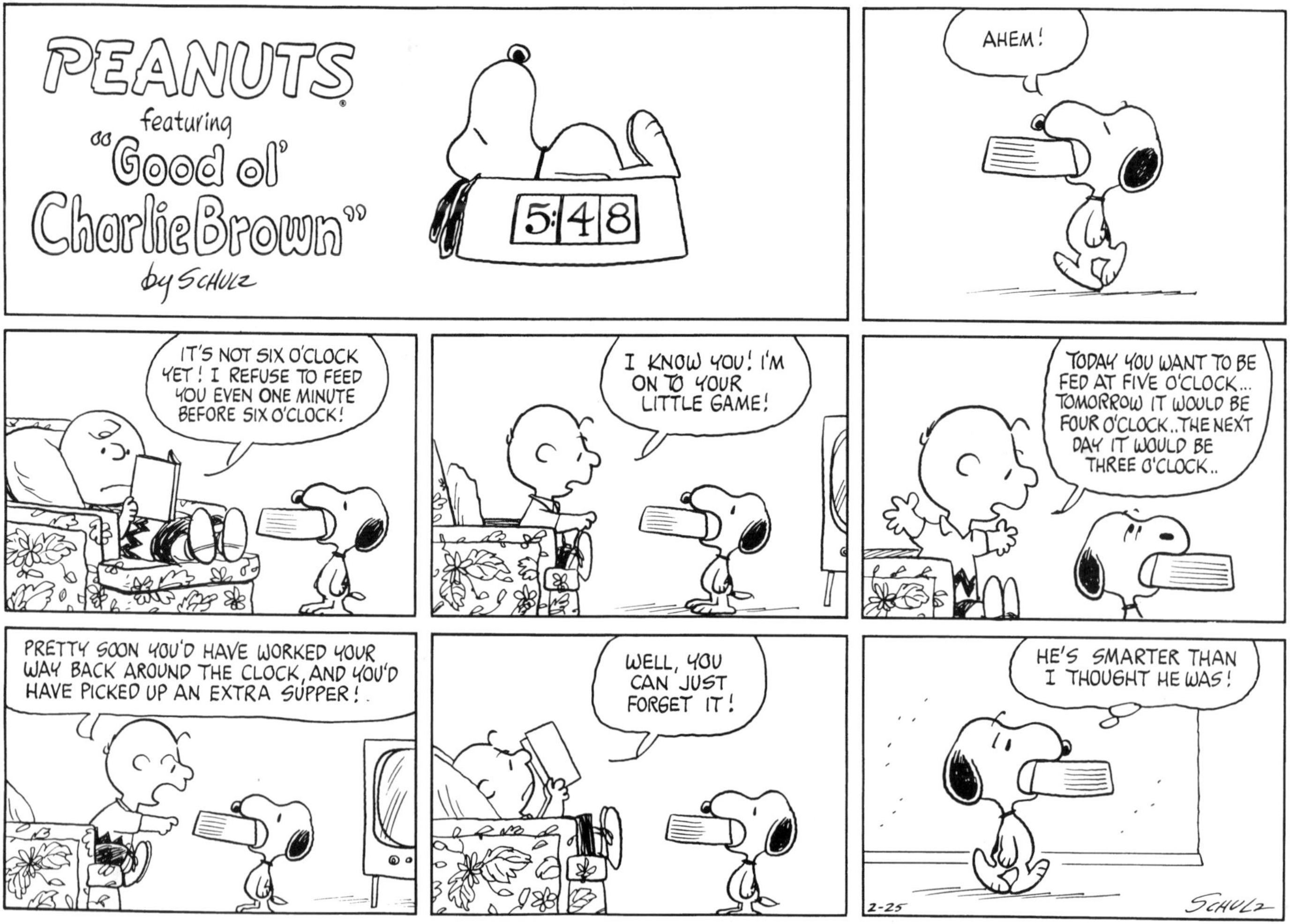
PEANUTS
featuring
"Good ol' Charlie Brown"
by SCHULZ
5:48
AHEM!
IT'S NOT SIX O'CLOCK YET! I REFUSE TO FEED YOU EVEN ONE MINUTE BEFORE SIX O'CLOCK!
I KNOW YOU! I'M ON TO YOUR LITTLE GAME!
TODAY YOU WANT TO BE FED AT FIVE O'CLOCK... TOMORROW IT WOULD BE FOUR O'CLOCK.. THE NEXT DAY IT WOULD BE THREE O'CLOCK..
PRETTY SOON YOU'D HAVE WORKED YOUR WAY BACK AROUND THE CLOCK, AND YOU'D HAVE PICKED UP AN EXTRA SUPPER!
WELL, YOU CAN JUST FORGET IT!
HE'S SMARTER THAN I THOUGHT HE WAS!
2-25
SCHULZ

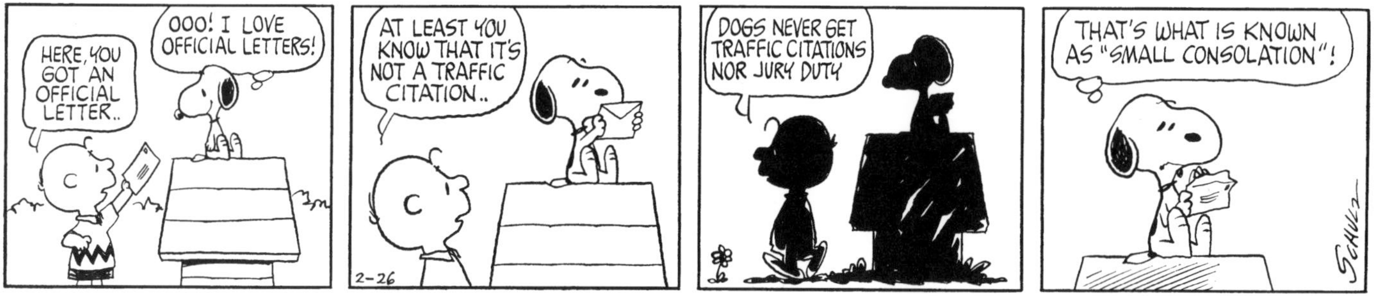
HERE, YOU GOT AN OFFICIAL LETTER..
OOO! I LOVE OFFICIAL LETTERS!
AT LEAST YOU KNOW THAT IT'S NOT A TRAFFIC CITATION..
2-26
DOGS NEVER GET TRAFFIC CITATIONS NOR JURY DUTY
THAT'S WHAT IS KNOWN AS "SMALL CONSOLATION"!
SCHULZ

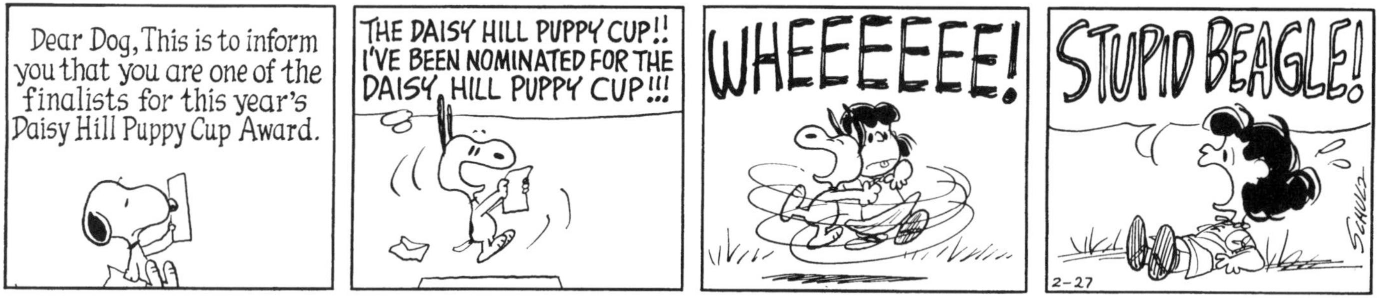
Dear Dog, This is to inform you that you are one of the finalists for this year's Daisy Hill Puppy Cup Award.
THE DAISY HILL PUPPY CUP!! I'VE BEEN NOMINATED FOR THE DAISY HILL PUPPY CUP!!!
WHEEEEEEE!
STUPID BEAGLE!
2-27
SCHULZ

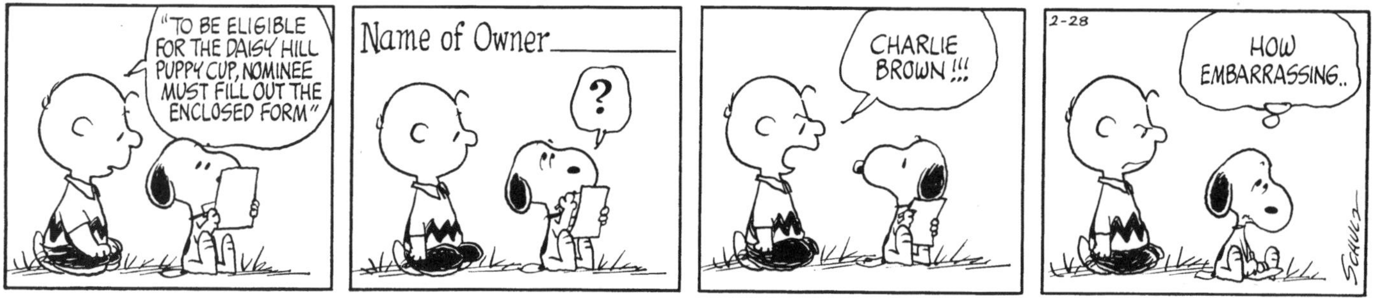
"TO BE ELIGIBLE FOR THE DAISY HILL PUPPY CUP, NOMINEE MUST FILL OUT THE ENCLOSED FORM"
Name of Owner
?
CHARLIE BROWN!!!
2-28
HOW EMBARRASSING..
SCHULZ

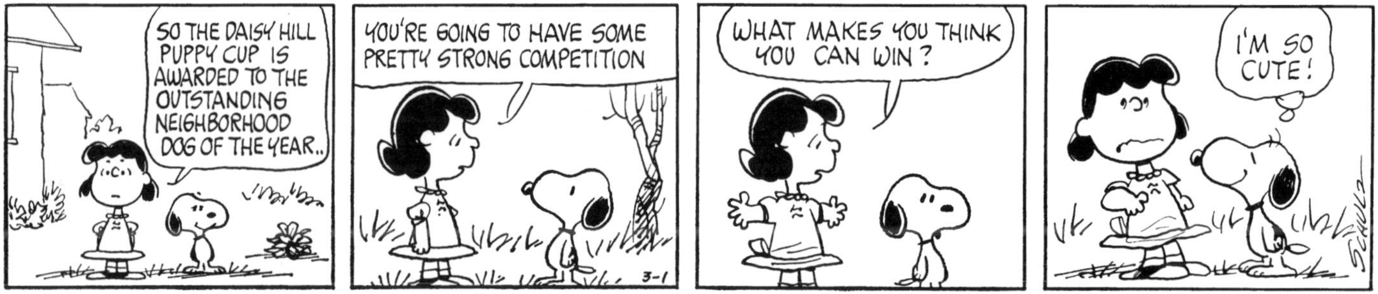
SO THE DAISY HILL PUPPY CUP IS AWARDED TO THE OUTSTANDING NEIGHBORHOOD DOG OF THE YEAR..
YOU'RE GOING TO HAVE SOME PRETTY STRONG COMPETITION
3-1
WHAT MAKES YOU THINK YOU CAN WIN?
I'M SO CUTE!

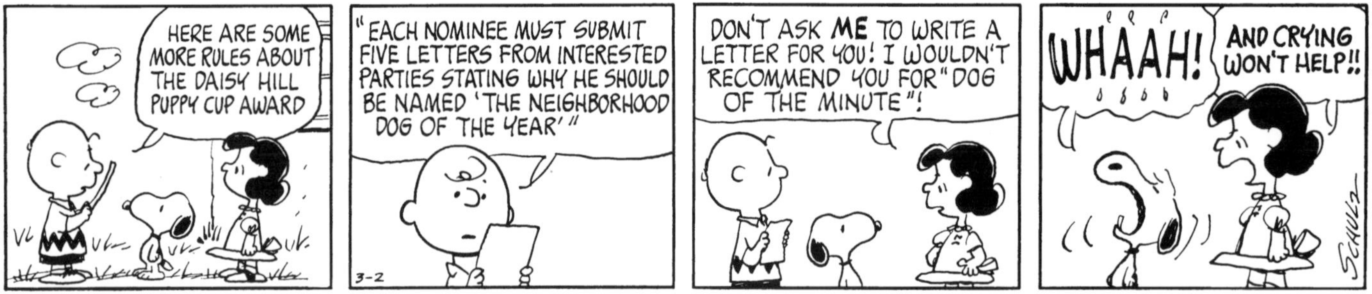
HERE ARE SOME MORE RULES ABOUT THE DAISY HILL PUPPY CUP AWARD
"EACH NOMINEE MUST SUBMIT FIVE LETTERS FROM INTERESTED PARTIES STATING WHY HE SHOULD BE NAMED 'THE NEIGHBORHOOD DOG OF THE YEAR'"
3-2
DON'T ASK **ME** TO WRITE A LETTER FOR YOU! I WOULDN'T RECOMMEND YOU FOR "DOG OF THE MINUTE"!
WHAAH!
AND CRYING WON'T HELP!!

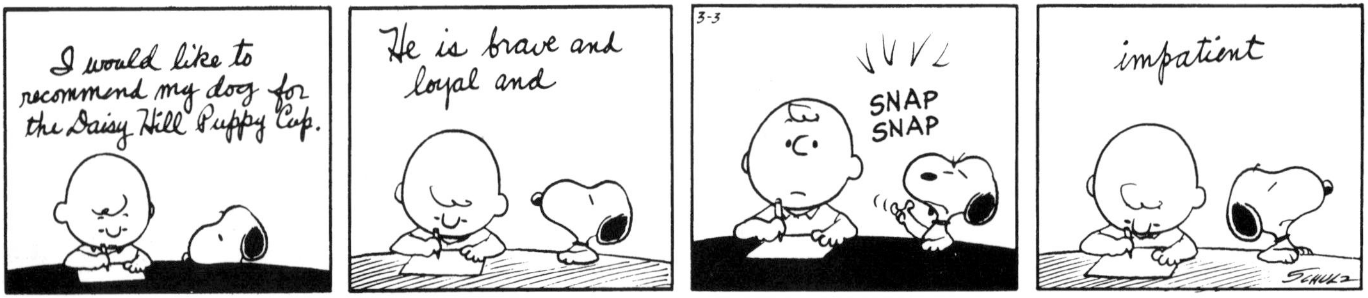
I would like to recommend my dog for the Daisy Hill Puppy Cup.
He is brave and loyal and
3-3
SNAP SNAP
impatient

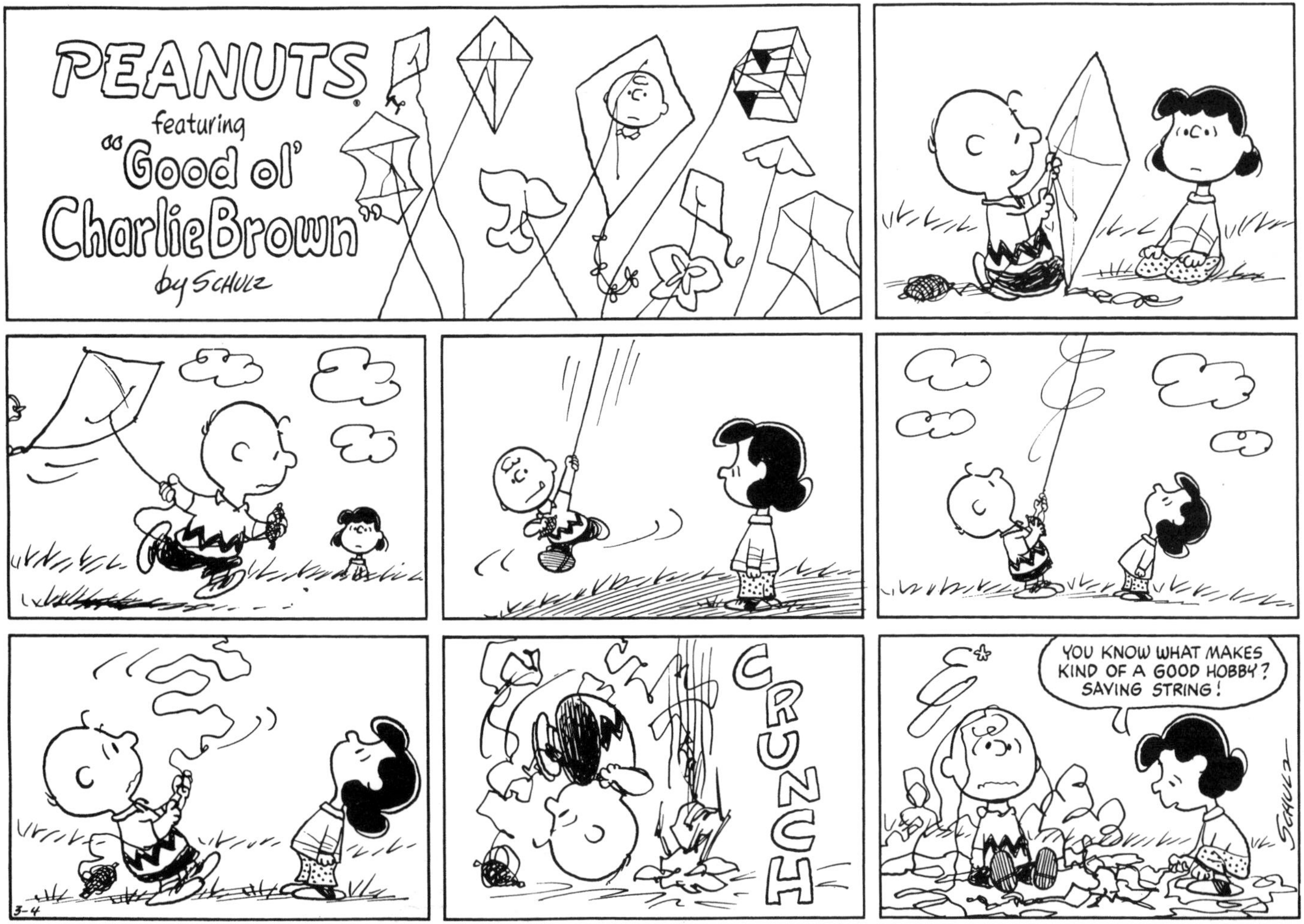
PEANUTS
featuring "Good ol' CharlieBrown"
by SCHULZ
CRUNCH
YOU KNOW WHAT MAKES KIND OF A GOOD HOBBY? SAVING STRING!
SCHULZ
3-4

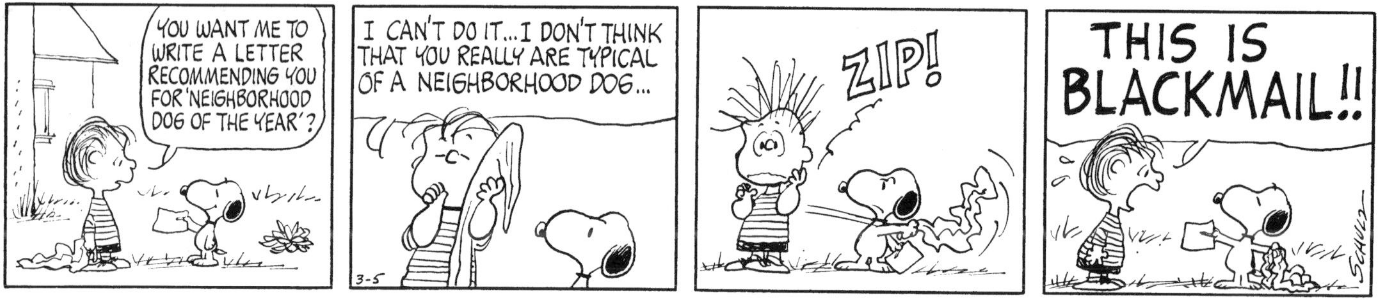
YOU WANT ME TO WRITE A LETTER RECOMMENDING YOU FOR 'NEIGHBORHOOD DOG OF THE YEAR'?
I CAN'T DO IT...I DON'T THINK THAT YOU REALLY ARE TYPICAL OF A NEIGHBORHOOD DOG...
3-5
ZIP!
THIS IS BLACKMAIL!!

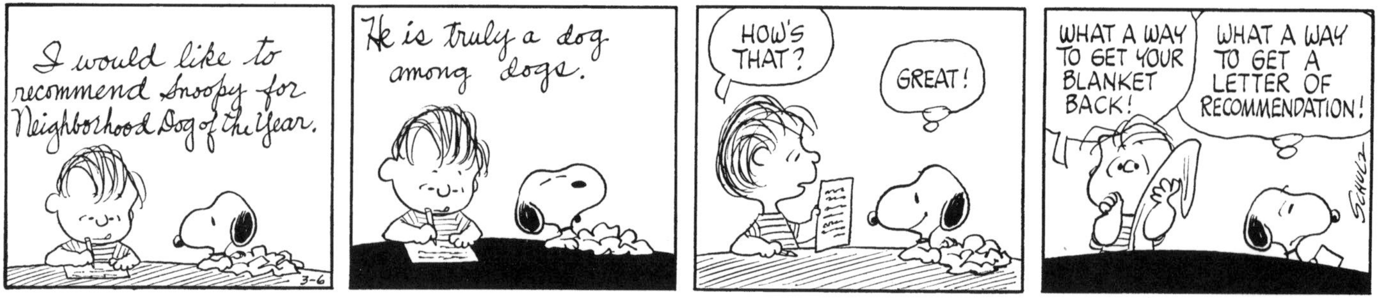
I would like to recommend Snoopy for Neighborhood Dog of the Year.
3-6
He is truly a dog among dogs.
HOW'S THAT?
GREAT!
WHAT A WAY TO GET YOUR BLANKET BACK!
WHAT A WAY TO GET A LETTER OF RECOMMENDATION!

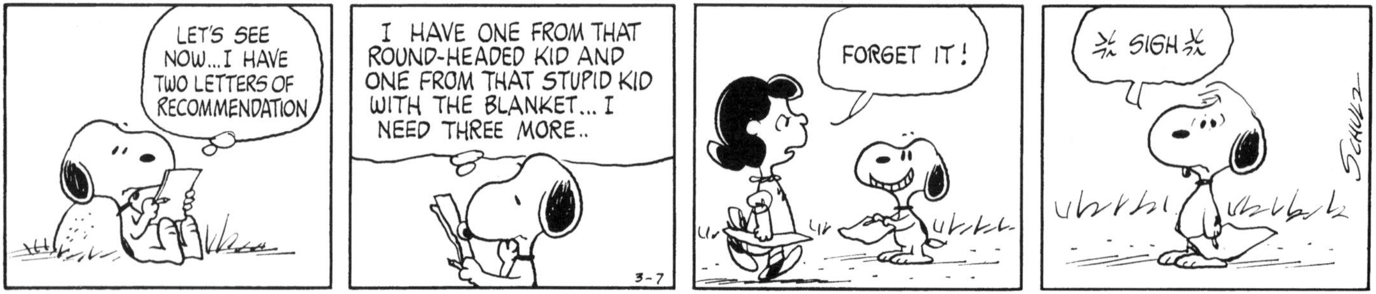
LET'S SEE NOW...I HAVE TWO LETTERS OF RECOMMENDATION
I HAVE ONE FROM THAT ROUND-HEADED KID AND ONE FROM THAT STUPID KID WITH THE BLANKET... I NEED THREE MORE..
3-7
FORGET IT!
SIGH

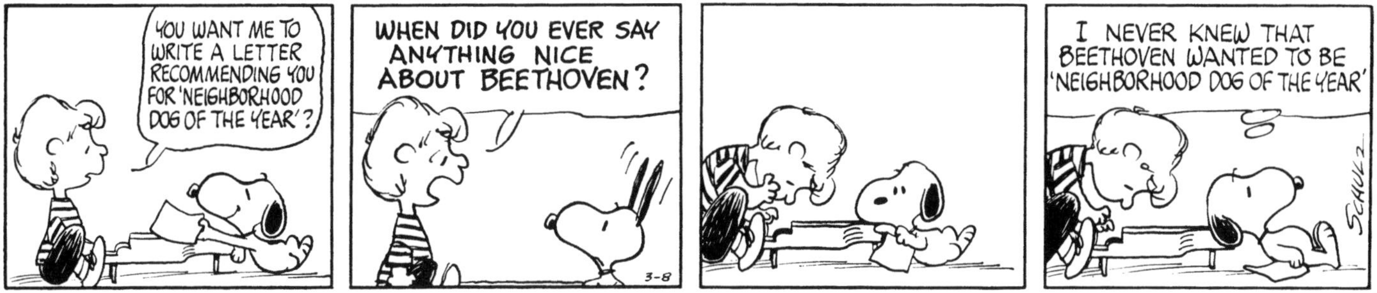

YOU WANT ME TO WRITE A LETTER RECOMMENDING YOU FOR 'NEIGHBORHOOD DOG OF THE YEAR'?
WHEN DID YOU EVER SAY ANYTHING NICE ABOUT BEETHOVEN?
3-8
I NEVER KNEW THAT BEETHOVEN WANTED TO BE 'NEIGHBORHOOD DOG OF THE YEAR'
SCHULZ

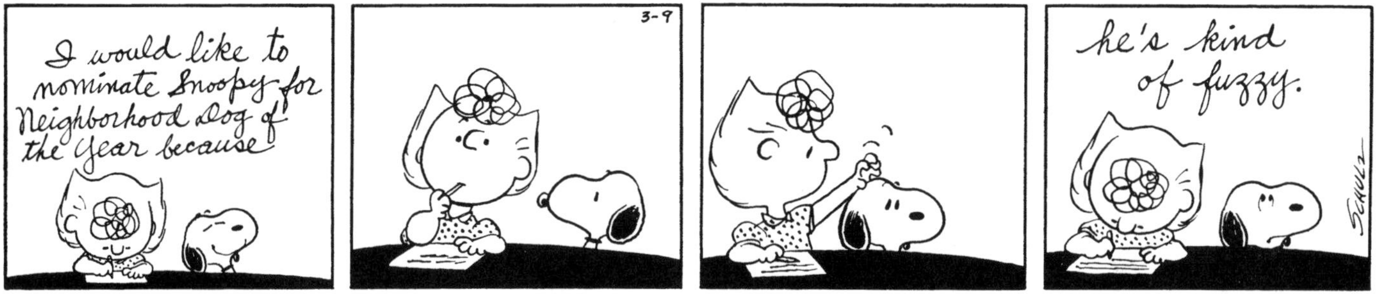

I would like to nominate Snoopy for Neighborhood Dog of the Year because
3-9
he's kind of fuzzy.
SCHULZ

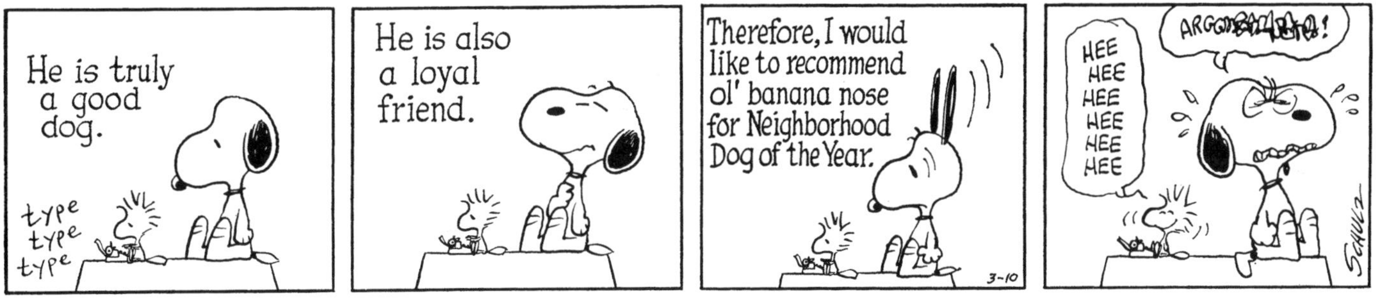

He is truly a good dog.
type type type
He is also a loyal friend.
Therefore, I would like to recommend ol' banana nose for Neighborhood Dog of the Year.
3-10
HEE HEE HEE HEE HEE HEE
SCHULZ

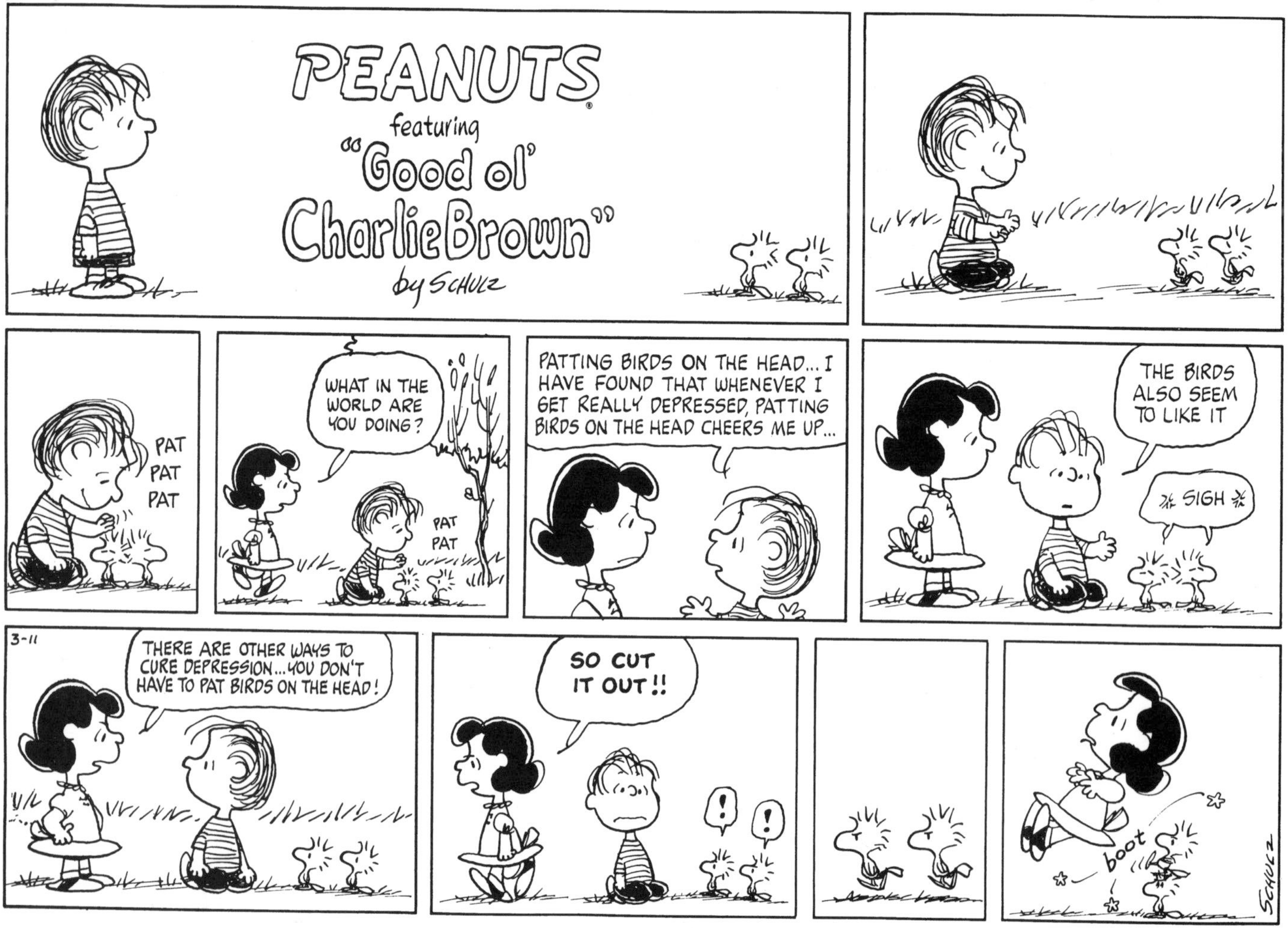
PEANUTS
featuring
"Good ol' CharlieBrown"
by SCHULZ
PAT PAT PAT
WHAT IN THE WORLD ARE YOU DOING?
PAT PAT
PATTING BIRDS ON THE HEAD... I HAVE FOUND THAT WHENEVER I GET REALLY DEPRESSED, PATTING BIRDS ON THE HEAD CHEERS ME UP...
THE BIRDS ALSO SEEM TO LIKE IT
SIGH
3-11
THERE ARE OTHER WAYS TO CURE DEPRESSION...YOU DON'T HAVE TO PAT BIRDS ON THE HEAD!
SO CUT IT OUT!!
!
!
boot
SCHULZ

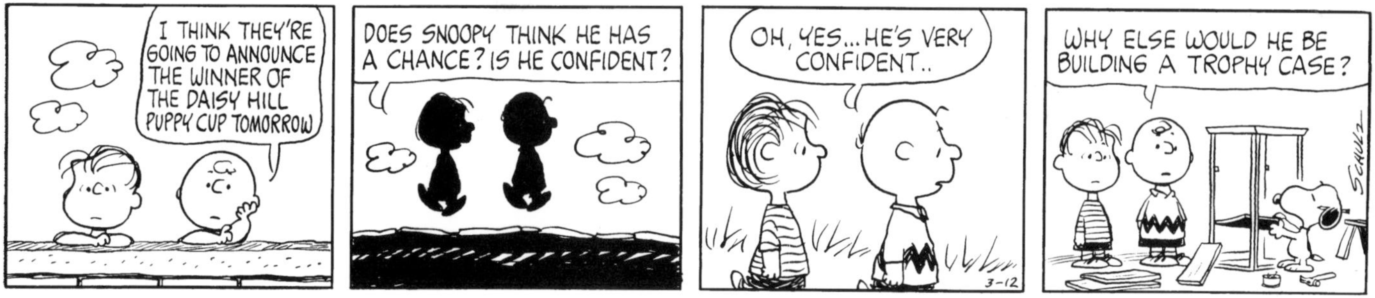
I THINK THEY'RE GOING TO ANNOUNCE THE WINNER OF THE DAISY HILL PUPPY CUP TOMORROW
DOES SNOOPY THINK HE HAS A CHANCE? IS HE CONFIDENT?
OH, YES... HE'S VERY CONFIDENT..
3-12
WHY ELSE WOULD HE BE BUILDING A TROPHY CASE?
SCHULZ

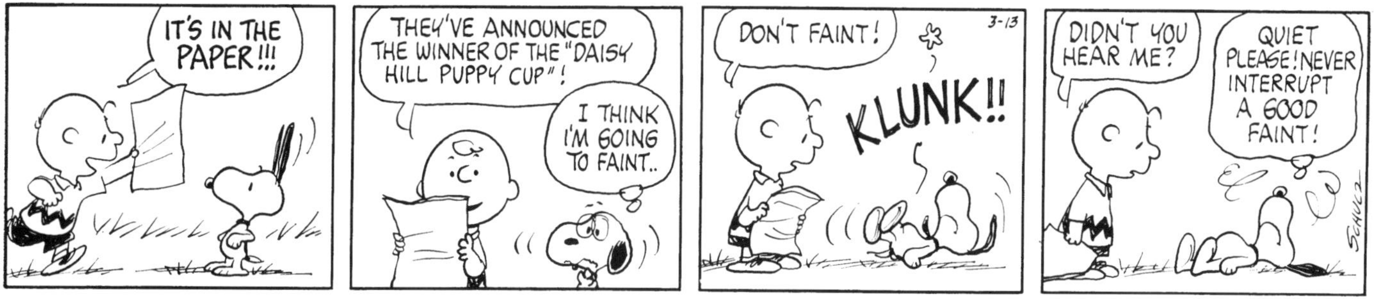
IT'S IN THE PAPER!!!
THEY'VE ANNOUNCED THE WINNER OF THE "DAISY HILL PUPPY CUP"!
I THINK I'M GOING TO FAINT..
DON'T FAINT!
3-13
KLUNK!!
DIDN'T YOU HEAR ME?
QUIET PLEASE! NEVER INTERRUPT A GOOD FAINT!
SCHULZ

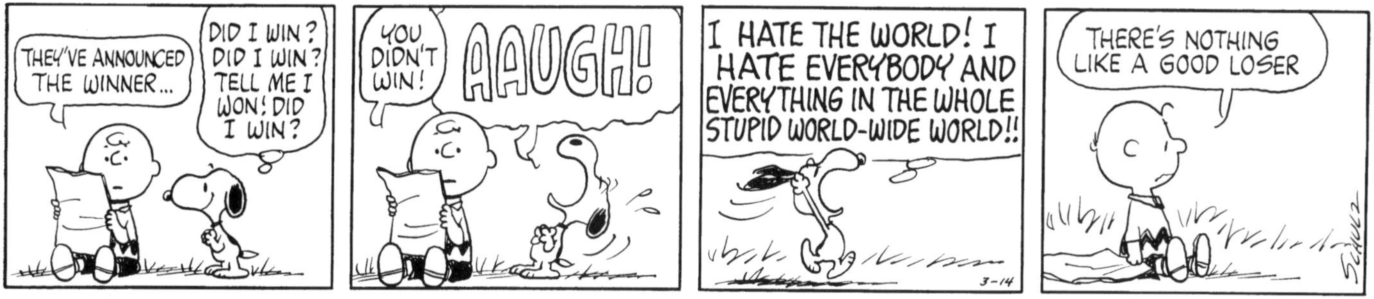
THEY'VE ANNOUNCED THE WINNER...
DID I WIN? DID I WIN? TELL ME I WON! DID I WIN?
YOU DIDN'T WIN!
AAUGH!
I HATE THE WORLD! I HATE EVERYBODY AND EVERYTHING IN THE WHOLE STUPID WORLD-WIDE WORLD!!
3-14
THERE'S NOTHING LIKE A GOOD LOSER
SCHULZ

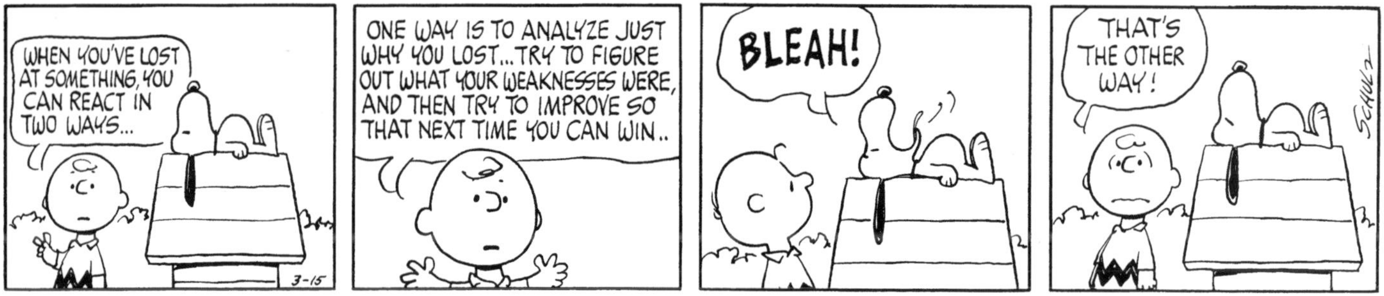
WHEN YOU'VE LOST AT SOMETHING, YOU CAN REACT IN TWO WAYS...
3-15
ONE WAY IS TO ANALYZE JUST WHY YOU LOST...TRY TO FIGURE OUT WHAT YOUR WEAKNESSES WERE, AND THEN TRY TO IMPROVE SO THAT NEXT TIME YOU CAN WIN..
BLEAH!
THAT'S THE OTHER WAY!
SCHULZ

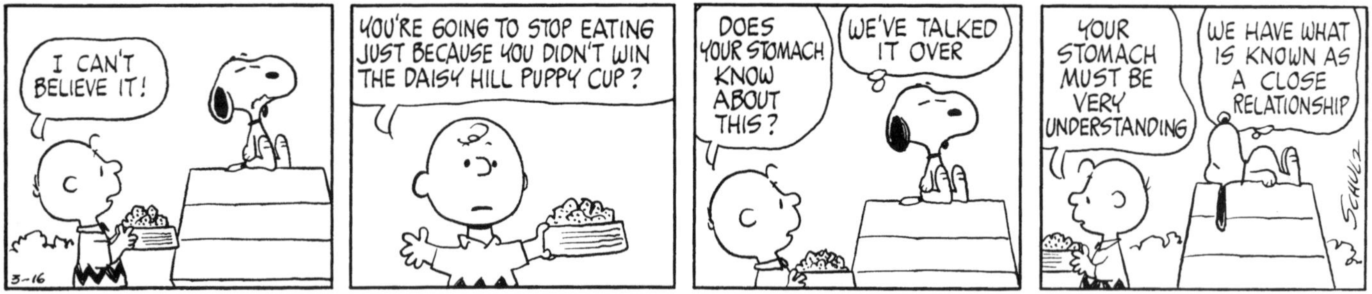
I CAN'T BELIEVE IT!
3-16
YOU'RE GOING TO STOP EATING JUST BECAUSE YOU DIDN'T WIN THE DAISY HILL PUPPY CUP?
DOES YOUR STOMACH KNOW ABOUT THIS?
WE'VE TALKED IT OVER
YOUR STOMACH MUST BE VERY UNDERSTANDING
WE HAVE WHAT IS KNOWN AS A CLOSE RELATIONSHIP
SCHULZ

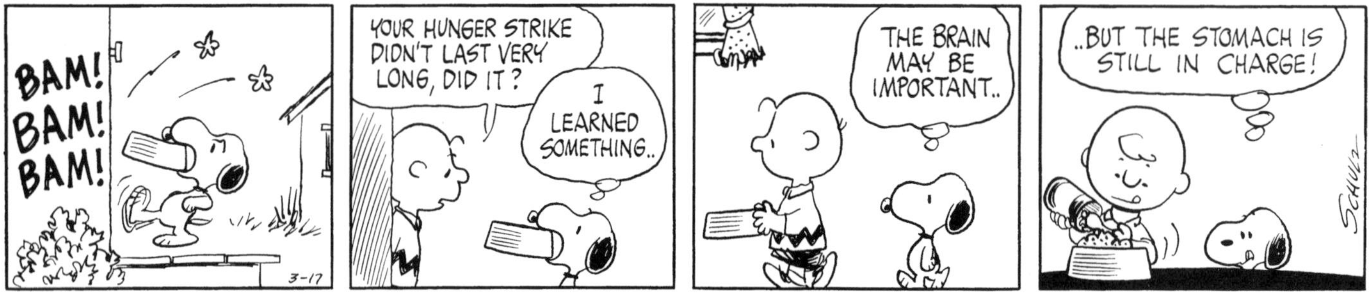
BAM! BAM! BAM!
3-17
YOUR HUNGER STRIKE DIDN'T LAST VERY LONG, DID IT?
I LEARNED SOMETHING..
THE BRAIN MAY BE IMPORTANT..
..BUT THE STOMACH IS STILL IN CHARGE!
SCHULZ

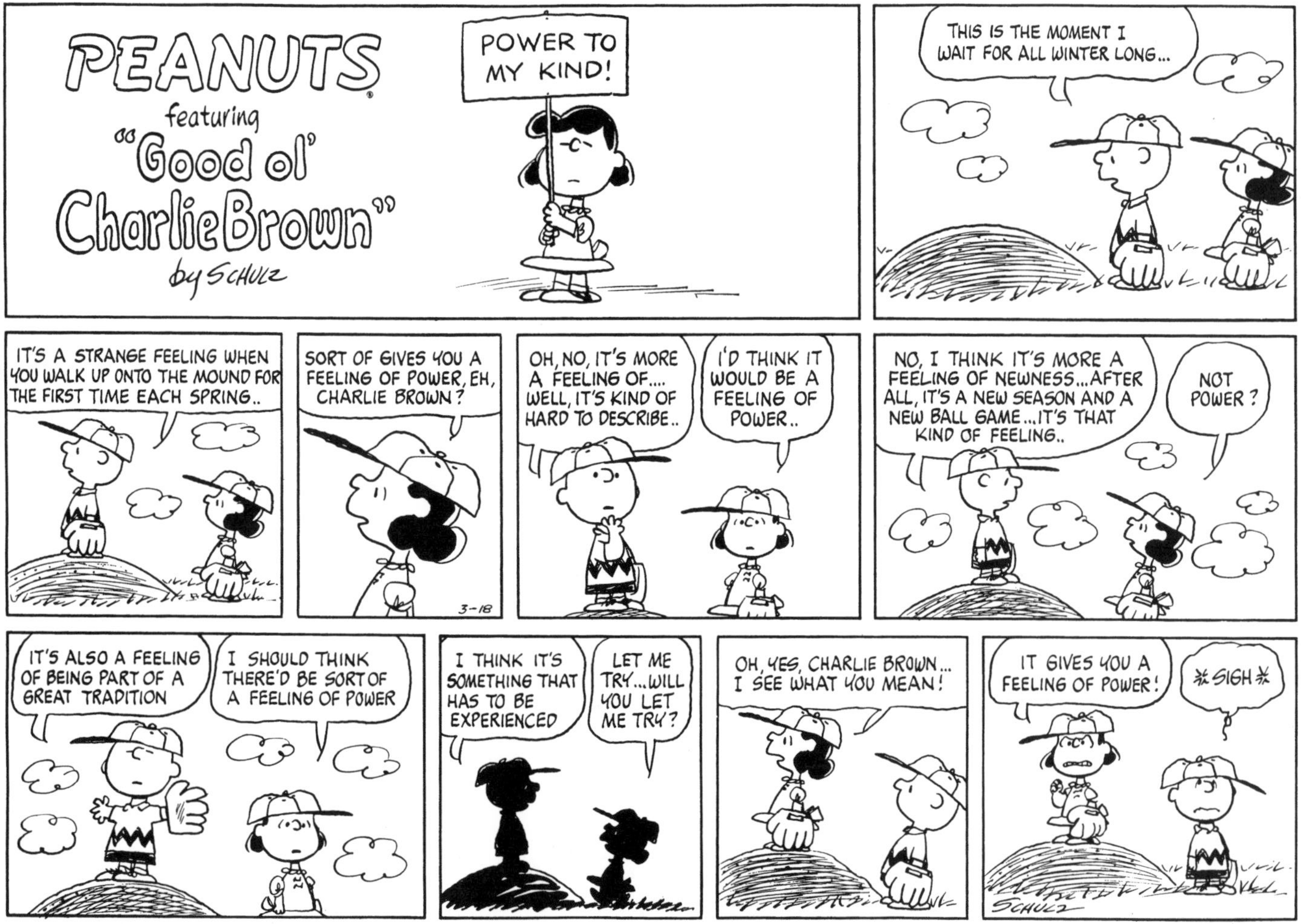
PEANUTS
featuring "Good ol' Charlie Brown"
by SCHULZ
POWER TO MY KIND!
THIS IS THE MOMENT I WAIT FOR ALL WINTER LONG...
IT'S A STRANGE FEELING WHEN YOU WALK UP ONTO THE MOUND FOR THE FIRST TIME EACH SPRING..
SORT OF GIVES YOU A FEELING OF POWER, EH, CHARLIE BROWN?
3-18
OH, NO, IT'S MORE A FEELING OF.... WELL, IT'S KIND OF HARD TO DESCRIBE..
I'D THINK IT WOULD BE A FEELING OF POWER..
NO, I THINK IT'S MORE A FEELING OF NEWNESS...AFTER ALL, IT'S A NEW SEASON AND A NEW BALL GAME...IT'S THAT KIND OF FEELING..
NOT POWER?
IT'S ALSO A FEELING OF BEING PART OF A GREAT TRADITION
I SHOULD THINK THERE'D BE SORT OF A FEELING OF POWER
I THINK IT'S SOMETHING THAT HAS TO BE EXPERIENCED
LET ME TRY...WILL YOU LET ME TRY?
OH, YES, CHARLIE BROWN... I SEE WHAT YOU MEAN!
IT GIVES YOU A FEELING OF POWER!
SIGH
SCHULZ

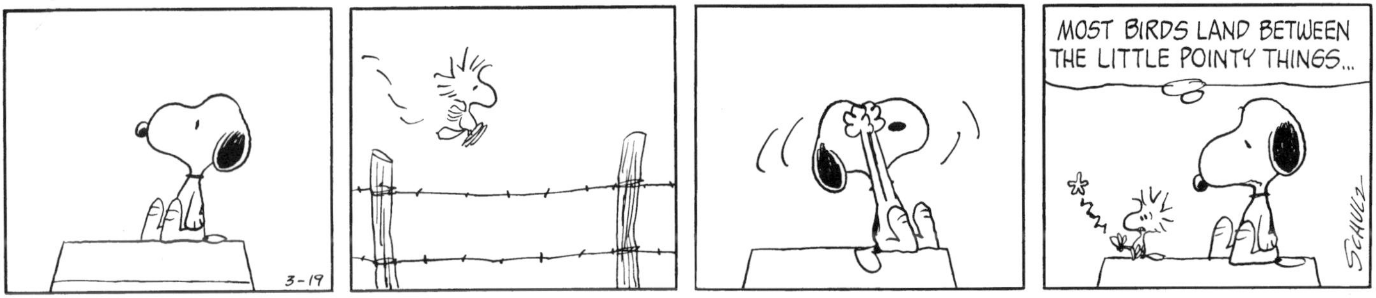
MOST BIRDS LAND BETWEEN THE LITTLE POINTY THINGS...

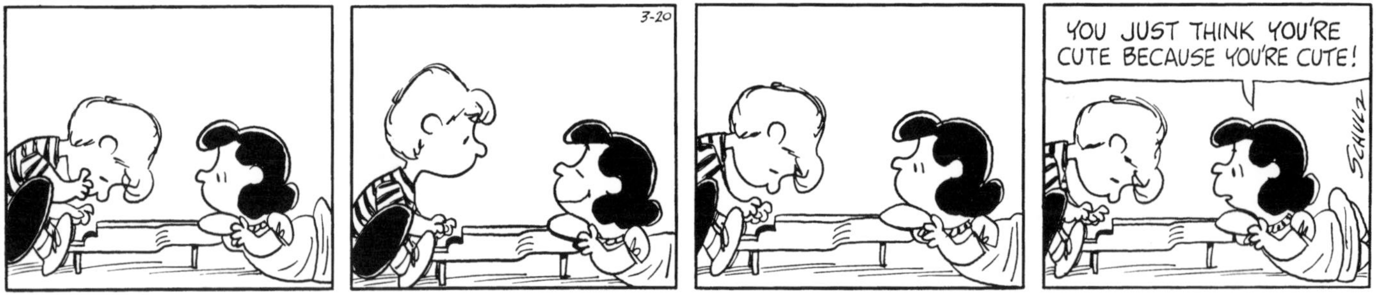
YOU JUST THINK YOU'RE CUTE BECAUSE YOU'RE CUTE!

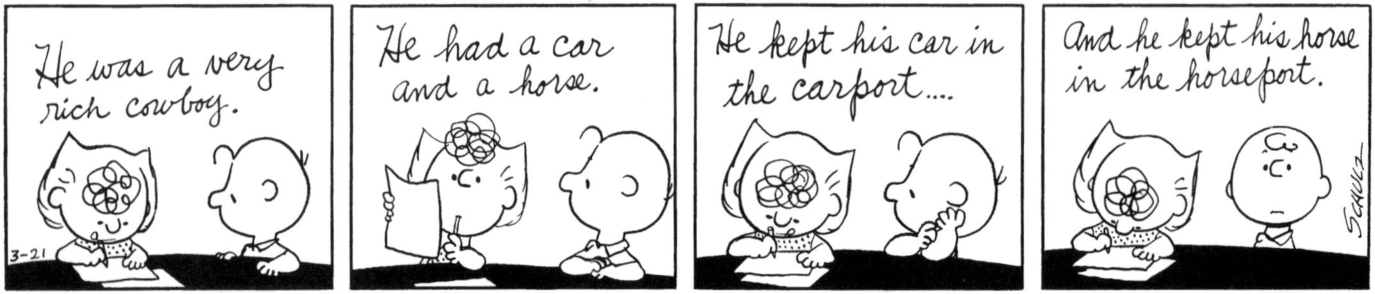
He was a very rich cowboy.
He had a car and a horse.
He kept his car in the carport....
And he kept his horse in the horseport.

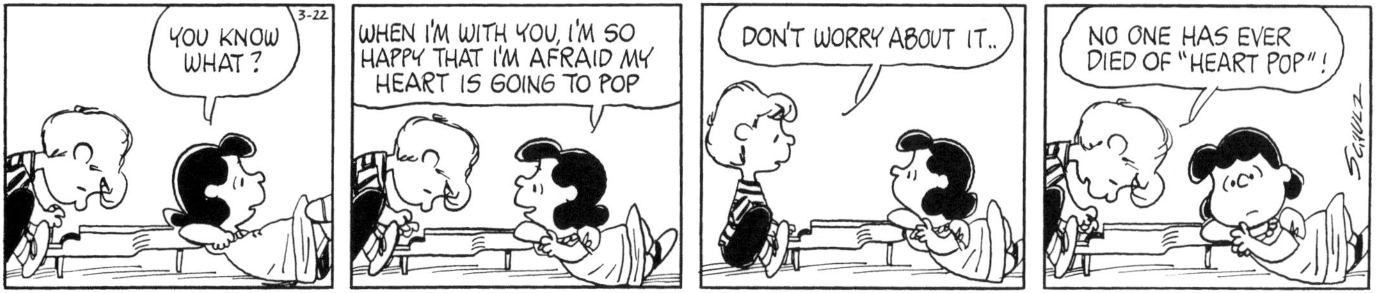
3-22
YOU KNOW WHAT?
WHEN I'M WITH YOU, I'M SO HAPPY THAT I'M AFRAID MY HEART IS GOING TO POP
DON'T WORRY ABOUT IT..
NO ONE HAS EVER DIED OF "HEART POP"!
SCHULZ

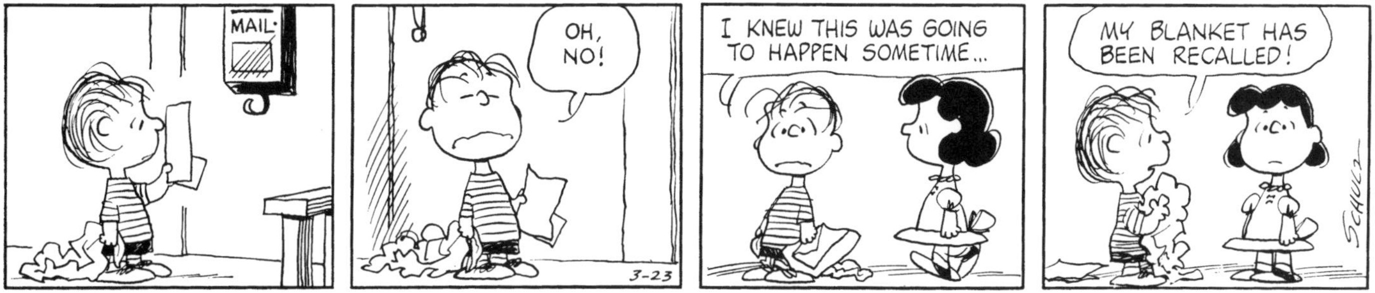
MAIL
OH, NO!
3-23
I KNEW THIS WAS GOING TO HAPPEN SOMETIME...
MY BLANKET HAS BEEN RECALLED!
SCHULZ

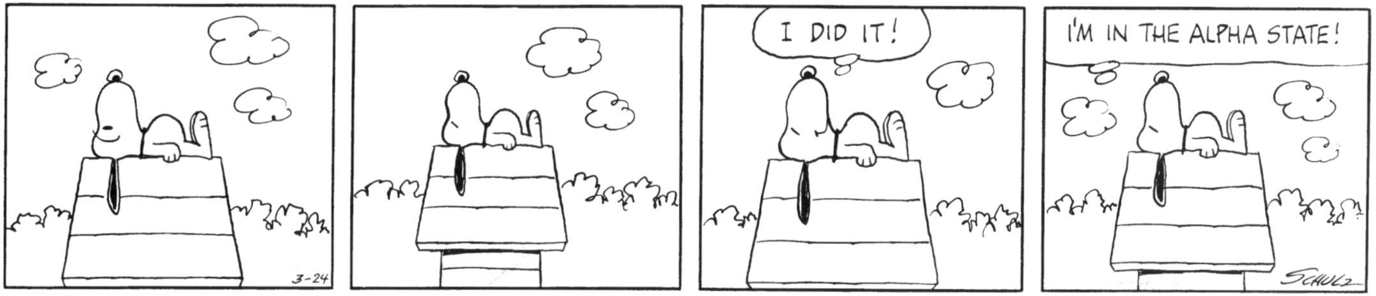
3-24
I DID IT!
I'M IN THE ALPHA STATE!
SCHULZ

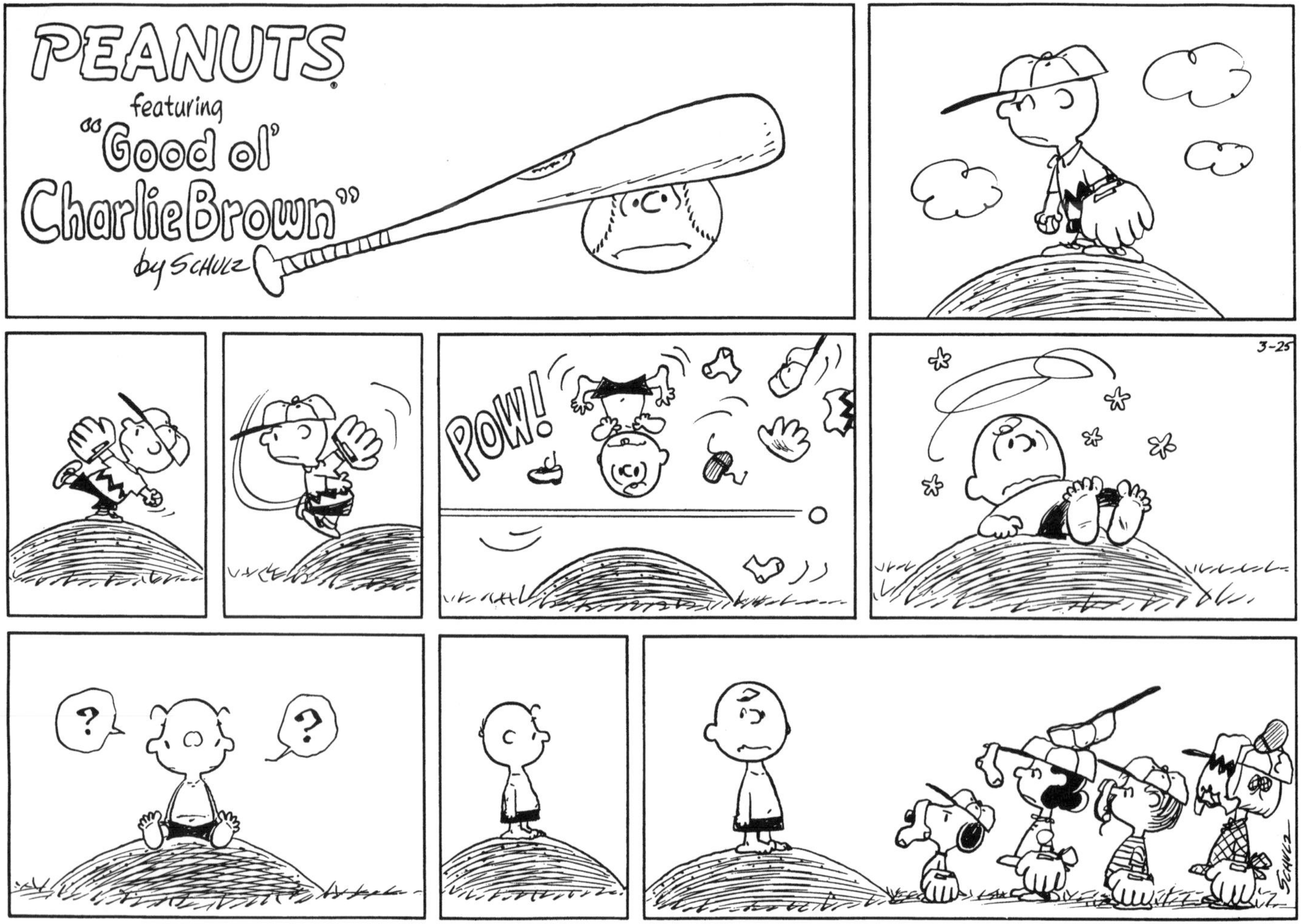

PEANUTS
featuring
"Good ol' CharlieBrown"
by SCHULZ
POW!
3-25
?
?
SCHULZ

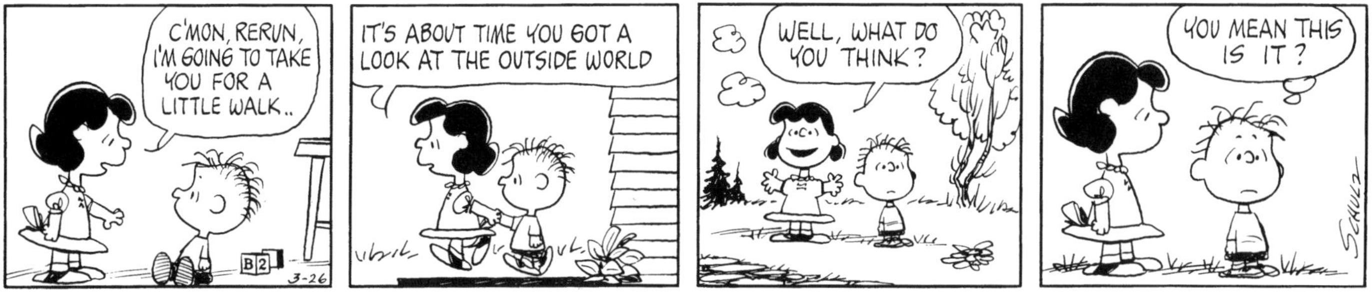
C'MON, RERUN, I'M GOING TO TAKE YOU FOR A LITTLE WALK..
3-26
IT'S ABOUT TIME YOU GOT A LOOK AT THE OUTSIDE WORLD
WELL, WHAT DO YOU THINK?
YOU MEAN THIS IS IT?

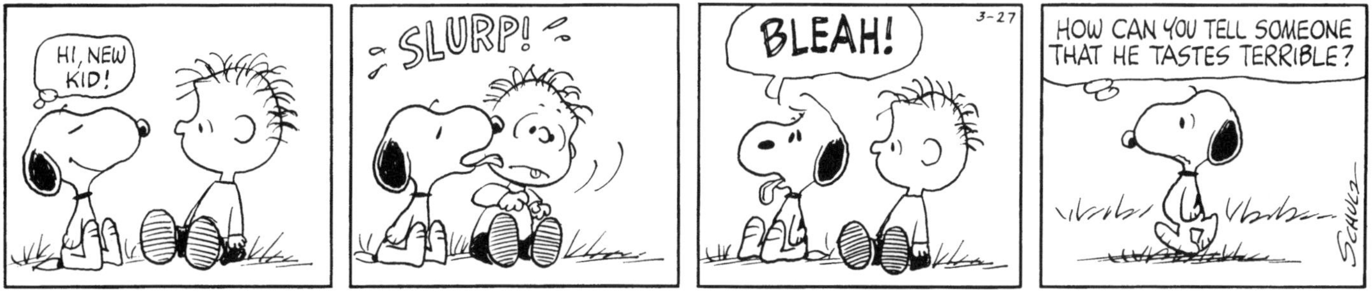
HI, NEW KID!
SLURP!
BLEAH!
3-27
HOW CAN YOU TELL SOMEONE THAT HE TASTES TERRIBLE?

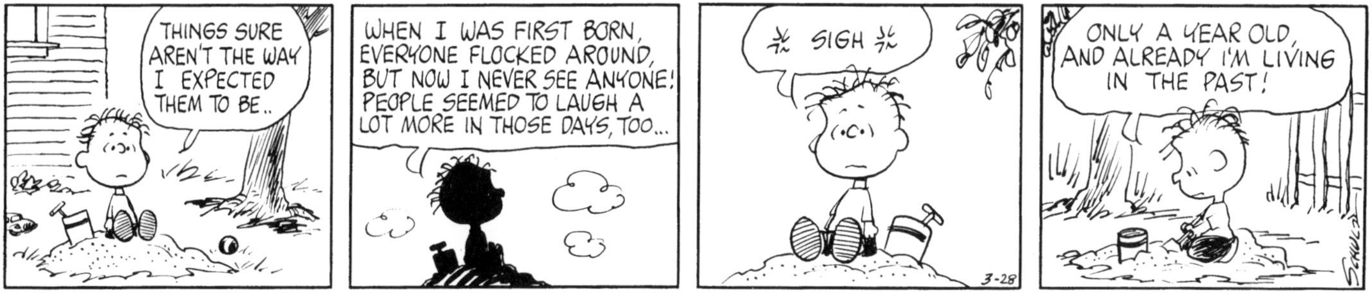
THINGS SURE AREN'T THE WAY I EXPECTED THEM TO BE..
WHEN I WAS FIRST BORN, EVERYONE FLOCKED AROUND, BUT NOW I NEVER SEE ANYONE! PEOPLE SEEMED TO LAUGH A LOT MORE IN THOSE DAYS, TOO...
SIGH
3-28
ONLY A YEAR OLD, AND ALREADY I'M LIVING IN THE PAST!

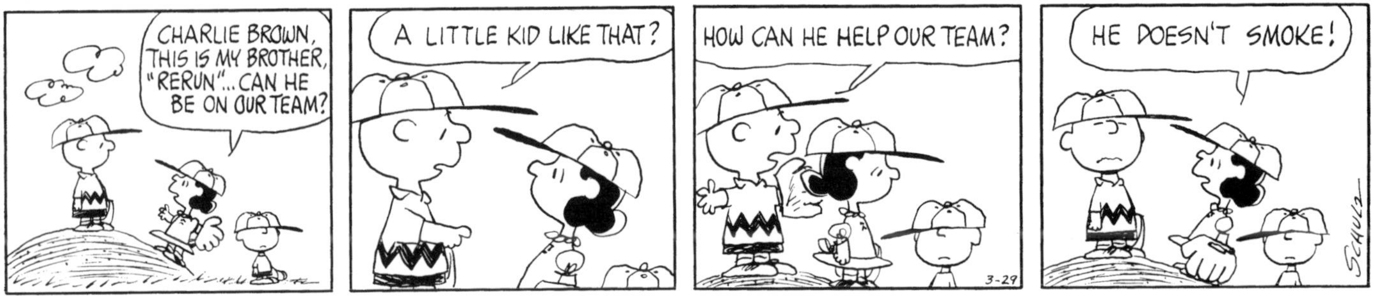

CHARLIE BROWN, THIS IS MY BROTHER, "RERUN"... CAN HE BE ON OUR TEAM?
A LITTLE KID LIKE THAT?
HOW CAN HE HELP OUR TEAM?
3-29
HE DOESN'T SMOKE!
SCHULZ

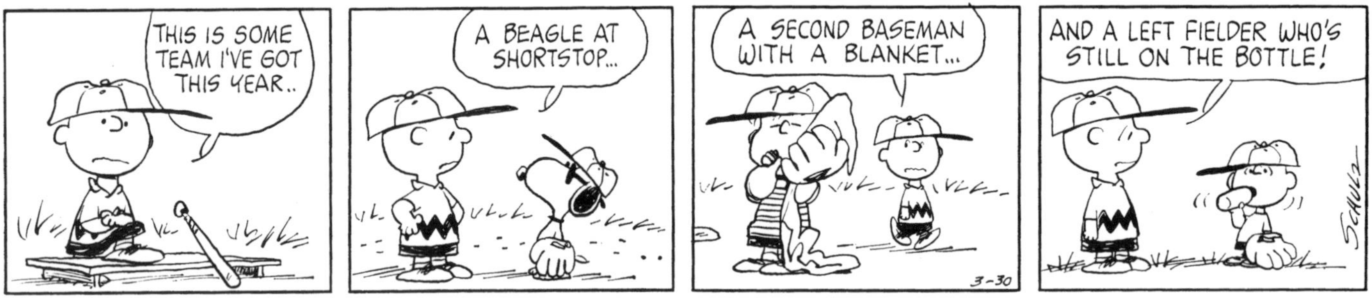

THIS IS SOME TEAM I'VE GOT THIS YEAR..
A BEAGLE AT SHORTSTOP...
A SECOND BASEMAN WITH A BLANKET...
3-30
AND A LEFT FIELDER WHO'S STILL ON THE BOTTLE!
SCHULZ

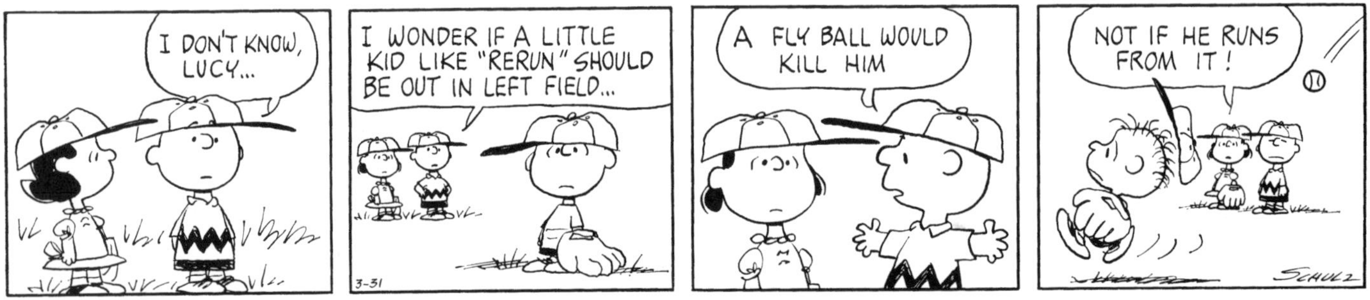

I DON'T KNOW, LUCY...
I WONDER IF A LITTLE KID LIKE "RERUN" SHOULD BE OUT IN LEFT FIELD...
3-31
A FLY BALL WOULD KILL HIM
NOT IF HE RUNS FROM IT!
SCHULZ

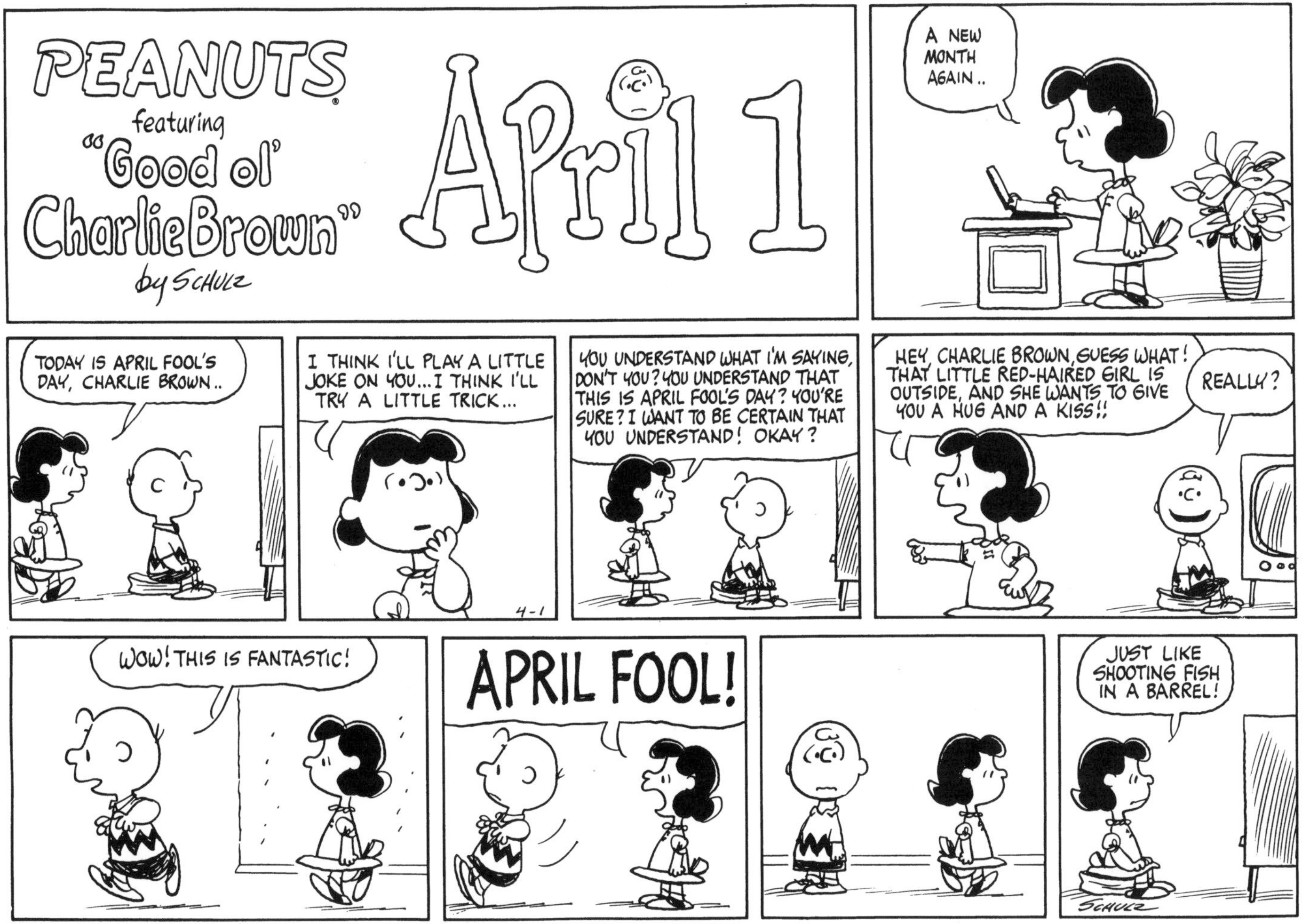
PEANUTS
featuring "Good ol' Charlie Brown"
by SCHULZ
April 1
A NEW MONTH AGAIN..
TODAY IS APRIL FOOL'S DAY, CHARLIE BROWN..
I THINK I'LL PLAY A LITTLE JOKE ON YOU...I THINK I'LL TRY A LITTLE TRICK...
4-1
YOU UNDERSTAND WHAT I'M SAYING, DON'T YOU? YOU UNDERSTAND THAT THIS IS APRIL FOOL'S DAY? YOU'RE SURE? I WANT TO BE CERTAIN THAT YOU UNDERSTAND! OKAY?
HEY, CHARLIE BROWN, GUESS WHAT! THAT LITTLE RED-HAIRED GIRL IS OUTSIDE, AND SHE WANTS TO GIVE YOU A HUG AND A KISS!!
REALLY?
WOW! THIS IS FANTASTIC!
APRIL FOOL!
JUST LIKE SHOOTING FISH IN A BARREL!
SCHULZ

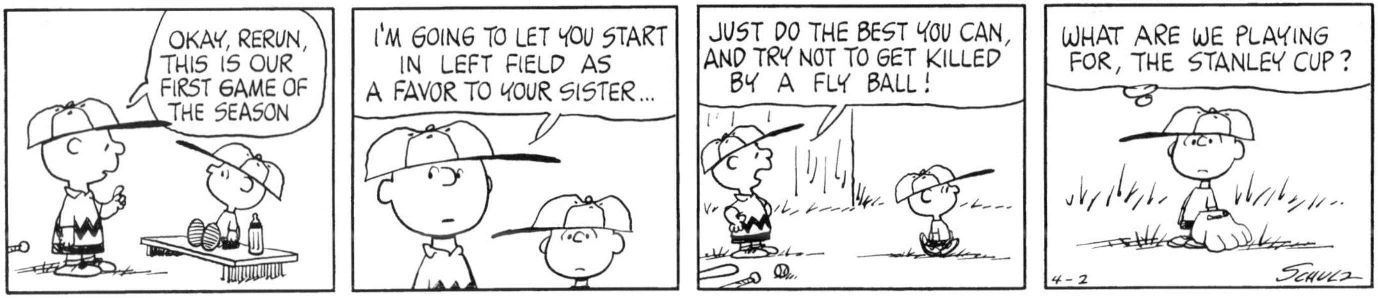
OKAY, RERUN, THIS IS OUR FIRST GAME OF THE SEASON
I'M GOING TO LET YOU START IN LEFT FIELD AS A FAVOR TO YOUR SISTER...
JUST DO THE BEST YOU CAN, AND TRY NOT TO GET KILLED BY A FLY BALL!
WHAT ARE WE PLAYING FOR, THE STANLEY CUP?
4-2
SCHULZ

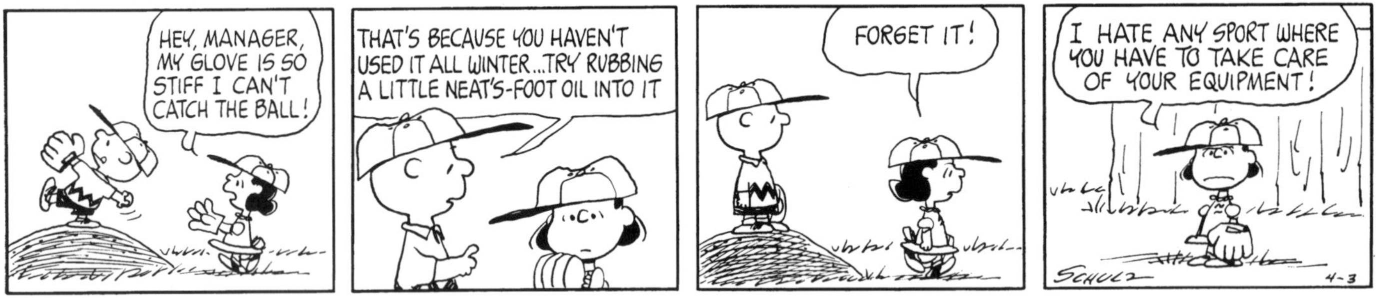
HEY, MANAGER, MY GLOVE IS SO STIFF I CAN'T CATCH THE BALL!
THAT'S BECAUSE YOU HAVEN'T USED IT ALL WINTER...TRY RUBBING A LITTLE NEAT'S-FOOT OIL INTO IT
FORGET IT!
I HATE ANY SPORT WHERE YOU HAVE TO TAKE CARE OF YOUR EQUIPMENT!
SCHULZ
4-3

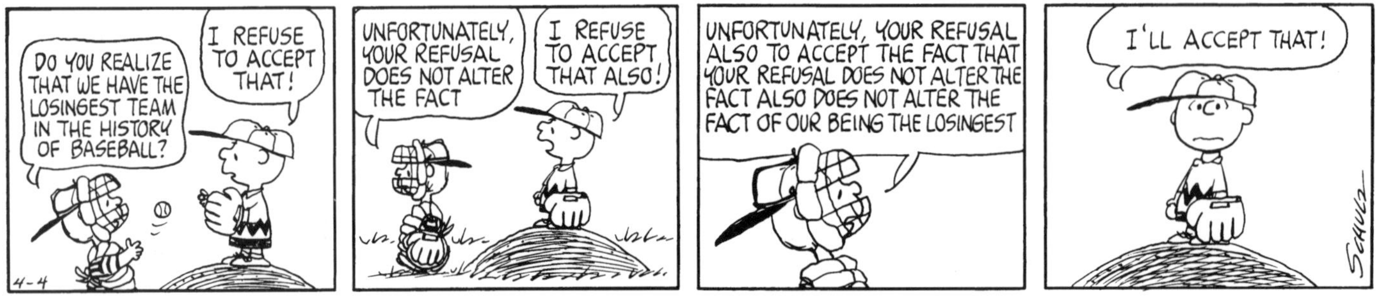
DO YOU REALIZE THAT WE HAVE THE LOSINGEST TEAM IN THE HISTORY OF BASEBALL?
I REFUSE TO ACCEPT THAT!
4-4
UNFORTUNATELY, YOUR REFUSAL DOES NOT ALTER THE FACT
I REFUSE TO ACCEPT THAT ALSO!
UNFORTUNATELY, YOUR REFUSAL ALSO TO ACCEPT THE FACT THAT YOUR REFUSAL DOES NOT ALTER THE FACT ALSO DOES NOT ALTER THE FACT OF OUR BEING THE LOSINGEST
I'LL ACCEPT THAT!
SCHULZ

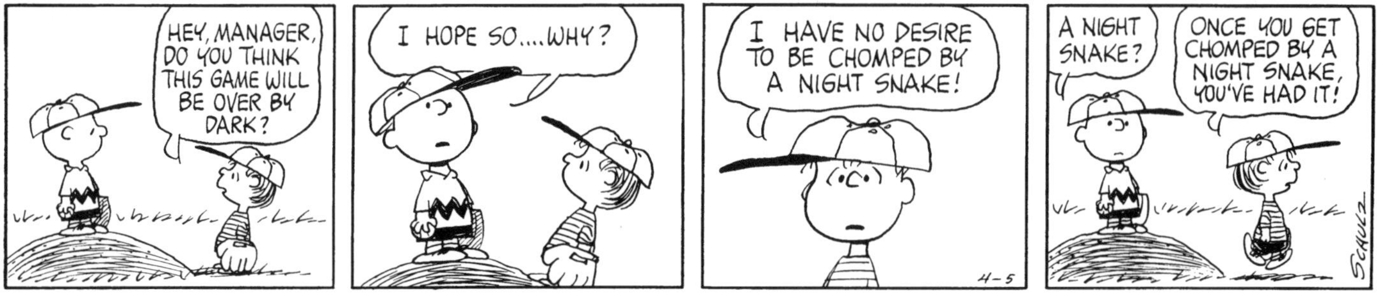
HEY, MANAGER, DO YOU THINK THIS GAME WILL BE OVER BY DARK?
I HOPE SO....WHY?
I HAVE NO DESIRE TO BE CHOMPED BY A NIGHT SNAKE!
4-5
A NIGHT SNAKE?
ONCE YOU GET CHOMPED BY A NIGHT SNAKE, YOU'VE HAD IT!

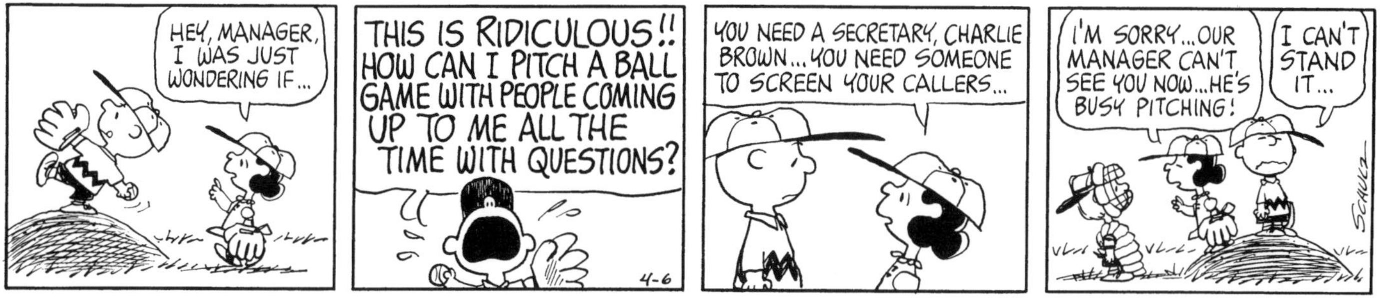
HEY, MANAGER, I WAS JUST WONDERING IF...
THIS IS RIDICULOUS!! HOW CAN I PITCH A BALL GAME WITH PEOPLE COMING UP TO ME ALL THE TIME WITH QUESTIONS?
4-6
YOU NEED A SECRETARY, CHARLIE BROWN... YOU NEED SOMEONE TO SCREEN YOUR CALLERS...
I'M SORRY...OUR MANAGER CAN'T SEE YOU NOW...HE'S BUSY PITCHING!
I CAN'T STAND IT...

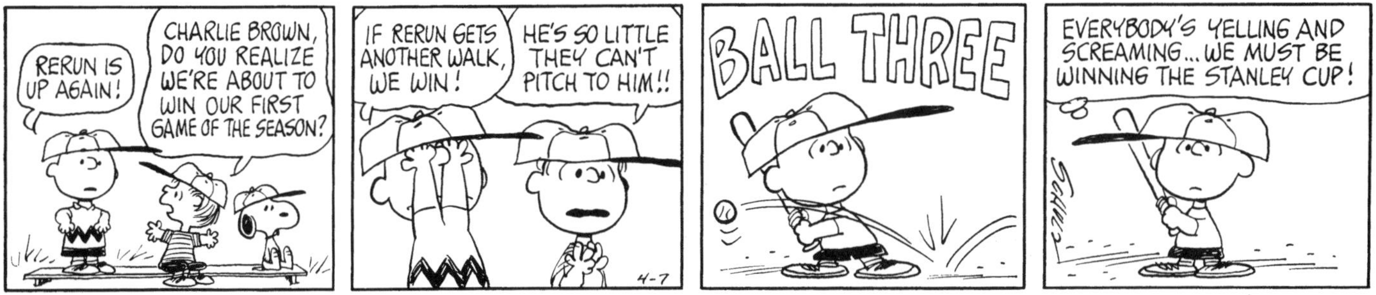
RERUN IS UP AGAIN!
CHARLIE BROWN, DO YOU REALIZE WE'RE ABOUT TO WIN OUR FIRST GAME OF THE SEASON?
IF RERUN GETS ANOTHER WALK, WE WIN!
HE'S SO LITTLE THEY CAN'T PITCH TO HIM!!
4-7
BALL THREE
EVERYBODY'S YELLING AND SCREAMING... WE MUST BE WINNING THE STANLEY CUP!

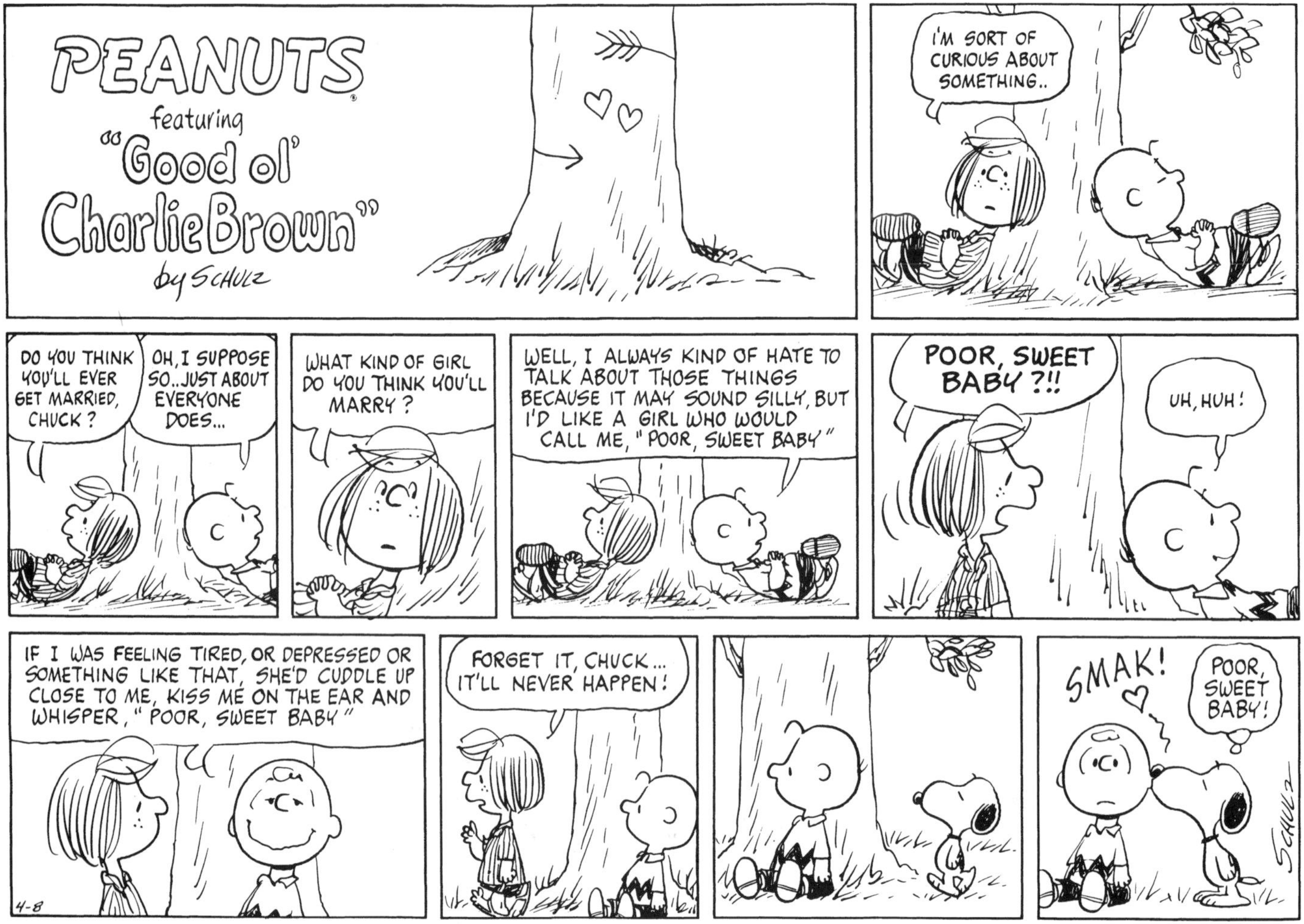
PEANUTS
featuring
"Good ol' Charlie Brown"
by SCHULZ
I'M SORT OF CURIOUS ABOUT SOMETHING..
DO YOU THINK YOU'LL EVER GET MARRIED, CHUCK?
OH, I SUPPOSE SO...JUST ABOUT EVERYONE DOES...
WHAT KIND OF GIRL DO YOU THINK YOU'LL MARRY?
WELL, I ALWAYS KIND OF HATE TO TALK ABOUT THOSE THINGS BECAUSE IT MAY SOUND SILLY, BUT I'D LIKE A GIRL WHO WOULD CALL ME, "POOR, SWEET BABY"
POOR, SWEET BABY?!!
UH, HUH!
IF I WAS FEELING TIRED, OR DEPRESSED OR SOMETHING LIKE THAT, SHE'D CUDDLE UP CLOSE TO ME, KISS ME ON THE EAR AND WHISPER, "POOR, SWEET BABY"
4-8
FORGET IT, CHUCK... IT'LL NEVER HAPPEN!
SMAK!
POOR, SWEET BABY!
SCHULZ

BALL FOUR!

WE WON! WE WON, CHARLIE BROWN!!

4-9

WE WON OUR FIRST GAME OF THE SEASON! WE FINALLY WON!! WE WON!! WE WON!!!

I THINK I'M GOING TO CRY...

WE **WON,** CHARLIE BROWN! C'MON, LET'S GO HOME, AND CELEBRATE!

NO! FIRST I HAVE TO WAIT FOR THE OPPOSING MANAGER TO COME OVER AND CONGRATULATE ME

4-10

EVERY YEAR I HAVE TO START THE SEASON BY GOING OVER AND CONGRATULATING THE OTHER MANAGER FOR BEATING US...THIS YEAR HE HAS TO COME TO **ME!** I'M GOING TO WAIT RIGHT HERE 'TIL HE COMES OVER AND CONGRATULATES ME...

WE WON OUR FIRST GAME OF THE SEASON... I CAN'T BELIEVE IT!

I WONDER HOW THE OTHER TEAM FEELS...

4-11

I DON'T KNOW...WHEN WE LOSE, I'M MISERABLE...WHEN WE WIN, I FEEL GUILTY!

1973

Page 43

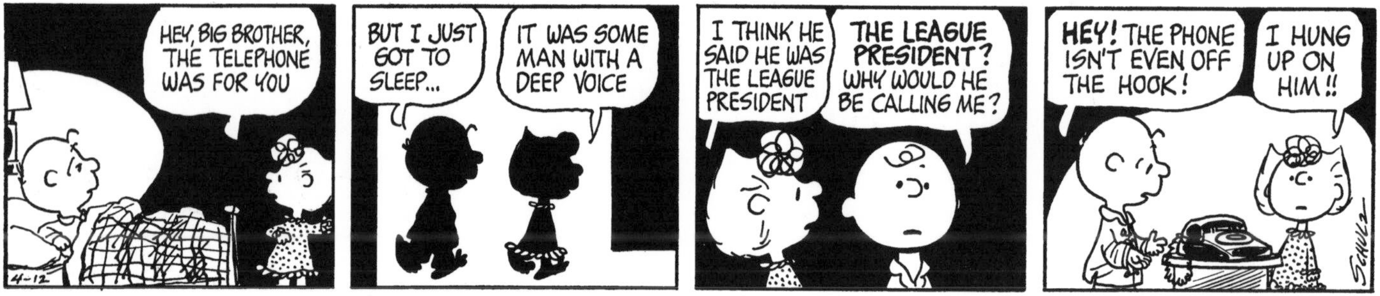
HEY, BIG BROTHER, THE TELEPHONE WAS FOR YOU
BUT I JUST GOT TO SLEEP...
IT WAS SOME MAN WITH A DEEP VOICE
I THINK HE SAID HE WAS THE LEAGUE PRESIDENT
THE LEAGUE PRESIDENT? WHY WOULD HE BE CALLING ME?
HEY! THE PHONE ISN'T EVEN OFF THE HOOK!
I HUNG UP ON HIM!!
SCHULZ
4-12

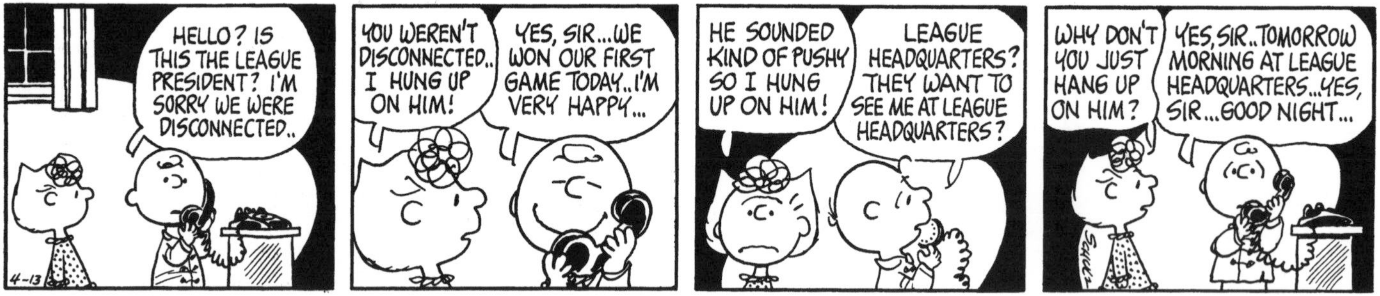
4-13
HELLO? IS THIS THE LEAGUE PRESIDENT? I'M SORRY WE WERE DISCONNECTED..
YOU WEREN'T DISCONNECTED.. I HUNG UP ON HIM!
YES, SIR...WE WON OUR FIRST GAME TODAY..I'M VERY HAPPY...
HE SOUNDED KIND OF PUSHY SO I HUNG UP ON HIM!
LEAGUE HEADQUARTERS? THEY WANT TO SEE ME AT LEAGUE HEADQUARTERS?
WHY DON'T YOU JUST HANG UP ON HIM?
YES, SIR..TOMORROW MORNING AT LEAGUE HEADQUARTERS...YES, SIR...GOOD NIGHT...
SCHULZ

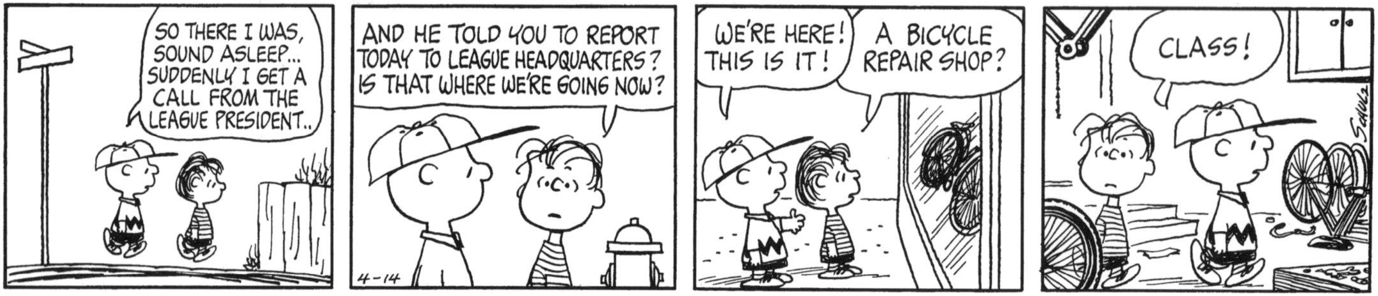
SO THERE I WAS, SOUND ASLEEP... SUDDENLY I GET A CALL FROM THE LEAGUE PRESIDENT..
AND HE TOLD YOU TO REPORT TODAY TO LEAGUE HEADQUARTERS? IS THAT WHERE WE'RE GOING NOW?
4-14
WE'RE HERE! THIS IS IT!
A BICYCLE REPAIR SHOP?
CLASS!
SCHULZ

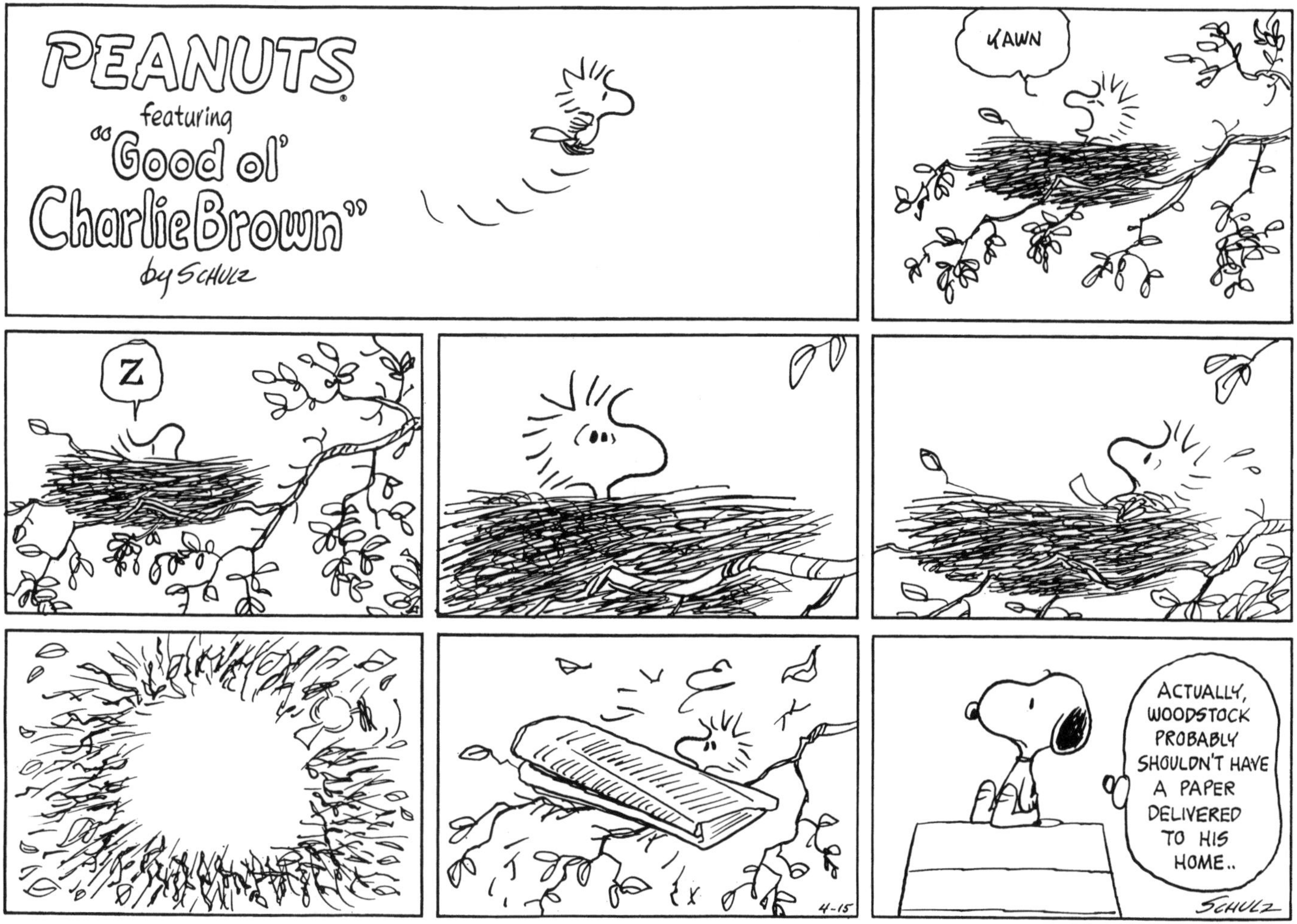
PEANUTS
featuring
"Good ol' Charlie Brown"
by SCHULZ
YAWN
Z
ACTUALLY, WOODSTOCK PROBABLY SHOULDN'T HAVE A PAPER DELIVERED TO HIS HOME..
4-15
SCHULZ

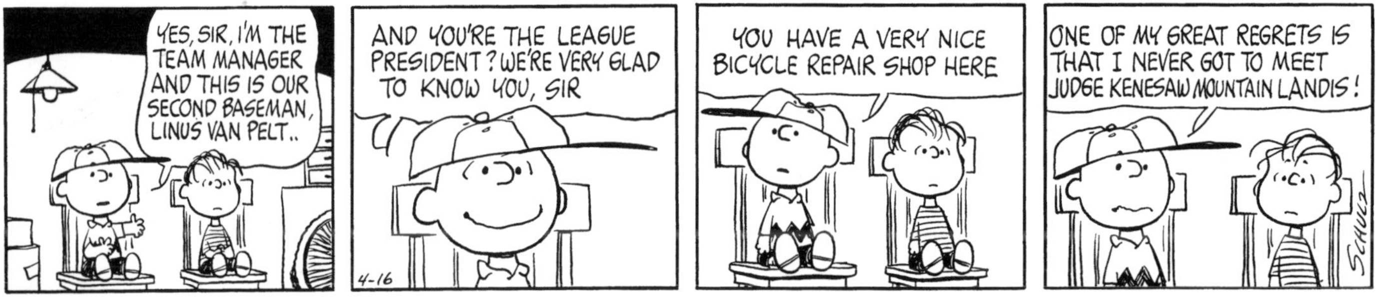
YES, SIR, I'M THE TEAM MANAGER AND THIS IS OUR SECOND BASEMAN, LINUS VAN PELT..
AND YOU'RE THE LEAGUE PRESIDENT? WE'RE VERY GLAD TO KNOW YOU, SIR
4-16
YOU HAVE A VERY NICE BICYCLE REPAIR SHOP HERE
ONE OF MY GREAT REGRETS IS THAT I NEVER GOT TO MEET JUDGE KENESAW MOUNTAIN LANDIS!
SCHULZ

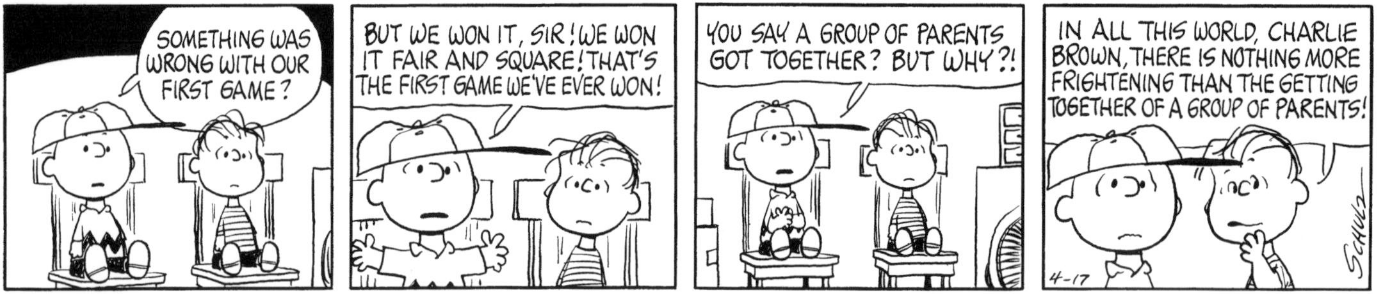
SOMETHING WAS WRONG WITH OUR FIRST GAME?
BUT WE WON IT, SIR! WE WON IT FAIR AND SQUARE! THAT'S THE FIRST GAME WE'VE EVER WON!
YOU SAY A GROUP OF PARENTS GOT TOGETHER? BUT WHY?!
IN ALL THIS WORLD, CHARLIE BROWN, THERE IS NOTHING MORE FRIGHTENING THAN THE GETTING TOGETHER OF A GROUP OF PARENTS!
4-17
SCHULZ

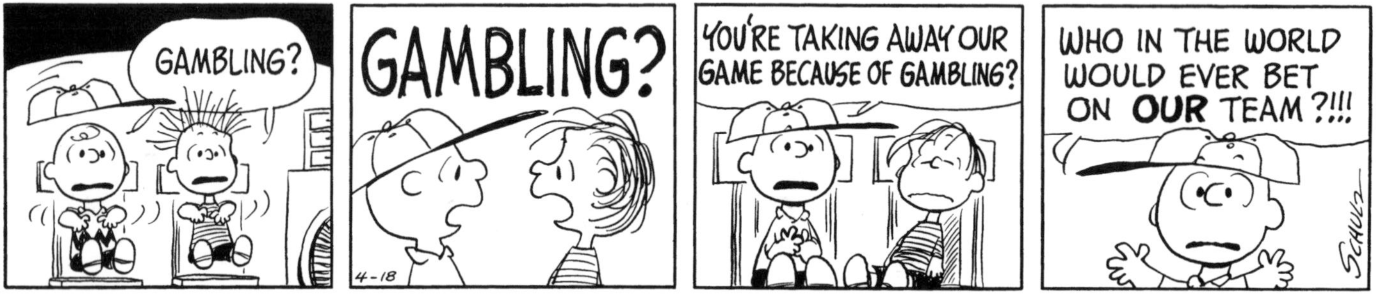
GAMBLING?
GAMBLING?
4-18
YOU'RE TAKING AWAY OUR GAME BECAUSE OF GAMBLING?
WHO IN THE WORLD WOULD EVER BET ON OUR TEAM?!!!
SCHULZ

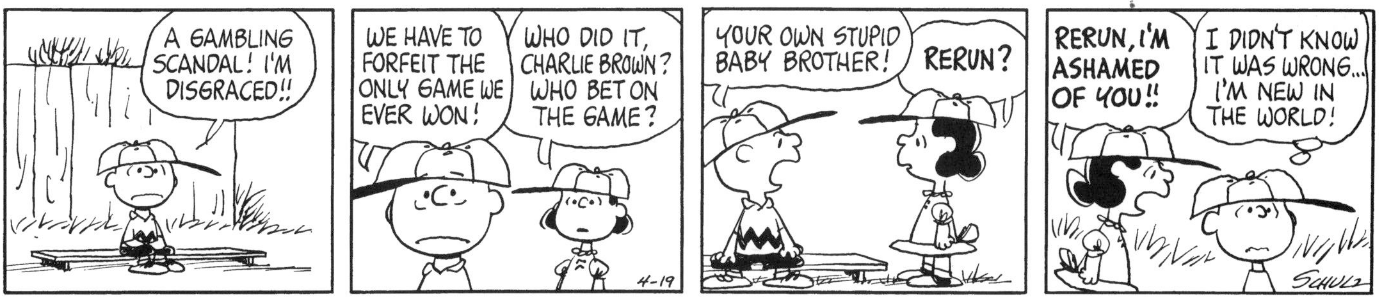
A GAMBLING SCANDAL! I'M DISGRACED!!
WE HAVE TO FORFEIT THE ONLY GAME WE EVER WON!
WHO DID IT, CHARLIE BROWN? WHO BET ON THE GAME?
4-19
YOUR OWN STUPID BABY BROTHER!
RERUN?
RERUN, I'M ASHAMED OF YOU!!
I DIDN'T KNOW IT WAS WRONG... I'M NEW IN THE WORLD!
SCHULZ

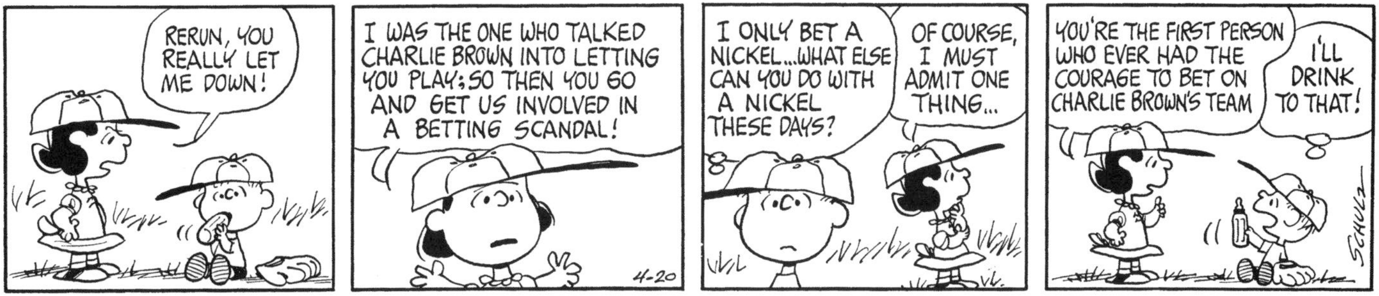
RERUN, YOU REALLY LET ME DOWN!
I WAS THE ONE WHO TALKED CHARLIE BROWN INTO LETTING YOU PLAY; SO THEN YOU GO AND GET US INVOLVED IN A BETTING SCANDAL!
4-20
I ONLY BET A NICKEL...WHAT ELSE CAN YOU DO WITH A NICKEL THESE DAYS?
OF COURSE, I MUST ADMIT ONE THING...
YOU'RE THE FIRST PERSON WHO EVER HAD THE COURAGE TO BET ON CHARLIE BROWN'S TEAM
I'LL DRINK TO THAT!
SCHULZ

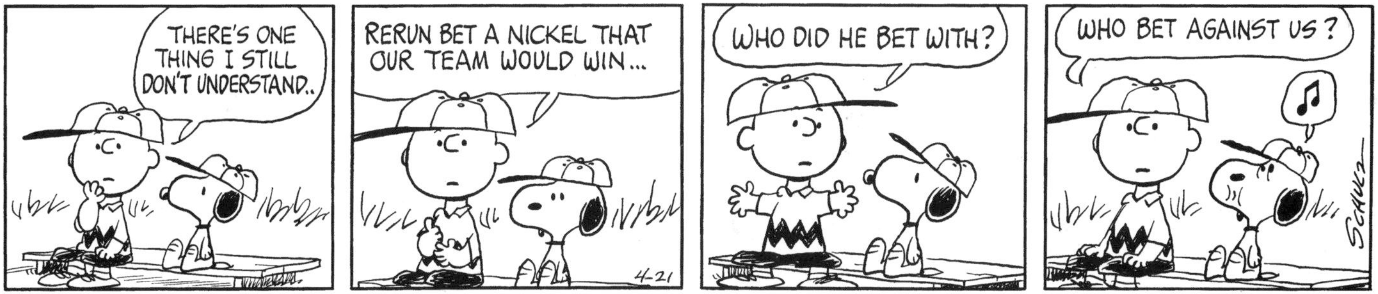
THERE'S ONE THING I STILL DON'T UNDERSTAND..
RERUN BET A NICKEL THAT OUR TEAM WOULD WIN...
4-21
WHO DID HE BET WITH?
WHO BET AGAINST US?
SCHULZ

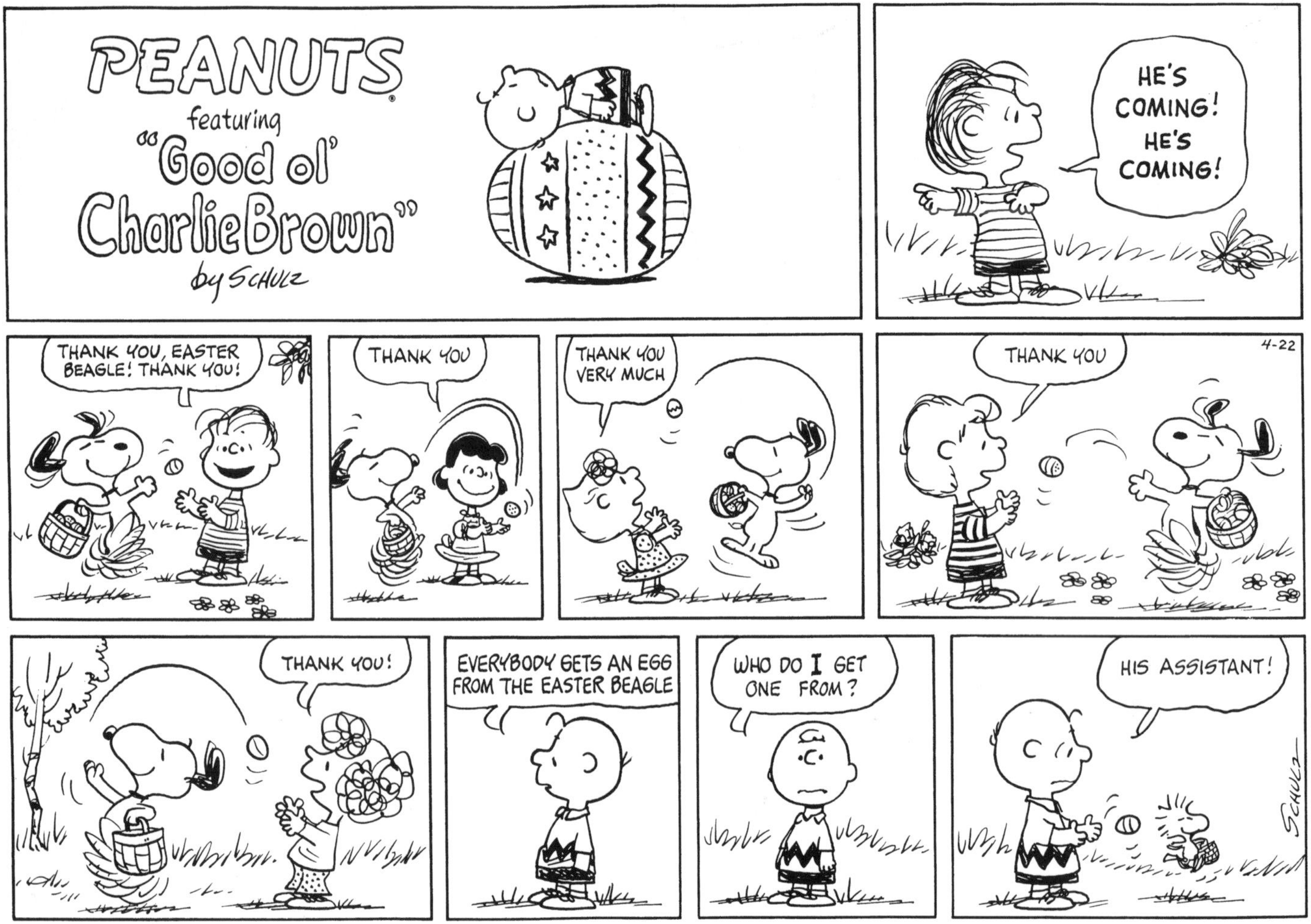
PEANUTS
featuring "Good ol' Charlie Brown"
by SCHULZ
HE'S COMING! HE'S COMING!
THANK YOU, EASTER BEAGLE! THANK YOU!
THANK YOU
THANK YOU VERY MUCH
4-22
THANK YOU
THANK YOU!
EVERYBODY GETS AN EGG FROM THE EASTER BEAGLE
WHO DO I GET ONE FROM?
HIS ASSISTANT!
SCHULZ

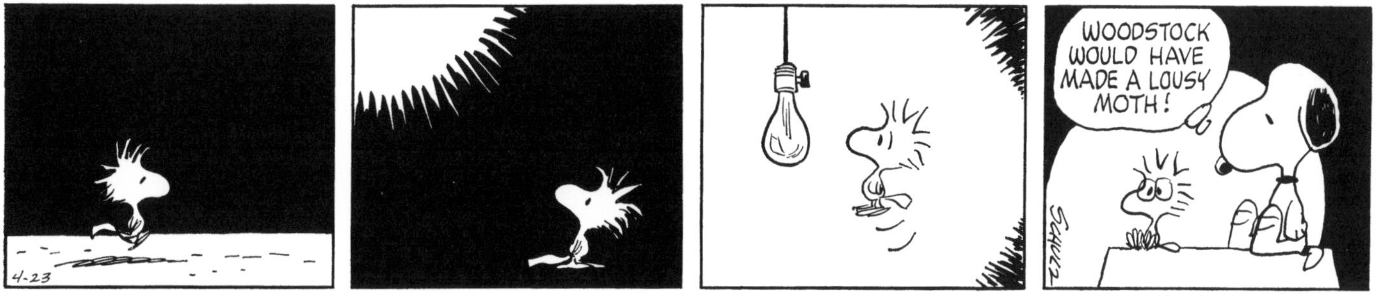
4-23
WOODSTOCK WOULD HAVE MADE A LOUSY MOTH!
SCHULZ

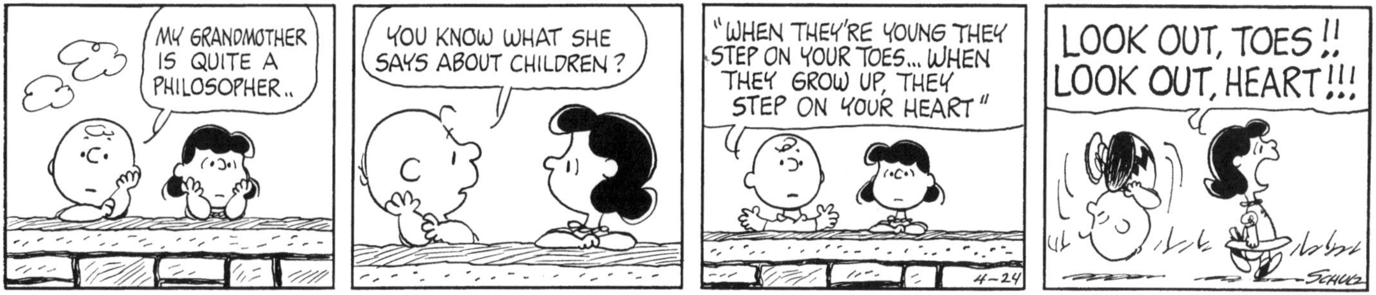
MY GRANDMOTHER IS QUITE A PHILOSOPHER..
YOU KNOW WHAT SHE SAYS ABOUT CHILDREN?
"WHEN THEY'RE YOUNG THEY STEP ON YOUR TOES... WHEN THEY GROW UP, THEY STEP ON YOUR HEART"
4-24
LOOK OUT, TOES!! LOOK OUT, HEART!!!
SCHULZ

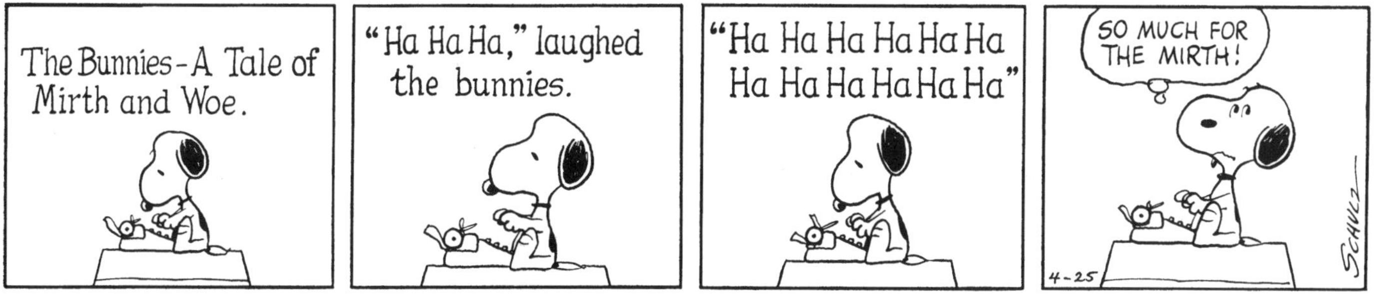
The Bunnies-A Tale of Mirth and Woe.
"Ha Ha Ha," laughed the bunnies.
"Ha Ha Ha Ha Ha Ha Ha Ha Ha Ha Ha Ha"
SO MUCH FOR THE MIRTH!
4-25
SCHULZ

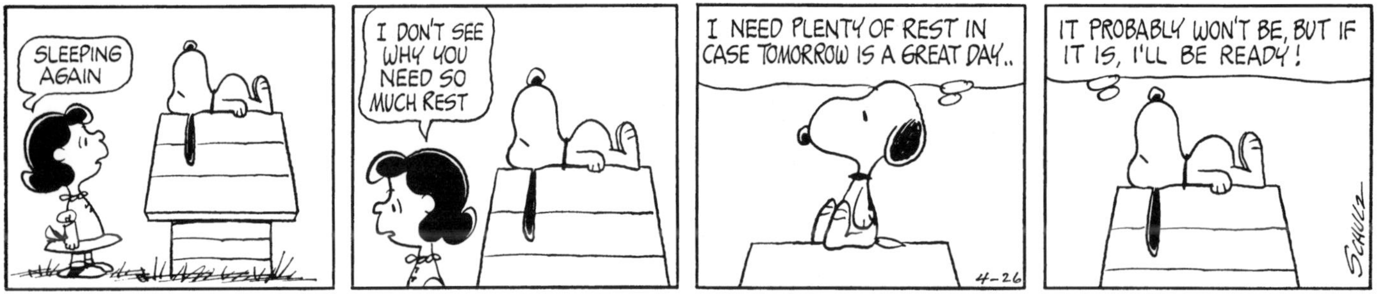
SLEEPING AGAIN
I DON'T SEE WHY YOU NEED SO MUCH REST
I NEED PLENTY OF REST IN CASE TOMORROW IS A GREAT DAY..
IT PROBABLY WON'T BE, BUT IF IT IS, I'LL BE READY!
4-26
SCHULZ

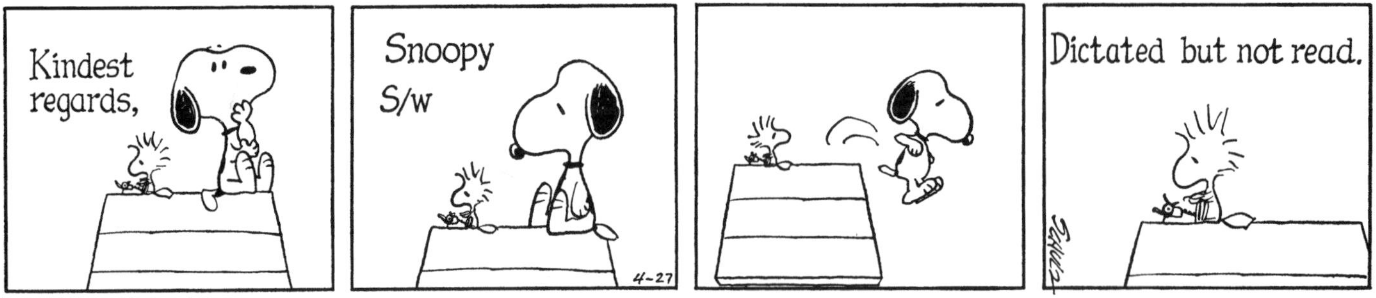
Kindest regards,
Snoopy
S/w
4-27
Dictated but not read.
SCHULZ

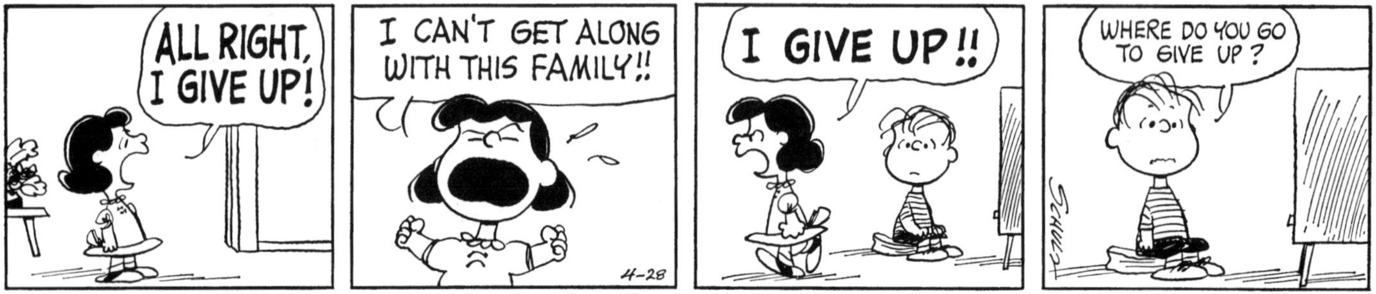
ALL RIGHT, I GIVE UP!
I CAN'T GET ALONG WITH THIS FAMILY!!
4-28
I GIVE UP!!
WHERE DO YOU GO TO GIVE UP?
SCHULZ

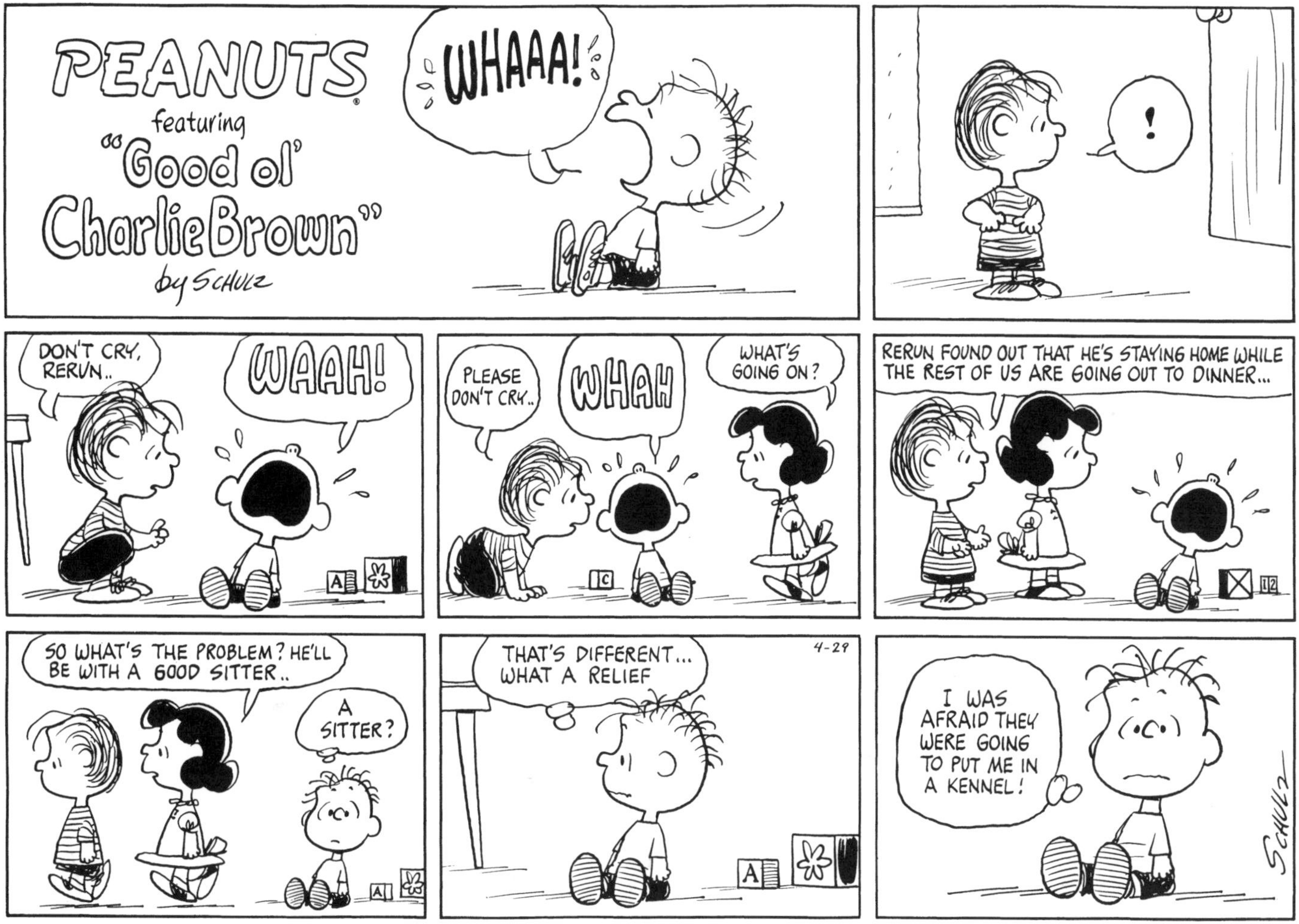
PEANUTS®
featuring "Good ol' CharlieBrown"
by SCHULZ
WHAAA!
!
DON'T CRY, RERUN..
WAAH!
PLEASE DON'T CRY..
WHAH
WHAT'S GOING ON?
RERUN FOUND OUT THAT HE'S STAYING HOME WHILE THE REST OF US ARE GOING OUT TO DINNER...
SO WHAT'S THE PROBLEM? HE'LL BE WITH A GOOD SITTER..
A SITTER?
4-29
THAT'S DIFFERENT... WHAT A RELIEF
I WAS AFRAID THEY WERE GOING TO PUT ME IN A KENNEL!
SCHULZ

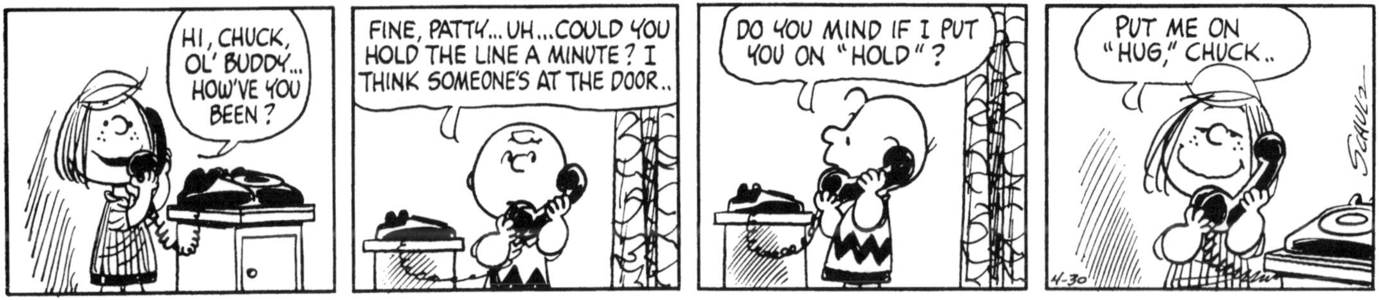
HI, CHUCK, OL' BUDDY... HOW'VE YOU BEEN?
FINE, PATTY... UH... COULD YOU HOLD THE LINE A MINUTE? I THINK SOMEONE'S AT THE DOOR..
DO YOU MIND IF I PUT YOU ON "HOLD"?
PUT ME ON "HUG," CHUCK..
4-30

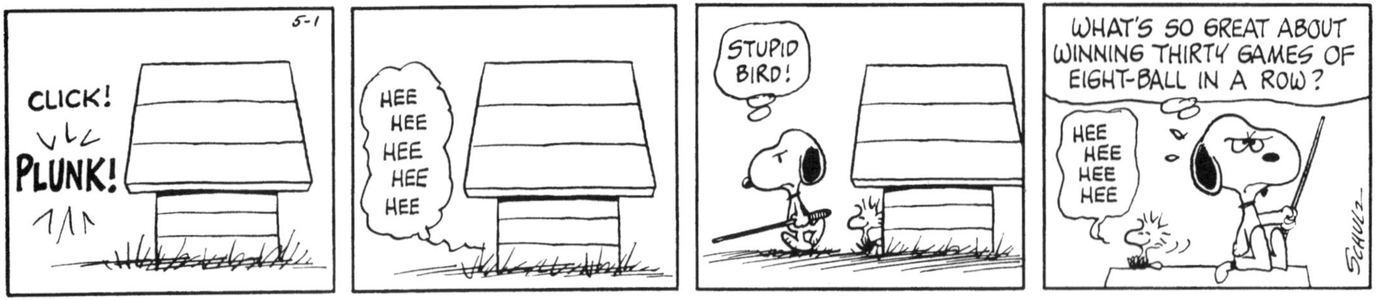
5-1
CLICK!
PLUNK!
HEE HEE HEE HEE HEE
STUPID BIRD!
WHAT'S SO GREAT ABOUT WINNING THIRTY GAMES OF EIGHT-BALL IN A ROW?
HEE HEE HEE HEE

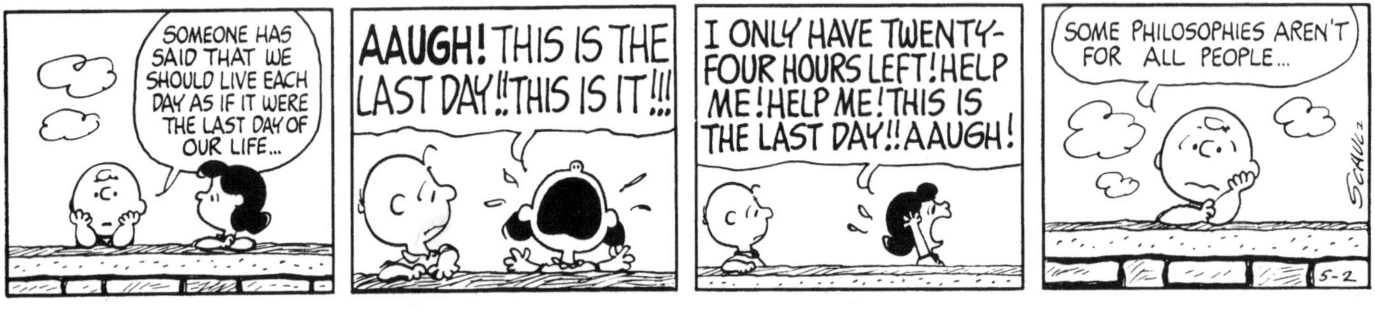
SOMEONE HAS SAID THAT WE SHOULD LIVE EACH DAY AS IF IT WERE THE LAST DAY OF OUR LIFE...
AAUGH! THIS IS THE LAST DAY!! THIS IS IT!!!
I ONLY HAVE TWENTY-FOUR HOURS LEFT! HELP ME! HELP ME! THIS IS THE LAST DAY!! AAUGH!
SOME PHILOSOPHIES AREN'T FOR ALL PEOPLE...
5-2

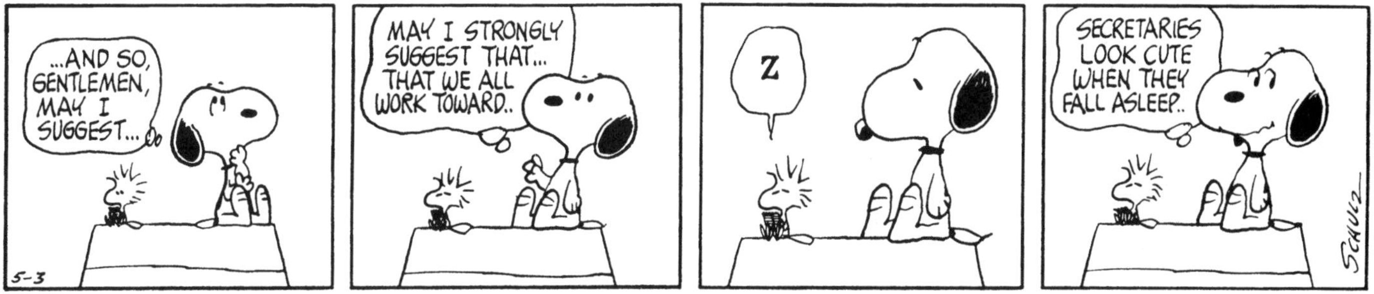
...AND SO, GENTLEMEN, MAY I SUGGEST...
5-3
MAY I STRONGLY SUGGEST THAT... THAT WE ALL WORK TOWARD..
Z
SECRETARIES LOOK CUTE WHEN THEY FALL ASLEEP..
SCHULZ

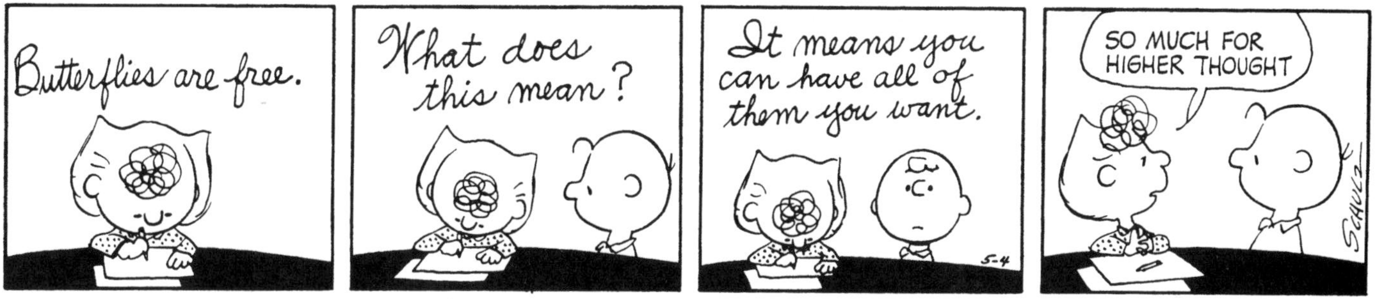
Butterflies are free.
What does this mean?
It means you can have all of them you want.
5-4
SO MUCH FOR HIGHER THOUGHT
SCHULZ

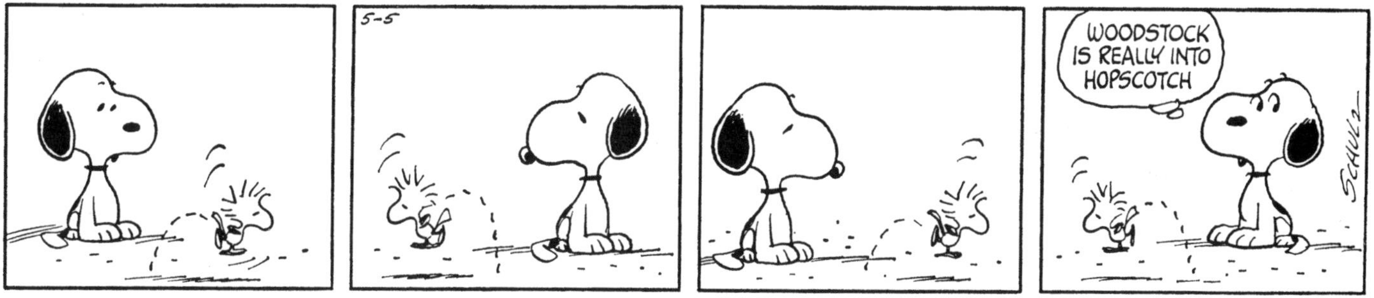
5-5
WOODSTOCK IS REALLY INTO HOPSCOTCH
SCHULZ

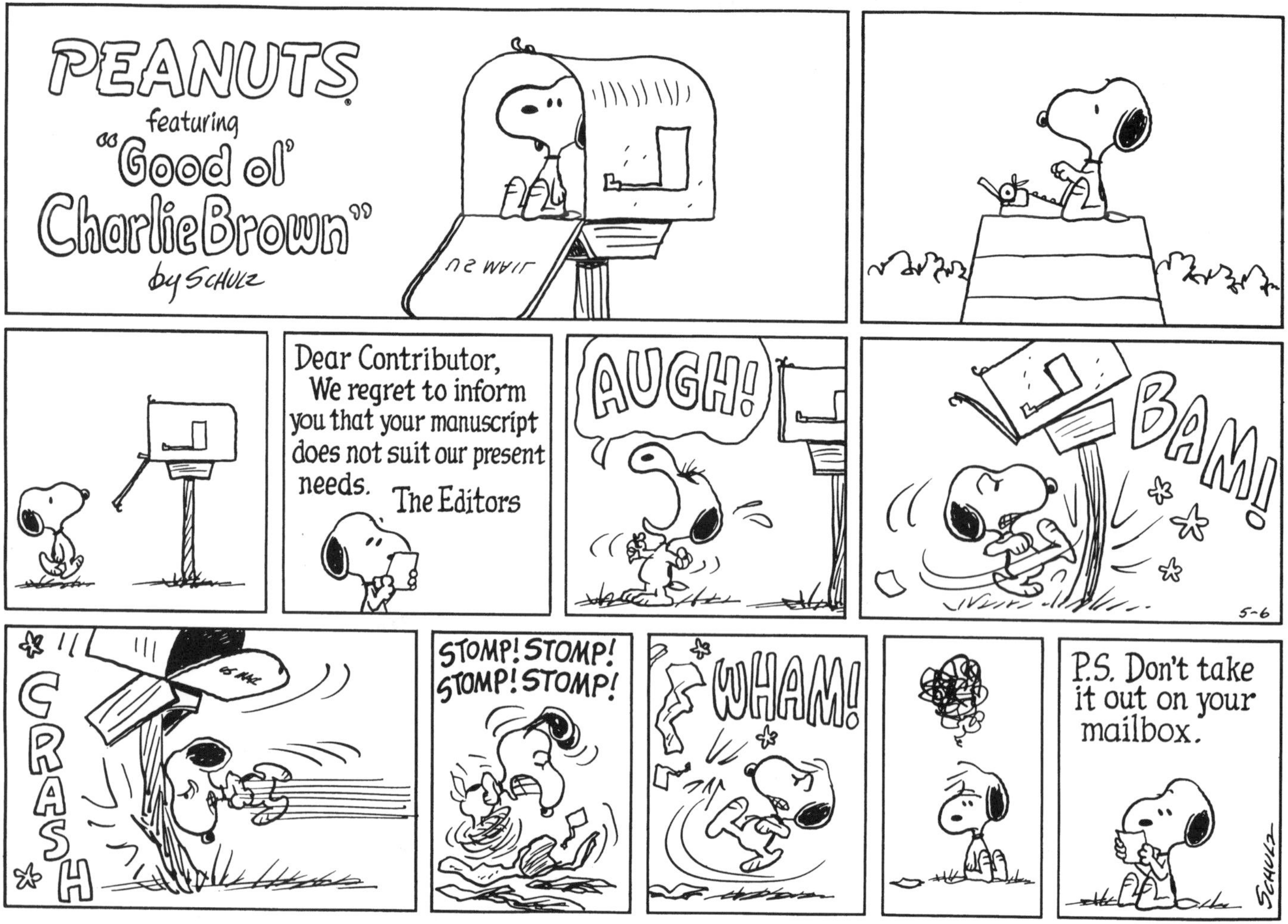
PEANUTS
featuring
"Good ol' CharlieBrown"
by SCHULZ
US MAIL
Dear Contributor,
We regret to inform you that your manuscript does not suit our present needs.
The Editors
AUGH!
BAM!
5-6
CRASH
STOMP! STOMP! STOMP! STOMP!
WHAM!
P.S. Don't take it out on your mailbox.
SCHULZ

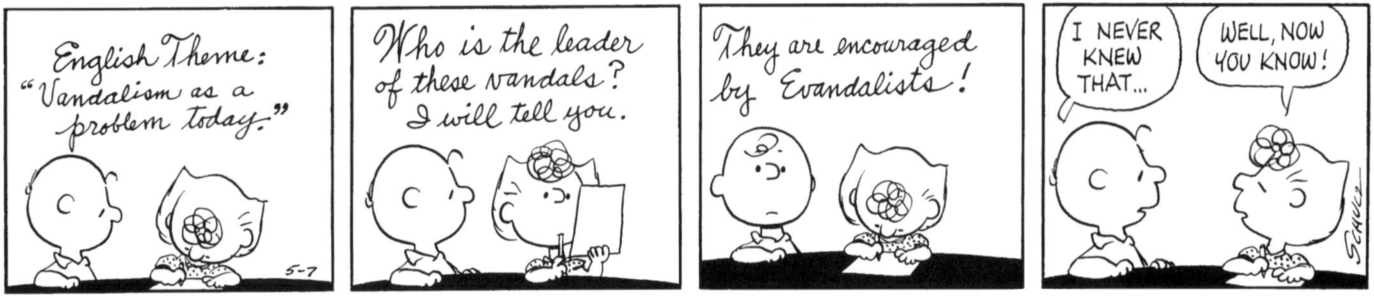
English Theme: "Vandalism as a problem today."
5-7
Who is the leader of these vandals? I will tell you.
They are encouraged by Evandalists!
I NEVER KNEW THAT...
WELL, NOW YOU KNOW!
SCHULZ

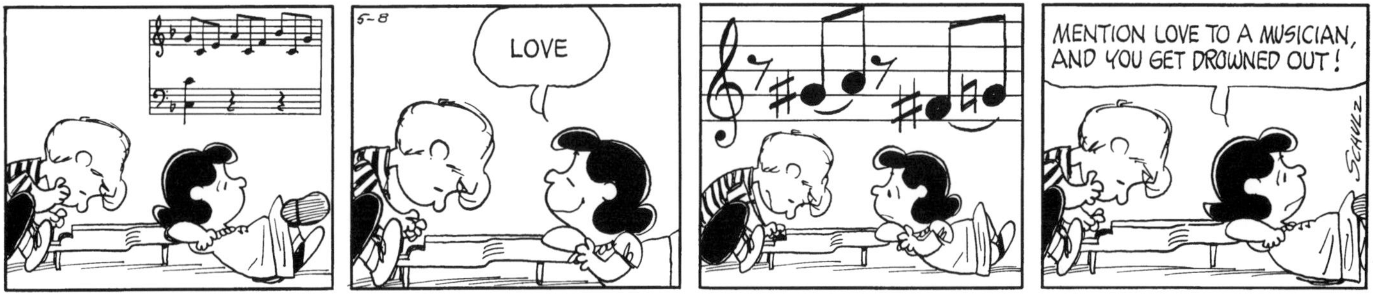
5-8
LOVE
MENTION LOVE TO A MUSICIAN, AND YOU GET DROWNED OUT!
SCHULZ

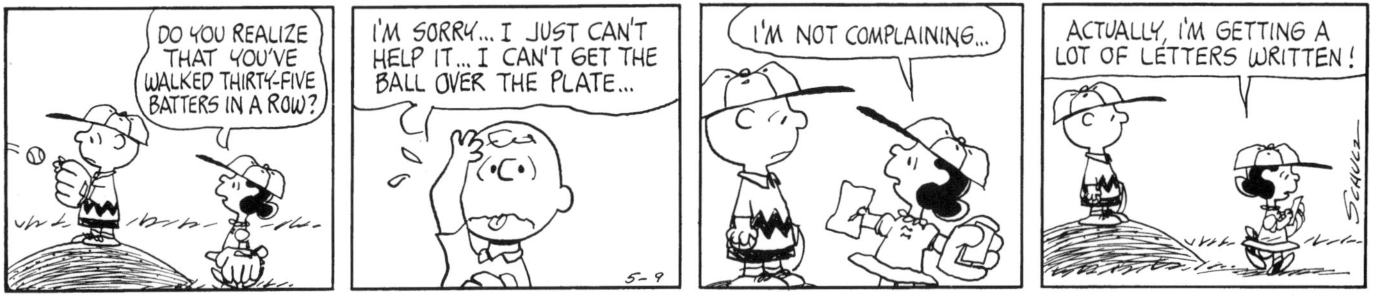
DO YOU REALIZE THAT YOU'VE WALKED THIRTY-FIVE BATTERS IN A ROW?
I'M SORRY... I JUST CAN'T HELP IT... I CAN'T GET THE BALL OVER THE PLATE...
5-9
I'M NOT COMPLAINING...
ACTUALLY, I'M GETTING A LOT OF LETTERS WRITTEN!
SCHULZ

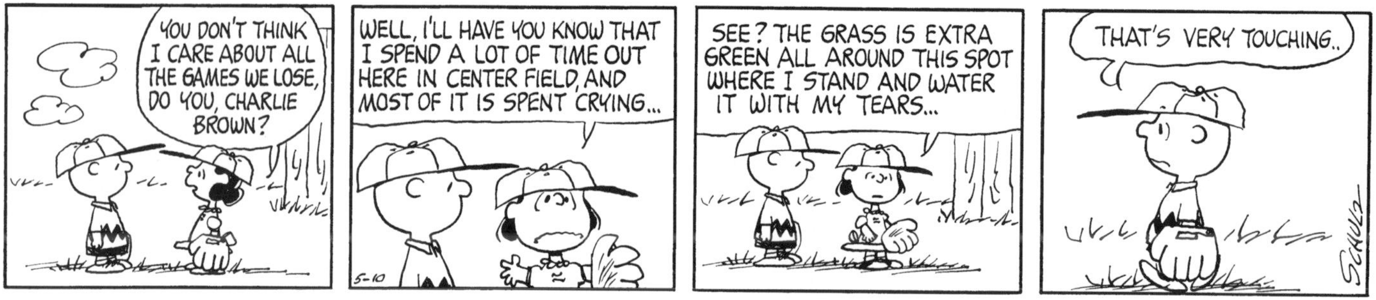
YOU DON'T THINK I CARE ABOUT ALL THE GAMES WE LOSE, DO YOU, CHARLIE BROWN?
WELL, I'LL HAVE YOU KNOW THAT I SPEND A LOT OF TIME OUT HERE IN CENTER FIELD, AND MOST OF IT IS SPENT CRYING...
5-10
SEE? THE GRASS IS EXTRA GREEN ALL AROUND THIS SPOT WHERE I STAND AND WATER IT WITH MY TEARS...
THAT'S VERY TOUCHING..
SCHULZ

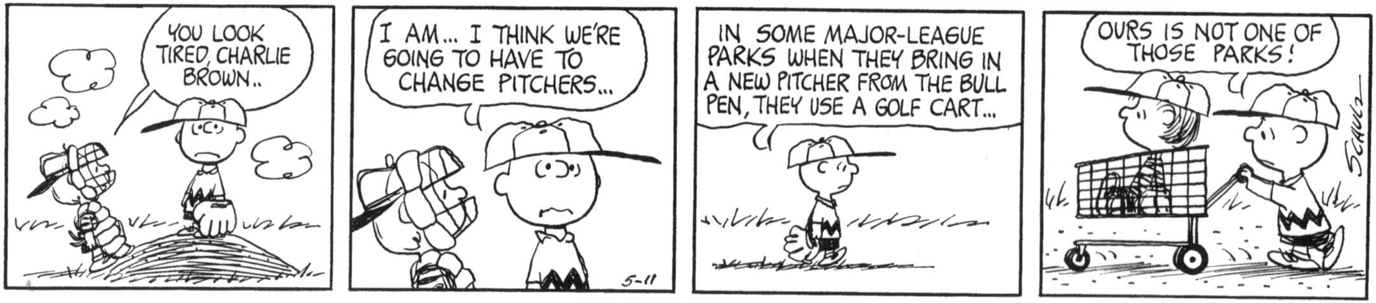
YOU LOOK TIRED, CHARLIE BROWN..
I AM... I THINK WE'RE GOING TO HAVE TO CHANGE PITCHERS...
5-11
IN SOME MAJOR-LEAGUE PARKS WHEN THEY BRING IN A NEW PITCHER FROM THE BULL PEN, THEY USE A GOLF CART...
OURS IS NOT ONE OF THOSE PARKS!
SCHULZ

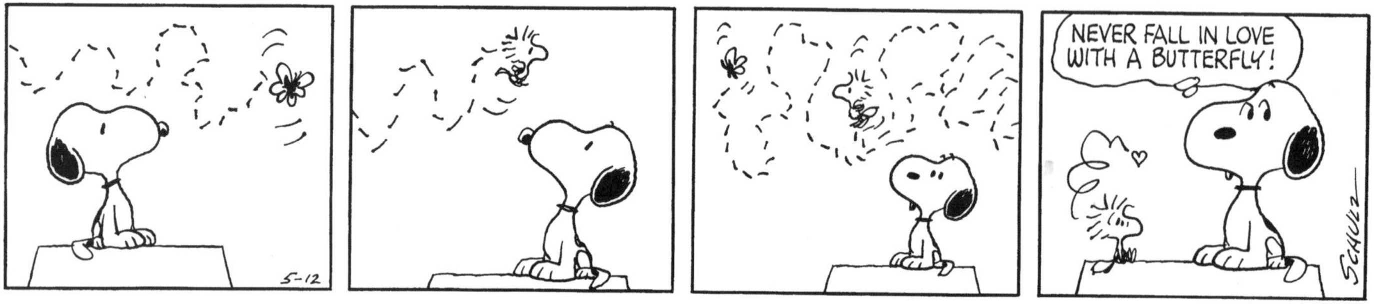
5-12
NEVER FALL IN LOVE WITH A BUTTERFLY!
SCHULZ

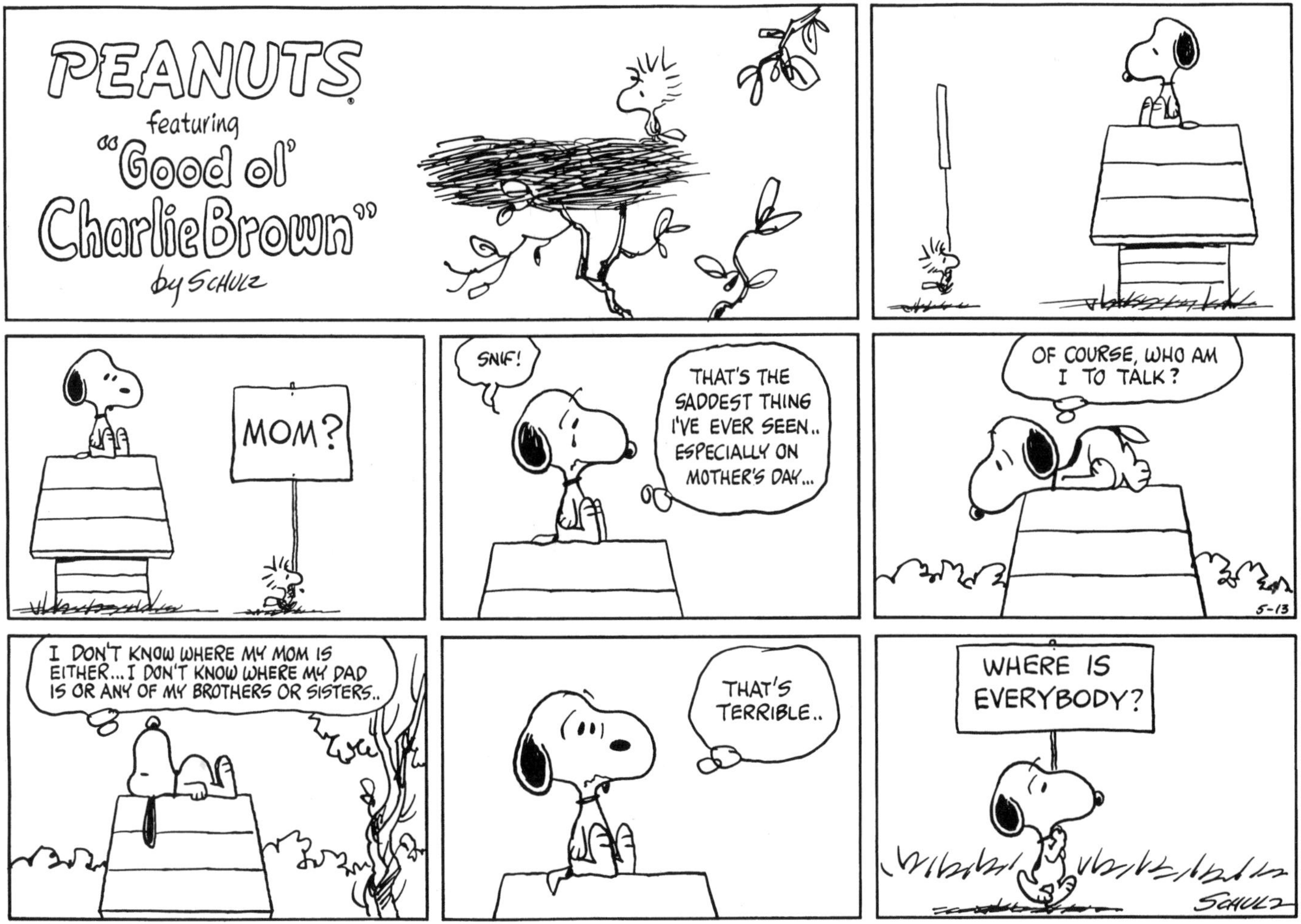
PEANUTS
featuring
"Good ol' CharlieBrown"
by SCHULZ
MOM?
SNIF!
THAT'S THE SADDEST THING I'VE EVER SEEN.. ESPECIALLY ON MOTHER'S DAY...
OF COURSE, WHO AM I TO TALK?
5-13
I DON'T KNOW WHERE MY MOM IS EITHER...I DON'T KNOW WHERE MY DAD IS OR ANY OF MY BROTHERS OR SISTERS..
THAT'S TERRIBLE..
WHERE IS EVERYBODY?
SCHULZ

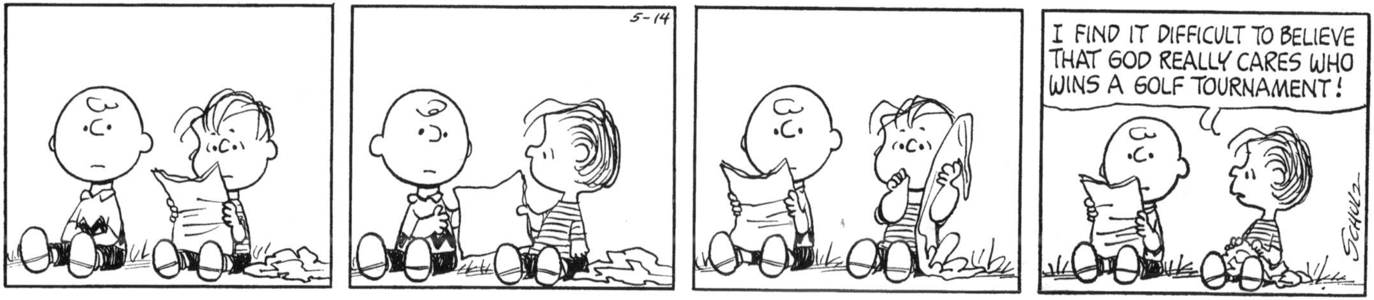
5-14
I FIND IT DIFFICULT TO BELIEVE THAT GOD REALLY CARES WHO WINS A GOLF TOURNAMENT!
SCHULZ

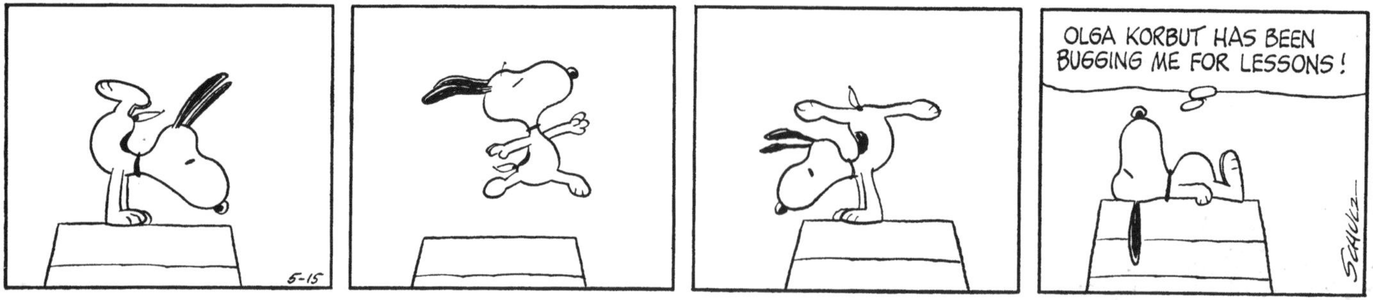
5-15
OLGA KORBUT HAS BEEN BUGGING ME FOR LESSONS!
SCHULZ

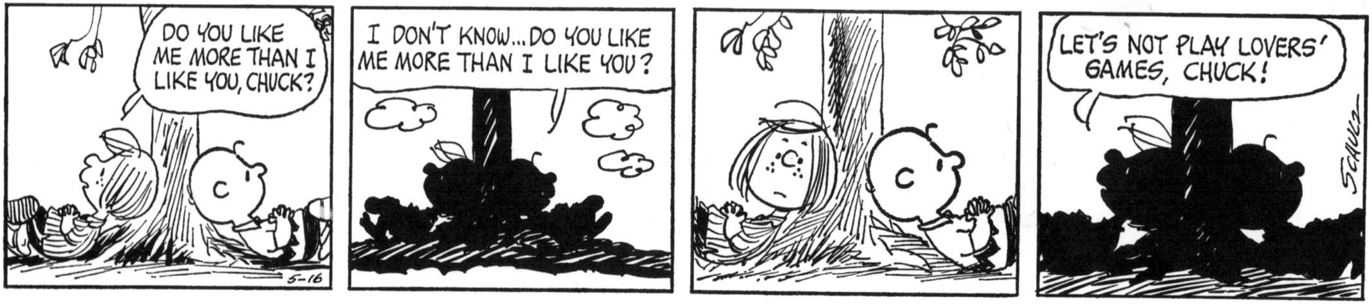
DO YOU LIKE ME MORE THAN I LIKE YOU, CHUCK?
5-16
I DON'T KNOW...DO YOU LIKE ME MORE THAN I LIKE YOU?
LET'S NOT PLAY LOVERS' GAMES, CHUCK!
SCHULZ

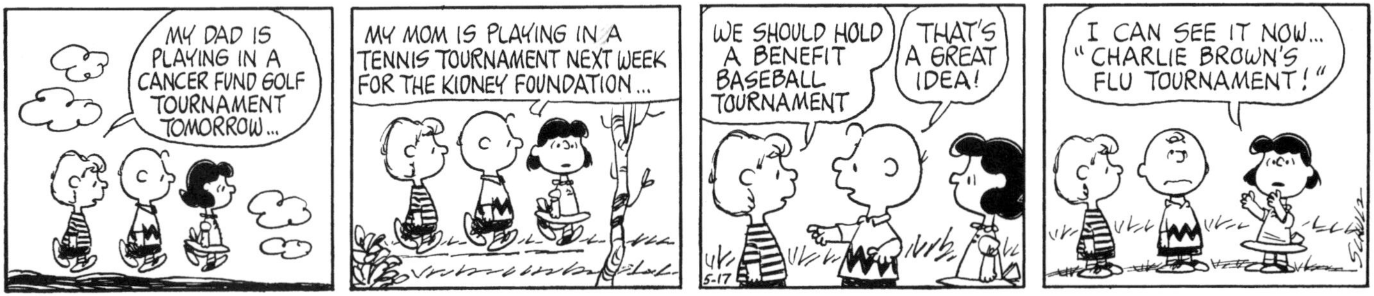
MY DAD IS PLAYING IN A CANCER FUND GOLF TOURNAMENT TOMORROW...
MY MOM IS PLAYING IN A TENNIS TOURNAMENT NEXT WEEK FOR THE KIDNEY FOUNDATION...
WE SHOULD HOLD A BENEFIT BASEBALL TOURNAMENT
THAT'S A GREAT IDEA!
I CAN SEE IT NOW... "CHARLIE BROWN'S FLU TOURNAMENT!"

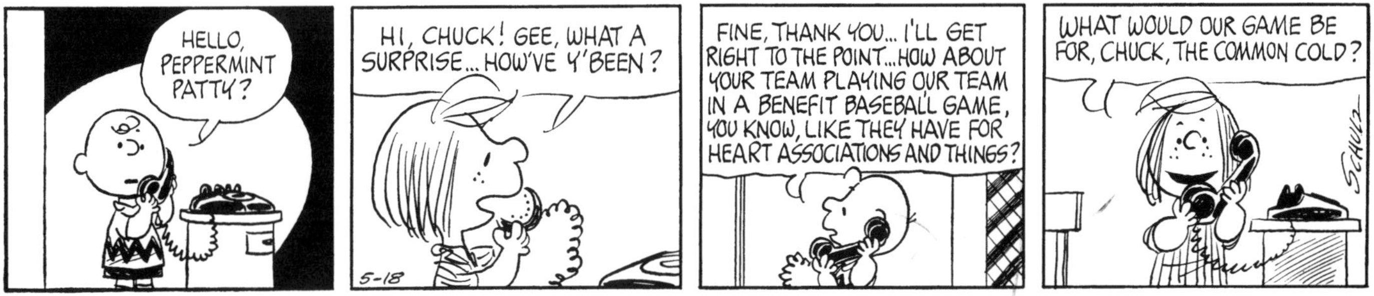
HELLO, PEPPERMINT PATTY?
HI, CHUCK! GEE, WHAT A SURPRISE... HOW'VE Y'BEEN?
FINE, THANK YOU... I'LL GET RIGHT TO THE POINT... HOW ABOUT YOUR TEAM PLAYING OUR TEAM IN A BENEFIT BASEBALL GAME, YOU KNOW, LIKE THEY HAVE FOR HEART ASSOCIATIONS AND THINGS?
WHAT WOULD OUR GAME BE FOR, CHUCK, THE COMMON COLD?

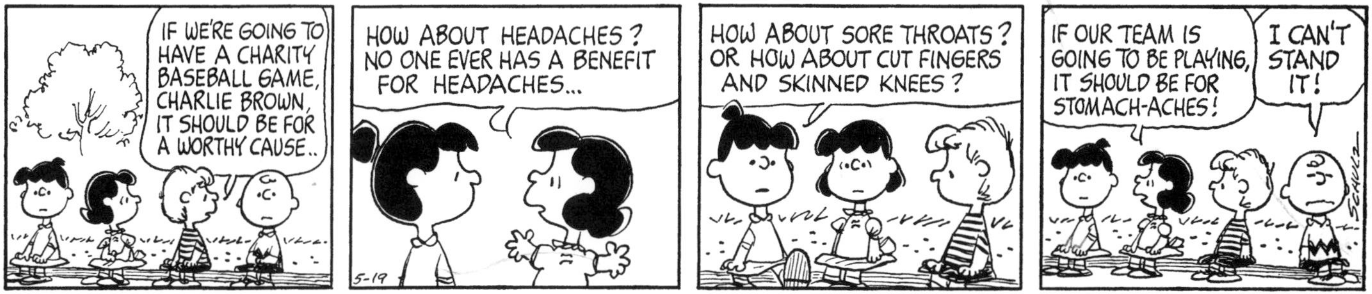
IF WE'RE GOING TO HAVE A CHARITY BASEBALL GAME, CHARLIE BROWN, IT SHOULD BE FOR A WORTHY CAUSE..
HOW ABOUT HEADACHES? NO ONE EVER HAS A BENEFIT FOR HEADACHES...
HOW ABOUT SORE THROATS? OR HOW ABOUT CUT FINGERS AND SKINNED KNEES?
IF OUR TEAM IS GOING TO BE PLAYING, IT SHOULD BE FOR STOMACH-ACHES!
I CAN'T STAND IT!

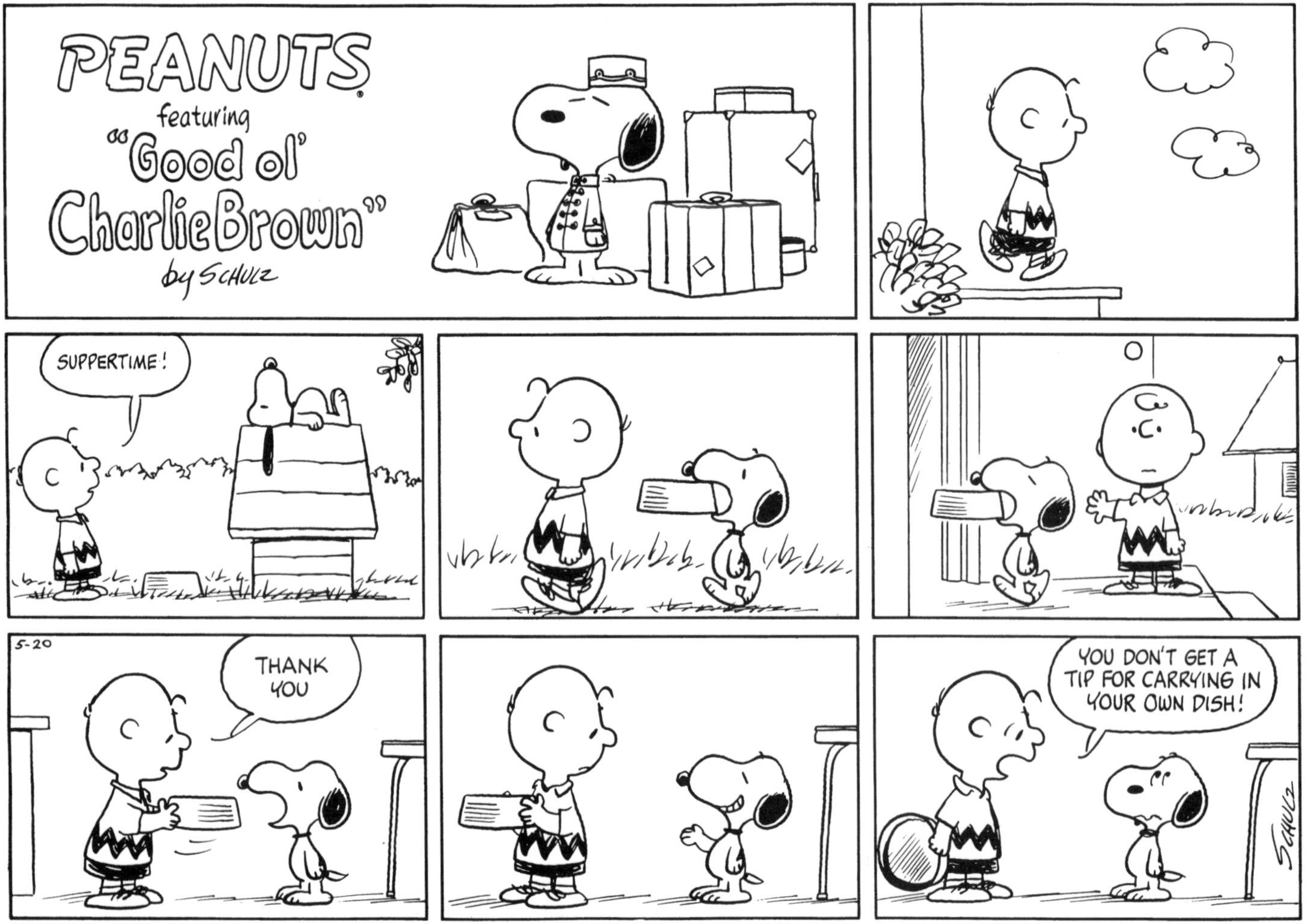
PEANUTS
featuring
"Good ol' Charlie Brown"
by SCHULZ
SUPPERTIME!
5-20
THANK YOU
YOU DON'T GET A TIP FOR CARRYING IN YOUR OWN DISH!
SCHULZ

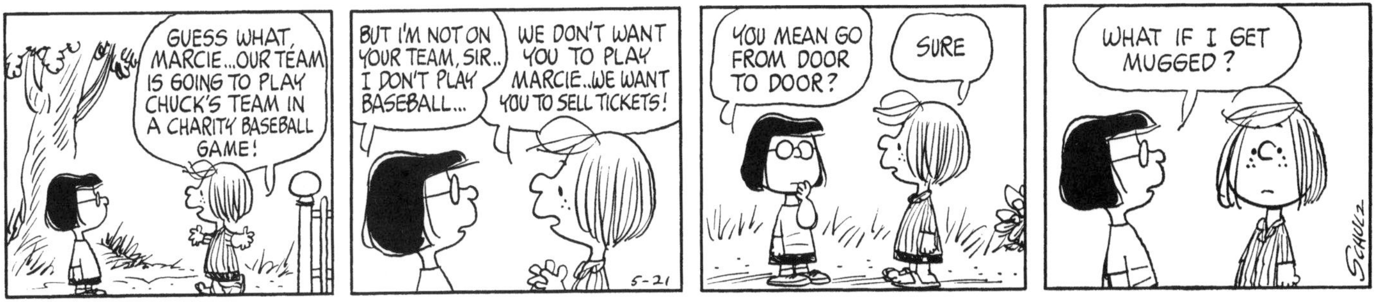
GUESS WHAT, MARCIE...OUR TEAM IS GOING TO PLAY CHUCK'S TEAM IN A CHARITY BASEBALL GAME!
BUT I'M NOT ON YOUR TEAM, SIR.. I DON'T PLAY BASEBALL...
WE DON'T WANT YOU TO PLAY MARCIE..WE WANT YOU TO SELL TICKETS!
5-21
YOU MEAN GO FROM DOOR TO DOOR?
SURE
WHAT IF I GET MUGGED?
SCHULZ

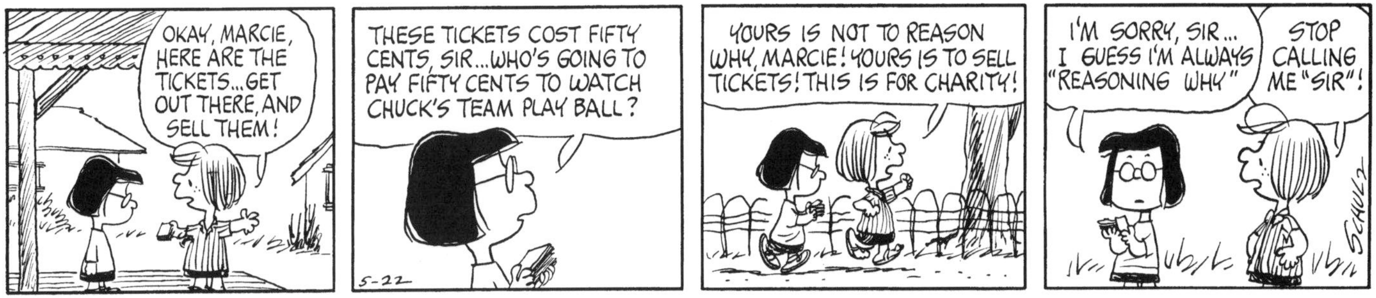
OKAY, MARCIE, HERE ARE THE TICKETS...GET OUT THERE, AND SELL THEM!
THESE TICKETS COST FIFTY CENTS, SIR...WHO'S GOING TO PAY FIFTY CENTS TO WATCH CHUCK'S TEAM PLAY BALL?
5-22
YOURS IS NOT TO REASON WHY, MARCIE! YOURS IS TO SELL TICKETS! THIS IS FOR CHARITY!
I'M SORRY, SIR... I GUESS I'M ALWAYS "REASONING WHY"
STOP CALLING ME "SIR"!
SCHULZ

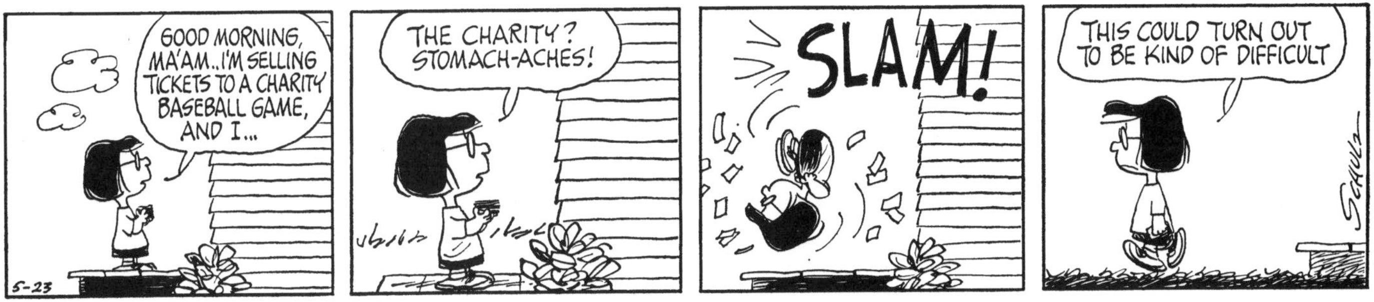
GOOD MORNING, MA'AM..I'M SELLING TICKETS TO A CHARITY BASEBALL GAME, AND I...
5-23
THE CHARITY? STOMACH-ACHES!
SLAM!
THIS COULD TURN OUT TO BE KIND OF DIFFICULT
SCHULZ

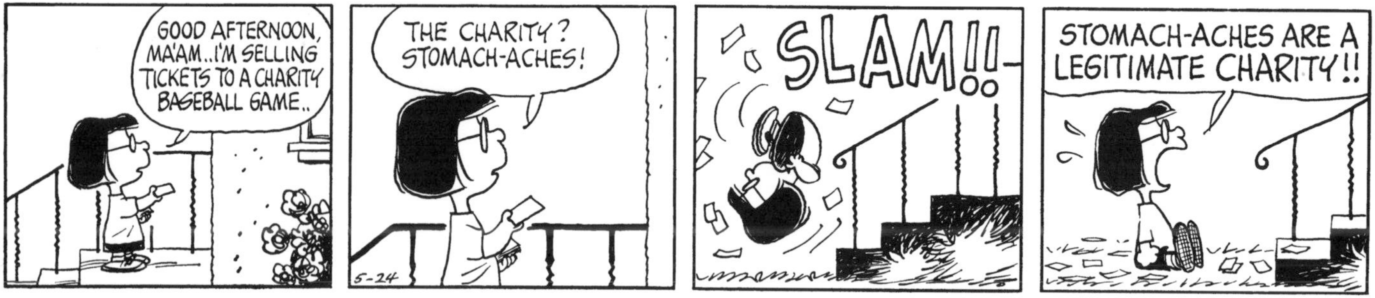
GOOD AFTERNOON, MA'AM.. I'M SELLING TICKETS TO A CHARITY BASEBALL GAME..
THE CHARITY? STOMACH-ACHES!
5-24
SLAM!!
STOMACH-ACHES ARE A LEGITIMATE CHARITY!!

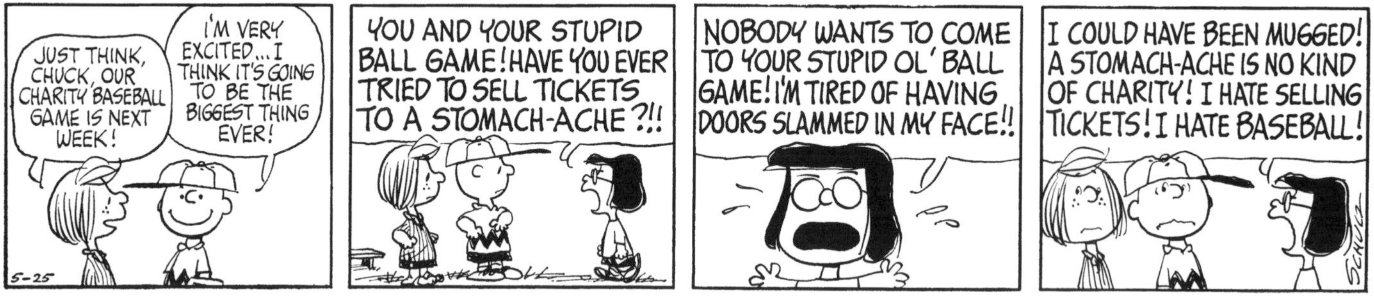
JUST THINK, CHUCK, OUR CHARITY BASEBALL GAME IS NEXT WEEK!
I'M VERY EXCITED... I THINK IT'S GOING TO BE THE BIGGEST THING EVER!
5-25
YOU AND YOUR STUPID BALL GAME! HAVE YOU EVER TRIED TO SELL TICKETS TO A STOMACH-ACHE?!!
NOBODY WANTS TO COME TO YOUR STUPID OL' BALL GAME! I'M TIRED OF HAVING DOORS SLAMMED IN MY FACE!!
I COULD HAVE BEEN MUGGED! A STOMACH-ACHE IS NO KIND OF CHARITY! I HATE SELLING TICKETS! I HATE BASEBALL!
SCHULZ

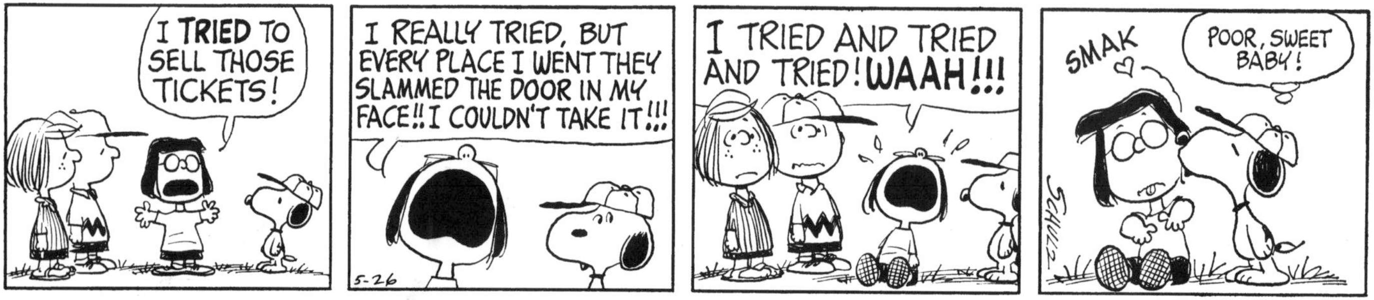
I **TRIED** TO SELL THOSE TICKETS!
I REALLY TRIED, BUT EVERY PLACE I WENT THEY SLAMMED THE DOOR IN MY FACE!! I COULDN'T TAKE IT!!!
5-26
I TRIED AND TRIED AND TRIED! **WAAH!!!**
SMAK
POOR, SWEET BABY!
SCHULZ

PEANUTS

featuring

"Good ol' CharlieBrown"

by Schulz

"Hi, pretty girl," he said.

"I love you," she said, and together they laughed. Then one day she said, "I hate you," and they cried. But not together.

"What happened to the love that we said would never die?" she asked. "It died," he said.

The first time he saw her she was playing tennis. The last time he saw her she was playing tennis.

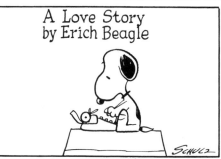

5-27

"Ours was a Love set," he said, "but we double-faulted." "You always talked a better game than you played," she said.

THAT'S VERY GOOD...NOW ALL YOU NEED IS A TITLE...

A Love Story
by Erich Beagle

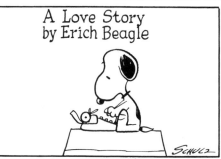

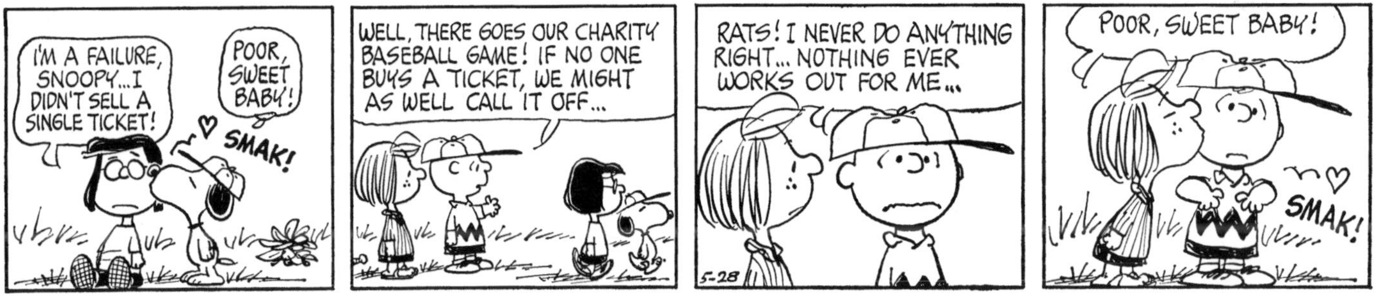
I'M A FAILURE, SNOOPY...I DIDN'T SELL A SINGLE TICKET!
POOR, SWEET BABY!
SMAK!
WELL, THERE GOES OUR CHARITY BASEBALL GAME! IF NO ONE BUYS A TICKET, WE MIGHT AS WELL CALL IT OFF...
RATS! I NEVER DO ANYTHING RIGHT... NOTHING EVER WORKS OUT FOR ME...
5-28
POOR, SWEET BABY!
SMAK!

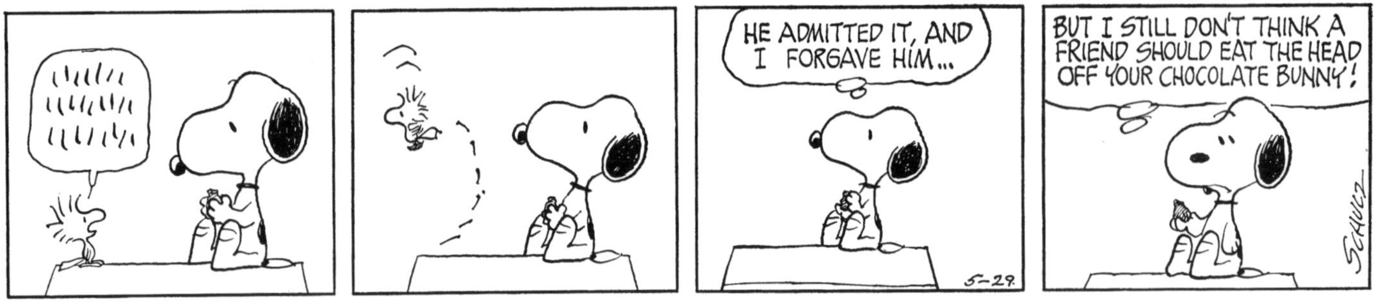
HE ADMITTED IT, AND I FORGAVE HIM...
5-29
BUT I STILL DON'T THINK A FRIEND SHOULD EAT THE HEAD OFF YOUR CHOCOLATE BUNNY!
SCHULZ

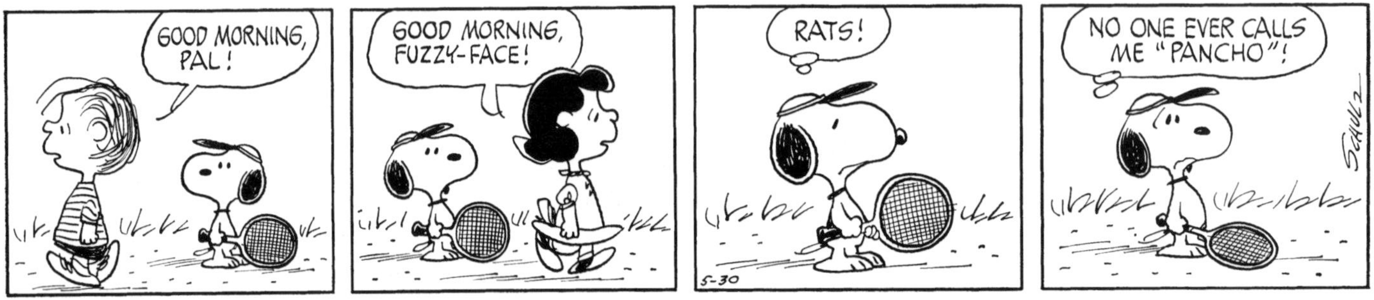
GOOD MORNING, PAL!
GOOD MORNING, FUZZY-FACE!
RATS!
5-30
NO ONE EVER CALLS ME "PANCHO"!
SCHULZ

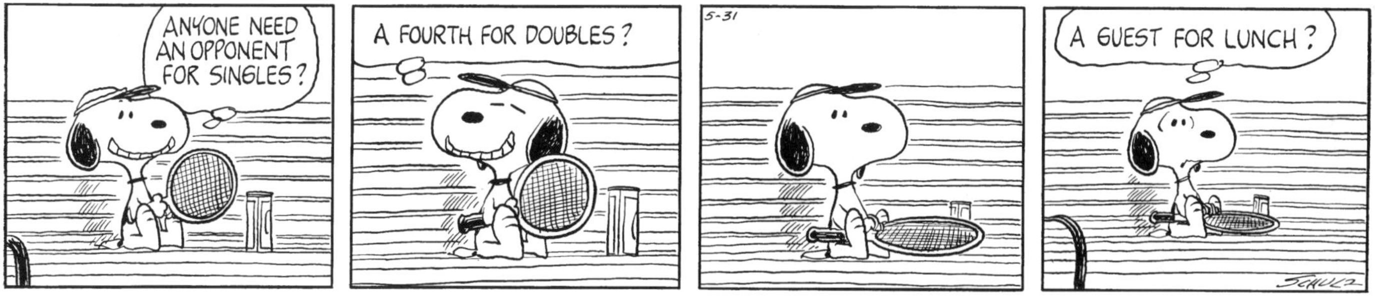
ANYONE NEED AN OPPONENT FOR SINGLES?
A FOURTH FOR DOUBLES?
A GUEST FOR LUNCH?

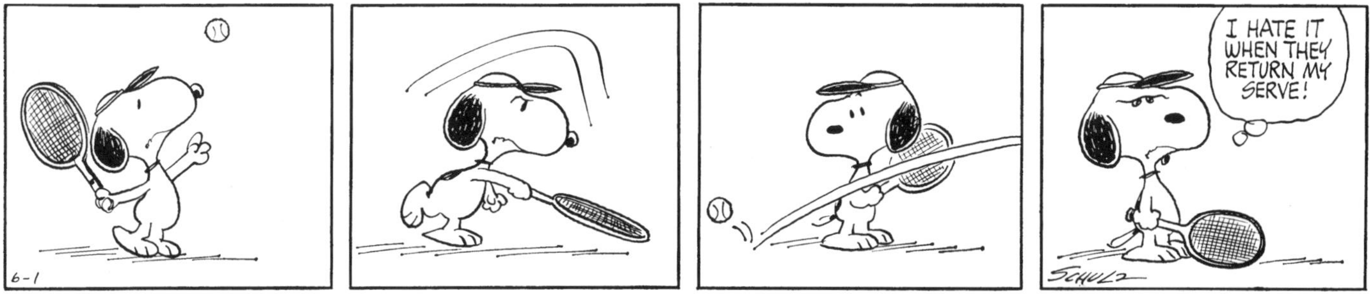
I HATE IT WHEN THEY RETURN MY SERVE!

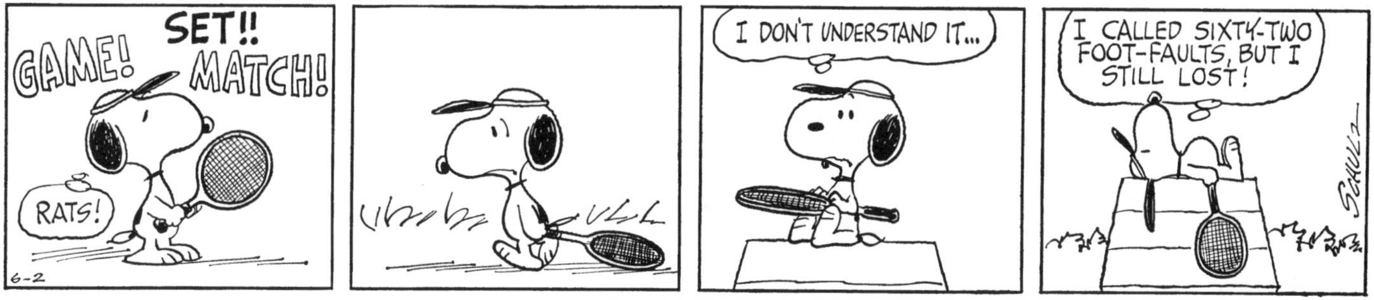
GAME!
SET!!
MATCH!
RATS!
I DON'T UNDERSTAND IT...
I CALLED SIXTY-TWO FOOT-FAULTS, BUT I STILL LOST!

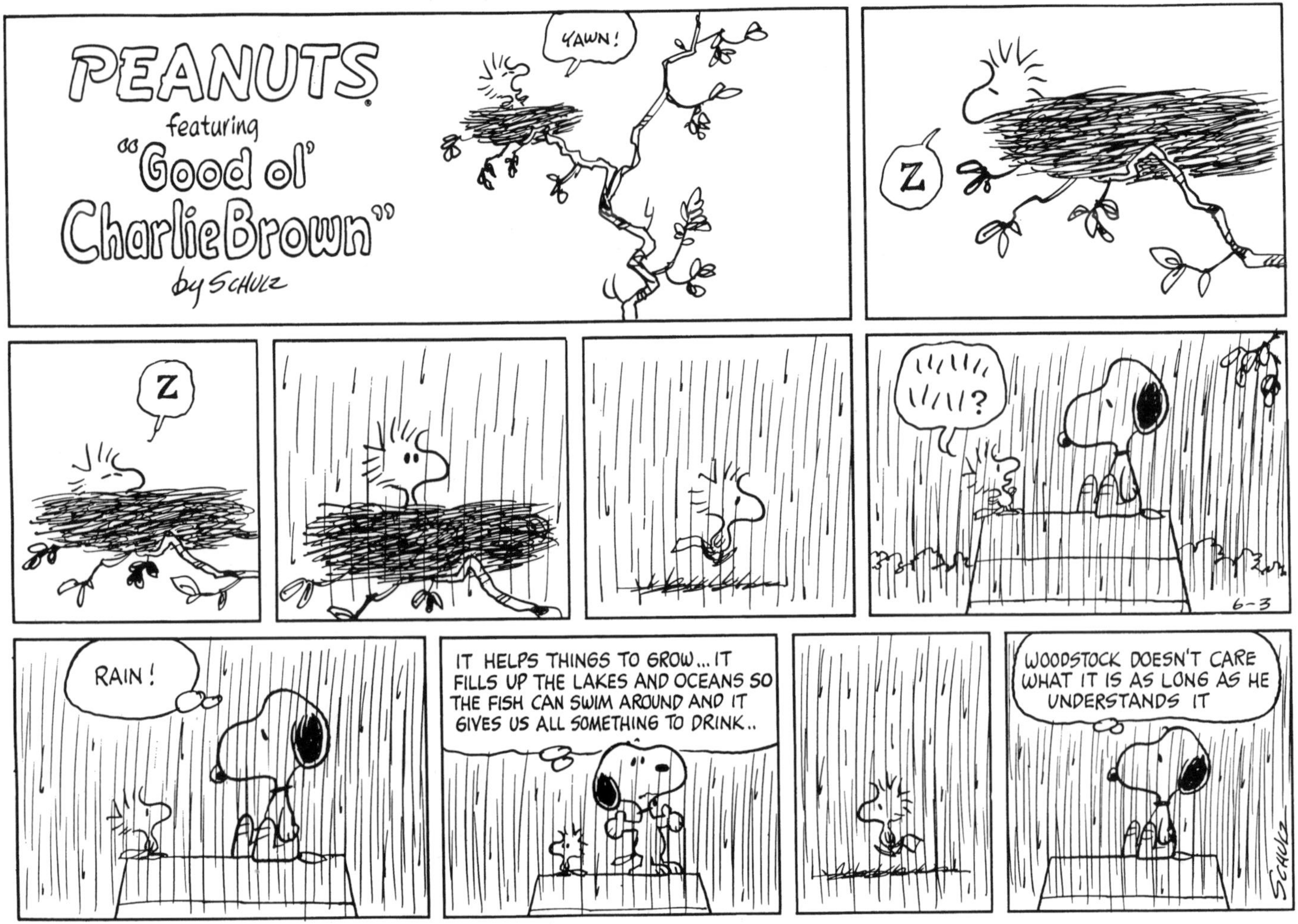
PEANUTS
featuring
"Good ol' CharlieBrown"
by SCHULZ
YAWN!
Z
Z
\\/\\?
6-3
RAIN!
IT HELPS THINGS TO GROW... IT FILLS UP THE LAKES AND OCEANS SO THE FISH CAN SWIM AROUND AND IT GIVES US ALL SOMETHING TO DRINK..
WOODSTOCK DOESN'T CARE WHAT IT IS AS LONG AS HE UNDERSTANDS IT
SCHULZ

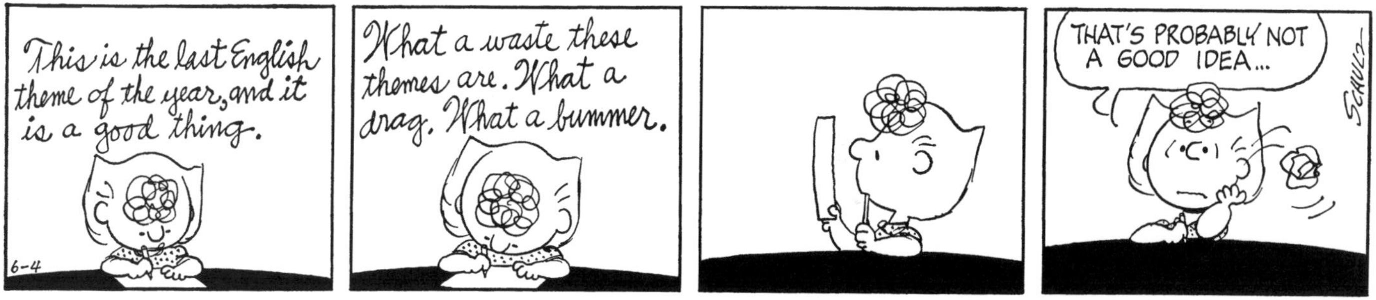
This is the last English theme of the year, and it is a good thing.
What a waste these themes are. What a drag. What a bummer.
THAT'S PROBABLY NOT A GOOD IDEA...

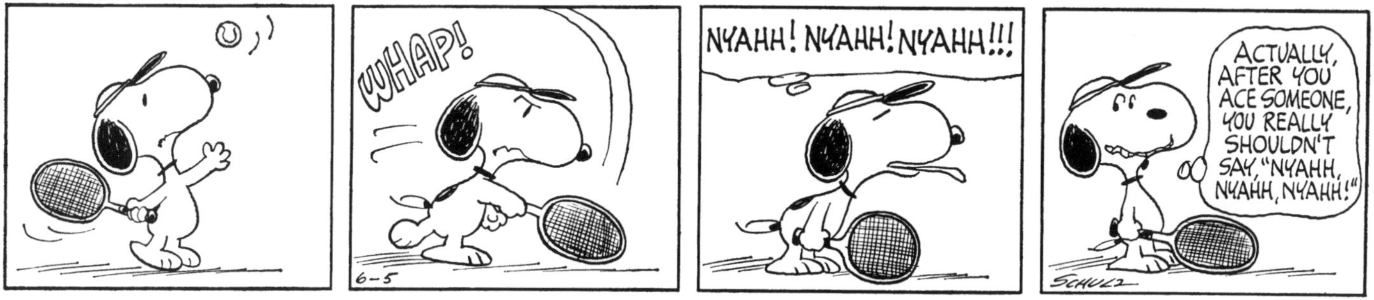
WHAP!
NYAHH! NYAHH! NYAHH!!!
ACTUALLY, AFTER YOU ACE SOMEONE, YOU REALLY SHOULDN'T SAY, "NYAHH, NYAHH, NYAHH!"

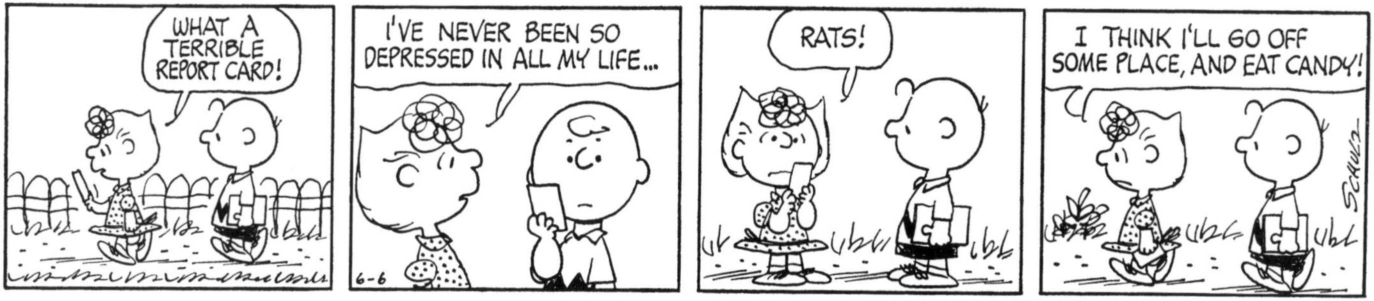
WHAT A TERRIBLE REPORT CARD!
I'VE NEVER BEEN SO DEPRESSED IN ALL MY LIFE...
RATS!
I THINK I'LL GO OFF SOME PLACE, AND EAT CANDY!

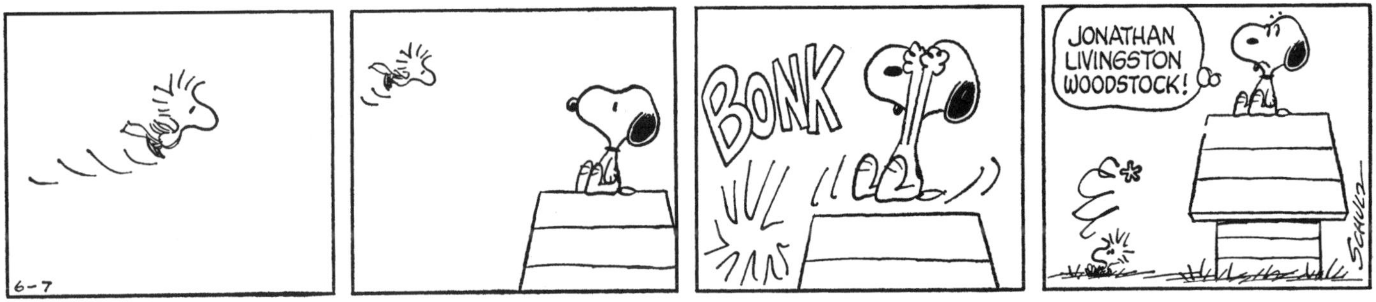
6-7
BONK
JONATHAN LIVINGSTON WOODSTOCK!
SCHULZ

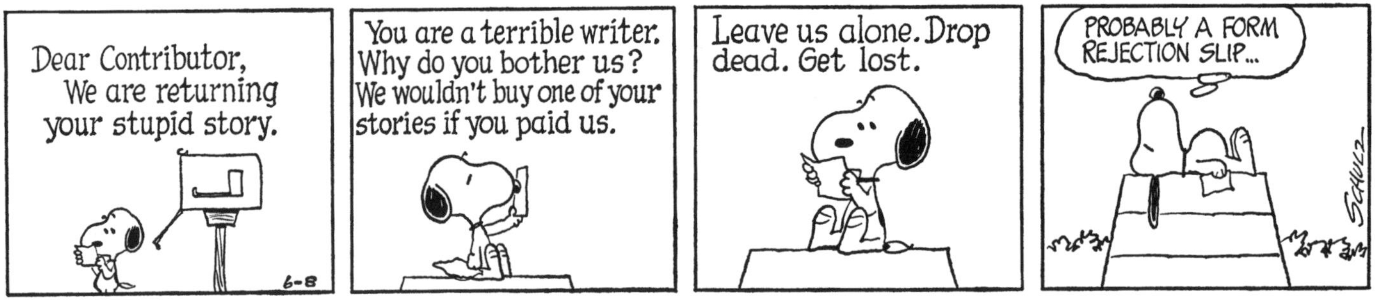
Dear Contributor,
We are returning your stupid story.
6-8
You are a terrible writer. Why do you bother us? We wouldn't buy one of your stories if you paid us.
Leave us alone. Drop dead. Get lost.
PROBABLY A FORM REJECTION SLIP...
SCHULZ

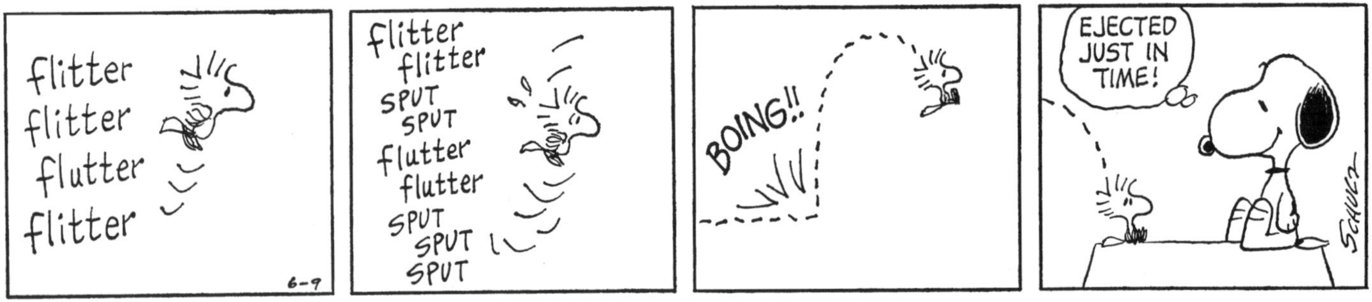
flitter flitter flutter flitter
6-9
flitter flitter SPUT SPUT flutter flutter SPUT SPUT SPUT
BOING!!
EJECTED JUST IN TIME!
SCHULZ

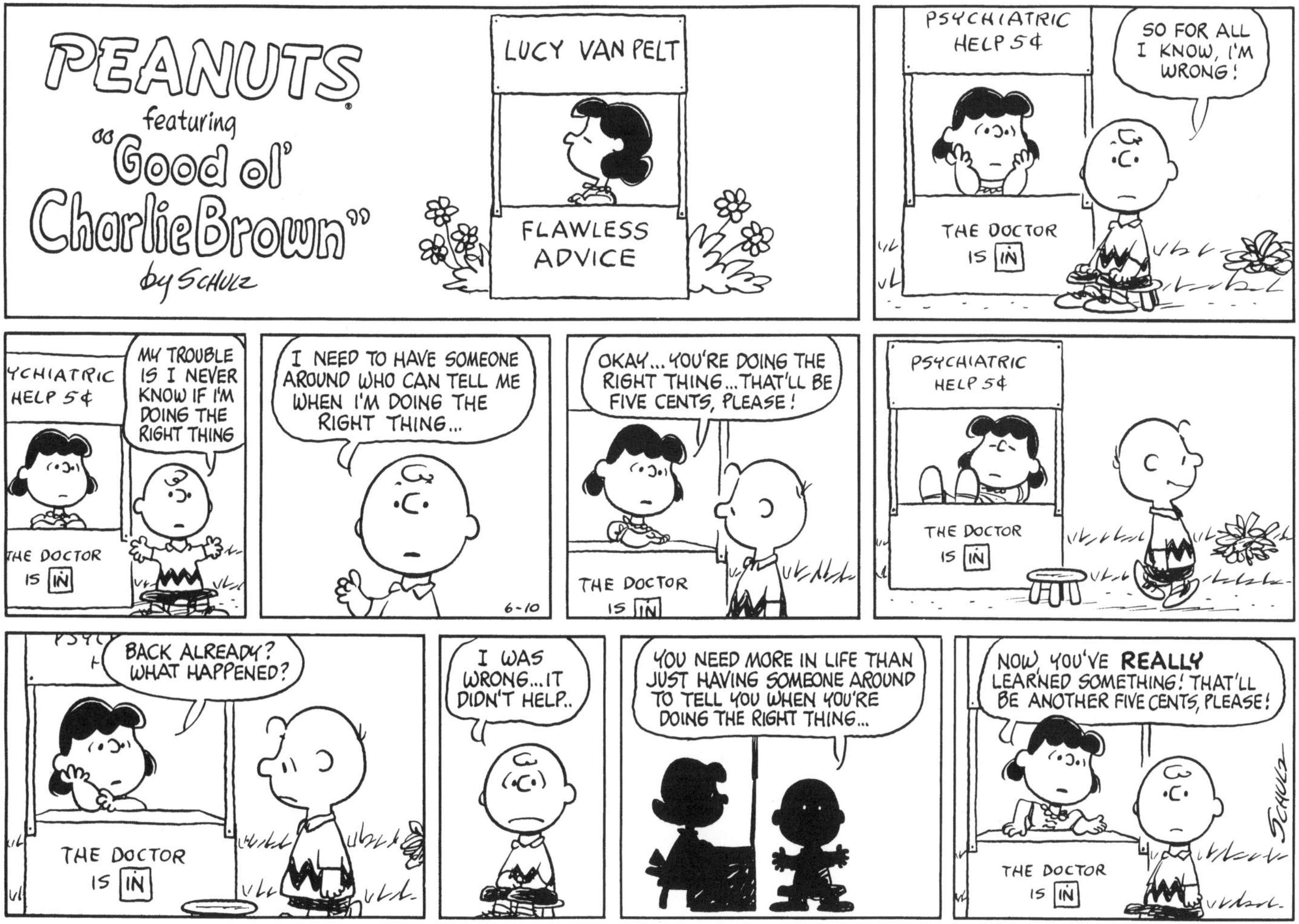
PEANUTS
featuring "Good ol' CharlieBrown"
by SCHULZ
LUCY VAN PELT
FLAWLESS ADVICE
PSYCHIATRIC HELP 5¢
SO FOR ALL I KNOW, I'M WRONG!
THE DOCTOR IS IN
YCHIATRIC HELP 5¢
MY TROUBLE IS I NEVER KNOW IF I'M DOING THE RIGHT THING
THE DOCTOR IS IN
I NEED TO HAVE SOMEONE AROUND WHO CAN TELL ME WHEN I'M DOING THE RIGHT THING...
6-10
OKAY... YOU'RE DOING THE RIGHT THING... THAT'LL BE FIVE CENTS, PLEASE!
THE DOCTOR IS IN
PSYCHIATRIC HELP 5¢
THE DOCTOR IS IN
BACK ALREADY? WHAT HAPPENED?
THE DOCTOR IS IN
I WAS WRONG... IT DIDN'T HELP..
YOU NEED MORE IN LIFE THAN JUST HAVING SOMEONE AROUND TO TELL YOU WHEN YOU'RE DOING THE RIGHT THING...
NOW, YOU'VE REALLY LEARNED SOMETHING! THAT'LL BE ANOTHER FIVE CENTS, PLEASE!
THE DOCTOR IS IN
SCHULZ

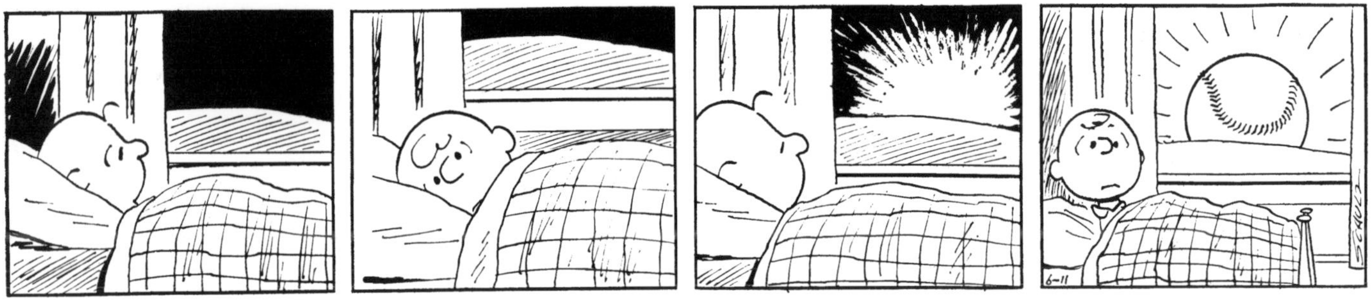
6-11
SCHULZ

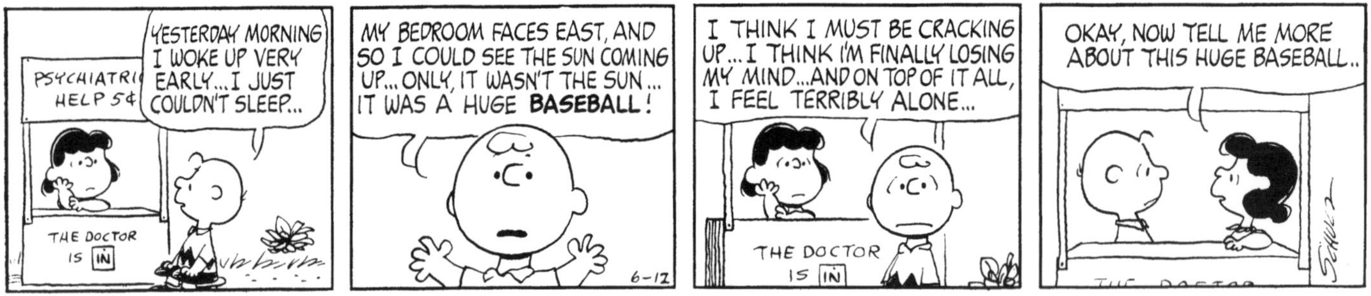
PSYCHIATRIC HELP 5¢
THE DOCTOR IS IN
YESTERDAY MORNING I WOKE UP VERY EARLY...I JUST COULDN'T SLEEP...
MY BEDROOM FACES EAST, AND SO I COULD SEE THE SUN COMING UP...ONLY, IT WASN'T THE SUN... IT WAS A HUGE **BASEBALL**!
6-12
I THINK I MUST BE CRACKING UP...I THINK I'M FINALLY LOSING MY MIND...AND ON TOP OF IT ALL, I FEEL TERRIBLY ALONE...
THE DOCTOR IS IN
OKAY, NOW TELL ME MORE ABOUT THIS HUGE BASEBALL..
SCHULZ

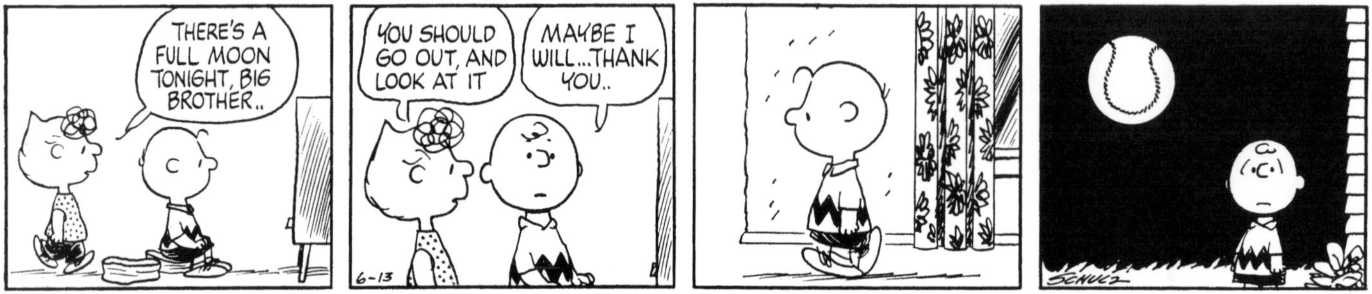
THERE'S A FULL MOON TONIGHT, BIG BROTHER..
YOU SHOULD GO OUT, AND LOOK AT IT
MAYBE I WILL...THANK YOU..
6-13
SCHULZ

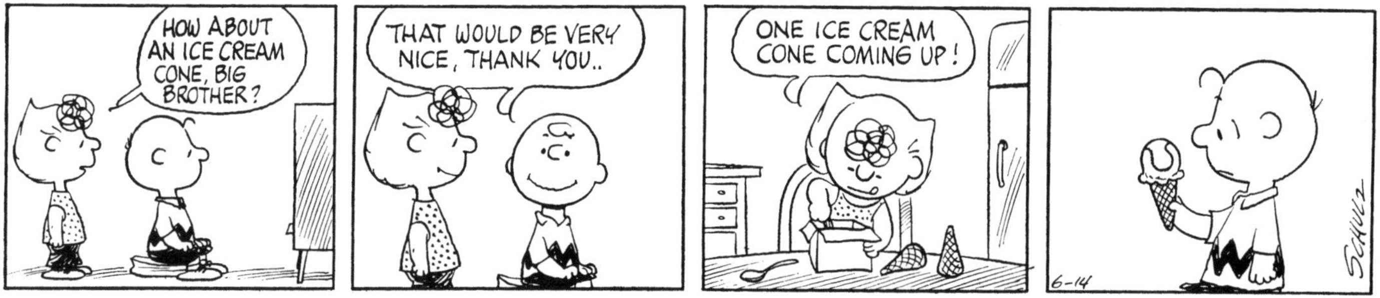
HOW ABOUT AN ICE CREAM CONE, BIG BROTHER?
THAT WOULD BE VERY NICE, THANK YOU..
ONE ICE CREAM CONE COMING UP!
6-14
SCHULZ

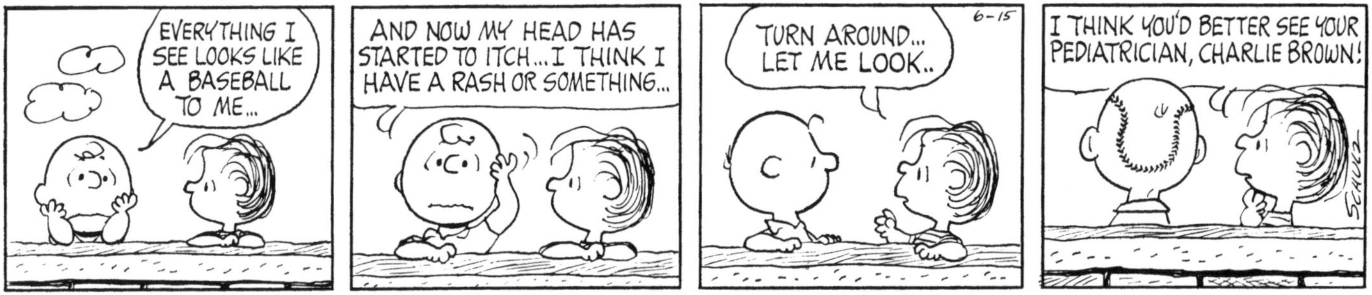
EVERYTHING I SEE LOOKS LIKE A BASEBALL TO ME...
AND NOW MY HEAD HAS STARTED TO ITCH...I THINK I HAVE A RASH OR SOMETHING...
6-15
TURN AROUND... LET ME LOOK..
I THINK YOU'D BETTER SEE YOUR PEDIATRICIAN, CHARLIE BROWN!
SCHULZ

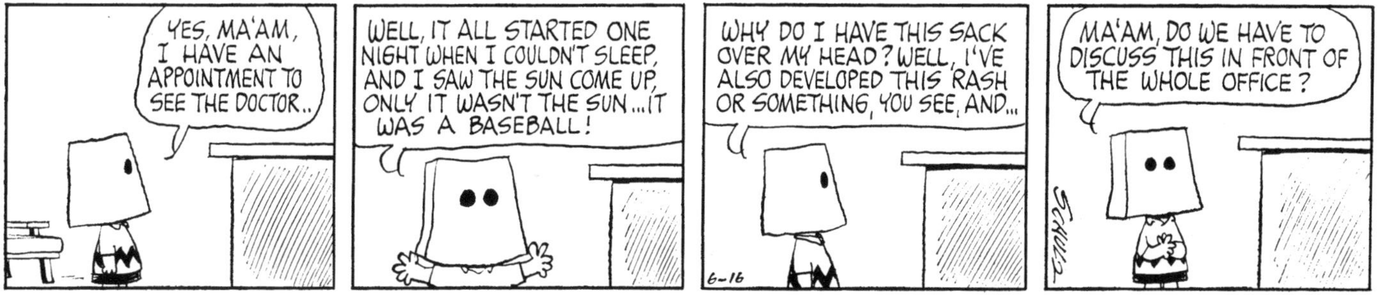
YES, MA'AM, I HAVE AN APPOINTMENT TO SEE THE DOCTOR..
WELL, IT ALL STARTED ONE NIGHT WHEN I COULDN'T SLEEP, AND I SAW THE SUN COME UP, ONLY IT WASN'T THE SUN...IT WAS A BASEBALL!
WHY DO I HAVE THIS SACK OVER MY HEAD? WELL, I'VE ALSO DEVELOPED THIS RASH OR SOMETHING, YOU SEE, AND...
6-16
SCHULZ
MA'AM, DO WE HAVE TO DISCUSS THIS IN FRONT OF THE WHOLE OFFICE?

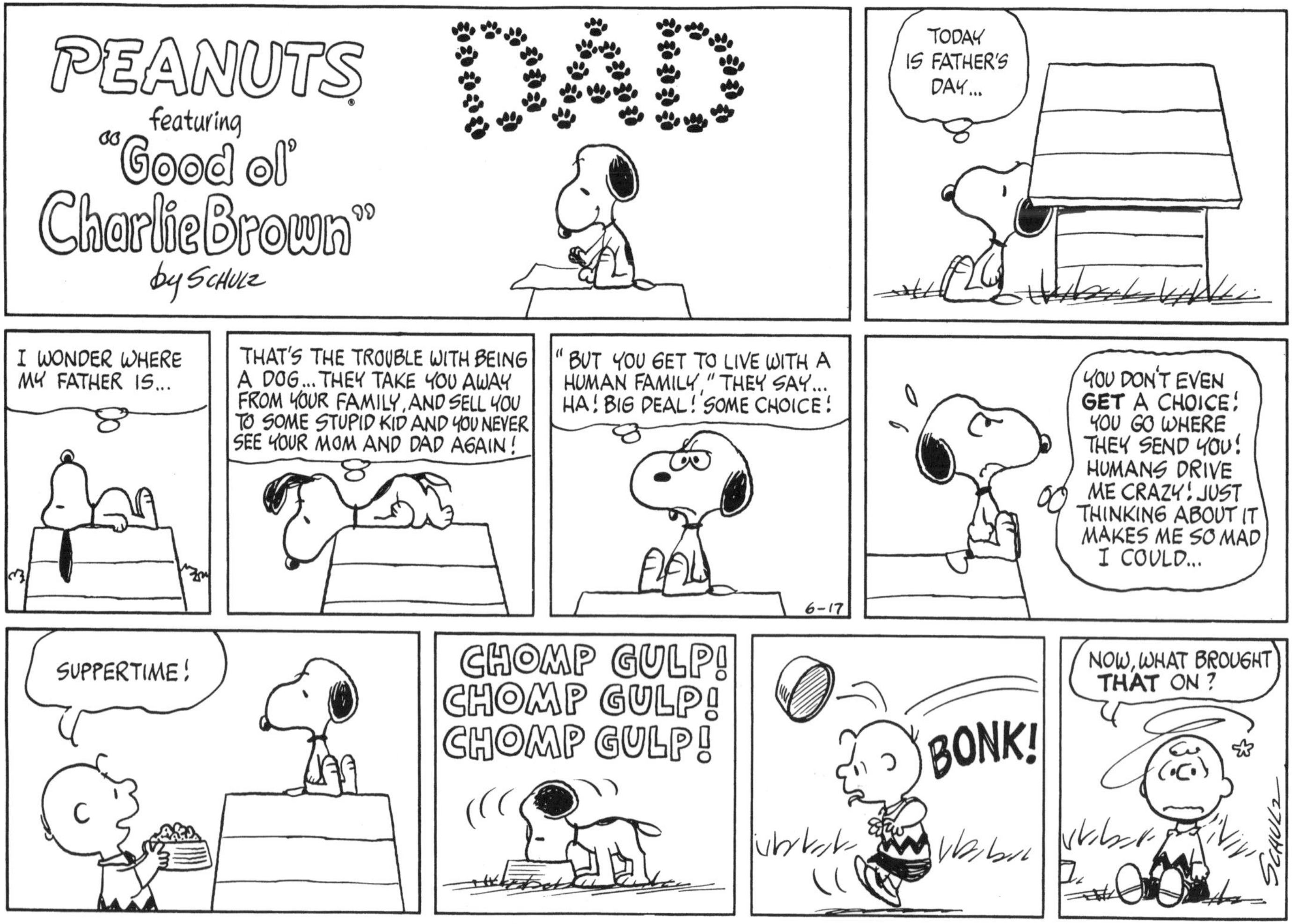
PEANUTS
featuring
"Good ol' CharlieBrown"
by SCHULZ
DAD
TODAY IS FATHER'S DAY...
I WONDER WHERE MY FATHER IS...
THAT'S THE TROUBLE WITH BEING A DOG... THEY TAKE YOU AWAY FROM YOUR FAMILY, AND SELL YOU TO SOME STUPID KID AND YOU NEVER SEE YOUR MOM AND DAD AGAIN!
"BUT YOU GET TO LIVE WITH A HUMAN FAMILY," THEY SAY... HA! BIG DEAL! SOME CHOICE!
6-17
YOU DON'T EVEN **GET** A CHOICE! YOU GO WHERE THEY SEND YOU! HUMANS DRIVE ME CRAZY! JUST THINKING ABOUT IT MAKES ME SO MAD I COULD...
SUPPERTIME!
CHOMP GULP! CHOMP GULP! CHOMP GULP!
BONK!
NOW, WHAT BROUGHT **THAT** ON?
SCHULZ

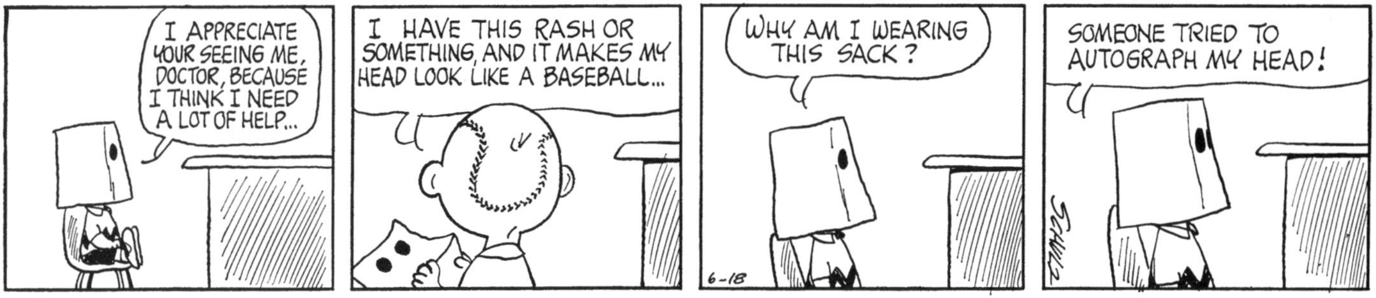
I APPRECIATE YOUR SEEING ME, DOCTOR, BECAUSE I THINK I NEED A LOT OF HELP...
I HAVE THIS RASH OR SOMETHING, AND IT MAKES MY HEAD LOOK LIKE A BASEBALL...
WHY AM I WEARING THIS SACK?
SOMEONE TRIED TO AUTOGRAPH MY HEAD!
6-18
SCHULZ

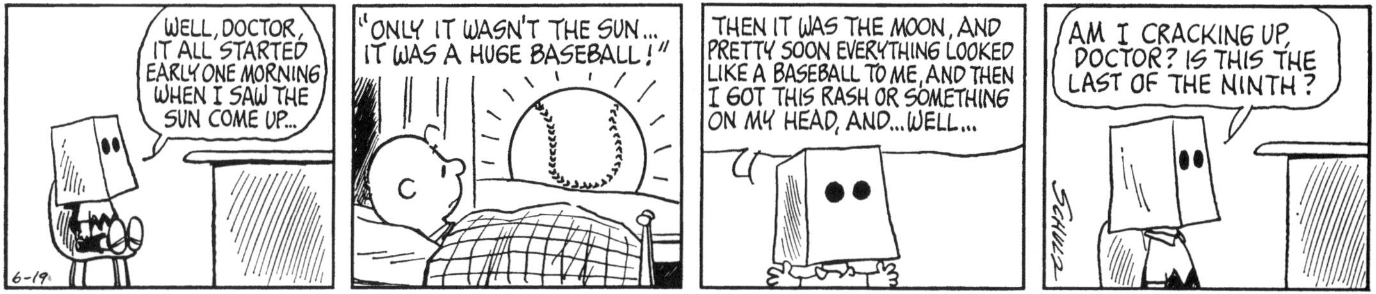
WELL, DOCTOR, IT ALL STARTED EARLY ONE MORNING WHEN I SAW THE SUN COME UP...
"ONLY IT WASN'T THE SUN... IT WAS A HUGE BASEBALL!"
THEN IT WAS THE MOON, AND PRETTY SOON EVERYTHING LOOKED LIKE A BASEBALL TO ME, AND THEN I GOT THIS RASH OR SOMETHING ON MY HEAD, AND...WELL...
AM I CRACKING UP, DOCTOR? IS THIS THE LAST OF THE NINTH?
6-19
SCHULZ

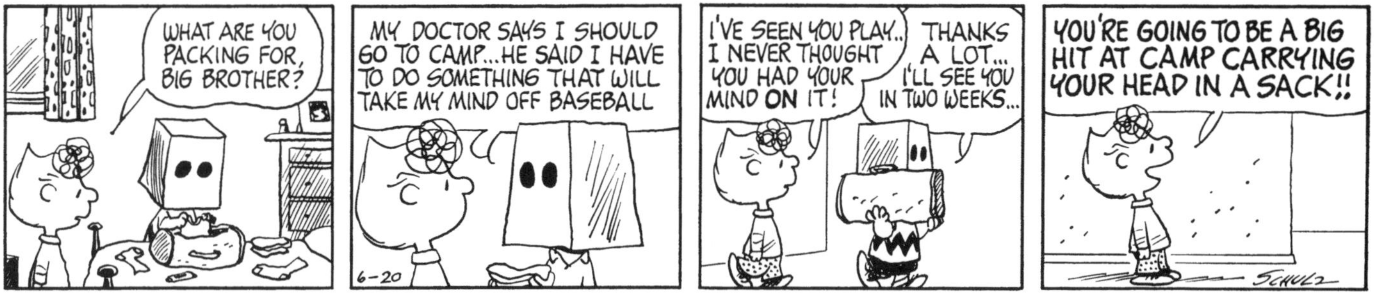
WHAT ARE YOU PACKING FOR, BIG BROTHER?
MY DOCTOR SAYS I SHOULD GO TO CAMP...HE SAID I HAVE TO DO SOMETHING THAT WILL TAKE MY MIND OFF BASEBALL
I'VE SEEN YOU PLAY.. I NEVER THOUGHT YOU HAD YOUR MIND ON IT!
THANKS A LOT... I'LL SEE YOU IN TWO WEEKS...
YOU'RE GOING TO BE A BIG HIT AT CAMP CARRYING YOUR HEAD IN A SACK!!
6-20
SCHULZ

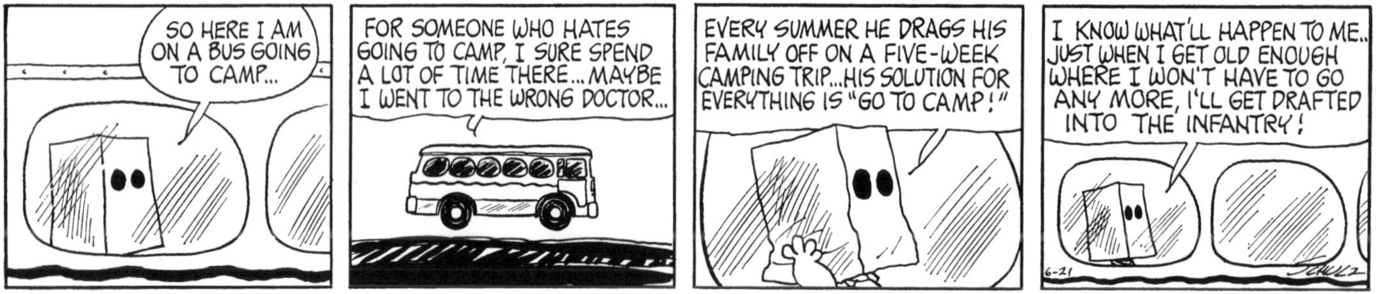
SO HERE I AM ON A BUS GOING TO CAMP...
FOR SOMEONE WHO HATES GOING TO CAMP, I SURE SPEND A LOT OF TIME THERE... MAYBE I WENT TO THE WRONG DOCTOR...
EVERY SUMMER HE DRAGS HIS FAMILY OFF ON A FIVE-WEEK CAMPING TRIP...HIS SOLUTION FOR EVERYTHING IS "GO TO CAMP!"
I KNOW WHAT'LL HAPPEN TO ME.. JUST WHEN I GET OLD ENOUGH WHERE I WON'T HAVE TO GO ANY MORE, I'LL GET DRAFTED INTO THE INFANTRY!
6-21
SCHULZ

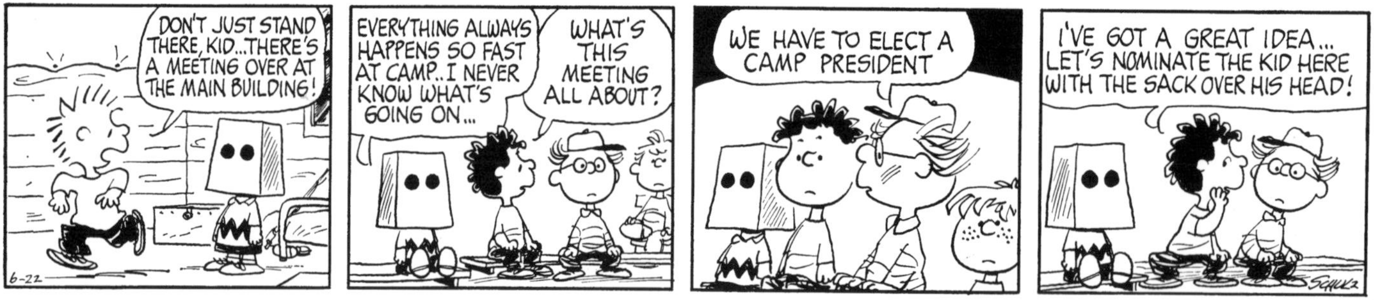
DON'T JUST STAND THERE, KID...THERE'S A MEETING OVER AT THE MAIN BUILDING!
6-22
EVERYTHING ALWAYS HAPPENS SO FAST AT CAMP..I NEVER KNOW WHAT'S GOING ON...
WHAT'S THIS MEETING ALL ABOUT?
WE HAVE TO ELECT A CAMP PRESIDENT
I'VE GOT A GREAT IDEA... LET'S NOMINATE THE KID HERE WITH THE SACK OVER HIS HEAD!
SCHULZ

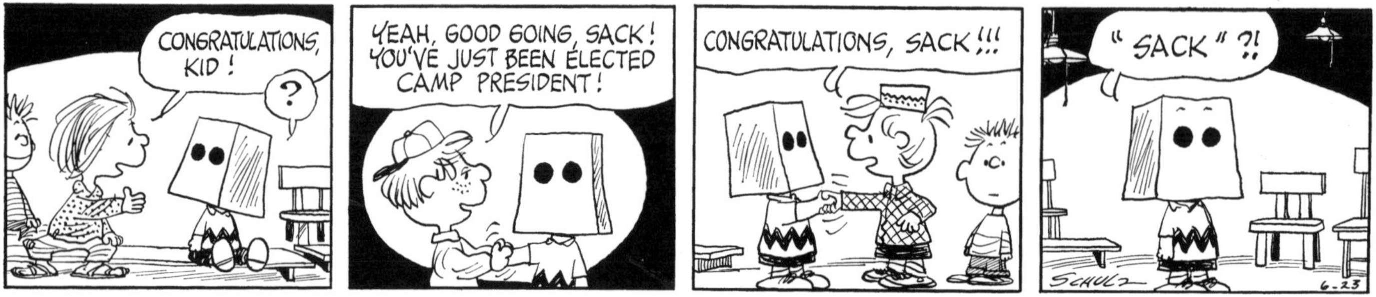
CONGRATULATIONS, KID!
?
YEAH, GOOD GOING, SACK! YOU'VE JUST BEEN ELECTED CAMP PRESIDENT!
CONGRATULATIONS, SACK!!!
"SACK"?!
SCHULZ
6-23

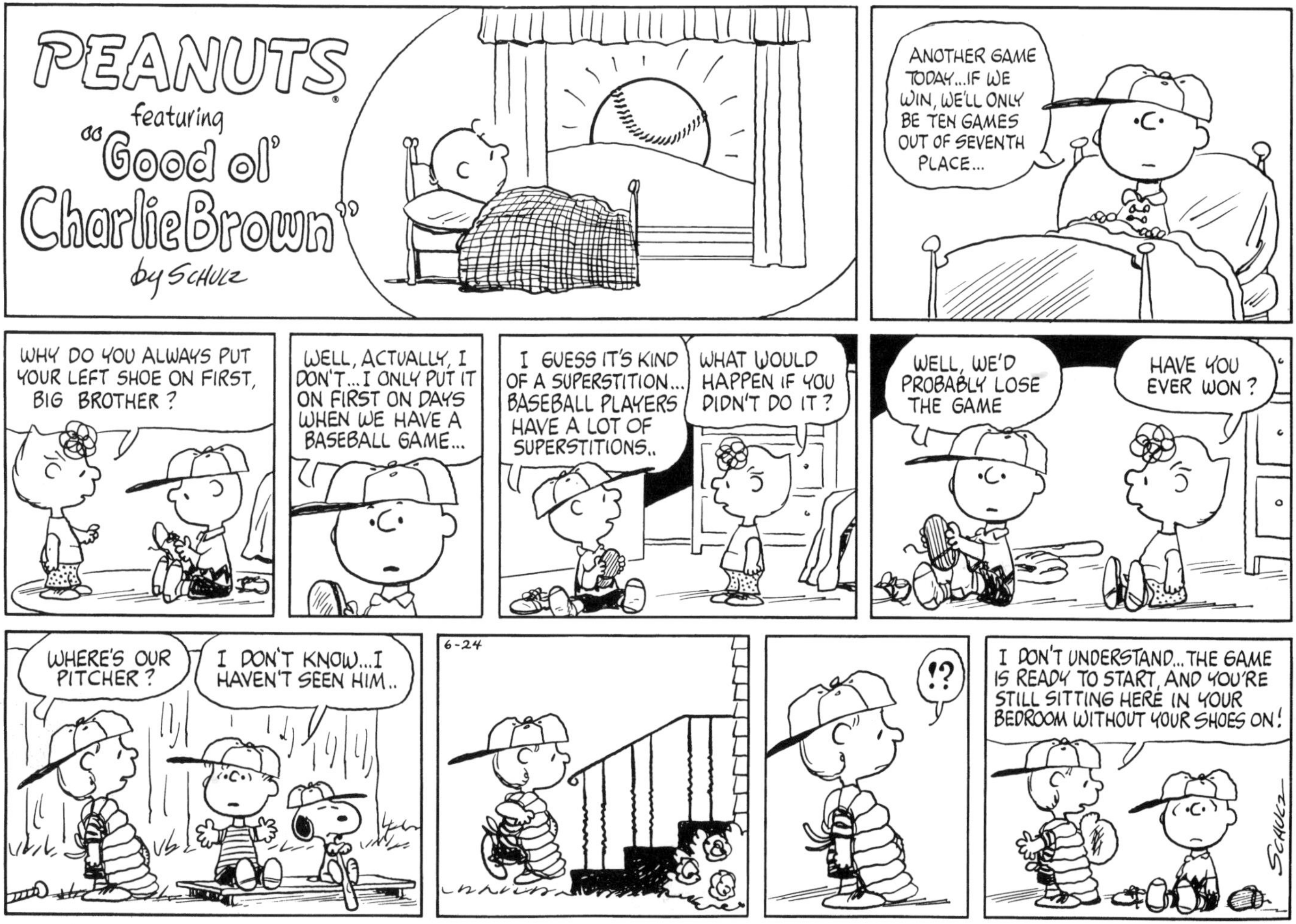
PEANUTS
featuring
"Good ol' Charlie Brown"
by SCHULZ
ANOTHER GAME TODAY...IF WE WIN, WE'LL ONLY BE TEN GAMES OUT OF SEVENTH PLACE...
WHY DO YOU ALWAYS PUT YOUR LEFT SHOE ON FIRST, BIG BROTHER ?
WELL, ACTUALLY, I DON'T...I ONLY PUT IT ON FIRST ON DAYS WHEN WE HAVE A BASEBALL GAME...
I GUESS IT'S KIND OF A SUPERSTITION... BASEBALL PLAYERS HAVE A LOT OF SUPERSTITIONS..
WHAT WOULD HAPPEN IF YOU DIDN'T DO IT ?
WELL, WE'D PROBABLY LOSE THE GAME
HAVE YOU EVER WON ?
WHERE'S OUR PITCHER ?
I DON'T KNOW...I HAVEN'T SEEN HIM..
6-24
!?
I DON'T UNDERSTAND...THE GAME IS READY TO START, AND YOU'RE STILL SITTING HERE IN YOUR BEDROOM WITHOUT YOUR SHOES ON!
SCHULZ

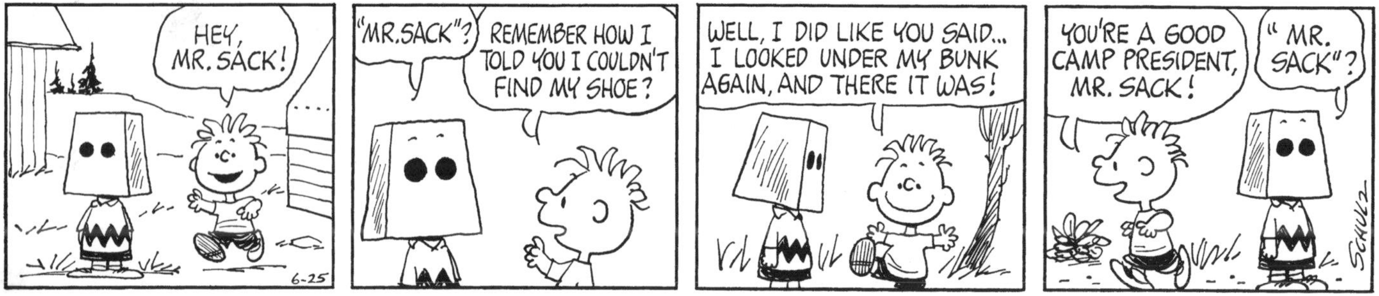
HEY, MR. SACK!
6-25
"MR.SACK"?
REMEMBER HOW I TOLD YOU I COULDN'T FIND MY SHOE?
WELL, I DID LIKE YOU SAID... I LOOKED UNDER MY BUNK AGAIN, AND THERE IT WAS!
YOU'RE A GOOD CAMP PRESIDENT, MR. SACK!
"MR. SACK"?
SCHULZ

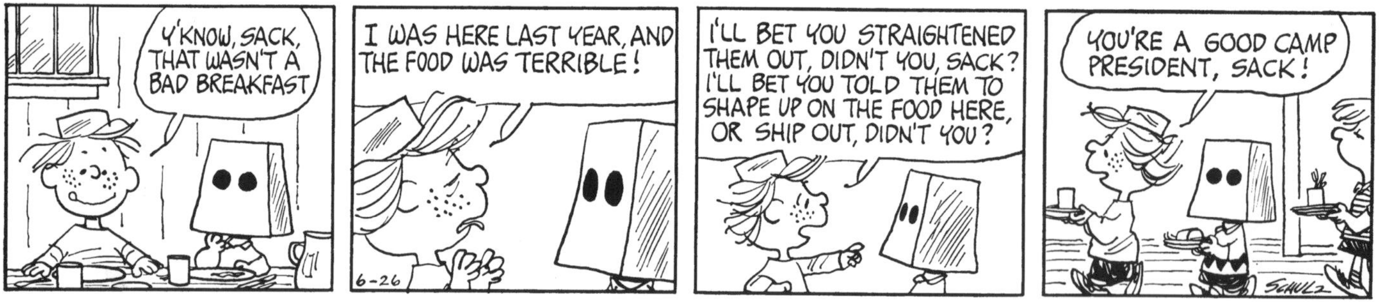
Y'KNOW, SACK, THAT WASN'T A BAD BREAKFAST
I WAS HERE LAST YEAR, AND THE FOOD WAS TERRIBLE!
6-26
I'LL BET YOU STRAIGHTENED THEM OUT, DIDN'T YOU, SACK? I'LL BET YOU TOLD THEM TO SHAPE UP ON THE FOOD HERE, OR SHIP OUT, DIDN'T YOU?
YOU'RE A GOOD CAMP PRESIDENT, SACK!
SCHULZ

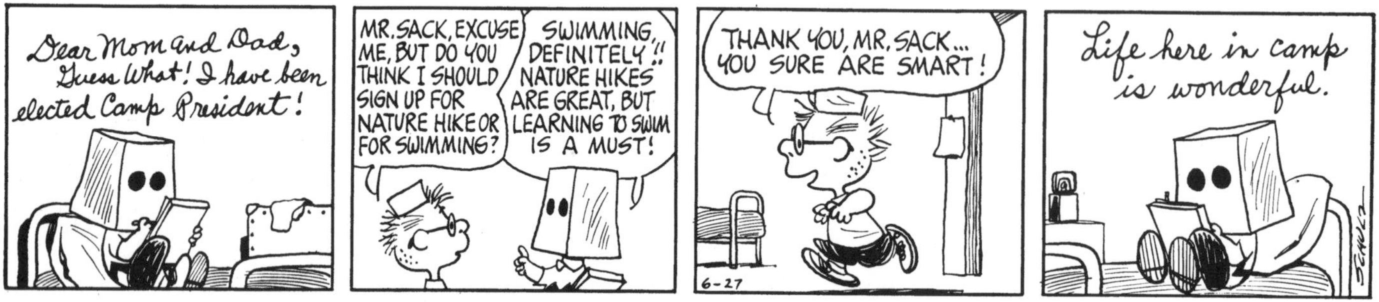
Dear Mom and Dad, Guess What! I have been elected Camp President!
MR. SACK, EXCUSE ME, BUT DO YOU THINK I SHOULD SIGN UP FOR NATURE HIKE OR FOR SWIMMING?
SWIMMING, DEFINITELY!! NATURE HIKES ARE GREAT, BUT LEARNING TO SWIM IS A MUST!
THANK YOU, MR. SACK... YOU SURE ARE SMART!
6-27
Life here in camp is wonderful.
SCHULZ

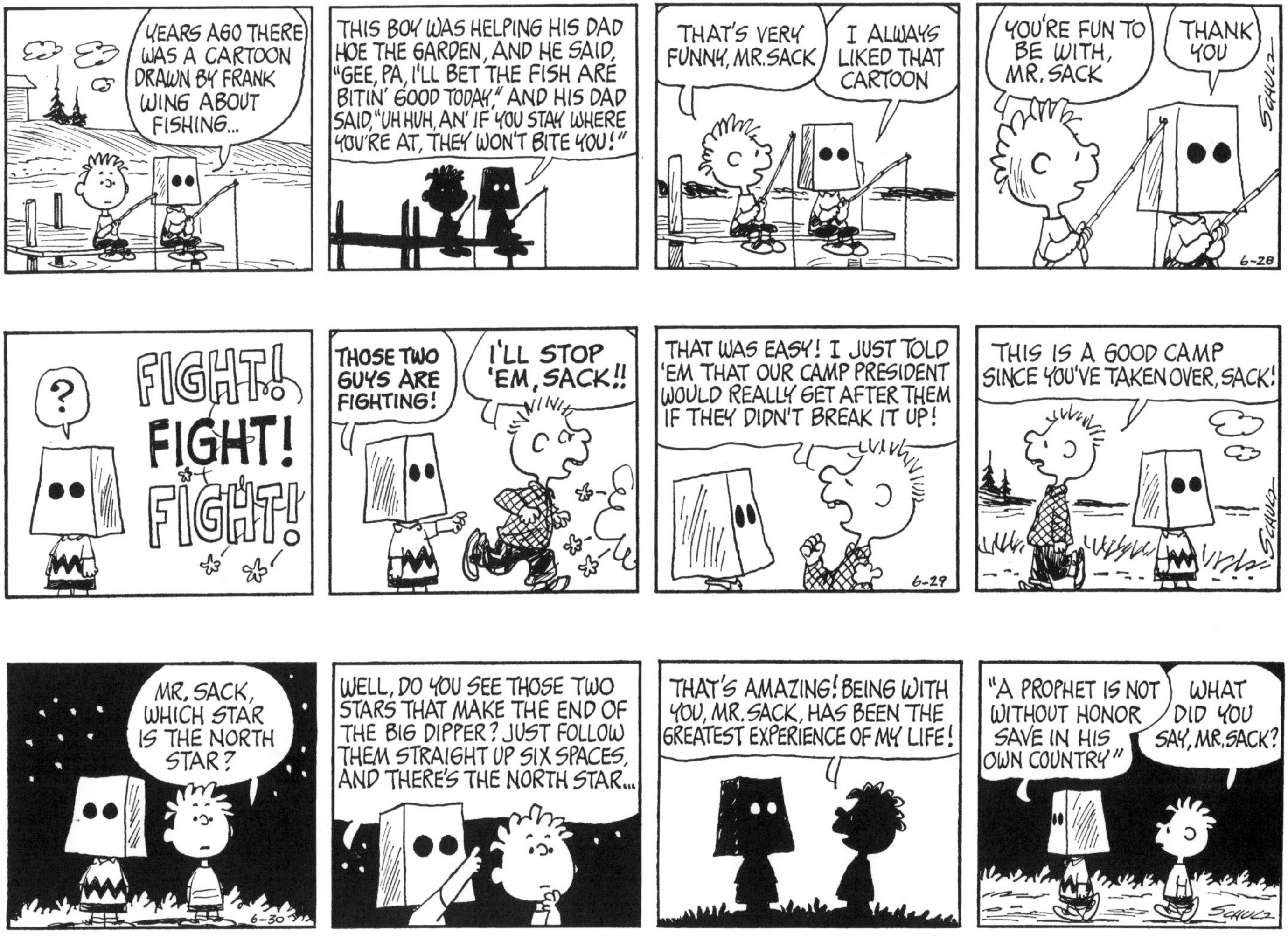
YEARS AGO THERE WAS A CARTOON DRAWN BY FRANK WING ABOUT FISHING...
THIS BOY WAS HELPING HIS DAD HOE THE GARDEN, AND HE SAID, "GEE, PA, I'LL BET THE FISH ARE BITIN' GOOD TODAY," AND HIS DAD SAID, "UH HUH, AN' IF YOU STAY WHERE YOU'RE AT, THEY WON'T BITE YOU!"
THAT'S VERY FUNNY, MR. SACK
I ALWAYS LIKED THAT CARTOON
YOU'RE FUN TO BE WITH, MR. SACK
THANK YOU
SCHULZ
6-28
?
FIGHT! FIGHT! FIGHT!
THOSE TWO GUYS ARE FIGHTING!
I'LL STOP 'EM, SACK!!
THAT WAS EASY! I JUST TOLD 'EM THAT OUR CAMP PRESIDENT WOULD REALLY GET AFTER THEM IF THEY DIDN'T BREAK IT UP!
6-29
THIS IS A GOOD CAMP SINCE YOU'VE TAKEN OVER, SACK!
SCHULZ
MR. SACK, WHICH STAR IS THE NORTH STAR?
6-30
WELL, DO YOU SEE THOSE TWO STARS THAT MAKE THE END OF THE BIG DIPPER? JUST FOLLOW THEM STRAIGHT UP SIX SPACES, AND THERE'S THE NORTH STAR...
THAT'S AMAZING! BEING WITH YOU, MR. SACK, HAS BEEN THE GREATEST EXPERIENCE OF MY LIFE!
"A PROPHET IS NOT WITHOUT HONOR SAVE IN HIS OWN COUNTRY"
WHAT DID YOU SAY, MR. SACK?
SCHULZ

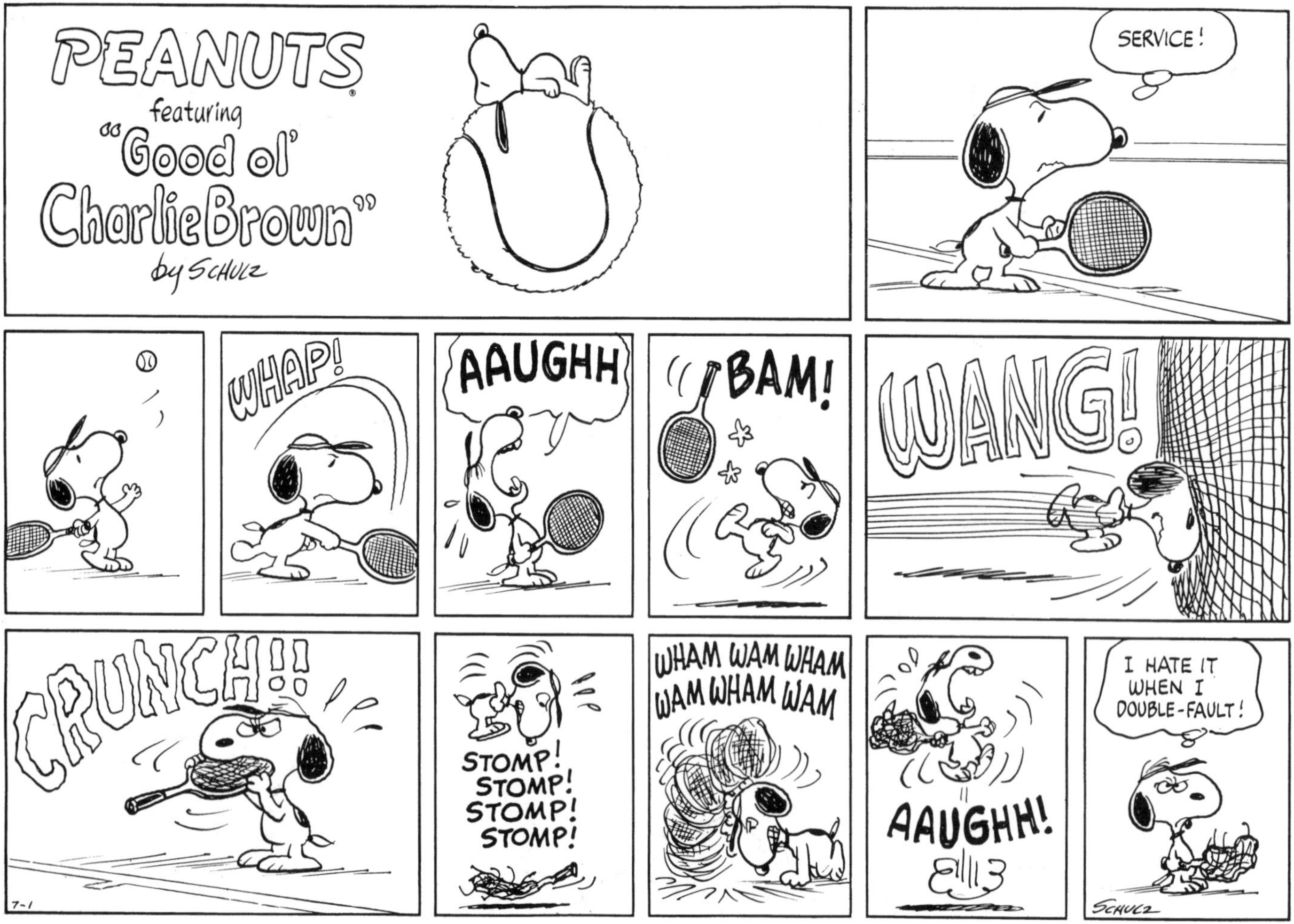
PEANUTS
featuring
"Good ol' CharlieBrown"
by SCHULZ
SERVICE!
WHAP!
AAUGHH
BAM!
WANG!
CRUNCH!!
7-1
STOMP! STOMP! STOMP! STOMP!
WHAM WAM WHAM WAM WHAM WAM
AAUGHH!
I HATE IT WHEN I DOUBLE-FAULT!
SCHULZ

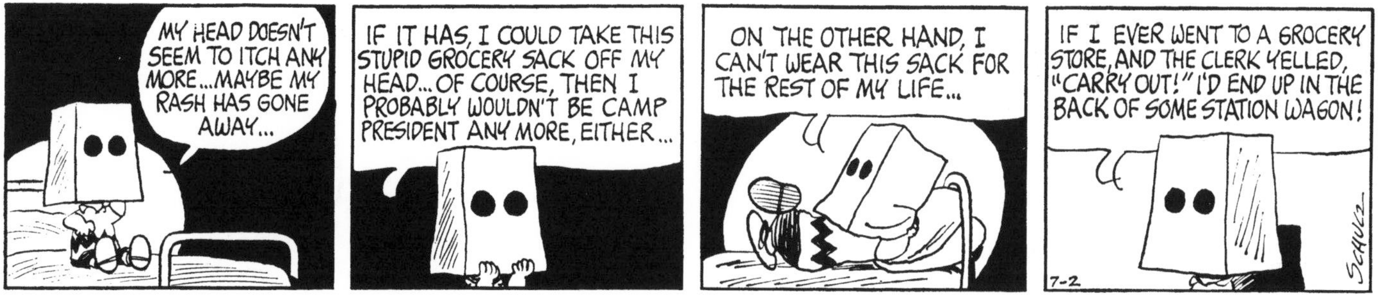
MY HEAD DOESN'T SEEM TO ITCH ANY MORE...MAYBE MY RASH HAS GONE AWAY...
IF IT HAS, I COULD TAKE THIS STUPID GROCERY SACK OFF MY HEAD...OF COURSE, THEN I PROBABLY WOULDN'T BE CAMP PRESIDENT ANY MORE, EITHER...
ON THE OTHER HAND, I CAN'T WEAR THIS SACK FOR THE REST OF MY LIFE...
IF I EVER WENT TO A GROCERY STORE, AND THE CLERK YELLED, "CARRY OUT!" I'D END UP IN THE BACK OF SOME STATION WAGON!
7-2
SCHULZ

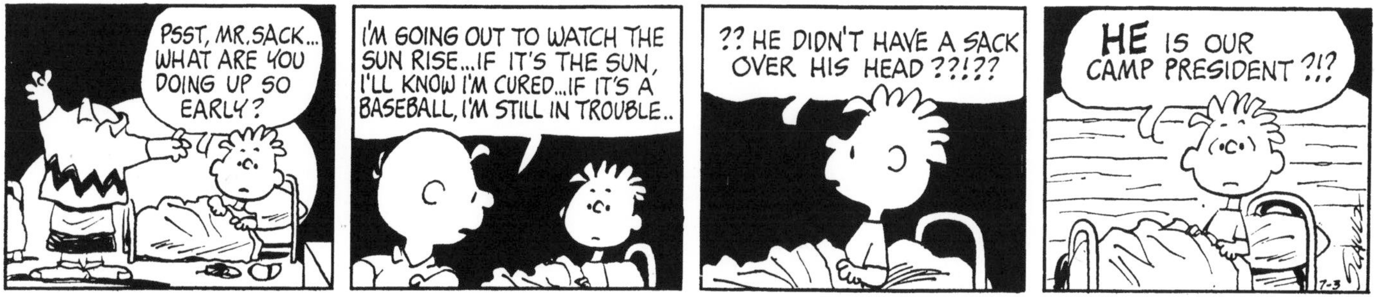
PSST, MR. SACK... WHAT ARE YOU DOING UP SO EARLY?
I'M GOING OUT TO WATCH THE SUN RISE...IF IT'S THE SUN, I'LL KNOW I'M CURED...IF IT'S A BASEBALL, I'M STILL IN TROUBLE..
?? HE DIDN'T HAVE A SACK OVER HIS HEAD ??!??
HE IS OUR CAMP PRESIDENT ?!?
7-3
SCHULZ

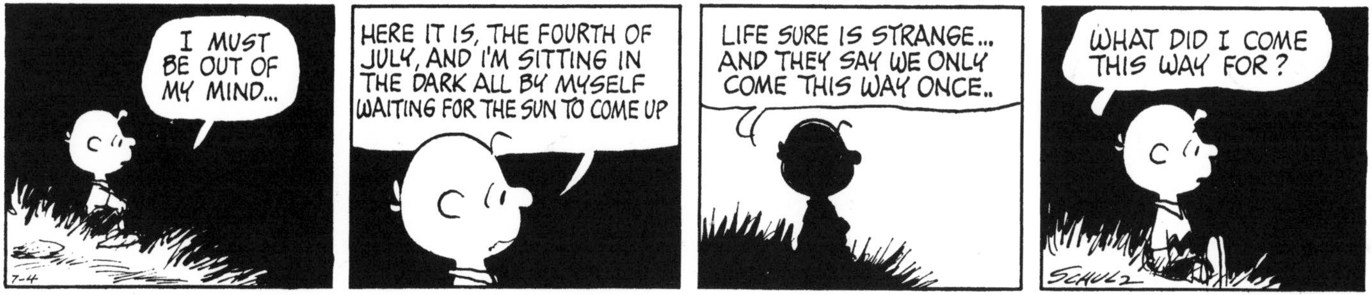
I MUST BE OUT OF MY MIND...
HERE IT IS, THE FOURTH OF JULY, AND I'M SITTING IN THE DARK ALL BY MYSELF WAITING FOR THE SUN TO COME UP
LIFE SURE IS STRANGE... AND THEY SAY WE ONLY COME THIS WAY ONCE..
WHAT DID I COME THIS WAY FOR?
7-4
SCHULZ

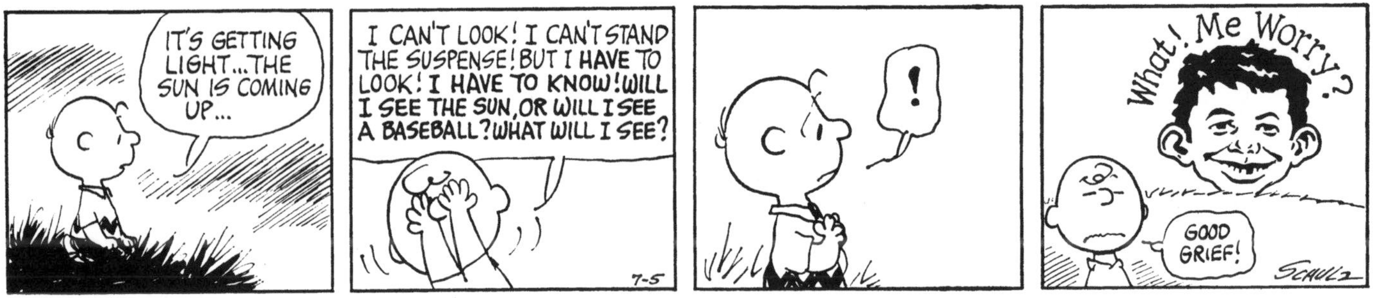
IT'S GETTING LIGHT...THE SUN IS COMING UP...
I CAN'T LOOK! I CAN'T STAND THE SUSPENSE! BUT I HAVE TO LOOK! I HAVE TO KNOW! WILL I SEE THE SUN, OR WILL I SEE A BASEBALL? WHAT WILL I SEE?
7-5
!
What! Me Worry?
GOOD GRIEF!
SCHULZ

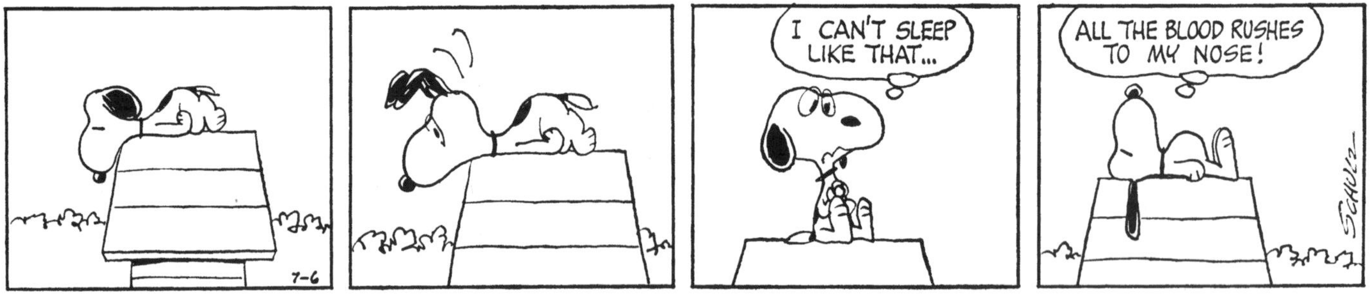
7-6
I CAN'T SLEEP LIKE THAT...
ALL THE BLOOD RUSHES TO MY NOSE!
SCHULZ

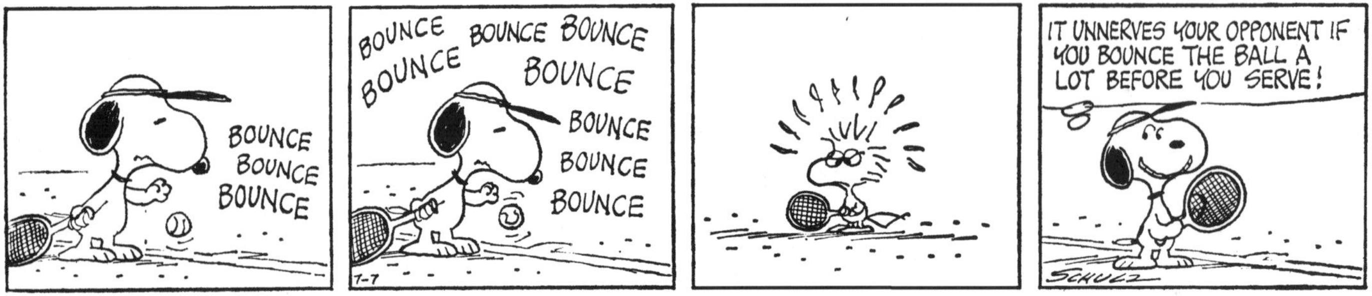
BOUNCE BOUNCE BOUNCE
BOUNCE BOUNCE BOUNCE BOUNCE BOUNCE BOUNCE BOUNCE BOUNCE
7-7
IT UNNERVES YOUR OPPONENT IF YOU BOUNCE THE BALL A LOT BEFORE YOU SERVE!
SCHULZ

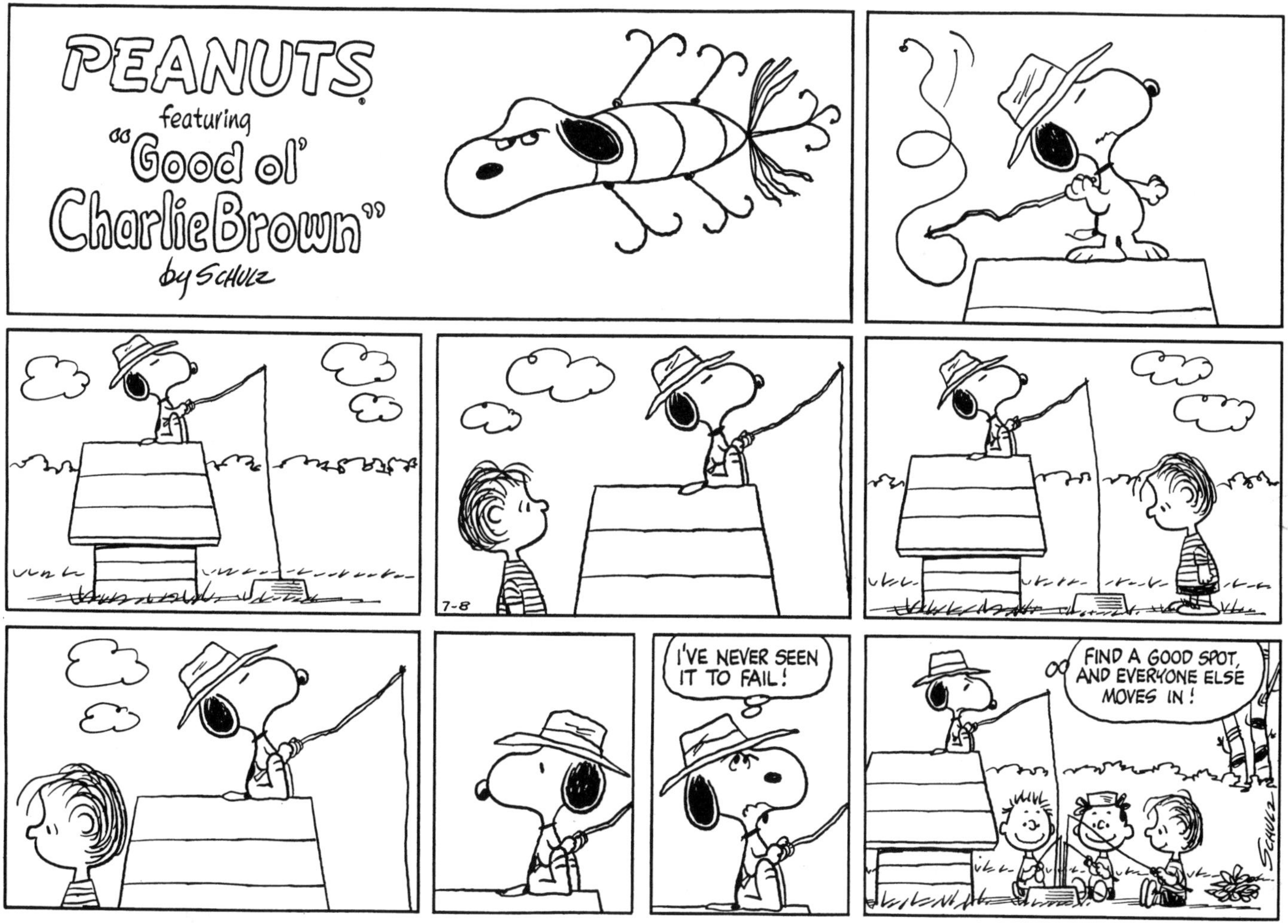
PEANUTS
featuring
"Good ol' Charlie Brown"
by SCHULZ
7-8
I'VE NEVER SEEN IT TO FAIL!
FIND A GOOD SPOT, AND EVERYONE ELSE MOVES IN!
SCHULZ

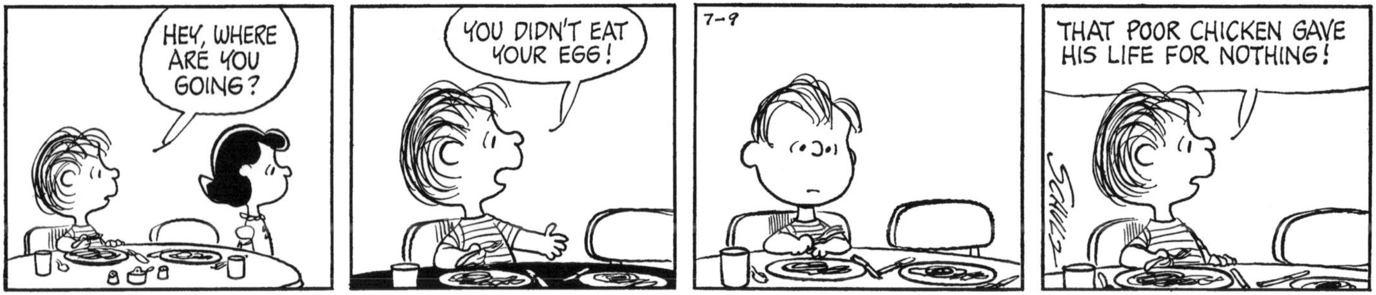
HEY, WHERE ARE YOU GOING?
YOU DIDN'T EAT YOUR EGG!
7-9
THAT POOR CHICKEN GAVE HIS LIFE FOR NOTHING!
SCHULZ

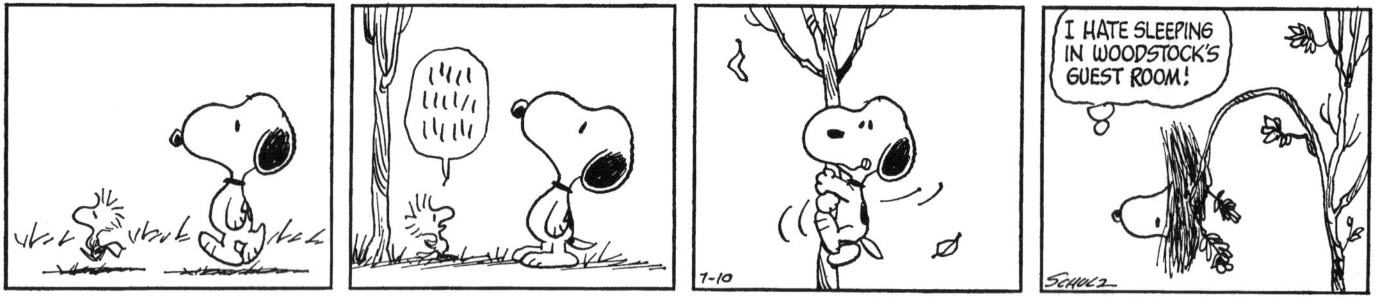
7-10
I HATE SLEEPING IN WOODSTOCK'S GUEST ROOM!
SCHULZ

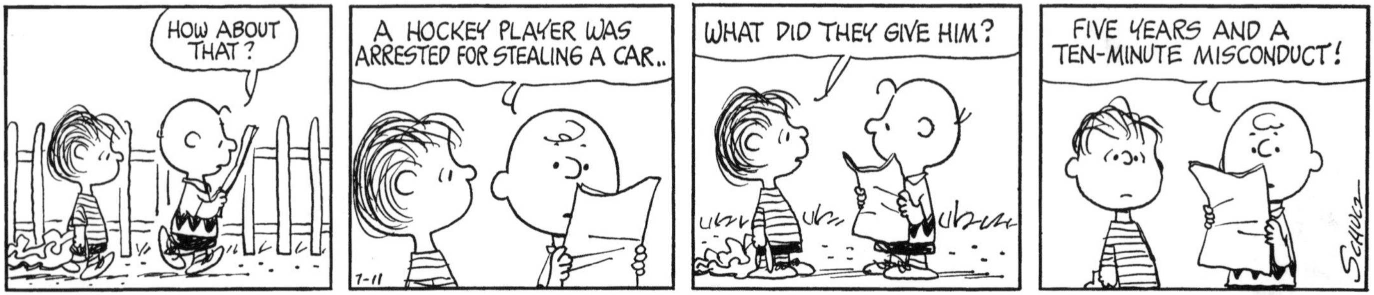
HOW ABOUT THAT?
A HOCKEY PLAYER WAS ARRESTED FOR STEALING A CAR..
7-11
WHAT DID THEY GIVE HIM?
FIVE YEARS AND A TEN-MINUTE MISCONDUCT!
SCHULZ

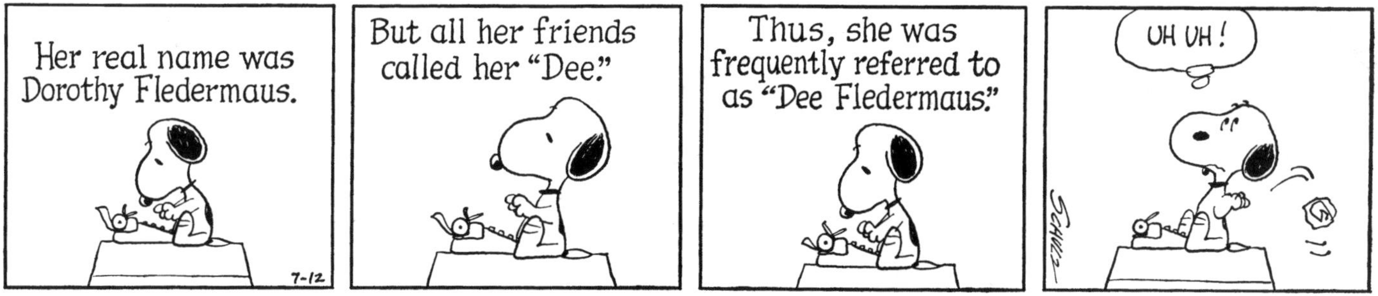
Her real name was Dorothy Fledermaus.
7-12
But all her friends called her "Dee."
Thus, she was frequently referred to as "Dee Fledermaus."
UH UH!

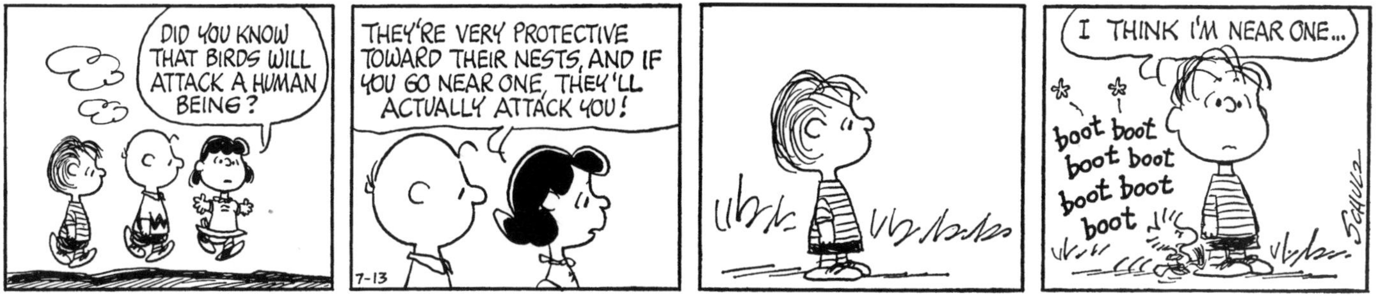
DID YOU KNOW THAT BIRDS WILL ATTACK A HUMAN BEING?
THEY'RE VERY PROTECTIVE TOWARD THEIR NESTS, AND IF YOU GO NEAR ONE, THEY'LL ACTUALLY ATTACK YOU!
7-13
I THINK I'M NEAR ONE...
boot boot boot boot boot boot boot

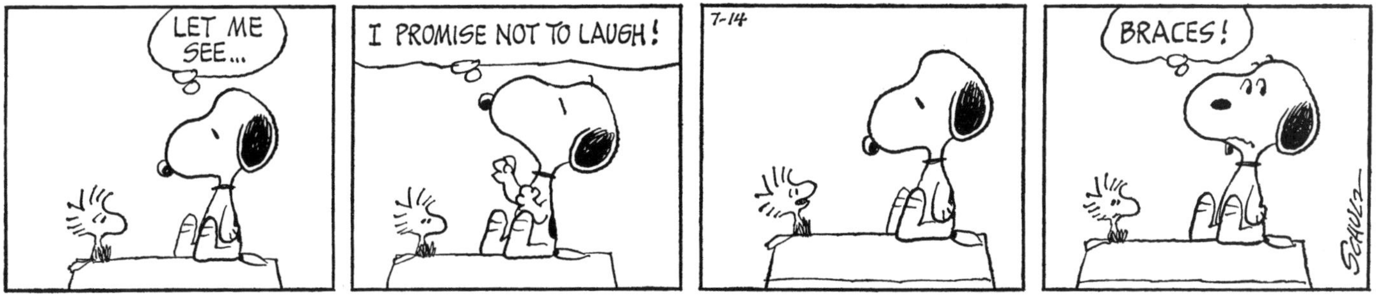
LET ME SEE...
I PROMISE NOT TO LAUGH!
7-14
BRACES!

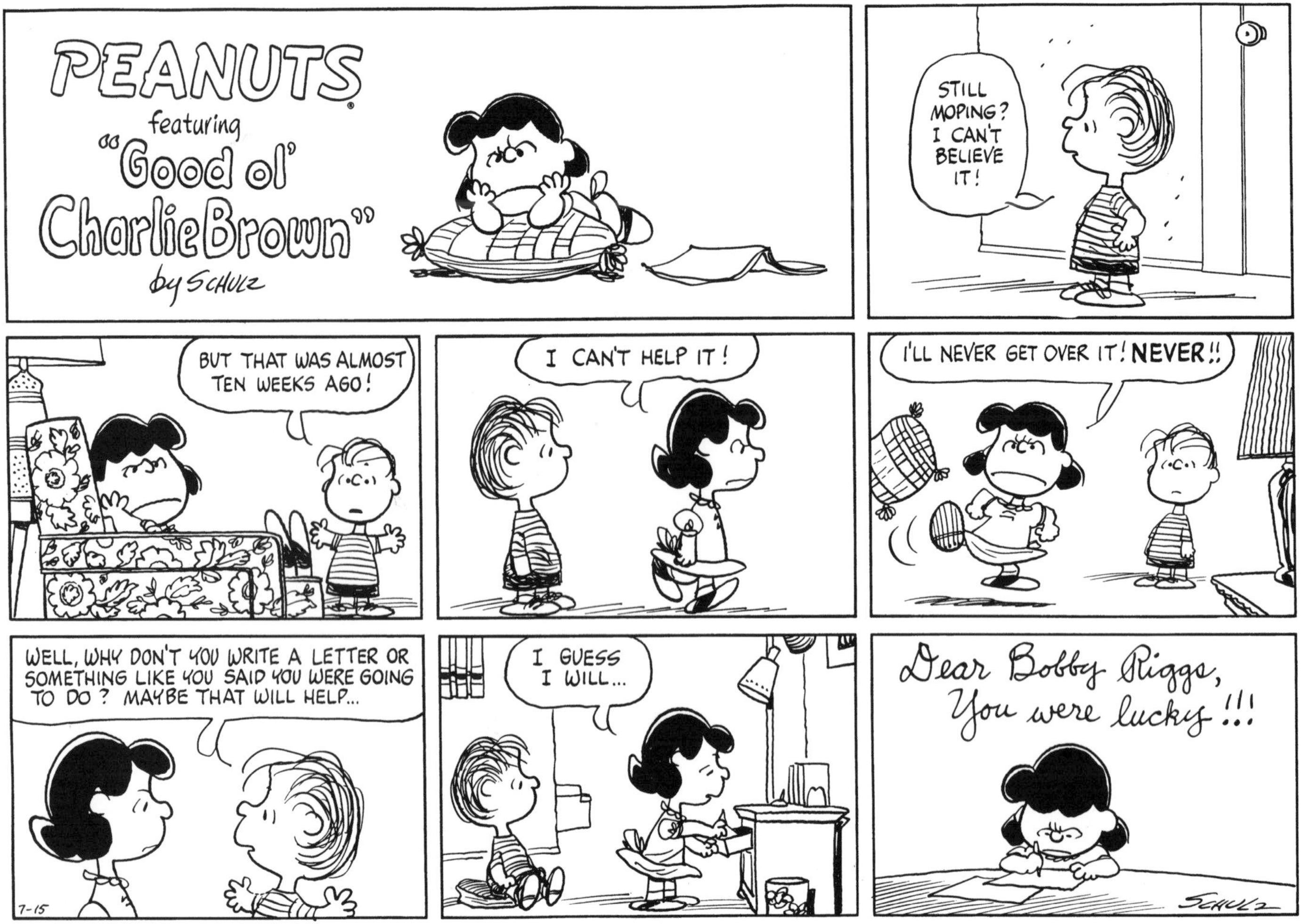
PEANUTS
featuring
"Good ol' Charlie Brown"
by SCHULZ
STILL MOPING? I CAN'T BELIEVE IT!
BUT THAT WAS ALMOST TEN WEEKS AGO!
I CAN'T HELP IT!
I'LL NEVER GET OVER IT! NEVER!!
WELL, WHY DON'T YOU WRITE A LETTER OR SOMETHING LIKE YOU SAID YOU WERE GOING TO DO? MAYBE THAT WILL HELP...
7-15
I GUESS I WILL...
Dear Bobby Riggs,
You were lucky!!!
SCHULZ

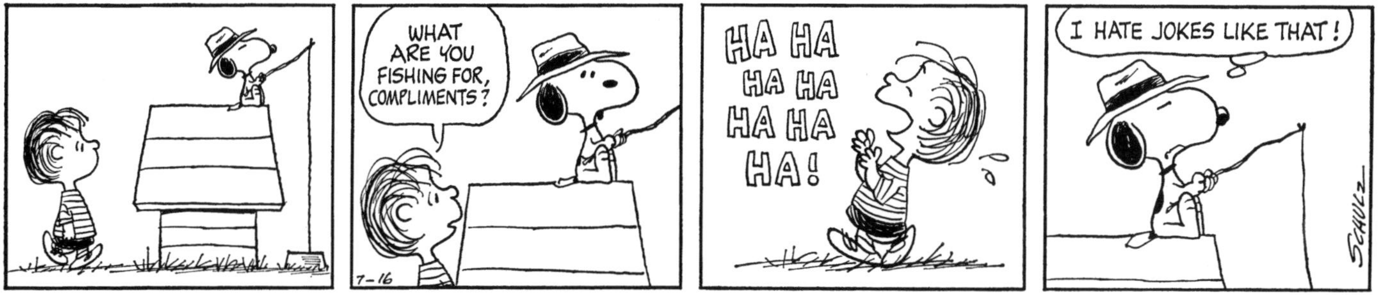
WHAT ARE YOU FISHING FOR, COMPLIMENTS?
7-16
HA HA HA HA HA HA HA!
I HATE JOKES LIKE THAT!
SCHULZ

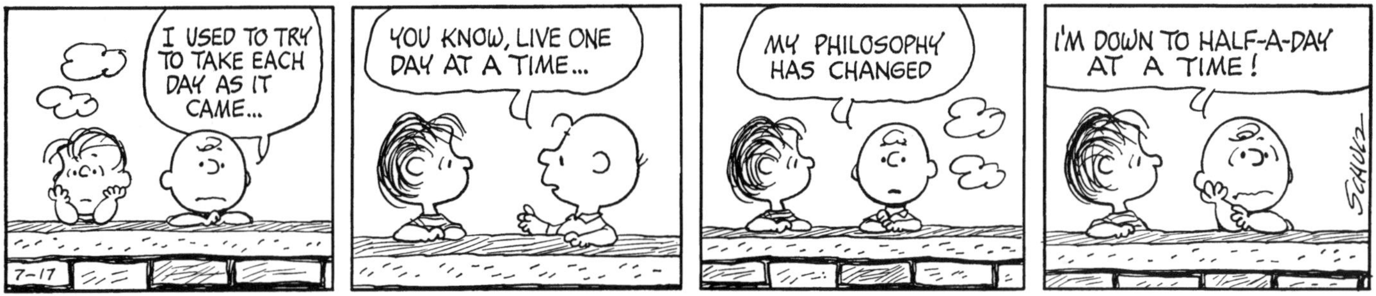
I USED TO TRY TO TAKE EACH DAY AS IT CAME...
7-17
YOU KNOW, LIVE ONE DAY AT A TIME...
MY PHILOSOPHY HAS CHANGED
I'M DOWN TO HALF-A-DAY AT A TIME!
SCHULZ

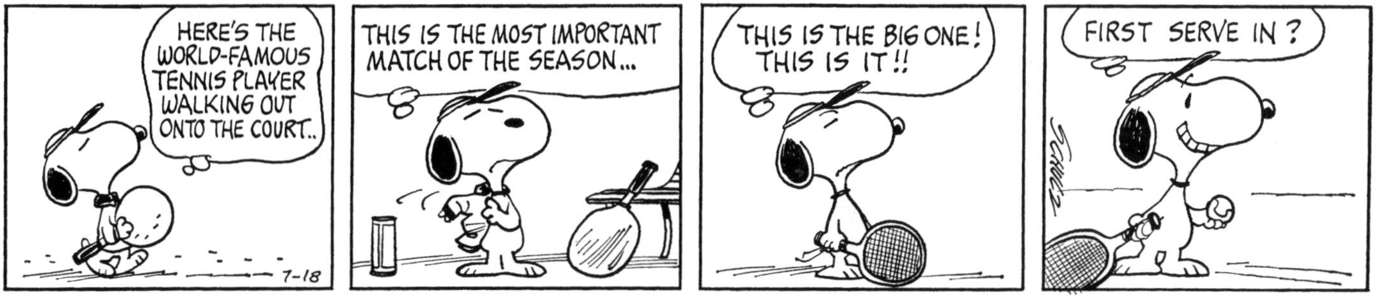
HERE'S THE WORLD-FAMOUS TENNIS PLAYER WALKING OUT ONTO THE COURT..
7-18
THIS IS THE MOST IMPORTANT MATCH OF THE SEASON...
THIS IS THE BIG ONE! THIS IS IT!!
SCHULZ
FIRST SERVE IN?

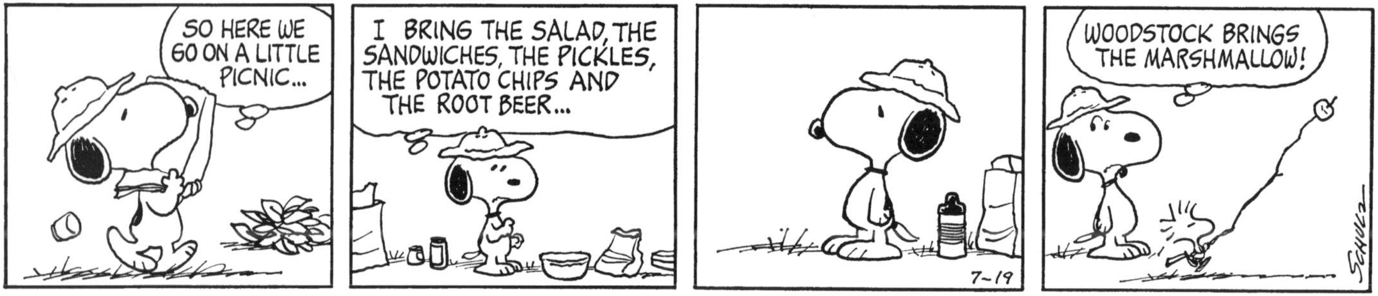
SO HERE WE GO ON A LITTLE PICNIC...
I BRING THE SALAD, THE SANDWICHES, THE PICKLES, THE POTATO CHIPS AND THE ROOT BEER...
WOODSTOCK BRINGS THE MARSHMALLOW!
7-19
SCHULZ

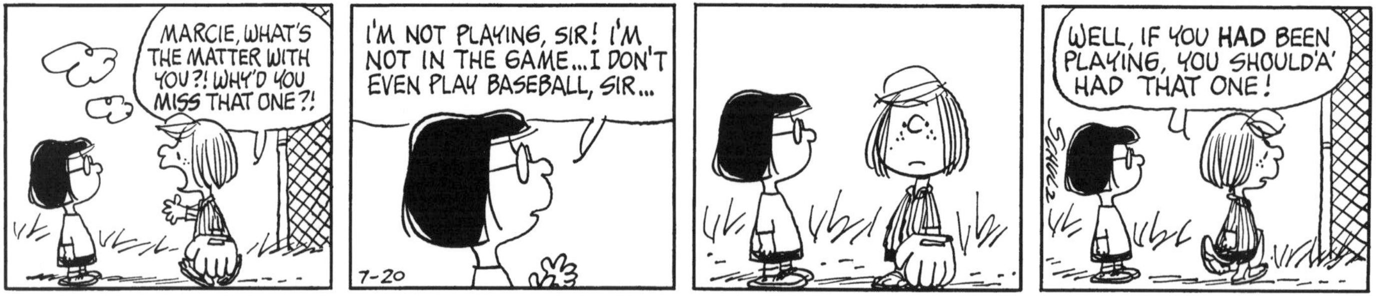
MARCIE, WHAT'S THE MATTER WITH YOU?! WHY'D YOU MISS THAT ONE?!
I'M NOT PLAYING, SIR! I'M NOT IN THE GAME...I DON'T EVEN PLAY BASEBALL, SIR...
7-20
WELL, IF YOU **HAD** BEEN PLAYING, YOU SHOULD'A' HAD THAT ONE!
SCHULZ

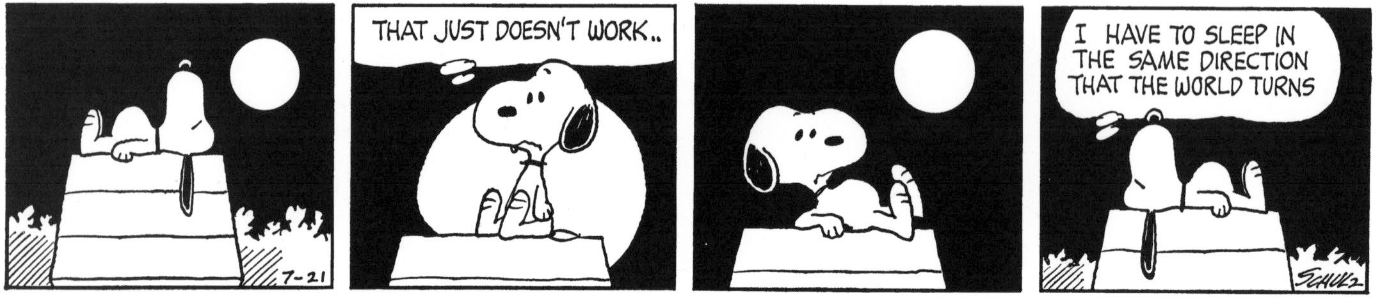
7-21
THAT JUST DOESN'T WORK..
I HAVE TO SLEEP IN THE SAME DIRECTION THAT THE WORLD TURNS
SCHULZ

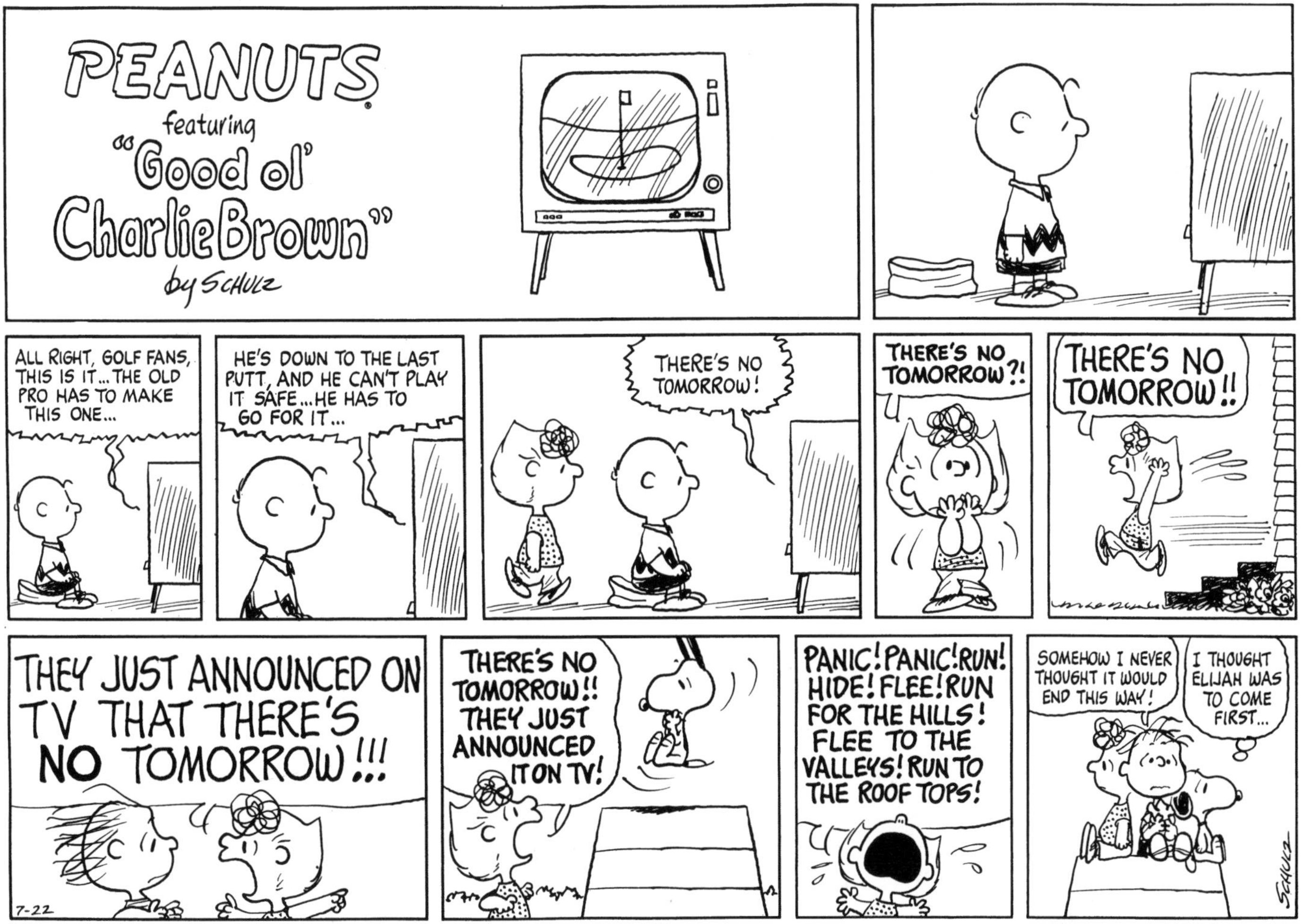
PEANUTS
featuring
"Good ol' Charlie Brown"
by SCHULZ
ALL RIGHT, GOLF FANS, THIS IS IT... THE OLD PRO HAS TO MAKE THIS ONE...
HE'S DOWN TO THE LAST PUTT, AND HE CAN'T PLAY IT SAFE...HE HAS TO GO FOR IT...
THERE'S NO TOMORROW!
THERE'S NO TOMORROW?!
THERE'S NO TOMORROW!!
THEY JUST ANNOUNCED ON TV THAT THERE'S NO TOMORROW!!!
7-22
THERE'S NO TOMORROW!! THEY JUST ANNOUNCED IT ON TV!
PANIC! PANIC! RUN! HIDE! FLEE! RUN FOR THE HILLS! FLEE TO THE VALLEYS! RUN TO THE ROOF TOPS!
SOMEHOW I NEVER THOUGHT IT WOULD END THIS WAY!
I THOUGHT ELIJAH WAS TO COME FIRST...
SCHULZ

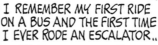

Panel 1: I REMEMBER THE CEREAL BOWL I HAD WHEN I WAS LITTLE..

Panel 2: I ALSO REMEMBER THE STROLLER THAT MOM USED TO PUSH ME IN, AND I REMEMBER THE PARK WE'D ALWAYS GO TO...

Panel 3: I REMEMBER MY FIRST RIDE ON A BUS AND THE FIRST TIME I EVER RODE AN ESCALATOR..

Panel 4: I HAVE A GOOD REMEMBERY!

Panel 5: I'VE BEEN ANXIOUS TO HAVE WOODSTOCK SEE MY NEW RACKET...

Panel 8: HOW DISAPPOINTING...HE HATES MY GUT!

Panel 9: I HAVE THE FEELING THAT I'M GROWING MORE BEAUTIFUL EVERY DAY

Panel 10: DO YOU REALIZE WHAT THAT MEANS?

Panel 11: IT MEANS THAT I AM THREE-HUNDRED AND SIXTY-FIVE TIMES MORE BEAUTIFUL TODAY THAN I WAS AT THIS TIME LAST YEAR....

Panel 12: WOW!!

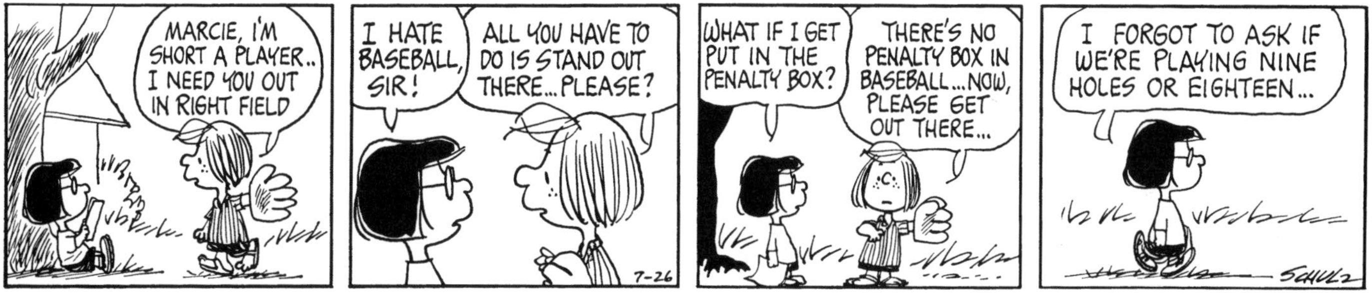
MARCIE, I'M SHORT A PLAYER.. I NEED YOU OUT IN RIGHT FIELD
I HATE BASEBALL, SIR!
ALL YOU HAVE TO DO IS STAND OUT THERE...PLEASE?
7-26
WHAT IF I GET PUT IN THE PENALTY BOX?
THERE'S NO PENALTY BOX IN BASEBALL...NOW, PLEASE GET OUT THERE...
I FORGOT TO ASK IF WE'RE PLAYING NINE HOLES OR EIGHTEEN...
SCHULZ

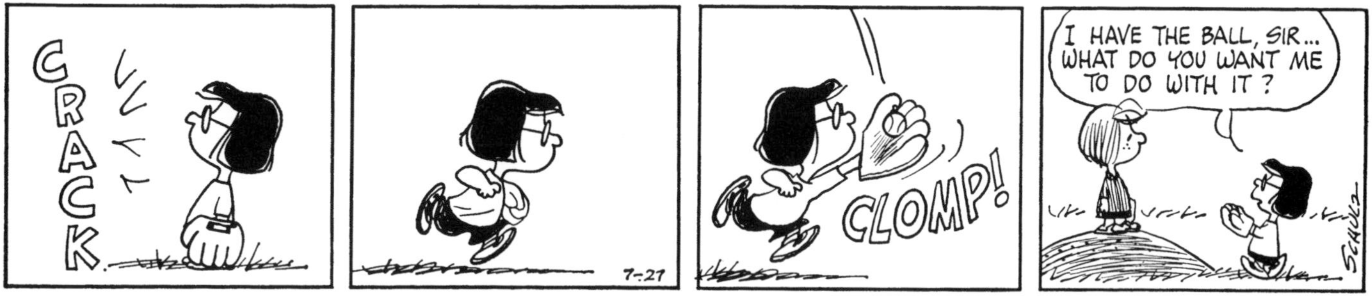
CRACK
7-27
CLOMP!
I HAVE THE BALL, SIR... WHAT DO YOU WANT ME TO DO WITH IT?
SCHULZ

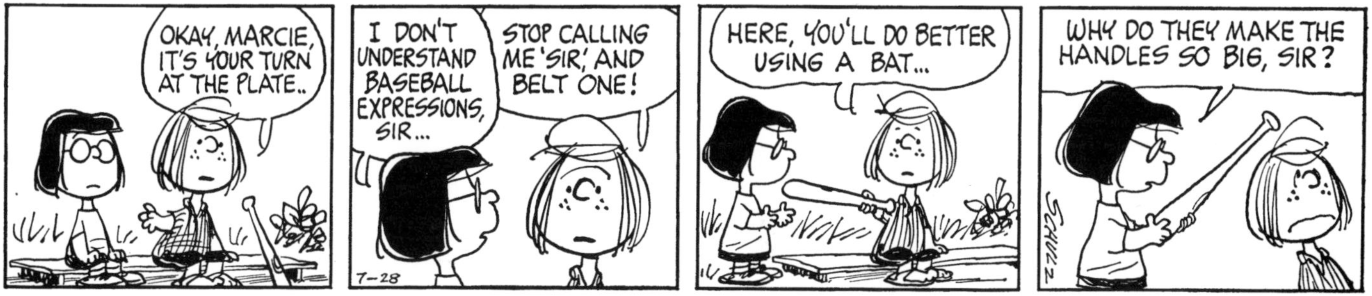
OKAY, MARCIE, IT'S YOUR TURN AT THE PLATE..
I DON'T UNDERSTAND BASEBALL EXPRESSIONS, SIR...
STOP CALLING ME 'SIR,' AND BELT ONE!
7-28
HERE, YOU'LL DO BETTER USING A BAT...
SCHULZ
WHY DO THEY MAKE THE HANDLES SO BIG, SIR?

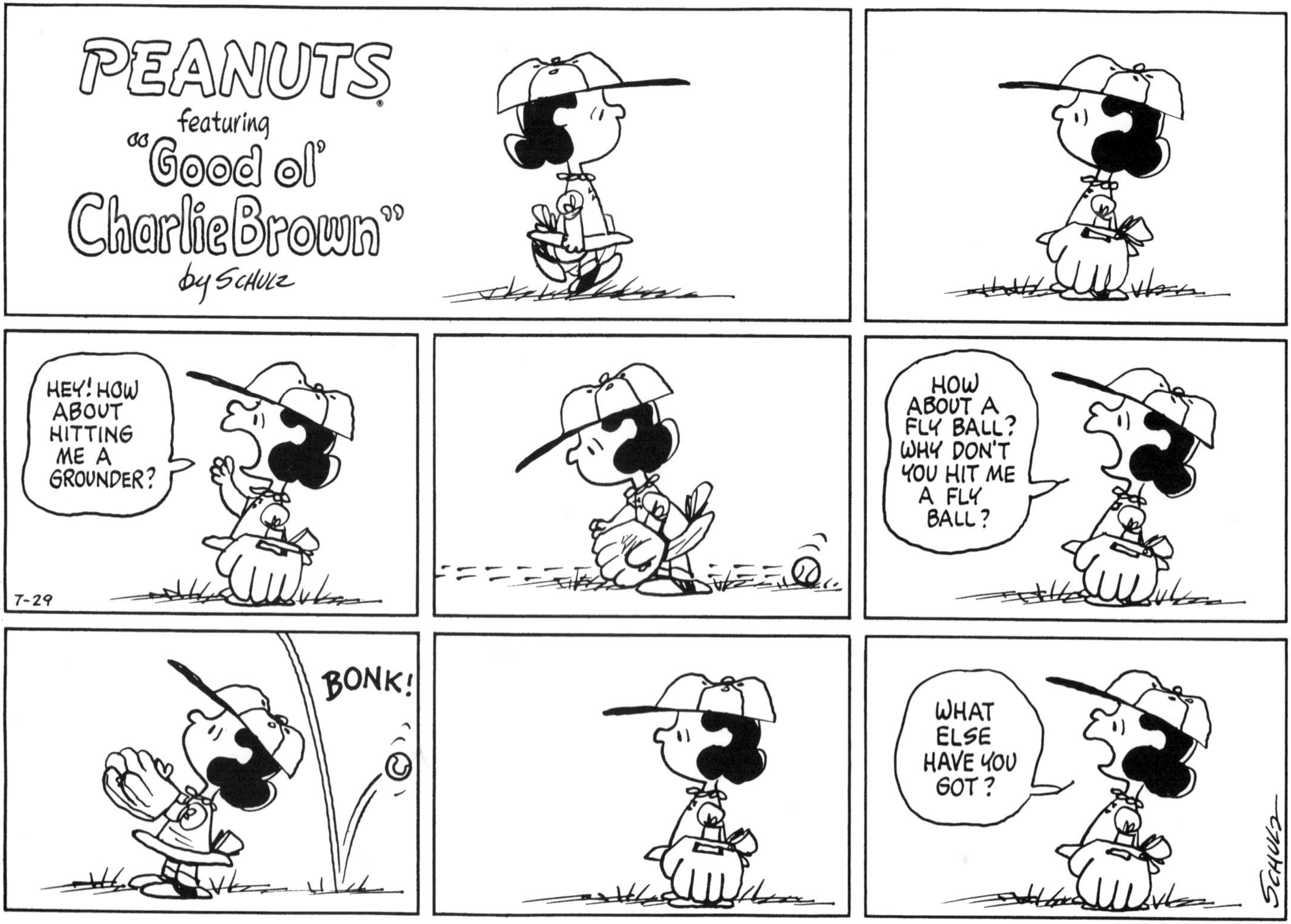
PEANUTS
featuring
"Good ol' Charlie Brown"
by SCHULZ
HEY! HOW ABOUT HITTING ME A GROUNDER?
7-29
HOW ABOUT A FLY BALL? WHY DON'T YOU HIT ME A FLY BALL?
BONK!
WHAT ELSE HAVE YOU GOT?
SCHULZ

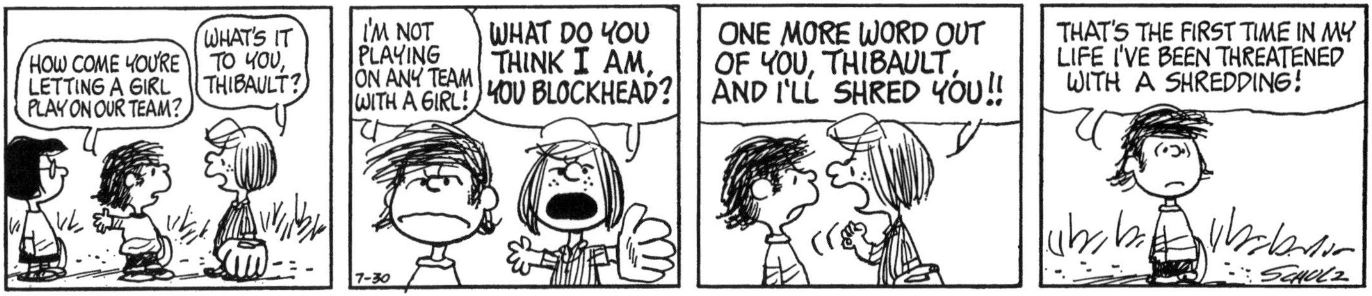
HOW COME YOU'RE LETTING A GIRL PLAY ON OUR TEAM?
WHAT'S IT TO YOU, THIBAULT?
I'M NOT PLAYING ON ANY TEAM WITH A GIRL!
WHAT DO YOU THINK I AM, YOU BLOCKHEAD?
7-30
ONE MORE WORD OUT OF YOU, THIBAULT, AND I'LL SHRED YOU!!
THAT'S THE FIRST TIME IN MY LIFE I'VE BEEN THREATENED WITH A SHREDDING!
SCHULZ

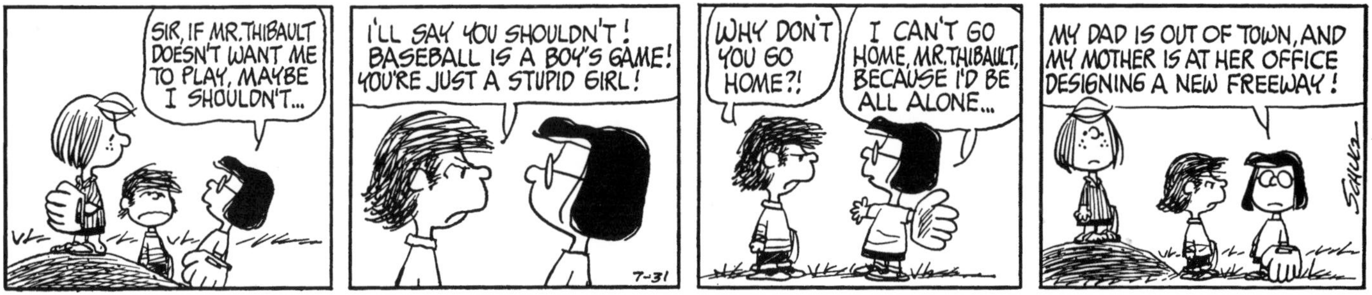
SIR, IF MR. THIBAULT DOESN'T WANT ME TO PLAY, MAYBE I SHOULDN'T...
I'LL SAY YOU SHOULDN'T! BASEBALL IS A BOY'S GAME! YOU'RE JUST A STUPID GIRL!
7-31
WHY DON'T YOU GO HOME?!
I CAN'T GO HOME, MR. THIBAULT, BECAUSE I'D BE ALL ALONE...
MY DAD IS OUT OF TOWN, AND MY MOTHER IS AT HER OFFICE DESIGNING A NEW FREEWAY!
SCHULZ

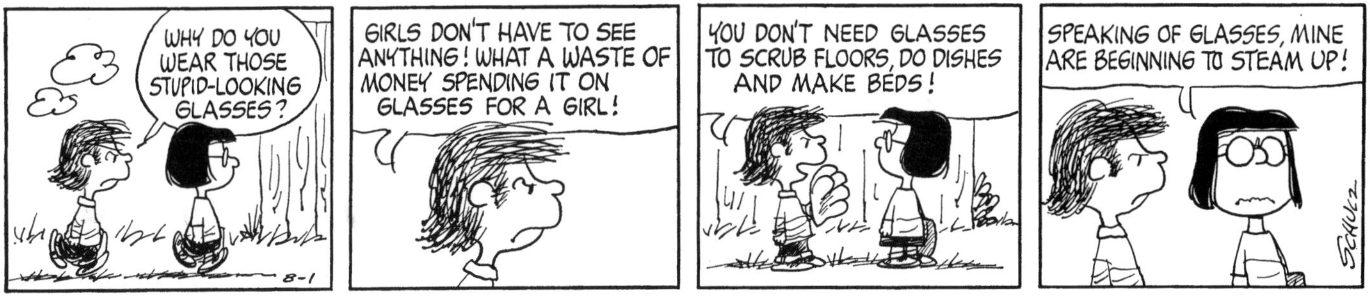
WHY DO YOU WEAR THOSE STUPID-LOOKING GLASSES?
8-1
GIRLS DON'T HAVE TO SEE ANYTHING! WHAT A WASTE OF MONEY SPENDING IT ON GLASSES FOR A GIRL!
YOU DON'T NEED GLASSES TO SCRUB FLOORS, DO DISHES AND MAKE BEDS!
SPEAKING OF GLASSES, MINE ARE BEGINNING TO STEAM UP!
SCHULZ

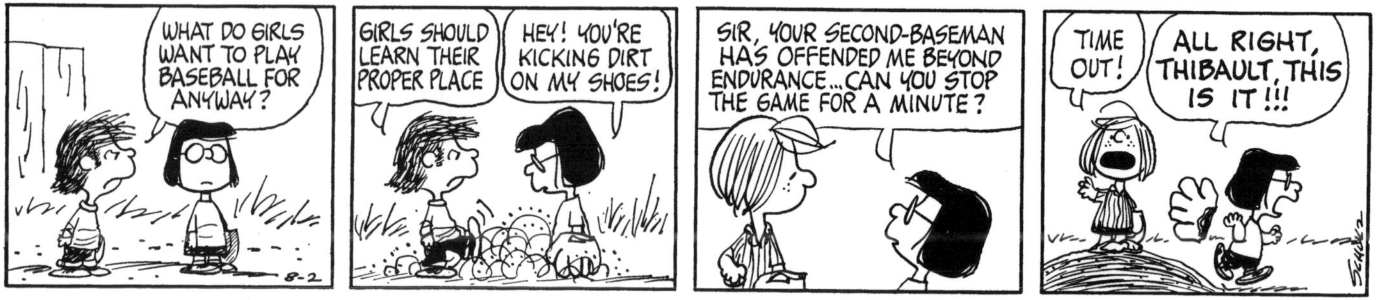
WHAT DO GIRLS WANT TO PLAY BASEBALL FOR ANYWAY?
GIRLS SHOULD LEARN THEIR PROPER PLACE
HEY! YOU'RE KICKING DIRT ON MY SHOES!
SIR, YOUR SECOND-BASEMAN HAS OFFENDED ME BEYOND ENDURANCE...CAN YOU STOP THE GAME FOR A MINUTE?
TIME OUT!
ALL RIGHT, THIBAULT, THIS IS IT!!!

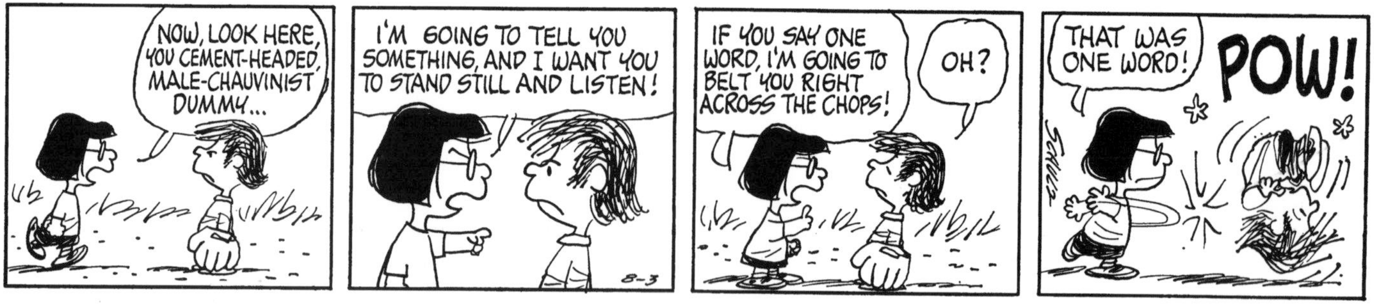
NOW, LOOK HERE, YOU CEMENT-HEADED, MALE-CHAUVINIST DUMMY...
I'M GOING TO TELL YOU SOMETHING, AND I WANT YOU TO STAND STILL AND LISTEN!
IF YOU SAY ONE WORD, I'M GOING TO BELT YOU RIGHT ACROSS THE CHOPS!
OH?
THAT WAS ONE WORD!
POW!

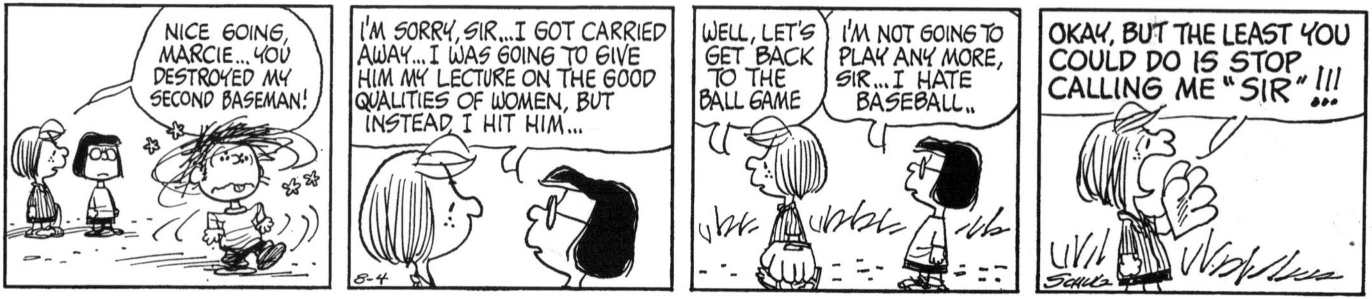
NICE GOING, MARCIE...YOU DESTROYED MY SECOND BASEMAN!
I'M SORRY, SIR...I GOT CARRIED AWAY...I WAS GOING TO GIVE HIM MY LECTURE ON THE GOOD QUALITIES OF WOMEN, BUT INSTEAD I HIT HIM...
WELL, LET'S GET BACK TO THE BALL GAME
I'M NOT GOING TO PLAY ANY MORE, SIR...I HATE BASEBALL..
OKAY, BUT THE LEAST YOU COULD DO IS STOP CALLING ME "SIR"!!!...

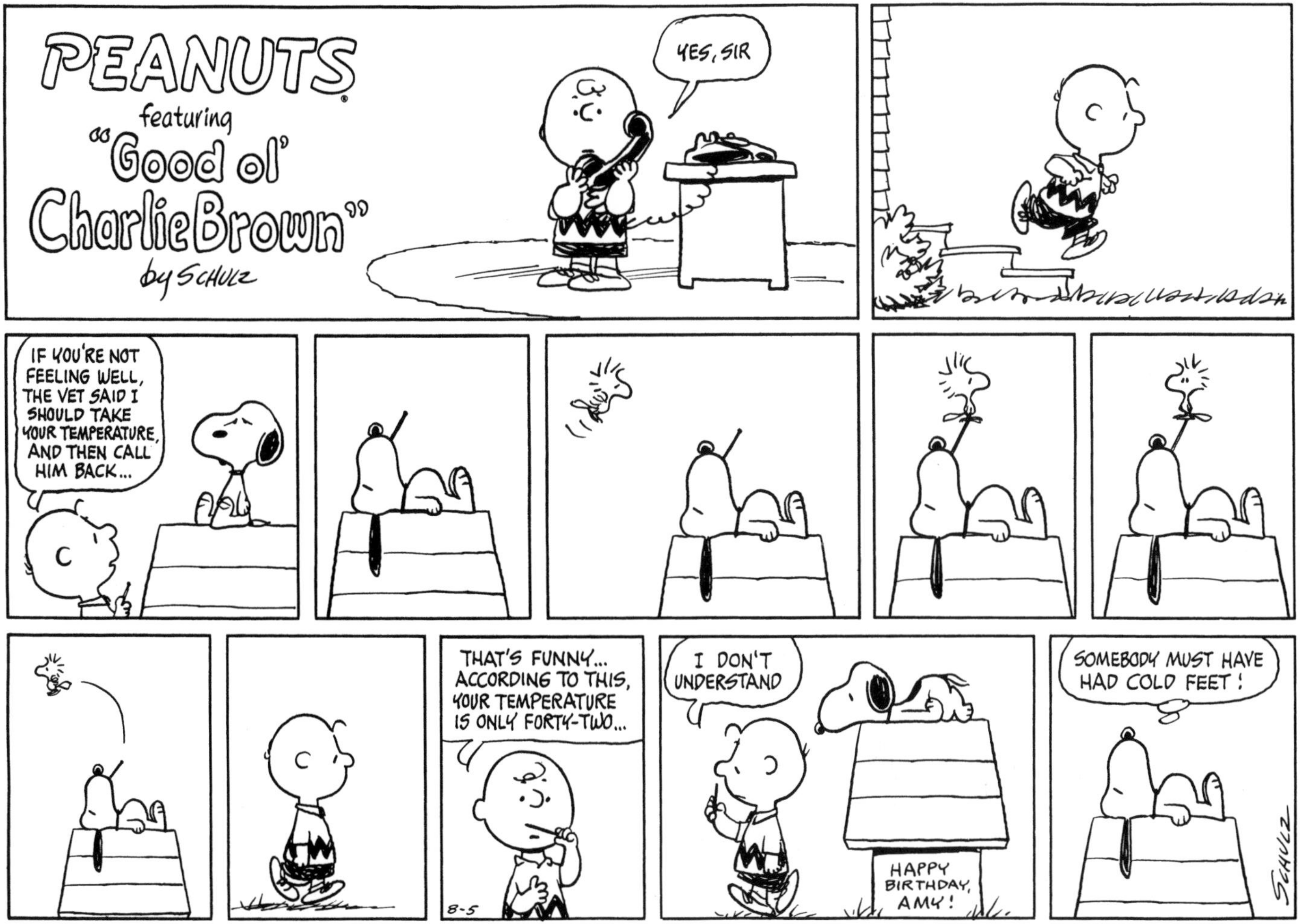
PEANUTS
featuring
"Good ol' Charlie Brown"
by SCHULZ
YES, SIR
IF YOU'RE NOT FEELING WELL, THE VET SAID I SHOULD TAKE YOUR TEMPERATURE, AND THEN CALL HIM BACK...
THAT'S FUNNY... ACCORDING TO THIS, YOUR TEMPERATURE IS ONLY FORTY-TWO...
8-5
I DON'T UNDERSTAND
HAPPY BIRTHDAY, AMY!
SOMEBODY MUST HAVE HAD COLD FEET!
SCHULZ

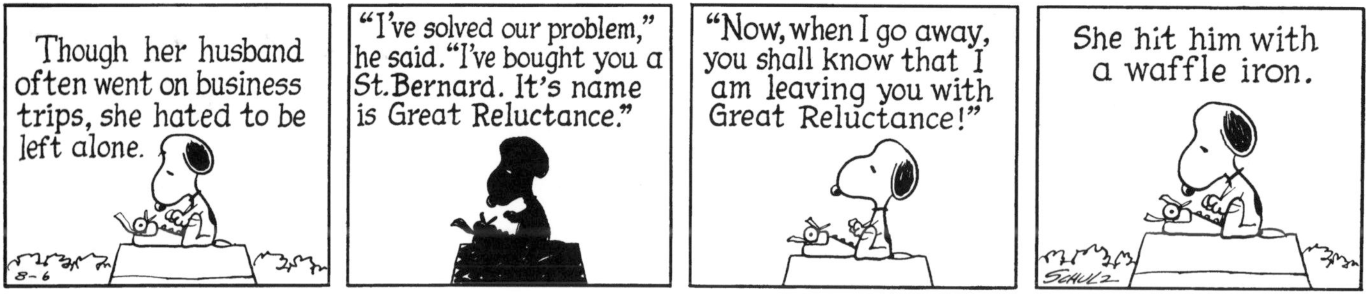
Though her husband often went on business trips, she hated to be left alone.
8-6
"I've solved our problem," he said. "I've bought you a St. Bernard. It's name is Great Reluctance."
"Now, when I go away, you shall know that I am leaving you with Great Reluctance!"
She hit him with a waffle iron.
SCHULZ

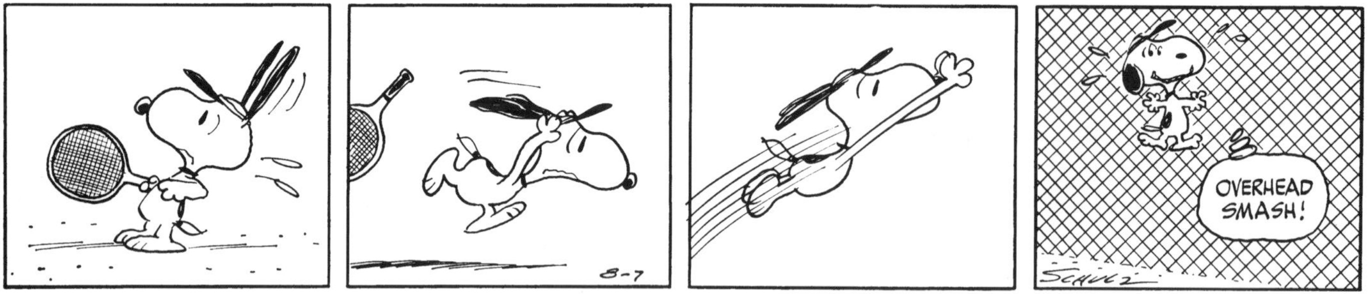
8-7
OVERHEAD SMASH!
SCHULZ

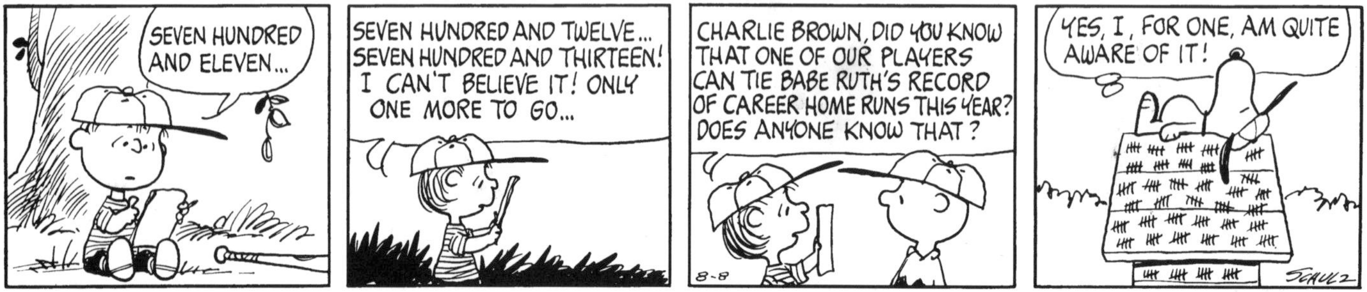
SEVEN HUNDRED AND ELEVEN...
SEVEN HUNDRED AND TWELVE... SEVEN HUNDRED AND THIRTEEN! I CAN'T BELIEVE IT! ONLY ONE MORE TO GO...
CHARLIE BROWN, DID YOU KNOW THAT ONE OF OUR PLAYERS CAN TIE BABE RUTH'S RECORD OF CAREER HOME RUNS THIS YEAR? DOES ANYONE KNOW THAT?
8-8
YES, I, FOR ONE, AM QUITE AWARE OF IT!
SCHULZ

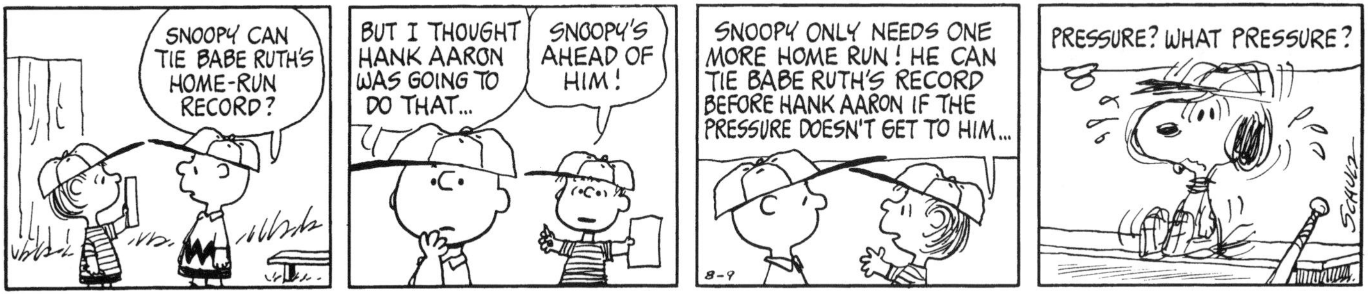

SNOOPY CAN TIE BABE RUTH'S HOME-RUN RECORD?
BUT I THOUGHT HANK AARON WAS GOING TO DO THAT...
SNOOPY'S AHEAD OF HIM!
SNOOPY ONLY NEEDS ONE MORE HOME RUN! HE CAN TIE BABE RUTH'S RECORD BEFORE HANK AARON IF THE PRESSURE DOESN'T GET TO HIM...
8-9
PRESSURE? WHAT PRESSURE?
SCHULZ

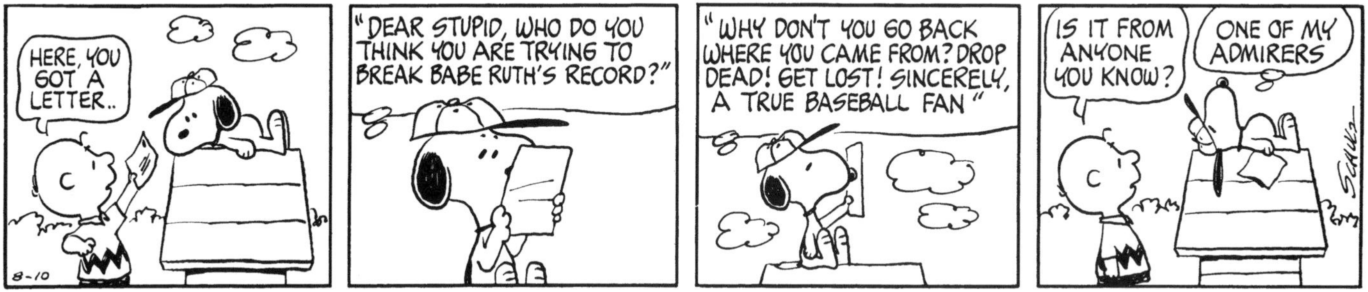

HERE, YOU GOT A LETTER..
8-10
"DEAR STUPID, WHO DO YOU THINK YOU ARE TRYING TO BREAK BABE RUTH'S RECORD?"
"WHY DON'T YOU GO BACK WHERE YOU CAME FROM? DROP DEAD! GET LOST! SINCERELY, A TRUE BASEBALL FAN"
IS IT FROM ANYONE YOU KNOW?
ONE OF MY ADMIRERS
SCHULZ

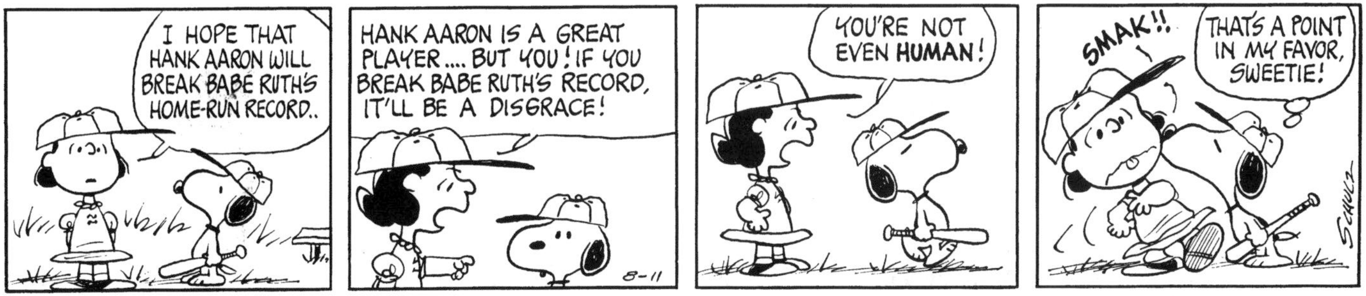

I HOPE THAT HANK AARON WILL BREAK BABE RUTH'S HOME-RUN RECORD..
HANK AARON IS A GREAT PLAYER.... BUT YOU! IF YOU BREAK BABE RUTH'S RECORD, IT'LL BE A DISGRACE!
8-11
YOU'RE NOT EVEN HUMAN!
SMAK!!
THAT'S A POINT IN MY FAVOR, SWEETIE!
SCHULZ

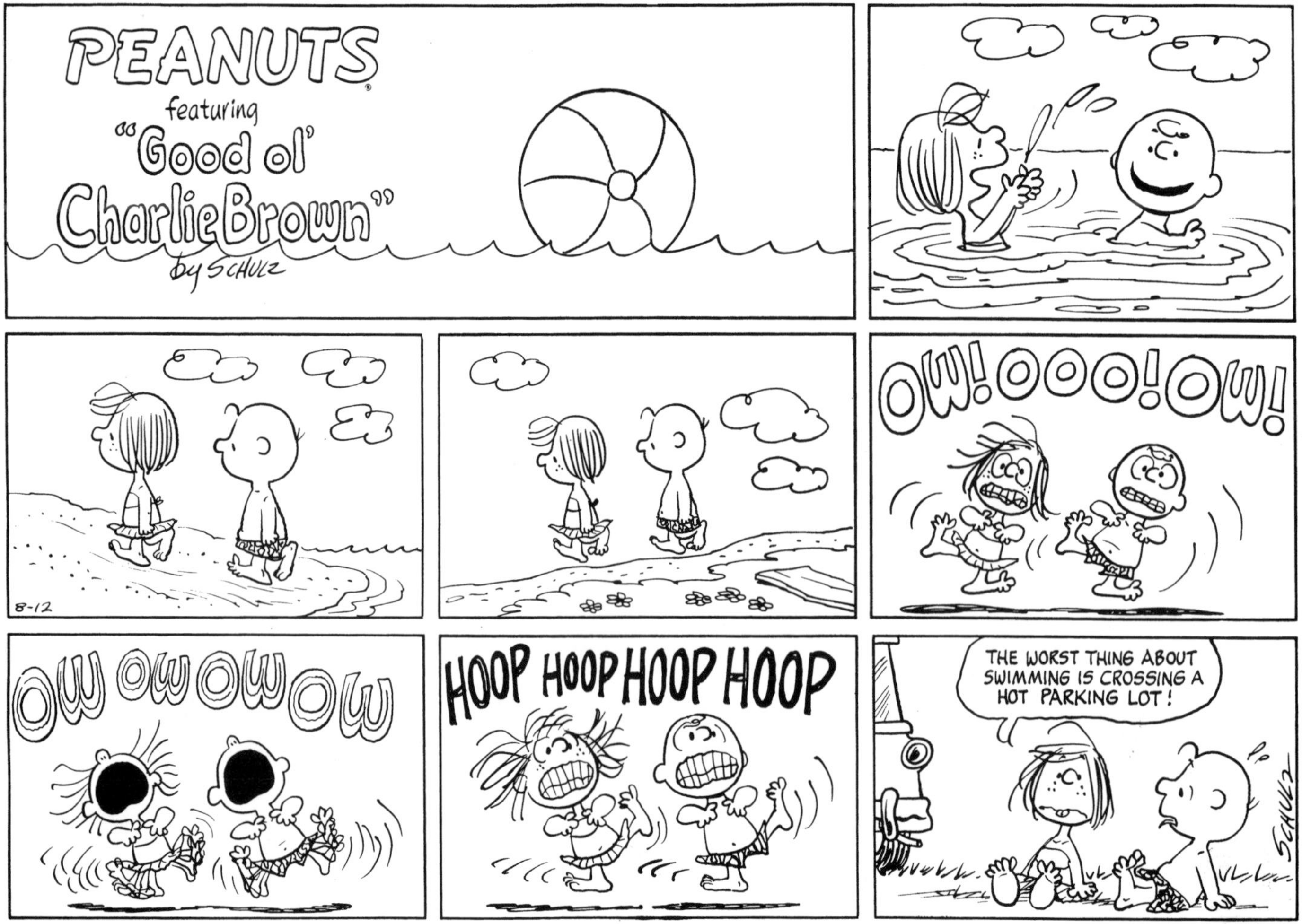
PEANUTS
featuring
"Good ol' CharlieBrown"
by SCHULZ
8-12
OW! OOO! OW!
OW OWOWOW
HOOP HOOP HOOP HOOP
THE WORST THING ABOUT SWIMMING IS CROSSING A HOT PARKING LOT!
SCHULZ

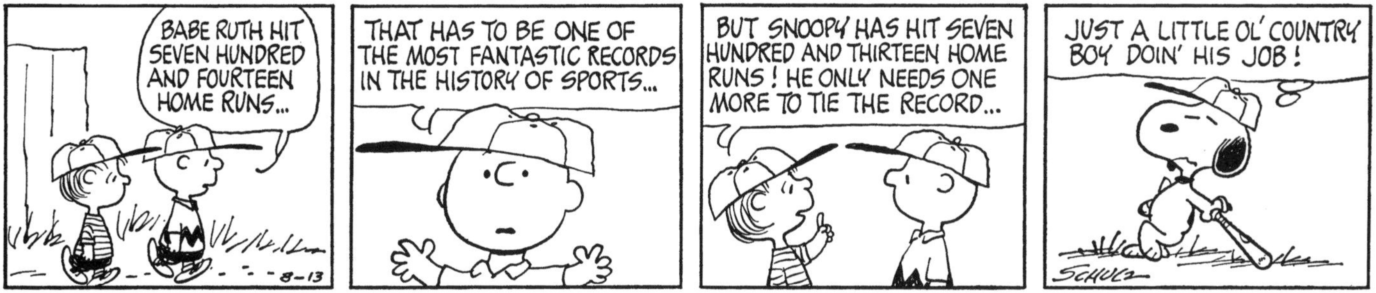
BABE RUTH HIT SEVEN HUNDRED AND FOURTEEN HOME RUNS...
8-13
THAT HAS TO BE ONE OF THE MOST FANTASTIC RECORDS IN THE HISTORY OF SPORTS...
BUT SNOOPY HAS HIT SEVEN HUNDRED AND THIRTEEN HOME RUNS! HE ONLY NEEDS ONE MORE TO TIE THE RECORD...
JUST A LITTLE OL' COUNTRY BOY DOIN' HIS JOB!
SCHULZ

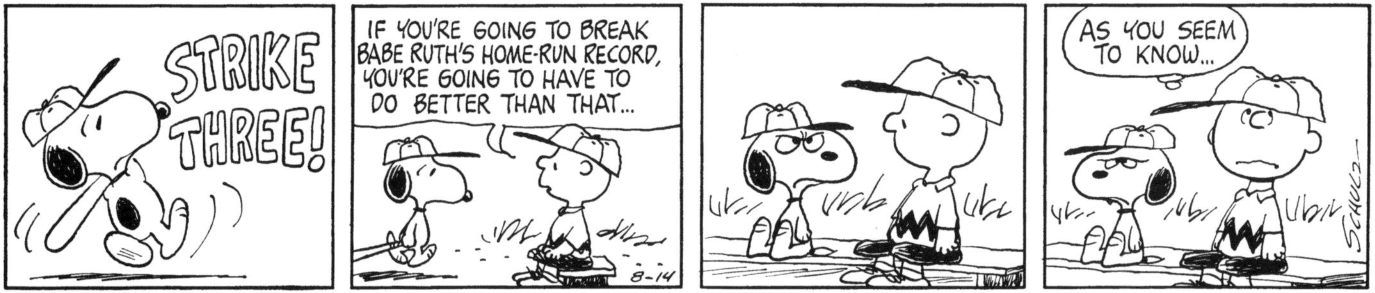
STRIKE THREE!
IF YOU'RE GOING TO BREAK BABE RUTH'S HOME-RUN RECORD, YOU'RE GOING TO HAVE TO DO BETTER THAN THAT...
8-14
AS YOU SEEM TO KNOW...
SCHULZ

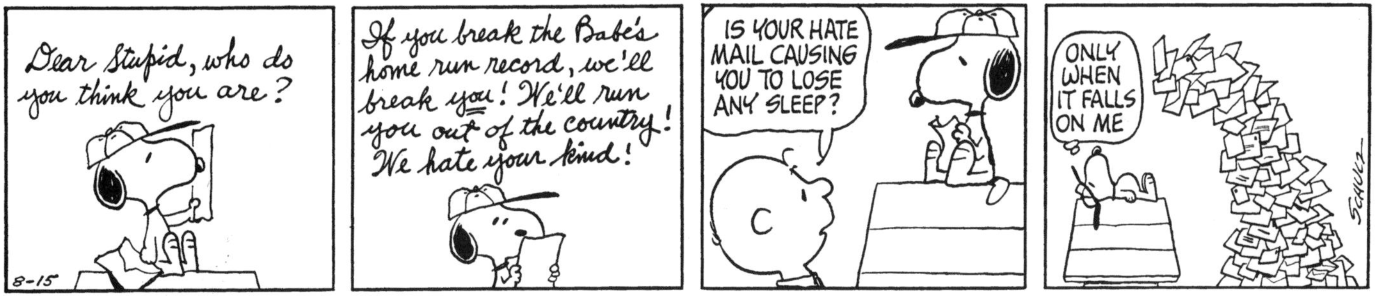
Dear Stupid, who do you think you are?
8-15
If you break the Babe's home run record, we'll break you! We'll run you out of the country! We hate your kind!
IS YOUR HATE MAIL CAUSING YOU TO LOSE ANY SLEEP?
ONLY WHEN IT FALLS ON ME
SCHULZ

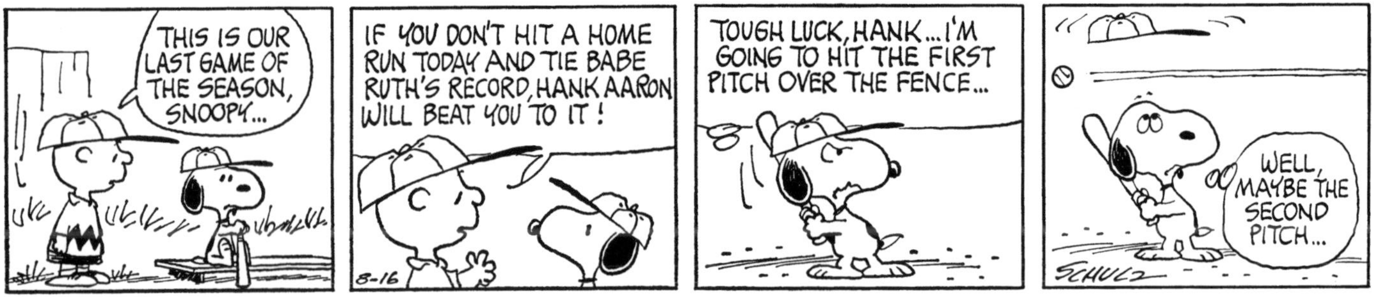
THIS IS OUR LAST GAME OF THE SEASON, SNOOPY...
IF YOU DON'T HIT A HOME RUN TODAY AND TIE BABE RUTH'S RECORD, HANK AARON WILL BEAT YOU TO IT!
8-16
TOUGH LUCK, HANK... I'M GOING TO HIT THE FIRST PITCH OVER THE FENCE...
WELL, MAYBE THE SECOND PITCH...
SCHULZ

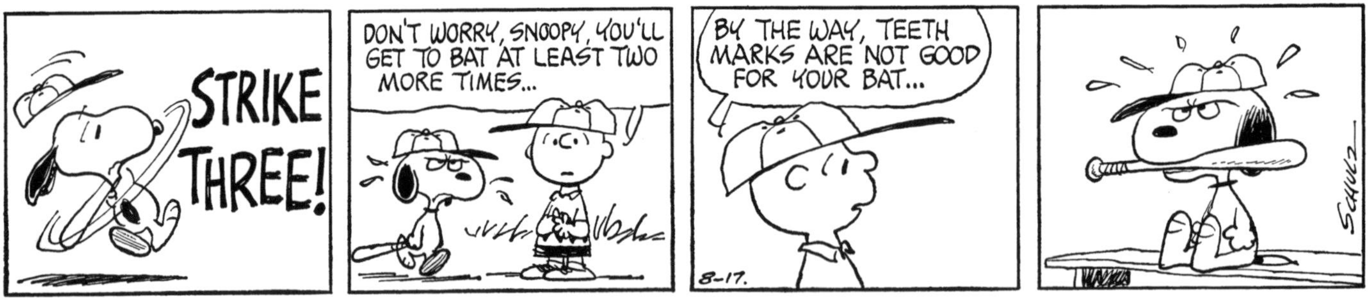
STRIKE THREE!
DON'T WORRY, SNOOPY, YOU'LL GET TO BAT AT LEAST TWO MORE TIMES...
BY THE WAY, TEETH MARKS ARE NOT GOOD FOR YOUR BAT...
8-17
SCHULZ

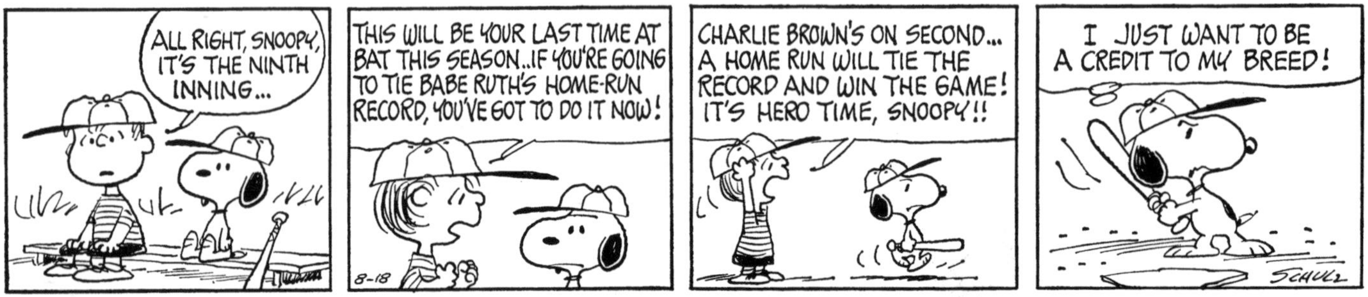
ALL RIGHT, SNOOPY, IT'S THE NINTH INNING...
THIS WILL BE YOUR LAST TIME AT BAT THIS SEASON..IF YOU'RE GOING TO TIE BABE RUTH'S HOME-RUN RECORD, YOU'VE GOT TO DO IT NOW!
8-18
CHARLIE BROWN'S ON SECOND... A HOME RUN WILL TIE THE RECORD AND WIN THE GAME! IT'S HERO TIME, SNOOPY!!
I JUST WANT TO BE A CREDIT TO MY BREED!
SCHULZ

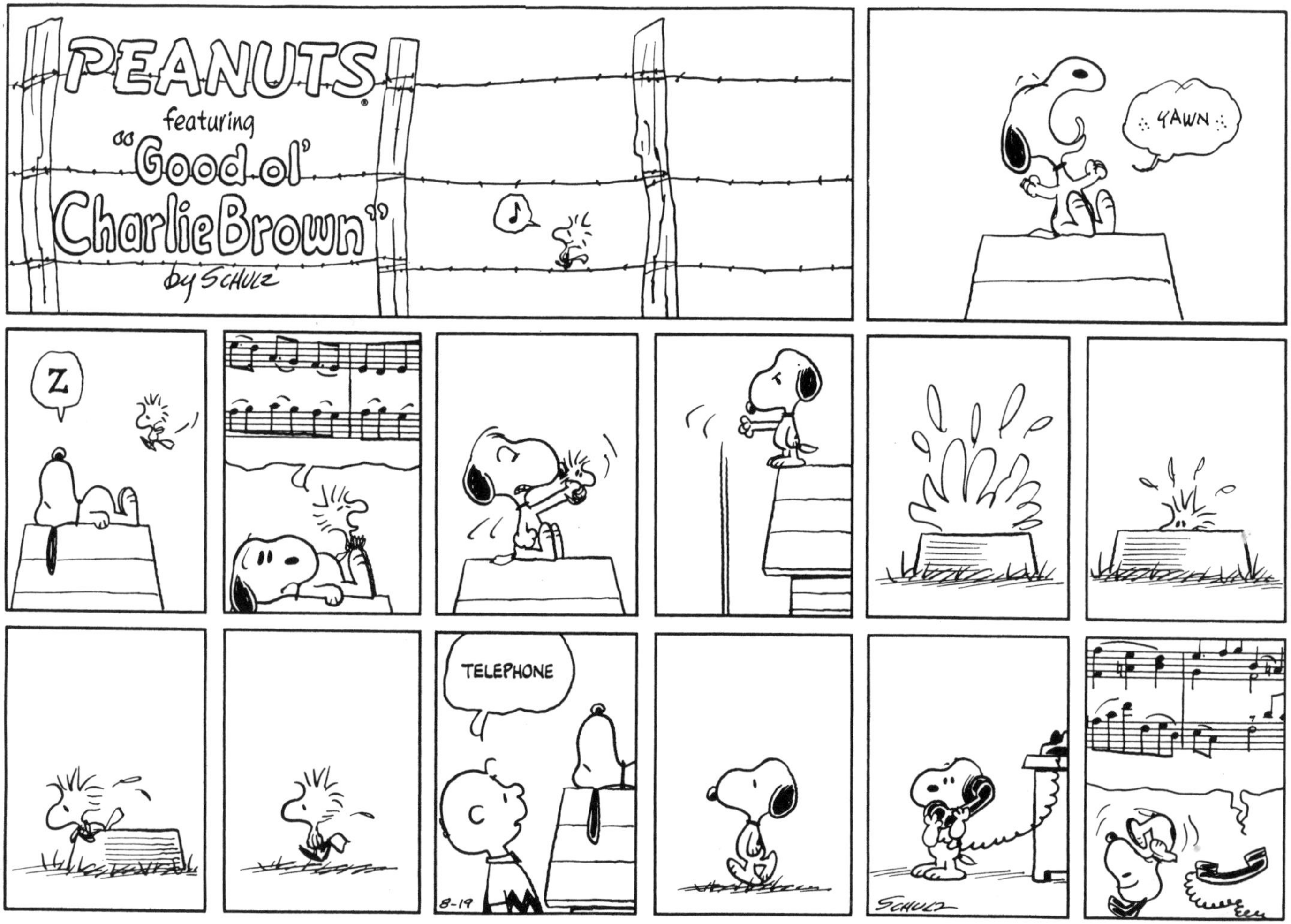
PEANUTS
featuring
"Good ol' Charlie Brown"
by SCHULZ
YAWN
Z
TELEPHONE
8-19
SCHULZ

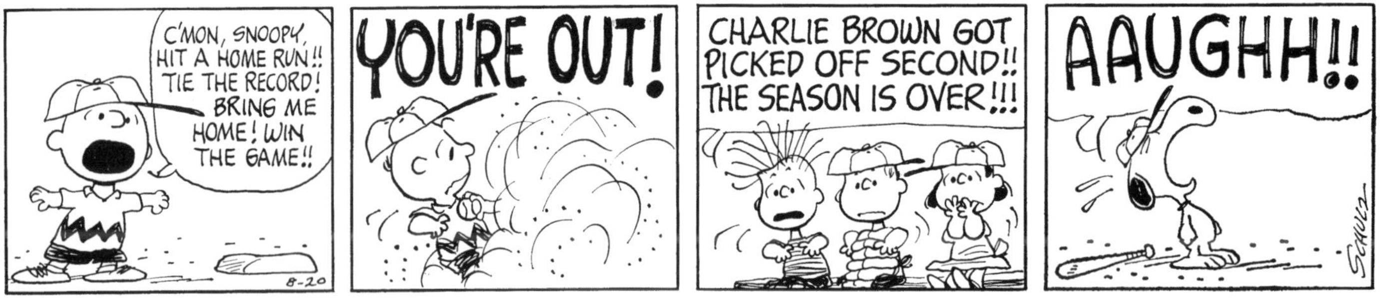
C'MON, SNOOPY, HIT A HOME RUN!! TIE THE RECORD! BRING ME HOME! WIN THE GAME!!
8-20
YOU'RE OUT!
CHARLIE BROWN GOT PICKED OFF SECOND!! THE SEASON IS OVER!!!
AAUGHH!!
SCHULZ

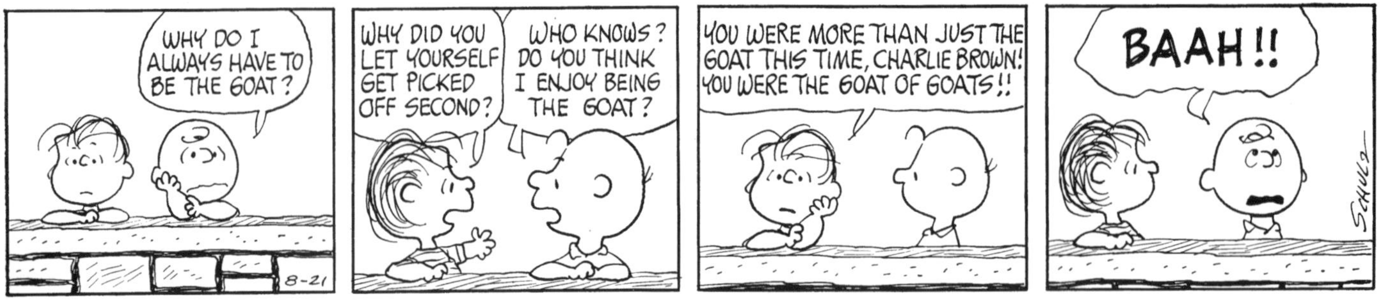
WHY DO I ALWAYS HAVE TO BE THE GOAT?
8-21
WHY DID YOU LET YOURSELF GET PICKED OFF SECOND?
WHO KNOWS? DO YOU THINK I ENJOY BEING THE GOAT?
YOU WERE MORE THAN JUST THE GOAT THIS TIME, CHARLIE BROWN! YOU WERE THE GOAT OF GOATS!!
BAAH!!
SCHULZ

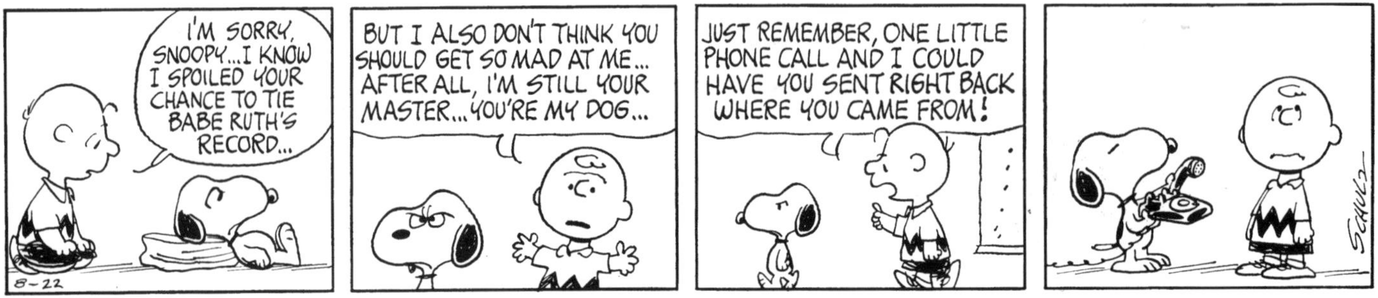
I'M SORRY, SNOOPY...I KNOW I SPOILED YOUR CHANCE TO TIE BABE RUTH'S RECORD...
8-22
BUT I ALSO DON'T THINK YOU SHOULD GET SO MAD AT ME... AFTER ALL, I'M STILL YOUR MASTER...YOU'RE MY DOG...
JUST REMEMBER, ONE LITTLE PHONE CALL AND I COULD HAVE YOU SENT RIGHT BACK WHERE YOU CAME FROM!
SCHULZ

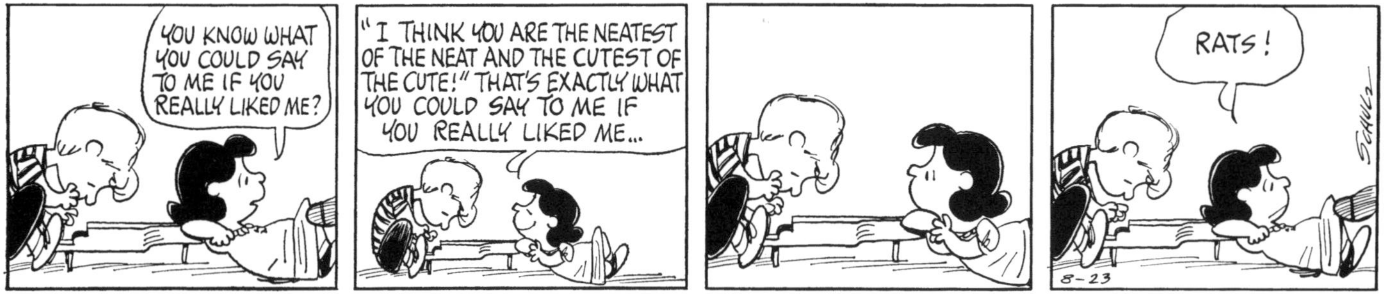
YOU KNOW WHAT YOU COULD SAY TO ME IF YOU REALLY LIKED ME?
"I THINK YOU ARE THE NEATEST OF THE NEAT AND THE CUTEST OF THE CUTE!" THAT'S EXACTLY WHAT YOU COULD SAY TO ME IF YOU REALLY LIKED ME...
RATS!
SCHULZ
8-23

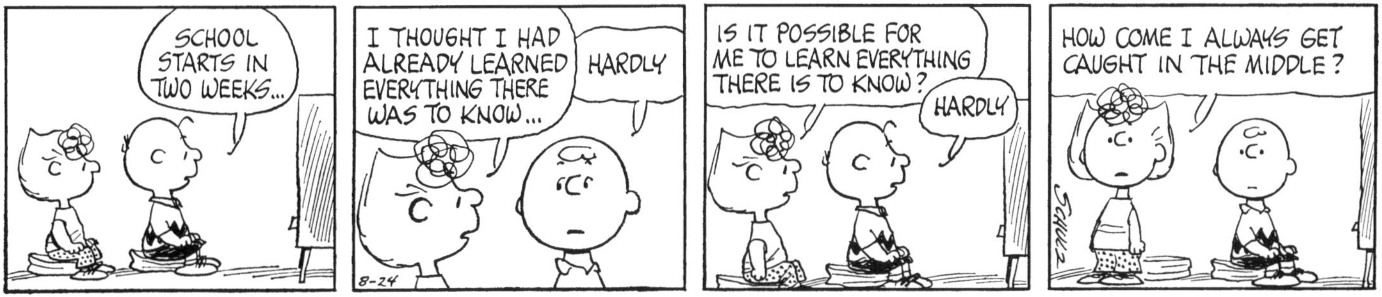
SCHOOL STARTS IN TWO WEEKS...
I THOUGHT I HAD ALREADY LEARNED EVERYTHING THERE WAS TO KNOW...
HARDLY
8-24
IS IT POSSIBLE FOR ME TO LEARN EVERYTHING THERE IS TO KNOW?
HARDLY
HOW COME I ALWAYS GET CAUGHT IN THE MIDDLE?
SCHULZ

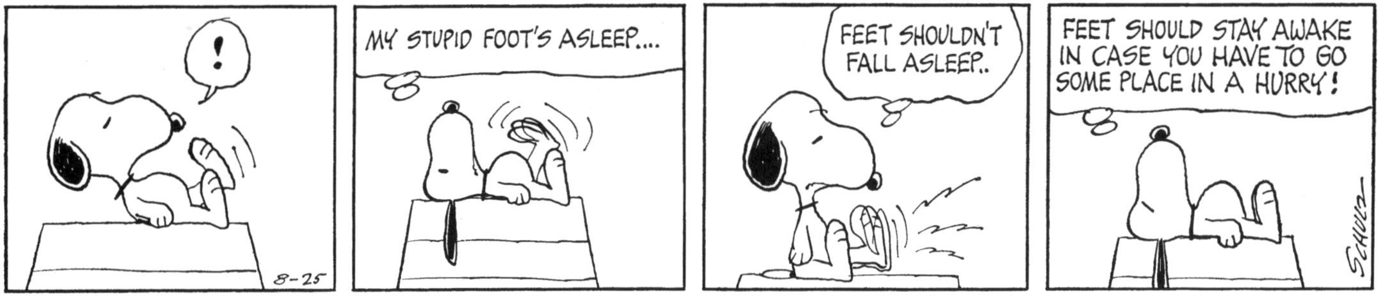
!
8-25
MY STUPID FOOT'S ASLEEP....
FEET SHOULDN'T FALL ASLEEP..
FEET SHOULD STAY AWAKE IN CASE YOU HAVE TO GO SOME PLACE IN A HURRY!
SCHULZ

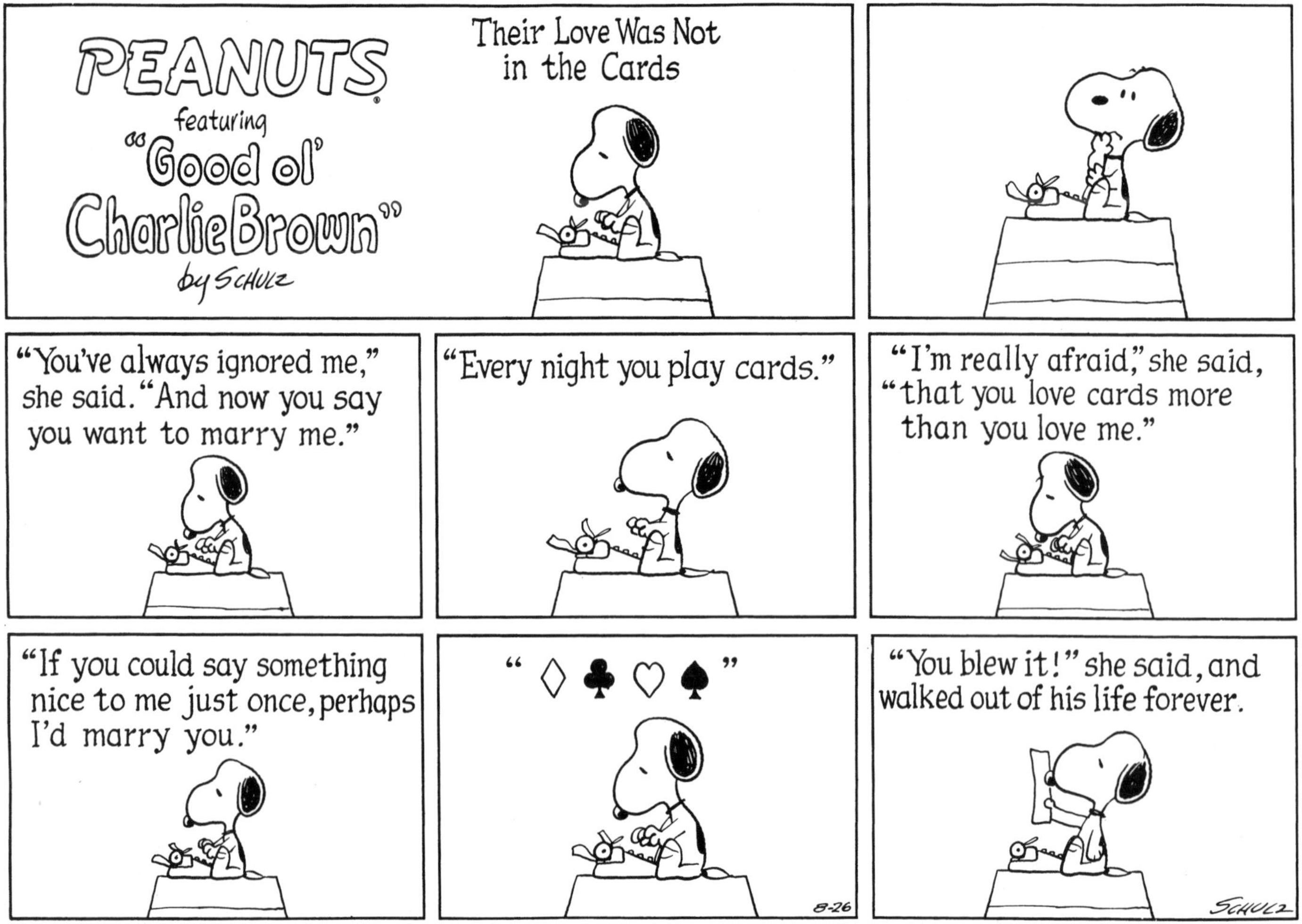
PEANUTS
featuring
"Good ol' Charlie Brown"
by SCHULZ
Their Love Was Not in the Cards
"You've always ignored me," she said. "And now you say you want to marry me."
"Every night you play cards."
"I'm really afraid," she said, "that you love cards more than you love me."
"If you could say something nice to me just once, perhaps I'd marry you."
" ♢ ♣ ♡ ♠ "
8-26
"You blew it!" she said, and walked out of his life forever.
SCHULZ

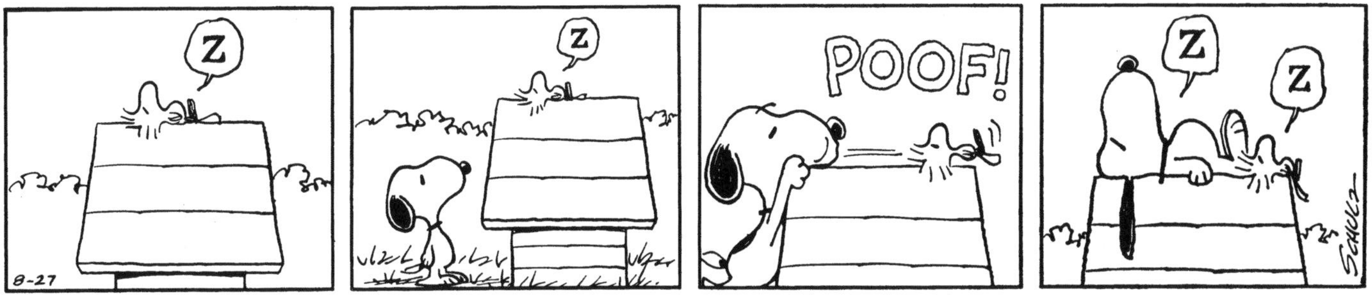
Z
8-27
Z
POOF!
Z
Z
SCHULZ

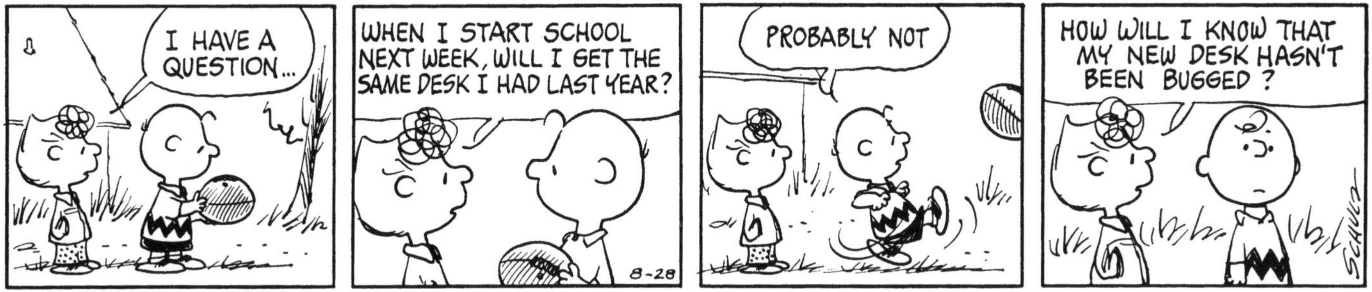
I HAVE A QUESTION...
WHEN I START SCHOOL NEXT WEEK, WILL I GET THE SAME DESK I HAD LAST YEAR?
8-28
PROBABLY NOT
HOW WILL I KNOW THAT MY NEW DESK HASN'T BEEN BUGGED ?
SCHULZ

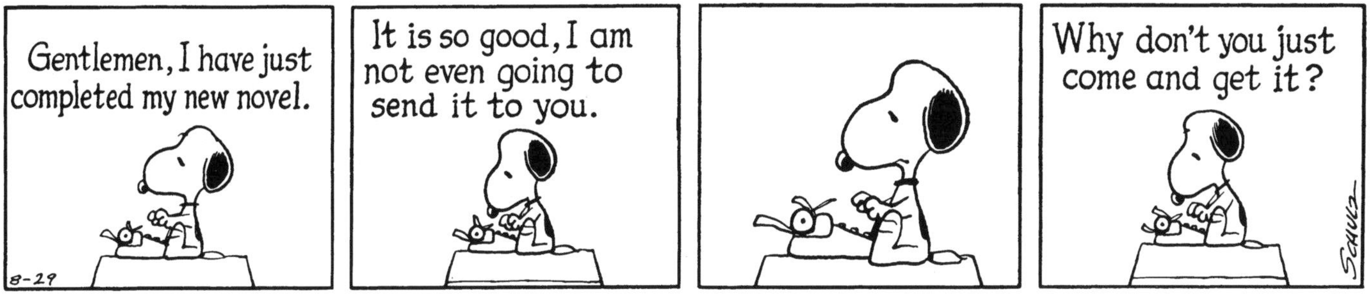
Gentlemen, I have just completed my new novel.
8-29
It is so good, I am not even going to send it to you.
Why don't you just come and get it?
SCHULZ

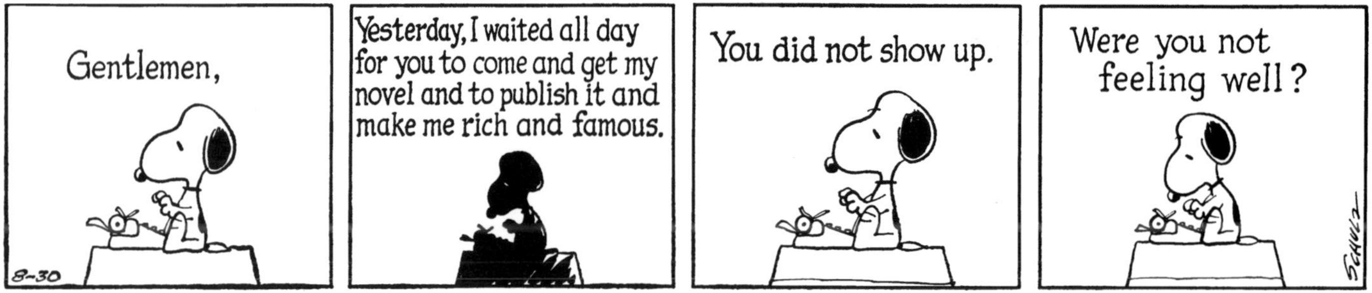
Gentlemen,
Yesterday, I waited all day for you to come and get my novel and to publish it and make me rich and famous.
You did not show up.
Were you not feeling well?
8-30
SCHULZ

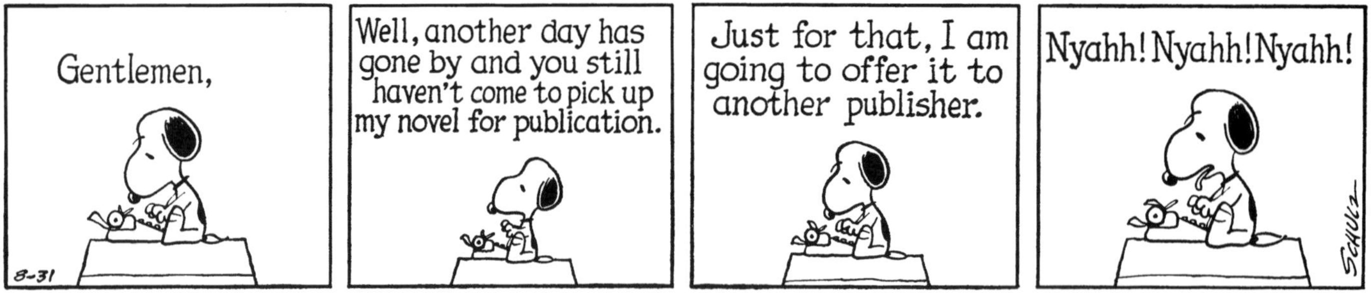
Gentlemen,
Well, another day has gone by and you still haven't come to pick up my novel for publication.
Just for that, I am going to offer it to another publisher.
Nyahh! Nyahh! Nyahh!
8-31
SCHULZ

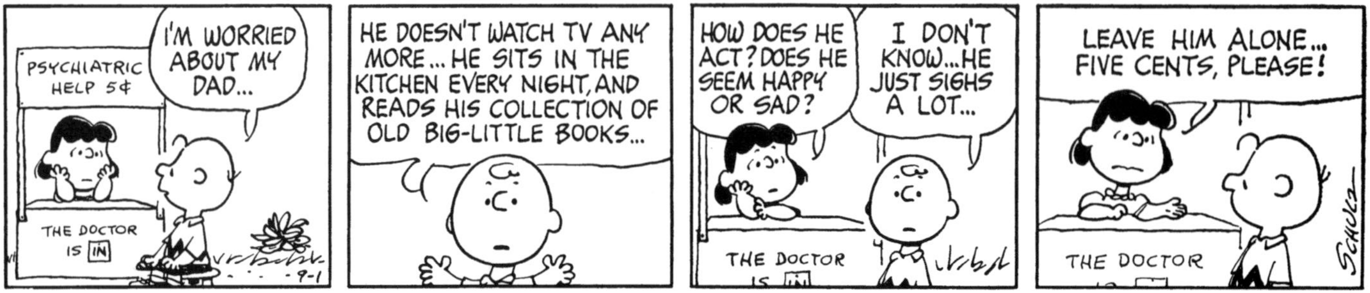
PSYCHIATRIC HELP 5¢
THE DOCTOR IS IN
I'M WORRIED ABOUT MY DAD...
9-1
HE DOESN'T WATCH TV ANY MORE... HE SITS IN THE KITCHEN EVERY NIGHT, AND READS HIS COLLECTION OF OLD BIG-LITTLE BOOKS...
HOW DOES HE ACT? DOES HE SEEM HAPPY OR SAD?
I DON'T KNOW... HE JUST SIGHS A LOT...
THE DOCTOR
LEAVE HIM ALONE... FIVE CENTS, PLEASE!
THE DOCTOR
SCHULZ

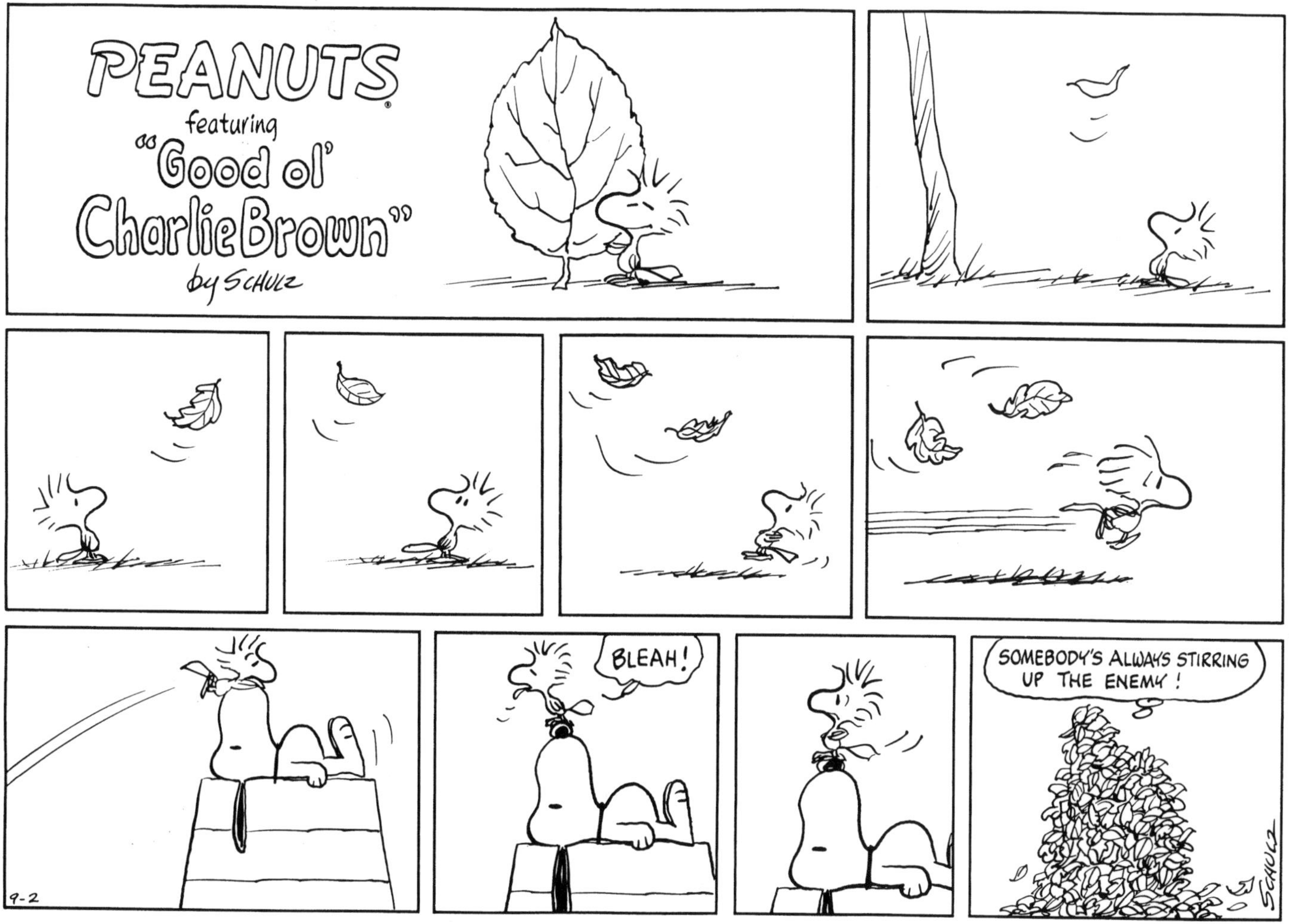
PEANUTS
featuring
"Good ol' CharlieBrown"
by SCHULZ
9-2
BLEAH!
SOMEBODY'S ALWAYS STIRRING UP THE ENEMY!
SCHULZ

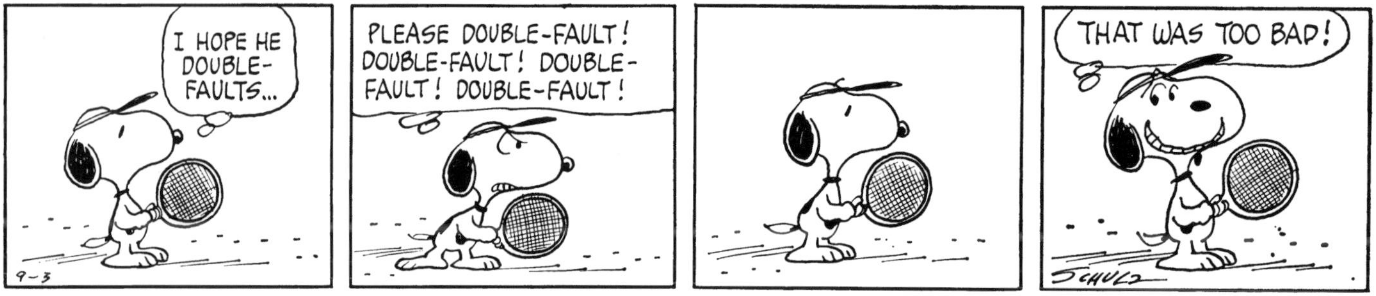
I HOPE HE DOUBLE-FAULTS...
9-3
PLEASE DOUBLE-FAULT! DOUBLE-FAULT! DOUBLE-FAULT! DOUBLE-FAULT!
THAT WAS TOO BAD!
SCHULZ

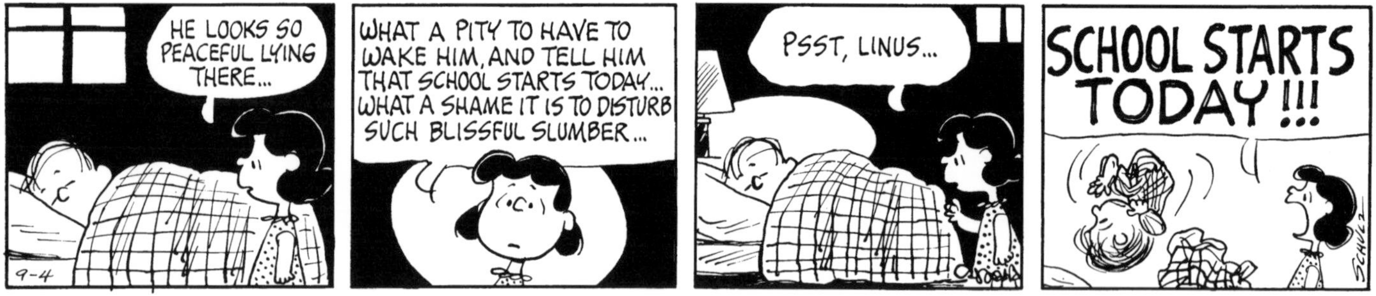
HE LOOKS SO PEACEFUL LYING THERE...
9-4
WHAT A PITY TO HAVE TO WAKE HIM, AND TELL HIM THAT SCHOOL STARTS TODAY... WHAT A SHAME IT IS TO DISTURB SUCH BLISSFUL SLUMBER...
PSST, LINUS...
SCHOOL STARTS TODAY!!!
SCHULZ

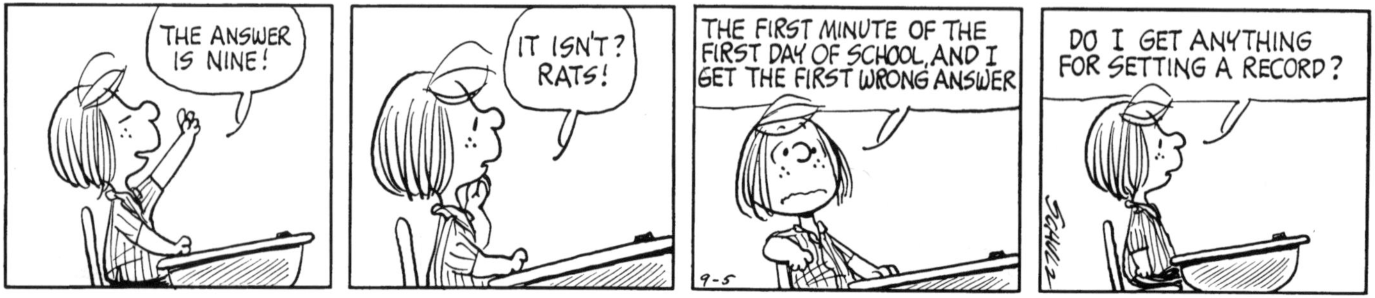
THE ANSWER IS NINE!
IT ISN'T? RATS!
THE FIRST MINUTE OF THE FIRST DAY OF SCHOOL, AND I GET THE FIRST WRONG ANSWER
9-5
SCHULZ
DO I GET ANYTHING FOR SETTING A RECORD?

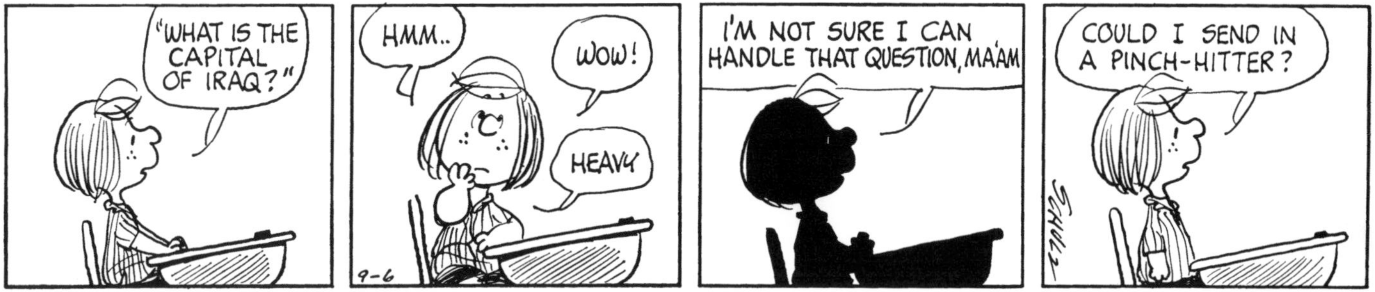
"WHAT IS THE CAPITAL OF IRAQ?"
HMM..
WOW!
HEAVY
I'M NOT SURE I CAN HANDLE THAT QUESTION, MA'AM
COULD I SEND IN A PINCH-HITTER?

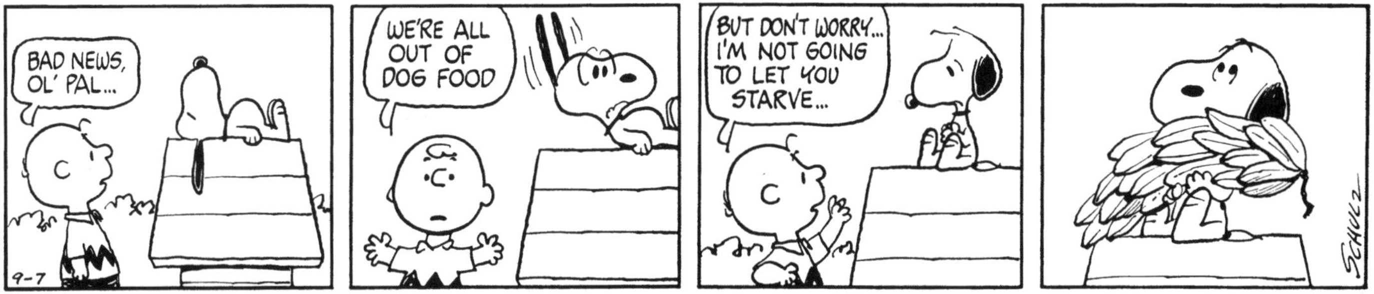
BAD NEWS, OL' PAL...
WE'RE ALL OUT OF DOG FOOD
BUT DON'T WORRY... I'M NOT GOING TO LET YOU STARVE...

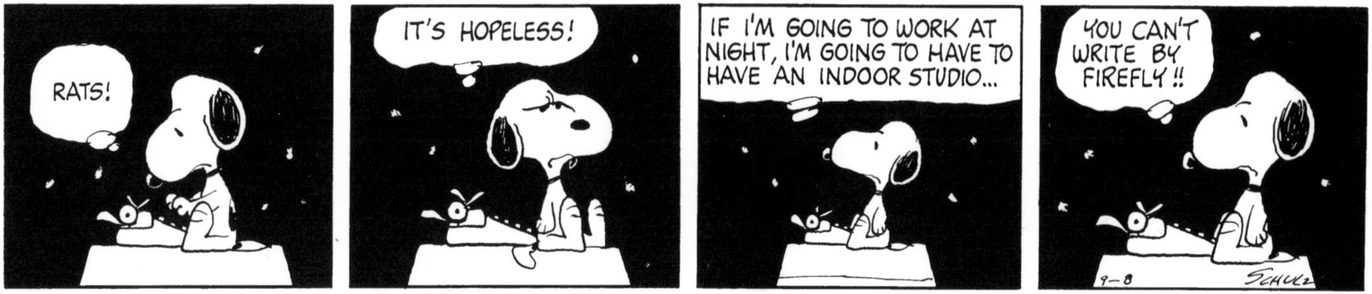
RATS!
IT'S HOPELESS!
IF I'M GOING TO WORK AT NIGHT, I'M GOING TO HAVE TO HAVE AN INDOOR STUDIO...
YOU CAN'T WRITE BY FIREFLY!!

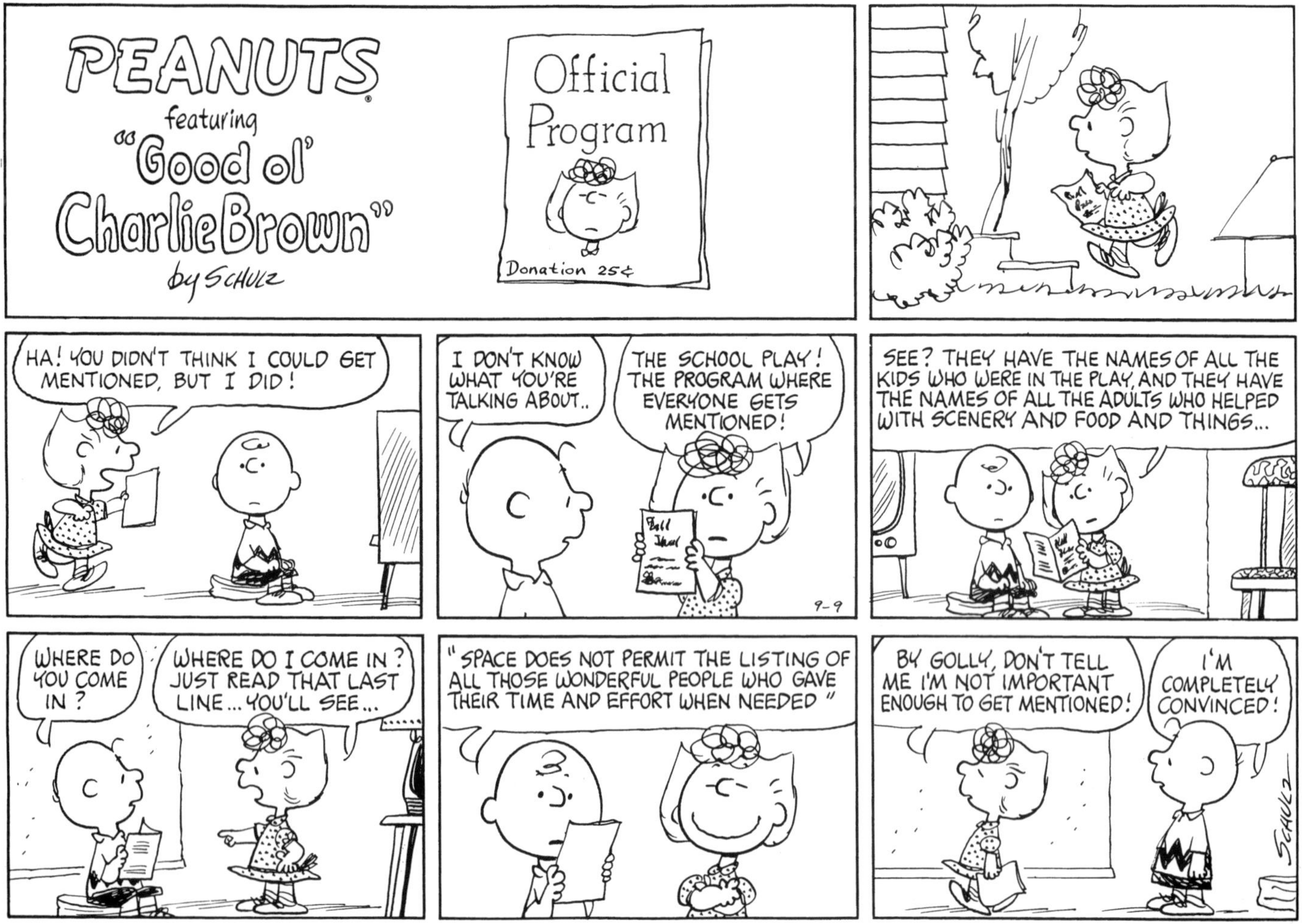
PEANUTS
featuring
"Good ol' Charlie Brown"
by SCHULZ
Official Program
Donation 25¢
HA! YOU DIDN'T THINK I COULD GET MENTIONED, BUT I DID!
I DON'T KNOW WHAT YOU'RE TALKING ABOUT..
THE SCHOOL PLAY! THE PROGRAM WHERE EVERYONE GETS MENTIONED!
9-9
SEE? THEY HAVE THE NAMES OF ALL THE KIDS WHO WERE IN THE PLAY, AND THEY HAVE THE NAMES OF ALL THE ADULTS WHO HELPED WITH SCENERY AND FOOD AND THINGS...
WHERE DO YOU COME IN?
WHERE DO I COME IN? JUST READ THAT LAST LINE... YOU'LL SEE...
"SPACE DOES NOT PERMIT THE LISTING OF ALL THOSE WONDERFUL PEOPLE WHO GAVE THEIR TIME AND EFFORT WHEN NEEDED"
BY GOLLY, DON'T TELL ME I'M NOT IMPORTANT ENOUGH TO GET MENTIONED!
I'M COMPLETELY CONVINCED!
SCHULZ

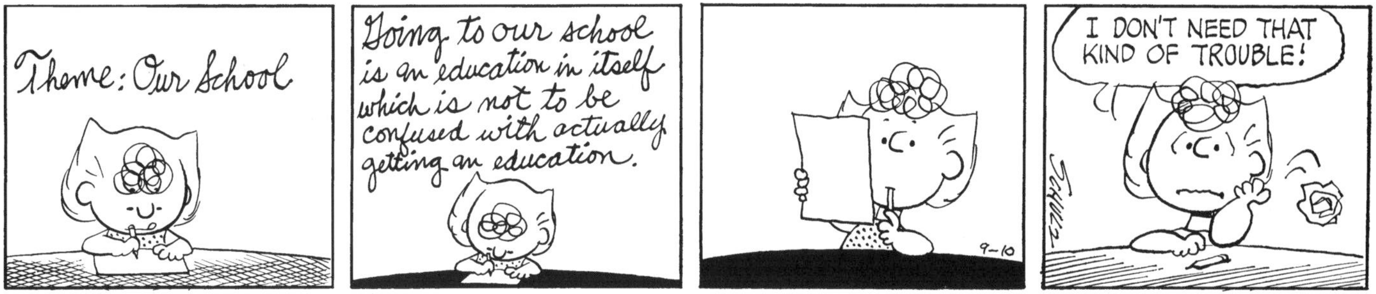
Theme: Our School
Going to our school is an education in itself which is not to be confused with actually getting an education.
I DON'T NEED THAT KIND OF TROUBLE!

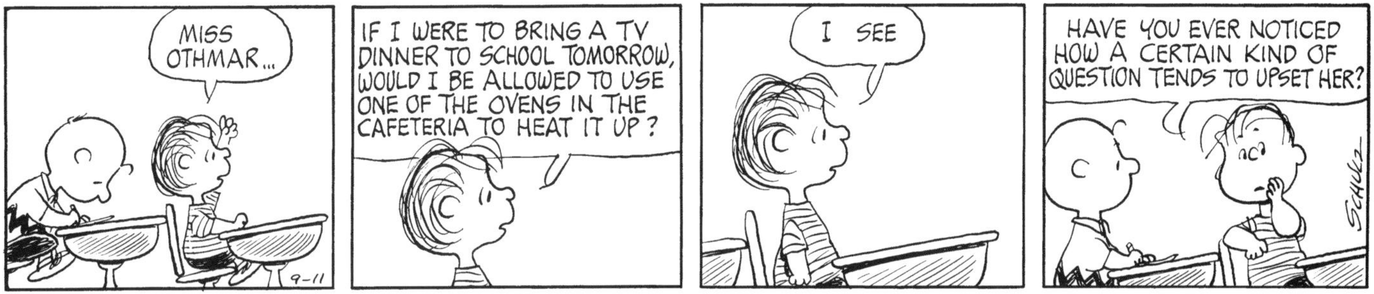
MISS OTHMAR...
IF I WERE TO BRING A TV DINNER TO SCHOOL TOMORROW, WOULD I BE ALLOWED TO USE ONE OF THE OVENS IN THE CAFETERIA TO HEAT IT UP?
I SEE
HAVE YOU EVER NOTICED HOW A CERTAIN KIND OF QUESTION TENDS TO UPSET HER?

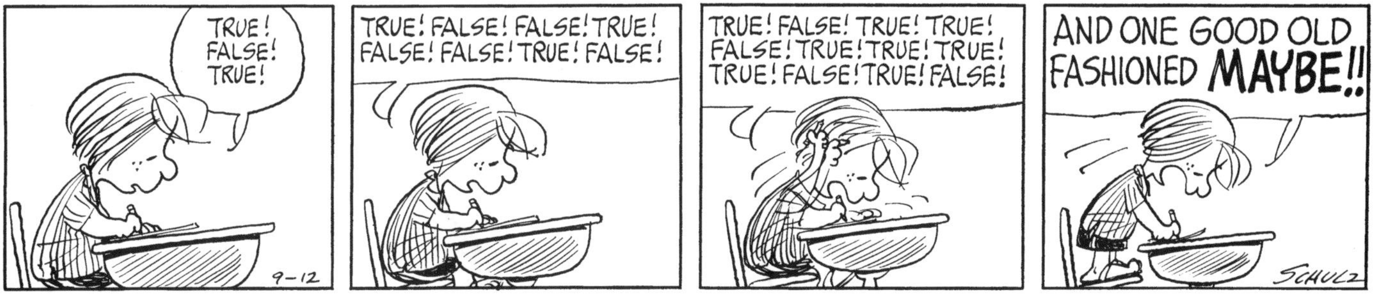
TRUE! FALSE! TRUE!
TRUE! FALSE! FALSE! TRUE! FALSE! FALSE! TRUE! FALSE!
TRUE! FALSE! TRUE! TRUE! FALSE! TRUE! TRUE! TRUE! TRUE! FALSE! TRUE! FALSE!
AND ONE GOOD OLD FASHIONED MAYBE!!

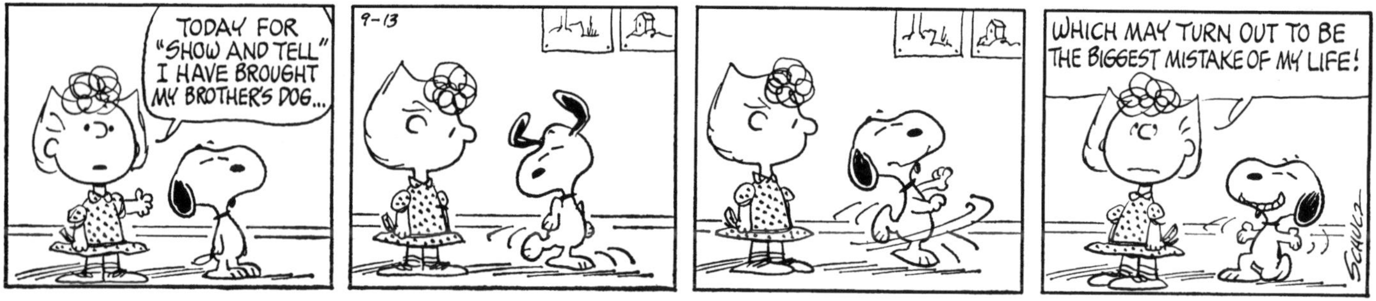
TODAY FOR "SHOW AND TELL" I HAVE BROUGHT MY BROTHER'S DOG...
9-13
WHICH MAY TURN OUT TO BE THE BIGGEST MISTAKE OF MY LIFE!
SCHULZ

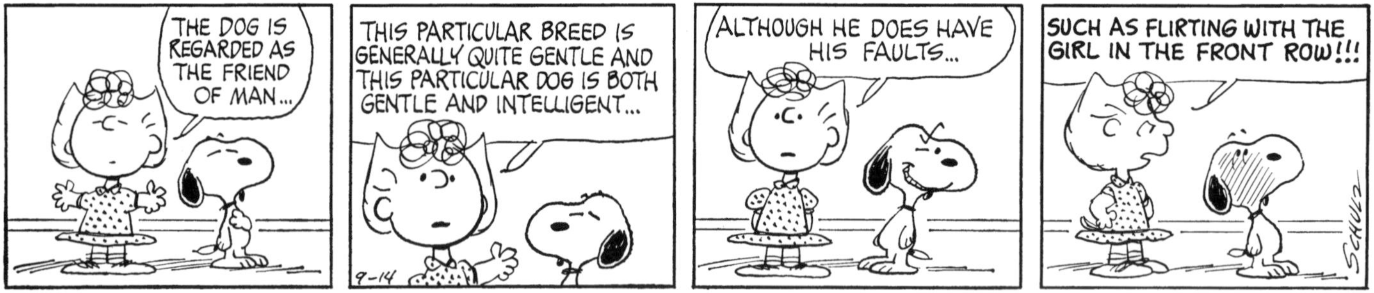
THE DOG IS REGARDED AS THE FRIEND OF MAN...
THIS PARTICULAR BREED IS GENERALLY QUITE GENTLE AND THIS PARTICULAR DOG IS BOTH GENTLE AND INTELLIGENT...
9-14
ALTHOUGH HE DOES HAVE HIS FAULTS...
SUCH AS FLIRTING WITH THE GIRL IN THE FRONT ROW!!!
SCHULZ

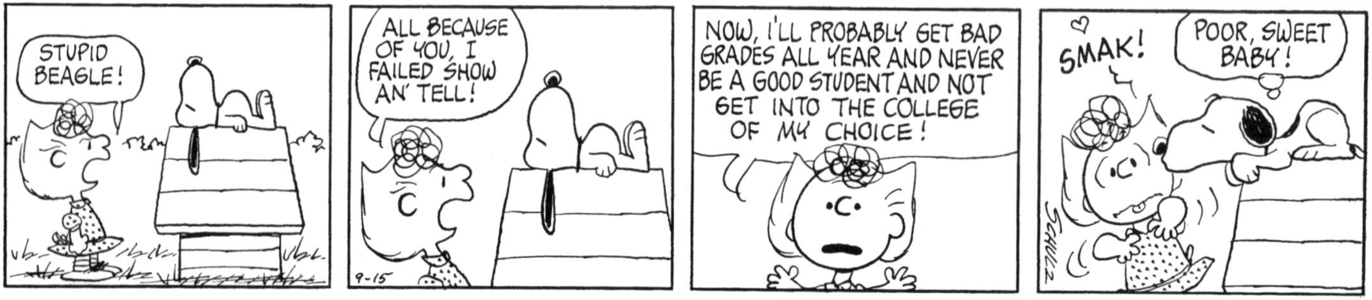
STUPID BEAGLE!
ALL BECAUSE OF YOU, I FAILED SHOW AN' TELL!
9-15
NOW, I'LL PROBABLY GET BAD GRADES ALL YEAR AND NEVER BE A GOOD STUDENT AND NOT GET INTO THE COLLEGE OF MY CHOICE!
SMAK!
POOR, SWEET BABY!
SCHULZ

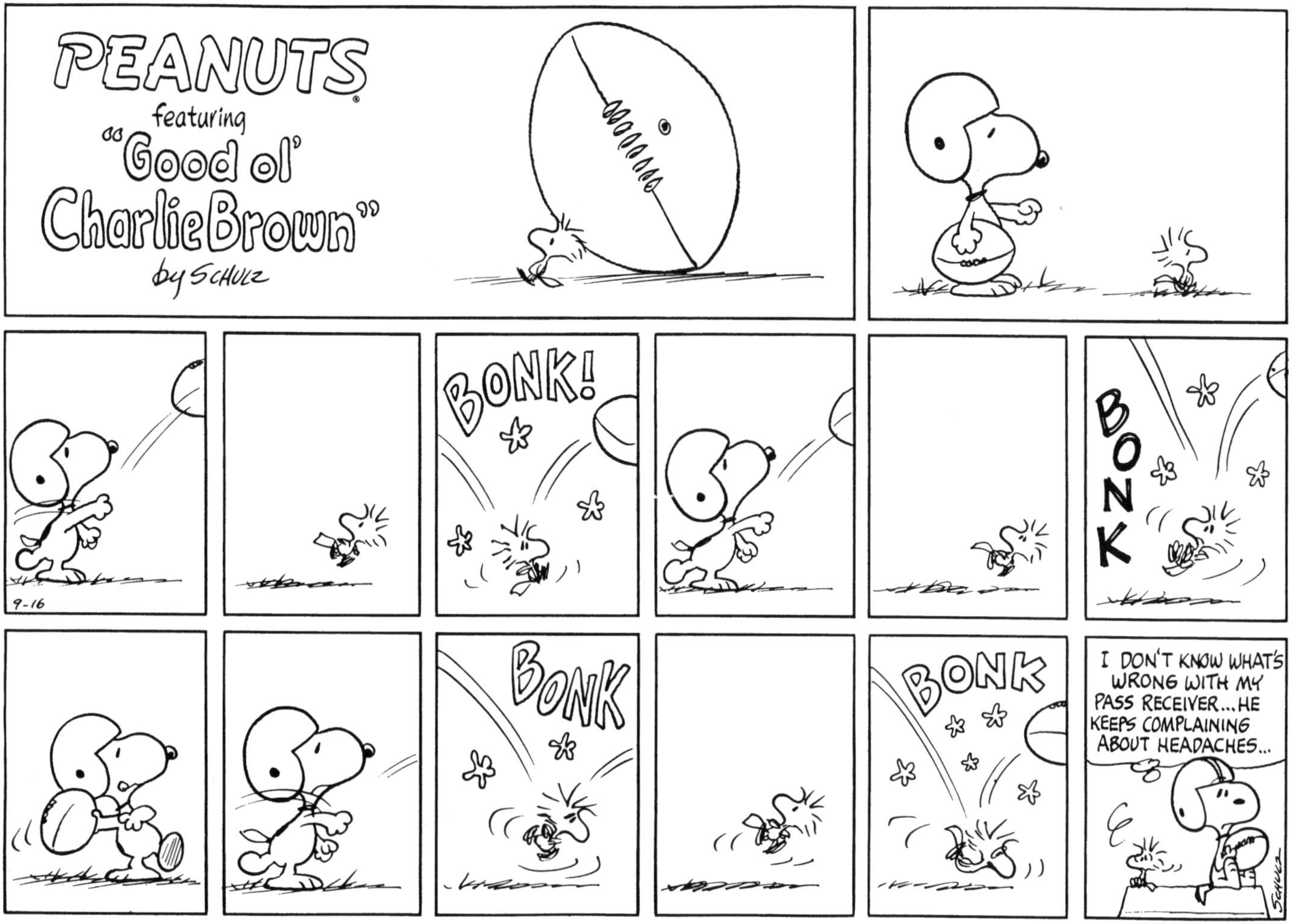
PEANUTS
featuring
"Good ol' CharlieBrown"
by SCHULZ
9-16
BONK!
BONK
BONK
BONK
I DON'T KNOW WHAT'S WRONG WITH MY PASS RECEIVER...HE KEEPS COMPLAINING ABOUT HEADACHES...
SCHULZ

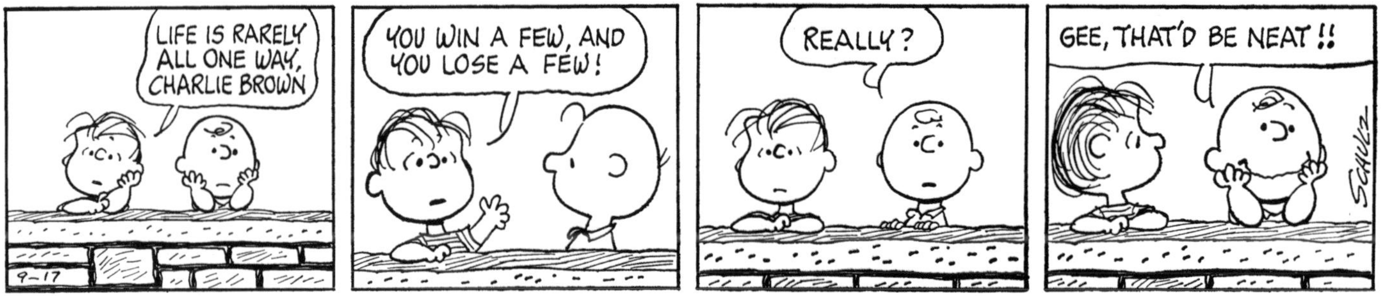
LIFE IS RARELY ALL ONE WAY, CHARLIE BROWN
YOU WIN A FEW, AND YOU LOSE A FEW!
REALLY?
GEE, THAT'D BE NEAT!!

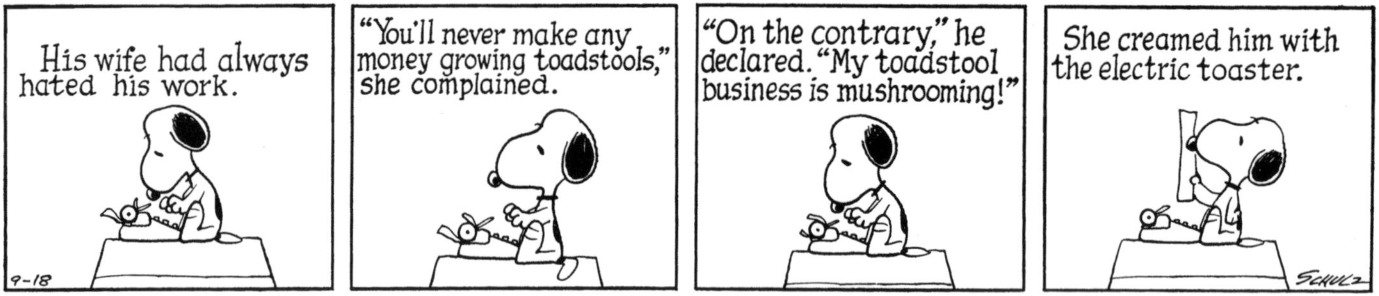
His wife had always hated his work.
"You'll never make any money growing toadstools," she complained.
"On the contrary," he declared. "My toadstool business is mushrooming!"
She creamed him with the electric toaster.

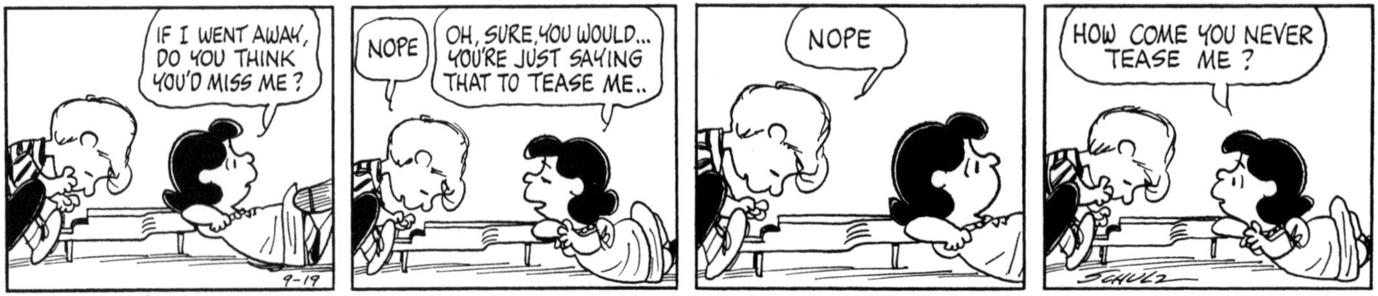
IF I WENT AWAY, DO YOU THINK YOU'D MISS ME?
NOPE
OH, SURE, YOU WOULD... YOU'RE JUST SAYING THAT TO TEASE ME..
NOPE
HOW COME YOU NEVER TEASE ME?

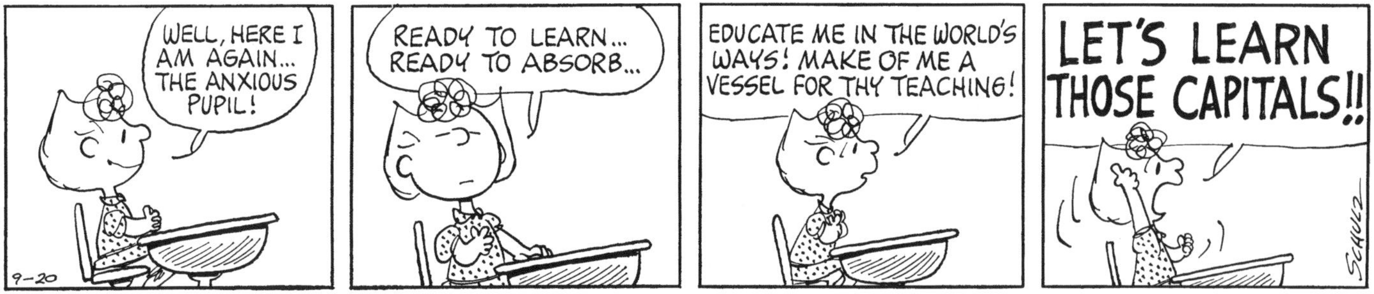
WELL, HERE I AM AGAIN... THE ANXIOUS PUPIL!
9-20
READY TO LEARN... READY TO ABSORB...
EDUCATE ME IN THE WORLD'S WAYS! MAKE OF ME A VESSEL FOR THY TEACHING!
LET'S LEARN THOSE CAPITALS!!
SCHULZ

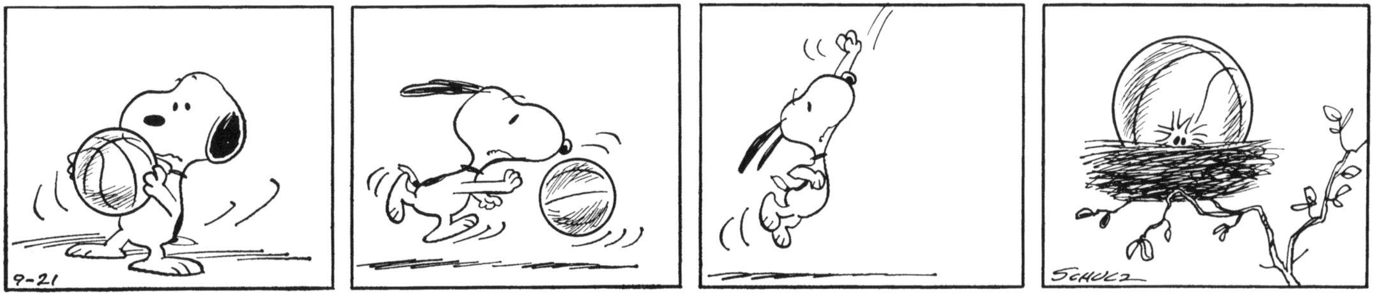
9-21
SCHULZ

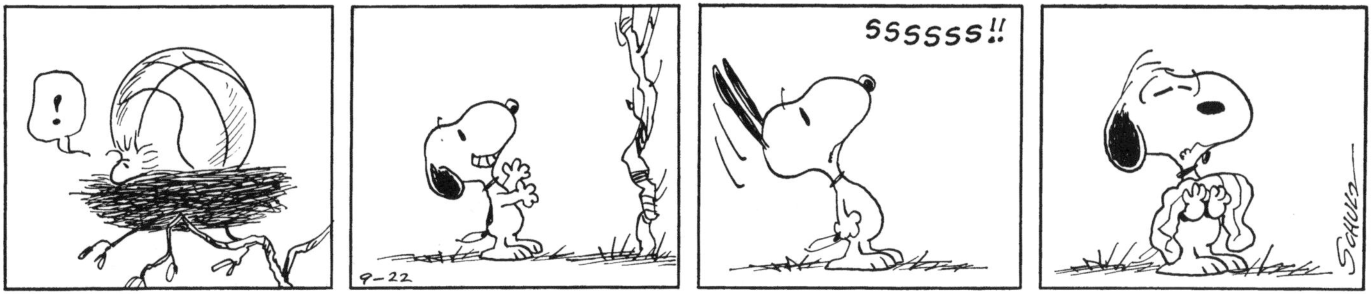
!
9-22
SSSSSS!!
SCHULZ

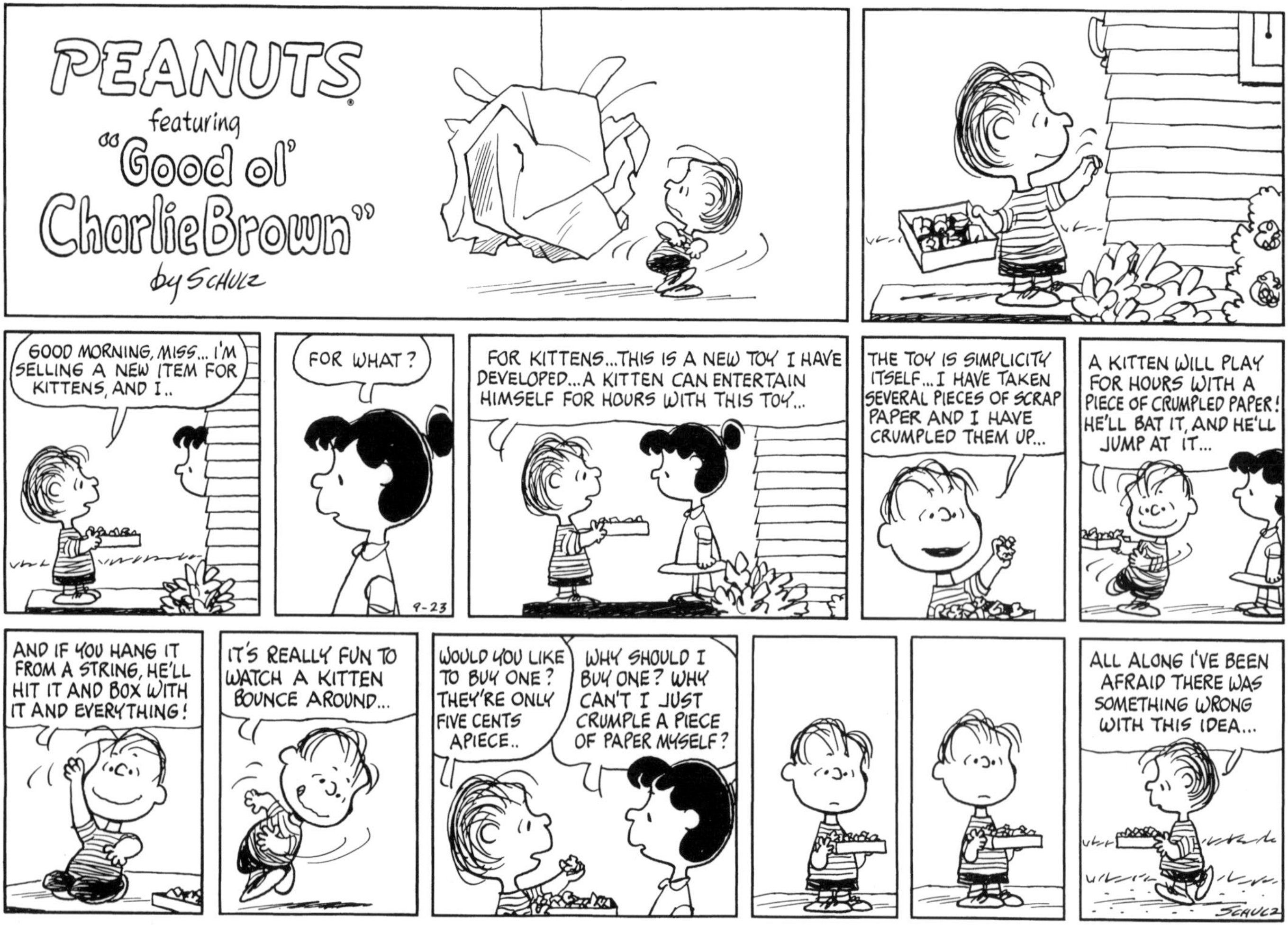
PEANUTS
featuring
"Good ol' Charlie Brown"
by SCHULZ
GOOD MORNING, MISS... I'M SELLING A NEW ITEM FOR KITTENS, AND I..
FOR WHAT?
9-23
FOR KITTENS...THIS IS A NEW TOY I HAVE DEVELOPED...A KITTEN CAN ENTERTAIN HIMSELF FOR HOURS WITH THIS TOY...
THE TOY IS SIMPLICITY ITSELF... I HAVE TAKEN SEVERAL PIECES OF SCRAP PAPER AND I HAVE CRUMPLED THEM UP...
A KITTEN WILL PLAY FOR HOURS WITH A PIECE OF CRUMPLED PAPER! HE'LL BAT IT, AND HE'LL JUMP AT IT...
AND IF YOU HANG IT FROM A STRING, HE'LL HIT IT AND BOX WITH IT AND EVERYTHING!
IT'S REALLY FUN TO WATCH A KITTEN BOUNCE AROUND...
WOULD YOU LIKE TO BUY ONE? THEY'RE ONLY FIVE CENTS APIECE..
WHY SHOULD I BUY ONE? WHY CAN'T I JUST CRUMPLE A PIECE OF PAPER MYSELF?
ALL ALONG I'VE BEEN AFRAID THERE WAS SOMETHING WRONG WITH THIS IDEA...
SCHULZ

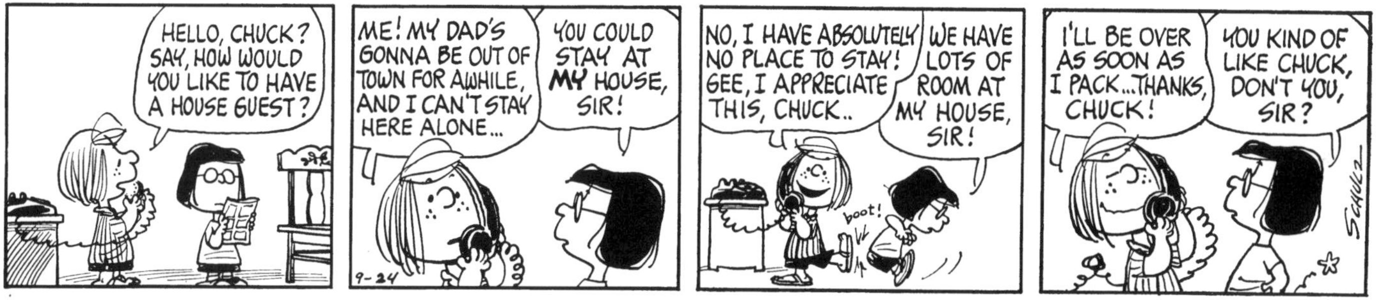
HELLO, CHUCK? SAY, HOW WOULD YOU LIKE TO HAVE A HOUSE GUEST?
ME! MY DAD'S GONNA BE OUT OF TOWN FOR AWHILE, AND I CAN'T STAY HERE ALONE...
YOU COULD STAY AT MY HOUSE, SIR!
9-24
NO, I HAVE ABSOLUTELY NO PLACE TO STAY! GEE, I APPRECIATE THIS, CHUCK..
WE HAVE LOTS OF ROOM AT MY HOUSE, SIR!
boot!
I'LL BE OVER AS SOON AS I PACK...THANKS, CHUCK!
YOU KIND OF LIKE CHUCK, DON'T YOU, SIR?
SCHULZ

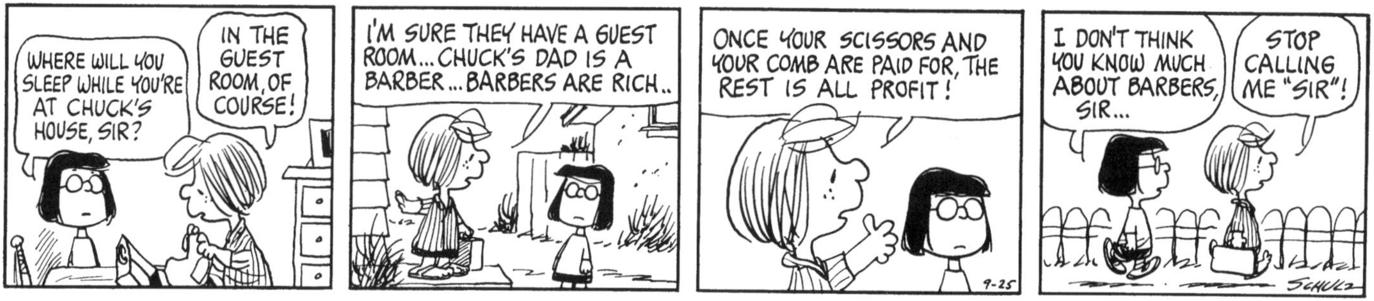
WHERE WILL YOU SLEEP WHILE YOU'RE AT CHUCK'S HOUSE, SIR?
IN THE GUEST ROOM, OF COURSE!
I'M SURE THEY HAVE A GUEST ROOM...CHUCK'S DAD IS A BARBER...BARBERS ARE RICH..
ONCE YOUR SCISSORS AND YOUR COMB ARE PAID FOR, THE REST IS ALL PROFIT!
9-25
I DON'T THINK YOU KNOW MUCH ABOUT BARBERS, SIR...
STOP CALLING ME "SIR"!
SCHULZ

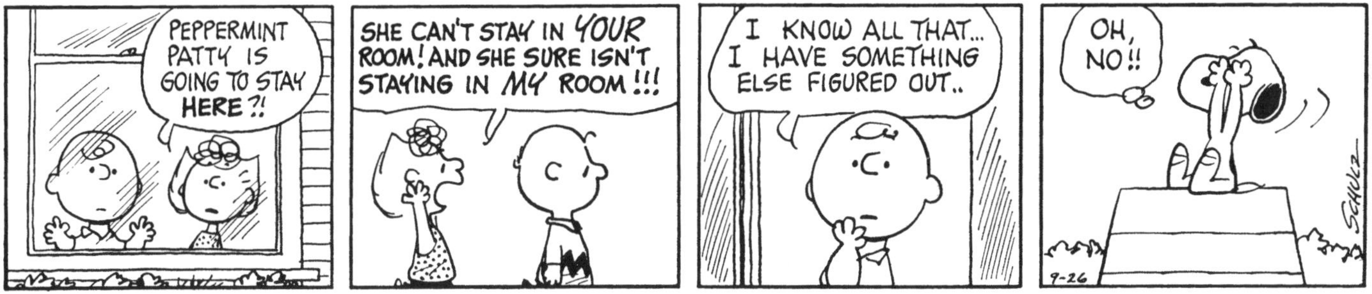
PEPPERMINT PATTY IS GOING TO STAY HERE?!
SHE CAN'T STAY IN YOUR ROOM! AND SHE SURE ISN'T STAYING IN MY ROOM!!!
I KNOW ALL THAT... I HAVE SOMETHING ELSE FIGURED OUT..
OH, NO!!
9-26
SCHULZ

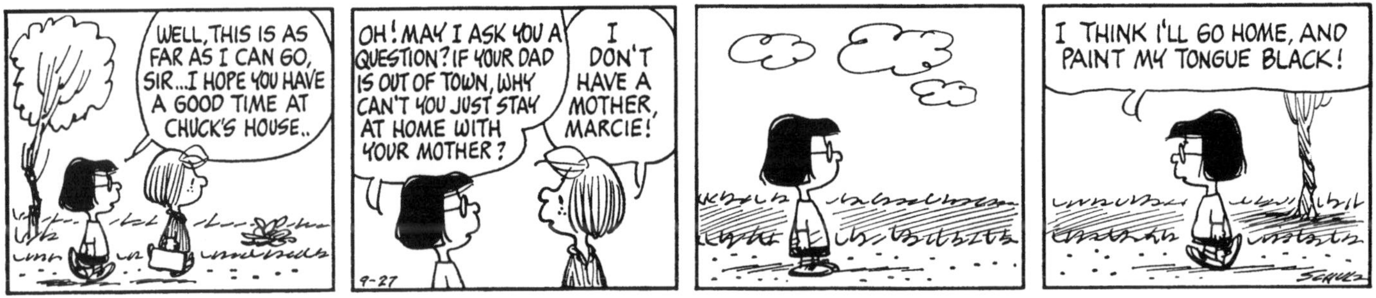
WELL, THIS IS AS FAR AS I CAN GO, SIR...I HOPE YOU HAVE A GOOD TIME AT CHUCK'S HOUSE..
OH! MAY I ASK YOU A QUESTION? IF YOUR DAD IS OUT OF TOWN, WHY CAN'T YOU JUST STAY AT HOME WITH YOUR MOTHER?
I DON'T HAVE A MOTHER, MARCIE!
9-27
I THINK I'LL GO HOME, AND PAINT MY TONGUE BLACK!
SCHULZ

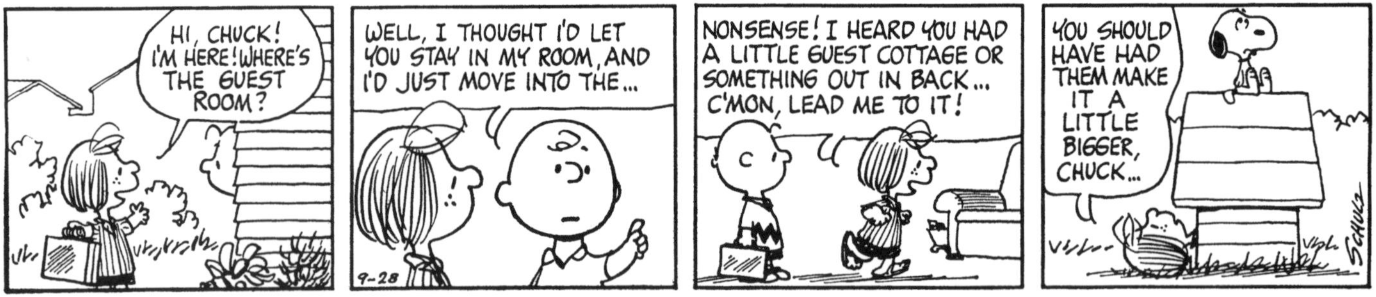
HI, CHUCK! I'M HERE! WHERE'S THE GUEST ROOM?
WELL, I THOUGHT I'D LET YOU STAY IN MY ROOM, AND I'D JUST MOVE INTO THE...
9-28
NONSENSE! I HEARD YOU HAD A LITTLE GUEST COTTAGE OR SOMETHING OUT IN BACK... C'MON, LEAD ME TO IT!
YOU SHOULD HAVE HAD THEM MAKE IT A LITTLE BIGGER, CHUCK...
SCHULZ

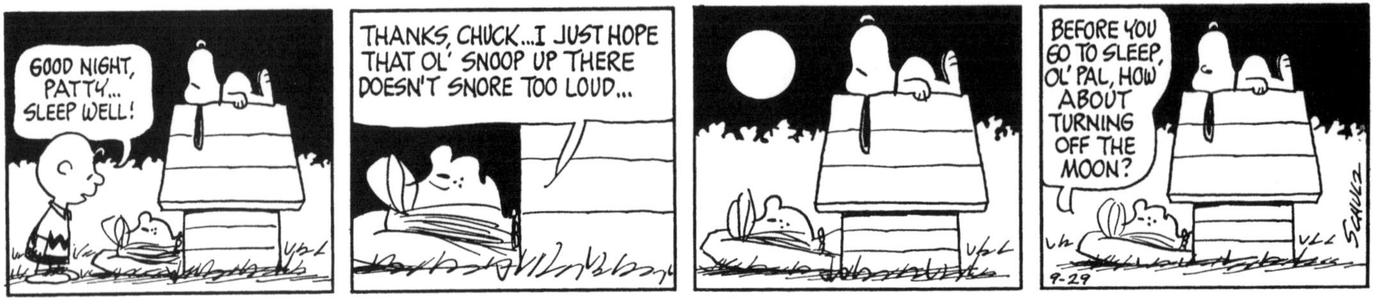
GOOD NIGHT, PATTY... SLEEP WELL!
THANKS, CHUCK...I JUST HOPE THAT OL' SNOOP UP THERE DOESN'T SNORE TOO LOUD...
BEFORE YOU GO TO SLEEP, OL' PAL, HOW ABOUT TURNING OFF THE MOON?
9-29
SCHULZ

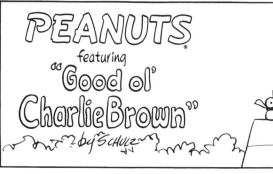

PEANUTS
featuring
"Good ol' Charlie Brown"
by SCHULZ

The last car drove away. It began to rain.

And so our hero's life ended as it had begun... a disaster.

"I never got any breaks," he had always complained.

He had wanted to be rich. He died poor. He wanted friends. He died friendless.

He wanted to be loved. He died unloved. He wanted laughter. He found only tears.

He wanted applause. He received boos. He wanted fame. He found only obscurity. He wanted answers. He found only questions.

I'M HAVING A HARD TIME ENDING THIS..

9-30

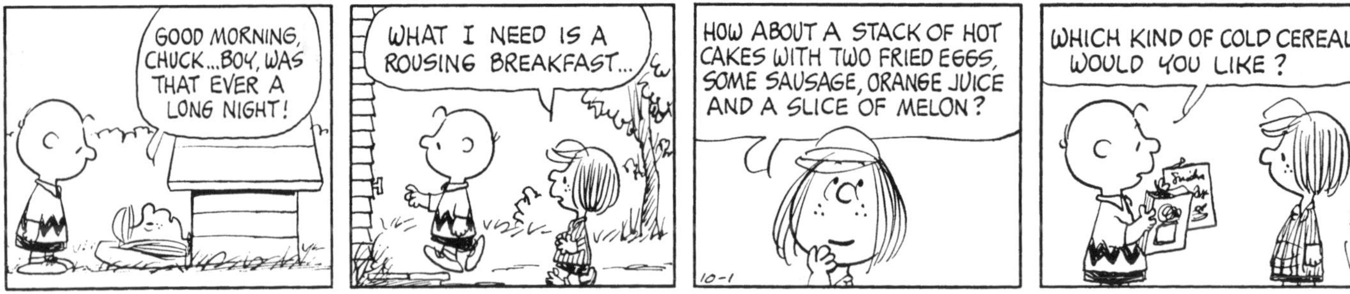
GOOD MORNING, CHUCK...BOY, WAS THAT EVER A LONG NIGHT!
WHAT I NEED IS A ROUSING BREAKFAST...
HOW ABOUT A STACK OF HOT CAKES WITH TWO FRIED EGGS, SOME SAUSAGE, ORANGE JUICE AND A SLICE OF MELON?
10-1
WHICH KIND OF COLD CEREAL WOULD YOU LIKE?
SCHULZ

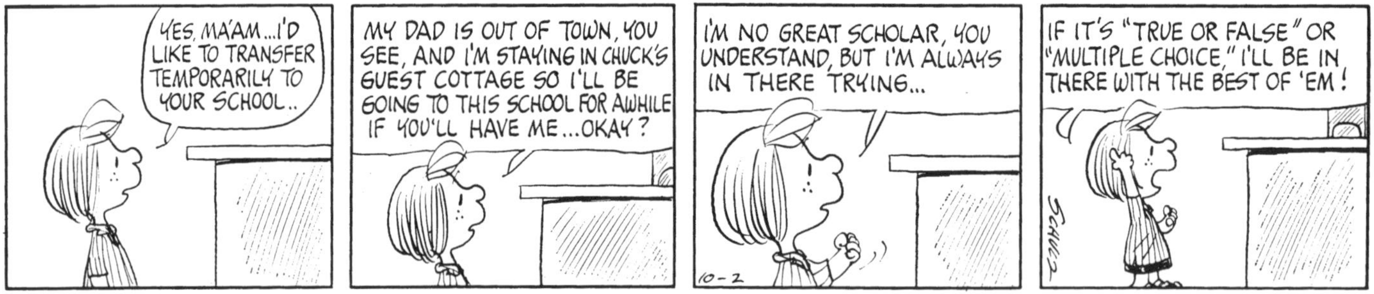
YES, MA'AM...I'D LIKE TO TRANSFER TEMPORARILY TO YOUR SCHOOL..
MY DAD IS OUT OF TOWN, YOU SEE, AND I'M STAYING IN CHUCK'S GUEST COTTAGE SO I'LL BE GOING TO THIS SCHOOL FOR AWHILE IF YOU'LL HAVE ME...OKAY?
I'M NO GREAT SCHOLAR, YOU UNDERSTAND, BUT I'M ALWAYS IN THERE TRYING...
10-2
IF IT'S "TRUE OR FALSE" OR "MULTIPLE CHOICE," I'LL BE IN THERE WITH THE BEST OF 'EM!
SCHULZ

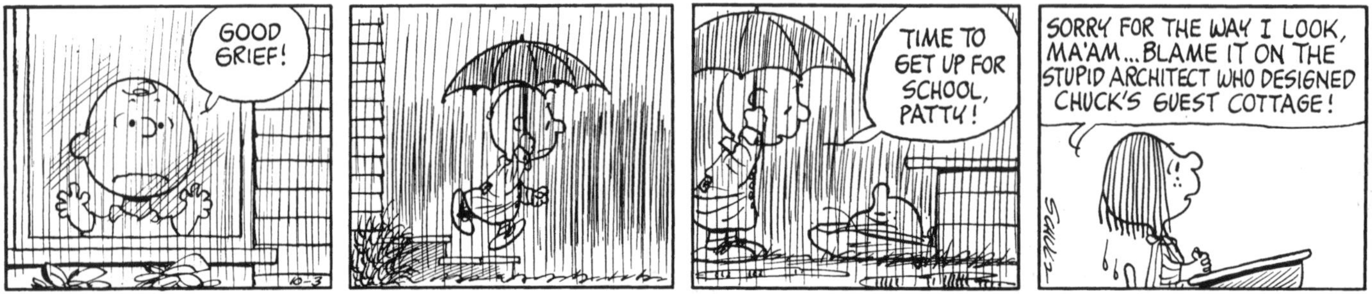
GOOD GRIEF!
10-3
TIME TO GET UP FOR SCHOOL, PATTY!
SORRY FOR THE WAY I LOOK, MA'AM...BLAME IT ON THE STUPID ARCHITECT WHO DESIGNED CHUCK'S GUEST COTTAGE!
SCHULZ

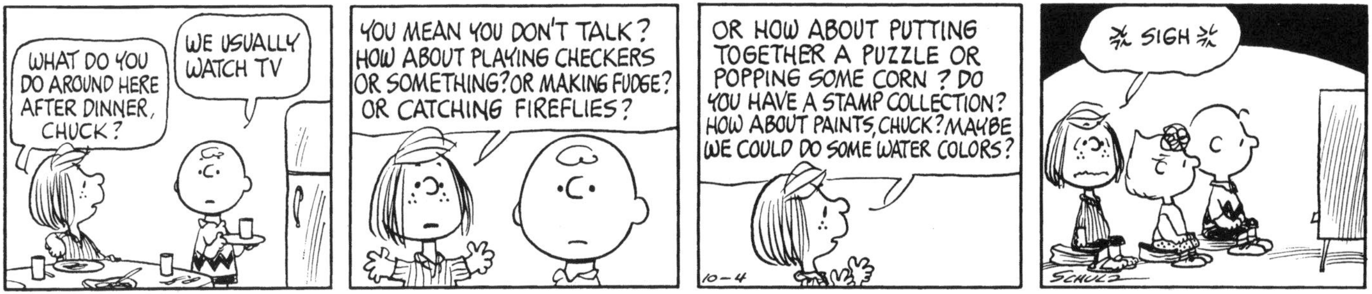
WHAT DO YOU DO AROUND HERE AFTER DINNER, CHUCK?
WE USUALLY WATCH TV
YOU MEAN YOU DON'T TALK? HOW ABOUT PLAYING CHECKERS OR SOMETHING? OR MAKING FUDGE? OR CATCHING FIREFLIES?
OR HOW ABOUT PUTTING TOGETHER A PUZZLE OR POPPING SOME CORN? DO YOU HAVE A STAMP COLLECTION? HOW ABOUT PAINTS, CHUCK? MAYBE WE COULD DO SOME WATER COLORS?
10-4
SIGH
SCHULZ

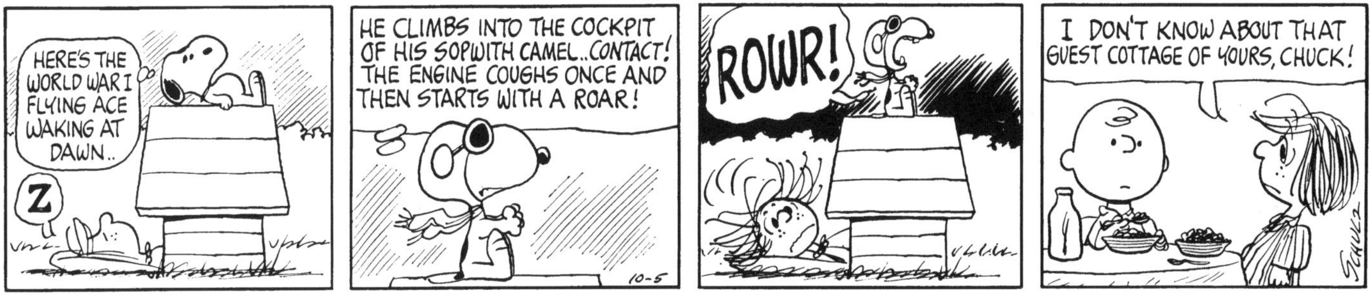
HERE'S THE WORLD WAR I FLYING ACE WAKING AT DAWN..
Z
HE CLIMBS INTO THE COCKPIT OF HIS SOPWITH CAMEL..CONTACT! THE ENGINE COUGHS ONCE AND THEN STARTS WITH A ROAR!
10-5
ROWR!
I DON'T KNOW ABOUT THAT GUEST COTTAGE OF YOURS, CHUCK!
SCHULZ

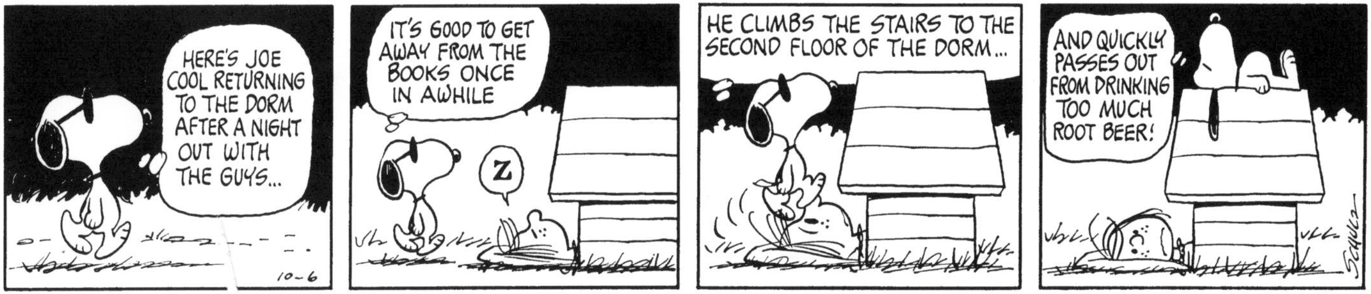
HERE'S JOE COOL RETURNING TO THE DORM AFTER A NIGHT OUT WITH THE GUYS...
10-6
IT'S GOOD TO GET AWAY FROM THE BOOKS ONCE IN AWHILE
Z
HE CLIMBS THE STAIRS TO THE SECOND FLOOR OF THE DORM...
AND QUICKLY PASSES OUT FROM DRINKING TOO MUCH ROOT BEER!
SCHULZ

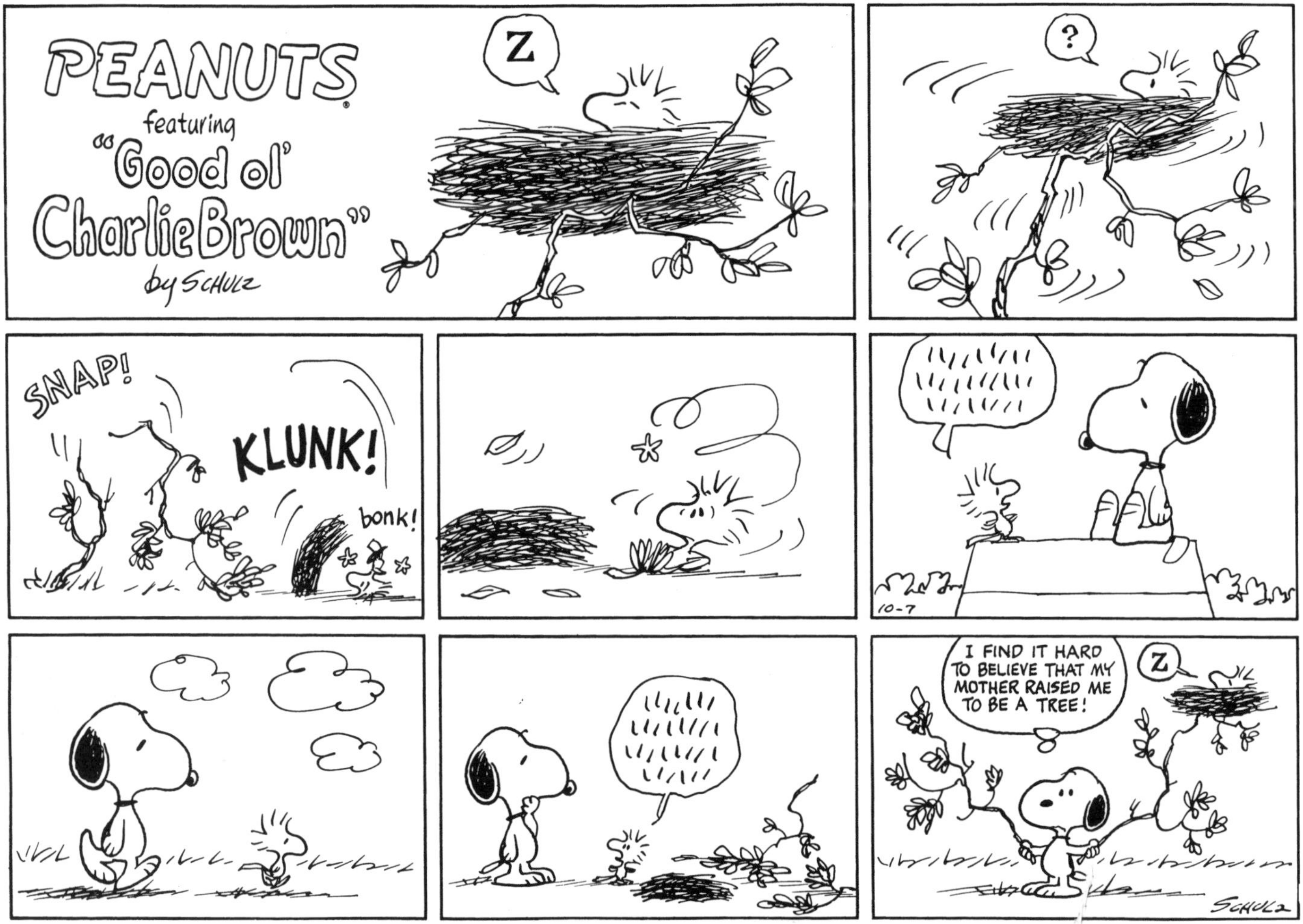
PEANUTS
featuring
"Good ol' Charlie Brown"
by SCHULZ
Z
?
SNAP!
KLUNK!
bonk!
10-7
I FIND IT HARD TO BELIEVE THAT MY MOTHER RAISED ME TO BE A TREE!
Z
SCHULZ

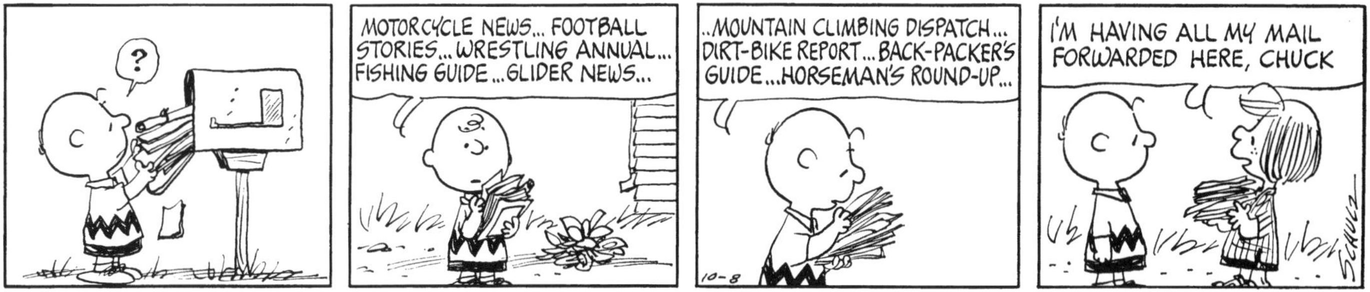
?
MOTORCYCLE NEWS... FOOTBALL STORIES... WRESTLING ANNUAL... FISHING GUIDE... GLIDER NEWS...
..MOUNTAIN CLIMBING DISPATCH... DIRT-BIKE REPORT... BACK-PACKER'S GUIDE... HORSEMAN'S ROUND-UP...
10-8
I'M HAVING ALL MY MAIL FORWARDED HERE, CHUCK
SCHULZ

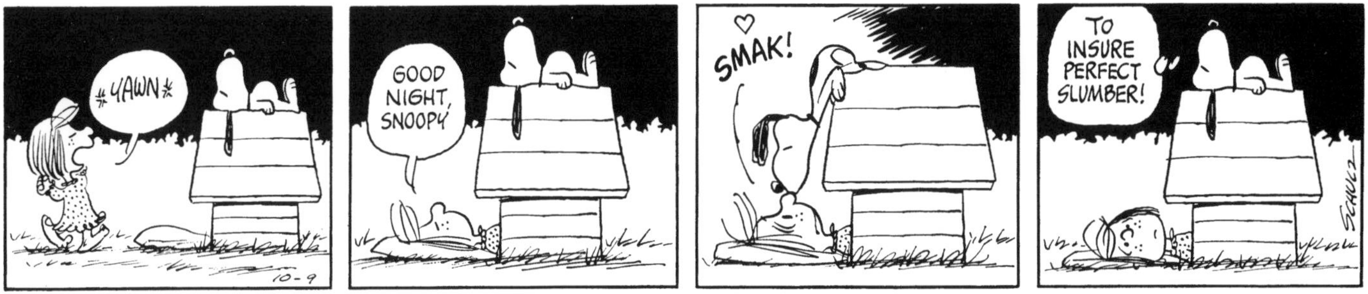
YAWN
10-9
GOOD NIGHT, SNOOPY
SMAK!
TO INSURE PERFECT SLUMBER!
SCHULZ

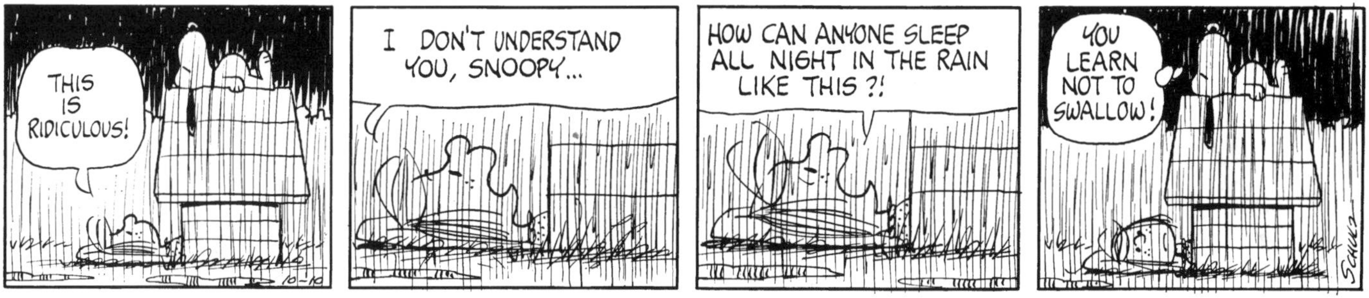
THIS IS RIDICULOUS!
10-10
I DON'T UNDERSTAND YOU, SNOOPY...
HOW CAN ANYONE SLEEP ALL NIGHT IN THE RAIN LIKE THIS?!
YOU LEARN NOT TO SWALLOW!
SCHULZ

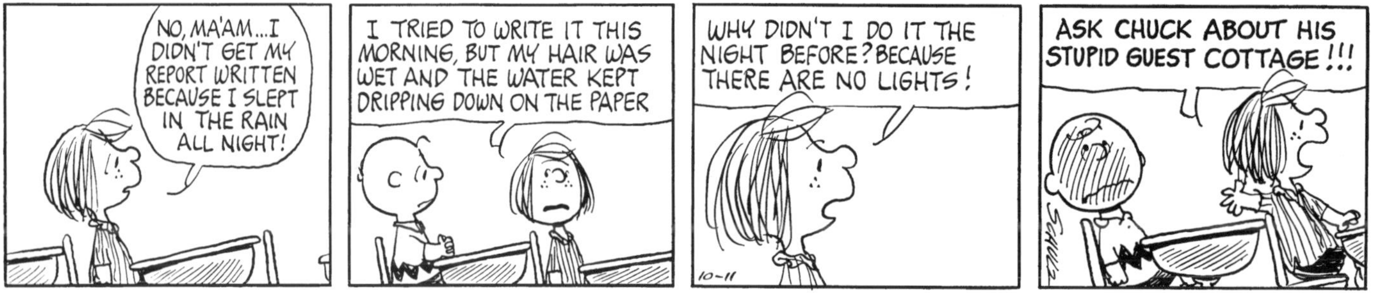
NO, MA'AM...I DIDN'T GET MY REPORT WRITTEN BECAUSE I SLEPT IN THE RAIN ALL NIGHT!
I TRIED TO WRITE IT THIS MORNING, BUT MY HAIR WAS WET AND THE WATER KEPT DRIPPING DOWN ON THE PAPER
WHY DIDN'T I DO IT THE NIGHT BEFORE? BECAUSE THERE ARE NO LIGHTS!
10-11
ASK CHUCK ABOUT HIS STUPID GUEST COTTAGE!!!
SCHULZ

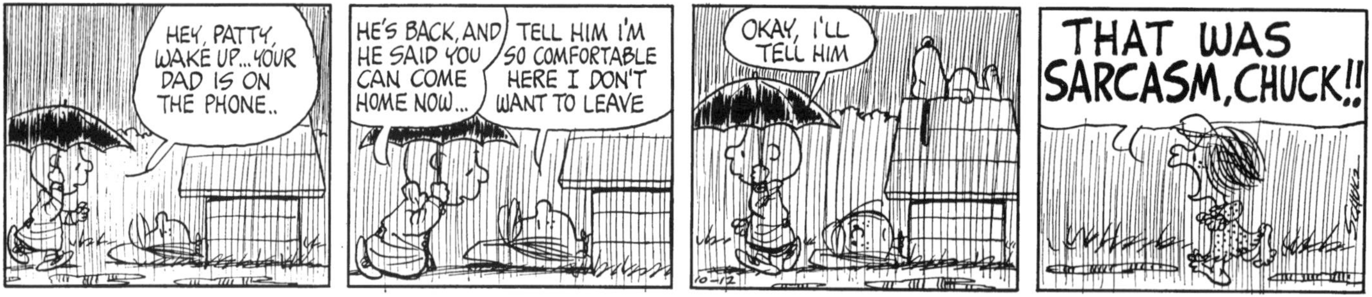
HEY, PATTY, WAKE UP...YOUR DAD IS ON THE PHONE..
HE'S BACK, AND HE SAID YOU CAN COME HOME NOW...
TELL HIM I'M SO COMFORTABLE HERE I DON'T WANT TO LEAVE
OKAY, I'LL TELL HIM
10-12
THAT WAS SARCASM, CHUCK!!
SCHULZ

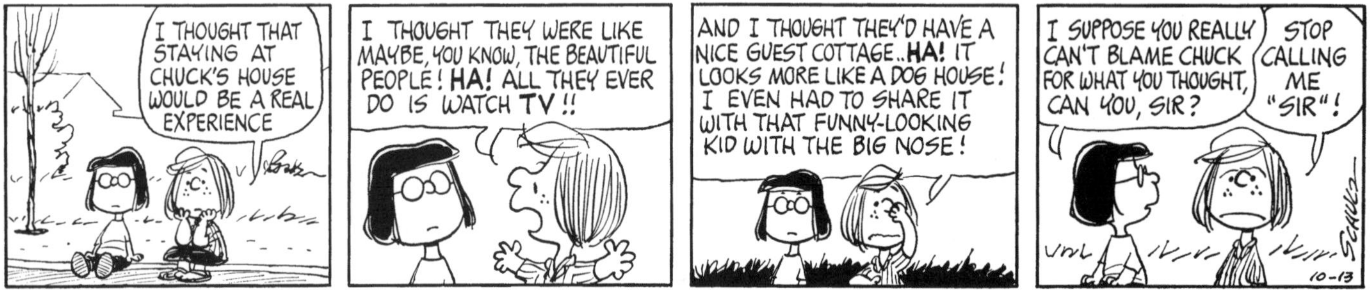
I THOUGHT THAT STAYING AT CHUCK'S HOUSE WOULD BE A REAL EXPERIENCE
I THOUGHT THEY WERE LIKE MAYBE, YOU KNOW, THE BEAUTIFUL PEOPLE! HA! ALL THEY EVER DO IS WATCH TV!!
AND I THOUGHT THEY'D HAVE A NICE GUEST COTTAGE..HA! IT LOOKS MORE LIKE A DOG HOUSE! I EVEN HAD TO SHARE IT WITH THAT FUNNY-LOOKING KID WITH THE BIG NOSE!
I SUPPOSE YOU REALLY CAN'T BLAME CHUCK FOR WHAT YOU THOUGHT, CAN YOU, SIR?
STOP CALLING ME "SIR"!
SCHULZ
10-13

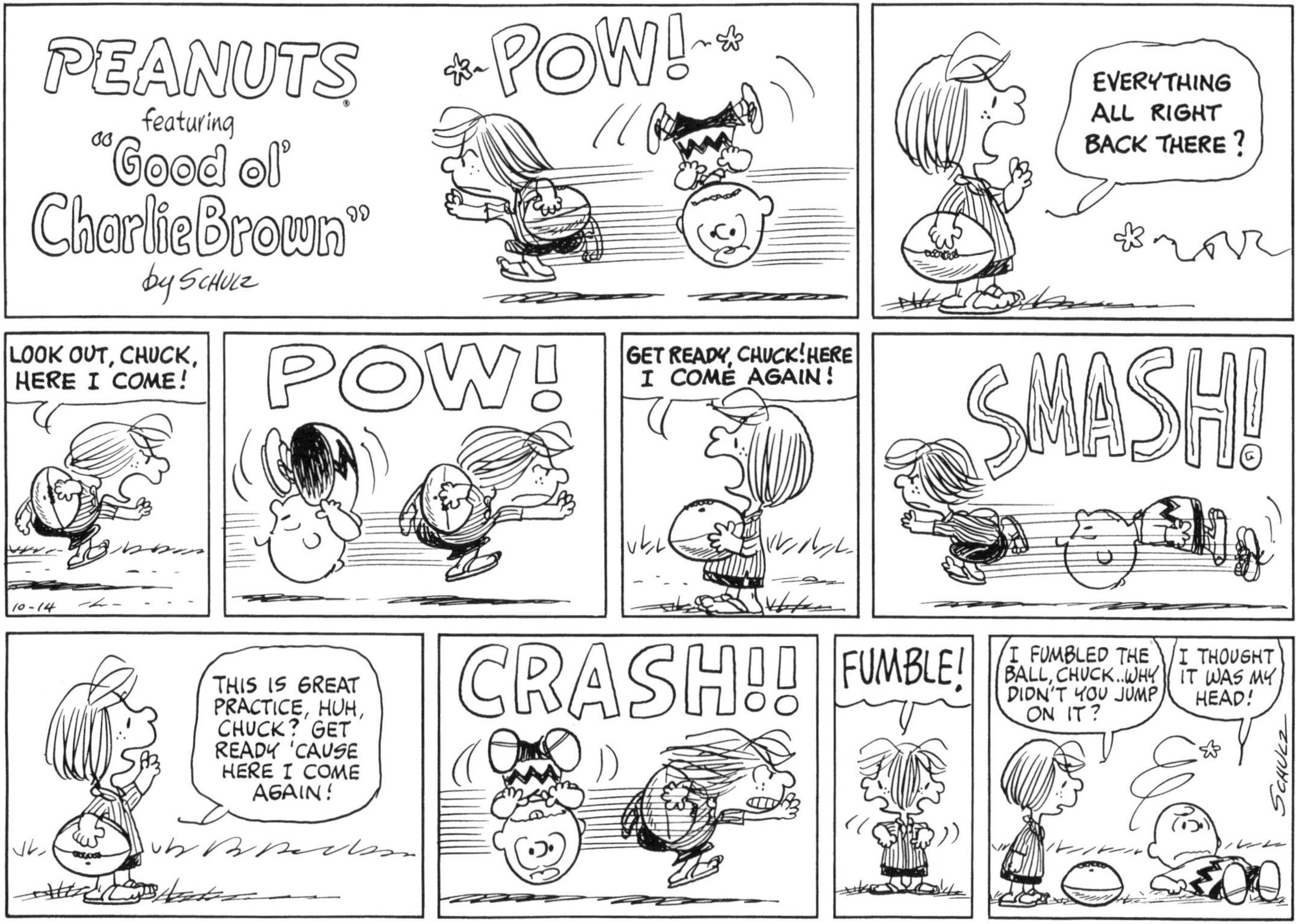
PEANUTS®
featuring
"Good ol' CharlieBrown"
by SCHULZ
POW!
EVERYTHING ALL RIGHT BACK THERE?
LOOK OUT, CHUCK, HERE I COME!
10-14
POW!
GET READY, CHUCK! HERE I COME AGAIN!
SMASH!
THIS IS GREAT PRACTICE, HUH, CHUCK? GET READY 'CAUSE HERE I COME AGAIN!
CRASH!!
FUMBLE!
I FUMBLED THE BALL, CHUCK..WHY DIDN'T YOU JUMP ON IT?
I THOUGHT IT WAS MY HEAD!
SCHULZ

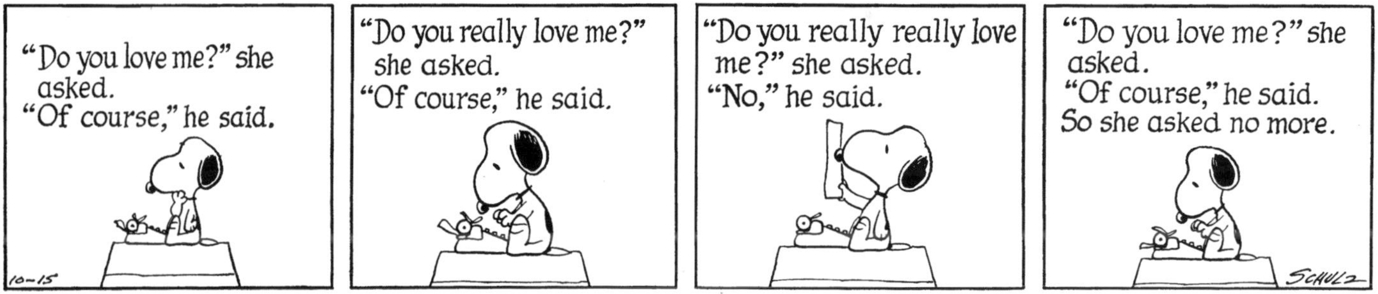
"Do you love me?" she asked.
"Of course," he said.
10-15
"Do you really love me?" she asked.
"Of course," he said.
"Do you really really love me?" she asked.
"No," he said.
"Do you love me?" she asked.
"Of course," he said.
So she asked no more.
SCHULZ

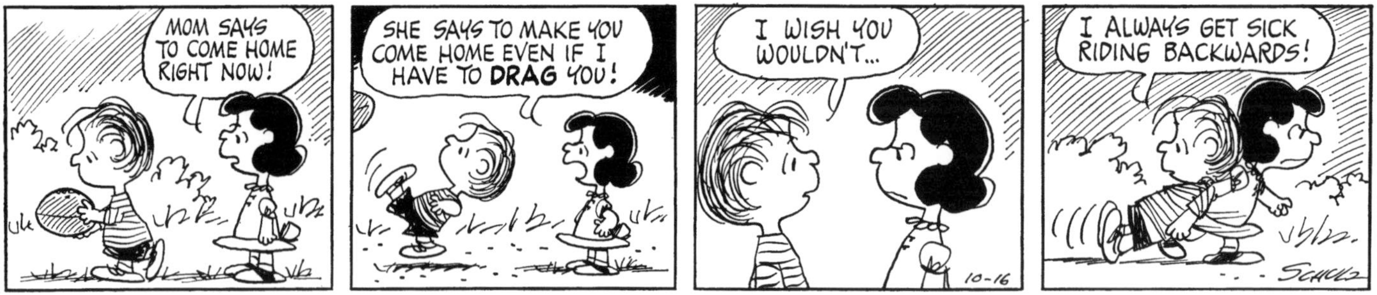
MOM SAYS TO COME HOME RIGHT NOW!
SHE SAYS TO MAKE YOU COME HOME EVEN IF I HAVE TO DRAG YOU!
I WISH YOU WOULDN'T...
10-16
I ALWAYS GET SICK RIDING BACKWARDS!
SCHULZ

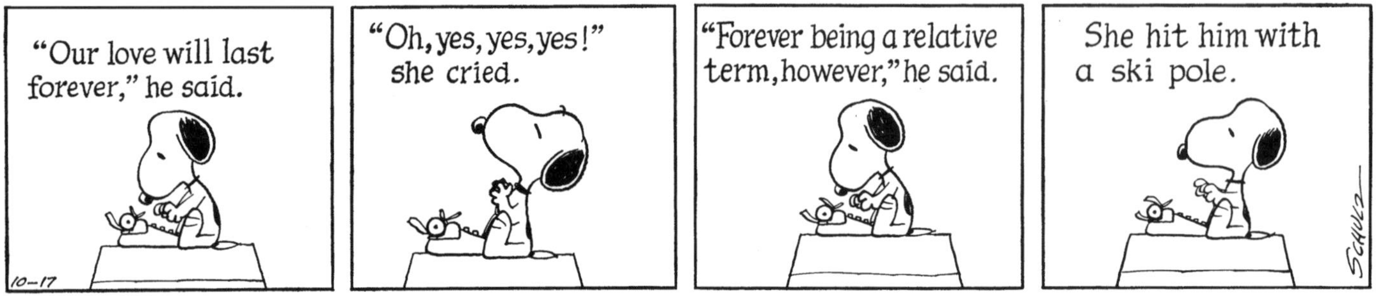
"Our love will last forever," he said.
10-17
"Oh, yes, yes, yes!" she cried.
"Forever being a relative term, however," he said.
She hit him with a ski pole.
SCHULZ

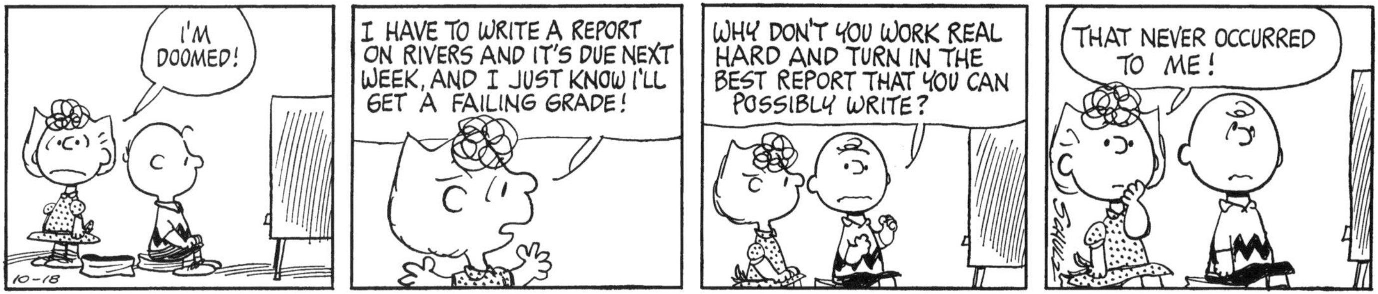
I'M DOOMED!
10-18
I HAVE TO WRITE A REPORT ON RIVERS AND IT'S DUE NEXT WEEK, AND I JUST KNOW I'LL GET A FAILING GRADE!
WHY DON'T YOU WORK REAL HARD AND TURN IN THE BEST REPORT THAT YOU CAN POSSIBLY WRITE?
THAT NEVER OCCURRED TO ME!
SCHULZ

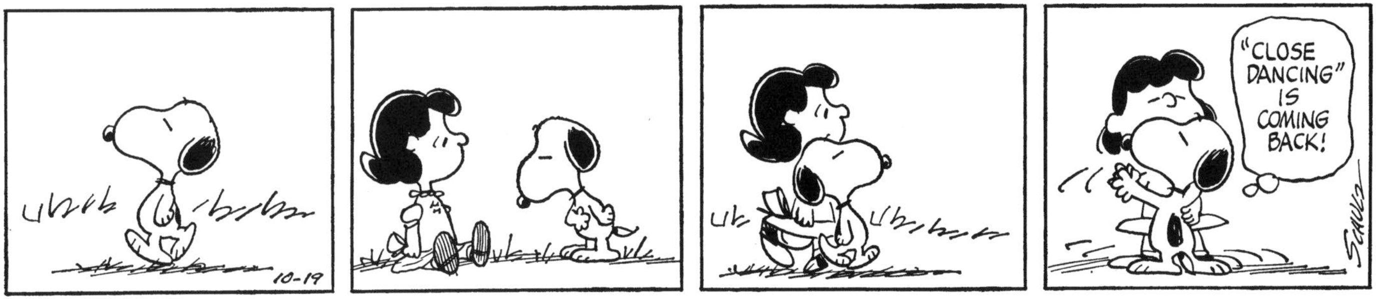
10-19
"CLOSE DANCING" IS COMING BACK!
SCHULZ

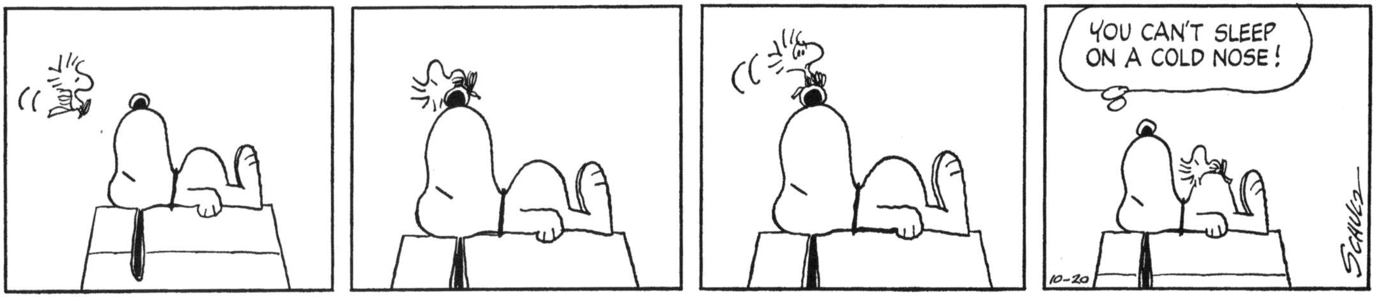
YOU CAN'T SLEEP ON A COLD NOSE!
10-20
SCHULZ

PEANUTS featuring "Good ol' Charlie Brown" by SCHULZ

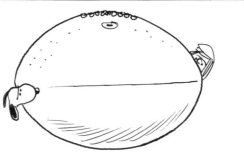

NOPE!

I'D LIKE TO HAVE YOU ON MY TEAM, CHUCK, BUT I JUST DON'T THINK YOU'RE GOOD ENOUGH...

IN FACT, I DON'T SEE ANYONE AROUND HERE WHO COULD COME UP TO MY STANDARD!

HOW ABOUT MY LINEBACKER OVER THERE? HE'S PRETTY GOOD

HIM?

OKAY, LET'S TRY HIM OUT..

HERE I COME, FELLA! STOP ME IF YOU CAN!!

FREIGHT TRAIN!!

CRUNCH! BONE-BREAKING RIB-SHAKING EAR-SPLITTING FLESH-TEARING EARTH SHATTERING TEETH RATTLING SMASH! SOUND OF GLASS BREAKING

10-21

GOOD SHOT, KID! HOW WOULD YOU LIKE TO PLAY FOR A DECENT TEAM?

SIGH

KEEP TALKING, SWEETIE..

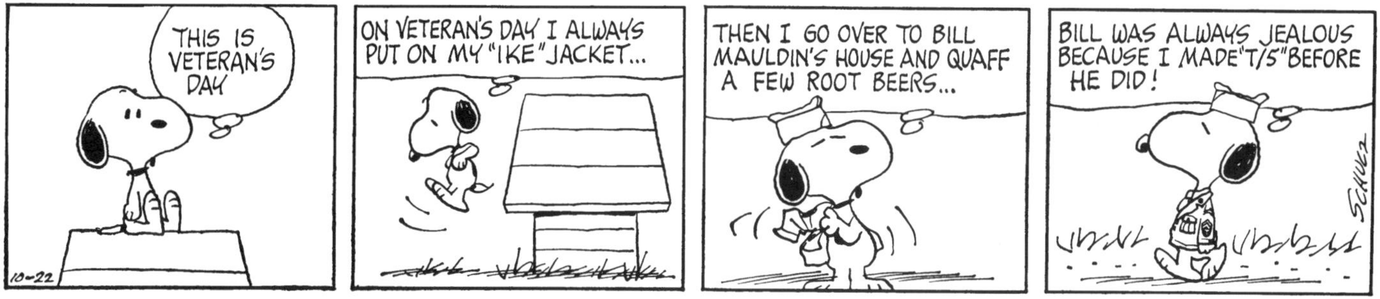
THIS IS VETERAN'S DAY
ON VETERAN'S DAY I ALWAYS PUT ON MY "IKE" JACKET...
THEN I GO OVER TO BILL MAULDIN'S HOUSE AND QUAFF A FEW ROOT BEERS...
BILL WAS ALWAYS JEALOUS BECAUSE I MADE "T/5" BEFORE HE DID!

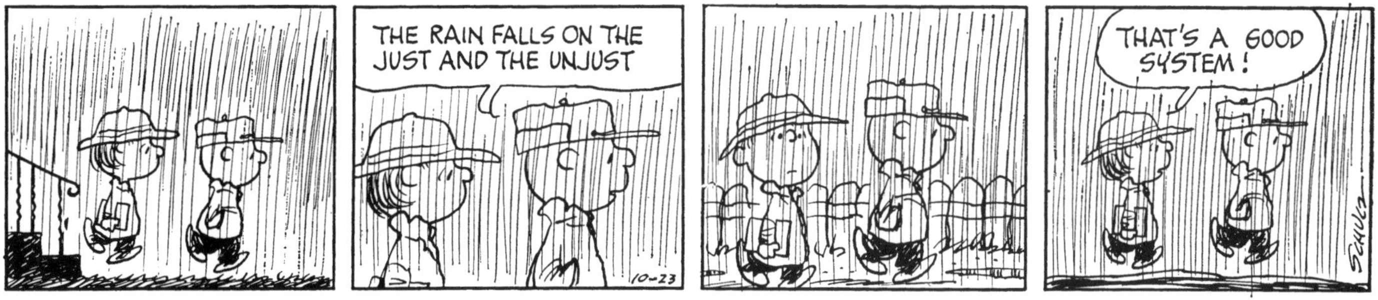
THE RAIN FALLS ON THE JUST AND THE UNJUST
THAT'S A GOOD SYSTEM!

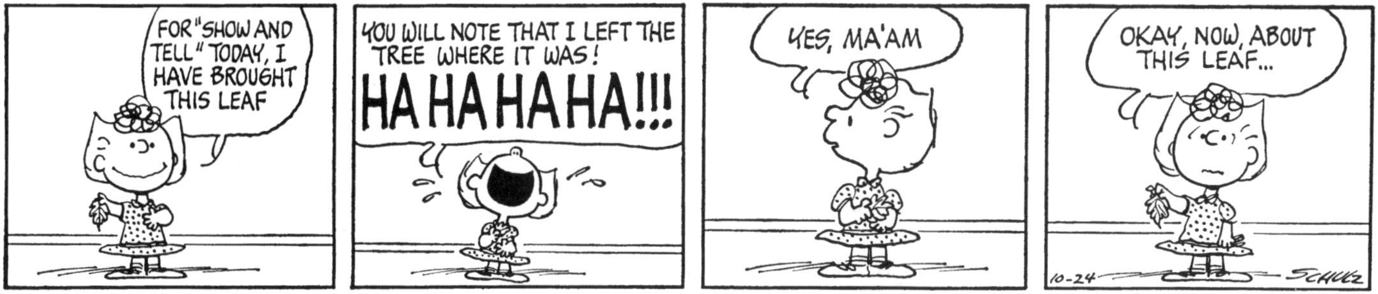
FOR "SHOW AND TELL" TODAY, I HAVE BROUGHT THIS LEAF
YOU WILL NOTE THAT I LEFT THE TREE WHERE IT WAS!
HA HA HA HA HA!!!
YES, MA'AM
OKAY, NOW, ABOUT THIS LEAF...

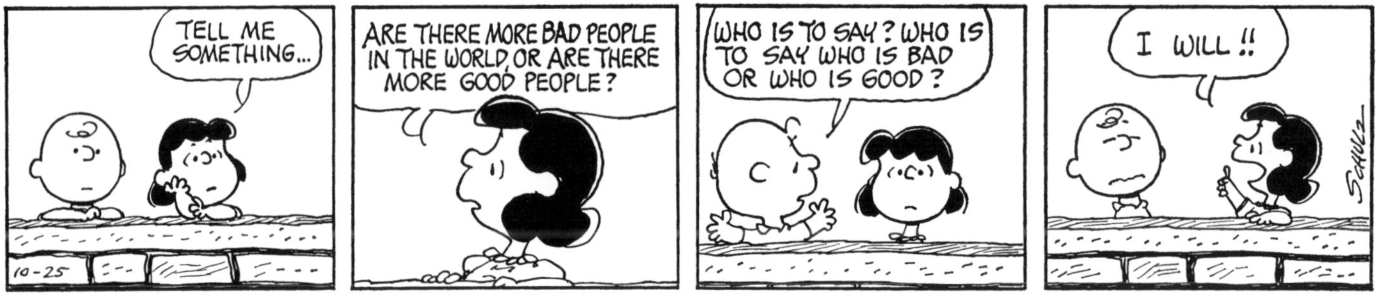
TELL ME SOMETHING...
ARE THERE MORE BAD PEOPLE IN THE WORLD, OR ARE THERE MORE GOOD PEOPLE?
WHO IS TO SAY? WHO IS TO SAY WHO IS BAD OR WHO IS GOOD?
I WILL!!
10-25
SCHULZ

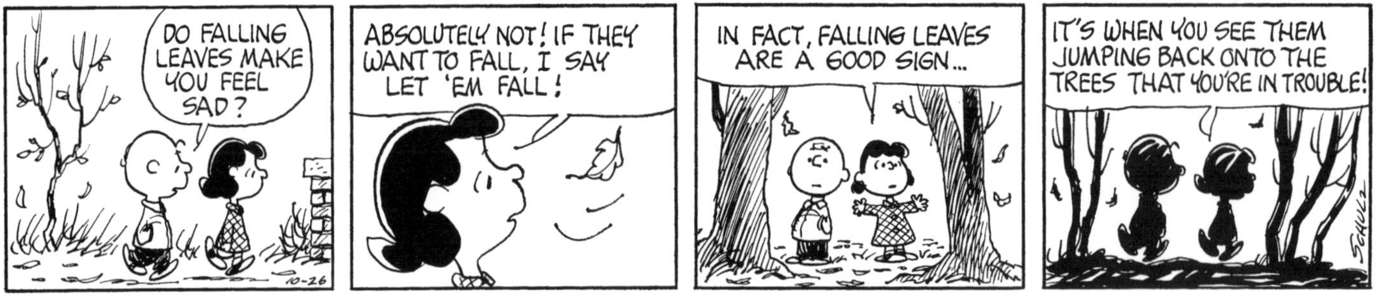
DO FALLING LEAVES MAKE YOU FEEL SAD?
ABSOLUTELY NOT! IF THEY WANT TO FALL, I SAY LET 'EM FALL!
IN FACT, FALLING LEAVES ARE A GOOD SIGN...
IT'S WHEN YOU SEE THEM JUMPING BACK ONTO THE TREES THAT YOU'RE IN TROUBLE!
10-26
SCHULZ

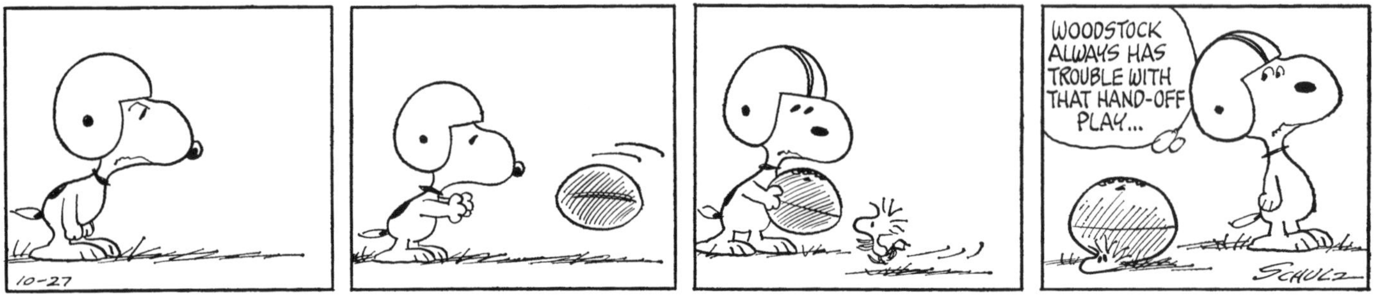
WOODSTOCK ALWAYS HAS TROUBLE WITH THAT HAND-OFF PLAY...
10-27
SCHULZ

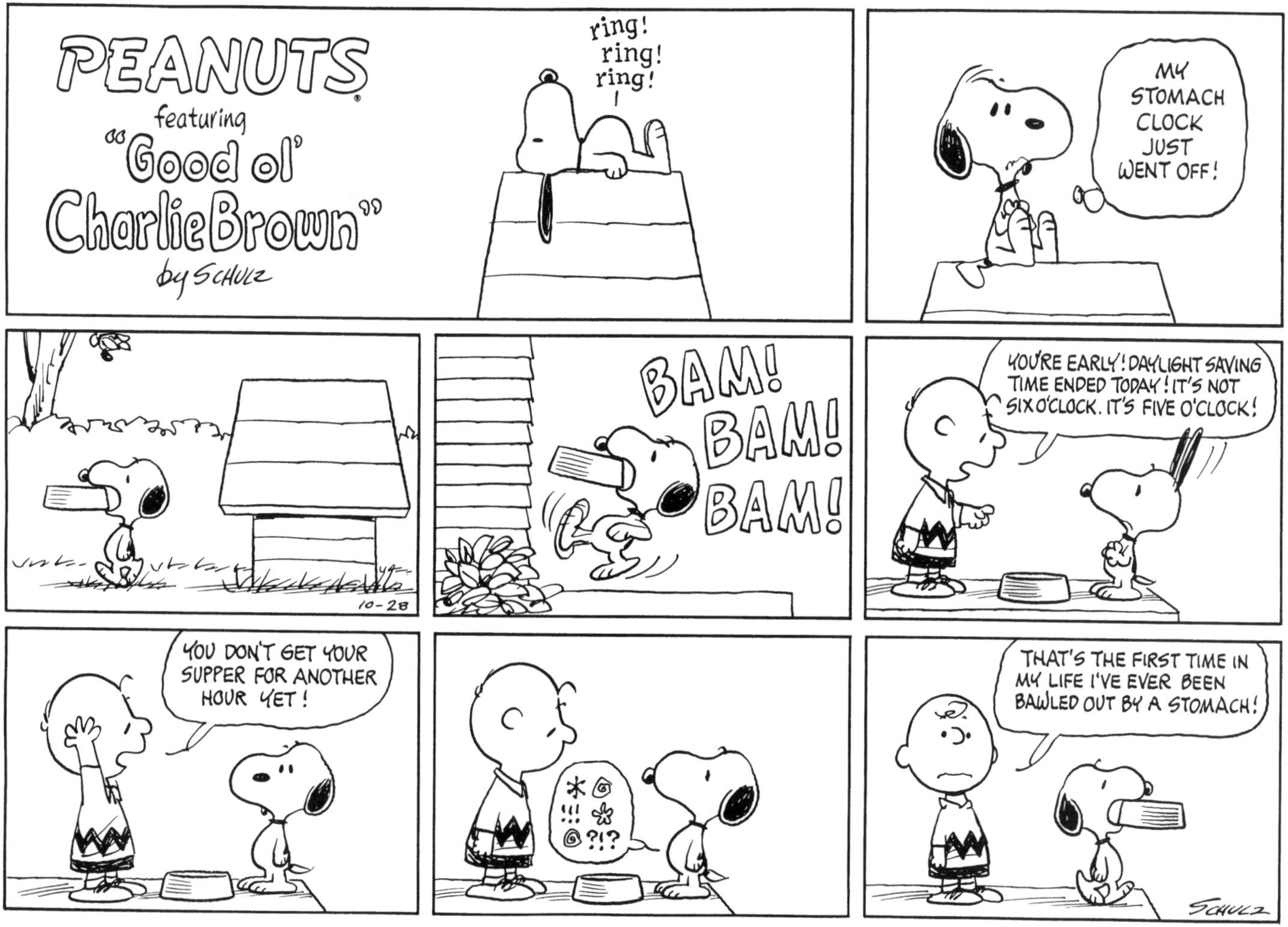
PEANUTS
featuring
"Good ol' Charlie Brown"
by SCHULZ
ring!
ring!
ring!
MY STOMACH CLOCK JUST WENT OFF!
10-28
BAM!
BAM!
BAM!
YOU'RE EARLY! DAYLIGHT SAVING TIME ENDED TODAY! IT'S NOT SIX O'CLOCK. IT'S FIVE O'CLOCK!
YOU DON'T GET YOUR SUPPER FOR ANOTHER HOUR YET!
!!!
?!?
THAT'S THE FIRST TIME IN MY LIFE I'VE EVER BEEN BAWLED OUT BY A STOMACH!
SCHULZ

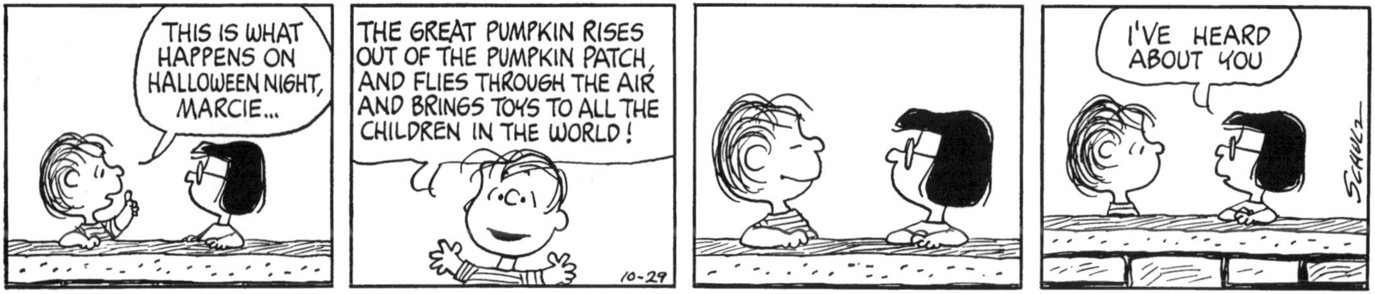
THIS IS WHAT HAPPENS ON HALLOWEEN NIGHT, MARCIE...
THE GREAT PUMPKIN RISES OUT OF THE PUMPKIN PATCH, AND FLIES THROUGH THE AIR AND BRINGS TOYS TO ALL THE CHILDREN IN THE WORLD!
10-29
I'VE HEARD ABOUT YOU
SCHULZ

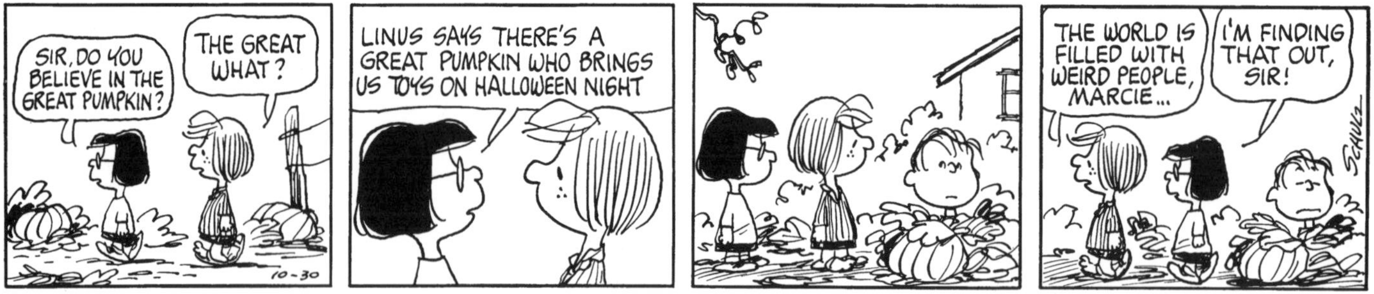
SIR, DO YOU BELIEVE IN THE GREAT PUMPKIN?
THE GREAT WHAT?
10-30
LINUS SAYS THERE'S A GREAT PUMPKIN WHO BRINGS US TOYS ON HALLOWEEN NIGHT
THE WORLD IS FILLED WITH WEIRD PEOPLE, MARCIE...
I'M FINDING THAT OUT, SIR!
SCHULZ

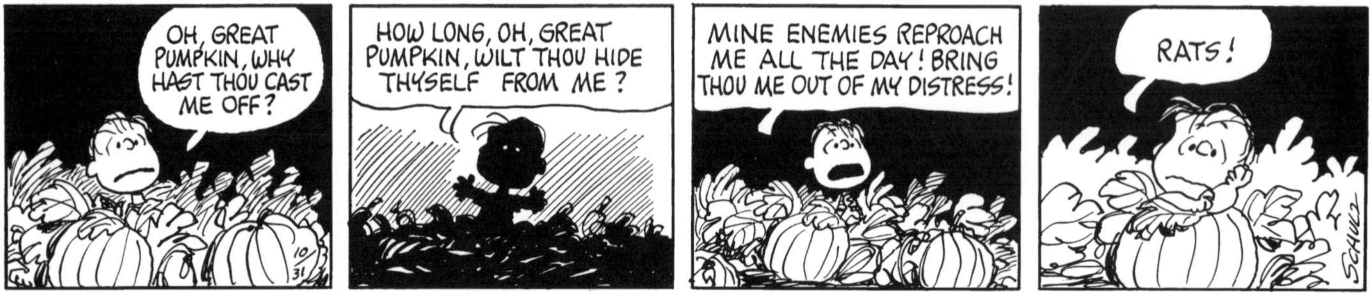
OH, GREAT PUMPKIN, WHY HAST THOU CAST ME OFF?
10/31
HOW LONG, OH, GREAT PUMPKIN, WILT THOU HIDE THYSELF FROM ME?
MINE ENEMIES REPROACH ME ALL THE DAY! BRING THOU ME OUT OF MY DISTRESS!
RATS!
SCHULZ

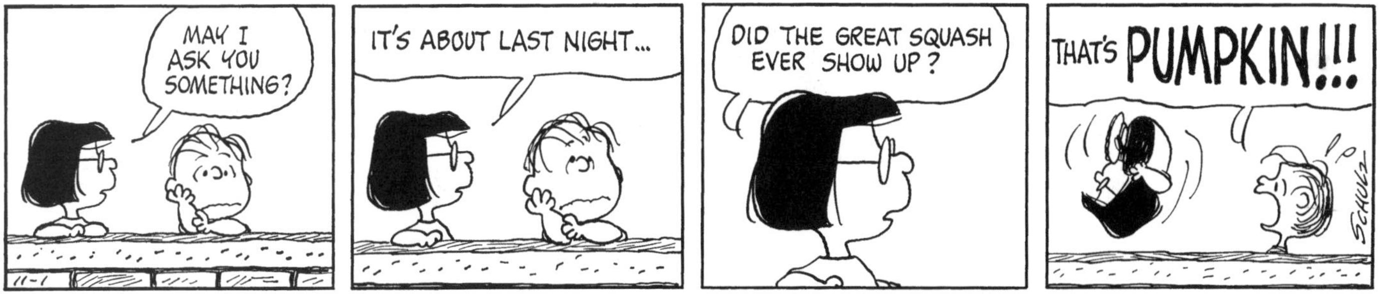
MAY I ASK YOU SOMETHING?
11-1
IT'S ABOUT LAST NIGHT...
DID THE GREAT SQUASH EVER SHOW UP?
THAT'S PUMPKIN!!!
SCHULZ

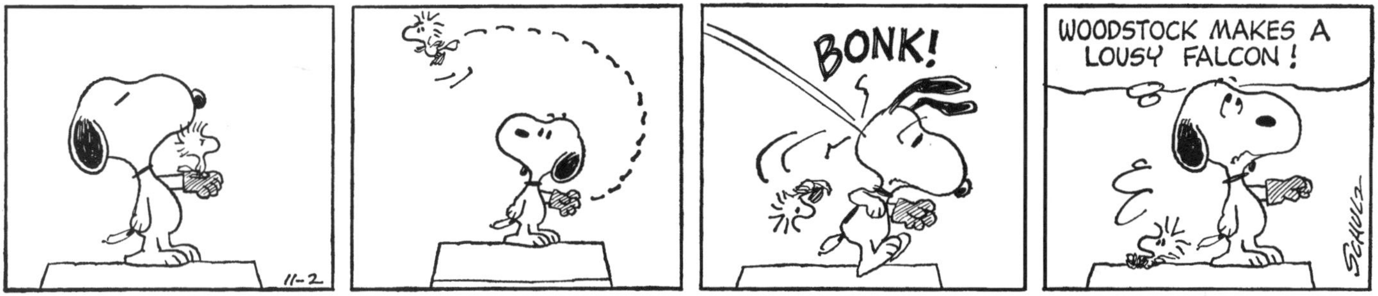
11-2
BONK!
WOODSTOCK MAKES A LOUSY FALCON!
SCHULZ

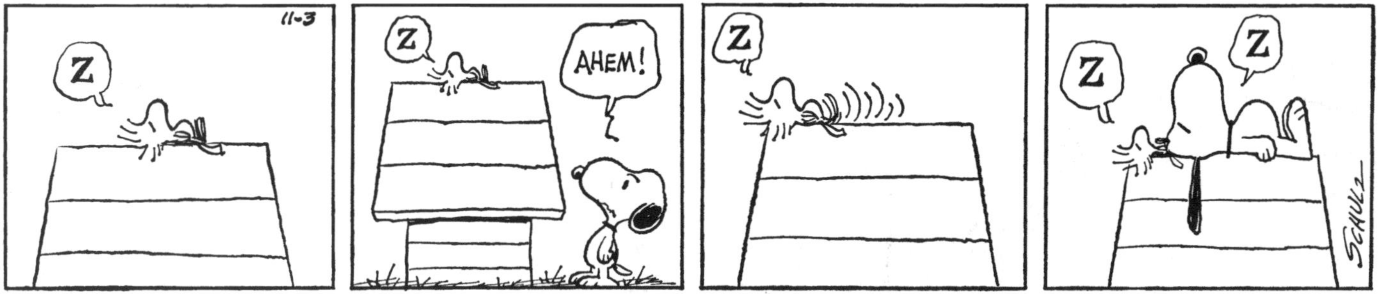
11-3
Z
Z
AHEM!
Z
Z
Z
SCHULZ

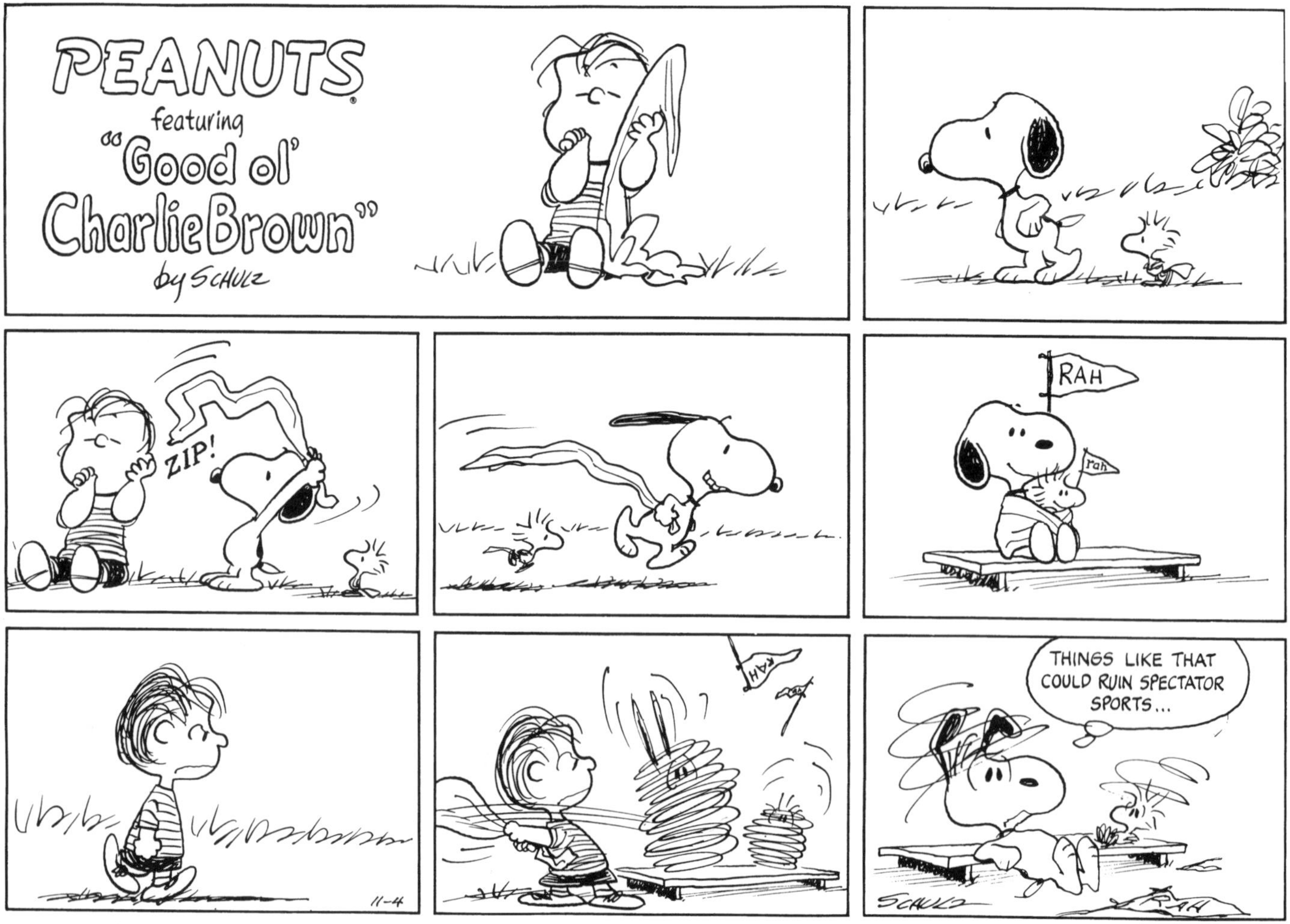
PEANUTS
featuring
"Good ol' CharlieBrown"
by SCHULZ
ZIP!
RAH
rah
11-4
RAH
THINGS LIKE THAT COULD RUIN SPECTATOR SPORTS...
SCHULZ
RAH

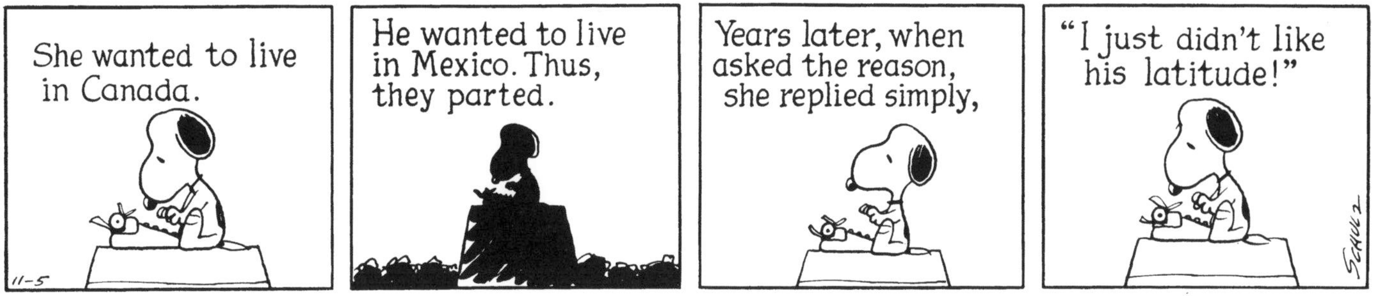
She wanted to live in Canada.
He wanted to live in Mexico. Thus, they parted.
Years later, when asked the reason, she replied simply,
"I just didn't like his latitude!"
11-5
SCHULZ

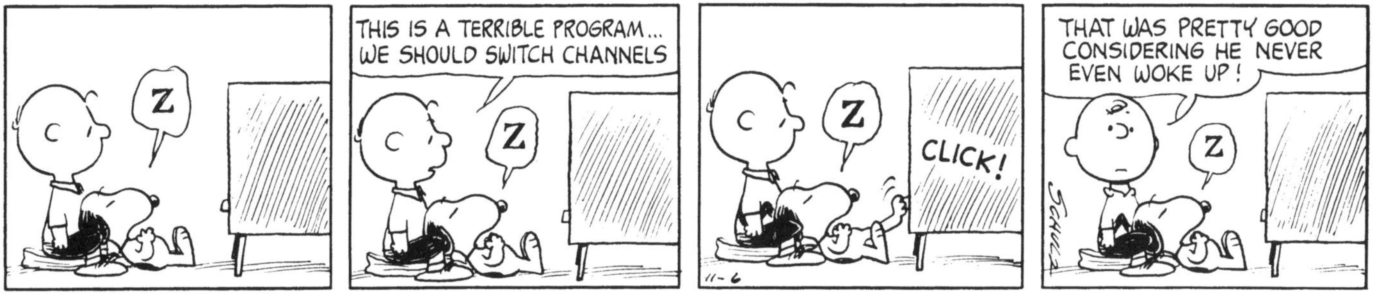
Z
THIS IS A TERRIBLE PROGRAM... WE SHOULD SWITCH CHANNELS
Z
Z
CLICK!
THAT WAS PRETTY GOOD CONSIDERING HE NEVER EVEN WOKE UP!
Z
11-6
SCHULZ

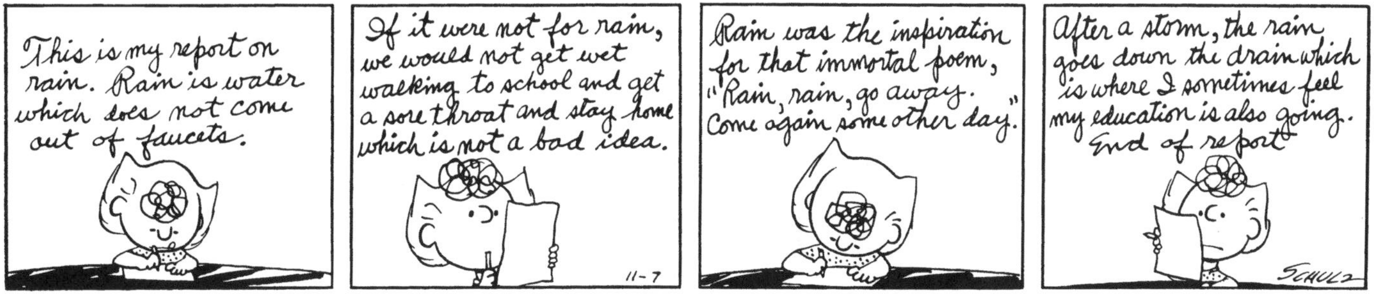
This is my report on rain. Rain is water which does not come out of faucets.
If it were not for rain, we would not get wet walking to school and get a sore throat and stay home which is not a bad idea.
Rain was the inspiration for that immortal poem, "Rain, rain, go away. Come again some other day."
After a storm, the rain goes down the drain which is where I sometimes feel my education is also going. End of report
11-7
SCHULZ

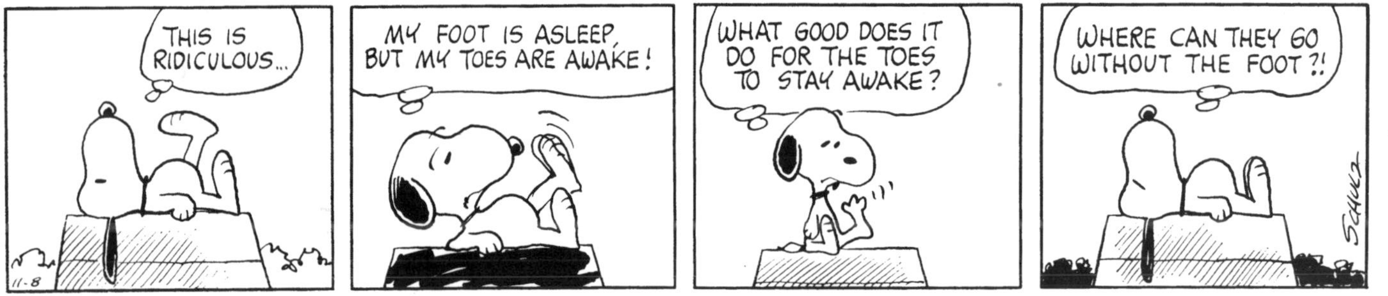
11-8
THIS IS RIDICULOUS...
MY FOOT IS ASLEEP, BUT MY TOES ARE AWAKE!
WHAT GOOD DOES IT DO FOR THE TOES TO STAY AWAKE?
WHERE CAN THEY GO WITHOUT THE FOOT?!
SCHULZ

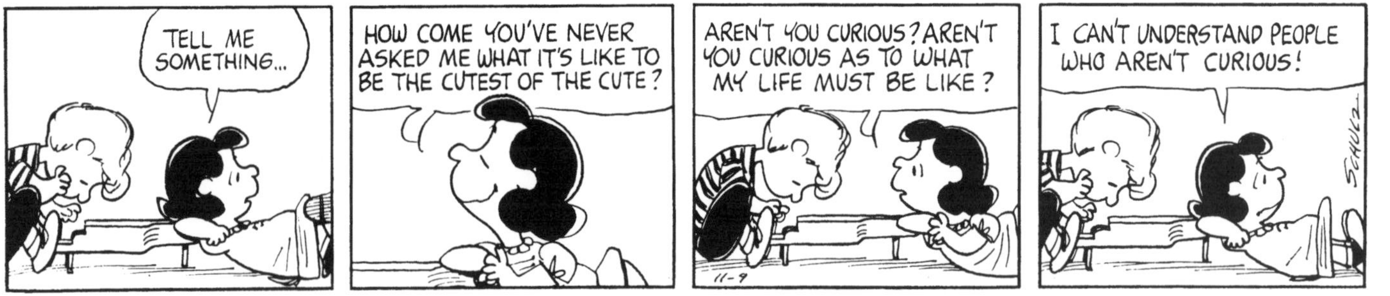
TELL ME SOMETHING...
HOW COME YOU'VE NEVER ASKED ME WHAT IT'S LIKE TO BE THE CUTEST OF THE CUTE?
11-9
AREN'T YOU CURIOUS? AREN'T YOU CURIOUS AS TO WHAT MY LIFE MUST BE LIKE?
I CAN'T UNDERSTAND PEOPLE WHO AREN'T CURIOUS!
SCHULZ

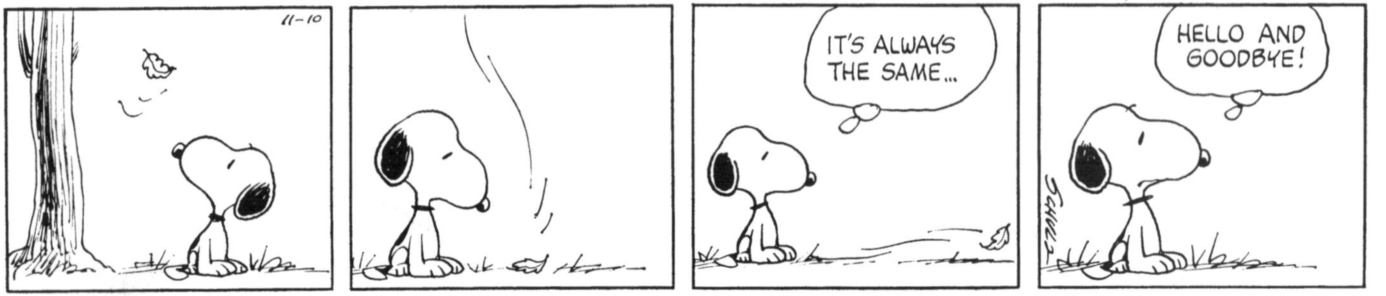
11-10
IT'S ALWAYS THE SAME...
SCHULZ
HELLO AND GOODBYE!

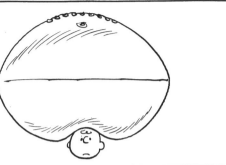

PEANUTS featuring "Good ol' Charlie Brown" by Schulz

DO YOU LIKE JOKES AND RIDDLES?

I GUESS SO...WHY?

I HAVE A RIDDLE FOR YOU, CHARLIE BROWN...WHAT ARE THE THREE THINGS IN LIFE THAT ARE CERTAIN?

DEATH AND TAXES!!

THAT'S ONLY TWO...

YOU'RE RIGHT...HMM...I KNOW WHAT THE THIRD ONE IS, BUT I JUST CAN'T SEEM TO THINK... DON'T TELL ME...

RATS! I SEEM TO HAVE A MENTAL BLOCK OR SOMETHING...

11-11

IT'S SO AGGRAVATING WHEN YOU'RE TRYING TO THINK OF SOMETHING, AND YOU...

NOW, I REMEMBER!

WHAM!

IT WAS SO OBVIOUS, CHARLIE BROWN!

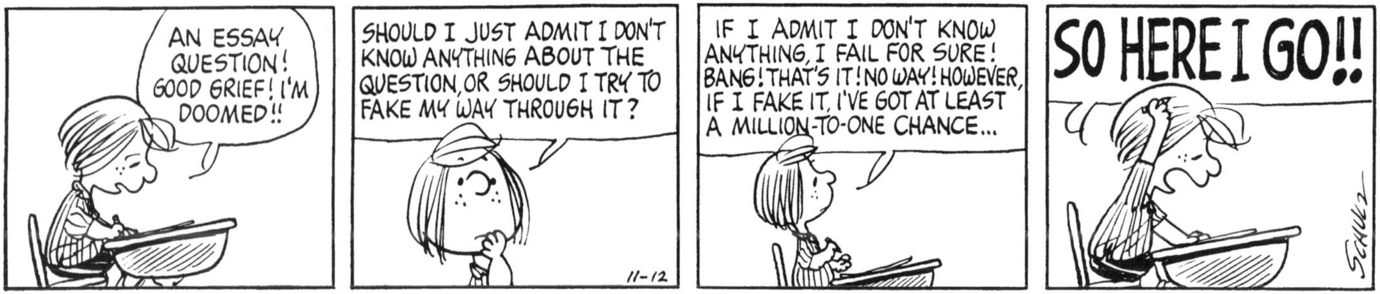
AN ESSAY QUESTION! GOOD GRIEF! I'M DOOMED!!
SHOULD I JUST ADMIT I DON'T KNOW ANYTHING ABOUT THE QUESTION, OR SHOULD I TRY TO FAKE MY WAY THROUGH IT?
11-12
IF I ADMIT I DON'T KNOW ANYTHING, I FAIL FOR SURE! BANG! THAT'S IT! NO WAY! HOWEVER, IF I FAKE IT, I'VE GOT AT LEAST A MILLION-TO-ONE CHANCE...
SO HERE I GO!!
SCHULZ

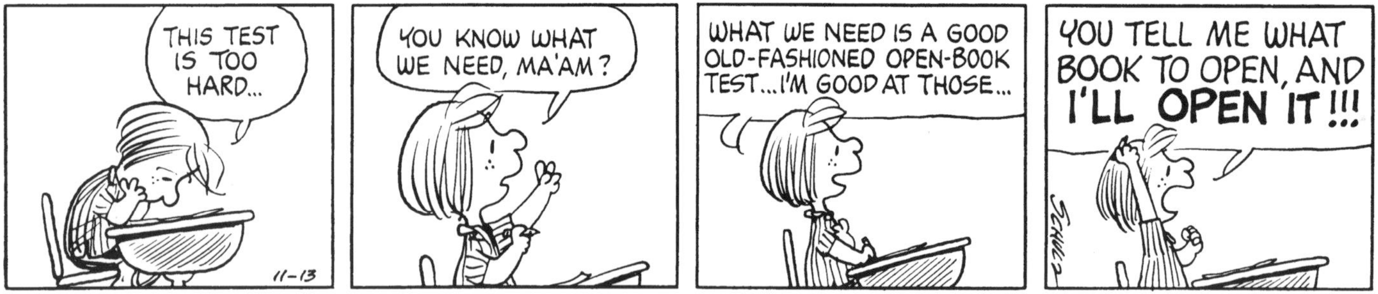
THIS TEST IS TOO HARD...
11-13
YOU KNOW WHAT WE NEED, MA'AM?
WHAT WE NEED IS A GOOD OLD-FASHIONED OPEN-BOOK TEST... I'M GOOD AT THOSE...
YOU TELL ME WHAT BOOK TO OPEN, AND I'LL OPEN IT!!!
SCHULZ

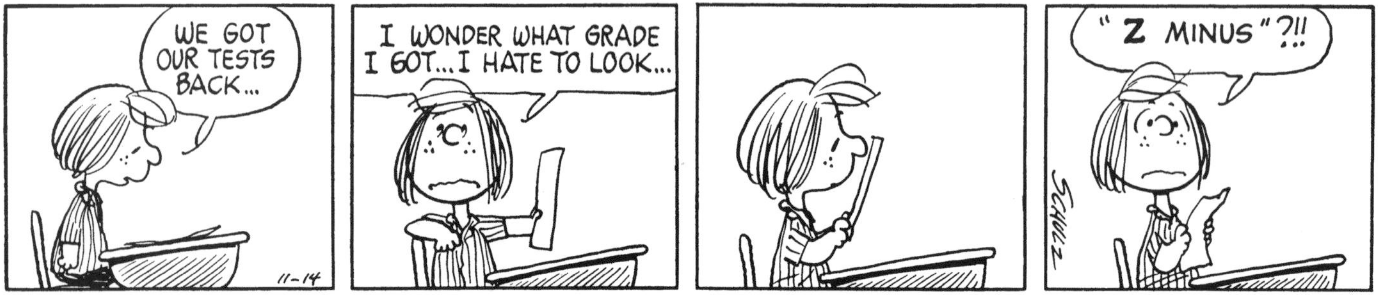
WE GOT OUR TESTS BACK...
11-14
I WONDER WHAT GRADE I GOT... I HATE TO LOOK...
SCHULZ
"Z MINUS"?!!

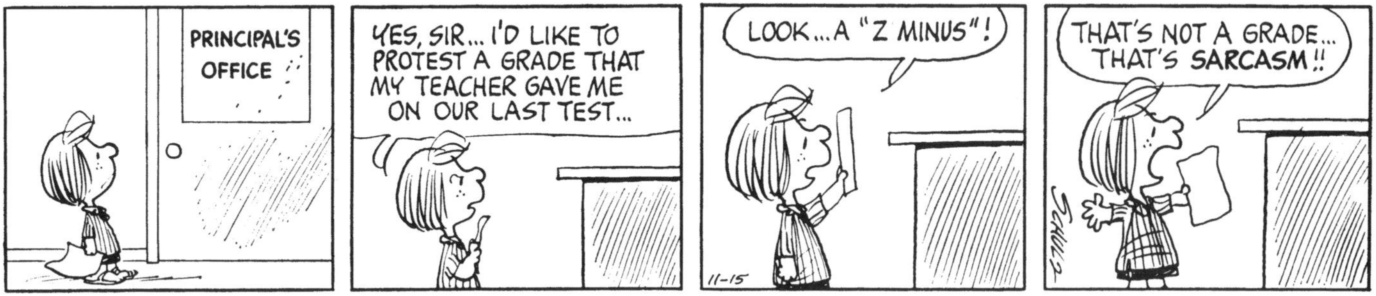
PRINCIPAL'S OFFICE
YES, SIR... I'D LIKE TO PROTEST A GRADE THAT MY TEACHER GAVE ME ON OUR LAST TEST...
LOOK...A "Z MINUS"!
THAT'S NOT A GRADE... THAT'S SARCASM!!

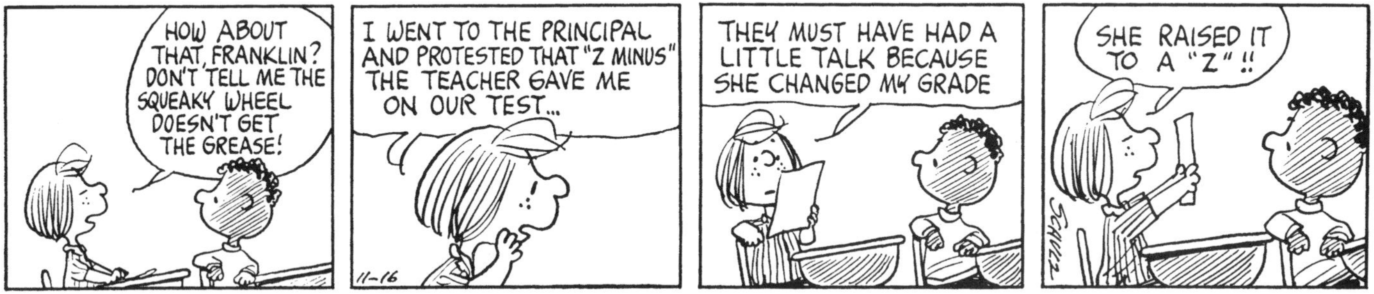
HOW ABOUT THAT, FRANKLIN? DON'T TELL ME THE SQUEAKY WHEEL DOESN'T GET THE GREASE!
I WENT TO THE PRINCIPAL AND PROTESTED THAT "Z MINUS" THE TEACHER GAVE ME ON OUR TEST...
THEY MUST HAVE HAD A LITTLE TALK BECAUSE SHE CHANGED MY GRADE
SHE RAISED IT TO A "Z"!!

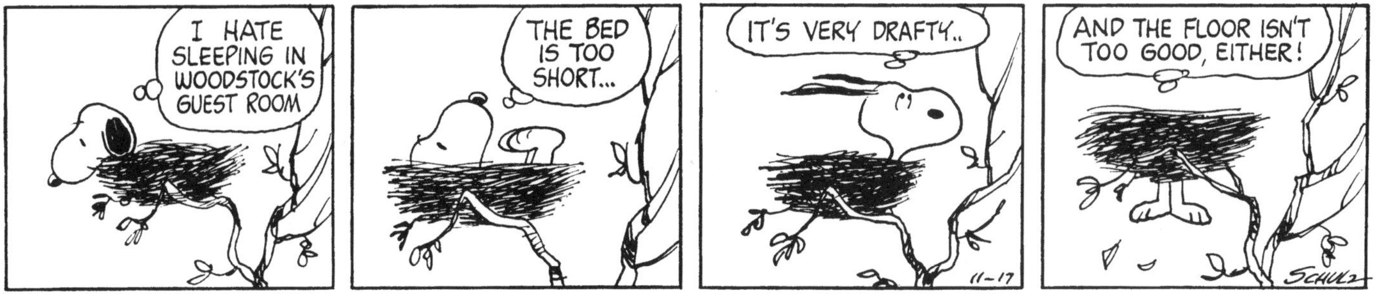
I HATE SLEEPING IN WOODSTOCK'S GUEST ROOM
THE BED IS TOO SHORT...
IT'S VERY DRAFTY..
AND THE FLOOR ISN'T TOO GOOD, EITHER!

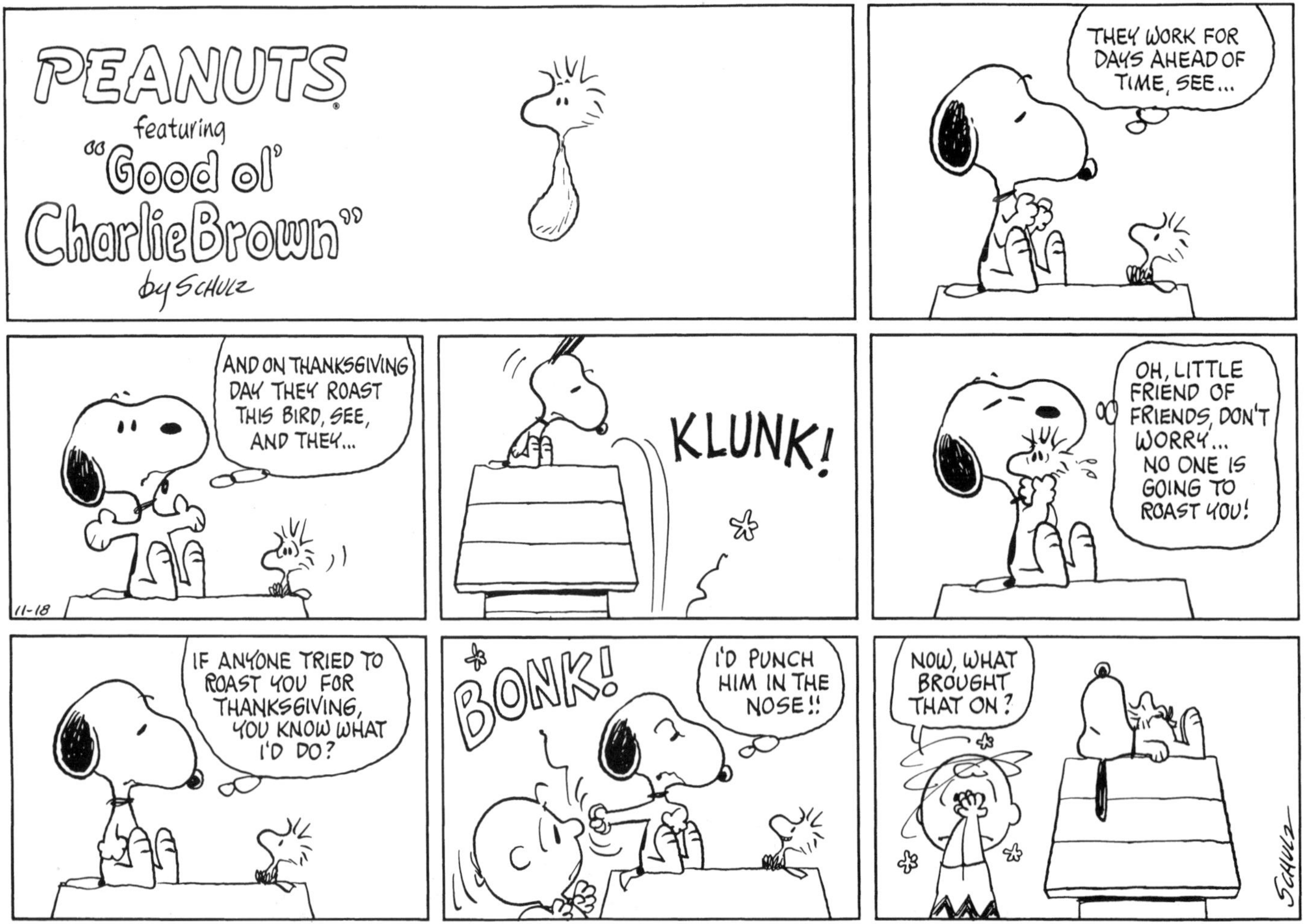
PEANUTS
featuring
"Good ol' CharlieBrown"
by SCHULZ
THEY WORK FOR DAYS AHEAD OF TIME, SEE...
AND ON THANKSGIVING DAY THEY ROAST THIS BIRD, SEE, AND THEY...
11-18
KLUNK!
OH, LITTLE FRIEND OF FRIENDS, DON'T WORRY... NO ONE IS GOING TO ROAST YOU!
IF ANYONE TRIED TO ROAST YOU FOR THANKSGIVING, YOU KNOW WHAT I'D DO?
BONK!
I'D PUNCH HIM IN THE NOSE!!
NOW, WHAT BROUGHT THAT ON?
SCHULZ

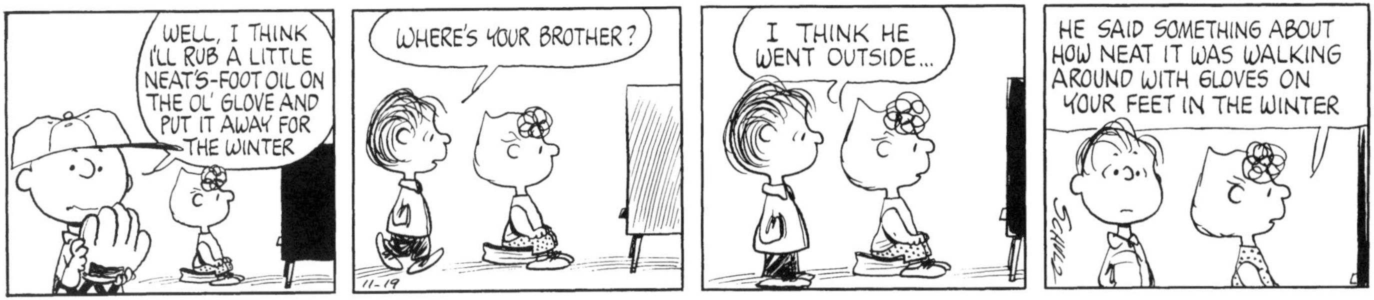
WELL, I THINK I'LL RUB A LITTLE NEAT'S-FOOT OIL ON THE OL' GLOVE AND PUT IT AWAY FOR THE WINTER
WHERE'S YOUR BROTHER?
I THINK HE WENT OUTSIDE...
HE SAID SOMETHING ABOUT HOW NEAT IT WAS WALKING AROUND WITH GLOVES ON YOUR FEET IN THE WINTER

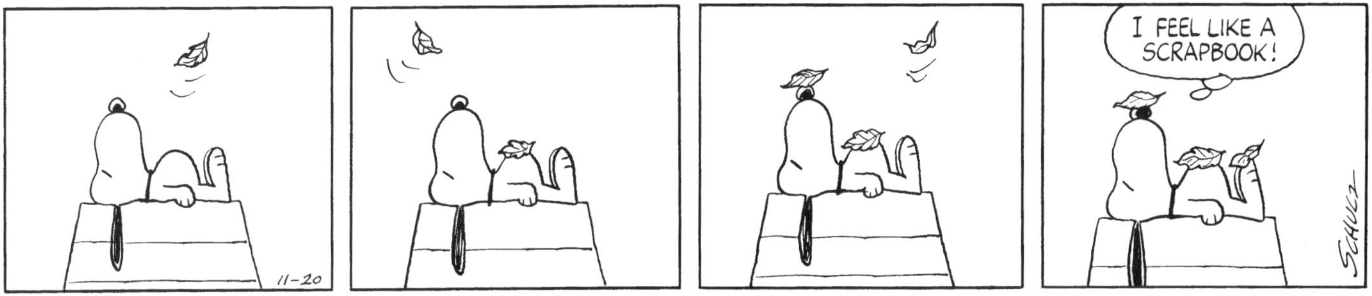
I FEEL LIKE A SCRAPBOOK!

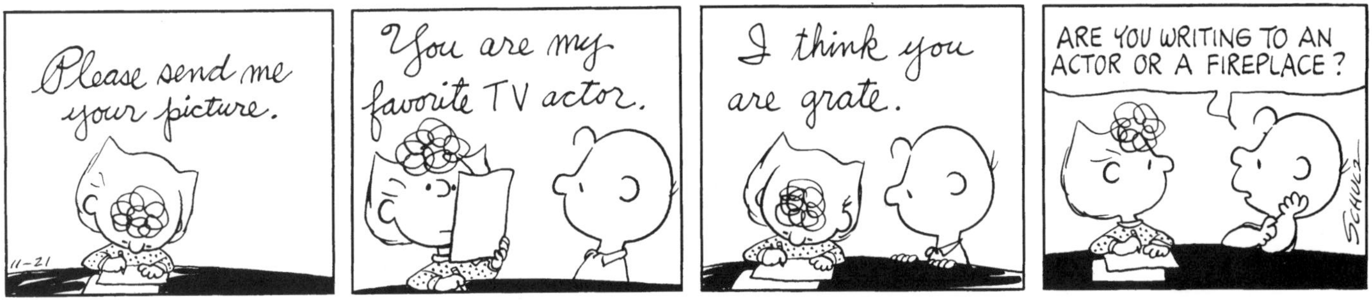
Please send me your picture.
You are my favorite TV actor.
I think you are grate.
ARE YOU WRITING TO AN ACTOR OR A FIREPLACE?

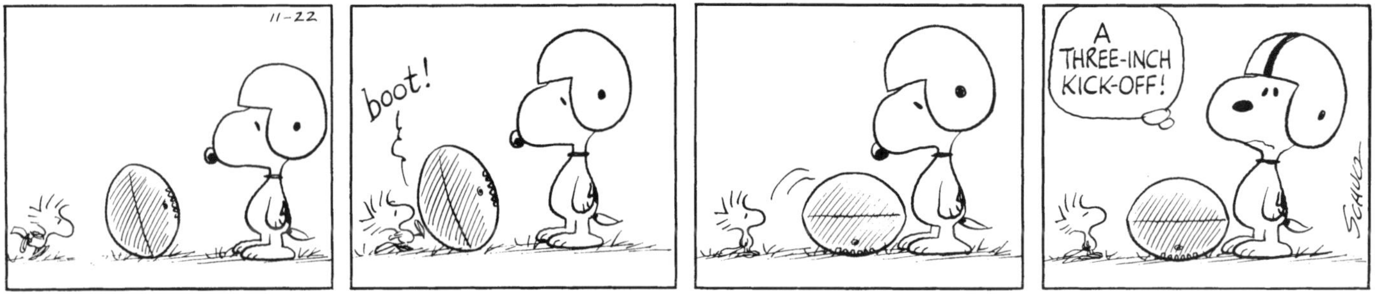
11-22
boot!
A THREE-INCH KICK-OFF!
SCHULZ

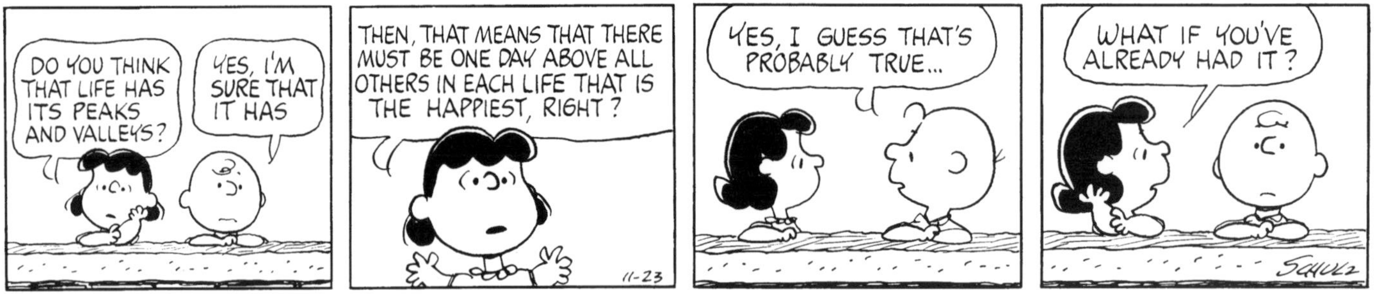
DO YOU THINK THAT LIFE HAS ITS PEAKS AND VALLEYS?
YES, I'M SURE THAT IT HAS
THEN, THAT MEANS THAT THERE MUST BE ONE DAY ABOVE ALL OTHERS IN EACH LIFE THAT IS THE HAPPIEST, RIGHT?
11-23
YES, I GUESS THAT'S PROBABLY TRUE...
WHAT IF YOU'VE ALREADY HAD IT?
SCHULZ

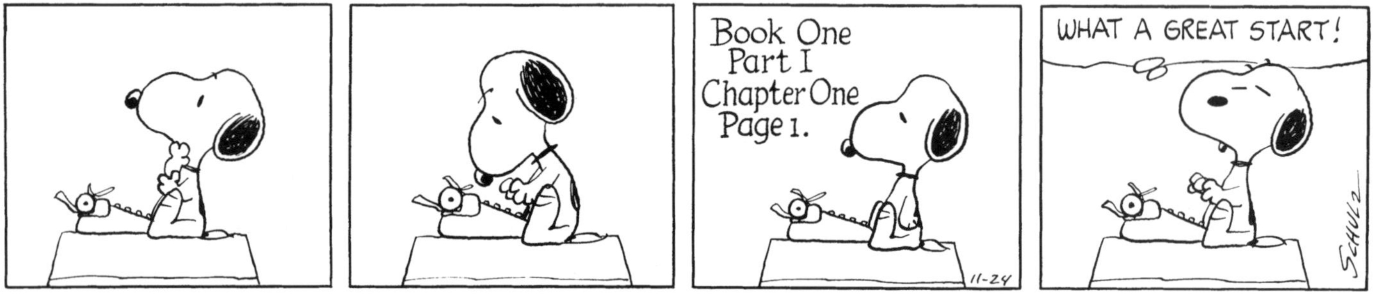
Book One
Part I
Chapter One
Page 1.
11-24
WHAT A GREAT START!
SCHULZ

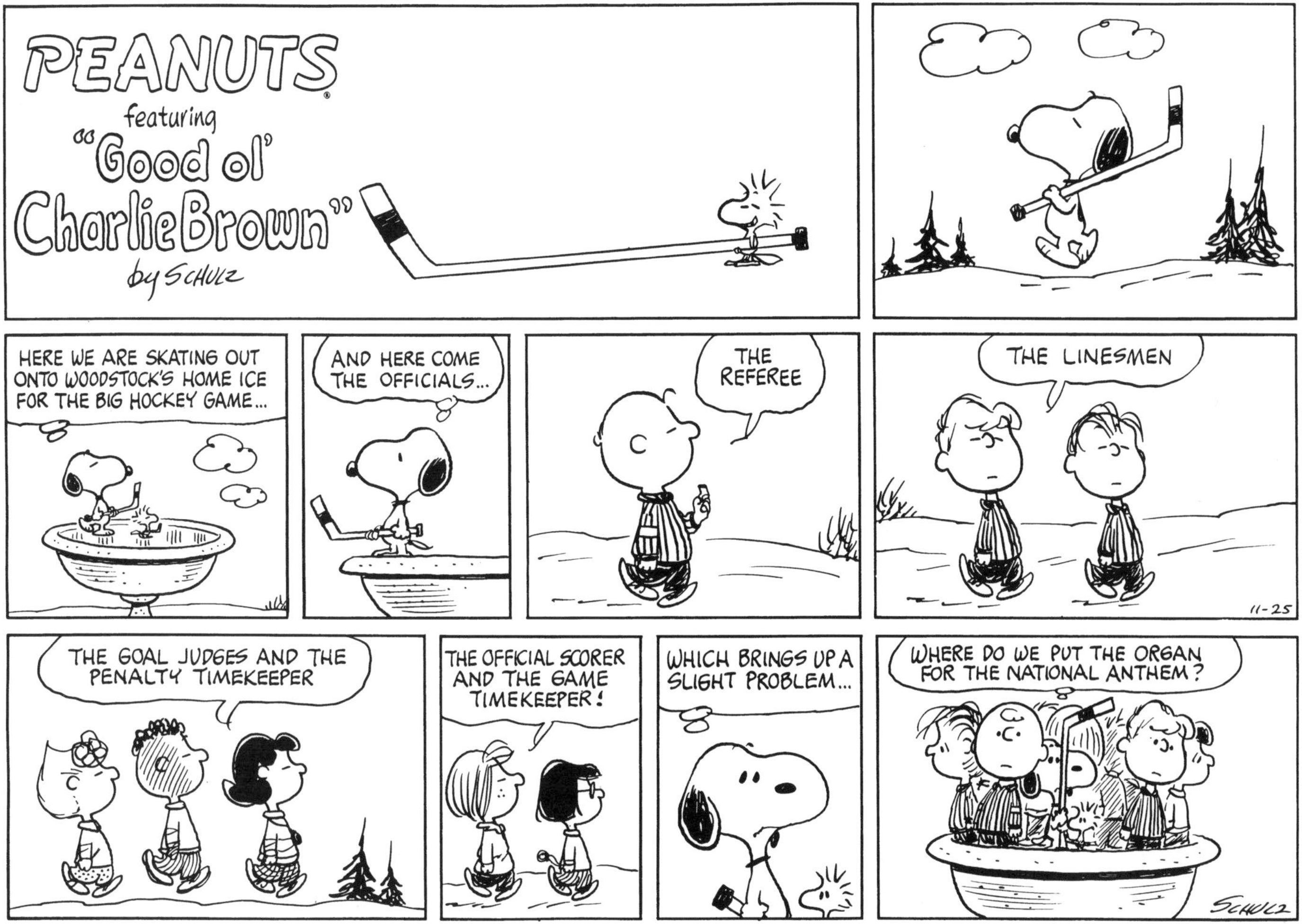
PEANUTS
featuring "Good ol' Charlie Brown"
by SCHULZ
HERE WE ARE SKATING OUT ONTO WOODSTOCK'S HOME ICE FOR THE BIG HOCKEY GAME...
AND HERE COME THE OFFICIALS...
THE REFEREE
THE LINESMEN
11-25
THE GOAL JUDGES AND THE PENALTY TIMEKEEPER
THE OFFICIAL SCORER AND THE GAME TIMEKEEPER!
WHICH BRINGS UP A SLIGHT PROBLEM...
WHERE DO WE PUT THE ORGAN FOR THE NATIONAL ANTHEM?
SCHULZ

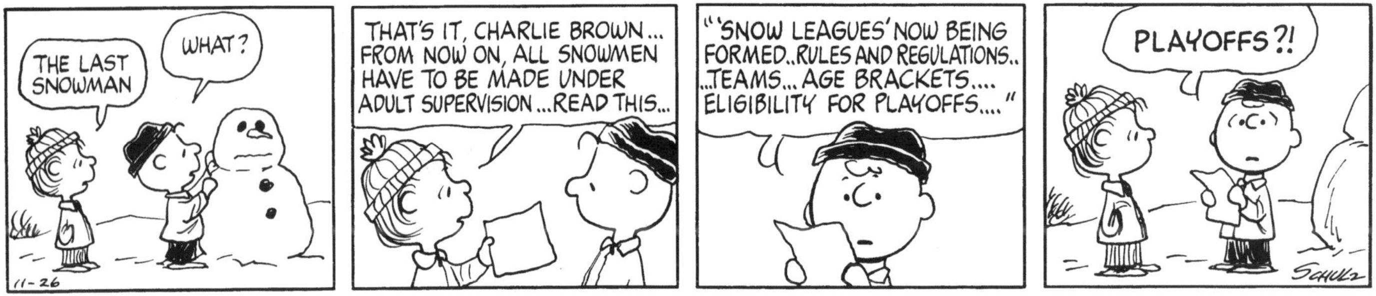
THE LAST SNOWMAN
WHAT?
THAT'S IT, CHARLIE BROWN... FROM NOW ON, ALL SNOWMEN HAVE TO BE MADE UNDER ADULT SUPERVISION...READ THIS...
"'SNOW LEAGUES' NOW BEING FORMED..RULES AND REGULATIONS.. ...TEAMS... AGE BRACKETS.... ELIGIBILITY FOR PLAYOFFS...."
PLAYOFFS?!
11-26

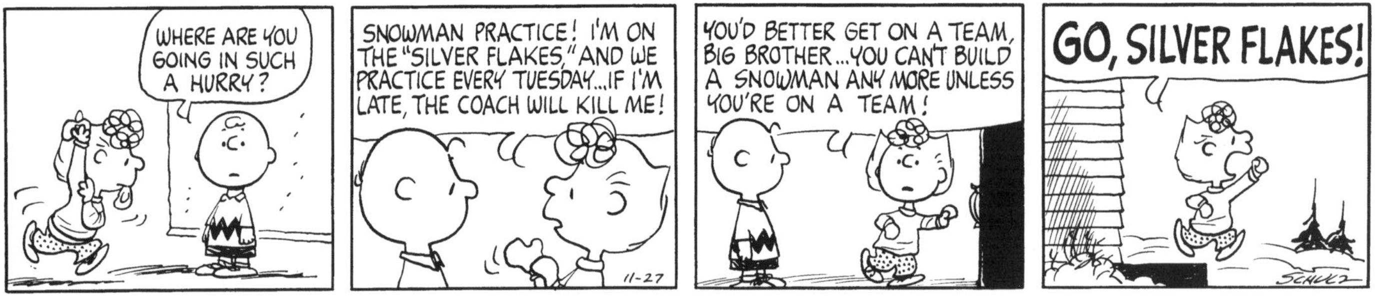
WHERE ARE YOU GOING IN SUCH A HURRY?
SNOWMAN PRACTICE! I'M ON THE "SILVER FLAKES," AND WE PRACTICE EVERY TUESDAY...IF I'M LATE, THE COACH WILL KILL ME!
YOU'D BETTER GET ON A TEAM, BIG BROTHER...YOU CAN'T BUILD A SNOWMAN ANY MORE UNLESS YOU'RE ON A TEAM!
GO, SILVER FLAKES!
11-27

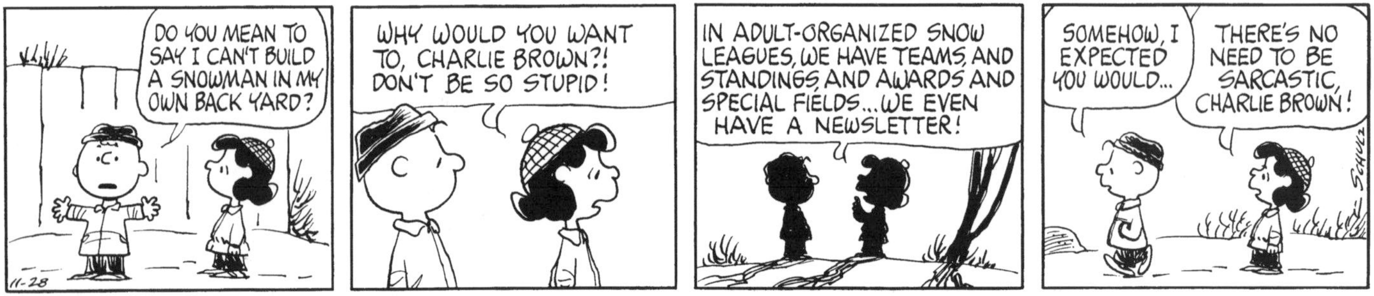
DO YOU MEAN TO SAY I CAN'T BUILD A SNOWMAN IN MY OWN BACK YARD?
WHY WOULD YOU WANT TO, CHARLIE BROWN?! DON'T BE SO STUPID!
IN ADULT-ORGANIZED SNOW LEAGUES, WE HAVE TEAMS AND STANDINGS AND AWARDS AND SPECIAL FIELDS...WE EVEN HAVE A NEWSLETTER!
SOMEHOW, I EXPECTED YOU WOULD...
THERE'S NO NEED TO BE SARCASTIC, CHARLIE BROWN!
11-28

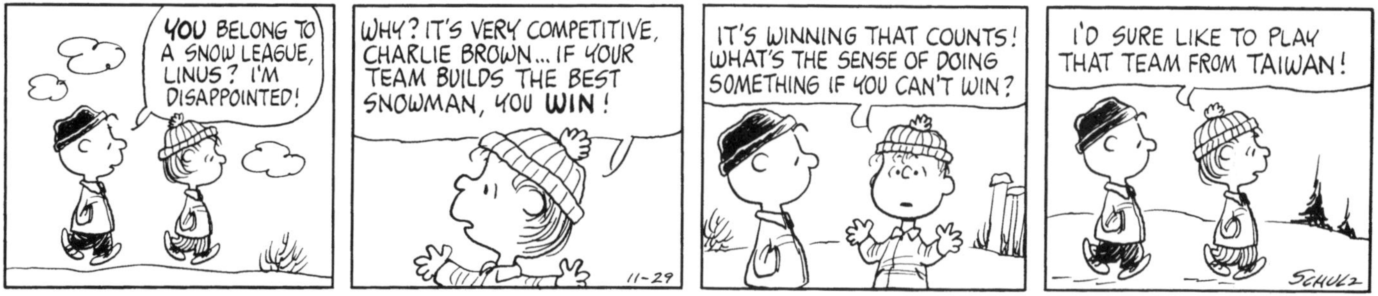
YOU BELONG TO A SNOW LEAGUE, LINUS? I'M DISAPPOINTED!
WHY? IT'S VERY COMPETITIVE, CHARLIE BROWN... IF YOUR TEAM BUILDS THE BEST SNOWMAN, YOU WIN!
11-29
IT'S WINNING THAT COUNTS! WHAT'S THE SENSE OF DOING SOMETHING IF YOU CAN'T WIN?
I'D SURE LIKE TO PLAY THAT TEAM FROM TAIWAN!
SCHULZ

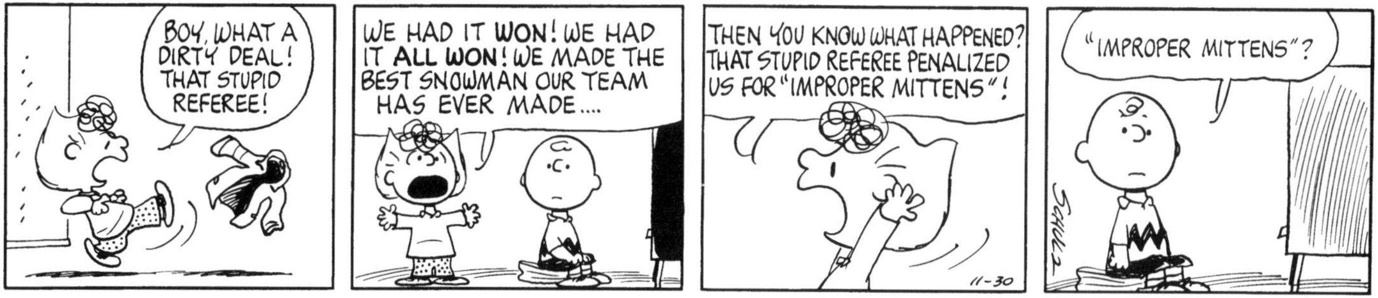
BOY, WHAT A DIRTY DEAL! THAT STUPID REFEREE!
WE HAD IT WON! WE HAD IT ALL WON! WE MADE THE BEST SNOWMAN OUR TEAM HAS EVER MADE....
THEN YOU KNOW WHAT HAPPENED? THAT STUPID REFEREE PENALIZED US FOR "IMPROPER MITTENS"!
11-30
"IMPROPER MITTENS"?
SCHULZ

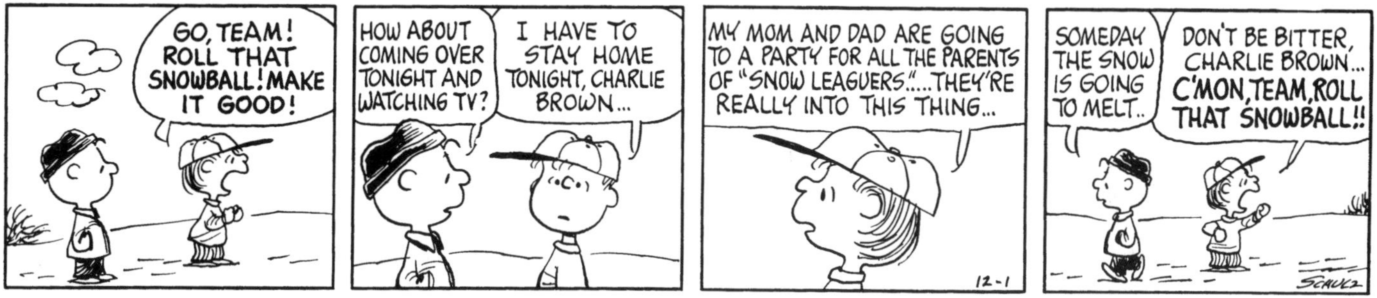
GO, TEAM! ROLL THAT SNOWBALL! MAKE IT GOOD!
HOW ABOUT COMING OVER TONIGHT AND WATCHING TV?
I HAVE TO STAY HOME TONIGHT, CHARLIE BROWN...
MY MOM AND DAD ARE GOING TO A PARTY FOR ALL THE PARENTS OF "SNOW LEAGUERS."... THEY'RE REALLY INTO THIS THING...
12-1
SOMEDAY THE SNOW IS GOING TO MELT..
DON'T BE BITTER, CHARLIE BROWN... C'MON, TEAM, ROLL THAT SNOWBALL!!
SCHULZ

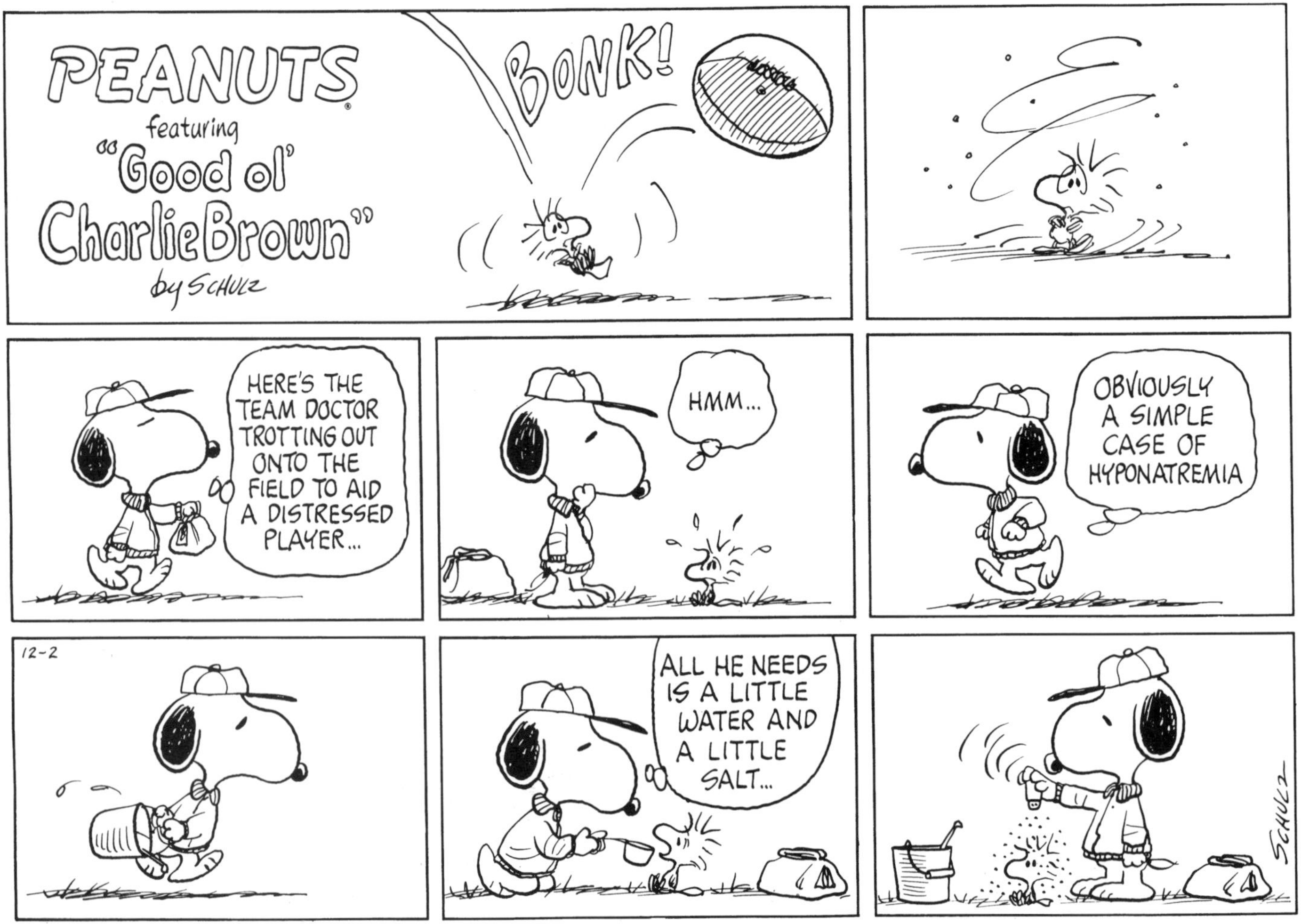
PEANUTS
featuring
"Good ol' Charlie Brown"
by SCHULZ
BONK!
HERE'S THE TEAM DOCTOR TROTTING OUT ONTO THE FIELD TO AID A DISTRESSED PLAYER...
HMM...
OBVIOUSLY A SIMPLE CASE OF HYPONATREMIA
12-2
ALL HE NEEDS IS A LITTLE WATER AND A LITTLE SALT...
SCHULZ

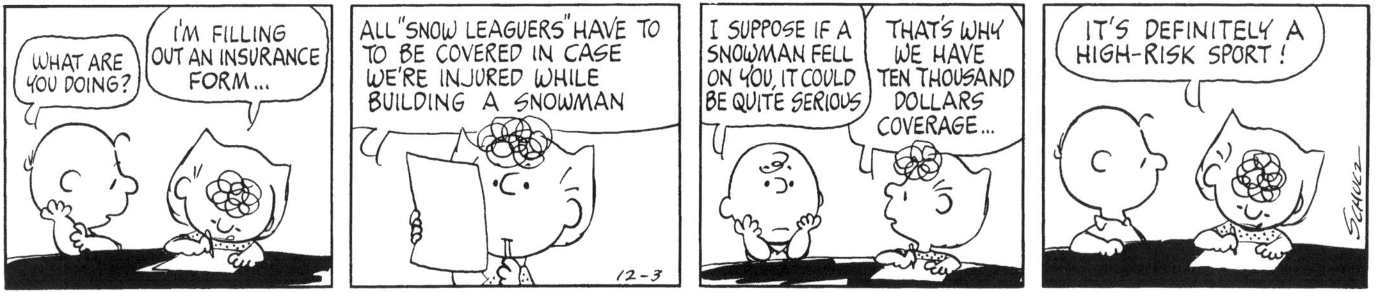
WHAT ARE YOU DOING?
I'M FILLING OUT AN INSURANCE FORM...
ALL "SNOW LEAGUERS" HAVE TO TO BE COVERED IN CASE WE'RE INJURED WHILE BUILDING A SNOWMAN
12-3
I SUPPOSE IF A SNOWMAN FELL ON YOU, IT COULD BE QUITE SERIOUS
THAT'S WHY WE HAVE TEN THOUSAND DOLLARS COVERAGE...
IT'S DEFINITELY A HIGH-RISK SPORT!
SCHULZ

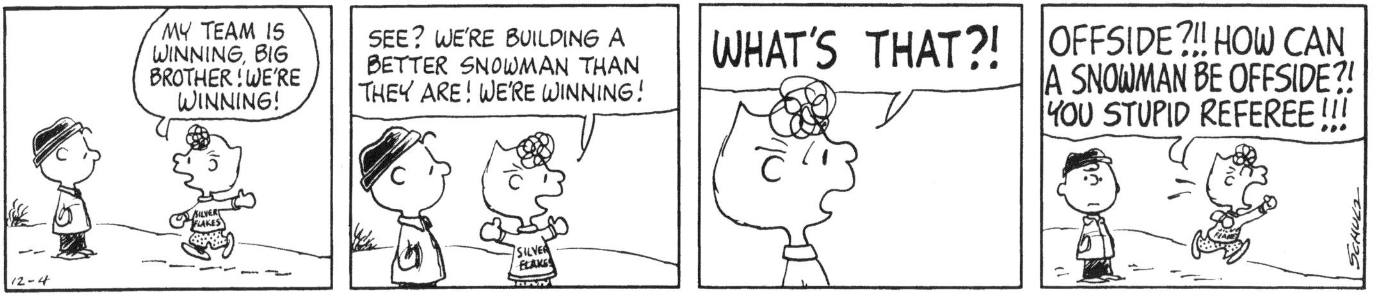
MY TEAM IS WINNING, BIG BROTHER! WE'RE WINNING!
SILVER FLAKES
12-4
SEE? WE'RE BUILDING A BETTER SNOWMAN THAN THEY ARE! WE'RE WINNING!
SILVER FLAKES
WHAT'S THAT?!
OFFSIDE?!! HOW CAN A SNOWMAN BE OFFSIDE?! YOU STUPID REFEREE!!!
SCHULZ

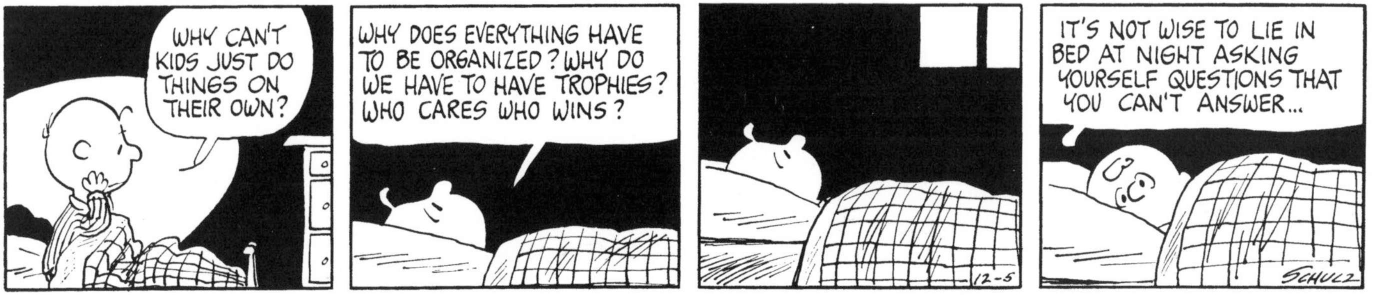
WHY CAN'T KIDS JUST DO THINGS ON THEIR OWN?
WHY DOES EVERYTHING HAVE TO BE ORGANIZED? WHY DO WE HAVE TO HAVE TROPHIES? WHO CARES WHO WINS?
12-5
IT'S NOT WISE TO LIE IN BED AT NIGHT ASKING YOURSELF QUESTIONS THAT YOU CAN'T ANSWER...
SCHULZ

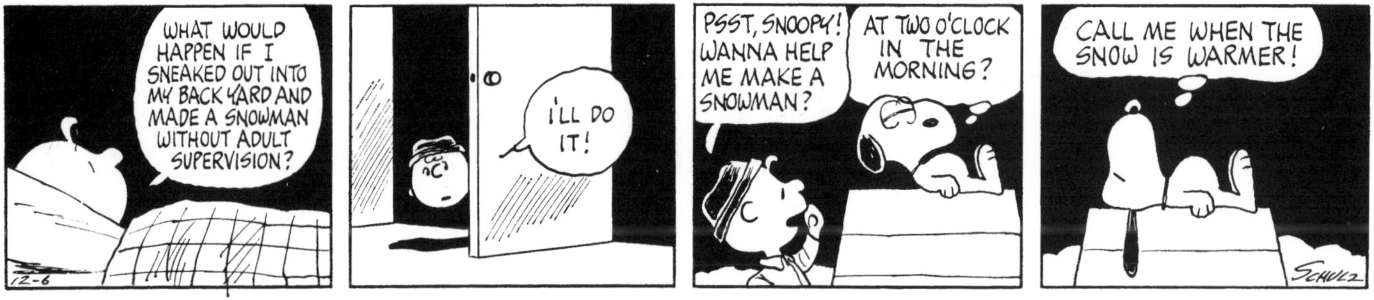
WHAT WOULD HAPPEN IF I SNEAKED OUT INTO MY BACK YARD AND MADE A SNOWMAN WITHOUT ADULT SUPERVISION?
12-6
I'LL DO IT!
PSST, SNOOPY! WANNA HELP ME MAKE A SNOWMAN?
AT TWO O'CLOCK IN THE MORNING?
CALL ME WHEN THE SNOW IS WARMER!
SCHULZ

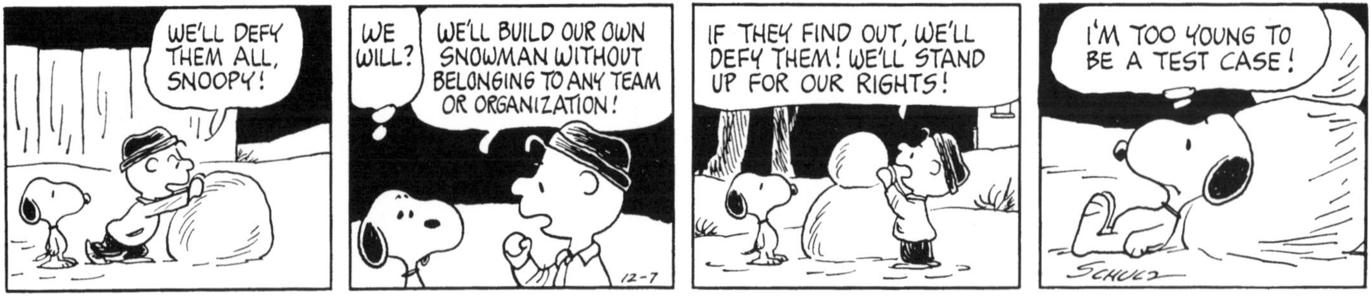
WE'LL DEFY THEM ALL, SNOOPY!
WE WILL?
WE'LL BUILD OUR OWN SNOWMAN WITHOUT BELONGING TO ANY TEAM OR ORGANIZATION!
12-7
IF THEY FIND OUT, WE'LL DEFY THEM! WE'LL STAND UP FOR OUR RIGHTS!
I'M TOO YOUNG TO BE A TEST CASE!
SCHULZ

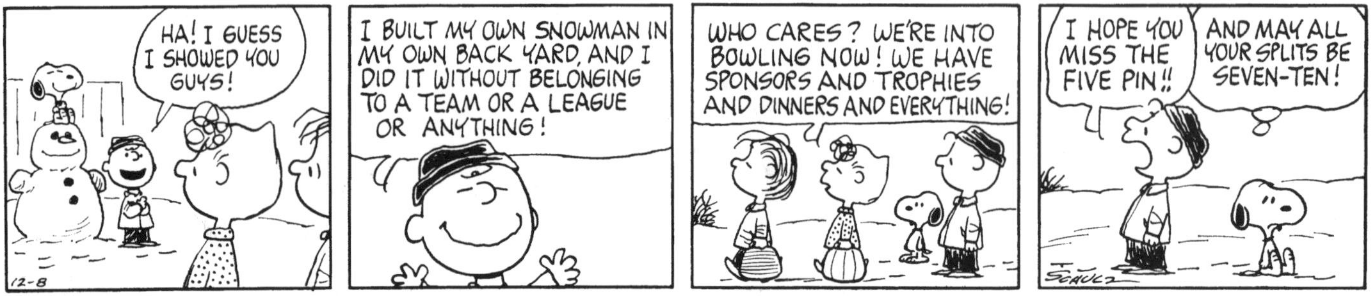
HA! I GUESS I SHOWED YOU GUYS!
12-8
I BUILT MY OWN SNOWMAN IN MY OWN BACK YARD, AND I DID IT WITHOUT BELONGING TO A TEAM OR A LEAGUE OR ANYTHING!
WHO CARES? WE'RE INTO BOWLING NOW! WE HAVE SPONSORS AND TROPHIES AND DINNERS AND EVERYTHING!
I HOPE YOU MISS THE FIVE PIN!!
AND MAY ALL YOUR SPLITS BE SEVEN-TEN!
SCHULZ

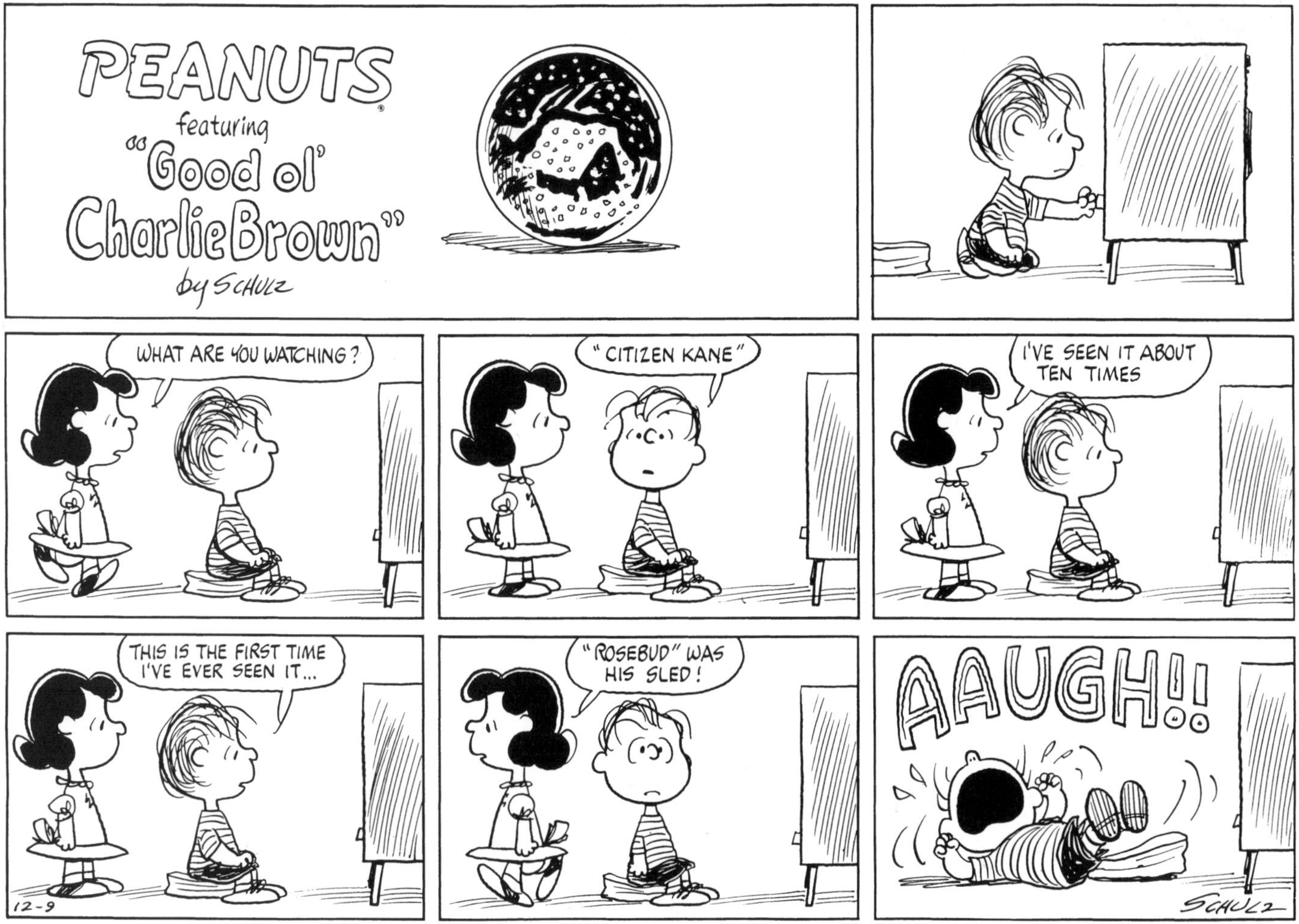
PEANUTS
featuring
"Good ol' Charlie Brown"
by SCHULZ
WHAT ARE YOU WATCHING?
"CITIZEN KANE"
I'VE SEEN IT ABOUT TEN TIMES
THIS IS THE FIRST TIME I'VE EVER SEEN IT...
"ROSEBUD" WAS HIS SLED!
AAUGH!!
12-9
SCHULZ

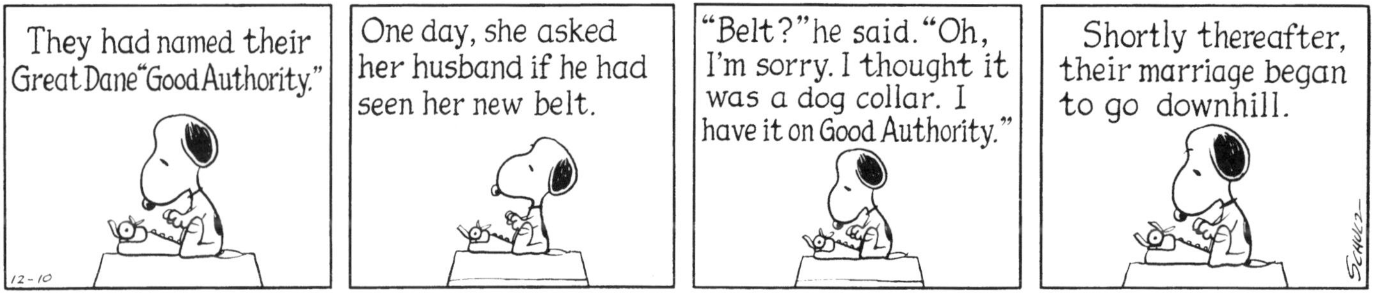
They had named their Great Dane "Good Authority."
One day, she asked her husband if he had seen her new belt.
"Belt?" he said. "Oh, I'm sorry. I thought it was a dog collar. I have it on Good Authority."
Shortly thereafter, their marriage began to go downhill.

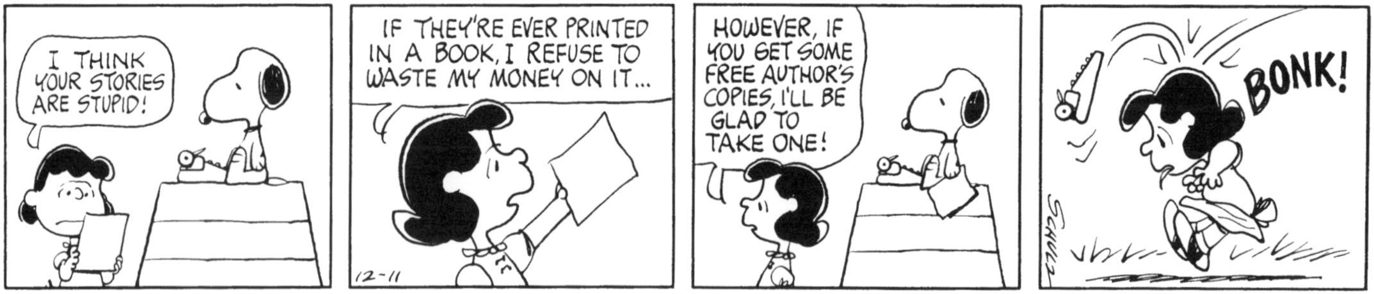
I THINK YOUR STORIES ARE STUPID!
IF THEY'RE EVER PRINTED IN A BOOK, I REFUSE TO WASTE MY MONEY ON IT...
HOWEVER, IF YOU GET SOME FREE AUTHOR'S COPIES, I'LL BE GLAD TO TAKE ONE!
BONK!

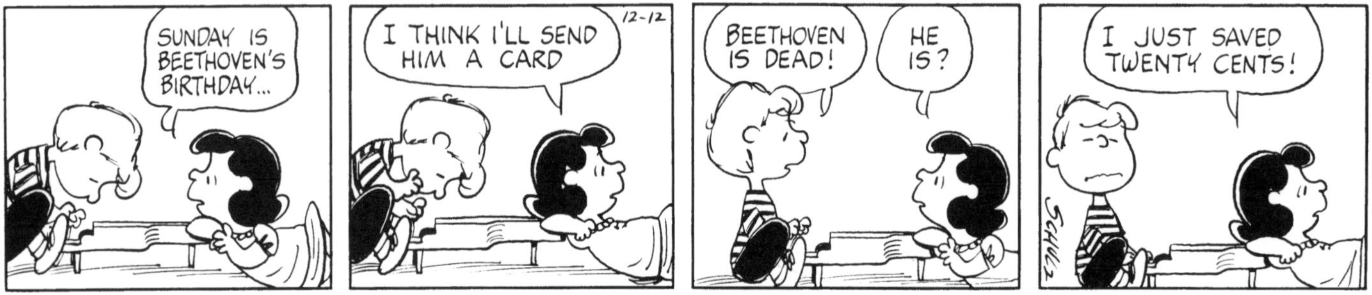
SUNDAY IS BEETHOVEN'S BIRTHDAY...
I THINK I'LL SEND HIM A CARD
BEETHOVEN IS DEAD!
HE IS?
I JUST SAVED TWENTY CENTS!

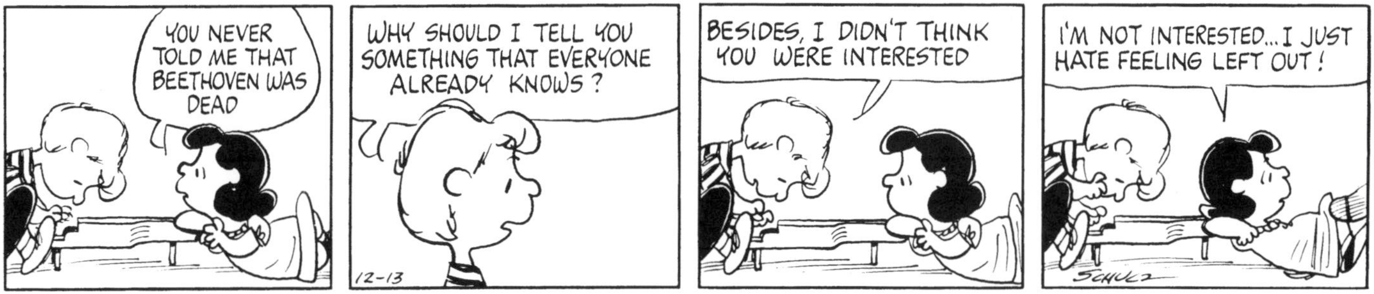
YOU NEVER TOLD ME THAT BEETHOVEN WAS DEAD
WHY SHOULD I TELL YOU SOMETHING THAT EVERYONE ALREADY KNOWS?
12-13
BESIDES, I DIDN'T THINK YOU WERE INTERESTED
I'M NOT INTERESTED... I JUST HATE FEELING LEFT OUT!
SCHULZ

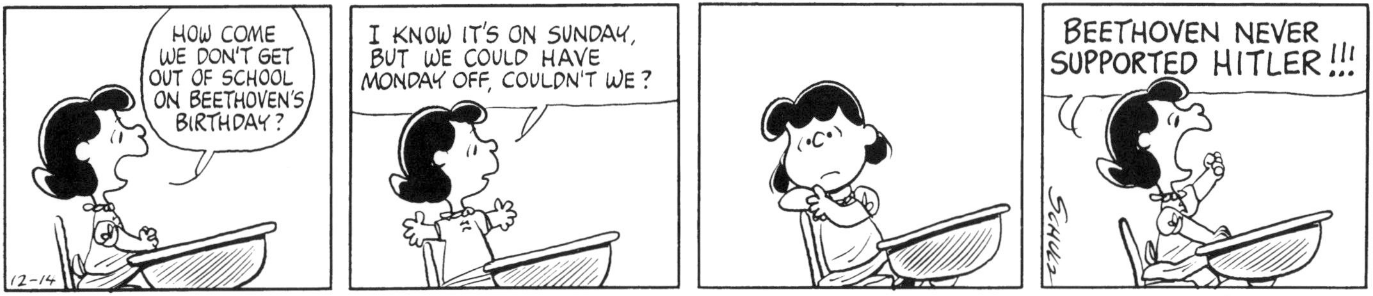
HOW COME WE DON'T GET OUT OF SCHOOL ON BEETHOVEN'S BIRTHDAY?
12-14
I KNOW IT'S ON SUNDAY, BUT WE COULD HAVE MONDAY OFF, COULDN'T WE?
BEETHOVEN NEVER SUPPORTED HITLER!!!
SCHULZ

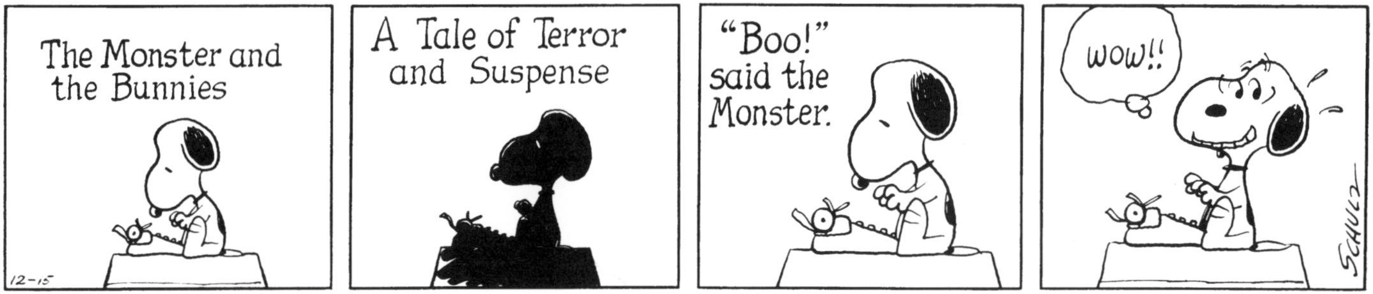
The Monster and the Bunnies
12-15
A Tale of Terror and Suspense
"Boo!" said the Monster.
WOW!!
SCHULZ

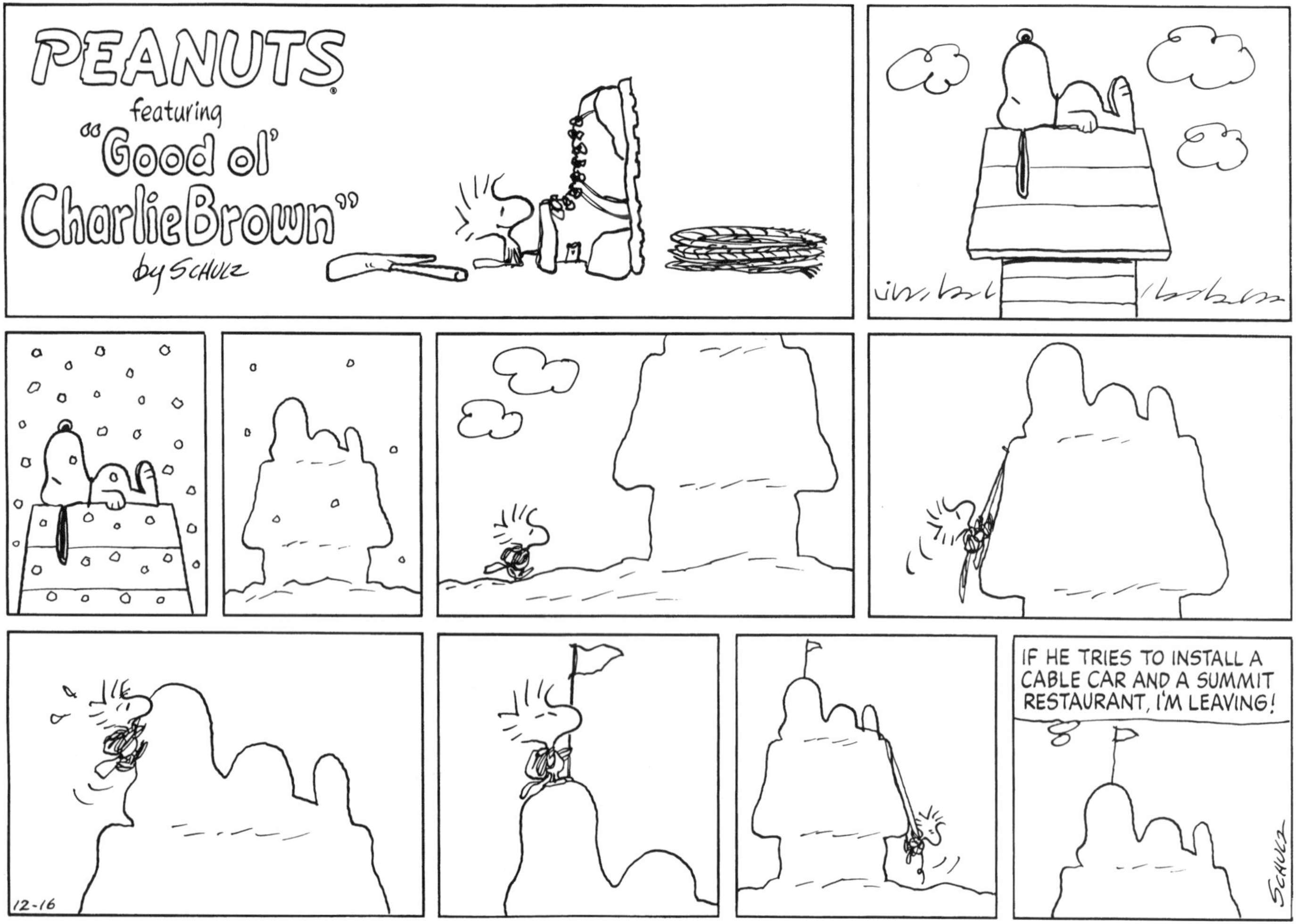
PEANUTS®
featuring
"Good ol' Charlie Brown"
by SCHULZ
12-16
IF HE TRIES TO INSTALL A CABLE CAR AND A SUMMIT RESTAURANT, I'M LEAVING!
SCHULZ

Dear Santa Claus, Do not bring me any presents this year.

I want my Christmas to be one of peace and love, not greed.

Getting a lot of presents is for the birds

!

THAT'S ONLY AN EXPRESSION!!

DON'T GIVE ME ANYTHING FOR CHRISTMAS THIS YEAR, BIG BROTHER...

ALL I WANT IS FOR EVERYONE TO HAVE PEACE, JOY AND LOVE

DO YOU REALLY MEAN THAT? ARE YOU SINCERE?

NO, I THINK I'VE FINALLY FLIPPED!

IF YOU'RE TYPING YOUR CHRISTMAS LIST, YOU CAN SCRATCH ME...I DON'T WANT ANY PRESENTS THIS YEAR

Linus van Pelt
Sally Brown

xSallyxBrownxxx

TAP TAP
TAP
TAP TAP
TAP TAP
TAP

SCRATCHING IS ONE THING... OBLITERATING IS ANOTHER!

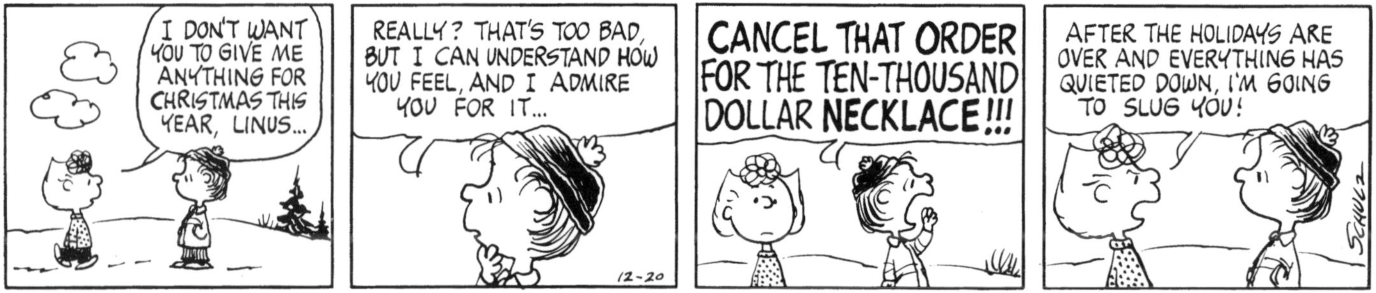
I DON'T WANT YOU TO GIVE ME ANYTHING FOR CHRISTMAS THIS YEAR, LINUS...
REALLY? THAT'S TOO BAD, BUT I CAN UNDERSTAND HOW YOU FEEL, AND I ADMIRE YOU FOR IT...
12-20
CANCEL THAT ORDER FOR THE TEN-THOUSAND DOLLAR NECKLACE!!!
AFTER THE HOLIDAYS ARE OVER AND EVERYTHING HAS QUIETED DOWN, I'M GOING TO SLUG YOU!
SCHULZ

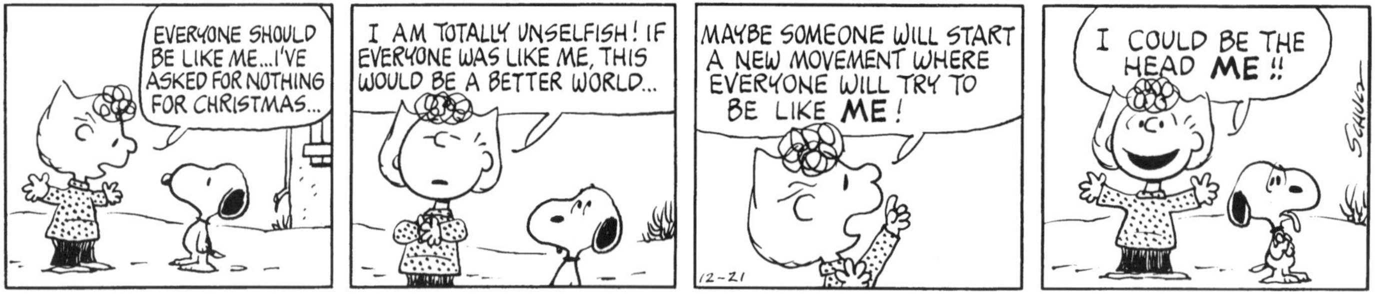
EVERYONE SHOULD BE LIKE ME...I'VE ASKED FOR NOTHING FOR CHRISTMAS...
I AM TOTALLY UNSELFISH! IF EVERYONE WAS LIKE ME, THIS WOULD BE A BETTER WORLD...
MAYBE SOMEONE WILL START A NEW MOVEMENT WHERE EVERYONE WILL TRY TO BE LIKE ME!
12-21
I COULD BE THE HEAD ME!!
SCHULZ

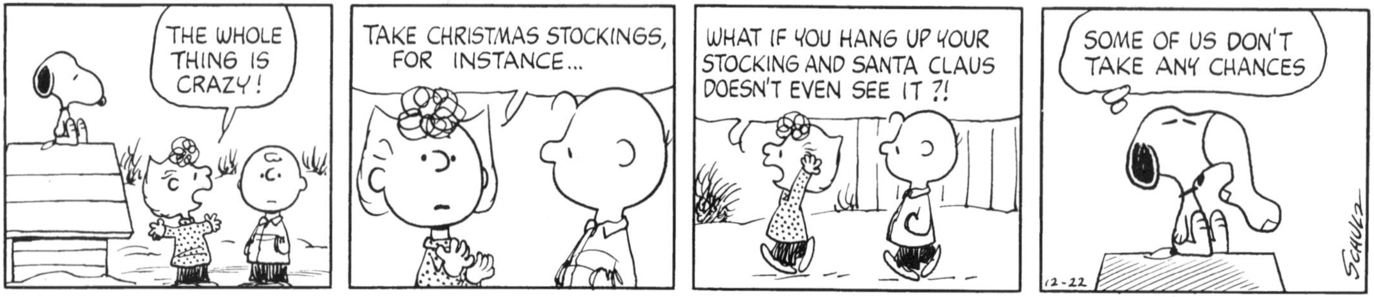
THE WHOLE THING IS CRAZY!
TAKE CHRISTMAS STOCKINGS, FOR INSTANCE...
WHAT IF YOU HANG UP YOUR STOCKING AND SANTA CLAUS DOESN'T EVEN SEE IT?!
SOME OF US DON'T TAKE ANY CHANCES
12-22
SCHULZ

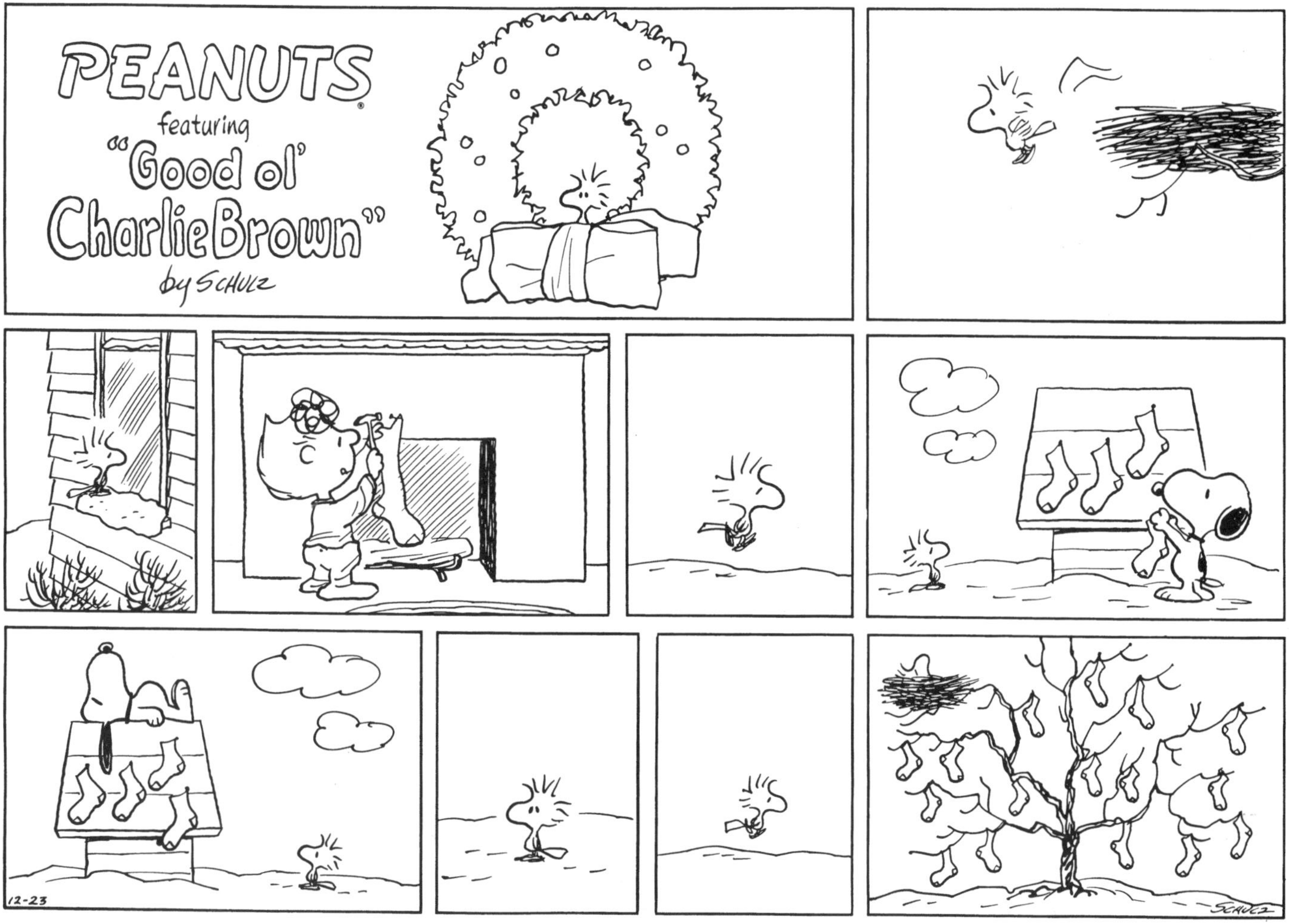
PEANUTS®
featuring
"Good ol' Charlie Brown"
by SCHULZ
12-23
SCHULZ

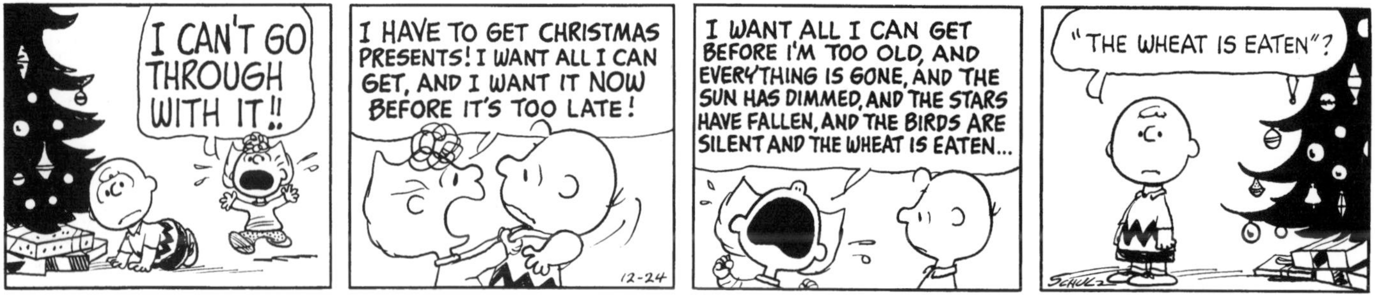
I CAN'T GO THROUGH WITH IT!!
I HAVE TO GET CHRISTMAS PRESENTS! I WANT ALL I CAN GET, AND I WANT IT NOW BEFORE IT'S TOO LATE!
12-24
I WANT ALL I CAN GET BEFORE I'M TOO OLD, AND EVERYTHING IS GONE, AND THE SUN HAS DIMMED, AND THE STARS HAVE FALLEN, AND THE BIRDS ARE SILENT AND THE WHEAT IS EATEN...
"THE WHEAT IS EATEN"?
SCHULZ

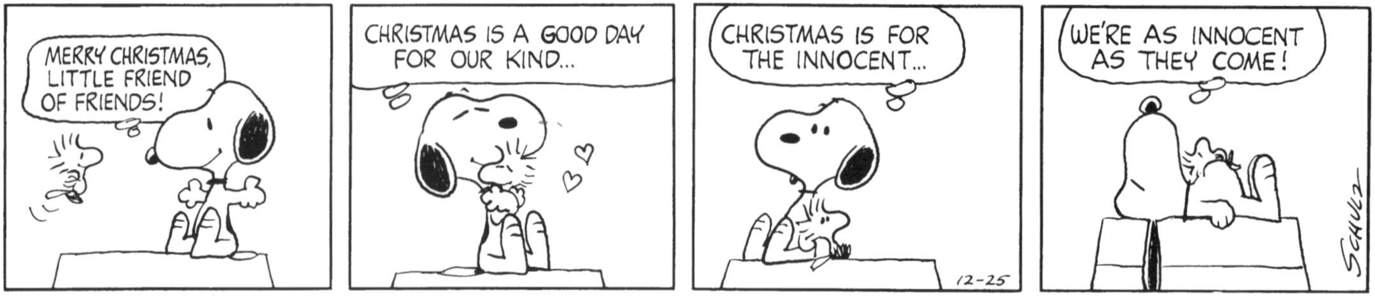
MERRY CHRISTMAS, LITTLE FRIEND OF FRIENDS!
CHRISTMAS IS A GOOD DAY FOR OUR KIND...
CHRISTMAS IS FOR THE INNOCENT...
12-25
WE'RE AS INNOCENT AS THEY COME!
SCHULZ

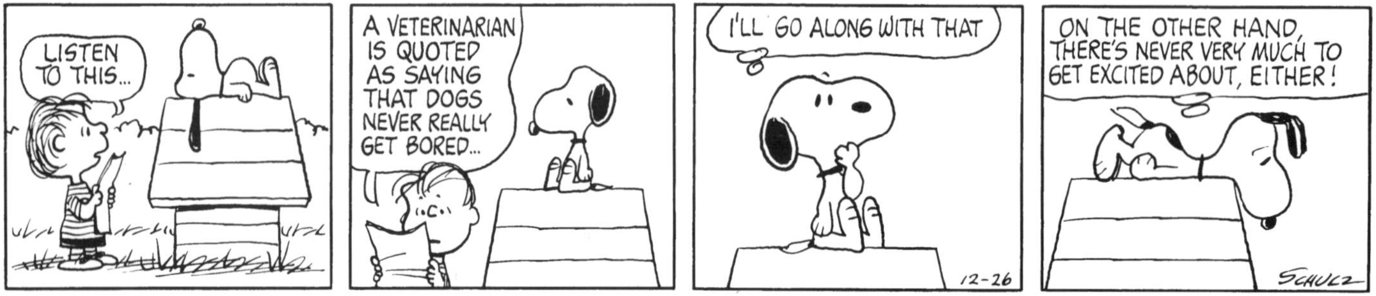
LISTEN TO THIS...
A VETERINARIAN IS QUOTED AS SAYING THAT DOGS NEVER REALLY GET BORED...
I'LL GO ALONG WITH THAT
12-26
ON THE OTHER HAND, THERE'S NEVER VERY MUCH TO GET EXCITED ABOUT, EITHER!
SCHULZ

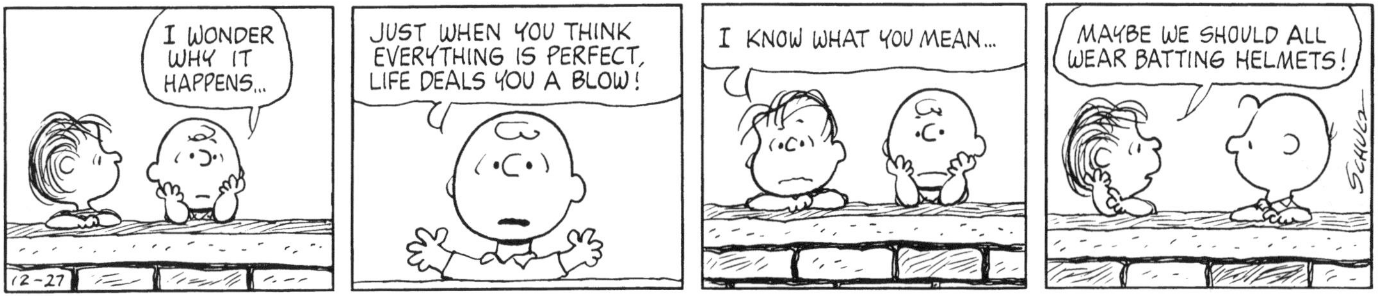
I WONDER WHY IT HAPPENS...
JUST WHEN YOU THINK EVERYTHING IS PERFECT, LIFE DEALS YOU A BLOW!
I KNOW WHAT YOU MEAN...
MAYBE WE SHOULD ALL WEAR BATTING HELMETS!
12-27
SCHULZ

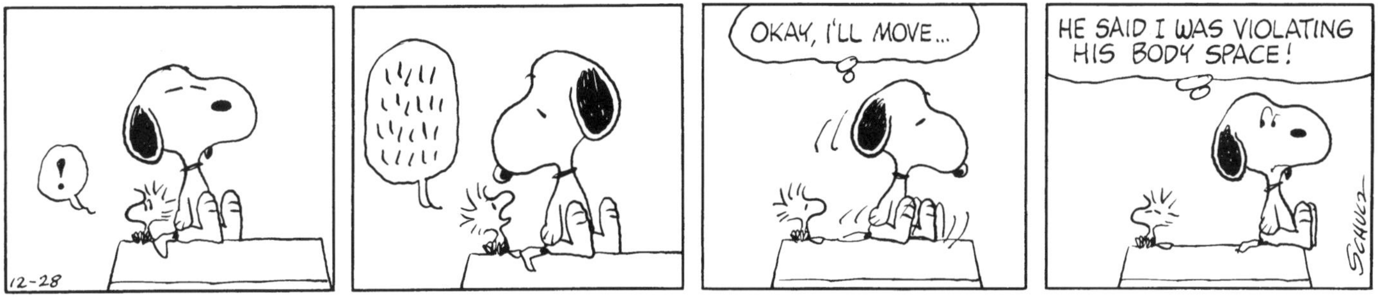
!
OKAY, I'LL MOVE...
HE SAID I WAS VIOLATING HIS BODY SPACE!
12-28
SCHULZ

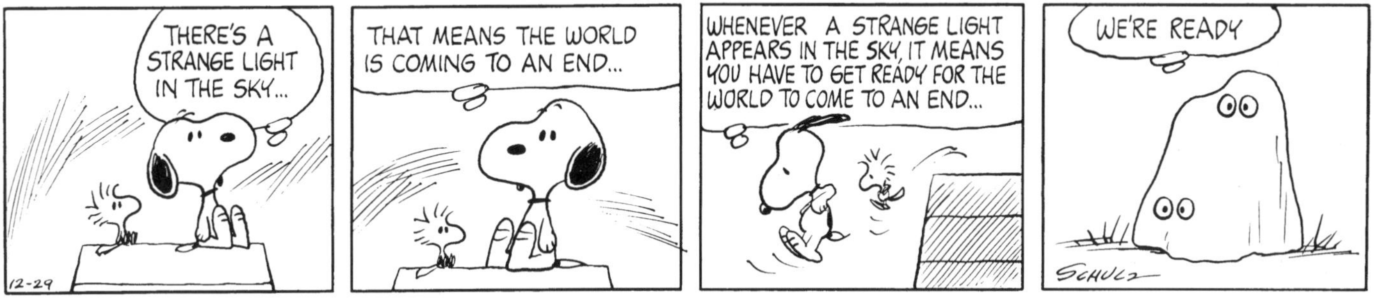
THERE'S A STRANGE LIGHT IN THE SKY...
THAT MEANS THE WORLD IS COMING TO AN END...
WHENEVER A STRANGE LIGHT APPEARS IN THE SKY, IT MEANS YOU HAVE TO GET READY FOR THE WORLD TO COME TO AN END...
WE'RE READY
12-29
SCHULZ

PEANUTS
featuring
"Good ol' CharlieBrown"
by Schulz

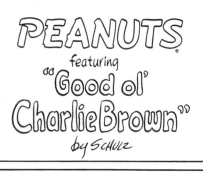

Winter had come again all too soon, and it was time for *Joe Jacket* to bring in his polar cows.

As he rode out from the barn, the first flakes of snow began to fall.

He looked up at the slate-gray sky and shivered.

12-30

The blizzard started quickly. A howling wind pounded the snow across the bleak prairie.

Joe Jacket hunched forward in the saddle, and urged his mount forward through the flying snow and screaming wind.

TELL MY PUBLISHERS NOT TO EXPECT A MANUSCRIPT UNTIL SPRING!

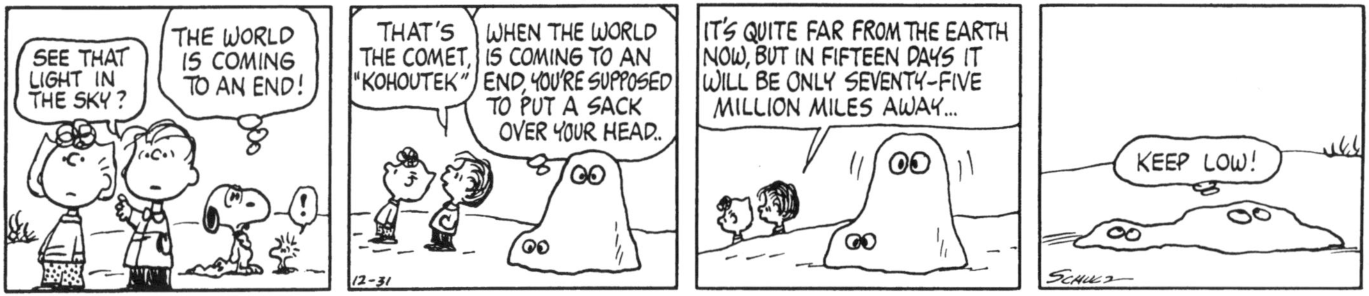
SEE THAT LIGHT IN THE SKY?
THE WORLD IS COMING TO AN END!
!
THAT'S THE COMET, "KOHOUTEK"
WHEN THE WORLD IS COMING TO AN END, YOU'RE SUPPOSED TO PUT A SACK OVER YOUR HEAD..
12-31
IT'S QUITE FAR FROM THE EARTH NOW, BUT IN FIFTEEN DAYS IT WILL BE ONLY SEVENTY-FIVE MILLION MILES AWAY...
KEEP LOW!
SCHULZ

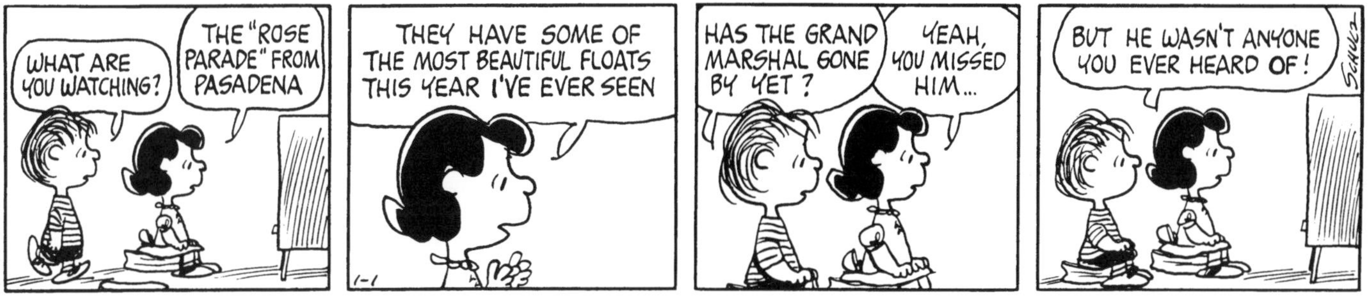
WHAT ARE YOU WATCHING?
THE "ROSE PARADE" FROM PASADENA
THEY HAVE SOME OF THE MOST BEAUTIFUL FLOATS THIS YEAR I'VE EVER SEEN
1-1
HAS THE GRAND MARSHAL GONE BY YET?
YEAH, YOU MISSED HIM...
BUT HE WASN'T ANYONE YOU EVER HEARD OF!
SCHULZ

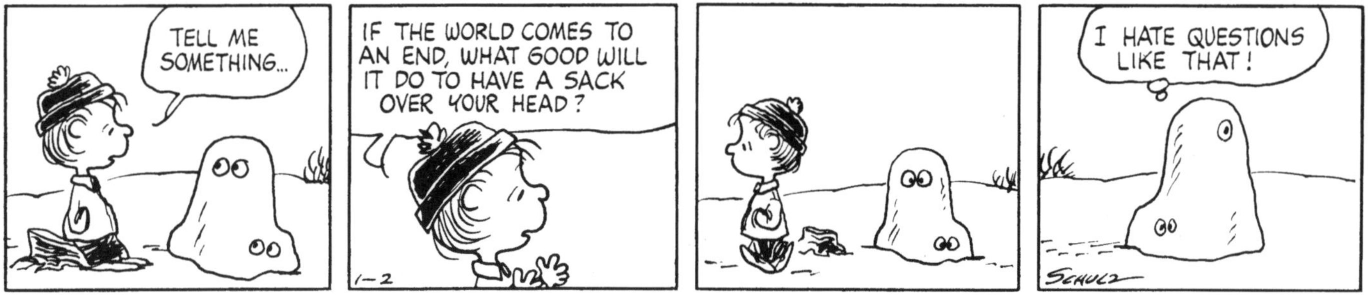
TELL ME SOMETHING...
IF THE WORLD COMES TO AN END, WHAT GOOD WILL IT DO TO HAVE A SACK OVER YOUR HEAD?
1-2
I HATE QUESTIONS LIKE THAT!
SCHULZ

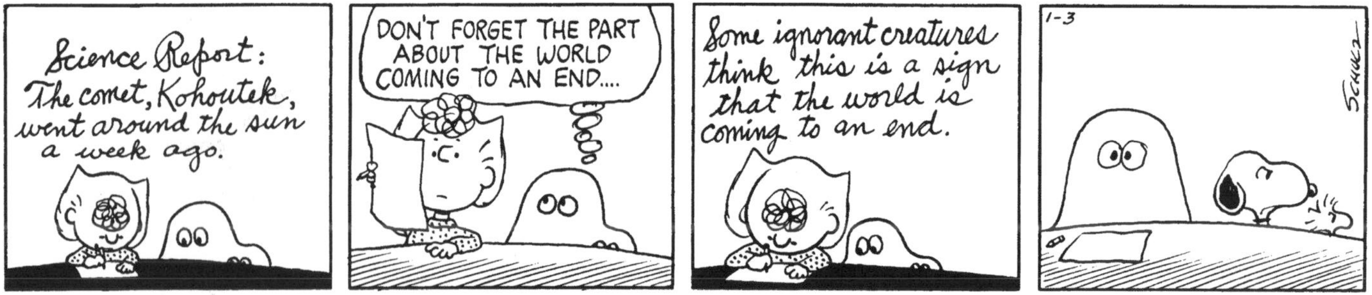
Science Report: The comet, Kohoutek, went around the sun a week ago.
DON'T FORGET THE PART ABOUT THE WORLD COMING TO AN END....
Some ignorant creatures think this is a sign that the world is coming to an end.

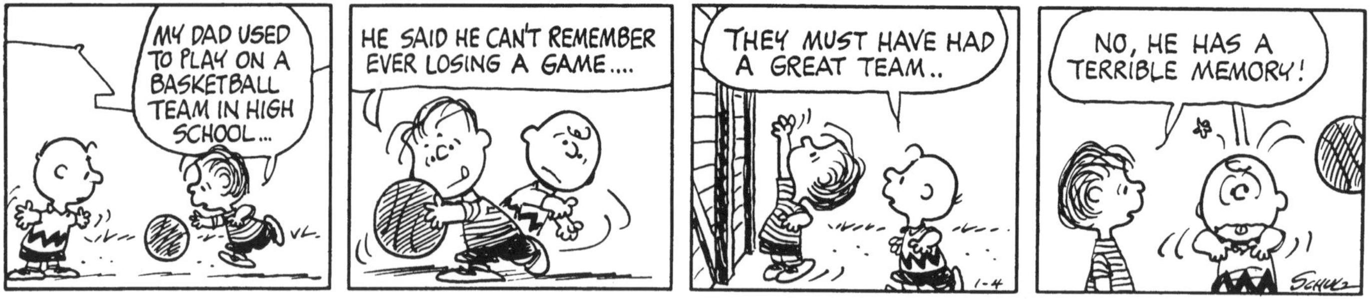
MY DAD USED TO PLAY ON A BASKETBALL TEAM IN HIGH SCHOOL...
HE SAID HE CAN'T REMEMBER EVER LOSING A GAME....
THEY MUST HAVE HAD A GREAT TEAM..
NO, HE HAS A TERRIBLE MEMORY!

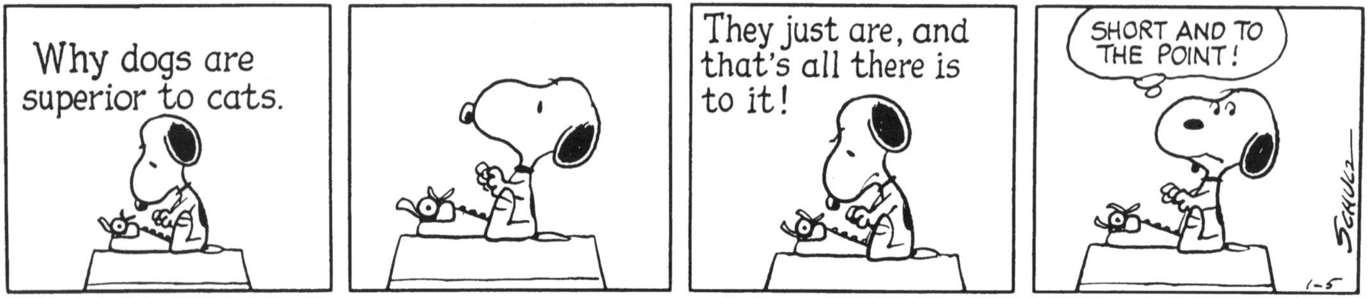
Why dogs are superior to cats.
They just are, and that's all there is to it!
SHORT AND TO THE POINT!

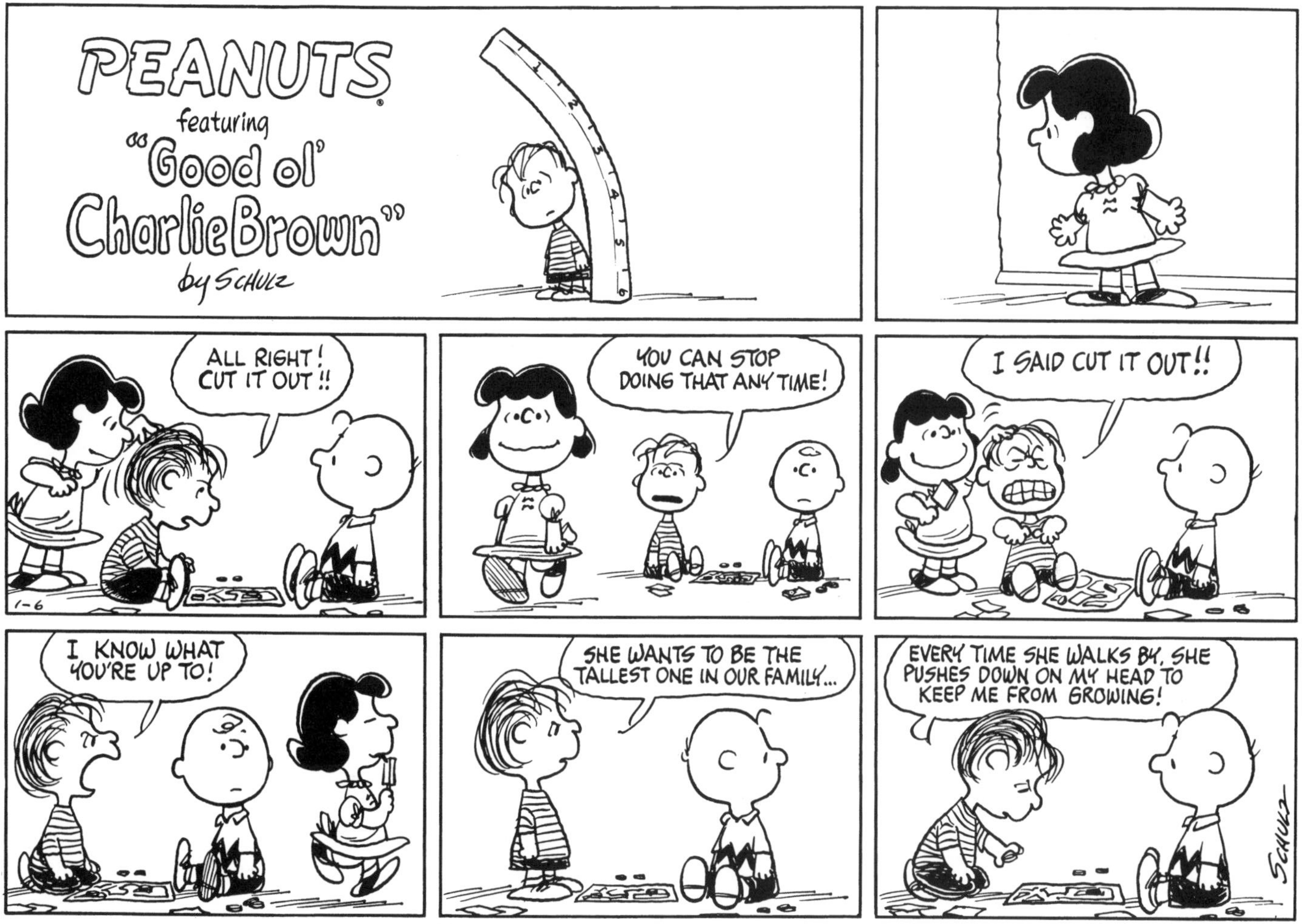
PEANUTS
featuring
"Good ol' Charlie Brown"
by SCHULZ
1-6
ALL RIGHT! CUT IT OUT!!
YOU CAN STOP DOING THAT ANY TIME!
I SAID CUT IT OUT!!
I KNOW WHAT YOU'RE UP TO!
SHE WANTS TO BE THE TALLEST ONE IN OUR FAMILY...
EVERY TIME SHE WALKS BY, SHE PUSHES DOWN ON MY HEAD TO KEEP ME FROM GROWING!
SCHULZ

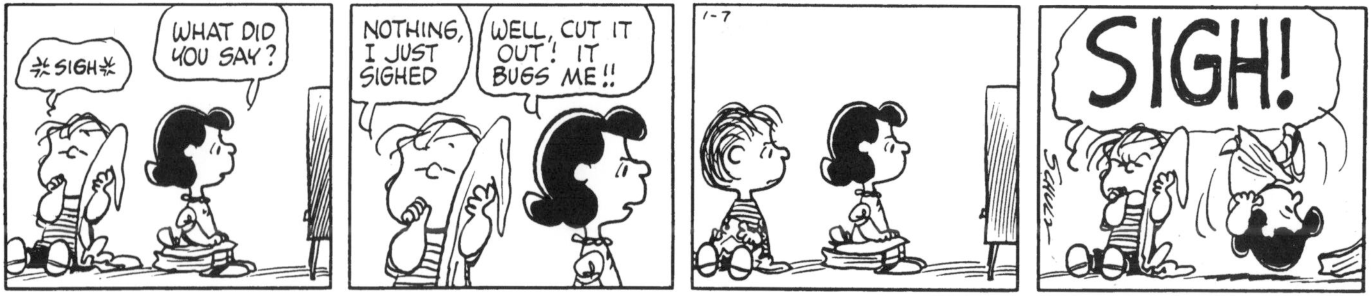

SIGH
WHAT DID YOU SAY?
NOTHING, I JUST SIGHED
WELL, CUT IT OUT! IT BUGS ME!!
1-7
SIGH!
SCHULZ

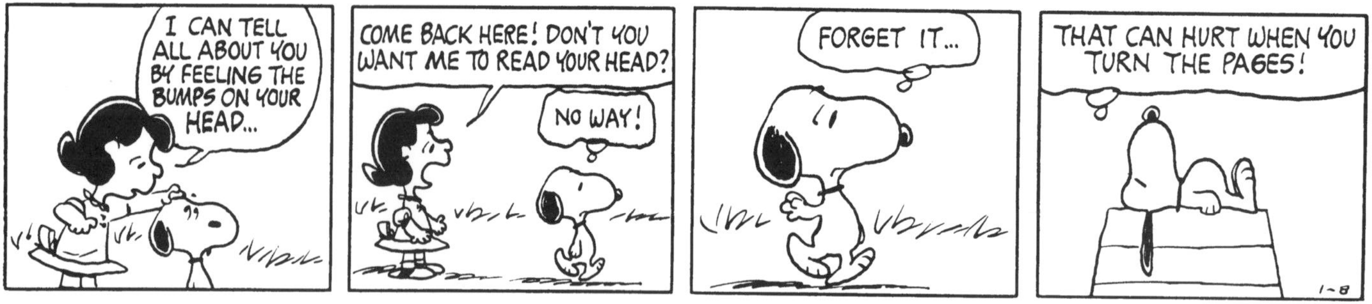

I CAN TELL ALL ABOUT YOU BY FEELING THE BUMPS ON YOUR HEAD...
COME BACK HERE! DON'T YOU WANT ME TO READ YOUR HEAD?
NO WAY!
FORGET IT...
THAT CAN HURT WHEN YOU TURN THE PAGES!
1-8

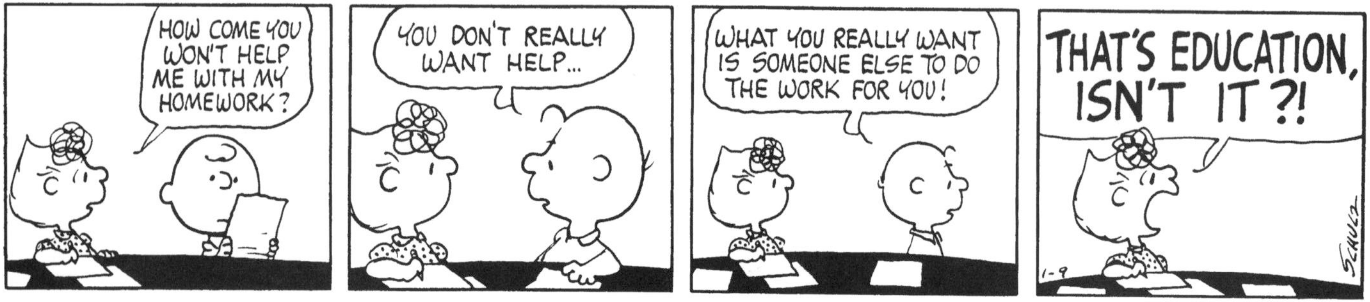

HOW COME YOU WON'T HELP ME WITH MY HOMEWORK?
YOU DON'T REALLY WANT HELP...
WHAT YOU REALLY WANT IS SOMEONE ELSE TO DO THE WORK FOR YOU!
1-9
THAT'S EDUCATION, ISN'T IT?!
SCHULZ

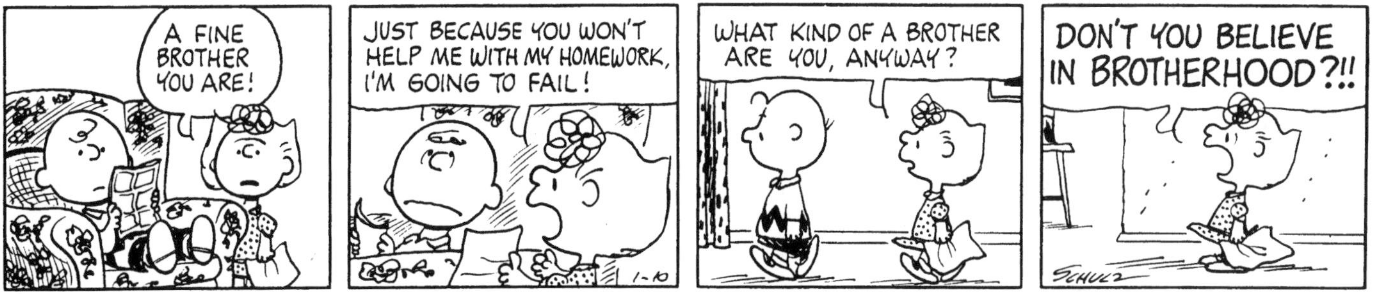
A FINE BROTHER YOU ARE!
JUST BECAUSE YOU WON'T HELP ME WITH MY HOMEWORK, I'M GOING TO FAIL!
WHAT KIND OF A BROTHER ARE YOU, ANYWAY?
DON'T YOU BELIEVE IN BROTHERHOOD?!!

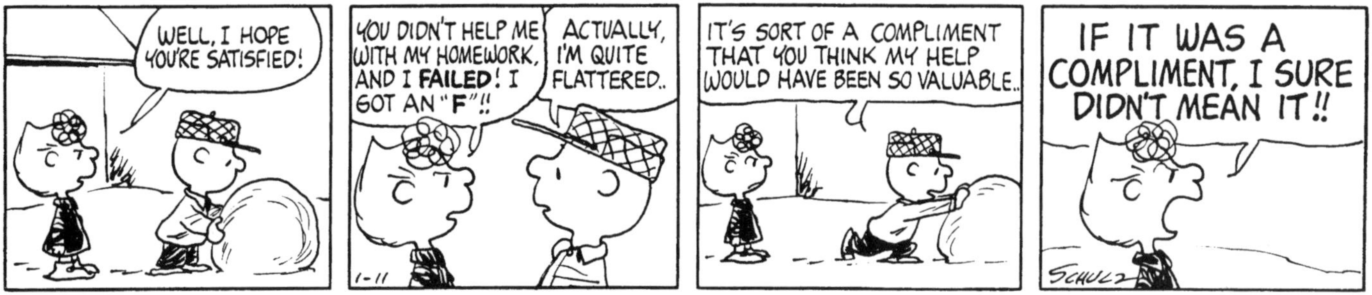
WELL, I HOPE YOU'RE SATISFIED!
YOU DIDN'T HELP ME WITH MY HOMEWORK, AND I **FAILED**! I GOT AN "**F**"!!
ACTUALLY, I'M QUITE FLATTERED..
IT'S SORT OF A COMPLIMENT THAT YOU THINK MY HELP WOULD HAVE BEEN SO VALUABLE..
IF IT WAS A COMPLIMENT, I SURE DIDN'T MEAN IT!!

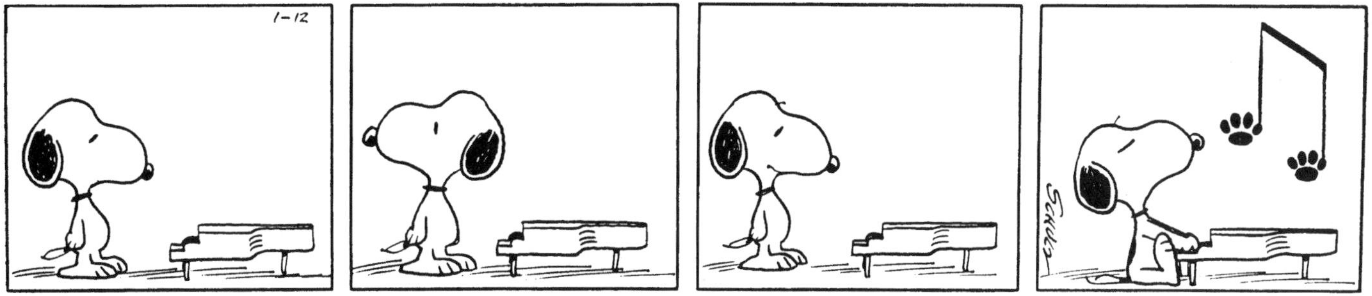

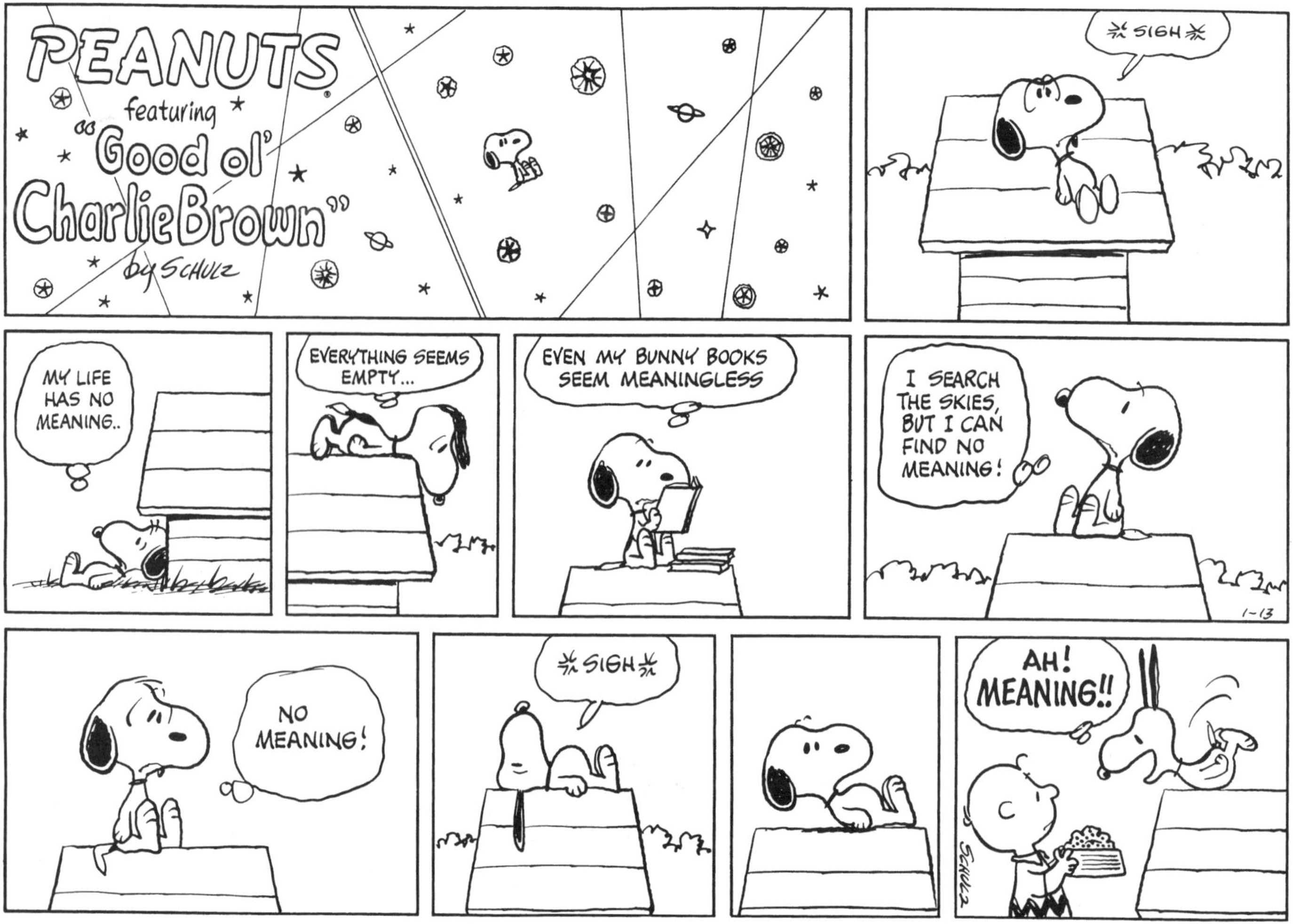
PEANUTS
featuring
"Good ol' Charlie Brown"
by SCHULZ
SIGH
MY LIFE HAS NO MEANING..
EVERYTHING SEEMS EMPTY...
EVEN MY BUNNY BOOKS SEEM MEANINGLESS
I SEARCH THE SKIES, BUT I CAN FIND NO MEANING!
1-13
NO MEANING!
SIGH
AH! MEANING!!
SCHULZ

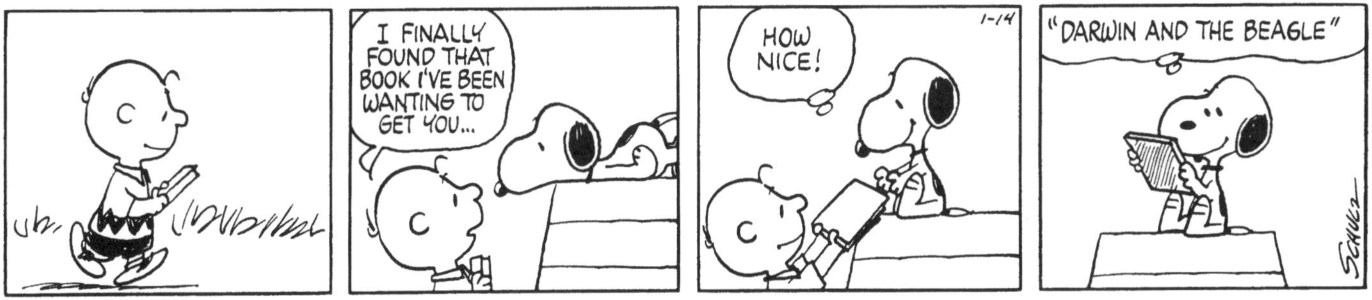
I FINALLY FOUND THAT BOOK I'VE BEEN WANTING TO GET YOU...
1-14
HOW NICE!
"DARWIN AND THE BEAGLE"

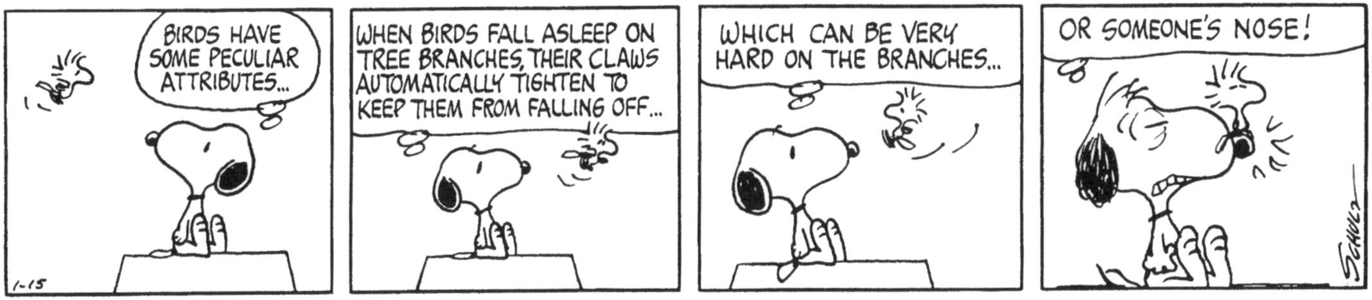
BIRDS HAVE SOME PECULIAR ATTRIBUTES...
1-15
WHEN BIRDS FALL ASLEEP ON TREE BRANCHES, THEIR CLAWS AUTOMATICALLY TIGHTEN TO KEEP THEM FROM FALLING OFF...
WHICH CAN BE VERY HARD ON THE BRANCHES...
OR SOMEONE'S NOSE!

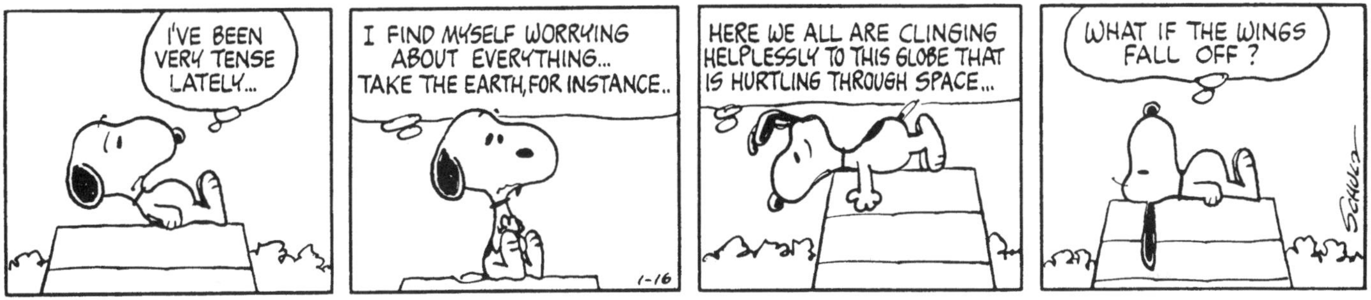
I'VE BEEN VERY TENSE LATELY...
I FIND MYSELF WORRYING ABOUT EVERYTHING... TAKE THE EARTH, FOR INSTANCE..
1-16
HERE WE ALL ARE CLINGING HELPLESSLY TO THIS GLOBE THAT IS HURTLING THROUGH SPACE...
WHAT IF THE WINGS FALL OFF?

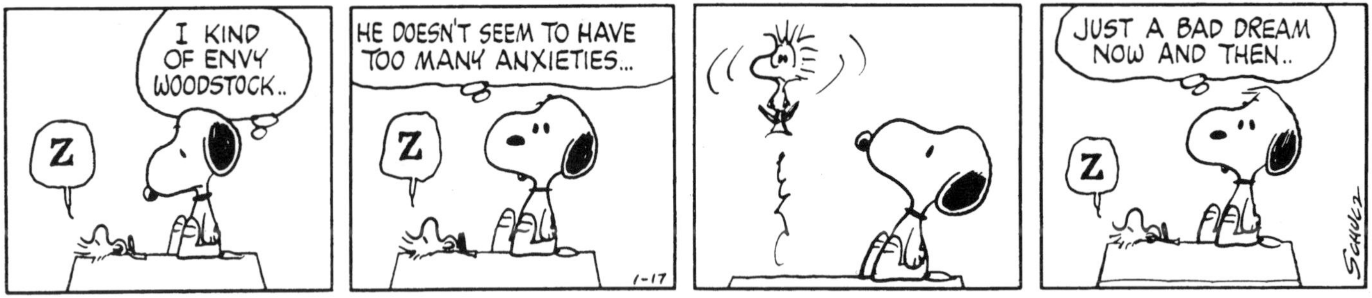
Z
I KIND OF ENVY WOODSTOCK..
Z
HE DOESN'T SEEM TO HAVE TOO MANY ANXIETIES...
1-17
JUST A BAD DREAM NOW AND THEN..
Z
SCHULZ

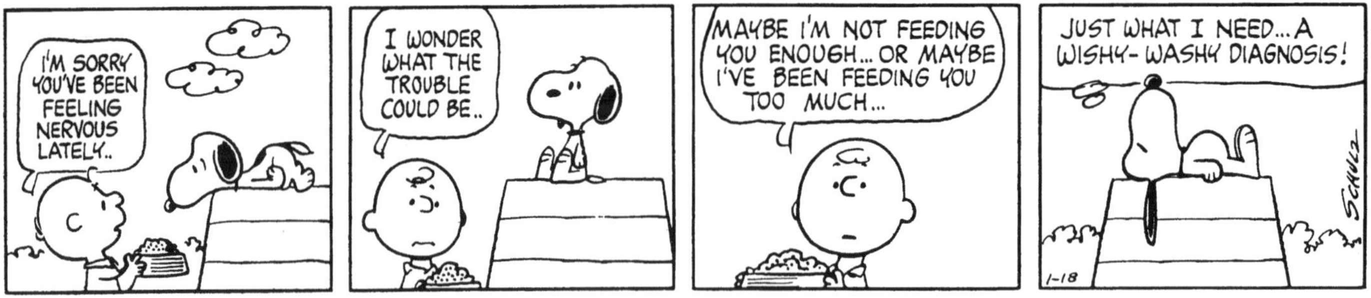
I'M SORRY YOU'VE BEEN FEELING NERVOUS LATELY..
I WONDER WHAT THE TROUBLE COULD BE..
MAYBE I'M NOT FEEDING YOU ENOUGH... OR MAYBE I'VE BEEN FEEDING YOU TOO MUCH...
JUST WHAT I NEED... A WISHY-WASHY DIAGNOSIS!
SCHULZ
1-18

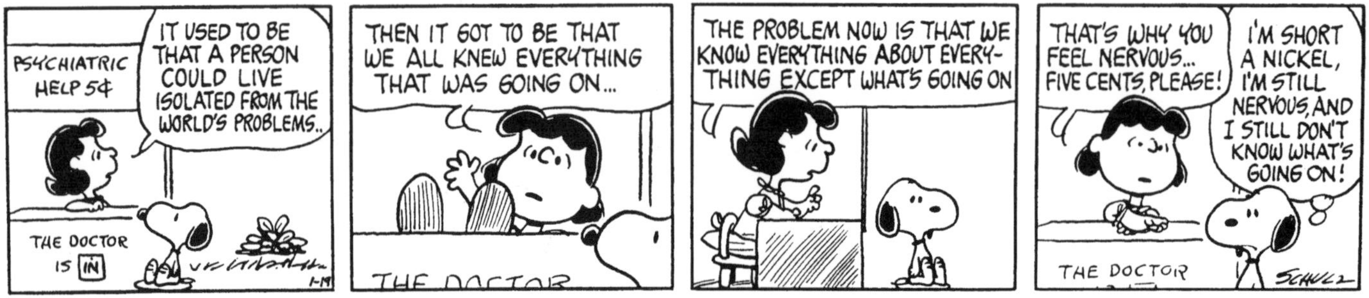
PSYCHIATRIC HELP 5¢
IT USED TO BE THAT A PERSON COULD LIVE ISOLATED FROM THE WORLD'S PROBLEMS..
THE DOCTOR IS IN
1-19
THEN IT GOT TO BE THAT WE ALL KNEW EVERYTHING THAT WAS GOING ON...
THE PROBLEM NOW IS THAT WE KNOW EVERYTHING ABOUT EVERYTHING EXCEPT WHAT'S GOING ON
THAT'S WHY YOU FEEL NERVOUS... FIVE CENTS, PLEASE!
I'M SHORT A NICKEL, I'M STILL NERVOUS, AND I STILL DON'T KNOW WHAT'S GOING ON!
THE DOCTOR
SCHULZ

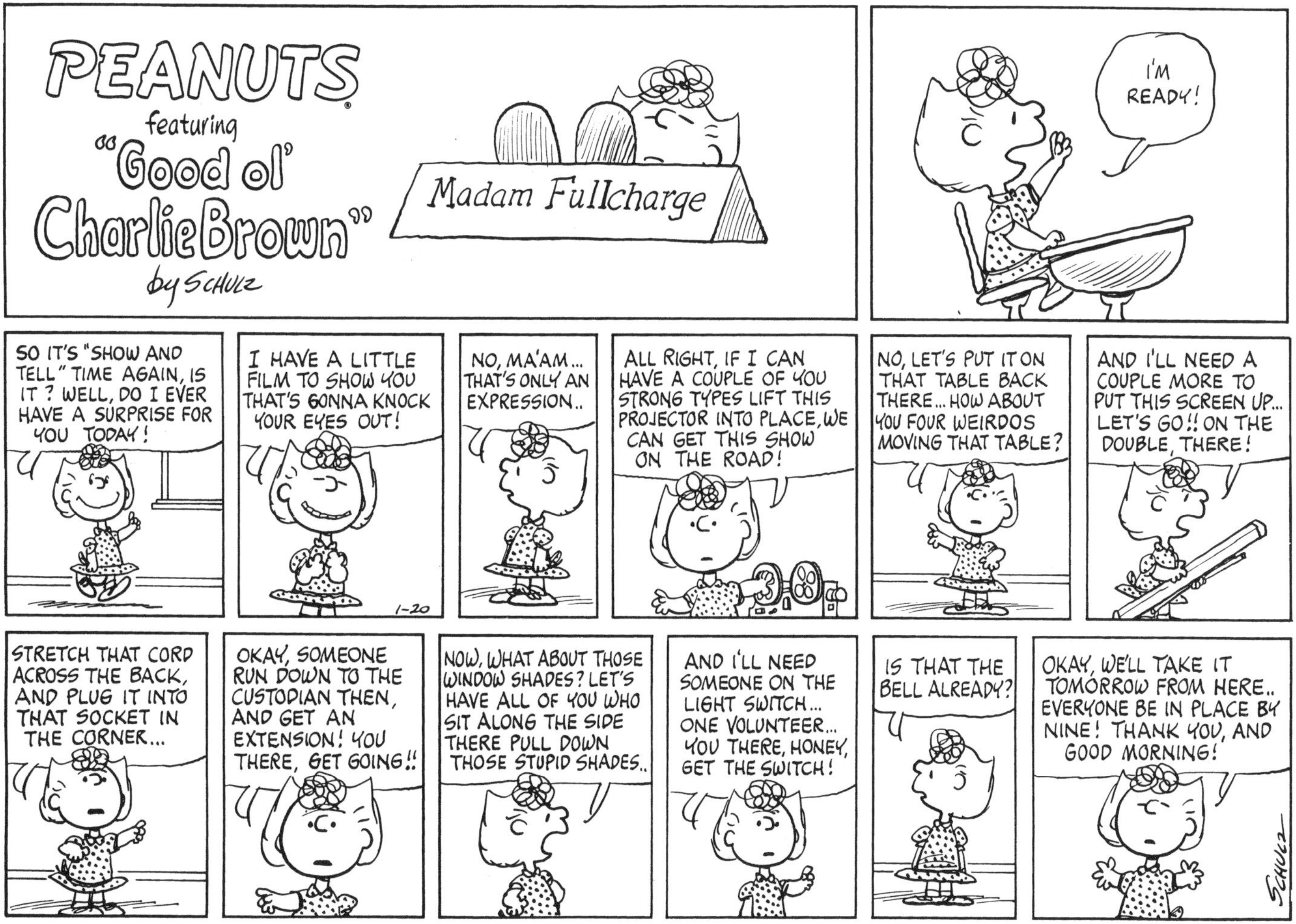
PEANUTS
featuring "Good ol' Charlie Brown"
by SCHULZ
Madam Fullcharge
I'M READY!
SO IT'S "SHOW AND TELL" TIME AGAIN, IS IT? WELL, DO I EVER HAVE A SURPRISE FOR YOU TODAY!
I HAVE A LITTLE FILM TO SHOW YOU THAT'S GONNA KNOCK YOUR EYES OUT!
1-20
NO, MA'AM... THAT'S ONLY AN EXPRESSION..
ALL RIGHT, IF I CAN HAVE A COUPLE OF YOU STRONG TYPES LIFT THIS PROJECTOR INTO PLACE, WE CAN GET THIS SHOW ON THE ROAD!
NO, LET'S PUT IT ON THAT TABLE BACK THERE... HOW ABOUT YOU FOUR WEIRDOS MOVING THAT TABLE?
AND I'LL NEED A COUPLE MORE TO PUT THIS SCREEN UP... LET'S GO!! ON THE DOUBLE, THERE!
STRETCH THAT CORD ACROSS THE BACK, AND PLUG IT INTO THAT SOCKET IN THE CORNER...
OKAY, SOMEONE RUN DOWN TO THE CUSTODIAN THEN, AND GET AN EXTENSION! YOU THERE, GET GOING!!
NOW, WHAT ABOUT THOSE WINDOW SHADES? LET'S HAVE ALL OF YOU WHO SIT ALONG THE SIDE THERE PULL DOWN THOSE STUPID SHADES..
AND I'LL NEED SOMEONE ON THE LIGHT SWITCH... ONE VOLUNTEER... YOU THERE, HONEY, GET THE SWITCH!
IS THAT THE BELL ALREADY?
OKAY, WE'LL TAKE IT TOMORROW FROM HERE.. EVERYONE BE IN PLACE BY NINE! THANK YOU, AND GOOD MORNING!
SCHULZ

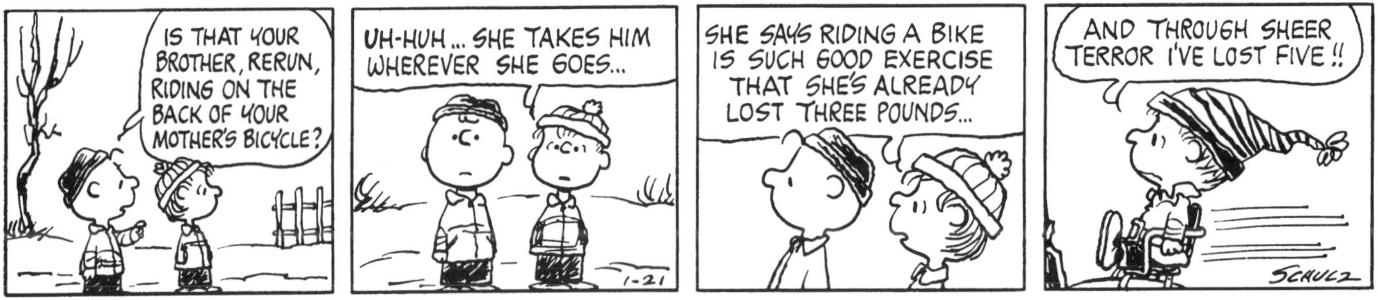
IS THAT YOUR BROTHER, RERUN, RIDING ON THE BACK OF YOUR MOTHER'S BICYCLE?
UH-HUH... SHE TAKES HIM WHEREVER SHE GOES...
1-21
SHE SAYS RIDING A BIKE IS SUCH GOOD EXERCISE THAT SHE'S ALREADY LOST THREE POUNDS...
AND THROUGH SHEER TERROR I'VE LOST FIVE!!
SCHULZ

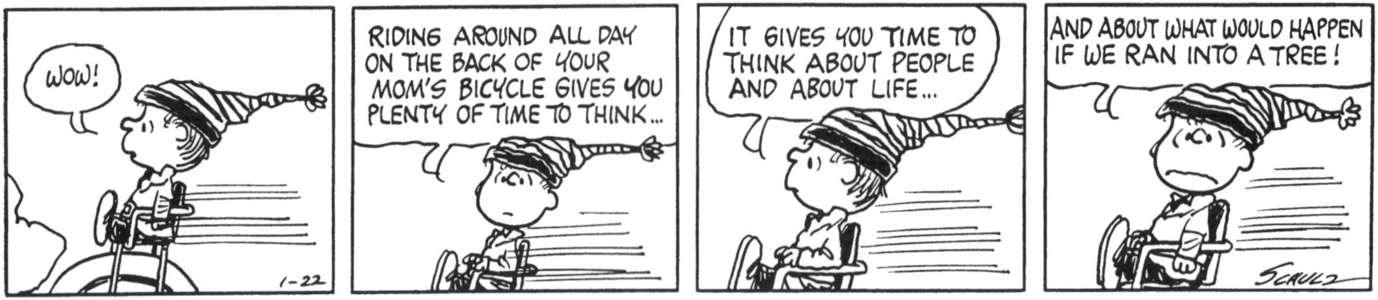
WOW!
1-22
RIDING AROUND ALL DAY ON THE BACK OF YOUR MOM'S BICYCLE GIVES YOU PLENTY OF TIME TO THINK...
IT GIVES YOU TIME TO THINK ABOUT PEOPLE AND ABOUT LIFE...
AND ABOUT WHAT WOULD HAPPEN IF WE RAN INTO A TREE!
SCHULZ

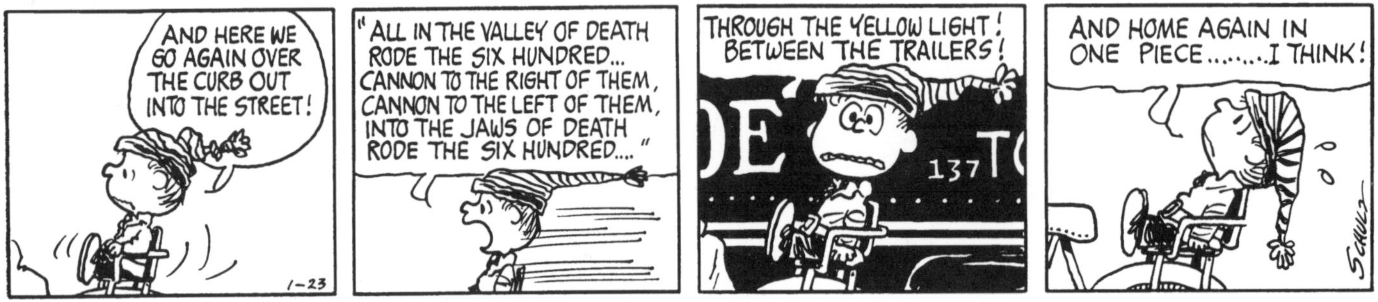
AND HERE WE GO AGAIN OVER THE CURB OUT INTO THE STREET!
1-23
"ALL IN THE VALLEY OF DEATH RODE THE SIX HUNDRED... CANNON TO THE RIGHT OF THEM, CANNON TO THE LEFT OF THEM, INTO THE JAWS OF DEATH RODE THE SIX HUNDRED...."
THROUGH THE YELLOW LIGHT! BETWEEN THE TRAILERS!
137
AND HOME AGAIN IN ONE PIECE.........I THINK!
SCHULZ

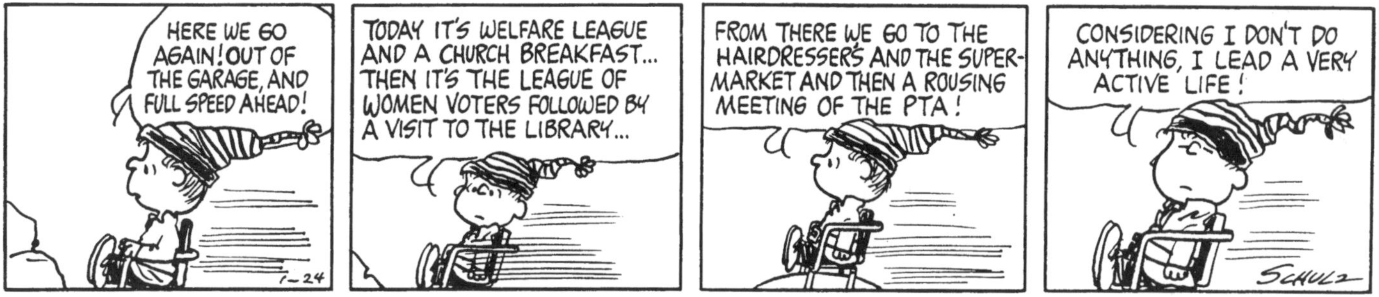
HERE WE GO AGAIN! OUT OF THE GARAGE, AND FULL SPEED AHEAD!
1-24
TODAY IT'S WELFARE LEAGUE AND A CHURCH BREAKFAST... THEN IT'S THE LEAGUE OF WOMEN VOTERS FOLLOWED BY A VISIT TO THE LIBRARY...
FROM THERE WE GO TO THE HAIRDRESSER'S AND THE SUPER-MARKET AND THEN A ROUSING MEETING OF THE PTA!
CONSIDERING I DON'T DO ANYTHING, I LEAD A VERY ACTIVE LIFE!
SCHULZ

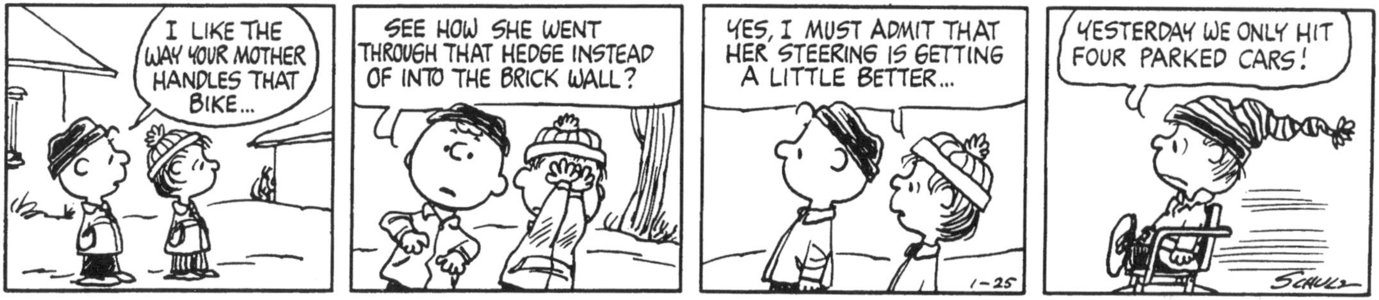
I LIKE THE WAY YOUR MOTHER HANDLES THAT BIKE...
SEE HOW SHE WENT THROUGH THAT HEDGE INSTEAD OF INTO THE BRICK WALL?
YES, I MUST ADMIT THAT HER STEERING IS GETTING A LITTLE BETTER...
1-25
YESTERDAY WE ONLY HIT FOUR PARKED CARS!
SCHULZ

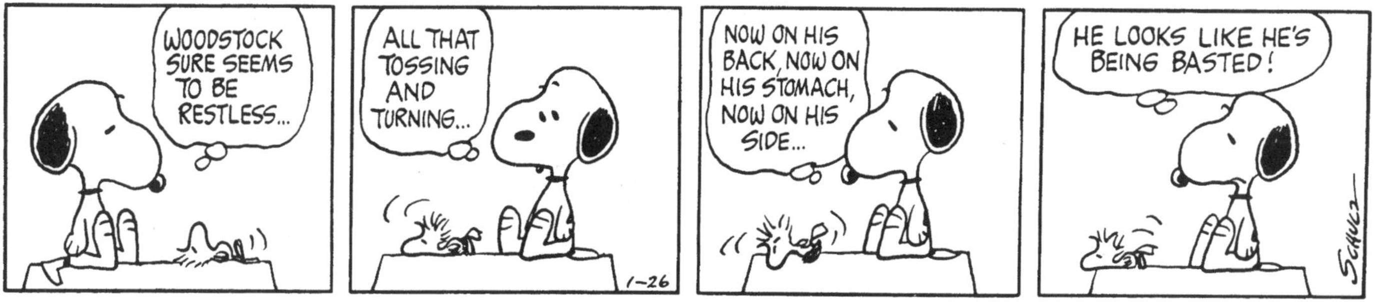
WOODSTOCK SURE SEEMS TO BE RESTLESS...
ALL THAT TOSSING AND TURNING...
1-26
NOW ON HIS BACK, NOW ON HIS STOMACH, NOW ON HIS SIDE...
HE LOOKS LIKE HE'S BEING BASTED!
SCHULZ

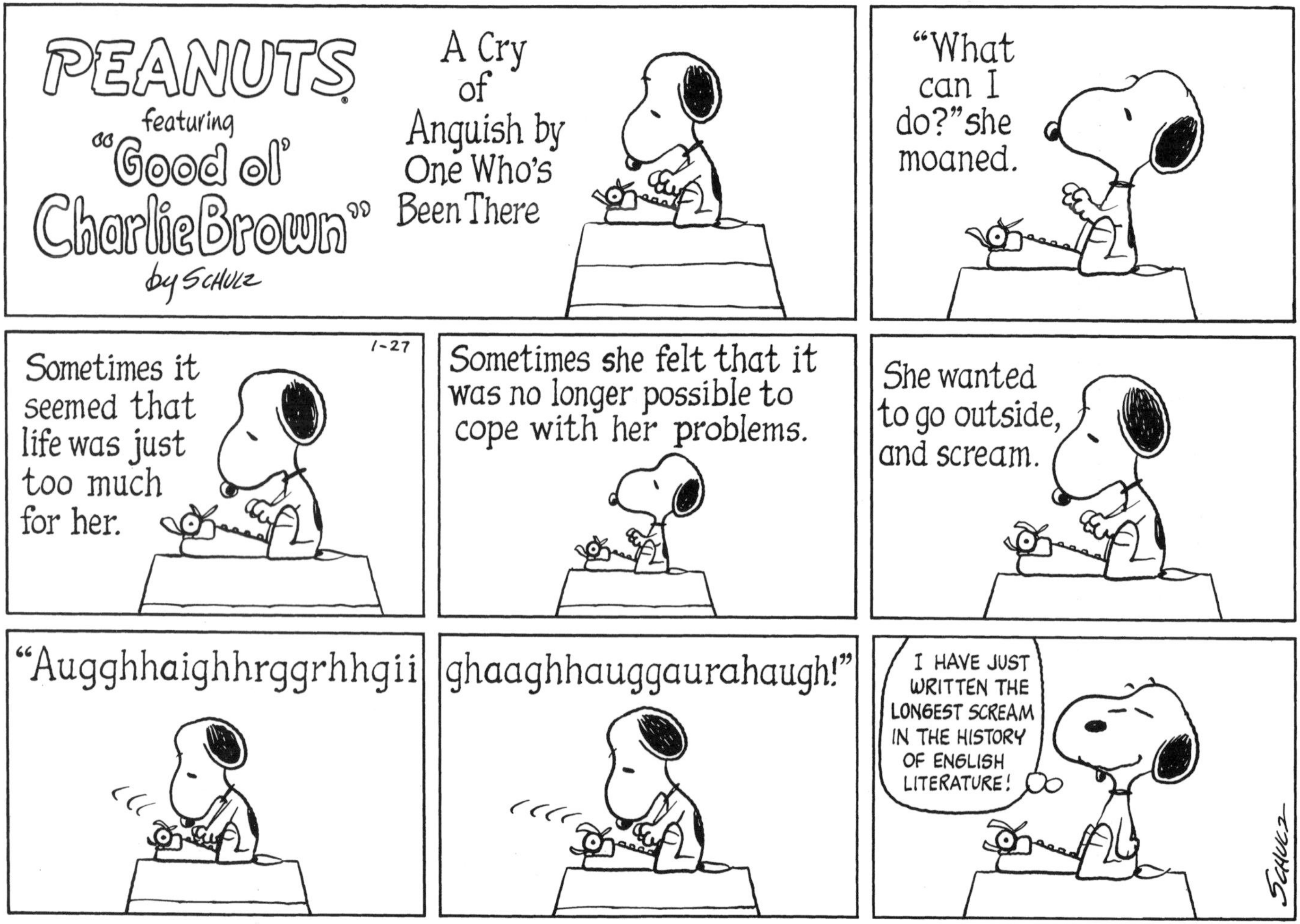
PEANUTS
featuring
"Good ol' Charlie Brown"
by SCHULZ
A Cry of Anguish by One Who's Been There
"What can I do?" she moaned.
1-27
Sometimes it seemed that life was just too much for her.
Sometimes she felt that it was no longer possible to cope with her problems.
She wanted to go outside, and scream.
"Augghhaighhrggrhhgii
ghaaghhauggaurahaugh!"
I HAVE JUST WRITTEN THE LONGEST SCREAM IN THE HISTORY OF ENGLISH LITERATURE!
SCHULZ

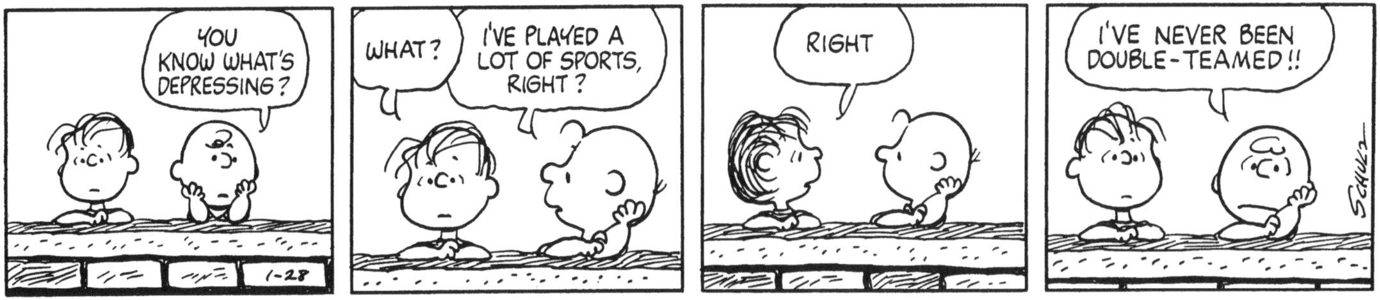
YOU KNOW WHAT'S DEPRESSING?
WHAT?
I'VE PLAYED A LOT OF SPORTS, RIGHT?
RIGHT
I'VE NEVER BEEN DOUBLE-TEAMED!!
1-28
SCHULZ

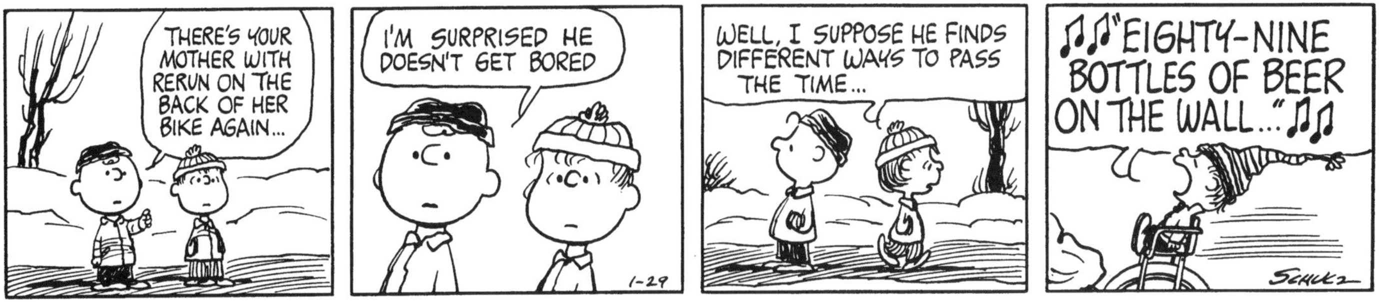
THERE'S YOUR MOTHER WITH RERUN ON THE BACK OF HER BIKE AGAIN...
I'M SURPRISED HE DOESN'T GET BORED
1-29
WELL, I SUPPOSE HE FINDS DIFFERENT WAYS TO PASS THE TIME...
"EIGHTY-NINE BOTTLES OF BEER ON THE WALL..."
SCHULZ

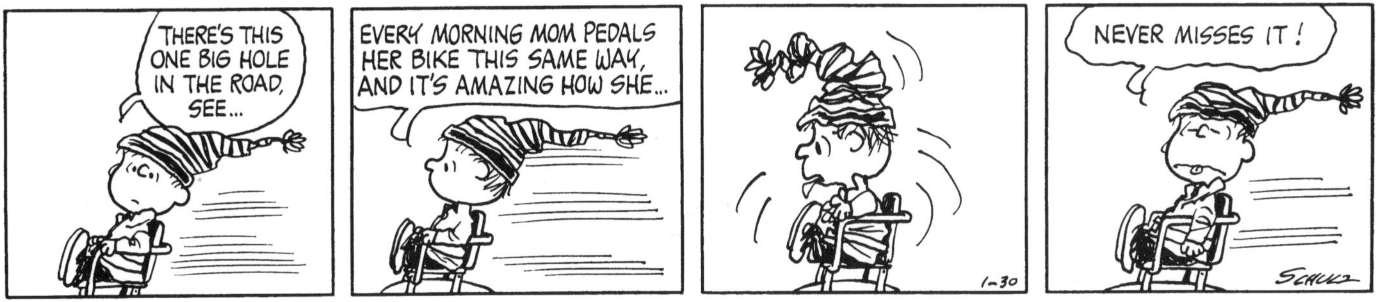
THERE'S THIS ONE BIG HOLE IN THE ROAD, SEE...
EVERY MORNING MOM PEDALS HER BIKE THIS SAME WAY, AND IT'S AMAZING HOW SHE...
1-30
NEVER MISSES IT!
SCHULZ

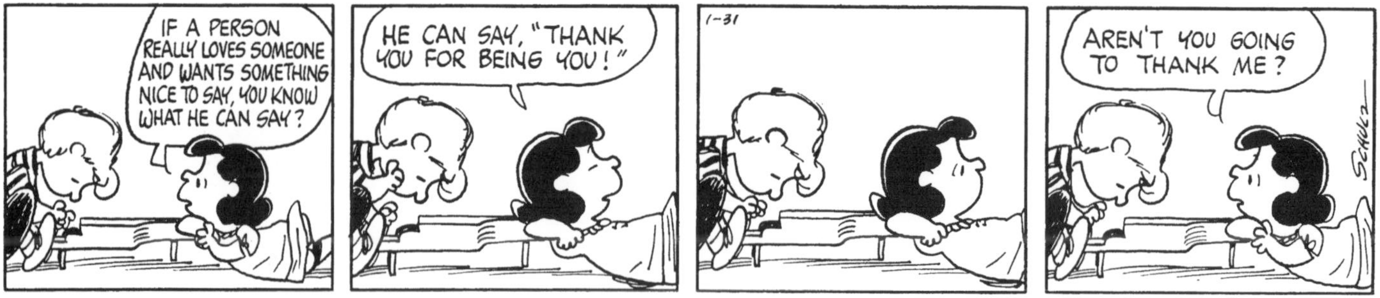
IF A PERSON REALLY LOVES SOMEONE AND WANTS SOMETHING NICE TO SAY, YOU KNOW WHAT HE CAN SAY?
HE CAN SAY, "THANK YOU FOR BEING YOU!"
1-31
AREN'T YOU GOING TO THANK ME?

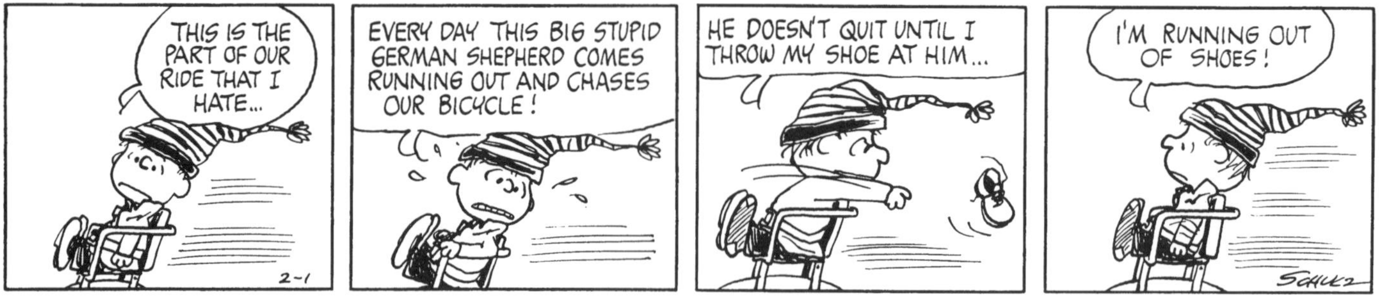
THIS IS THE PART OF OUR RIDE THAT I HATE...
2-1
EVERY DAY THIS BIG STUPID GERMAN SHEPHERD COMES RUNNING OUT AND CHASES OUR BICYCLE!
HE DOESN'T QUIT UNTIL I THROW MY SHOE AT HIM...
I'M RUNNING OUT OF SHOES!

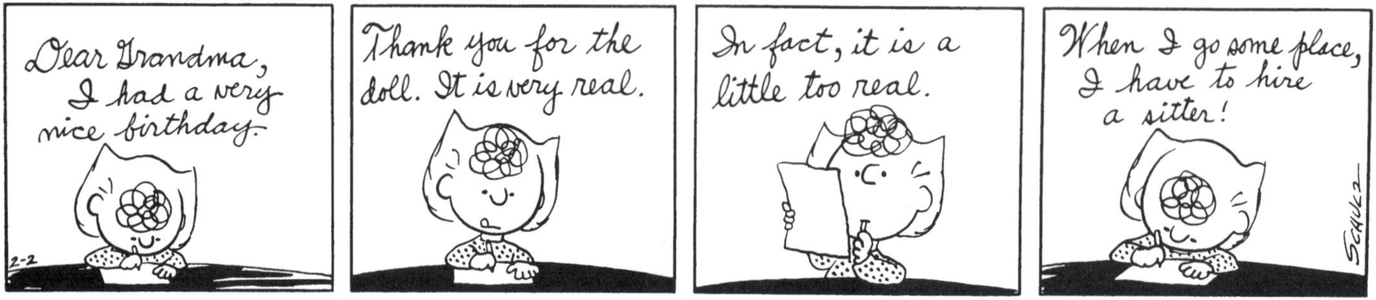
Dear Grandma, I had a very nice birthday.
2-2
Thank you for the doll. It is very real.
In fact, it is a little too real.
When I go some place, I have to hire a sitter!

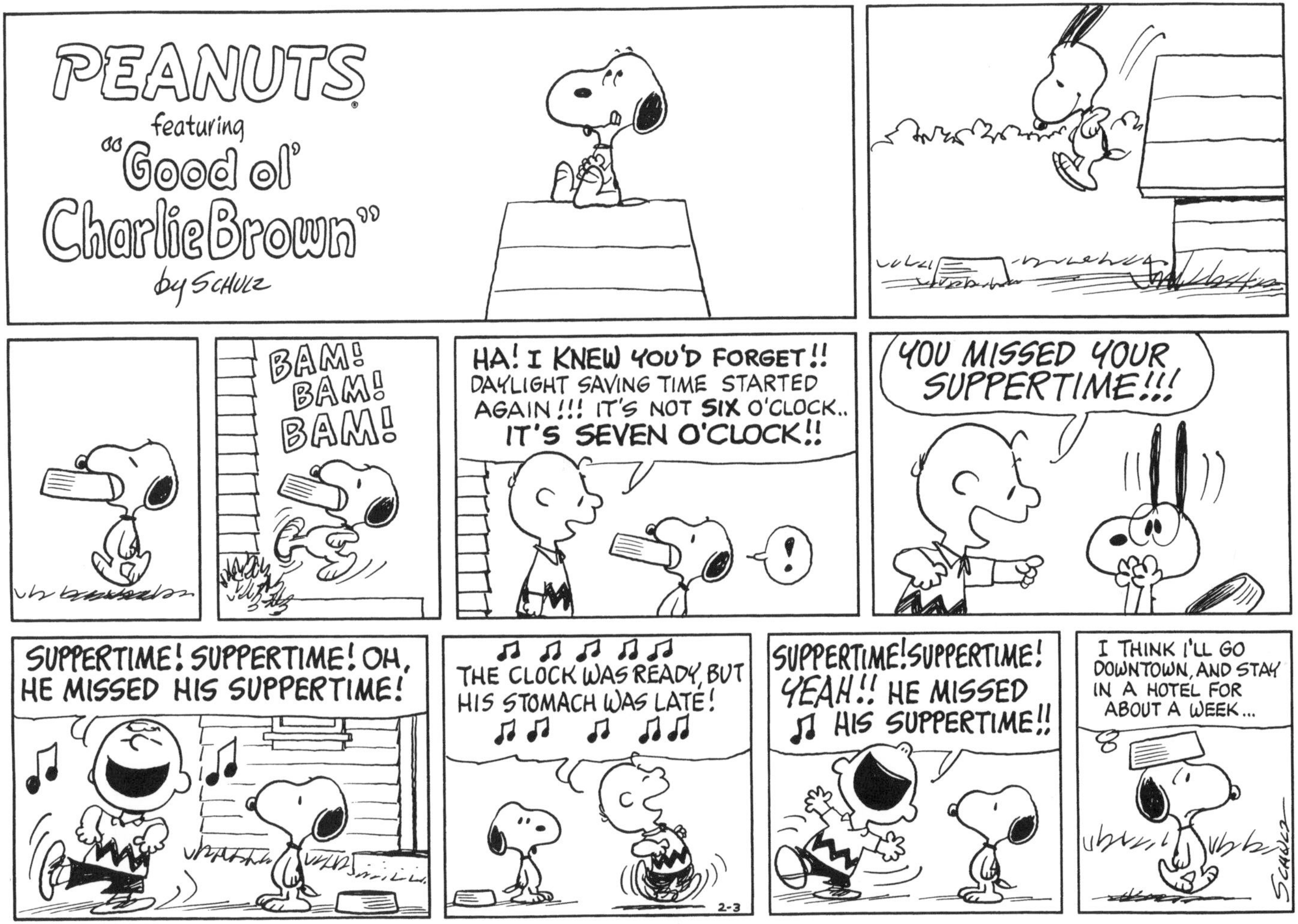
PEANUTS
featuring
"Good ol' Charlie Brown"
by SCHULZ
BAM! BAM! BAM!
HA! I KNEW YOU'D FORGET!! DAYLIGHT SAVING TIME STARTED AGAIN!!! IT'S NOT SIX O'CLOCK.. IT'S SEVEN O'CLOCK!!
!
YOU MISSED YOUR SUPPERTIME!!!
SUPPERTIME! SUPPERTIME! OH, HE MISSED HIS SUPPERTIME!
THE CLOCK WAS READY, BUT HIS STOMACH WAS LATE!
2-3
SUPPERTIME! SUPPERTIME! YEAH!! HE MISSED HIS SUPPERTIME!!
I THINK I'LL GO DOWNTOWN, AND STAY IN A HOTEL FOR ABOUT A WEEK...
SCHULZ

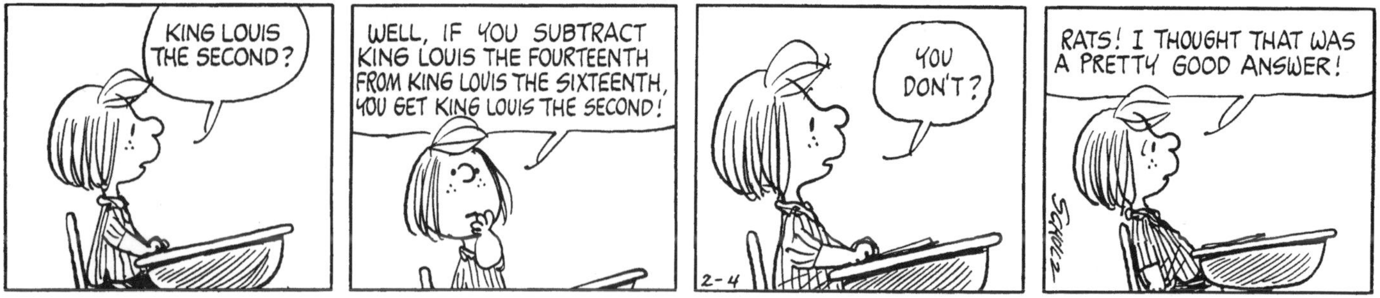

KING LOUIS THE SECOND?
WELL, IF YOU SUBTRACT KING LOUIS THE FOURTEENTH FROM KING LOUIS THE SIXTEENTH, YOU GET KING LOUIS THE SECOND!
2-4
YOU DON'T?
RATS! I THOUGHT THAT WAS A PRETTY GOOD ANSWER!
SCHULZ

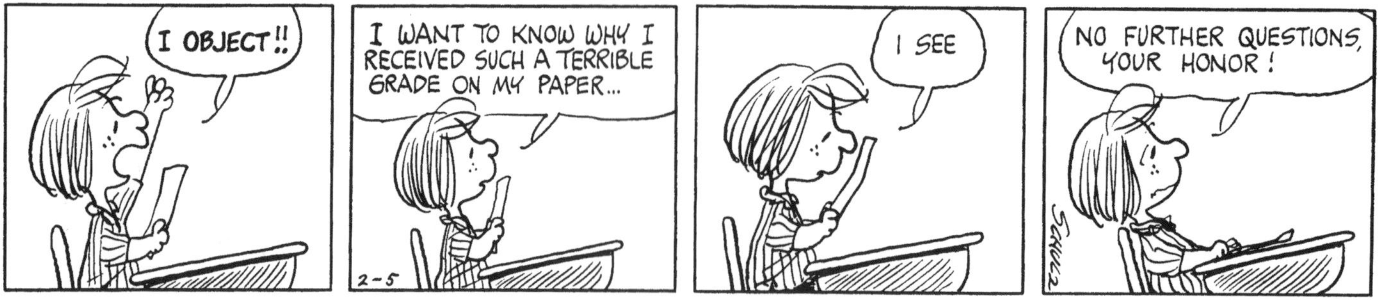

I OBJECT!!
I WANT TO KNOW WHY I RECEIVED SUCH A TERRIBLE GRADE ON MY PAPER...
2-5
I SEE
NO FURTHER QUESTIONS, YOUR HONOR!
SCHULZ

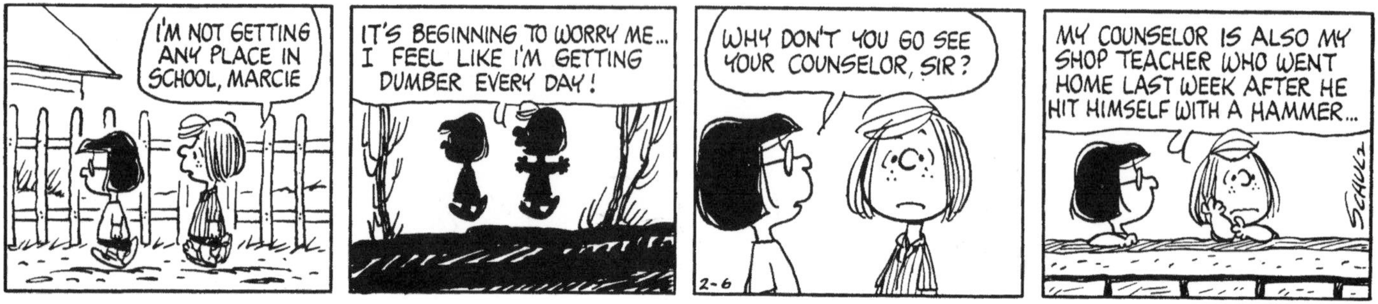

I'M NOT GETTING ANY PLACE IN SCHOOL, MARCIE
IT'S BEGINNING TO WORRY ME... I FEEL LIKE I'M GETTING DUMBER EVERY DAY!
WHY DON'T YOU GO SEE YOUR COUNSELOR, SIR?
2-6
MY COUNSELOR IS ALSO MY SHOP TEACHER WHO WENT HOME LAST WEEK AFTER HE HIT HIMSELF WITH A HAMMER...
SCHULZ

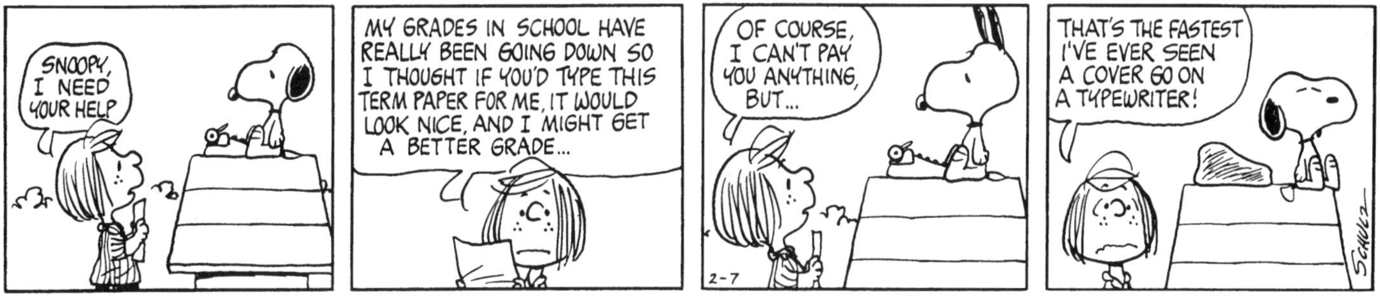
SNOOPY, I NEED YOUR HELP
MY GRADES IN SCHOOL HAVE REALLY BEEN GOING DOWN SO I THOUGHT IF YOU'D TYPE THIS TERM PAPER FOR ME, IT WOULD LOOK NICE, AND I MIGHT GET A BETTER GRADE...
OF COURSE, I CAN'T PAY YOU ANYTHING, BUT...
THAT'S THE FASTEST I'VE EVER SEEN A COVER GO ON A TYPEWRITER!

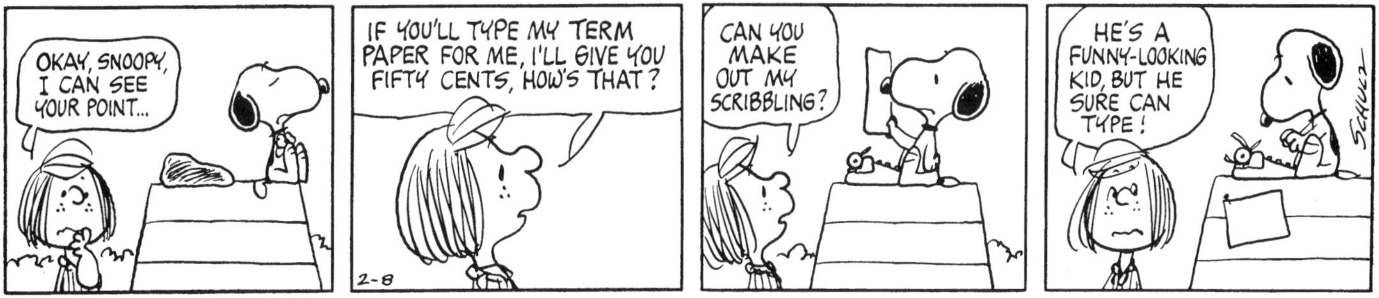
OKAY, SNOOPY, I CAN SEE YOUR POINT...
IF YOU'LL TYPE MY TERM PAPER FOR ME, I'LL GIVE YOU FIFTY CENTS, HOW'S THAT?
CAN YOU MAKE OUT MY SCRIBBLING?
HE'S A FUNNY-LOOKING KID, BUT HE SURE CAN TYPE!

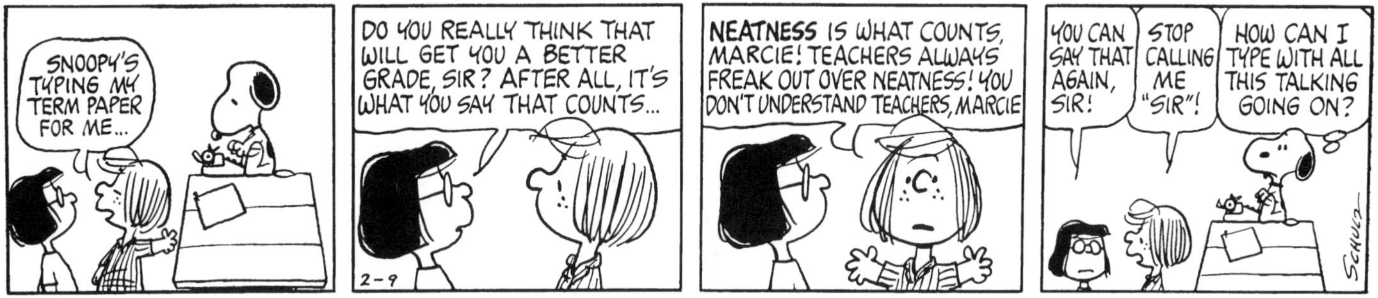
SNOOPY'S TYPING MY TERM PAPER FOR ME...
DO YOU REALLY THINK THAT WILL GET YOU A BETTER GRADE, SIR? AFTER ALL, IT'S WHAT YOU SAY THAT COUNTS...
NEATNESS IS WHAT COUNTS, MARCIE! TEACHERS ALWAYS FREAK OUT OVER NEATNESS! YOU DON'T UNDERSTAND TEACHERS, MARCIE
YOU CAN SAY THAT AGAIN, SIR!
STOP CALLING ME "SIR"!
HOW CAN I TYPE WITH ALL THIS TALKING GOING ON?

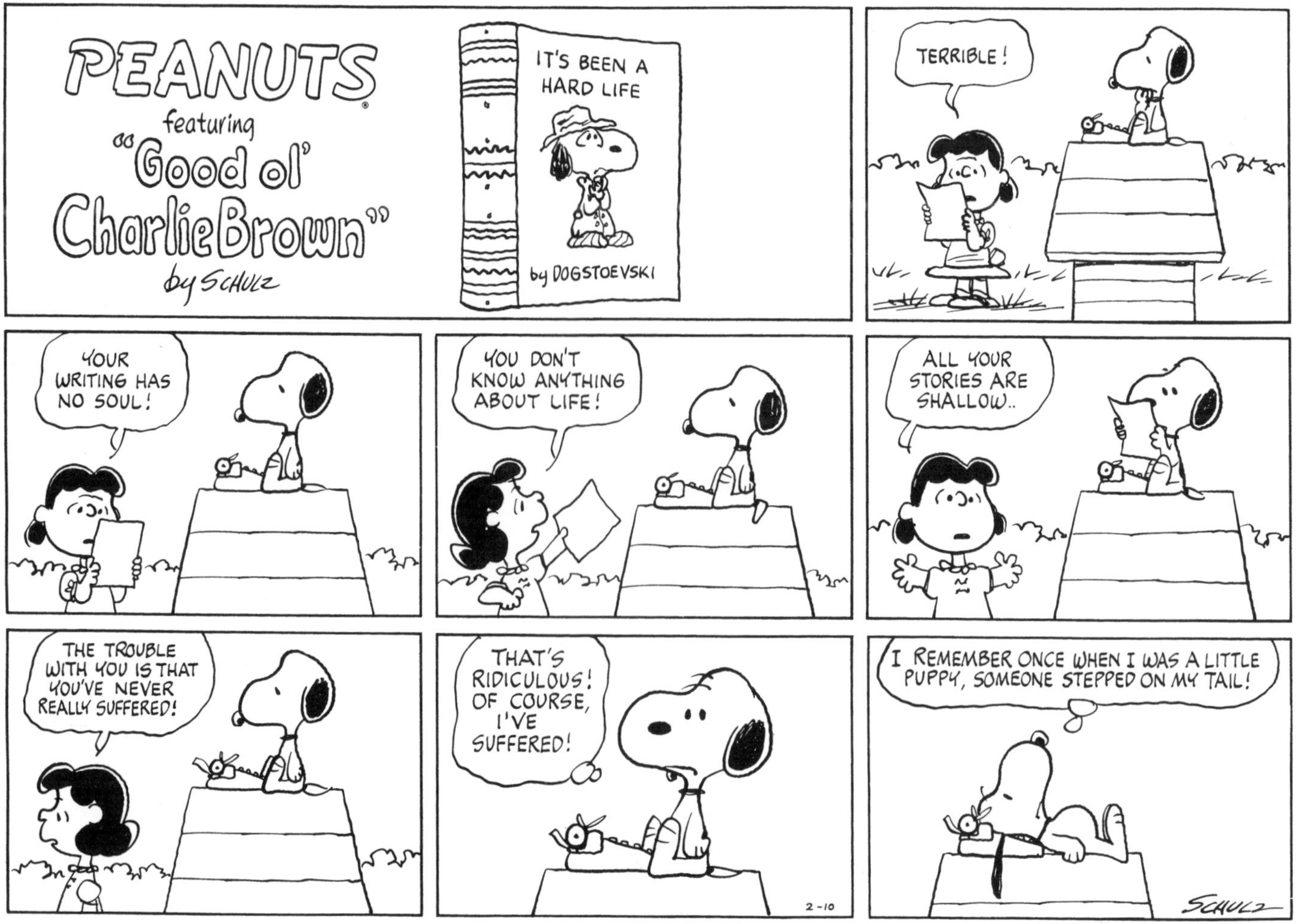
PEANUTS
featuring
"Good ol' CharlieBrown"
by SCHULZ
IT'S BEEN A HARD LIFE
by DOGSTOEVSKI
TERRIBLE!
YOUR WRITING HAS NO SOUL!
YOU DON'T KNOW ANYTHING ABOUT LIFE!
ALL YOUR STORIES ARE SHALLOW..
THE TROUBLE WITH YOU IS THAT YOU'VE NEVER REALLY SUFFERED!
THAT'S RIDICULOUS! OF COURSE, I'VE SUFFERED!
2-10
I REMEMBER ONCE WHEN I WAS A LITTLE PUPPY, SOMEONE STEPPED ON MY TAIL!
SCHULZ

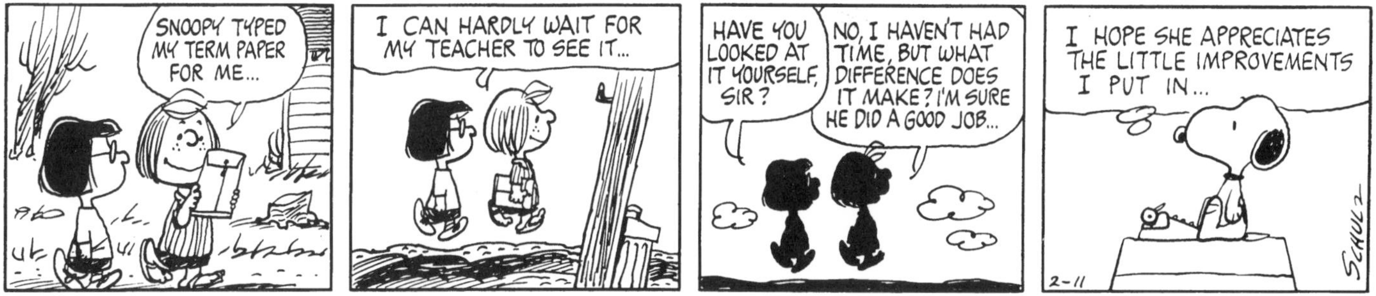
SNOOPY TYPED MY TERM PAPER FOR ME...
I CAN HARDLY WAIT FOR MY TEACHER TO SEE IT...
HAVE YOU LOOKED AT IT YOURSELF, SIR?
NO, I HAVEN'T HAD TIME, BUT WHAT DIFFERENCE DOES IT MAKE? I'M SURE HE DID A GOOD JOB...
I HOPE SHE APPRECIATES THE LITTLE IMPROVEMENTS I PUT IN...
2-11
SCHULZ

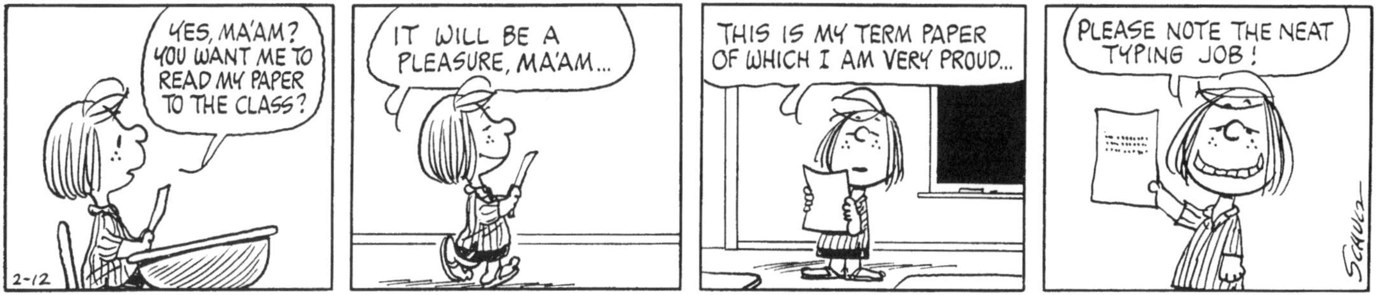
YES, MA'AM? YOU WANT ME TO READ MY PAPER TO THE CLASS?
2-12
IT WILL BE A PLEASURE, MA'AM...
THIS IS MY TERM PAPER OF WHICH I AM VERY PROUD...
PLEASE NOTE THE NEAT TYPING JOB!
SCHULZ

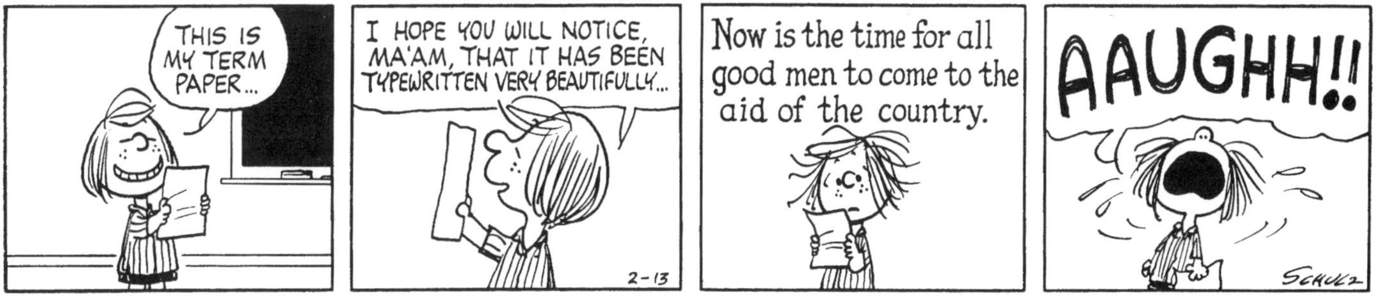
THIS IS MY TERM PAPER...
I HOPE YOU WILL NOTICE, MA'AM, THAT IT HAS BEEN TYPEWRITTEN VERY BEAUTIFULLY...
2-13
Now is the time for all good men to come to the aid of the country.
AAUGHH!!
SCHULZ

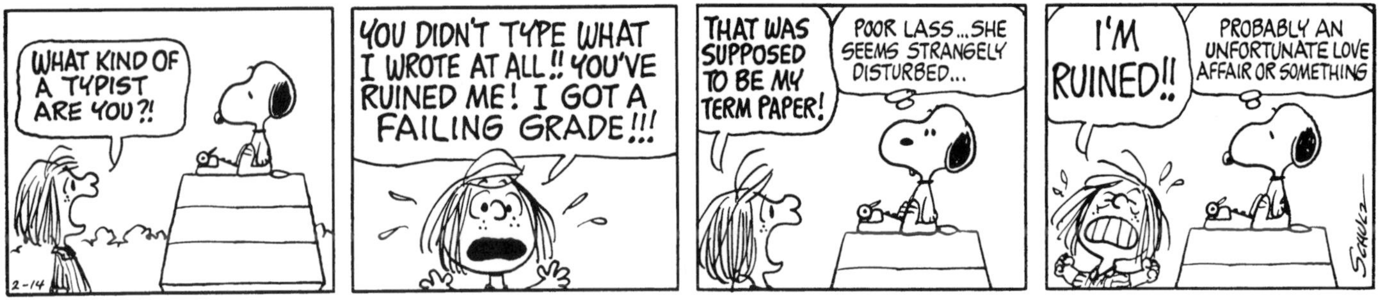
WHAT KIND OF A TYPIST ARE YOU?!
2-14
YOU DIDN'T TYPE WHAT I WROTE AT ALL!! YOU'VE RUINED ME! I GOT A FAILING GRADE!!!
THAT WAS SUPPOSED TO BE MY TERM PAPER!
POOR LASS...SHE SEEMS STRANGELY DISTURBED...
I'M RUINED!!
PROBABLY AN UNFORTUNATE LOVE AFFAIR OR SOMETHING

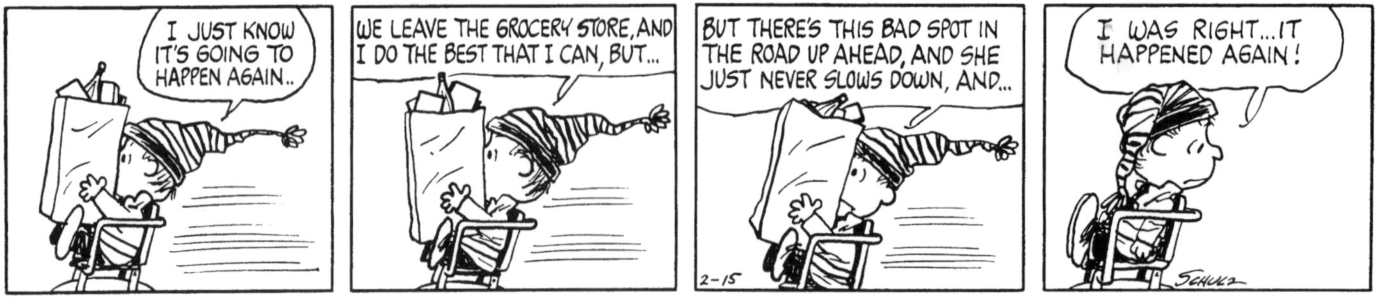
I JUST KNOW IT'S GOING TO HAPPEN AGAIN..
WE LEAVE THE GROCERY STORE, AND I DO THE BEST THAT I CAN, BUT...
BUT THERE'S THIS BAD SPOT IN THE ROAD UP AHEAD, AND SHE JUST NEVER SLOWS DOWN, AND...
2-15
I WAS RIGHT...IT HAPPENED AGAIN!

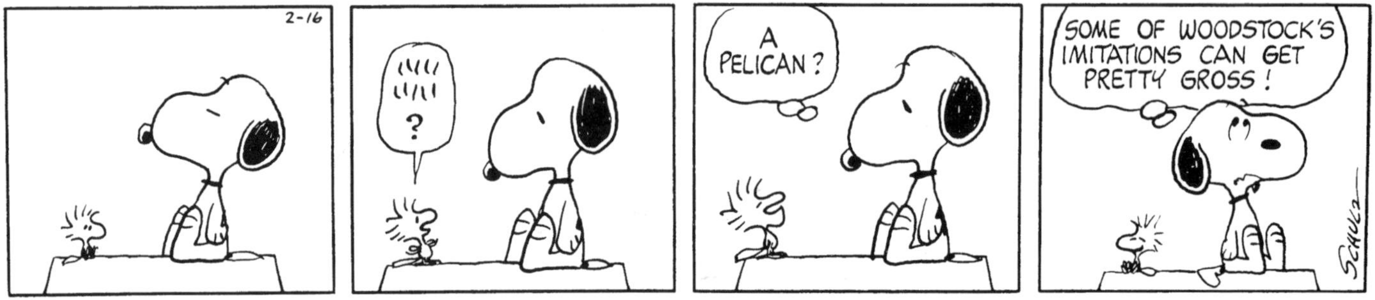
2-16
?
A PELICAN?
SOME OF WOODSTOCK'S IMITATIONS CAN GET PRETTY GROSS!

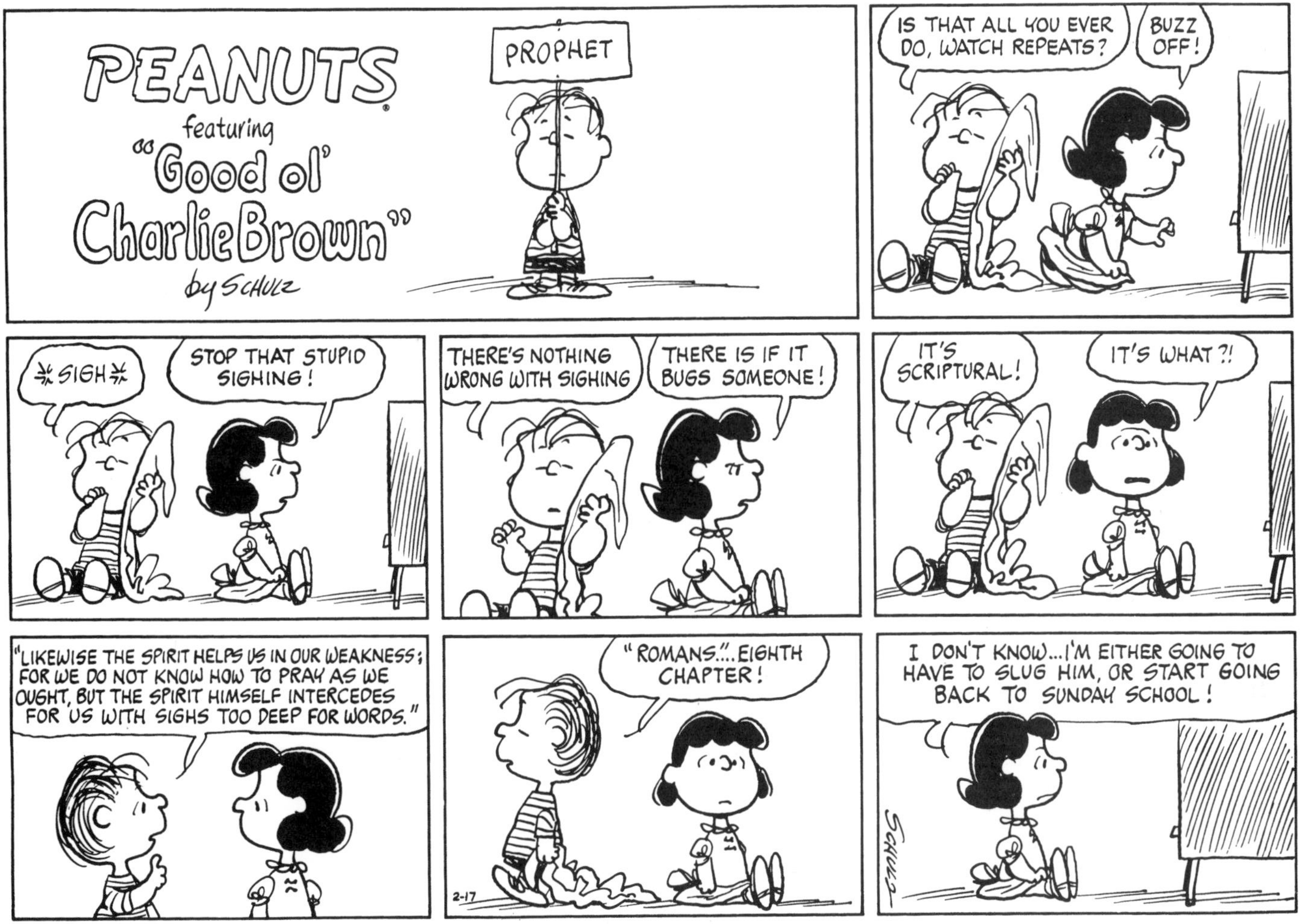
PEANUTS
featuring "Good ol' CharlieBrown"
by SCHULZ
PROPHET
IS THAT ALL YOU EVER DO, WATCH REPEATS?
BUZZ OFF!
SIGH
STOP THAT STUPID SIGHING!
THERE'S NOTHING WRONG WITH SIGHING
THERE IS IF IT BUGS SOMEONE!
IT'S SCRIPTURAL!
IT'S WHAT?!
"LIKEWISE THE SPIRIT HELPS US IN OUR WEAKNESS; FOR WE DO NOT KNOW HOW TO PRAY AS WE OUGHT, BUT THE SPIRIT HIMSELF INTERCEDES FOR US WITH SIGHS TOO DEEP FOR WORDS."
"ROMANS"...EIGHTH CHAPTER!
2-17
I DON'T KNOW...I'M EITHER GOING TO HAVE TO SLUG HIM, OR START GOING BACK TO SUNDAY SCHOOL!
SCHULZ

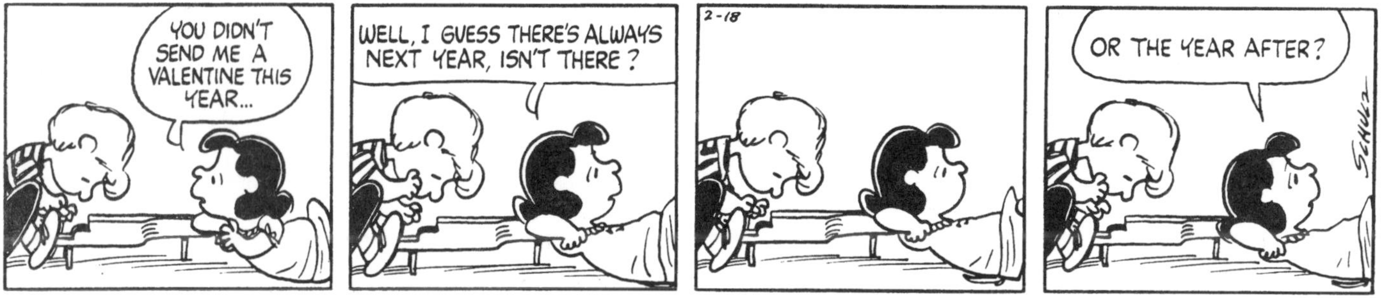
YOU DIDN'T SEND ME A VALENTINE THIS YEAR...
WELL, I GUESS THERE'S ALWAYS NEXT YEAR, ISN'T THERE ?
2-18
OR THE YEAR AFTER?
SCHULZ

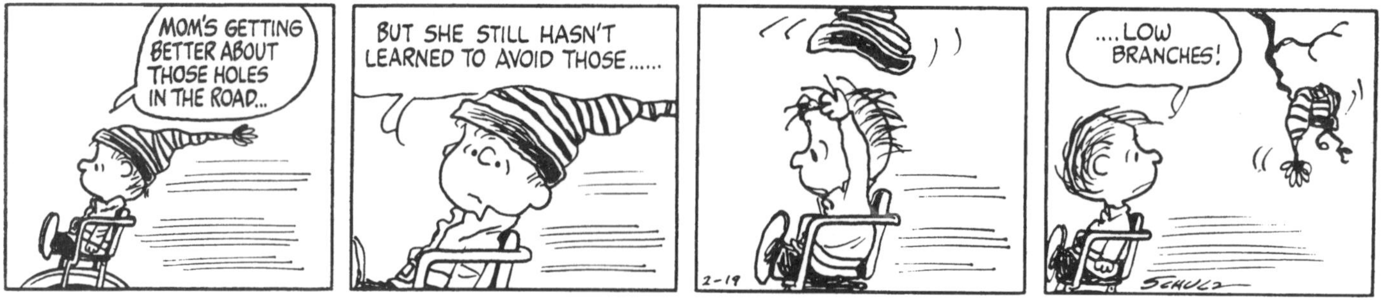
MOM'S GETTING BETTER ABOUT THOSE HOLES IN THE ROAD...
BUT SHE STILL HASN'T LEARNED TO AVOID THOSE......
2-19
....LOW BRANCHES!
SCHULZ

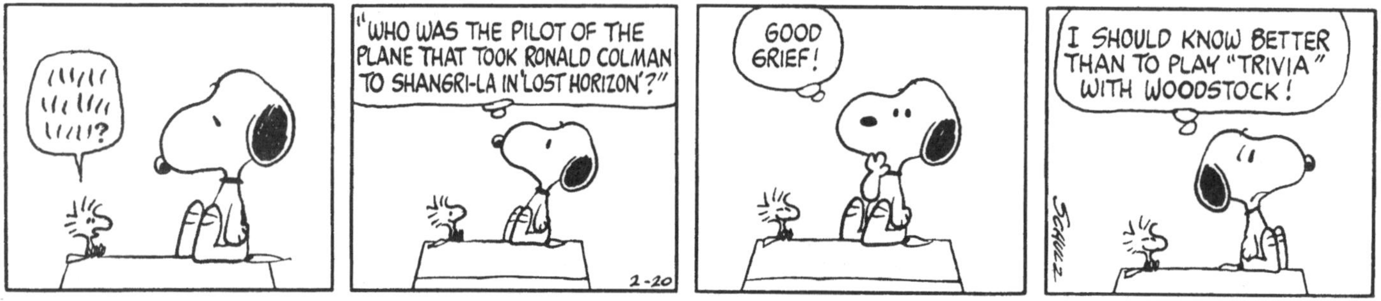
"WHO WAS THE PILOT OF THE PLANE THAT TOOK RONALD COLMAN TO SHANGRI-LA IN 'LOST HORIZON'?"
2-20
GOOD GRIEF!
I SHOULD KNOW BETTER THAN TO PLAY "TRIVIA" WITH WOODSTOCK!
SCHULZ

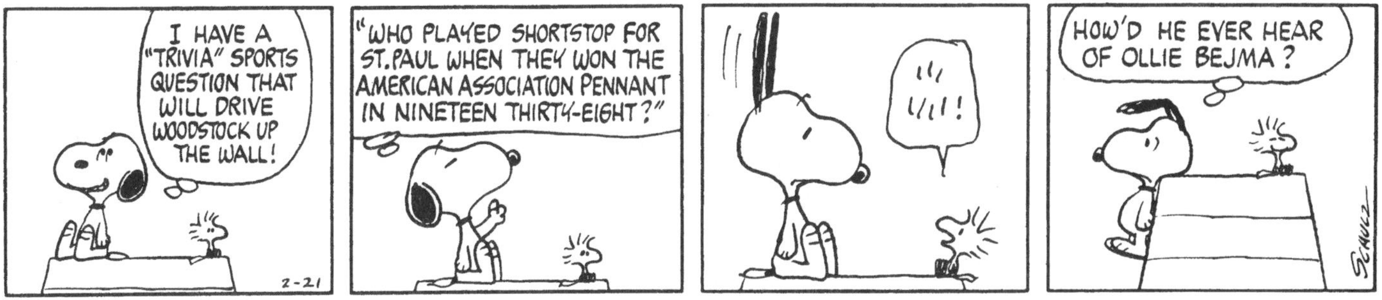
I HAVE A "TRIVIA" SPORTS QUESTION THAT WILL DRIVE WOODSTOCK UP THE WALL!
2-21
"WHO PLAYED SHORTSTOP FOR ST. PAUL WHEN THEY WON THE AMERICAN ASSOCIATION PENNANT IN NINETEEN THIRTY-EIGHT?"
HOW'D HE EVER HEAR OF OLLIE BEJMA?
SCHULZ

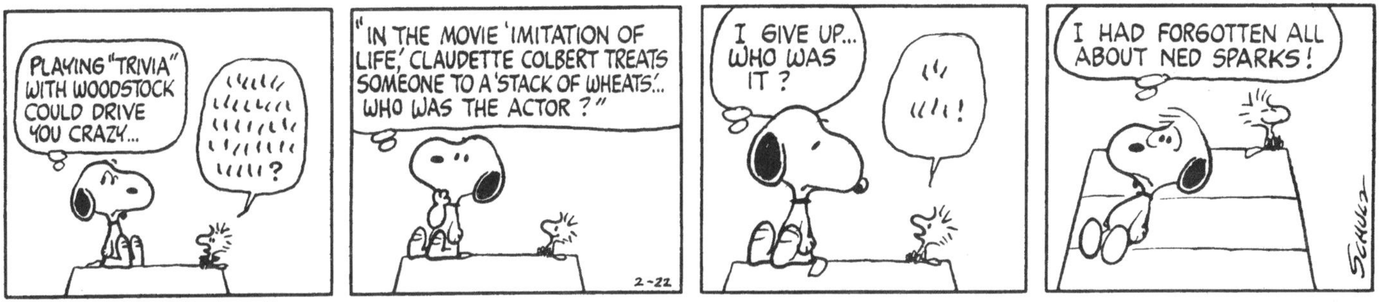
PLAYING "TRIVIA" WITH WOODSTOCK COULD DRIVE YOU CRAZY...
"IN THE MOVIE 'IMITATION OF LIFE,' CLAUDETTE COLBERT TREATS SOMEONE TO A 'STACK OF WHEATS'... WHO WAS THE ACTOR?"
2-22
I GIVE UP... WHO WAS IT?
I HAD FORGOTTEN ALL ABOUT NED SPARKS!
SCHULZ

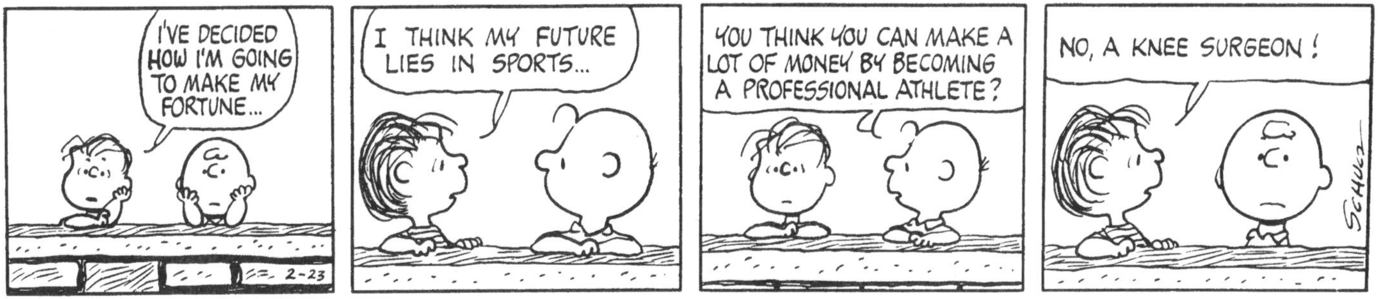
I'VE DECIDED HOW I'M GOING TO MAKE MY FORTUNE...
2-23
I THINK MY FUTURE LIES IN SPORTS...
YOU THINK YOU CAN MAKE A LOT OF MONEY BY BECOMING A PROFESSIONAL ATHLETE?
NO, A KNEE SURGEON!
SCHULZ

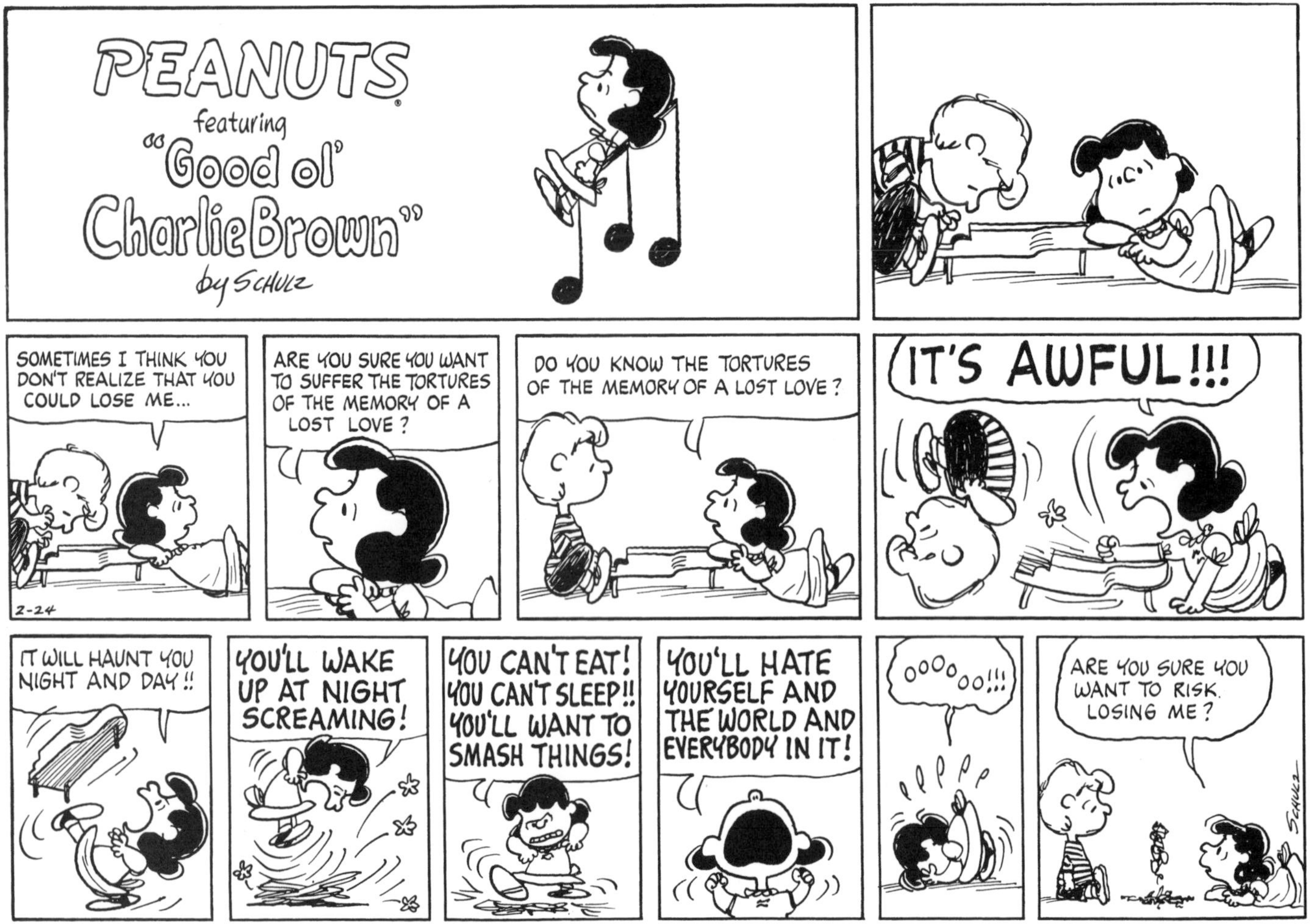
PEANUTS
featuring
"Good ol' Charlie Brown"
by SCHULZ
SOMETIMES I THINK YOU DON'T REALIZE THAT YOU COULD LOSE ME...
2-24
ARE YOU SURE YOU WANT TO SUFFER THE TORTURES OF THE MEMORY OF A LOST LOVE?
DO YOU KNOW THE TORTURES OF THE MEMORY OF A LOST LOVE?
IT'S AWFUL!!!
IT WILL HAUNT YOU NIGHT AND DAY!!
YOU'LL WAKE UP AT NIGHT SCREAMING!
YOU CAN'T EAT! YOU CAN'T SLEEP!! YOU'LL WANT TO SMASH THINGS!
YOU'LL HATE YOURSELF AND THE WORLD AND EVERYBODY IN IT!
OOOOOO!!!
ARE YOU SURE YOU WANT TO RISK LOSING ME?
SCHULZ

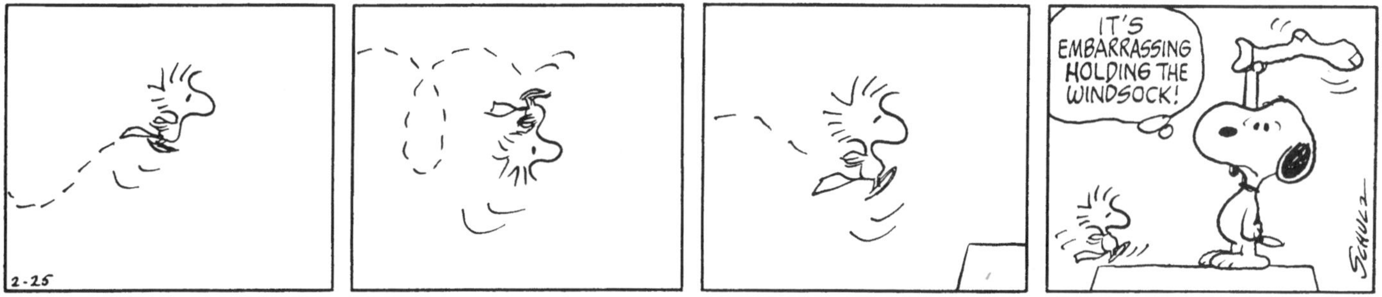
2-25
IT'S EMBARRASSING HOLDING THE WINDSOCK!
SCHULZ

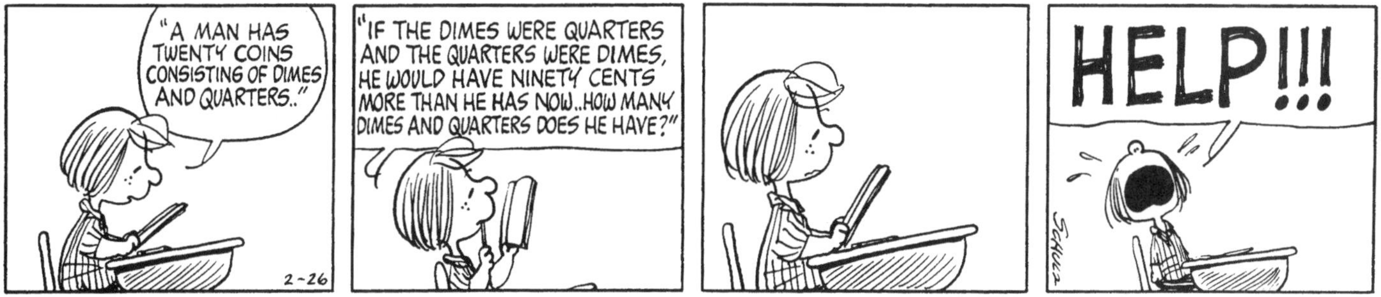
"A MAN HAS TWENTY COINS CONSISTING OF DIMES AND QUARTERS.."
2-26
"IF THE DIMES WERE QUARTERS AND THE QUARTERS WERE DIMES, HE WOULD HAVE NINETY CENTS MORE THAN HE HAS NOW..HOW MANY DIMES AND QUARTERS DOES HE HAVE?"
HELP!!!
SCHULZ

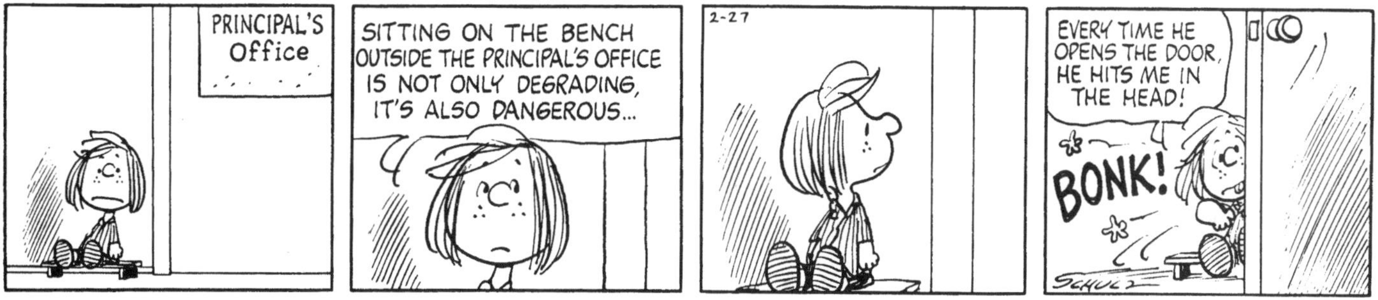
PRINCIPAL'S Office
SITTING ON THE BENCH OUTSIDE THE PRINCIPAL'S OFFICE IS NOT ONLY DEGRADING, IT'S ALSO DANGEROUS...
2-27
EVERY TIME HE OPENS THE DOOR, HE HITS ME IN THE HEAD!
BONK!
SCHULZ

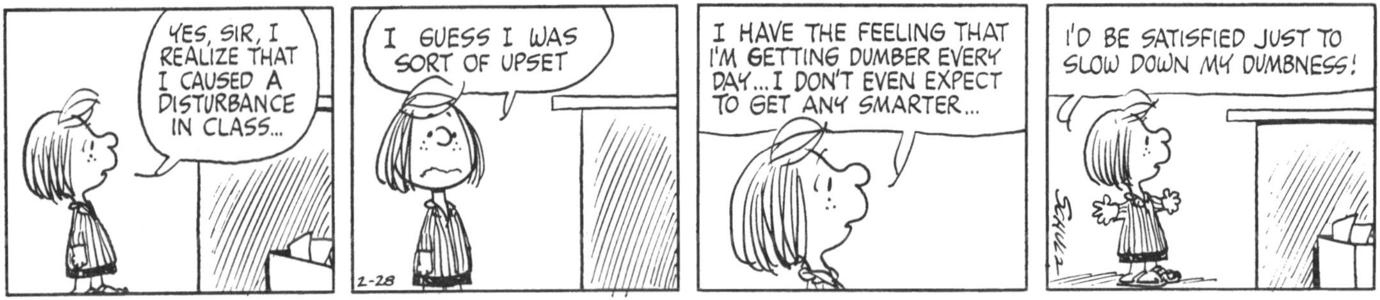
YES, SIR, I REALIZE THAT I CAUSED A DISTURBANCE IN CLASS...
I GUESS I WAS SORT OF UPSET
2-28
I HAVE THE FEELING THAT I'M GETTING DUMBER EVERY DAY...I DON'T EVEN EXPECT TO GET ANY SMARTER...
I'D BE SATISFIED JUST TO SLOW DOWN MY DUMBNESS!

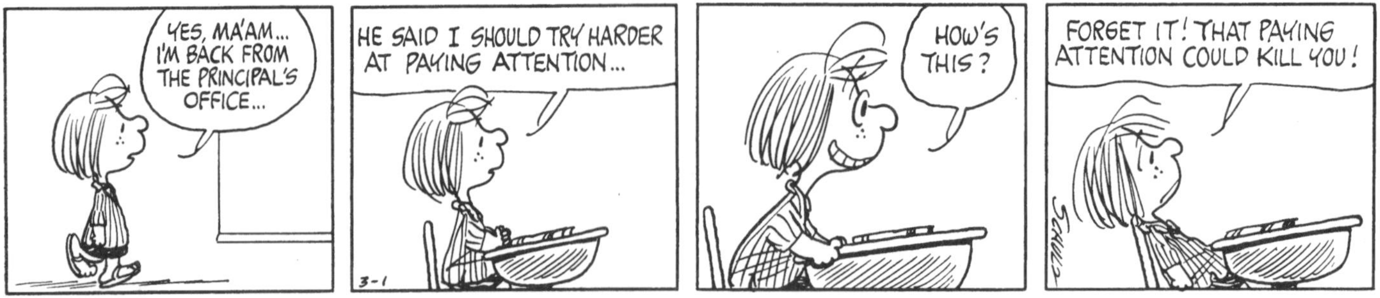
YES, MA'AM... I'M BACK FROM THE PRINCIPAL'S OFFICE...
HE SAID I SHOULD TRY HARDER AT PAYING ATTENTION...
3-1
HOW'S THIS?
FORGET IT! THAT PAYING ATTENTION COULD KILL YOU!

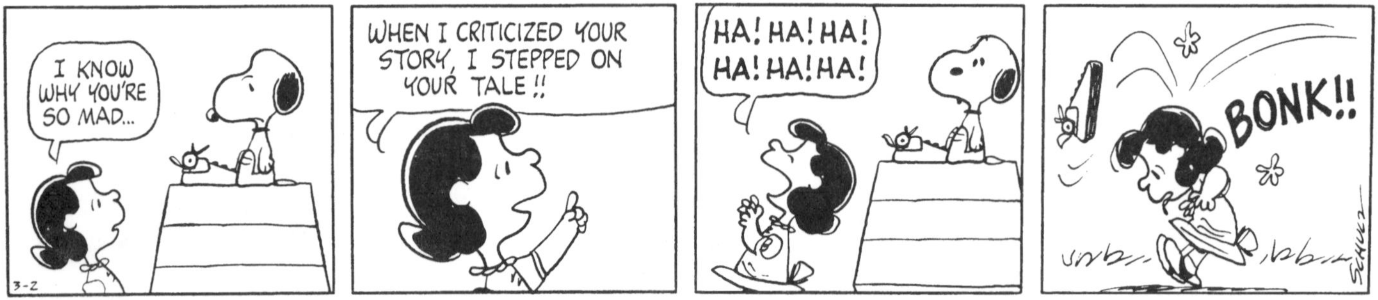
I KNOW WHY YOU'RE SO MAD...
3-2
WHEN I CRITICIZED YOUR STORY, I STEPPED ON YOUR TALE!!
HA! HA! HA! HA! HA! HA!
BONK!!

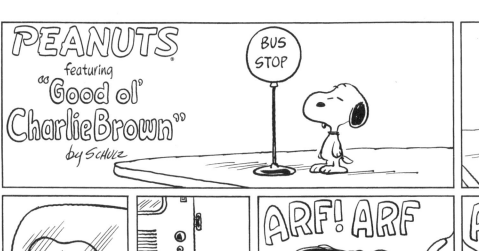

PEANUTS featuring "Good ol' CharlieBrown" by Schulz

BUS STOP

AT LAST!

ARF! ARF
ARF! ARF!

ARF! ARF!
ARF! ARF!!

3-3

THAT'S THE TROUBLE WITH LIVING IN A QUIET NEIGHBORHOOD...

I HAVE TO TAKE A BUS ALL THE WAY DOWNTOWN WHEN I WANT TO CHASE CARS!

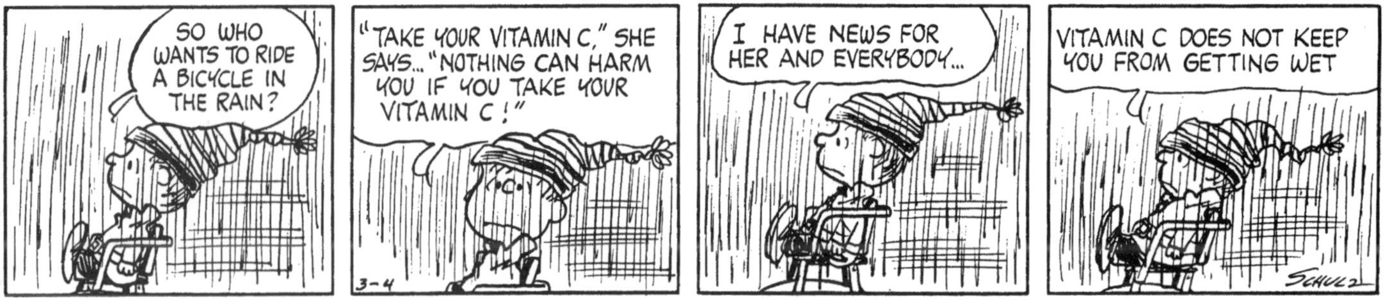
SO WHO WANTS TO RIDE A BICYCLE IN THE RAIN?
"TAKE YOUR VITAMIN C," SHE SAYS... "NOTHING CAN HARM YOU IF YOU TAKE YOUR VITAMIN C!"
3-4
I HAVE NEWS FOR HER AND EVERYBODY...
VITAMIN C DOES NOT KEEP YOU FROM GETTING WET
SCHULZ

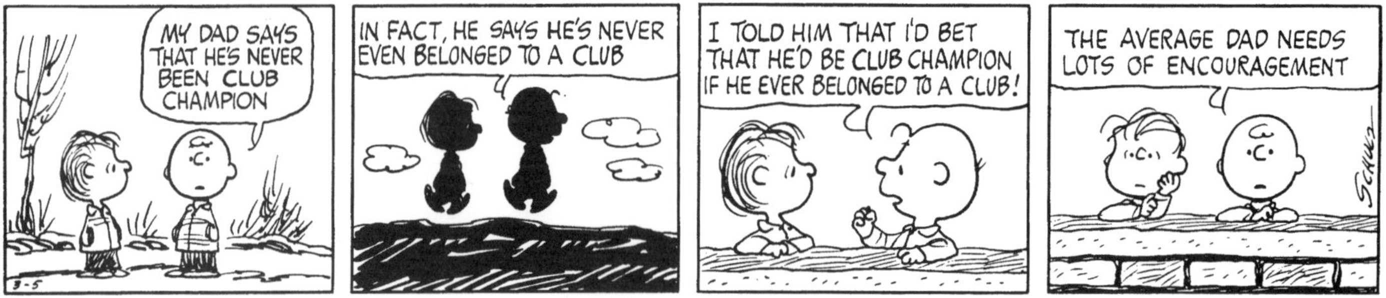
MY DAD SAYS THAT HE'S NEVER BEEN CLUB CHAMPION
3-5
IN FACT, HE SAYS HE'S NEVER EVEN BELONGED TO A CLUB
I TOLD HIM THAT I'D BET THAT HE'D BE CLUB CHAMPION IF HE EVER BELONGED TO A CLUB!
THE AVERAGE DAD NEEDS LOTS OF ENCOURAGEMENT
SCHULZ

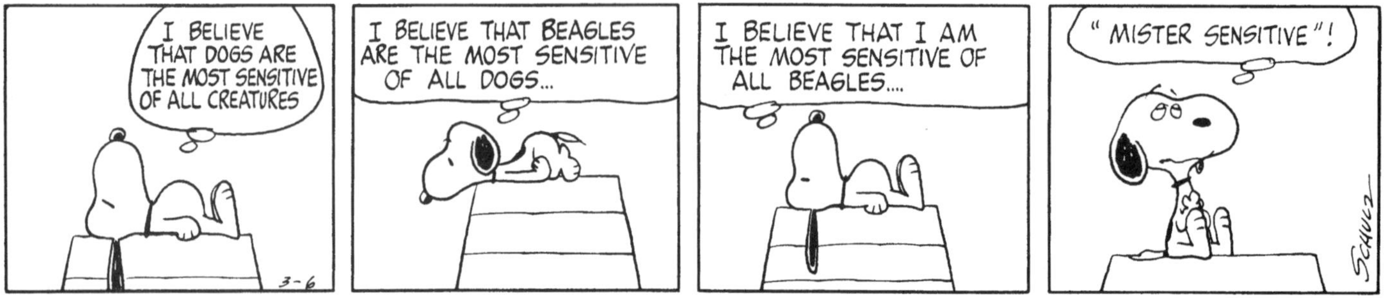
I BELIEVE THAT DOGS ARE THE MOST SENSITIVE OF ALL CREATURES
3-6
I BELIEVE THAT BEAGLES ARE THE MOST SENSITIVE OF ALL DOGS...
I BELIEVE THAT I AM THE MOST SENSITIVE OF ALL BEAGLES....
"MISTER SENSITIVE"!
SCHULZ

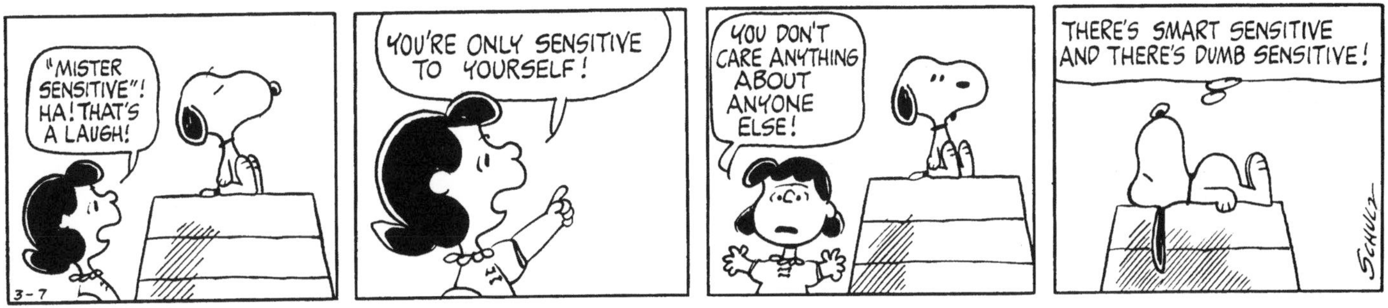
"MISTER SENSITIVE"! HA! THAT'S A LAUGH!
YOU'RE ONLY SENSITIVE TO YOURSELF!
YOU DON'T CARE ANYTHING ABOUT ANYONE ELSE!
THERE'S SMART SENSITIVE AND THERE'S DUMB SENSITIVE!

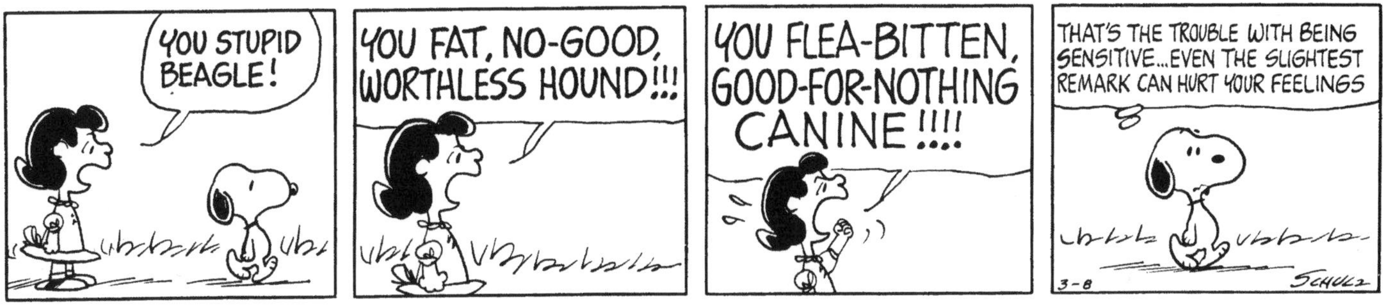
YOU STUPID BEAGLE!
YOU FAT, NO-GOOD, WORTHLESS HOUND!!!
YOU FLEA-BITTEN, GOOD-FOR-NOTHING CANINE!!!!
THAT'S THE TROUBLE WITH BEING SENSITIVE...EVEN THE SLIGHTEST REMARK CAN HURT YOUR FEELINGS

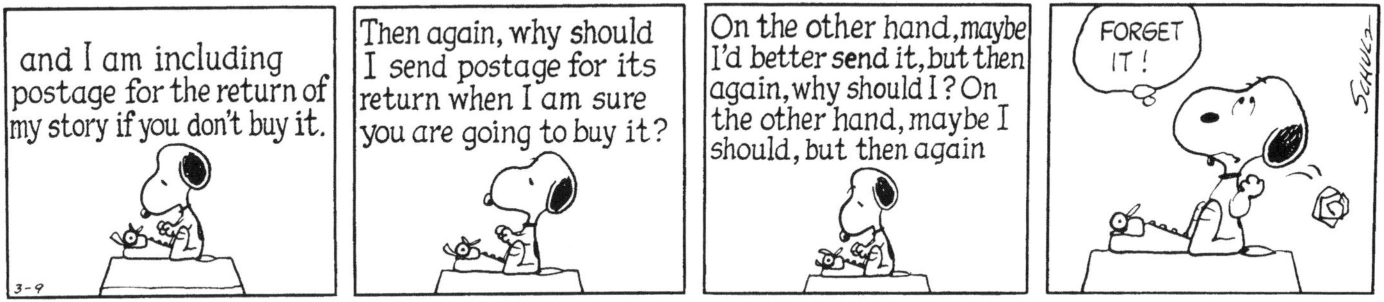
and I am including postage for the return of my story if you don't buy it.
Then again, why should I send postage for its return when I am sure you are going to buy it?
On the other hand, maybe I'd better send it, but then again, why should I? On the other hand, maybe I should, but then again
FORGET IT!

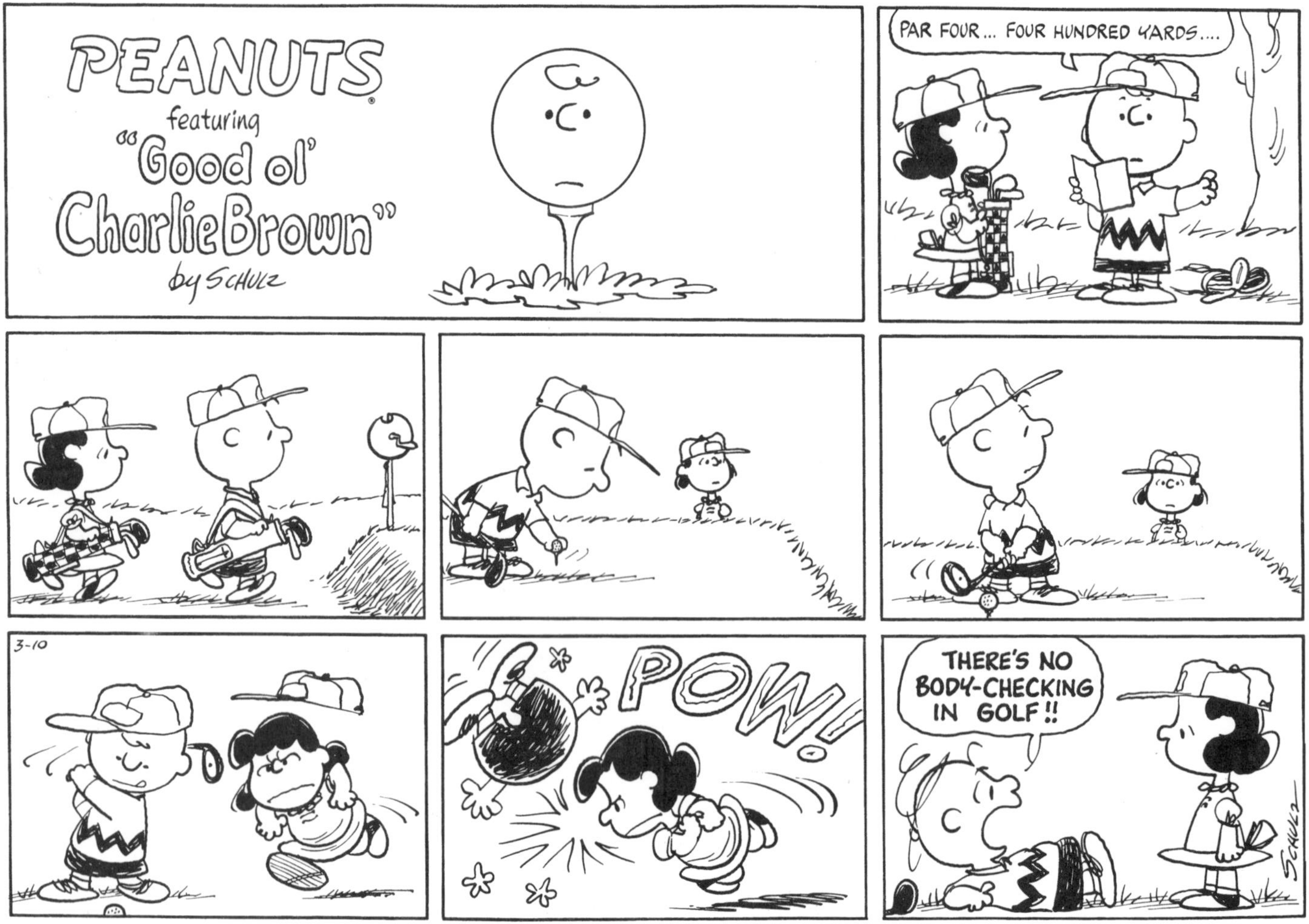
PEANUTS®
featuring "Good ol' Charlie Brown"
by SCHULZ
PAR FOUR... FOUR HUNDRED YARDS....
3-10
POW!
THERE'S NO BODY-CHECKING IN GOLF!!
SCHULZ

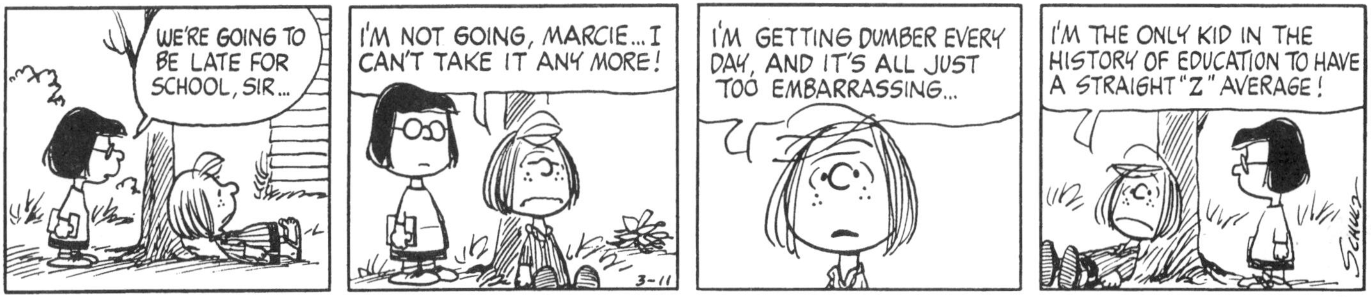
WE'RE GOING TO BE LATE FOR SCHOOL, SIR...
I'M NOT GOING, MARCIE... I CAN'T TAKE IT ANY MORE!
I'M GETTING DUMBER EVERY DAY, AND IT'S ALL JUST TOO EMBARRASSING...
I'M THE ONLY KID IN THE HISTORY OF EDUCATION TO HAVE A STRAIGHT "Z" AVERAGE!

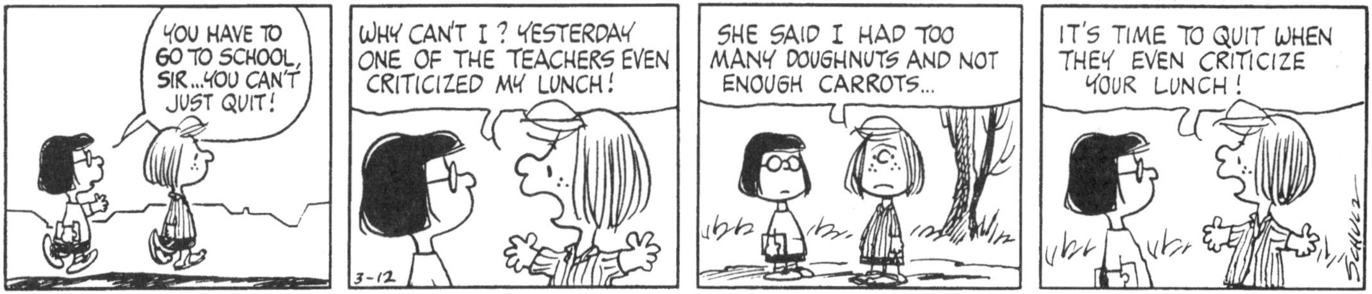
YOU HAVE TO GO TO SCHOOL, SIR...YOU CAN'T JUST QUIT!
WHY CAN'T I? YESTERDAY ONE OF THE TEACHERS EVEN CRITICIZED MY LUNCH!
SHE SAID I HAD TOO MANY DOUGHNUTS AND NOT ENOUGH CARROTS...
IT'S TIME TO QUIT WHEN THEY EVEN CRITICIZE YOUR LUNCH!

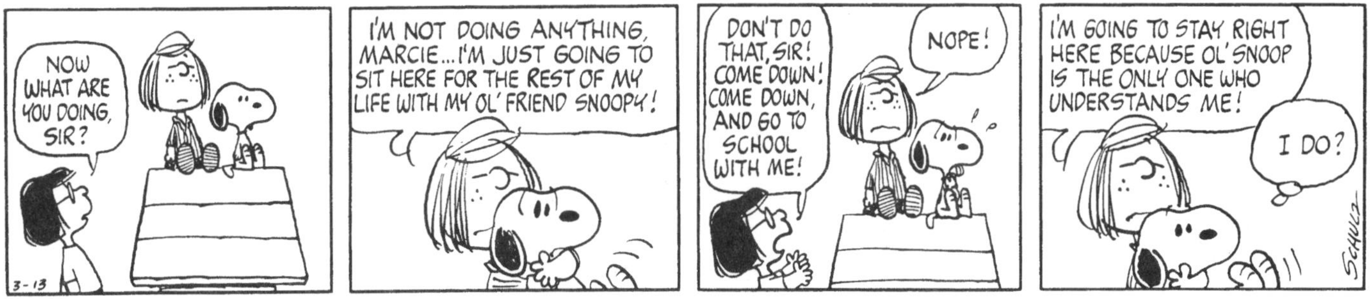
NOW WHAT ARE YOU DOING, SIR?
I'M NOT DOING ANYTHING, MARCIE...I'M JUST GOING TO SIT HERE FOR THE REST OF MY LIFE WITH MY OL' FRIEND SNOOPY!
DON'T DO THAT, SIR! COME DOWN! COME DOWN, AND GO TO SCHOOL WITH ME!
NOPE!
I'M GOING TO STAY RIGHT HERE BECAUSE OL' SNOOP IS THE ONLY ONE WHO UNDERSTANDS ME!
I DO?

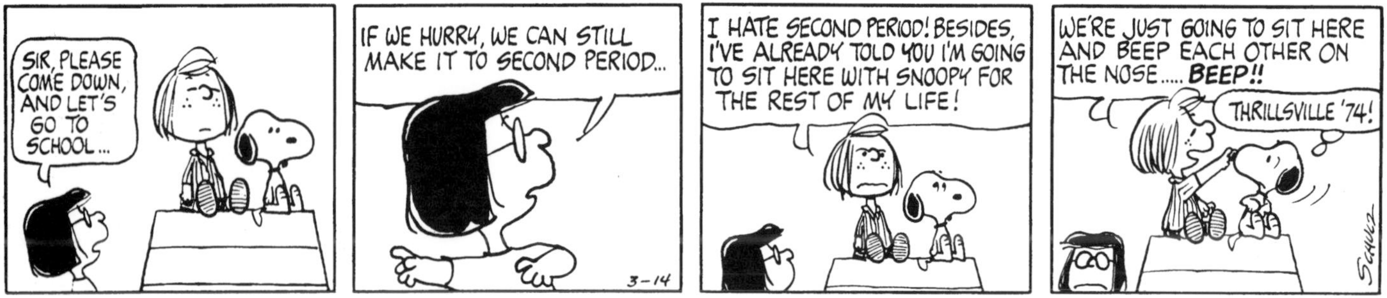
SIR, PLEASE COME DOWN, AND LET'S GO TO SCHOOL...
IF WE HURRY, WE CAN STILL MAKE IT TO SECOND PERIOD...
3-14
I HATE SECOND PERIOD! BESIDES, I'VE ALREADY TOLD YOU I'M GOING TO SIT HERE WITH SNOOPY FOR THE REST OF MY LIFE!
WE'RE JUST GOING TO SIT HERE AND BEEP EACH OTHER ON THE NOSE..... BEEP!!
THRILLSVILLE '74!
SCHULZ

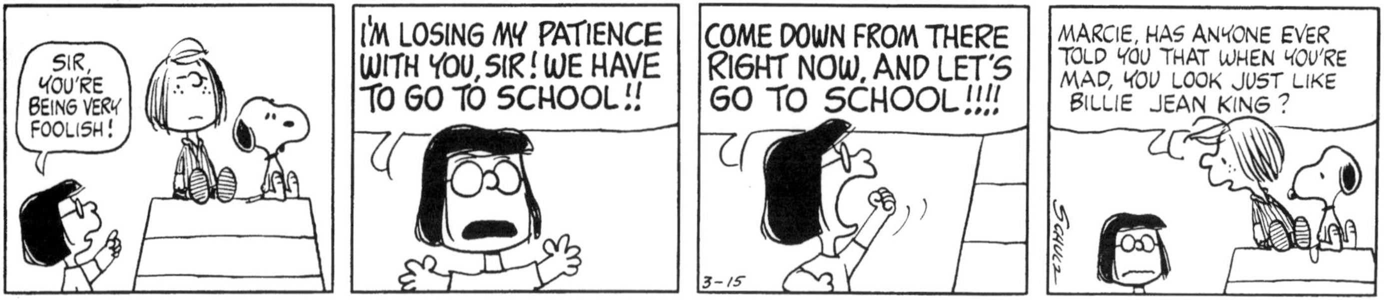
SIR, YOU'RE BEING VERY FOOLISH!
I'M LOSING MY PATIENCE WITH YOU, SIR! WE HAVE TO GO TO SCHOOL!!
COME DOWN FROM THERE RIGHT NOW, AND LET'S GO TO SCHOOL!!!!
3-15
MARCIE, HAS ANYONE EVER TOLD YOU THAT WHEN YOU'RE MAD, YOU LOOK JUST LIKE BILLIE JEAN KING?
SCHULZ

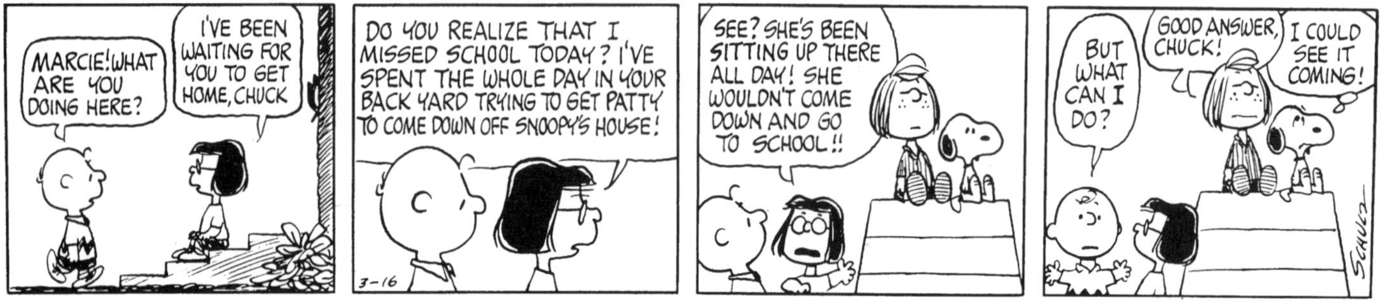
MARCIE! WHAT ARE YOU DOING HERE?
I'VE BEEN WAITING FOR YOU TO GET HOME, CHUCK
DO YOU REALIZE THAT I MISSED SCHOOL TODAY? I'VE SPENT THE WHOLE DAY IN YOUR BACK YARD TRYING TO GET PATTY TO COME DOWN OFF SNOOPY'S HOUSE!
3-16
SEE? SHE'S BEEN SITTING UP THERE ALL DAY! SHE WOULDN'T COME DOWN AND GO TO SCHOOL!!
BUT WHAT CAN I DO?
GOOD ANSWER, CHUCK!
I COULD SEE IT COMING!
SCHULZ

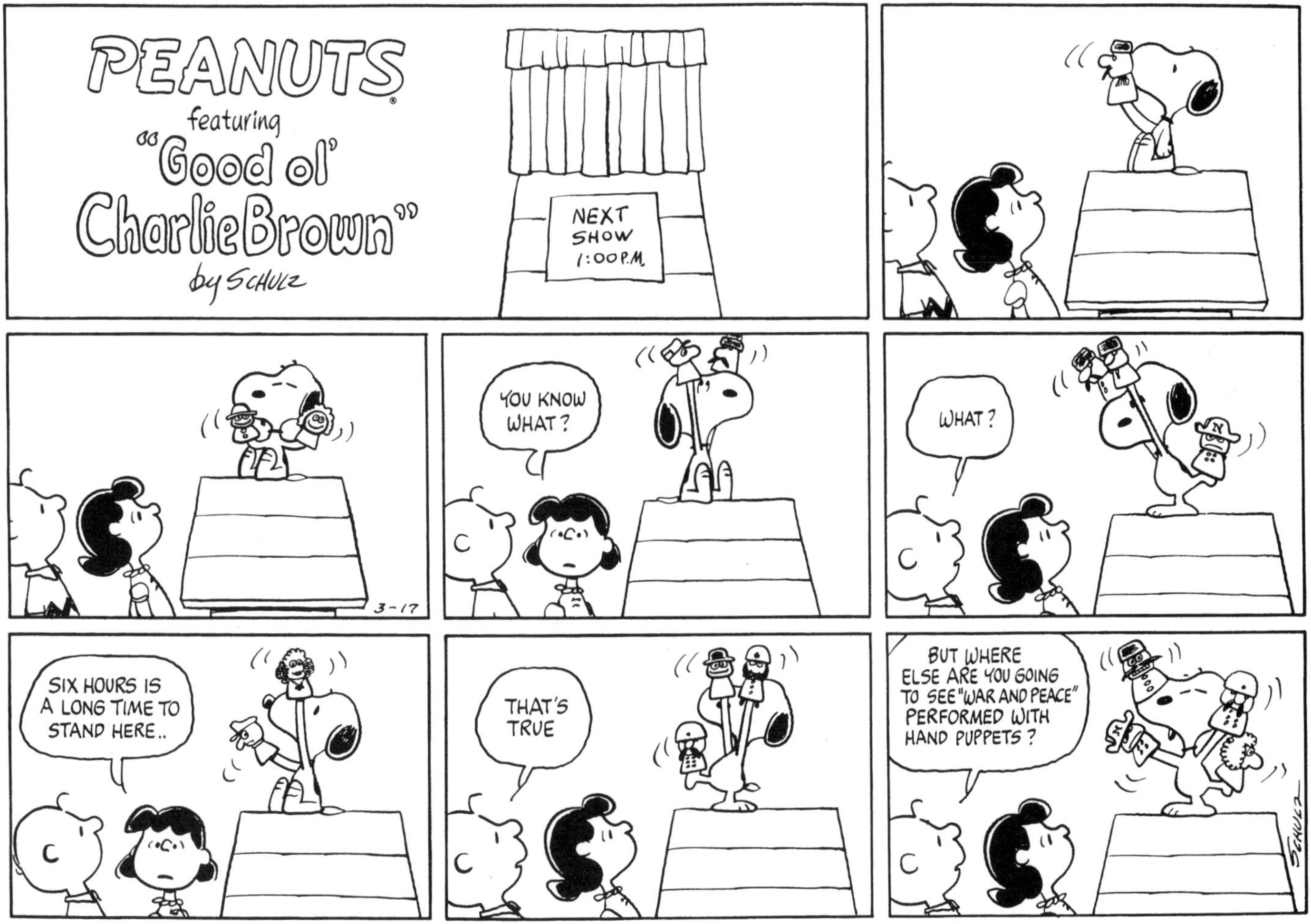
PEANUTS
featuring
"Good ol' CharlieBrown"
by SCHULZ
NEXT SHOW 1:00 P.M.
3-17
YOU KNOW WHAT?
WHAT?
SIX HOURS IS A LONG TIME TO STAND HERE..
THAT'S TRUE
BUT WHERE ELSE ARE YOU GOING TO SEE "WAR AND PEACE" PERFORMED WITH HAND PUPPETS?
SCHULZ

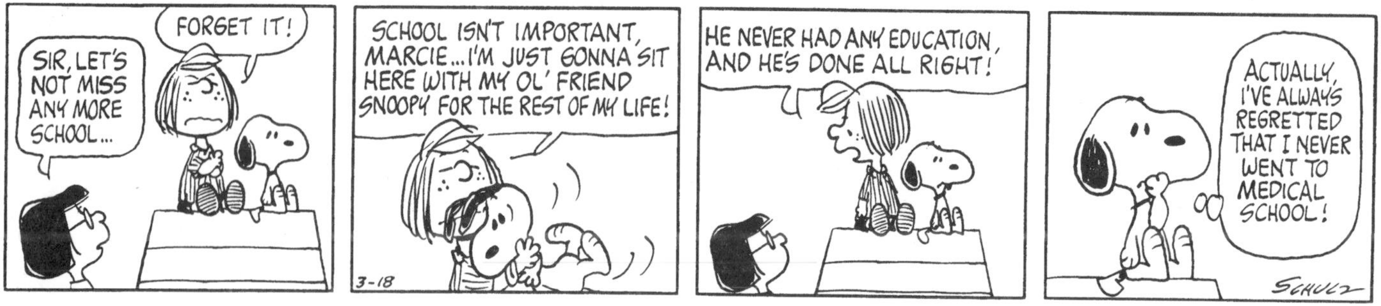
SIR, LET'S NOT MISS ANY MORE SCHOOL...
FORGET IT!
SCHOOL ISN'T IMPORTANT, MARCIE...I'M JUST GONNA SIT HERE WITH MY OL' FRIEND SNOOPY FOR THE REST OF MY LIFE!
3-18
HE NEVER HAD ANY EDUCATION, AND HE'S DONE ALL RIGHT!
ACTUALLY, I'VE ALWAYS REGRETTED THAT I NEVER WENT TO MEDICAL SCHOOL!

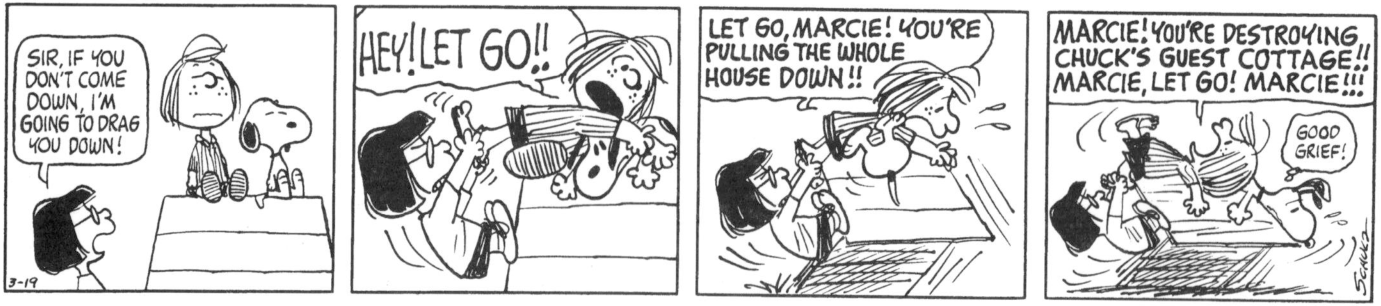
SIR, IF YOU DON'T COME DOWN, I'M GOING TO DRAG YOU DOWN!
3-19
HEY! LET GO!!
LET GO, MARCIE! YOU'RE PULLING THE WHOLE HOUSE DOWN!!
MARCIE! YOU'RE DESTROYING CHUCK'S GUEST COTTAGE!! MARCIE, LET GO! MARCIE!!!
GOOD GRIEF!

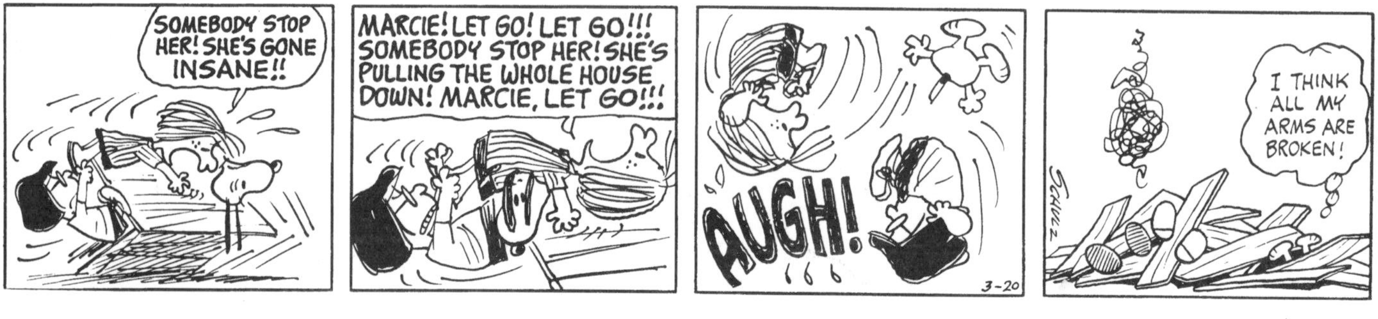
SOMEBODY STOP HER! SHE'S GONE INSANE!!
MARCIE! LET GO! LET GO!!! SOMEBODY STOP HER! SHE'S PULLING THE WHOLE HOUSE DOWN! MARCIE, LET GO!!!
AUGH!
3-20
I THINK ALL MY ARMS ARE BROKEN!

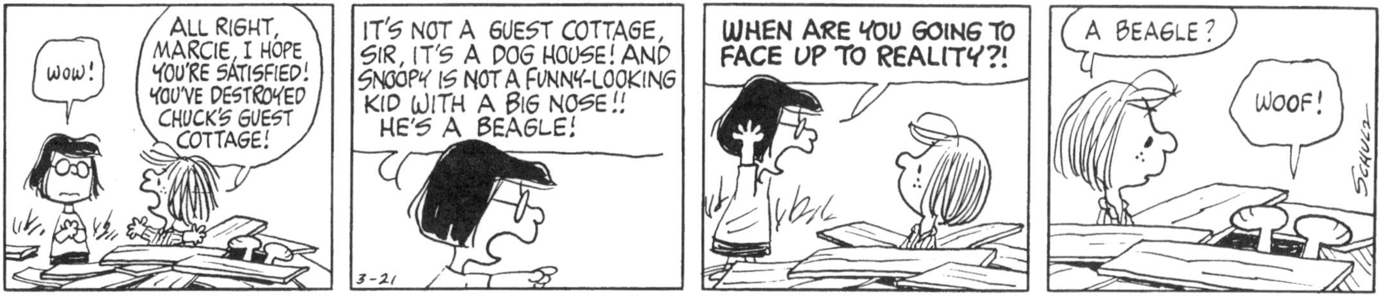
WOW!
ALL RIGHT, MARCIE, I HOPE YOU'RE SATISFIED! YOU'VE DESTROYED CHUCK'S GUEST COTTAGE!
IT'S NOT A GUEST COTTAGE, SIR, IT'S A DOG HOUSE! AND SNOOPY IS NOT A FUNNY-LOOKING KID WITH A BIG NOSE!! HE'S A BEAGLE!
3-21
WHEN ARE YOU GOING TO FACE UP TO REALITY?!
A BEAGLE?
WOOF!
SCHULZ

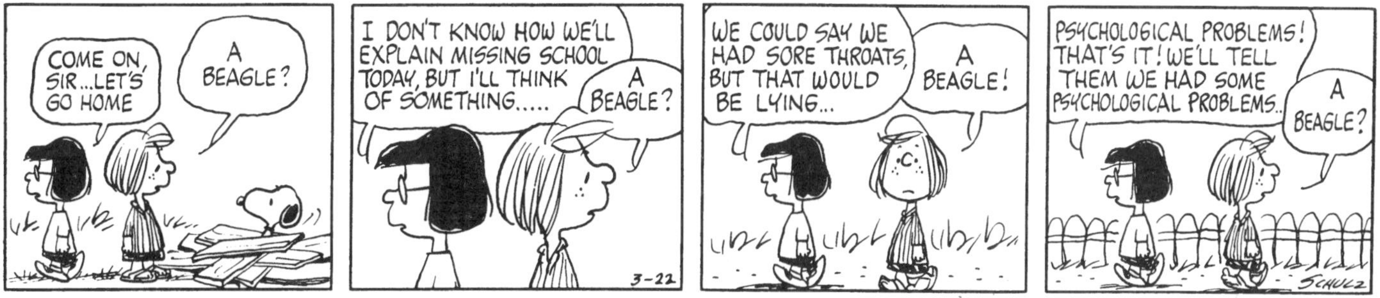
COME ON, SIR...LET'S GO HOME
A BEAGLE?
I DON'T KNOW HOW WE'LL EXPLAIN MISSING SCHOOL TODAY, BUT I'LL THINK OF SOMETHING.....
A BEAGLE?
3-22
WE COULD SAY WE HAD SORE THROATS, BUT THAT WOULD BE LYING...
A BEAGLE!
PSYCHOLOGICAL PROBLEMS! THAT'S IT! WE'LL TELL THEM WE HAD SOME PSYCHOLOGICAL PROBLEMS..
A BEAGLE?
SCHULZ

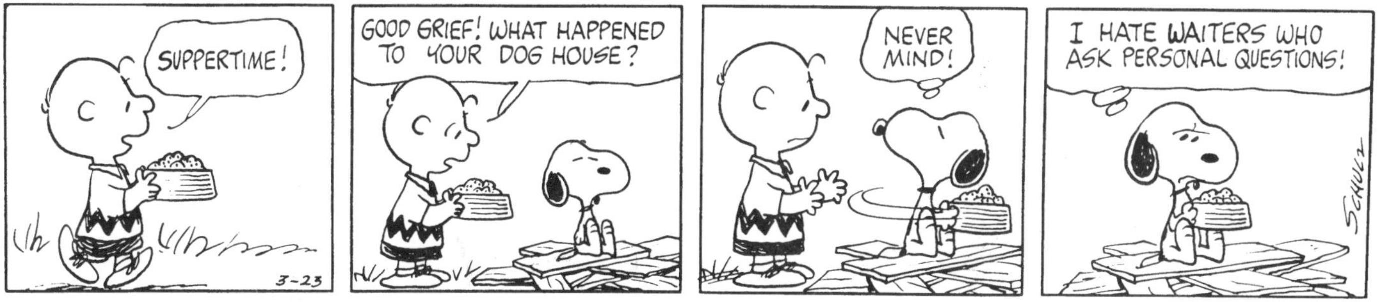
SUPPERTIME!
3-23
GOOD GRIEF! WHAT HAPPENED TO YOUR DOG HOUSE?
NEVER MIND!
I HATE WAITERS WHO ASK PERSONAL QUESTIONS!
SCHULZ

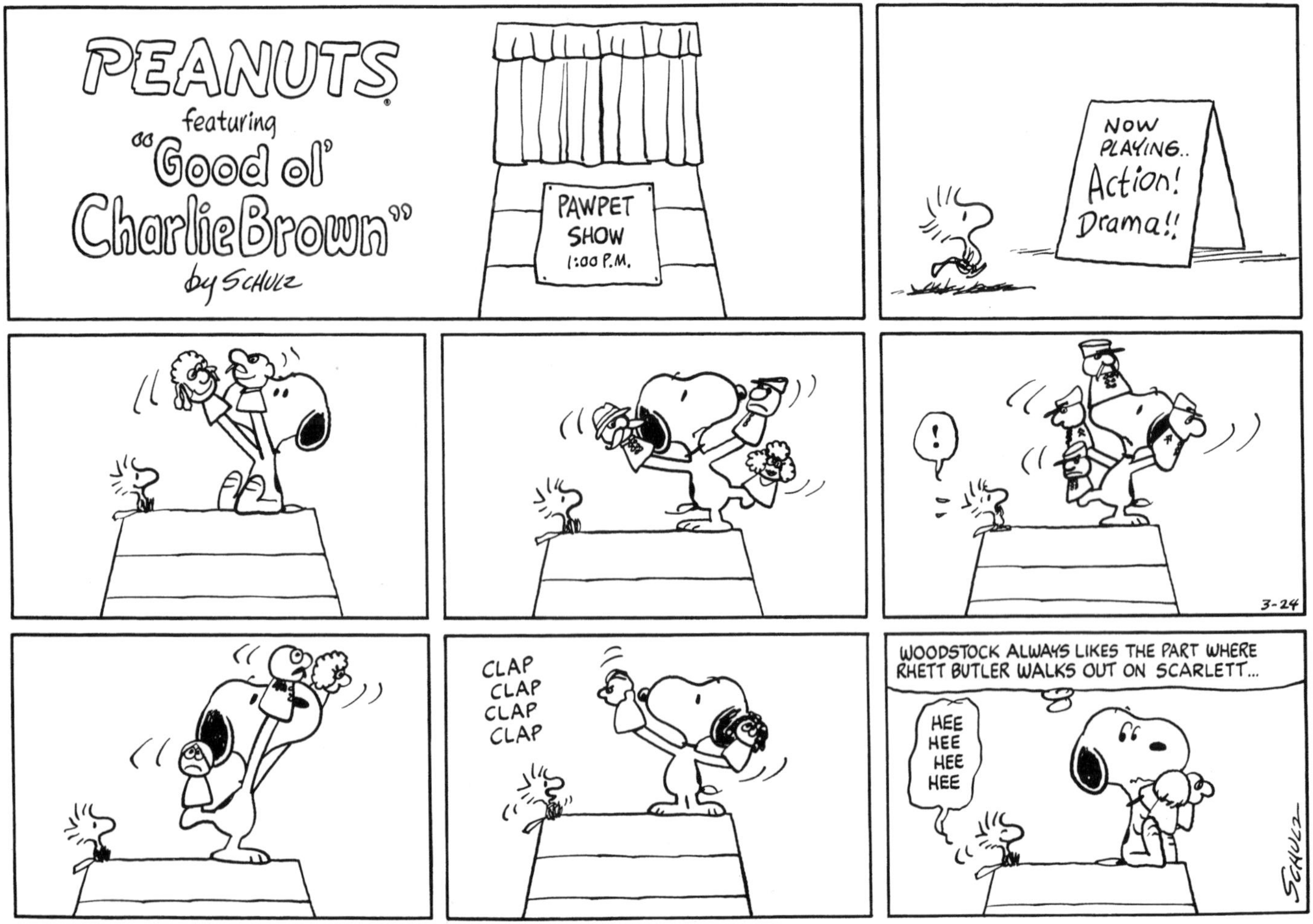
PEANUTS
featuring
"Good ol' Charlie Brown"
by SCHULZ
PAWPET SHOW 1:00 P.M.
NOW PLAYING.. Action! Drama!!
!
3-24
CLAP CLAP CLAP CLAP
WOODSTOCK ALWAYS LIKES THE PART WHERE RHETT BUTLER WALKS OUT ON SCARLETT...
HEE HEE HEE HEE
SCHULZ

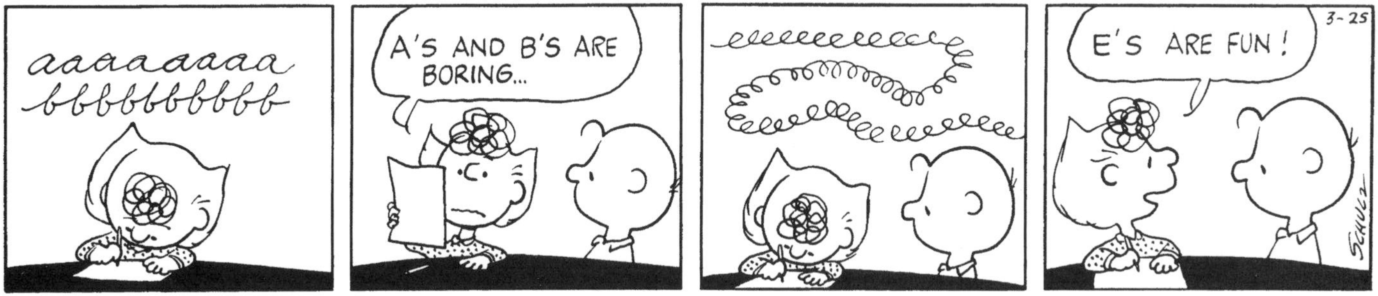
A'S AND B'S ARE BORING...
E'S ARE FUN!
3-25
SCHULZ

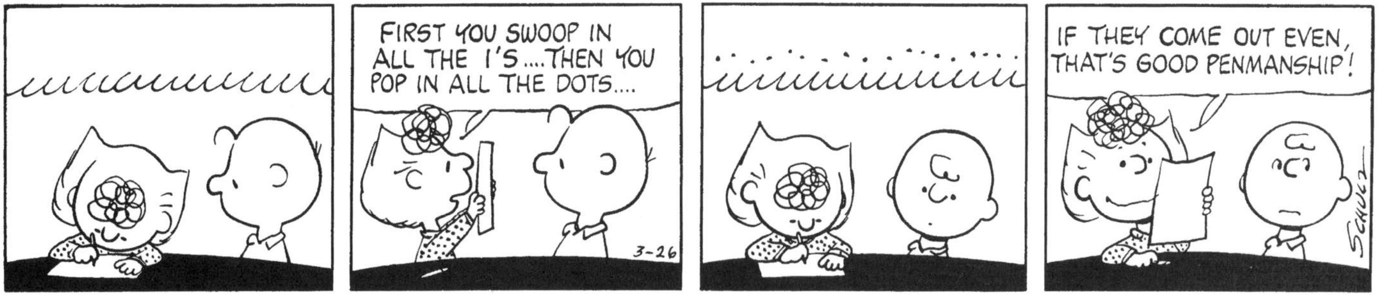
FIRST YOU SWOOP IN ALL THE I'S....THEN YOU POP IN ALL THE DOTS....
3-26
IF THEY COME OUT EVEN, THAT'S GOOD PENMANSHIP!
SCHULZ

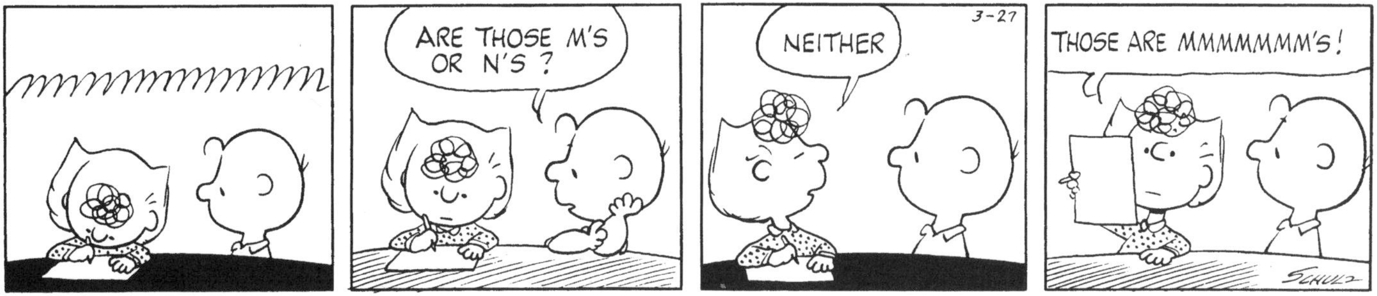
ARE THOSE M'S OR N'S ?
3-27
NEITHER
THOSE ARE MMMMMMM'S!
SCHULZ

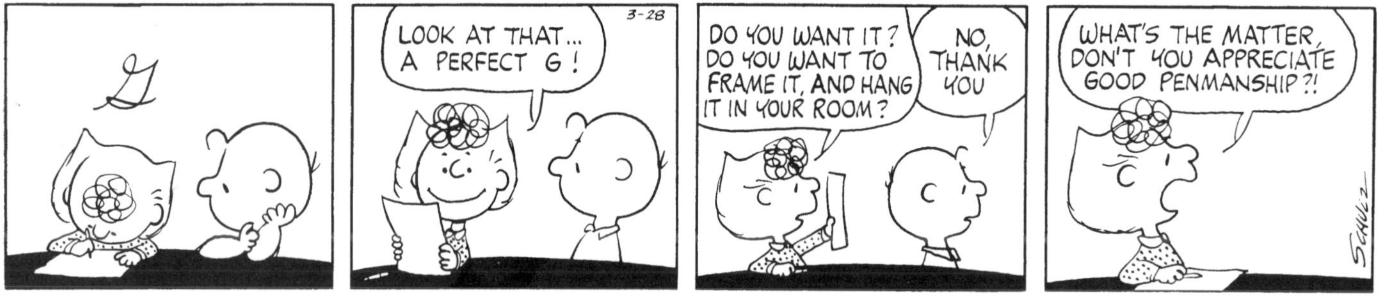
G
3-28
LOOK AT THAT... A PERFECT G!
DO YOU WANT IT? DO YOU WANT TO FRAME IT, AND HANG IT IN YOUR ROOM?
NO, THANK YOU
WHAT'S THE MATTER, DON'T YOU APPRECIATE GOOD PENMANSHIP?!
SCHULZ

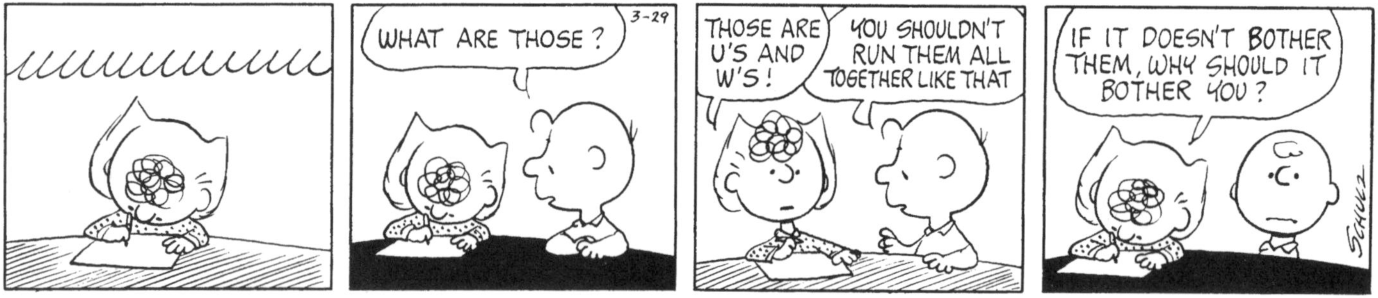
uuuuuuuuuuuuu
3-29
WHAT ARE THOSE?
THOSE ARE U'S AND W'S!
YOU SHOULDN'T RUN THEM ALL TOGETHER LIKE THAT
IF IT DOESN'T BOTHER THEM, WHY SHOULD IT BOTHER YOU?
SCHULZ

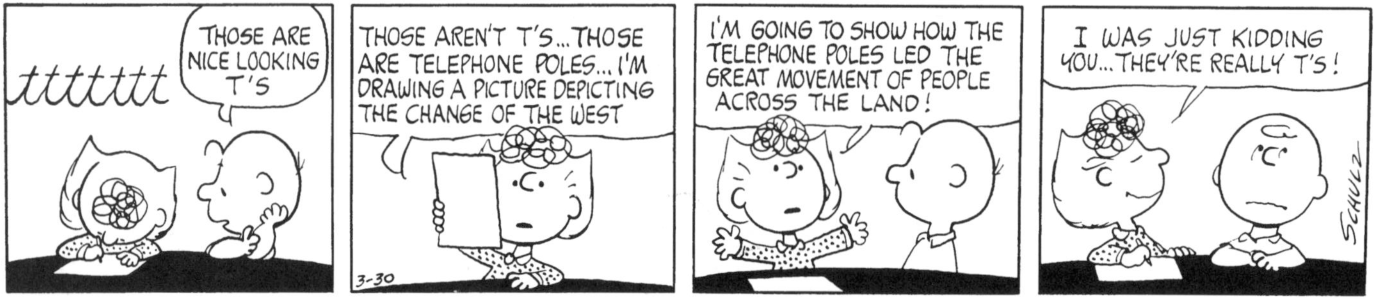
ttttttt
THOSE ARE NICE LOOKING T'S
THOSE AREN'T T'S...THOSE ARE TELEPHONE POLES...I'M DRAWING A PICTURE DEPICTING THE CHANGE OF THE WEST
3-30
I'M GOING TO SHOW HOW THE TELEPHONE POLES LED THE GREAT MOVEMENT OF PEOPLE ACROSS THE LAND!
I WAS JUST KIDDING YOU...THEY'RE REALLY T'S!
SCHULZ

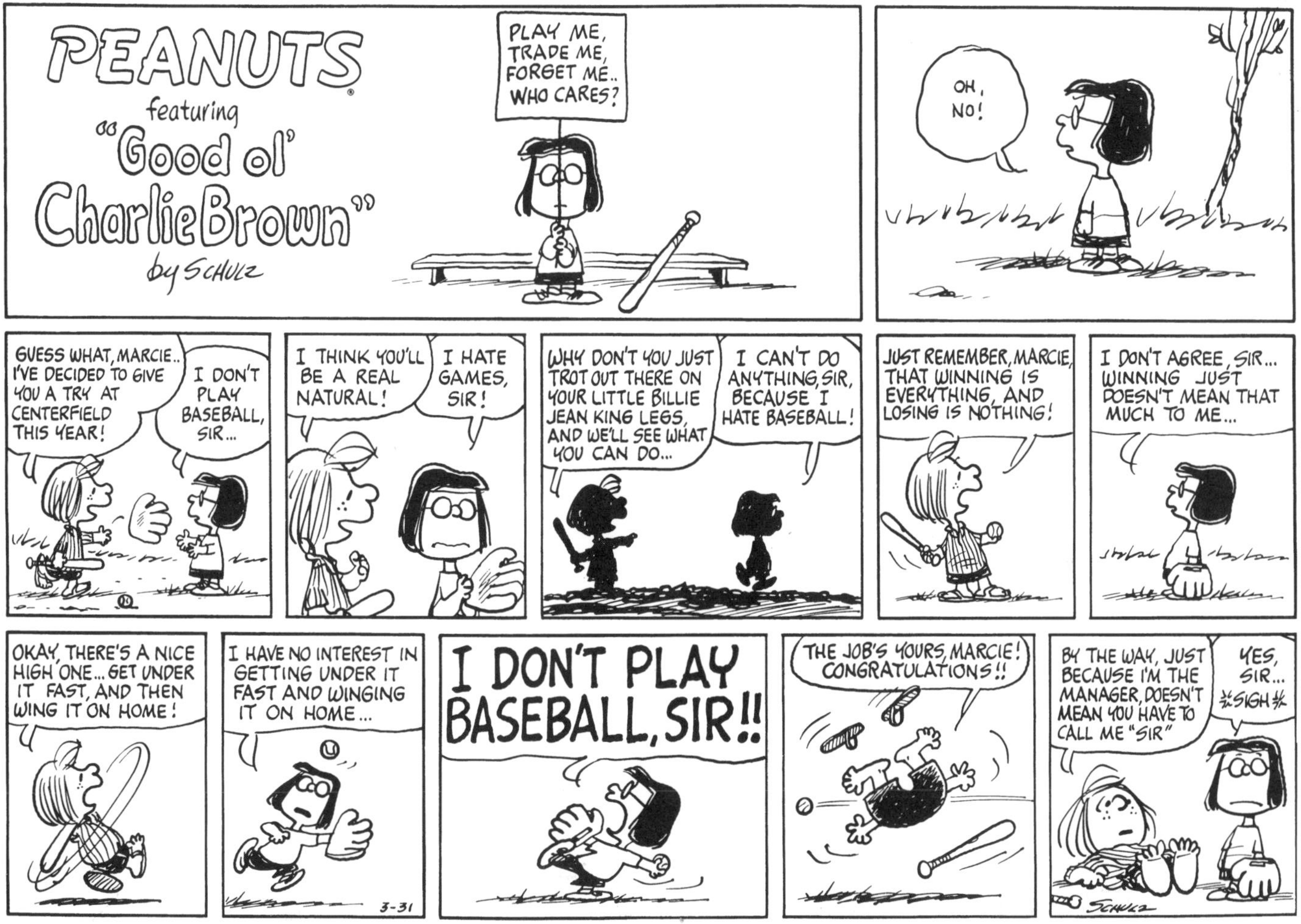
PEANUTS
featuring
"Good ol' CharlieBrown"
by SCHULZ
PLAY ME, TRADE ME, FORGET ME.. WHO CARES?
OH, NO!
GUESS WHAT, MARCIE.. I'VE DECIDED TO GIVE YOU A TRY AT CENTERFIELD THIS YEAR!
I DON'T PLAY BASEBALL, SIR...
I THINK YOU'LL BE A REAL NATURAL!
I HATE GAMES, SIR!
WHY DON'T YOU JUST TROT OUT THERE ON YOUR LITTLE BILLIE JEAN KING LEGS, AND WE'LL SEE WHAT YOU CAN DO...
I CAN'T DO ANYTHING, SIR, BECAUSE I HATE BASEBALL!
JUST REMEMBER, MARCIE, THAT WINNING IS EVERYTHING, AND LOSING IS NOTHING!
I DON'T AGREE, SIR... WINNING JUST DOESN'T MEAN THAT MUCH TO ME...
OKAY, THERE'S A NICE HIGH ONE... GET UNDER IT FAST, AND THEN WING IT ON HOME!
I HAVE NO INTEREST IN GETTING UNDER IT FAST AND WINGING IT ON HOME...
3-31
I DON'T PLAY BASEBALL, SIR!!
THE JOB'S YOURS, MARCIE! CONGRATULATIONS!!
BY THE WAY, JUST BECAUSE I'M THE MANAGER, DOESN'T MEAN YOU HAVE TO CALL ME "SIR"
YES, SIR... *SIGH*
SCHULZ

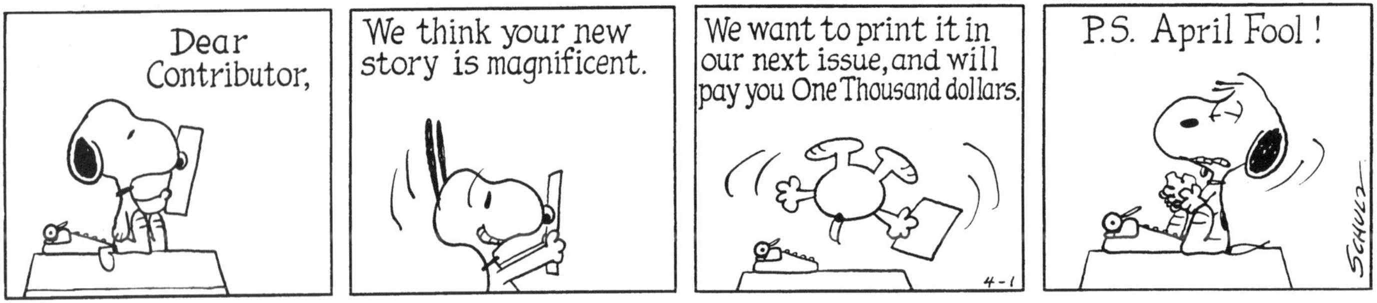
Dear Contributor,
We think your new story is magnificent.
We want to print it in our next issue, and will pay you One Thousand dollars.
4-1
P.S. April Fool!
SCHULZ

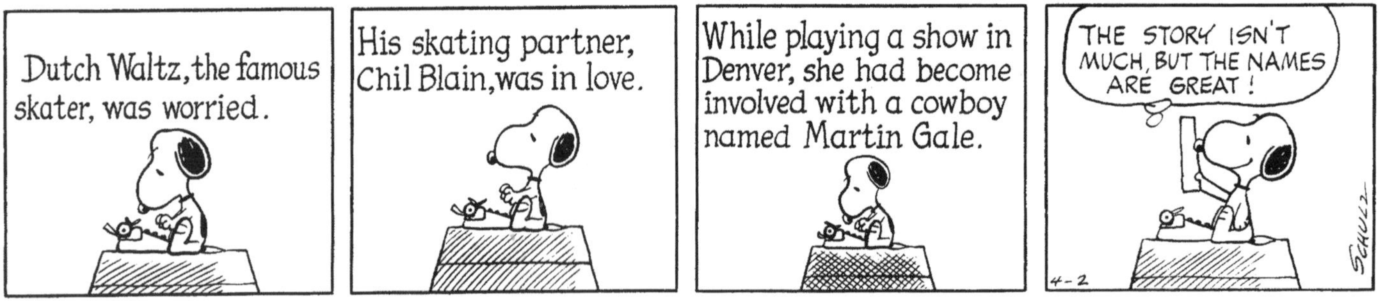
Dutch Waltz, the famous skater, was worried.
His skating partner, Chil Blain, was in love.
While playing a show in Denver, she had become involved with a cowboy named Martin Gale.
THE STORY ISN'T MUCH, BUT THE NAMES ARE GREAT!
4-2
SCHULZ

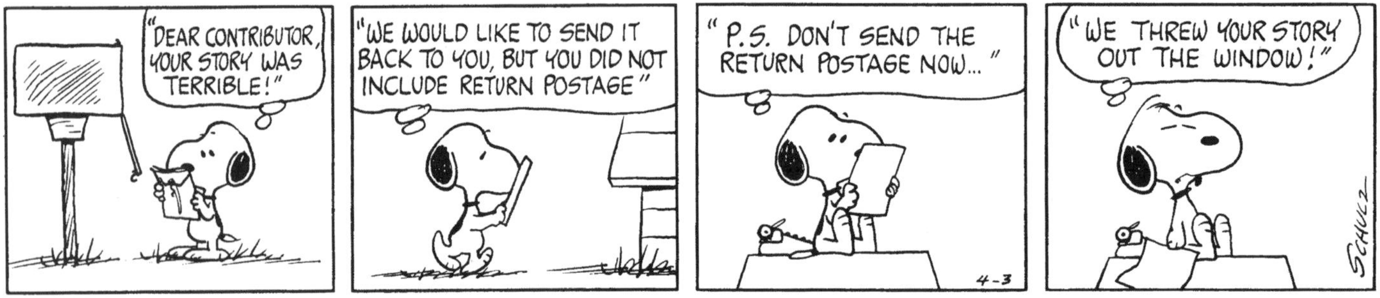
"DEAR CONTRIBUTOR, YOUR STORY WAS TERRIBLE!"
"WE WOULD LIKE TO SEND IT BACK TO YOU, BUT YOU DID NOT INCLUDE RETURN POSTAGE"
"P.S. DON'T SEND THE RETURN POSTAGE NOW..."
4-3
"WE THREW YOUR STORY OUT THE WINDOW!"
SCHULZ

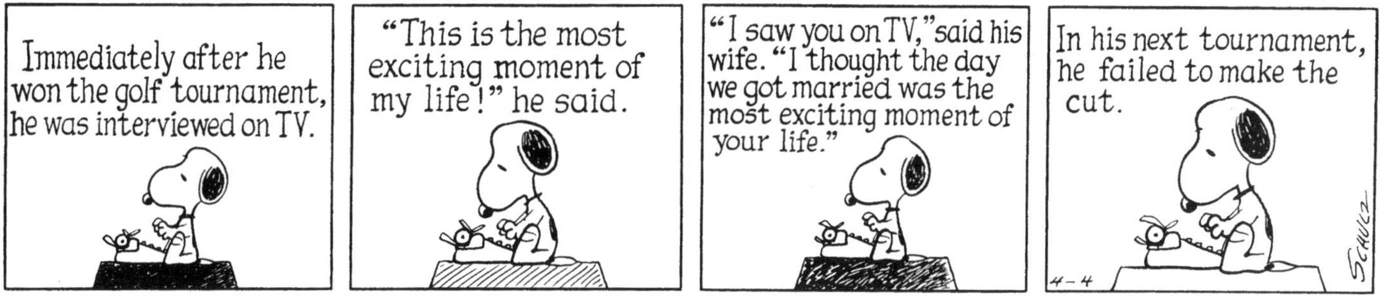
Immediately after he won the golf tournament, he was interviewed on TV.
"This is the most exciting moment of my life!" he said.
"I saw you on TV," said his wife. "I thought the day we got married was the most exciting moment of your life."
In his next tournament, he failed to make the cut.
4-4
SCHULZ

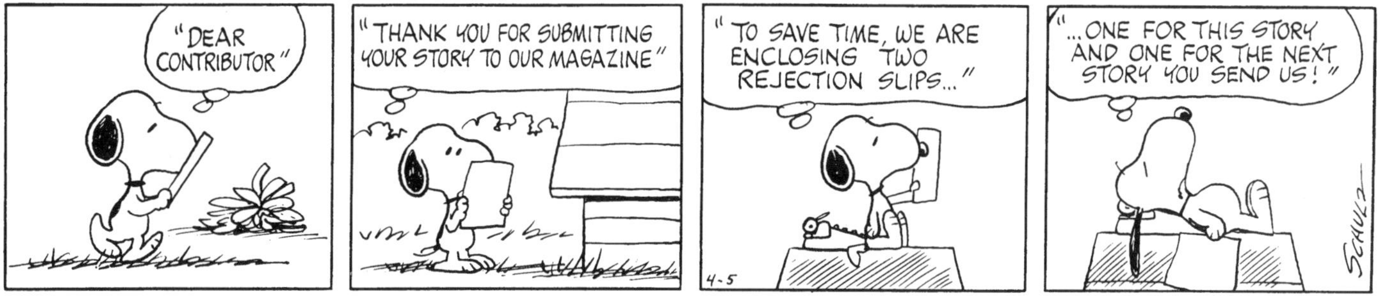
"DEAR CONTRIBUTOR"
"THANK YOU FOR SUBMITTING YOUR STORY TO OUR MAGAZINE"
"TO SAVE TIME, WE ARE ENCLOSING TWO REJECTION SLIPS..."
4-5
"...ONE FOR THIS STORY AND ONE FOR THE NEXT STORY YOU SEND US!"
SCHULZ

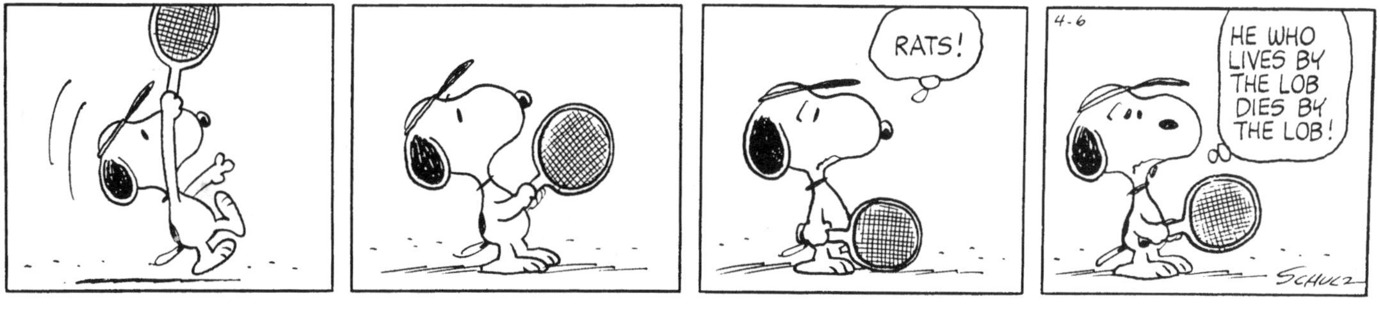
RATS!
4-6
HE WHO LIVES BY THE LOB DIES BY THE LOB!
SCHULZ

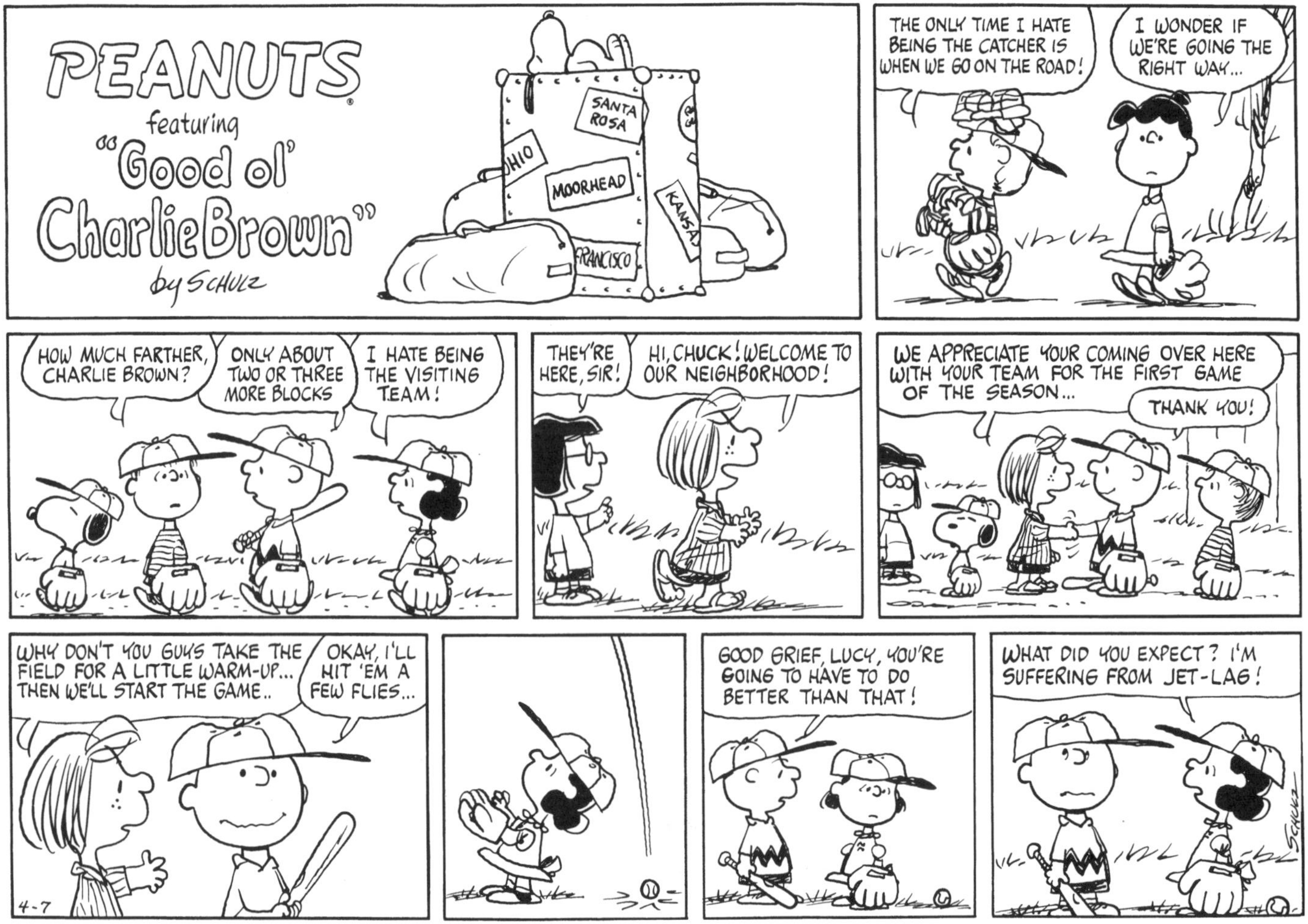
PEANUTS
featuring "Good ol' CharlieBrown"
by SCHULZ
SANTA ROSA
OHIO
MOORHEAD
KANSAS
FRANCISCO
THE ONLY TIME I HATE BEING THE CATCHER IS WHEN WE GO ON THE ROAD!
I WONDER IF WE'RE GOING THE RIGHT WAY...
HOW MUCH FARTHER, CHARLIE BROWN?
ONLY ABOUT TWO OR THREE MORE BLOCKS
I HATE BEING THE VISITING TEAM!
THEY'RE HERE, SIR!
HI, CHUCK! WELCOME TO OUR NEIGHBORHOOD!
WE APPRECIATE YOUR COMING OVER HERE WITH YOUR TEAM FOR THE FIRST GAME OF THE SEASON...
THANK YOU!
WHY DON'T YOU GUYS TAKE THE FIELD FOR A LITTLE WARM-UP... THEN WE'LL START THE GAME..
OKAY, I'LL HIT 'EM A FEW FLIES...
4-7
GOOD GRIEF, LUCY, YOU'RE GOING TO HAVE TO DO BETTER THAN THAT!
WHAT DID YOU EXPECT? I'M SUFFERING FROM JET-LAG!
SCHULZ

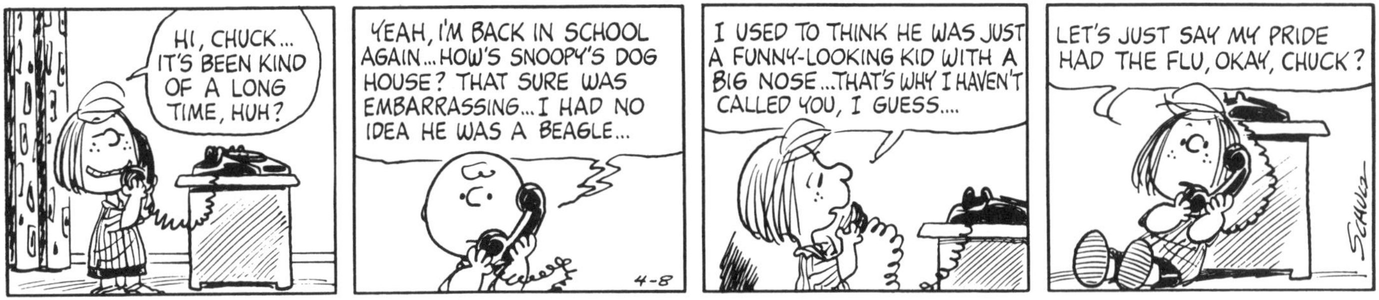
HI, CHUCK... IT'S BEEN KIND OF A LONG TIME, HUH?
YEAH, I'M BACK IN SCHOOL AGAIN... HOW'S SNOOPY'S DOG HOUSE? THAT SURE WAS EMBARRASSING... I HAD NO IDEA HE WAS A BEAGLE...
4-8
I USED TO THINK HE WAS JUST A FUNNY-LOOKING KID WITH A BIG NOSE... THAT'S WHY I HAVEN'T CALLED YOU, I GUESS....
LET'S JUST SAY MY PRIDE HAD THE FLU, OKAY, CHUCK?
SCHULZ

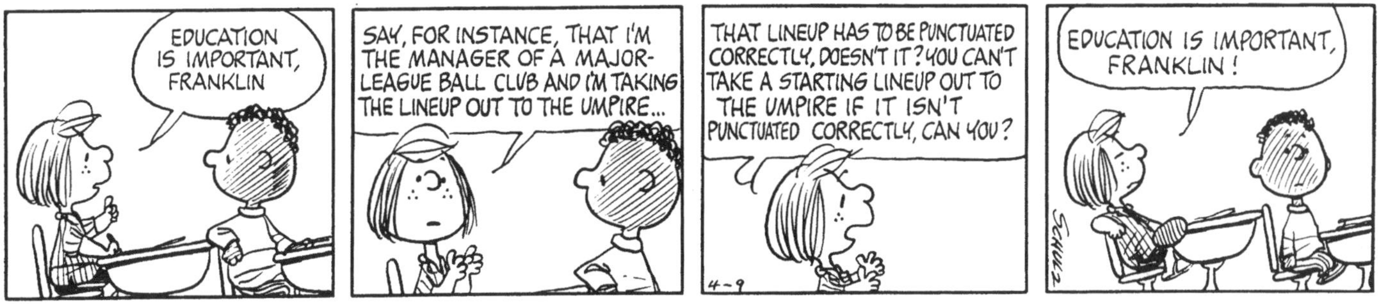
EDUCATION IS IMPORTANT, FRANKLIN
SAY, FOR INSTANCE, THAT I'M THE MANAGER OF A MAJOR-LEAGUE BALL CLUB AND I'M TAKING THE LINEUP OUT TO THE UMPIRE...
THAT LINEUP HAS TO BE PUNCTUATED CORRECTLY, DOESN'T IT? YOU CAN'T TAKE A STARTING LINEUP OUT TO THE UMPIRE IF IT ISN'T PUNCTUATED CORRECTLY, CAN YOU?
4-9
EDUCATION IS IMPORTANT, FRANKLIN!
SCHULZ

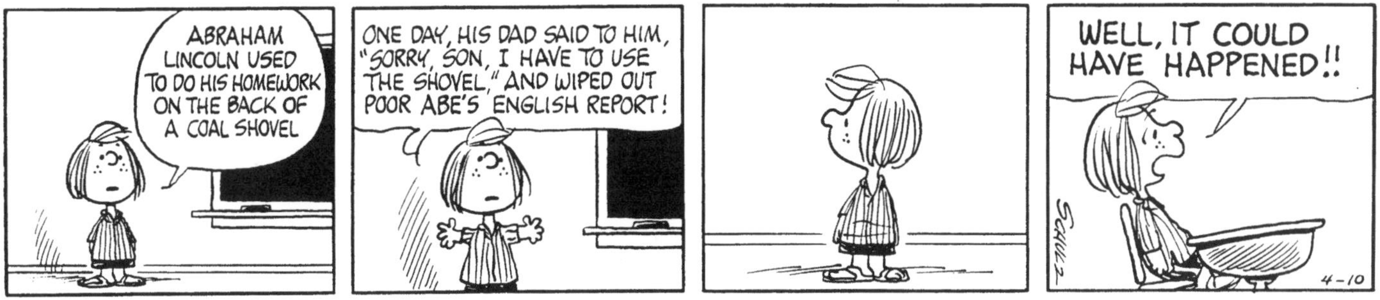
ABRAHAM LINCOLN USED TO DO HIS HOMEWORK ON THE BACK OF A COAL SHOVEL
ONE DAY, HIS DAD SAID TO HIM, "SORRY, SON, I HAVE TO USE THE SHOVEL," AND WIPED OUT POOR ABE'S ENGLISH REPORT!
WELL, IT COULD HAVE HAPPENED!!
SCHULZ
4-10

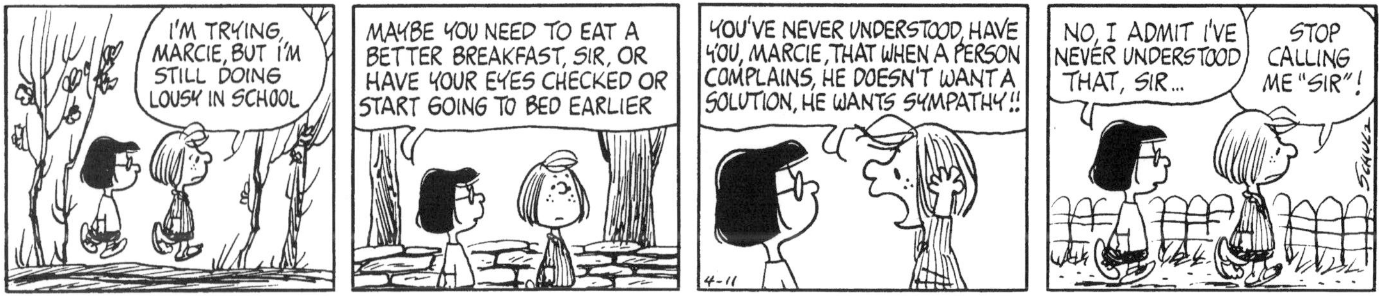
I'M TRYING, MARCIE, BUT I'M STILL DOING LOUSY IN SCHOOL
MAYBE YOU NEED TO EAT A BETTER BREAKFAST, SIR, OR HAVE YOUR EYES CHECKED OR START GOING TO BED EARLIER
YOU'VE NEVER UNDERSTOOD, HAVE YOU, MARCIE, THAT WHEN A PERSON COMPLAINS, HE DOESN'T WANT A SOLUTION, HE WANTS SYMPATHY!!
4-11
NO, I ADMIT I'VE NEVER UNDERSTOOD THAT, SIR...
STOP CALLING ME "SIR"!
SCHULZ

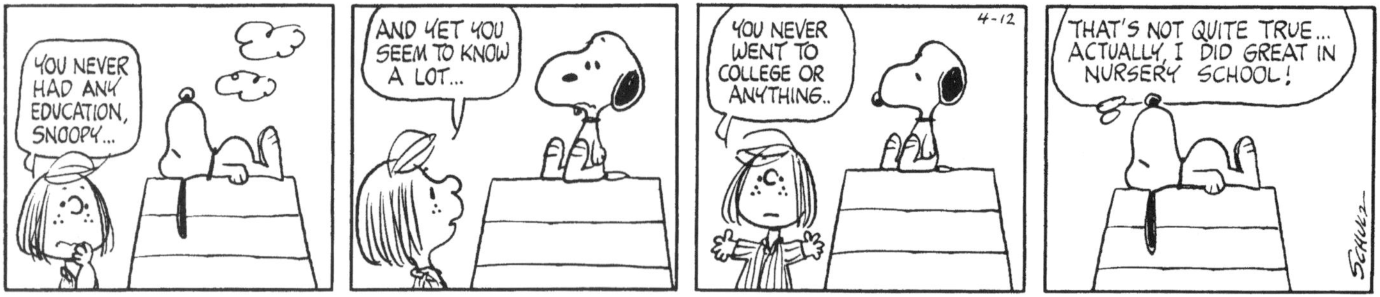
YOU NEVER HAD ANY EDUCATION, SNOOPY...
AND YET YOU SEEM TO KNOW A LOT...
4-12
YOU NEVER WENT TO COLLEGE OR ANYTHING..
THAT'S NOT QUITE TRUE... ACTUALLY, I DID GREAT IN NURSERY SCHOOL!
SCHULZ

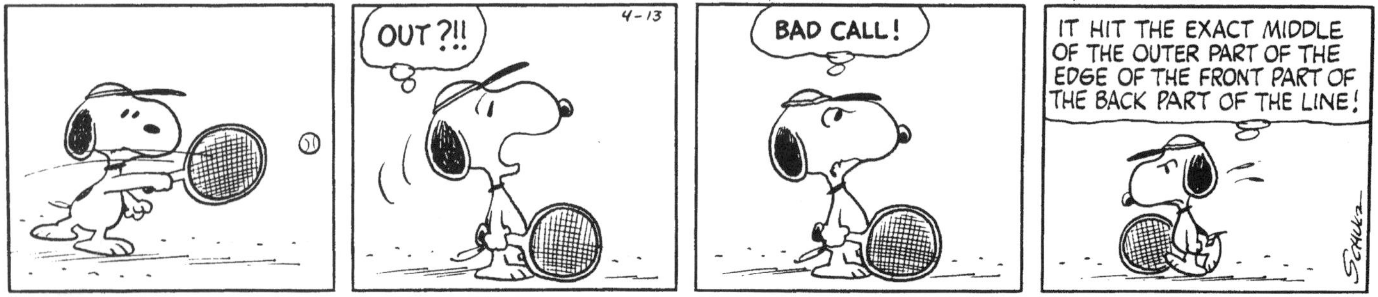
4-13
OUT?!!
BAD CALL!
IT HIT THE EXACT MIDDLE OF THE OUTER PART OF THE EDGE OF THE FRONT PART OF THE BACK PART OF THE LINE!
SCHULZ

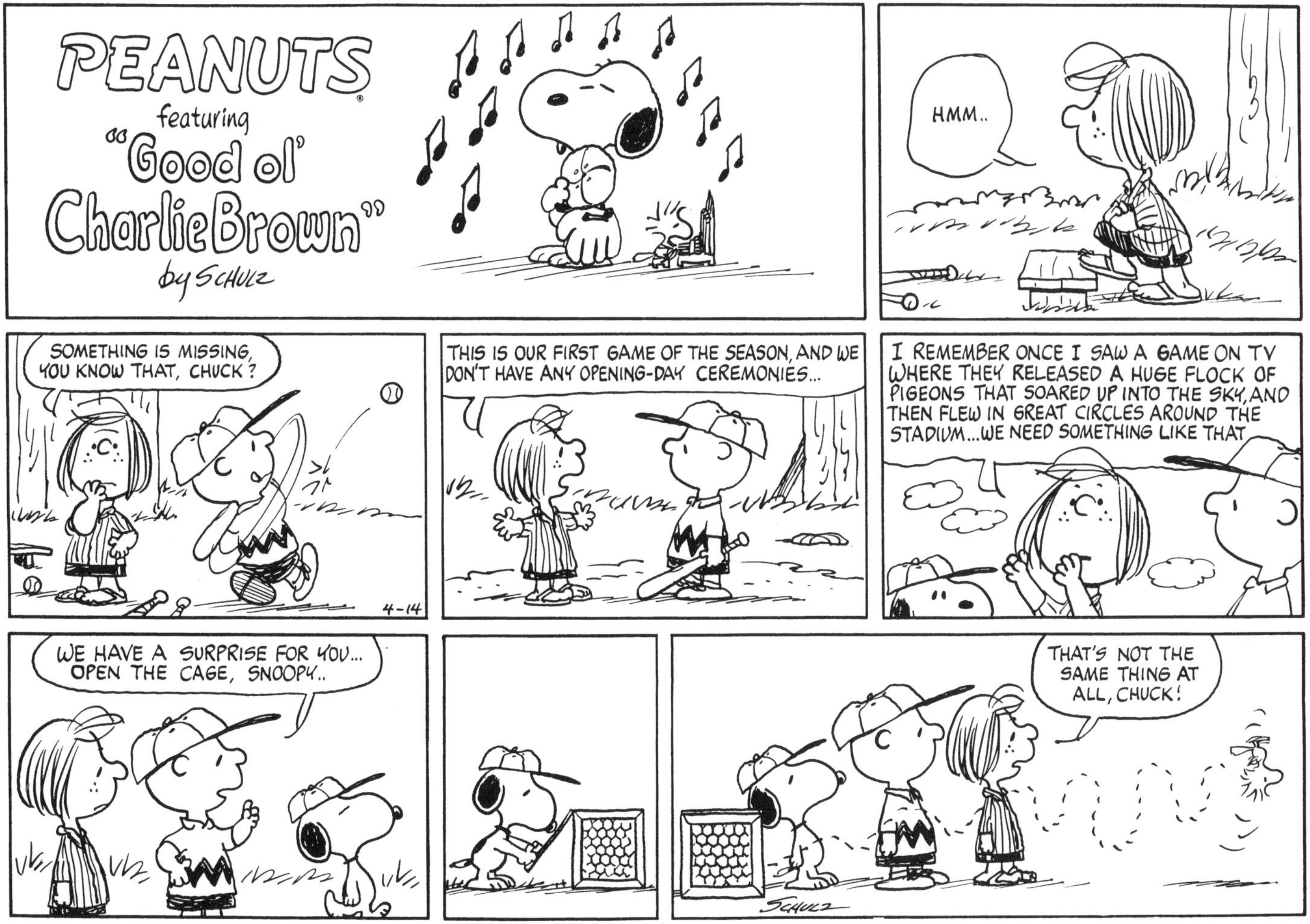
PEANUTS
featuring
"Good ol' Charlie Brown"
by SCHULZ
HMM..
SOMETHING IS MISSING, YOU KNOW THAT, CHUCK?
4-14
THIS IS OUR FIRST GAME OF THE SEASON, AND WE DON'T HAVE ANY OPENING-DAY CEREMONIES...
I REMEMBER ONCE I SAW A GAME ON TV WHERE THEY RELEASED A HUGE FLOCK OF PIGEONS THAT SOARED UP INTO THE SKY, AND THEN FLEW IN GREAT CIRCLES AROUND THE STADIUM...WE NEED SOMETHING LIKE THAT
WE HAVE A SURPRISE FOR YOU... OPEN THE CAGE, SNOOPY..
THAT'S NOT THE SAME THING AT ALL, CHUCK!
SCHULZ

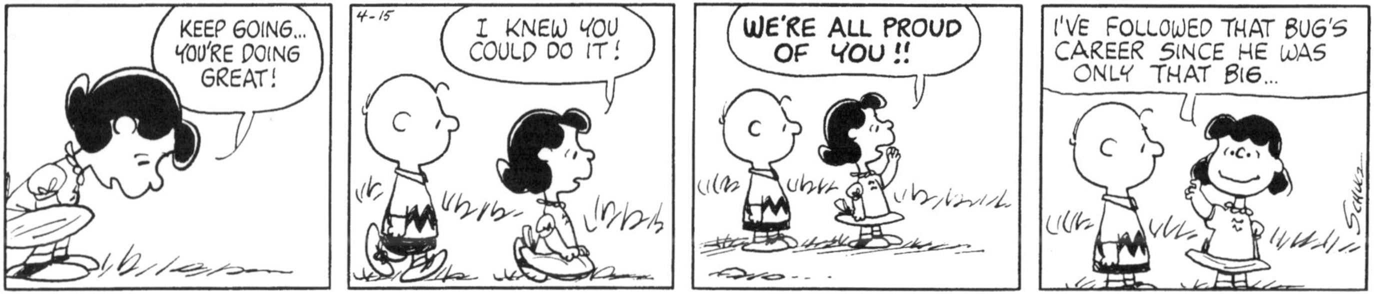
KEEP GOING... YOU'RE DOING GREAT!
4-15
I KNEW YOU COULD DO IT!
WE'RE ALL PROUD OF YOU!!
I'VE FOLLOWED THAT BUG'S CAREER SINCE HE WAS ONLY THAT BIG...
SCHULZ

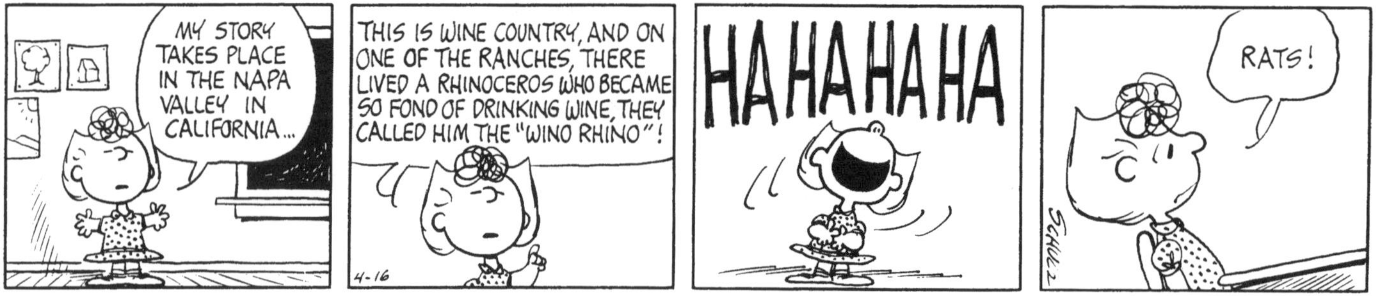
MY STORY TAKES PLACE IN THE NAPA VALLEY IN CALIFORNIA...
THIS IS WINE COUNTRY, AND ON ONE OF THE RANCHES, THERE LIVED A RHINOCEROS WHO BECAME SO FOND OF DRINKING WINE, THEY CALLED HIM THE "WINO RHINO"!
4-16
HAHAHAHA
RATS!
SCHULZ

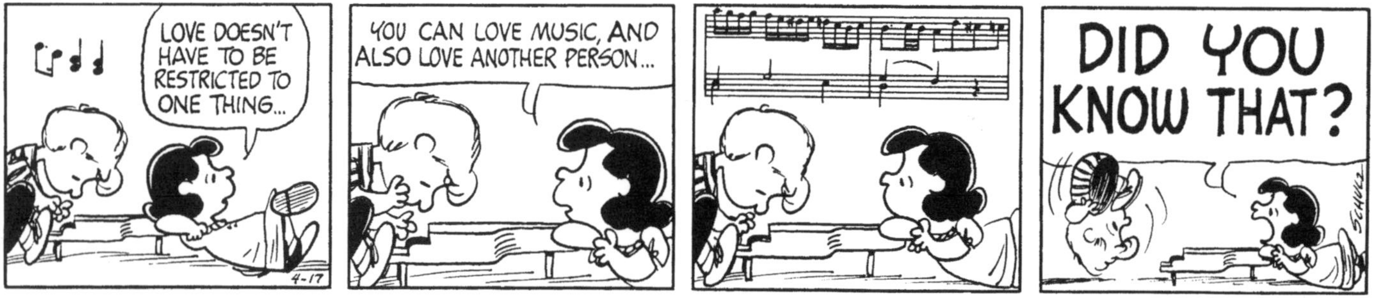
LOVE DOESN'T HAVE TO BE RESTRICTED TO ONE THING...
4-17
YOU CAN LOVE MUSIC, AND ALSO LOVE ANOTHER PERSON...
DID YOU KNOW THAT?
SCHULZ

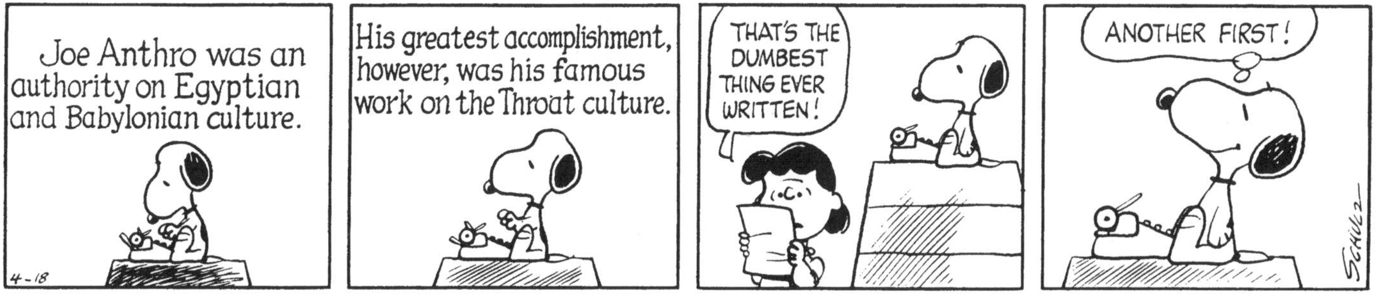
Joe Anthro was an authority on Egyptian and Babylonian culture.
His greatest accomplishment, however, was his famous work on the Throat culture.
THAT'S THE DUMBEST THING EVER WRITTEN!
ANOTHER FIRST!
4-18
SCHULZ

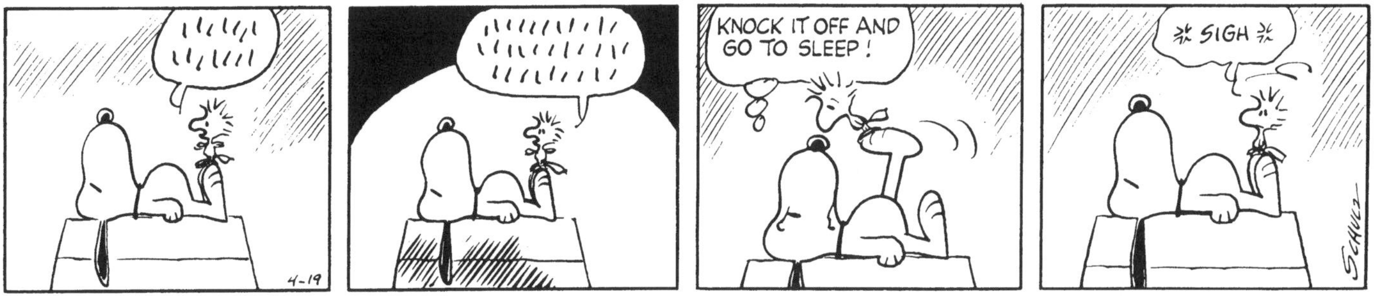
KNOCK IT OFF AND GO TO SLEEP!
SIGH
4-19
SCHULZ

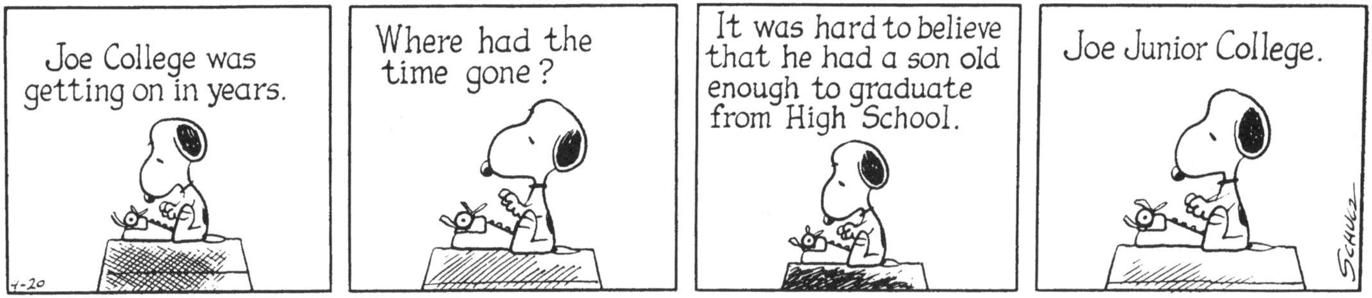
Joe College was getting on in years.
Where had the time gone?
It was hard to believe that he had a son old enough to graduate from High School.
Joe Junior College.
4-20
SCHULZ

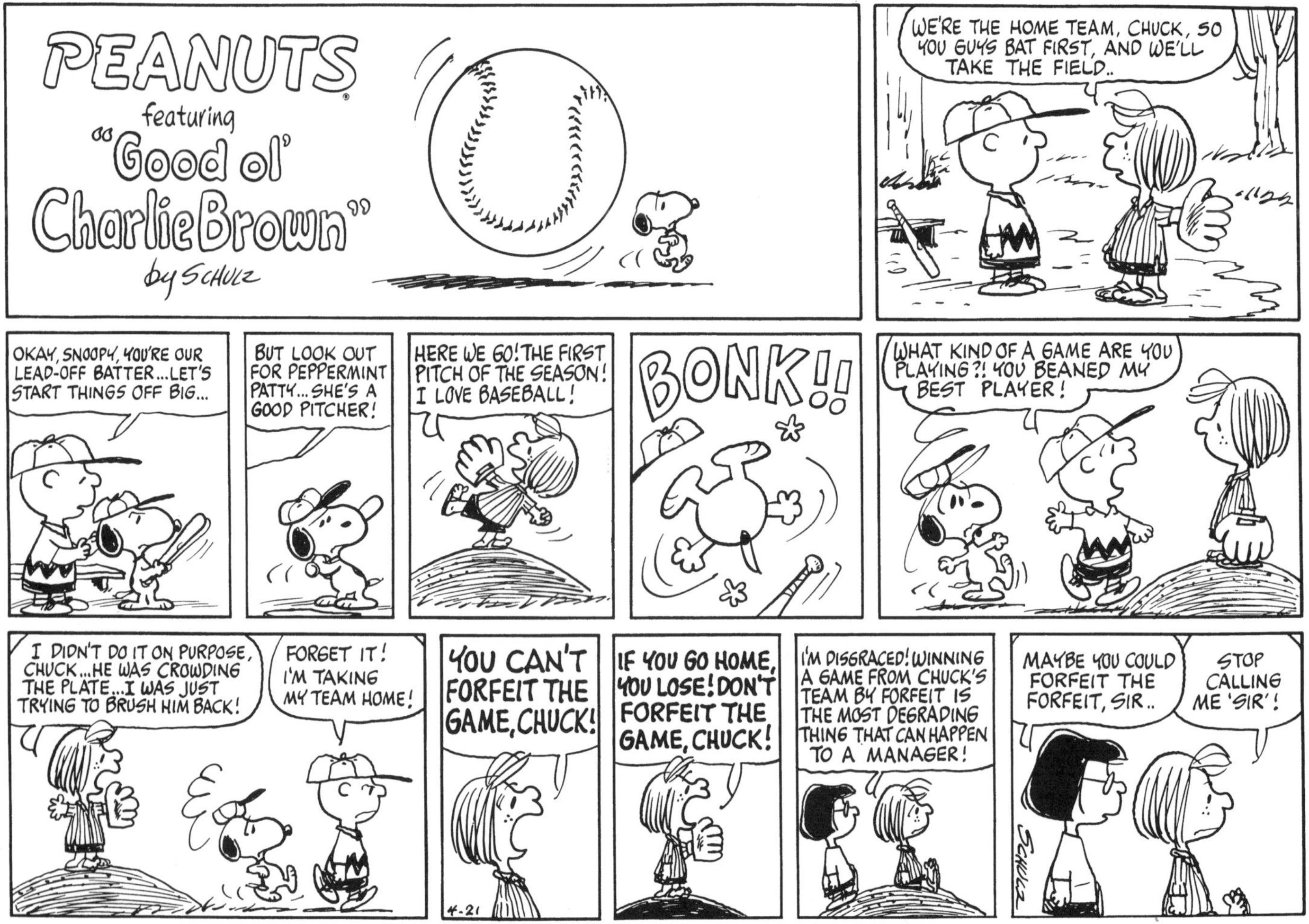
PEANUTS
featuring
"Good ol' Charlie Brown"
by SCHULZ
WE'RE THE HOME TEAM, CHUCK, SO YOU GUYS BAT FIRST, AND WE'LL TAKE THE FIELD..
OKAY, SNOOPY, YOU'RE OUR LEAD-OFF BATTER...LET'S START THINGS OFF BIG...
BUT LOOK OUT FOR PEPPERMINT PATTY... SHE'S A GOOD PITCHER!
HERE WE GO! THE FIRST PITCH OF THE SEASON! I LOVE BASEBALL!
BONK!!
WHAT KIND OF A GAME ARE YOU PLAYING?! YOU BEANED MY BEST PLAYER!
I DIDN'T DO IT ON PURPOSE, CHUCK...HE WAS CROWDING THE PLATE...I WAS JUST TRYING TO BRUSH HIM BACK!
FORGET IT! I'M TAKING MY TEAM HOME!
YOU CAN'T FORFEIT THE GAME, CHUCK!
4-21
IF YOU GO HOME, YOU LOSE! DON'T FORFEIT THE GAME, CHUCK!
I'M DISGRACED! WINNING A GAME FROM CHUCK'S TEAM BY FORFEIT IS THE MOST DEGRADING THING THAT CAN HAPPEN TO A MANAGER!
MAYBE YOU COULD FORFEIT THE FORFEIT, SIR..
STOP CALLING ME 'SIR'!
SCHULZ

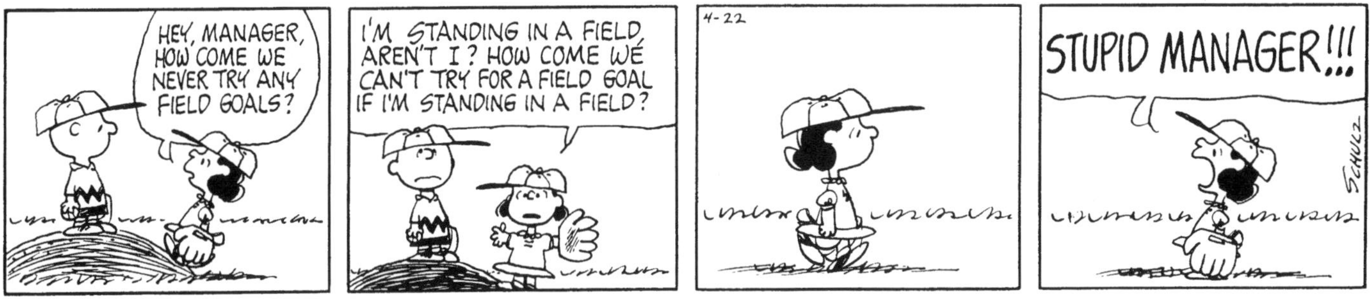
HEY, MANAGER, HOW COME WE NEVER TRY ANY FIELD GOALS?
I'M STANDING IN A FIELD, AREN'T I? HOW COME WE CAN'T TRY FOR A FIELD GOAL IF I'M STANDING IN A FIELD?
4-22
STUPID MANAGER!!!
SCHULZ

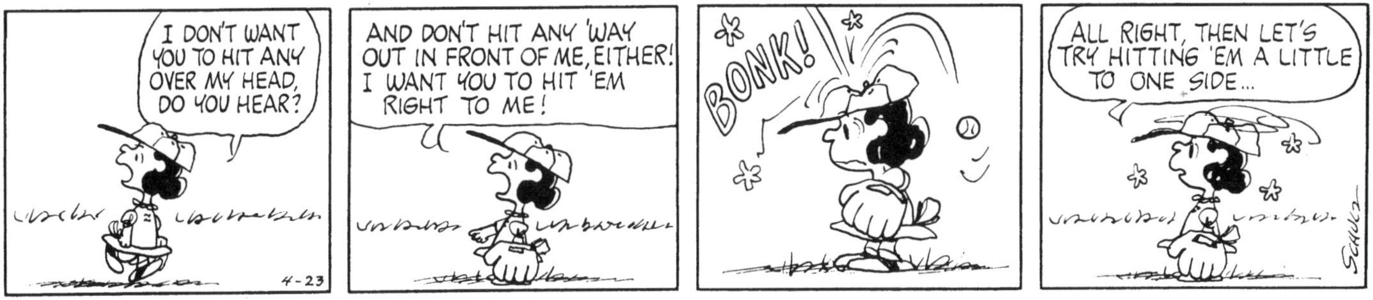
I DON'T WANT YOU TO HIT ANY OVER MY HEAD, DO YOU HEAR?
4-23
AND DON'T HIT ANY 'WAY OUT IN FRONT OF ME, EITHER! I WANT YOU TO HIT 'EM RIGHT TO ME!
BONK!
ALL RIGHT, THEN LET'S TRY HITTING 'EM A LITTLE TO ONE SIDE...
SCHULZ

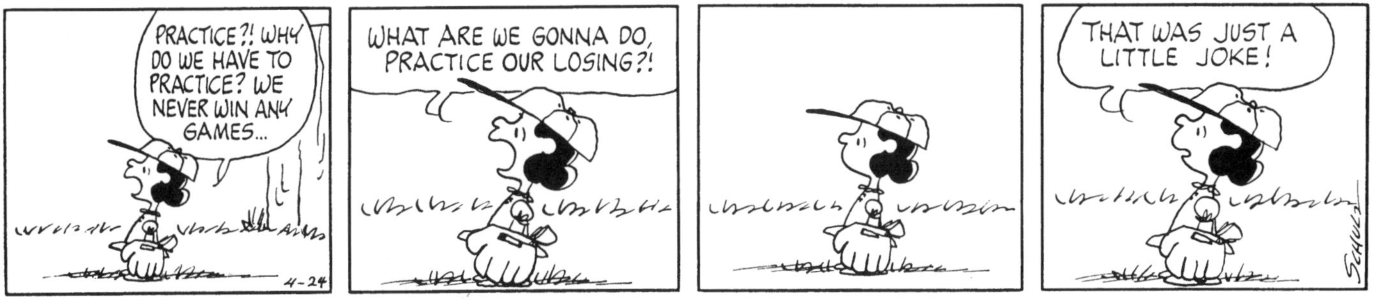
PRACTICE?! WHY DO WE HAVE TO PRACTICE? WE NEVER WIN ANY GAMES...
4-24
WHAT ARE WE GONNA DO, PRACTICE OUR LOSING?!
THAT WAS JUST A LITTLE JOKE!
SCHULZ

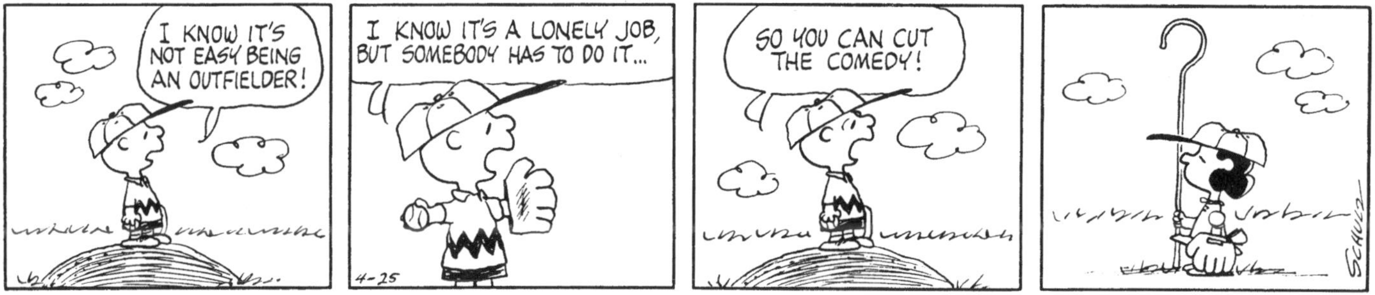
I KNOW IT'S NOT EASY BEING AN OUTFIELDER!
I KNOW IT'S A LONELY JOB, BUT SOMEBODY HAS TO DO IT...
4-25
SO YOU CAN CUT THE COMEDY!
SCHULZ

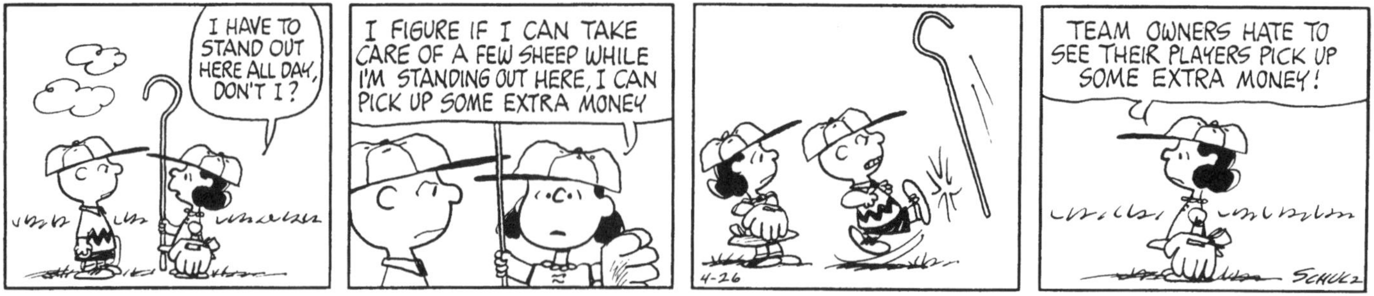
I HAVE TO STAND OUT HERE ALL DAY, DON'T I?
I FIGURE IF I CAN TAKE CARE OF A FEW SHEEP WHILE I'M STANDING OUT HERE, I CAN PICK UP SOME EXTRA MONEY
4-26
TEAM OWNERS HATE TO SEE THEIR PLAYERS PICK UP SOME EXTRA MONEY!
SCHULZ

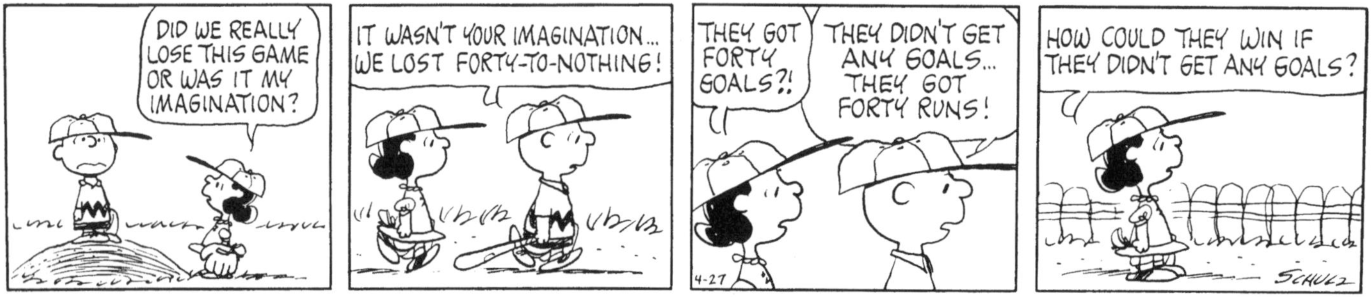
DID WE REALLY LOSE THIS GAME OR WAS IT MY IMAGINATION?
IT WASN'T YOUR IMAGINATION... WE LOST FORTY-TO-NOTHING!
THEY GOT FORTY GOALS?!
THEY DIDN'T GET ANY GOALS... THEY GOT FORTY RUNS!
4-27
HOW COULD THEY WIN IF THEY DIDN'T GET ANY GOALS?
SCHULZ

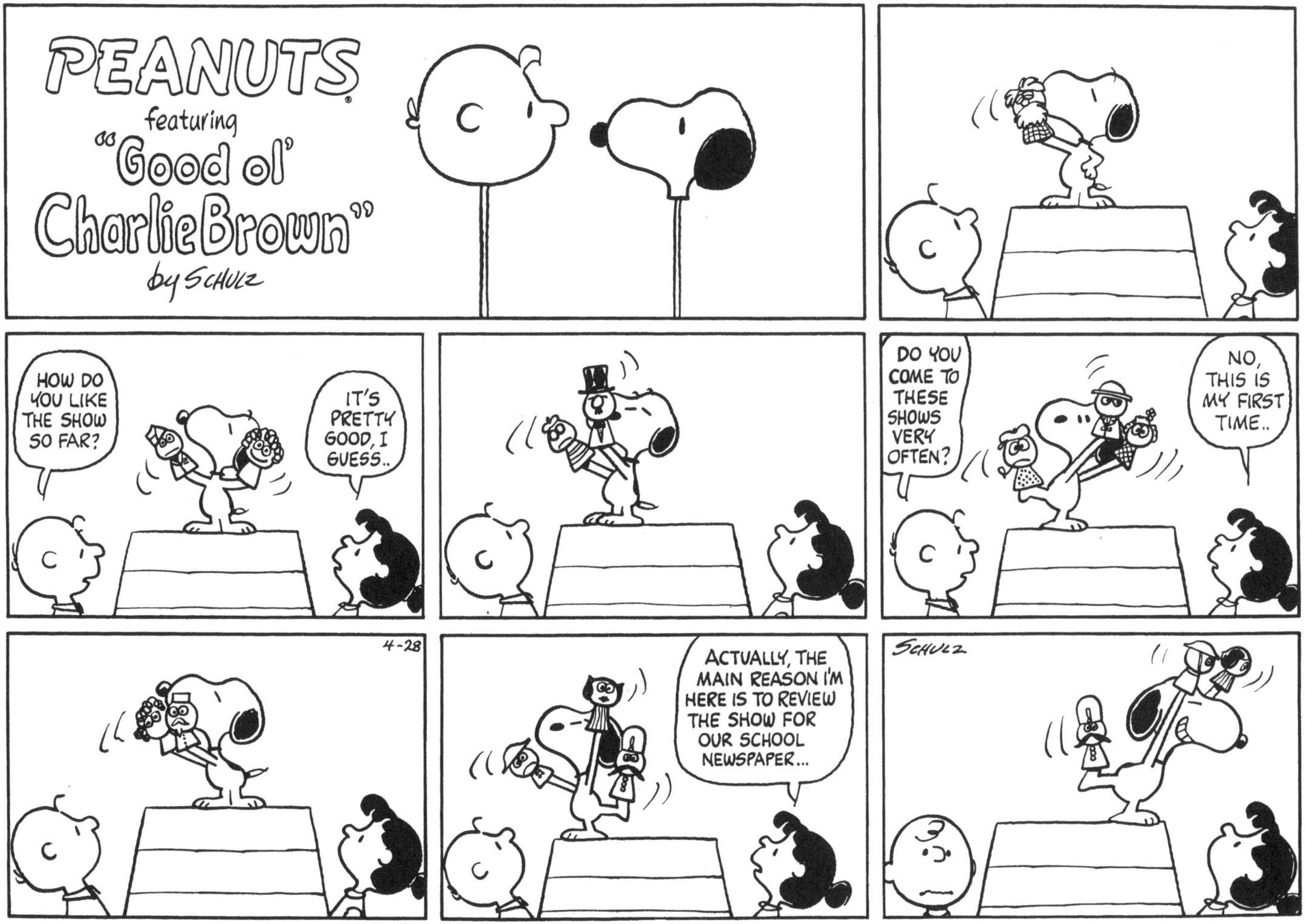
PEANUTS
featuring
"Good ol' CharlieBrown"
by SCHULZ
HOW DO YOU LIKE THE SHOW SO FAR?
IT'S PRETTY GOOD, I GUESS..
DO YOU COME TO THESE SHOWS VERY OFTEN?
NO, THIS IS MY FIRST TIME..
4-28
ACTUALLY, THE MAIN REASON I'M HERE IS TO REVIEW THE SHOW FOR OUR SCHOOL NEWSPAPER...
SCHULZ

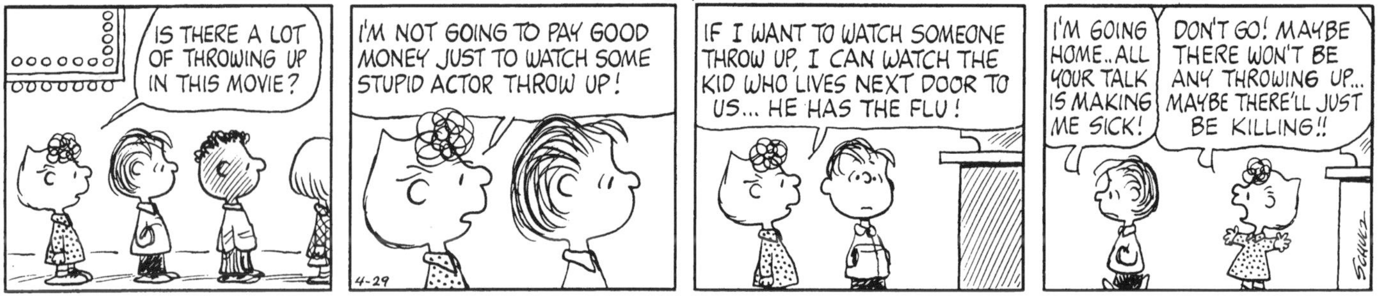
IS THERE A LOT OF THROWING UP IN THIS MOVIE?
I'M NOT GOING TO PAY GOOD MONEY JUST TO WATCH SOME STUPID ACTOR THROW UP!
4-29
IF I WANT TO WATCH SOMEONE THROW UP, I CAN WATCH THE KID WHO LIVES NEXT DOOR TO US... HE HAS THE FLU!
I'M GOING HOME..ALL YOUR TALK IS MAKING ME SICK!
DON'T GO! MAYBE THERE WON'T BE ANY THROWING UP... MAYBE THERE'LL JUST BE KILLING!!
SCHULZ

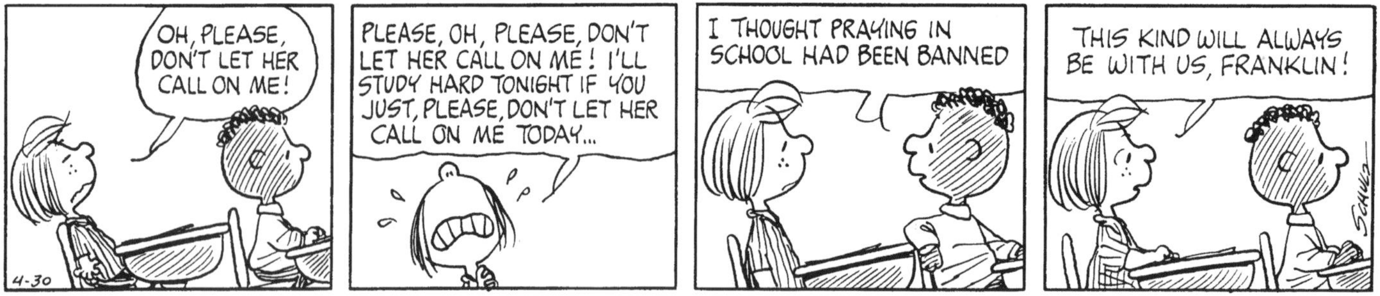
OH, PLEASE, DON'T LET HER CALL ON ME!
4-30
PLEASE, OH, PLEASE, DON'T LET HER CALL ON ME! I'LL STUDY HARD TONIGHT IF YOU JUST, PLEASE, DON'T LET HER CALL ON ME TODAY...
I THOUGHT PRAYING IN SCHOOL HAD BEEN BANNED
THIS KIND WILL ALWAYS BE WITH US, FRANKLIN!
SCHULZ

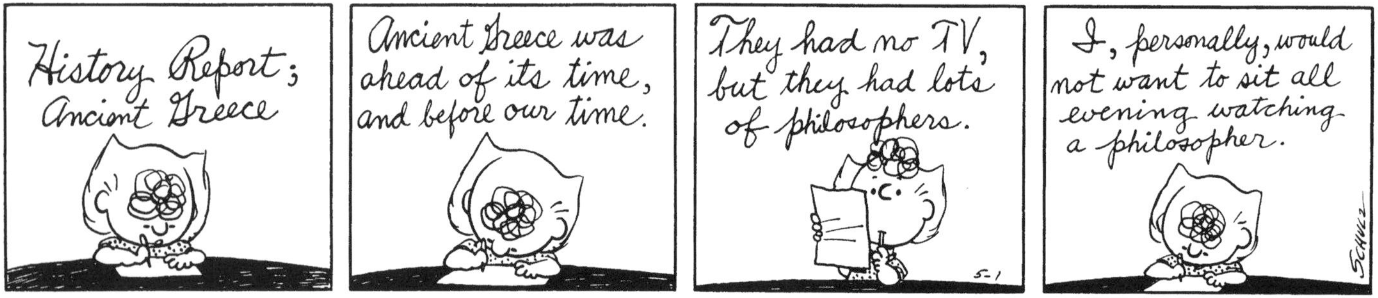
History Report; Ancient Greece
Ancient Greece was ahead of its time, and before our time.
They had no TV, but they had lots of philosophers.
5-1
I, personally, would not want to sit all evening watching a philosopher.
SCHULZ

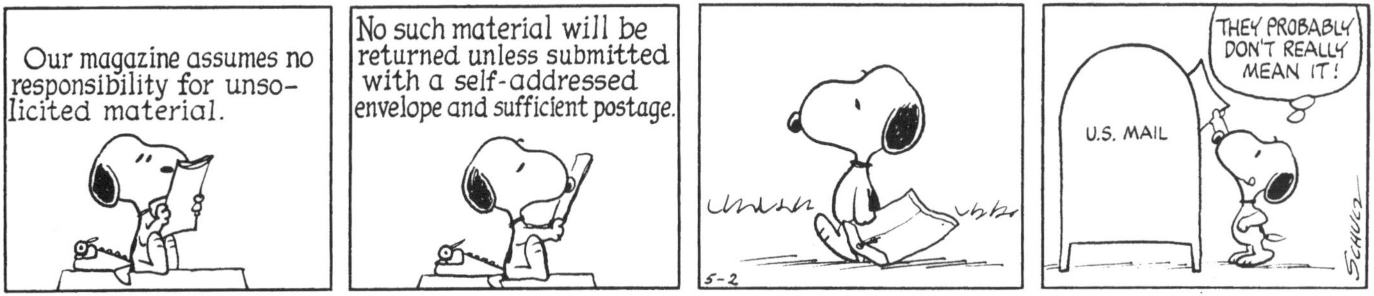
Our magazine assumes no responsibility for unsolicited material.
No such material will be returned unless submitted with a self-addressed envelope and sufficient postage.
5-2
U.S. MAIL
THEY PROBABLY DON'T REALLY MEAN IT!
SCHULZ

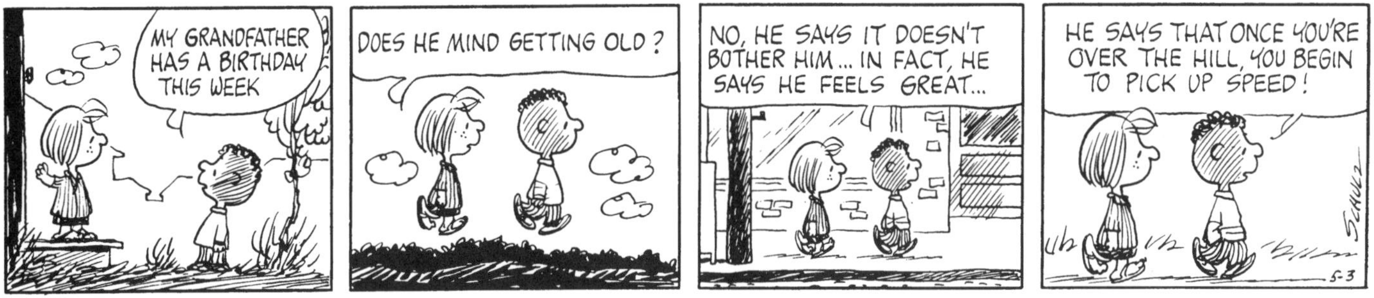
MY GRANDFATHER HAS A BIRTHDAY THIS WEEK
DOES HE MIND GETTING OLD?
NO, HE SAYS IT DOESN'T BOTHER HIM... IN FACT, HE SAYS HE FEELS GREAT...
HE SAYS THAT ONCE YOU'RE OVER THE HILL, YOU BEGIN TO PICK UP SPEED!
SCHULZ
5-3

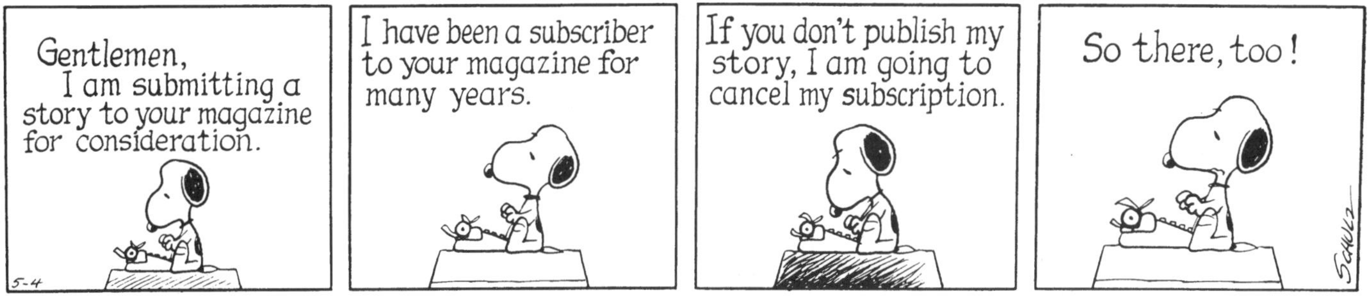
Gentlemen,
I am submitting a story to your magazine for consideration.
5-4
I have been a subscriber to your magazine for many years.
If you don't publish my story, I am going to cancel my subscription.
So there, too!
SCHULZ

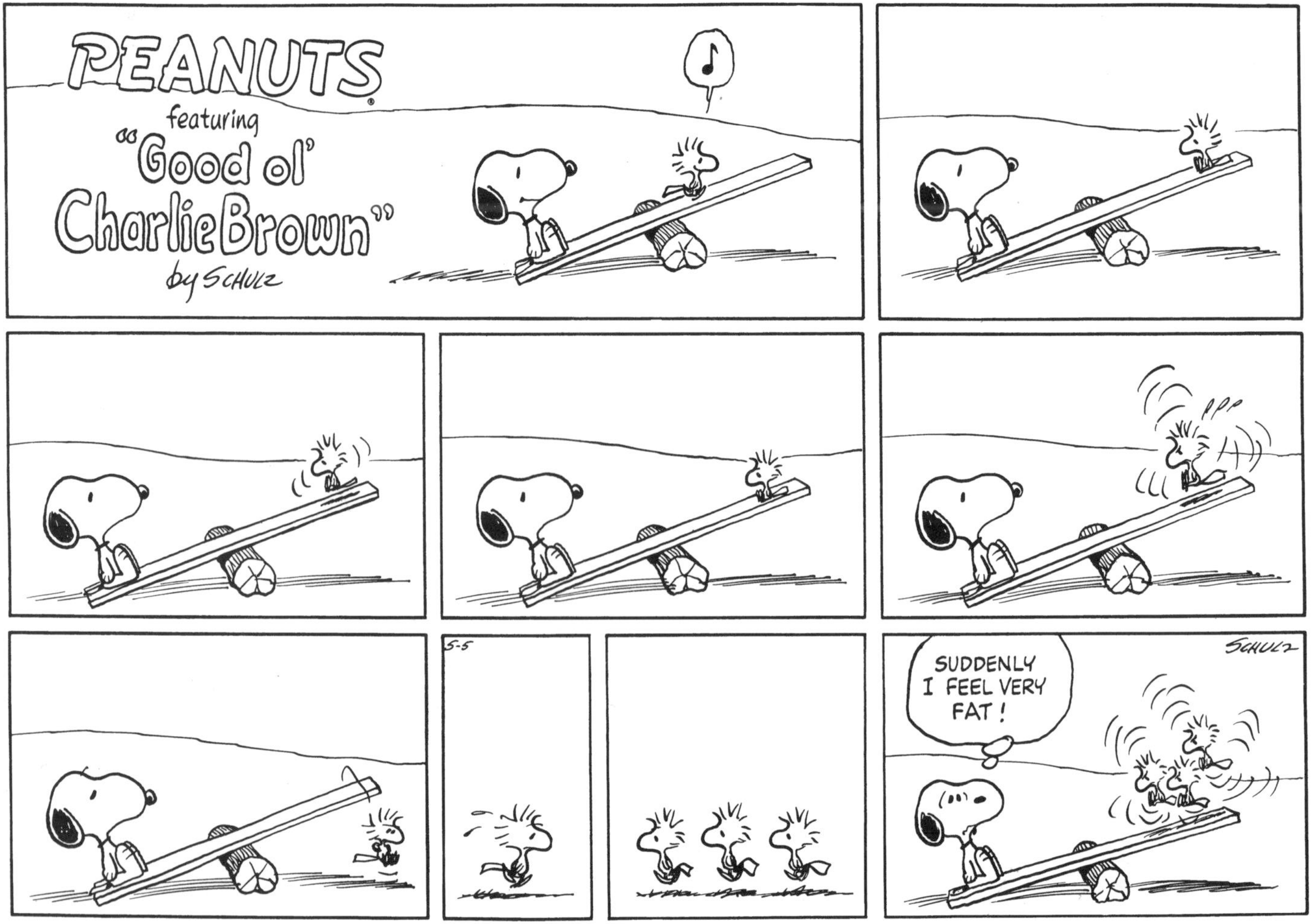
PEANUTS
featuring
"Good ol' Charlie Brown"
by SCHULZ
5-5
SCHULZ
SUDDENLY I FEEL VERY FAT!

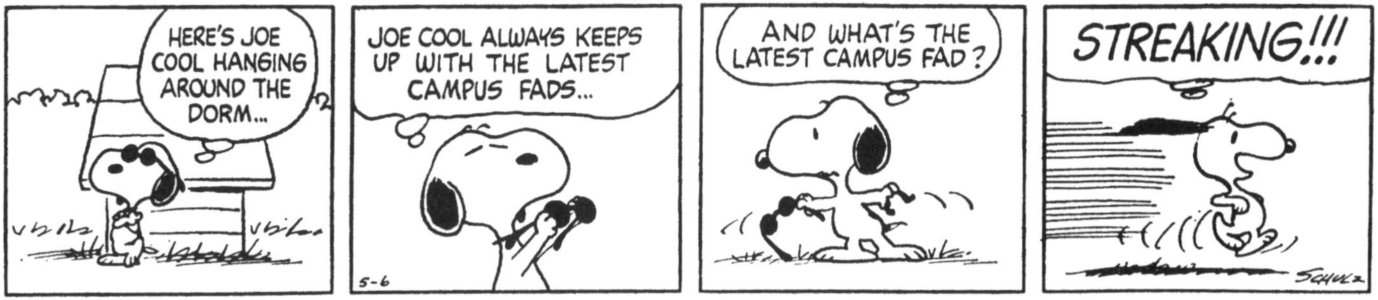
HERE'S JOE COOL HANGING AROUND THE DORM...
JOE COOL ALWAYS KEEPS UP WITH THE LATEST CAMPUS FADS...
5-6
AND WHAT'S THE LATEST CAMPUS FAD?
STREAKING!!!

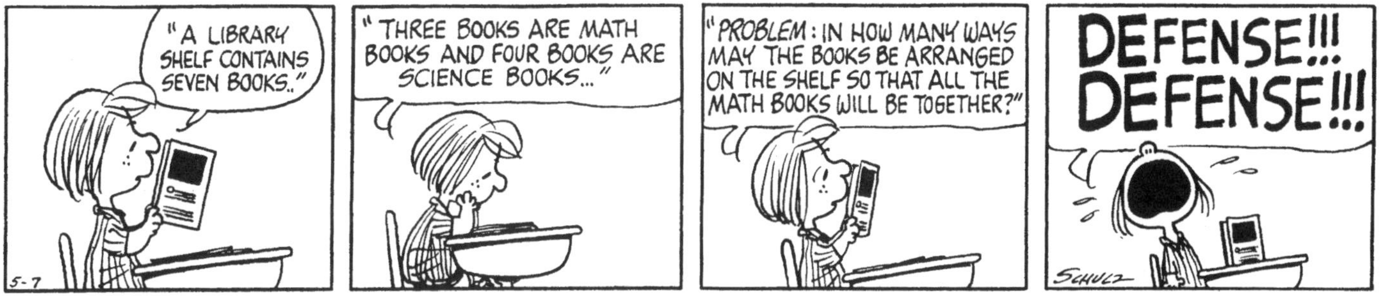
"A LIBRARY SHELF CONTAINS SEVEN BOOKS.."
5-7
"THREE BOOKS ARE MATH BOOKS AND FOUR BOOKS ARE SCIENCE BOOKS..."
"PROBLEM: IN HOW MANY WAYS MAY THE BOOKS BE ARRANGED ON THE SHELF SO THAT ALL THE MATH BOOKS WILL BE TOGETHER?"
DEFENSE!!! DEFENSE!!!

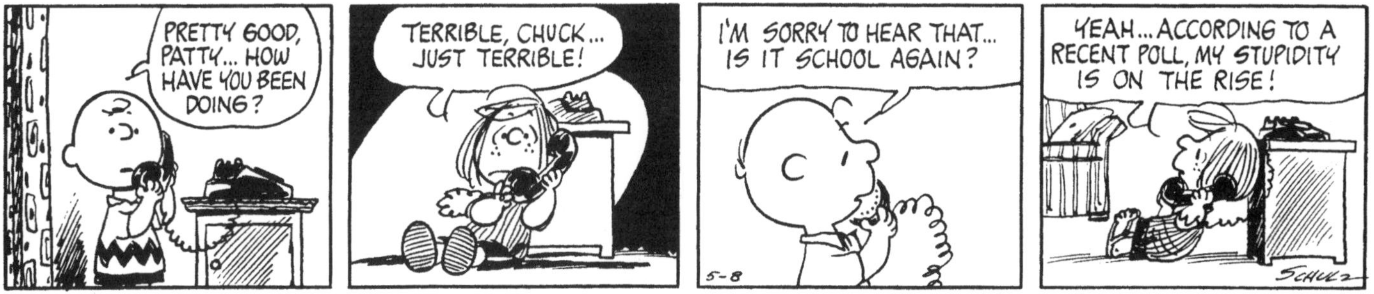
PRETTY GOOD, PATTY... HOW HAVE YOU BEEN DOING?
TERRIBLE, CHUCK... JUST TERRIBLE!
I'M SORRY TO HEAR THAT... IS IT SCHOOL AGAIN?
5-8
YEAH... ACCORDING TO A RECENT POLL, MY STUPIDITY IS ON THE RISE!

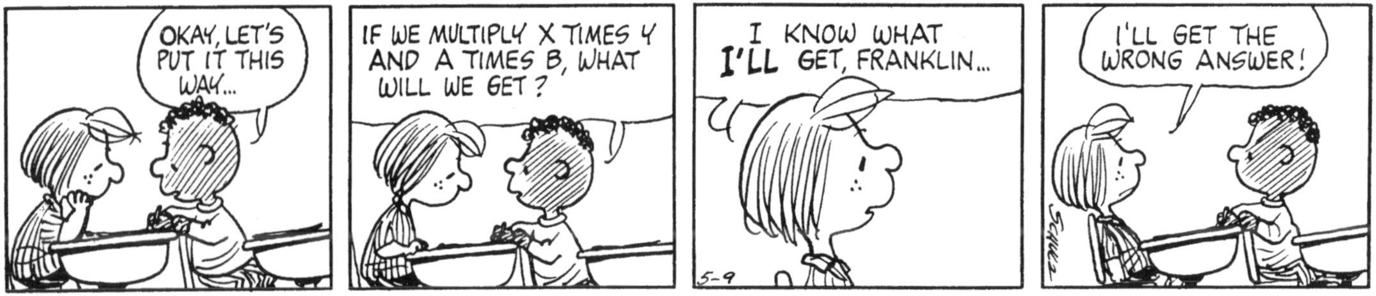
OKAY, LET'S PUT IT THIS WAY...
IF WE MULTIPLY X TIMES Y AND A TIMES B, WHAT WILL WE GET?
I KNOW WHAT I'LL GET, FRANKLIN...
I'LL GET THE WRONG ANSWER!
5-9
SCHULZ

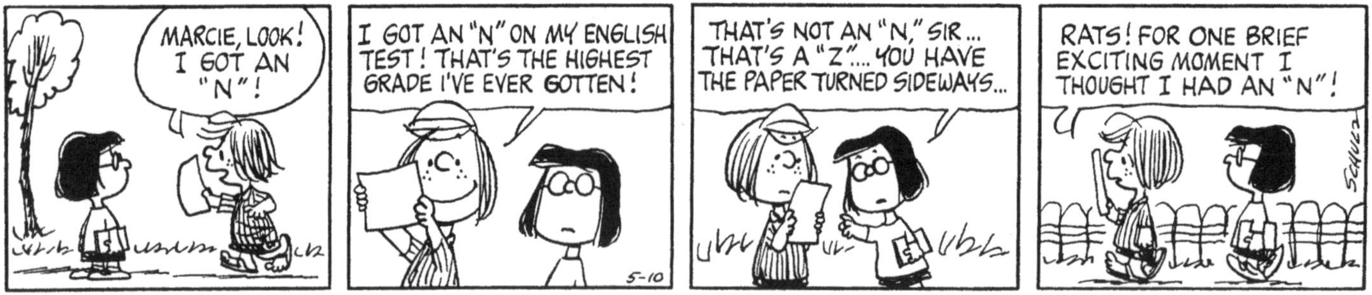
MARCIE, LOOK! I GOT AN "N"!
I GOT AN "N" ON MY ENGLISH TEST! THAT'S THE HIGHEST GRADE I'VE EVER GOTTEN!
5-10
THAT'S NOT AN "N," SIR... THAT'S A "Z".... YOU HAVE THE PAPER TURNED SIDEWAYS...
RATS! FOR ONE BRIEF EXCITING MOMENT I THOUGHT I HAD AN "N"!
SCHULZ

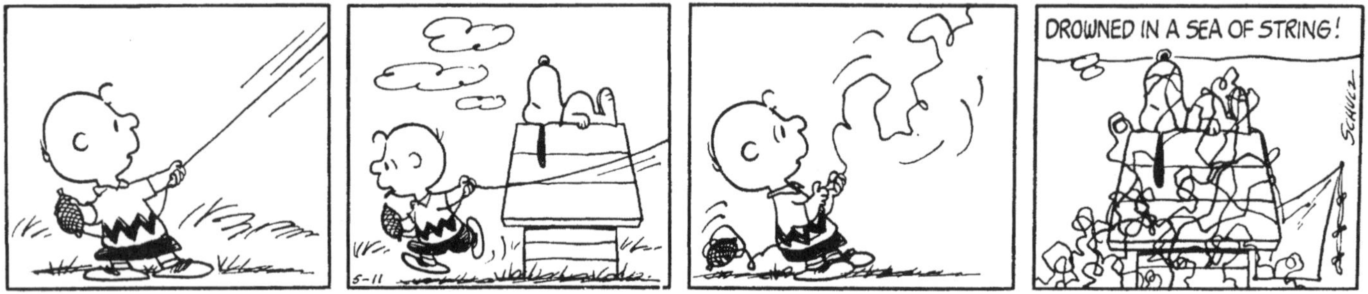
5-11
DROWNED IN A SEA OF STRING!
SCHULZ

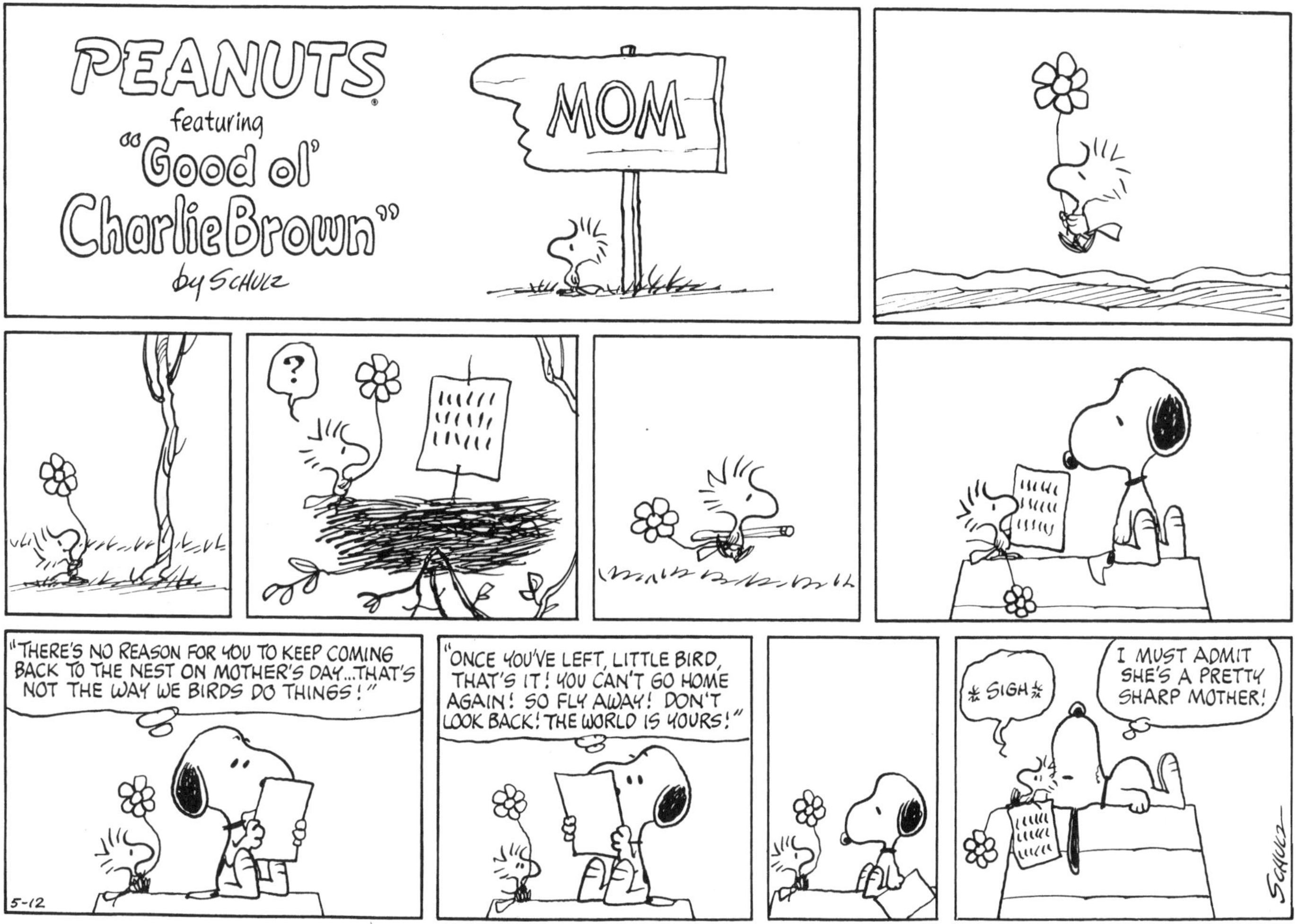

PEANUTS
featuring
"Good ol' CharlieBrown"
by SCHULZ
MOM
?
"THERE'S NO REASON FOR YOU TO KEEP COMING BACK TO THE NEST ON MOTHER'S DAY...THAT'S NOT THE WAY WE BIRDS DO THINGS!"
5-12
"ONCE YOU'VE LEFT, LITTLE BIRD, THAT'S IT! YOU CAN'T GO HOME AGAIN! SO FLY AWAY! DON'T LOOK BACK! THE WORLD IS YOURS!"
* SIGH *
I MUST ADMIT SHE'S A PRETTY SHARP MOTHER!
SCHULZ

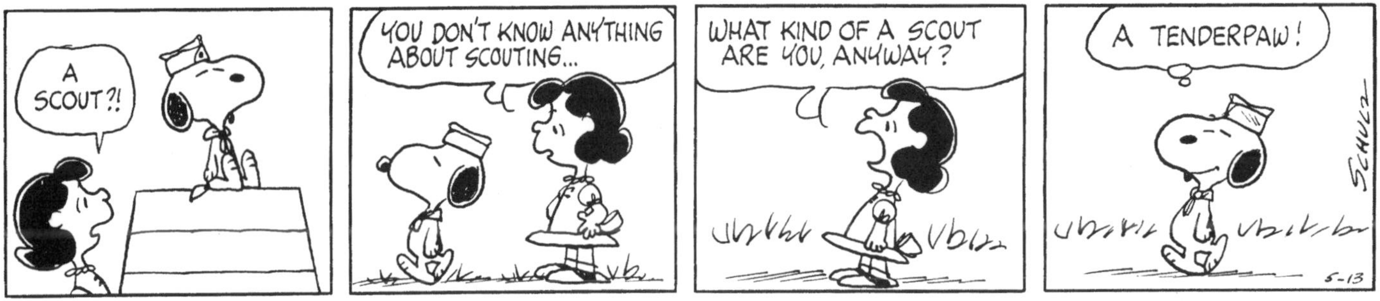
A SCOUT?!
YOU DON'T KNOW ANYTHING ABOUT SCOUTING...
WHAT KIND OF A SCOUT ARE YOU, ANYWAY?
A TENDERPAW!
SCHULZ
5-13

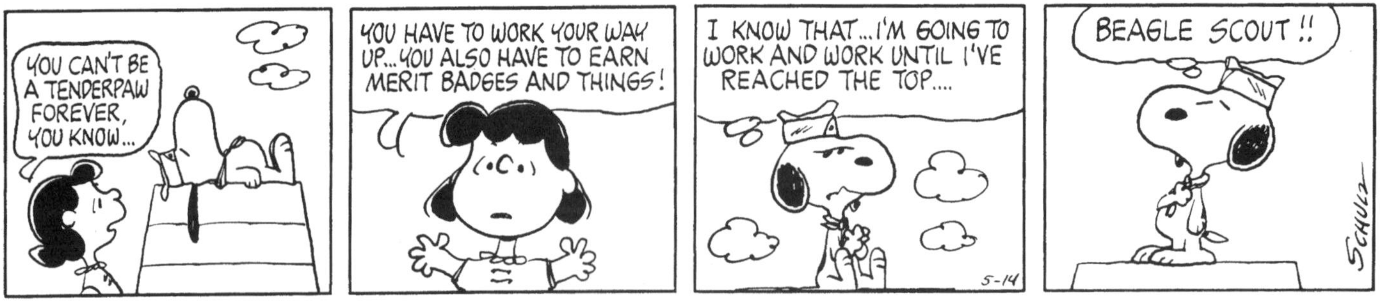
YOU CAN'T BE A TENDERPAW FOREVER, YOU KNOW...
YOU HAVE TO WORK YOUR WAY UP...YOU ALSO HAVE TO EARN MERIT BADGES AND THINGS!
I KNOW THAT...I'M GOING TO WORK AND WORK UNTIL I'VE REACHED THE TOP....
5-14
BEAGLE SCOUT!!
SCHULZ

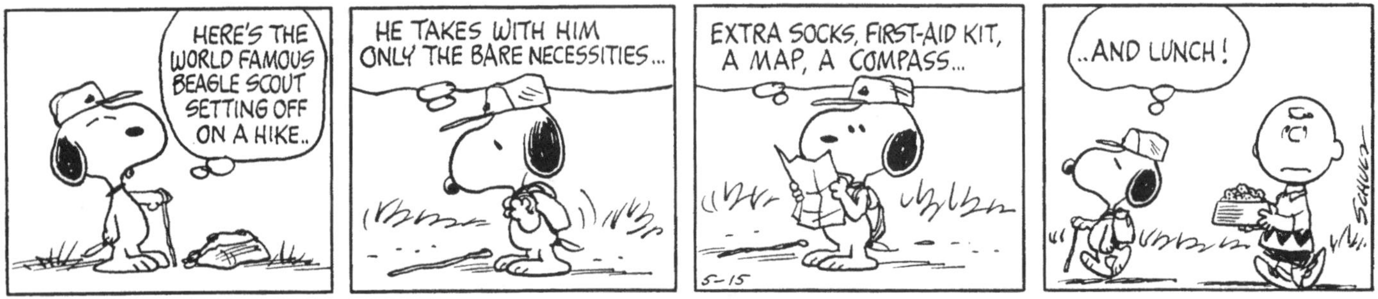
HERE'S THE WORLD FAMOUS BEAGLE SCOUT SETTING OFF ON A HIKE..
HE TAKES WITH HIM ONLY THE BARE NECESSITIES...
EXTRA SOCKS, FIRST-AID KIT, A MAP, A COMPASS...
5-15
..AND LUNCH!
SCHULZ

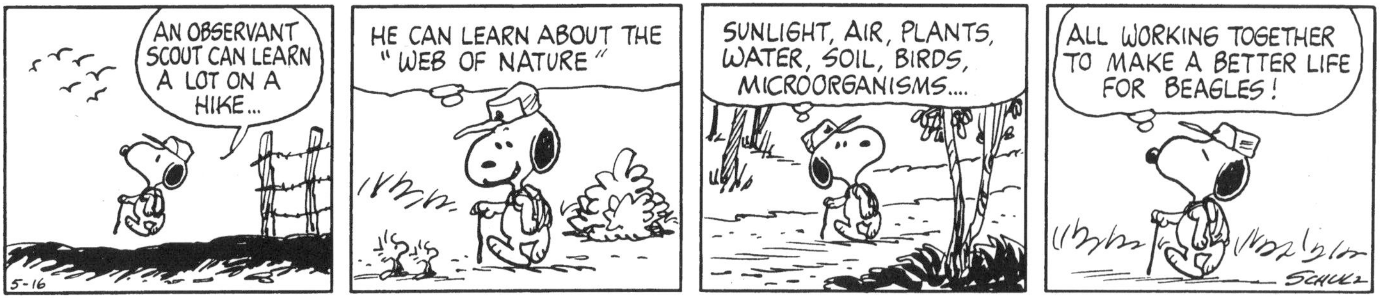
AN OBSERVANT SCOUT CAN LEARN A LOT ON A HIKE...
HE CAN LEARN ABOUT THE "WEB OF NATURE"
SUNLIGHT, AIR, PLANTS, WATER, SOIL, BIRDS, MICROORGANISMS....
ALL WORKING TOGETHER TO MAKE A BETTER LIFE FOR BEAGLES!
5-16
SCHULZ

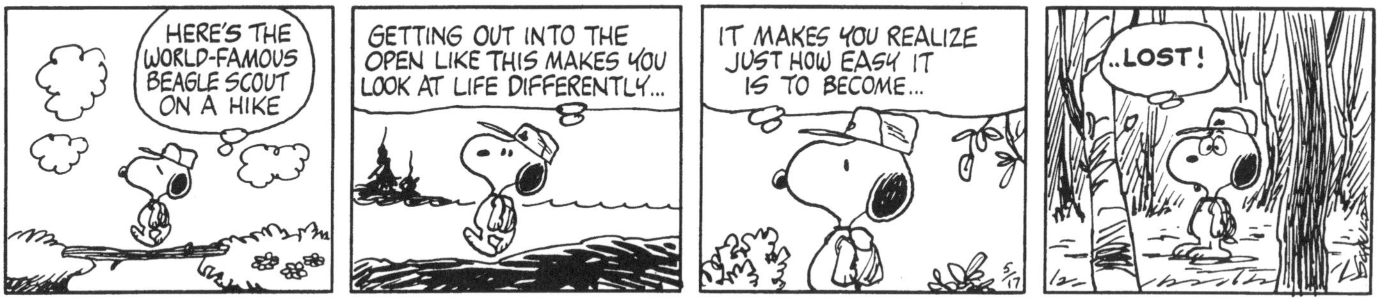
HERE'S THE WORLD-FAMOUS BEAGLE SCOUT ON A HIKE
GETTING OUT INTO THE OPEN LIKE THIS MAKES YOU LOOK AT LIFE DIFFERENTLY...
IT MAKES YOU REALIZE JUST HOW EASY IT IS TO BECOME...
..LOST!
5/17

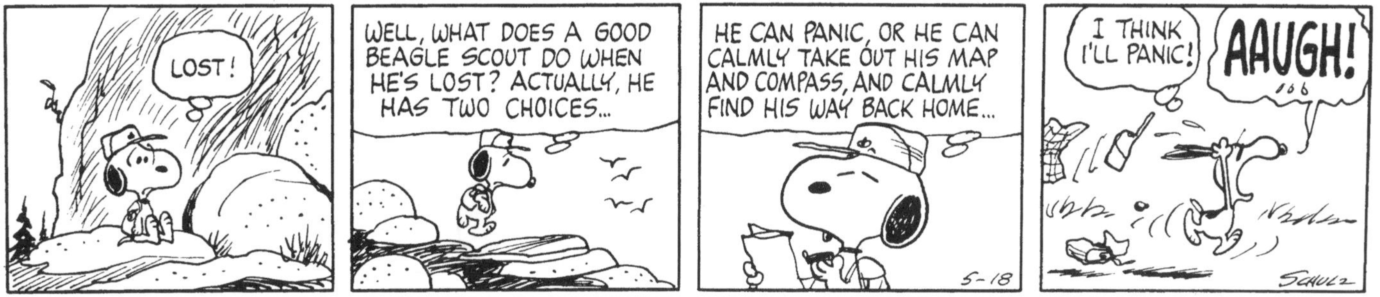
LOST!
WELL, WHAT DOES A GOOD BEAGLE SCOUT DO WHEN HE'S LOST? ACTUALLY, HE HAS TWO CHOICES...
HE CAN PANIC, OR HE CAN CALMLY TAKE OUT HIS MAP AND COMPASS, AND CALMLY FIND HIS WAY BACK HOME...
5-18
I THINK I'LL PANIC!
AAUGH!
SCHULZ

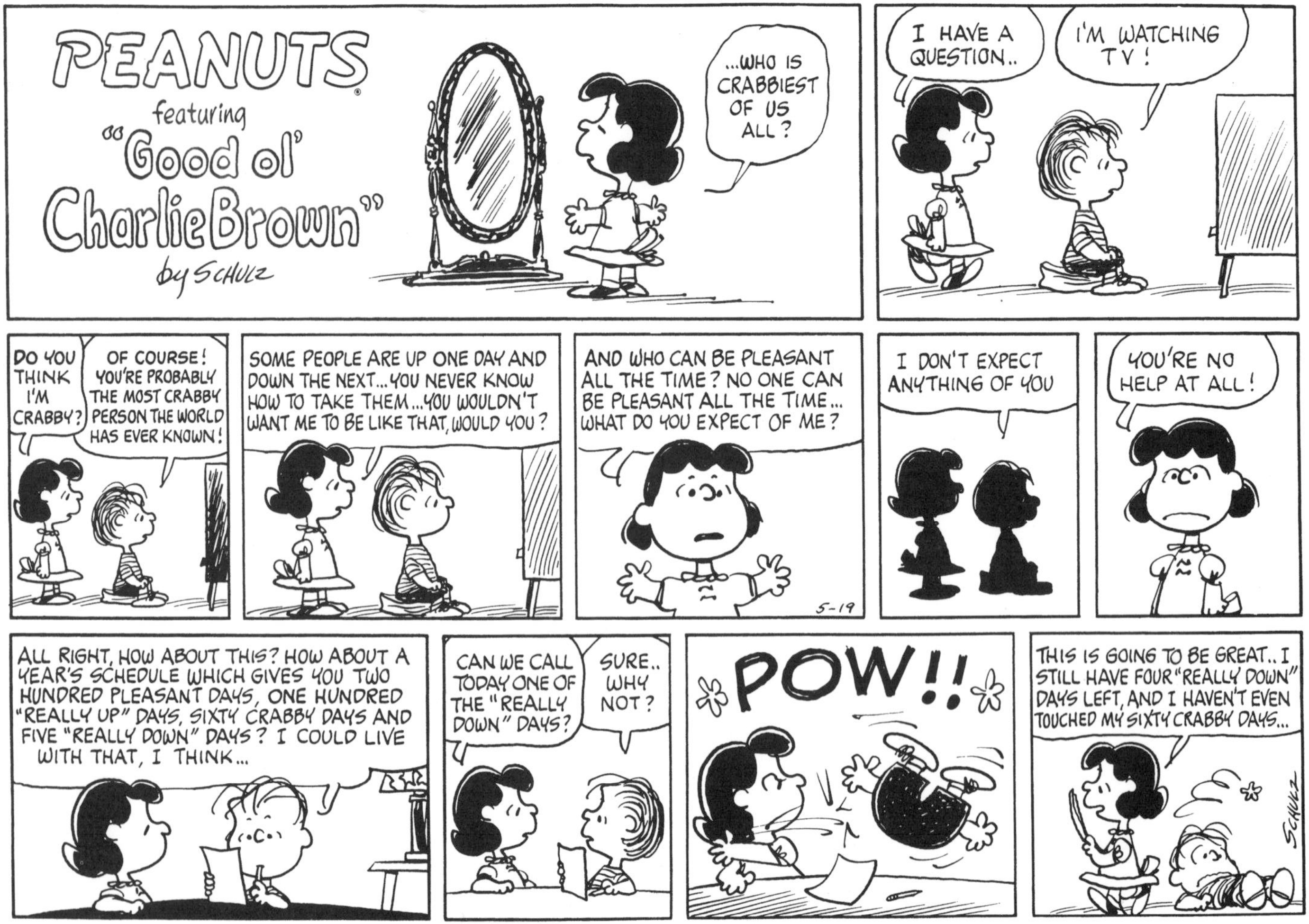
PEANUTS
featuring "Good ol' Charlie Brown"
by SCHULZ
...WHO IS CRABBIEST OF US ALL?
I HAVE A QUESTION..
I'M WATCHING TV!
DO YOU THINK I'M CRABBY?
OF COURSE! YOU'RE PROBABLY THE MOST CRABBY PERSON THE WORLD HAS EVER KNOWN!
SOME PEOPLE ARE UP ONE DAY AND DOWN THE NEXT...YOU NEVER KNOW HOW TO TAKE THEM...YOU WOULDN'T WANT ME TO BE LIKE THAT, WOULD YOU?
AND WHO CAN BE PLEASANT ALL THE TIME? NO ONE CAN BE PLEASANT ALL THE TIME... WHAT DO YOU EXPECT OF ME?
5-19
I DON'T EXPECT ANYTHING OF YOU
YOU'RE NO HELP AT ALL!
ALL RIGHT, HOW ABOUT THIS? HOW ABOUT A YEAR'S SCHEDULE WHICH GIVES YOU TWO HUNDRED PLEASANT DAYS, ONE HUNDRED "REALLY UP" DAYS, SIXTY CRABBY DAYS AND FIVE "REALLY DOWN" DAYS? I COULD LIVE WITH THAT, I THINK...
CAN WE CALL TODAY ONE OF THE "REALLY DOWN" DAYS?
SURE.. WHY NOT?
POW!!
THIS IS GOING TO BE GREAT.. I STILL HAVE FOUR "REALLY DOWN" DAYS LEFT, AND I HAVEN'T EVEN TOUCHED MY SIXTY CRABBY DAYS...
SCHULZ

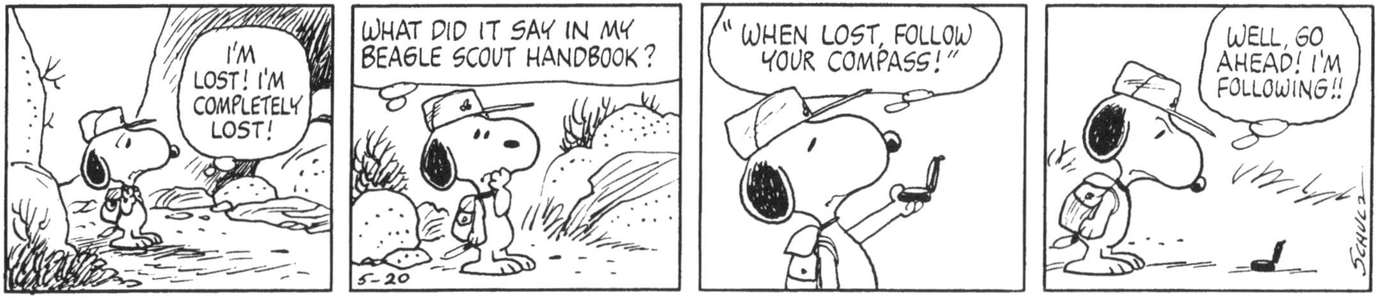
I'M LOST! I'M COMPLETELY LOST!
WHAT DID IT SAY IN MY BEAGLE SCOUT HANDBOOK?
5-20
" WHEN LOST, FOLLOW YOUR COMPASS!"
WELL, GO AHEAD! I'M FOLLOWING!!
SCHULZ

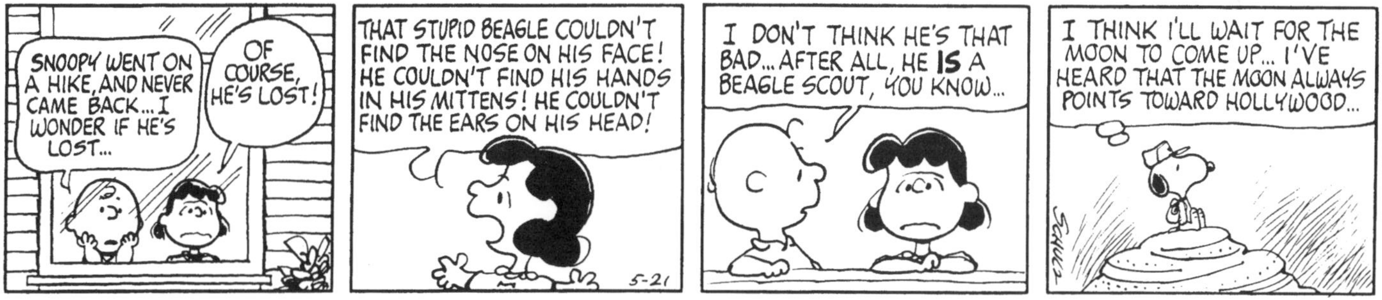
SNOOPY WENT ON A HIKE, AND NEVER CAME BACK... I WONDER IF HE'S LOST...
OF COURSE, HE'S LOST!
THAT STUPID BEAGLE COULDN'T FIND THE NOSE ON HIS FACE! HE COULDN'T FIND HIS HANDS IN HIS MITTENS! HE COULDN'T FIND THE EARS ON HIS HEAD!
5-21
I DON'T THINK HE'S THAT BAD... AFTER ALL, HE **IS** A BEAGLE SCOUT, YOU KNOW...
I THINK I'LL WAIT FOR THE MOON TO COME UP... I'VE HEARD THAT THE MOON ALWAYS POINTS TOWARD HOLLYWOOD...
SCHULZ

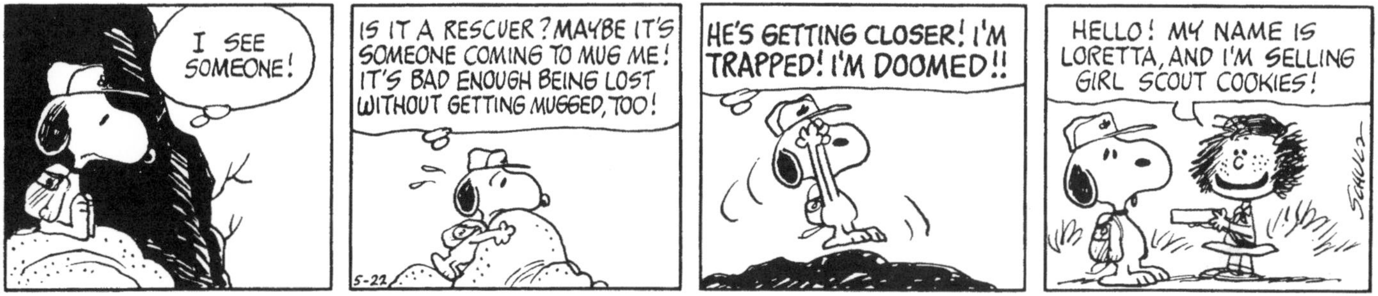
I SEE SOMEONE!
IS IT A RESCUER? MAYBE IT'S SOMEONE COMING TO MUG ME! IT'S BAD ENOUGH BEING LOST WITHOUT GETTING MUGGED, TOO!
5-22
HE'S GETTING CLOSER! I'M TRAPPED! I'M DOOMED!!
HELLO! MY NAME IS LORETTA, AND I'M SELLING GIRL SCOUT COOKIES!
SCHULZ

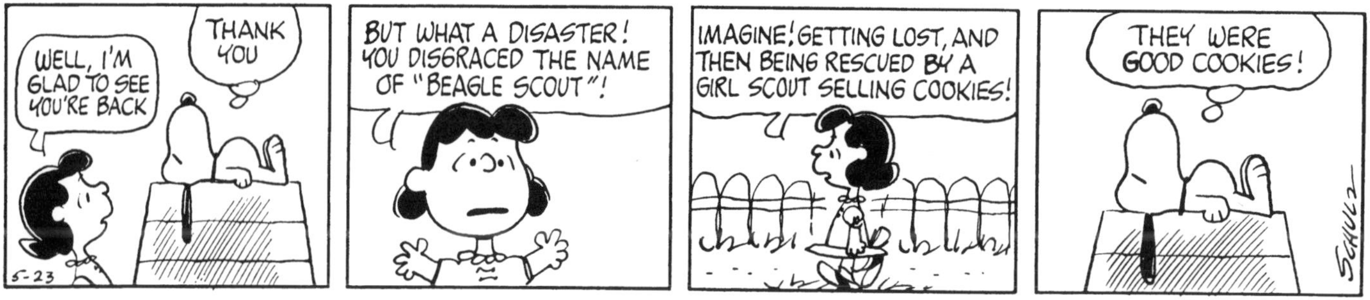
WELL, I'M GLAD TO SEE YOU'RE BACK
THANK YOU
5-23
BUT WHAT A DISASTER! YOU DISGRACED THE NAME OF "BEAGLE SCOUT"!
IMAGINE! GETTING LOST, AND THEN BEING RESCUED BY A GIRL SCOUT SELLING COOKIES!
THEY WERE GOOD COOKIES!
SCHULZ

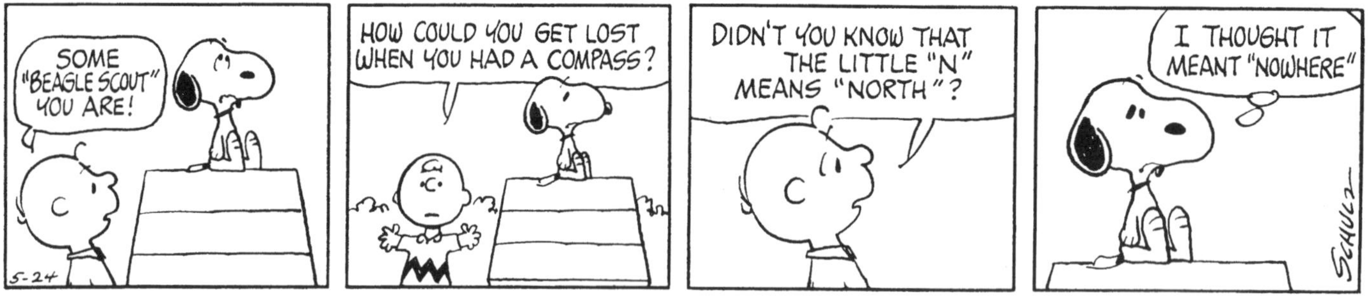
SOME "BEAGLE SCOUT" YOU ARE!
5-24
HOW COULD YOU GET LOST WHEN YOU HAD A COMPASS?
DIDN'T YOU KNOW THAT THE LITTLE "N" MEANS "NORTH"?
I THOUGHT IT MEANT "NOWHERE"
SCHULZ

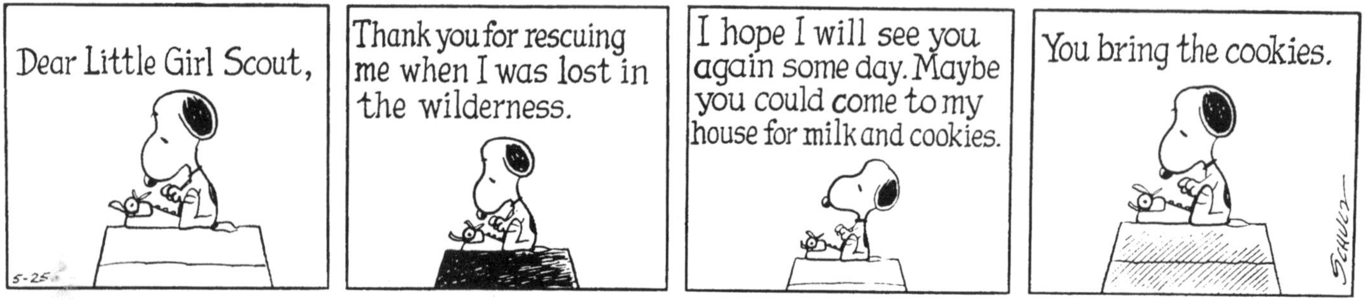
Dear Little Girl Scout,
5-25
Thank you for rescuing me when I was lost in the wilderness.
I hope I will see you again some day. Maybe you could come to my house for milk and cookies.
You bring the cookies.
SCHULZ

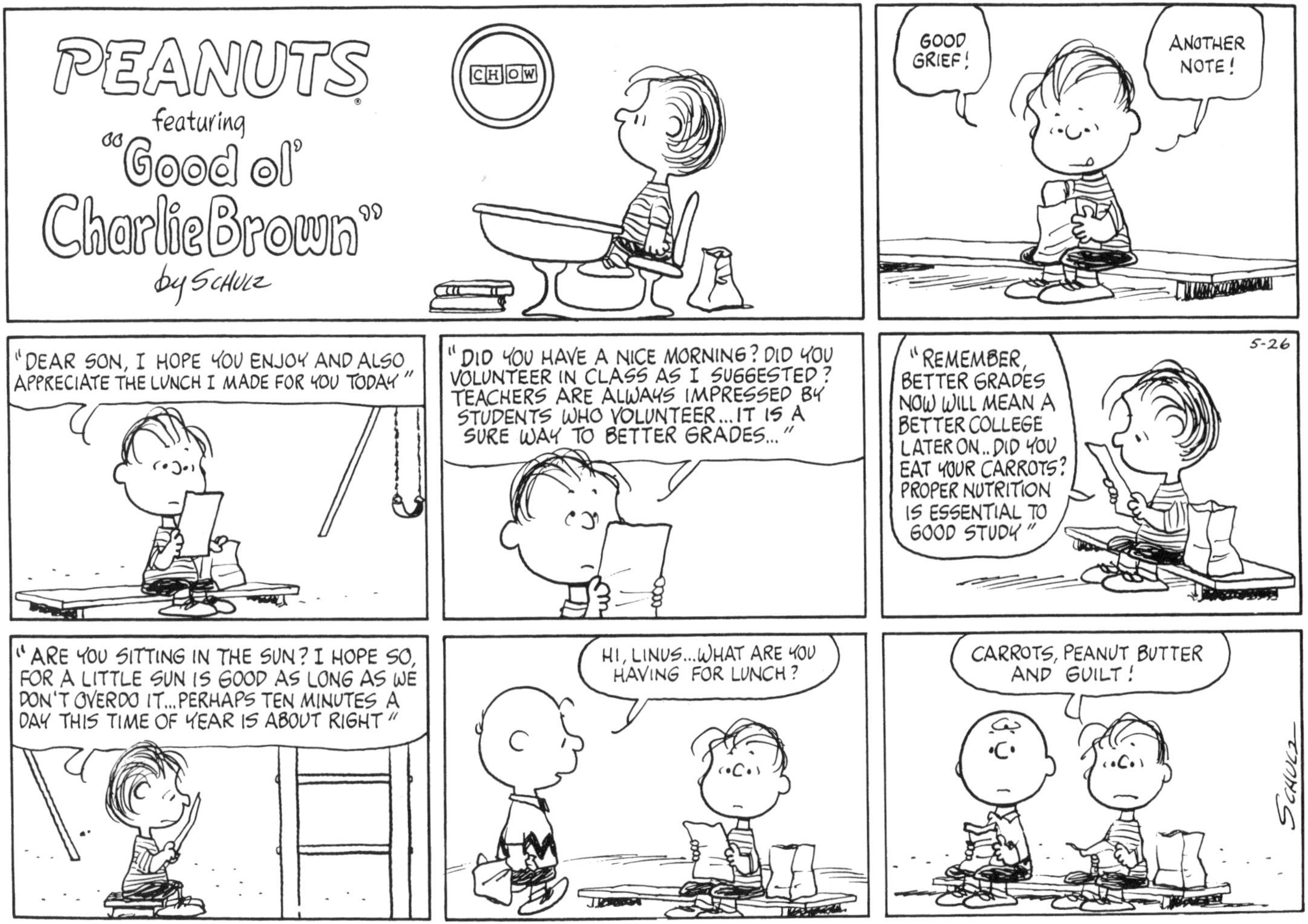
PEANUTS
featuring
"Good ol' Charlie Brown"
by SCHULZ
CHOW
GOOD GRIEF!
ANOTHER NOTE!
"DEAR SON, I HOPE YOU ENJOY AND ALSO APPRECIATE THE LUNCH I MADE FOR YOU TODAY"
"DID YOU HAVE A NICE MORNING? DID YOU VOLUNTEER IN CLASS AS I SUGGESTED? TEACHERS ARE ALWAYS IMPRESSED BY STUDENTS WHO VOLUNTEER...IT IS A SURE WAY TO BETTER GRADES..."
5-26
"REMEMBER, BETTER GRADES NOW WILL MEAN A BETTER COLLEGE LATER ON..DID YOU EAT YOUR CARROTS? PROPER NUTRITION IS ESSENTIAL TO GOOD STUDY"
"ARE YOU SITTING IN THE SUN? I HOPE SO, FOR A LITTLE SUN IS GOOD AS LONG AS WE DON'T OVERDO IT...PERHAPS TEN MINUTES A DAY THIS TIME OF YEAR IS ABOUT RIGHT"
HI, LINUS...WHAT ARE YOU HAVING FOR LUNCH?
CARROTS, PEANUT BUTTER AND GUILT!
SCHULZ

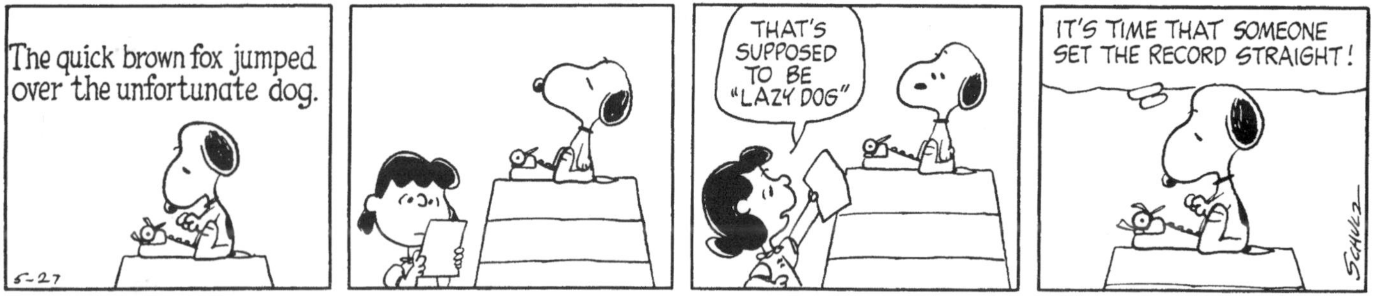
The quick brown fox jumped over the unfortunate dog.
5-27
THAT'S SUPPOSED TO BE "LAZY DOG"
IT'S TIME THAT SOMEONE SET THE RECORD STRAIGHT!
SCHULZ

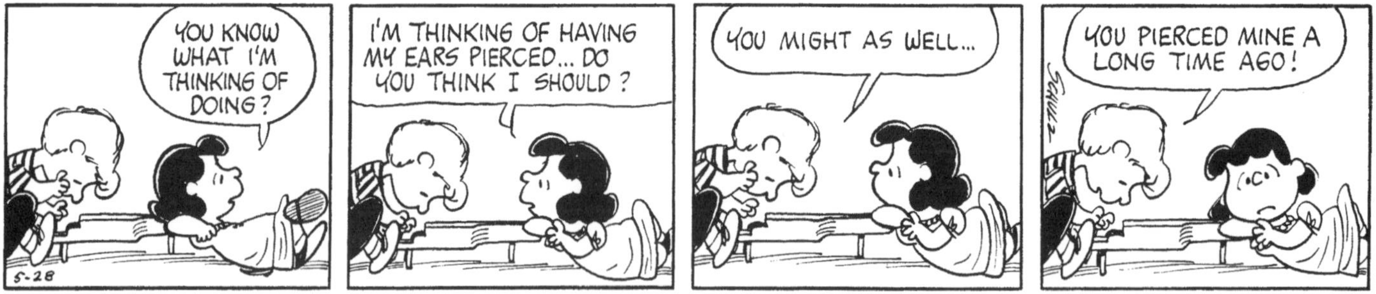
YOU KNOW WHAT I'M THINKING OF DOING?
5-28
I'M THINKING OF HAVING MY EARS PIERCED... DO YOU THINK I SHOULD?
YOU MIGHT AS WELL...
YOU PIERCED MINE A LONG TIME AGO!
SCHULZ

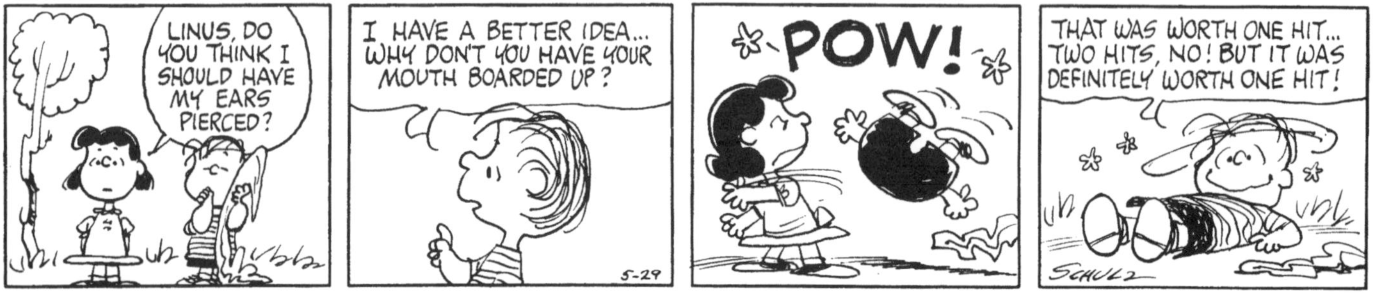
LINUS, DO YOU THINK I SHOULD HAVE MY EARS PIERCED?
I HAVE A BETTER IDEA... WHY DON'T YOU HAVE YOUR MOUTH BOARDED UP?
5-29
POW!
THAT WAS WORTH ONE HIT... TWO HITS, NO! BUT IT WAS DEFINITELY WORTH ONE HIT!
SCHULZ

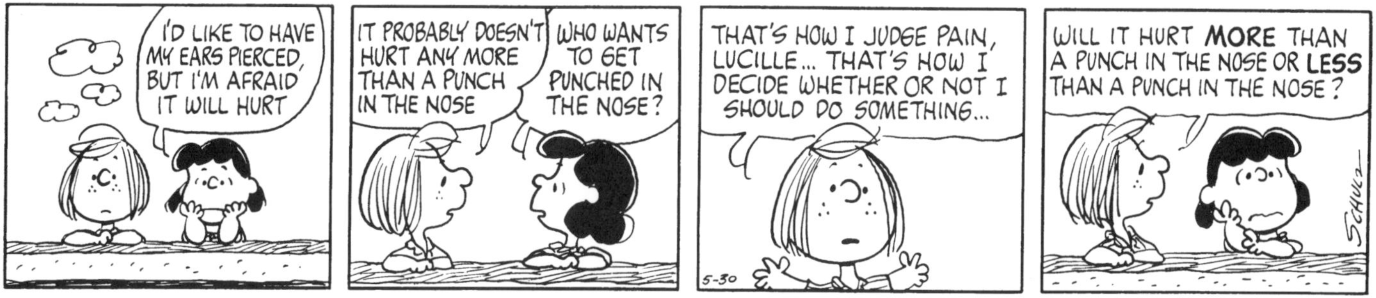
I'D LIKE TO HAVE MY EARS PIERCED, BUT I'M AFRAID IT WILL HURT
IT PROBABLY DOESN'T HURT ANY MORE THAN A PUNCH IN THE NOSE
WHO WANTS TO GET PUNCHED IN THE NOSE?
THAT'S HOW I JUDGE PAIN, LUCILLE... THAT'S HOW I DECIDE WHETHER OR NOT I SHOULD DO SOMETHING...
5-30
WILL IT HURT **MORE** THAN A PUNCH IN THE NOSE OR **LESS** THAN A PUNCH IN THE NOSE?
SCHULZ

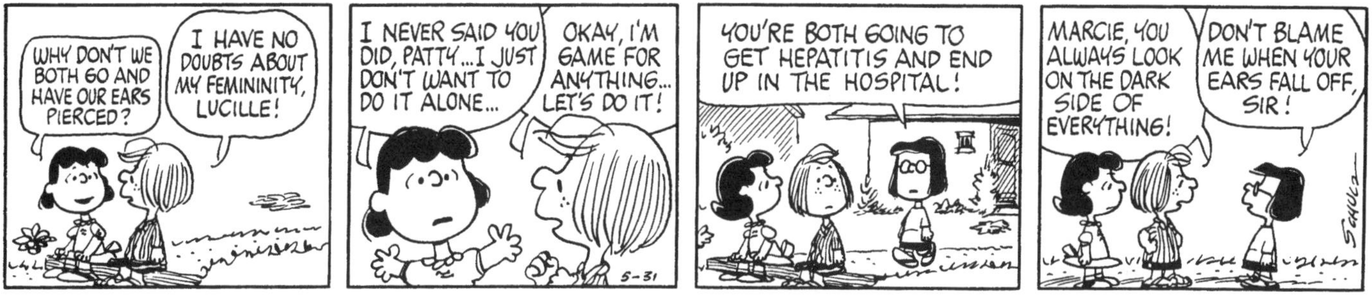
WHY DON'T WE BOTH GO AND HAVE OUR EARS PIERCED?
I HAVE NO DOUBTS ABOUT MY FEMININITY, LUCILLE!
I NEVER SAID YOU DID, PATTY...I JUST DON'T WANT TO DO IT ALONE...
OKAY, I'M GAME FOR ANYTHING... LET'S DO IT!
5-31
YOU'RE BOTH GOING TO GET HEPATITIS AND END UP IN THE HOSPITAL!
MARCIE, YOU ALWAYS LOOK ON THE DARK SIDE OF EVERYTHING!
DON'T BLAME ME WHEN YOUR EARS FALL OFF, SIR!
SCHULZ

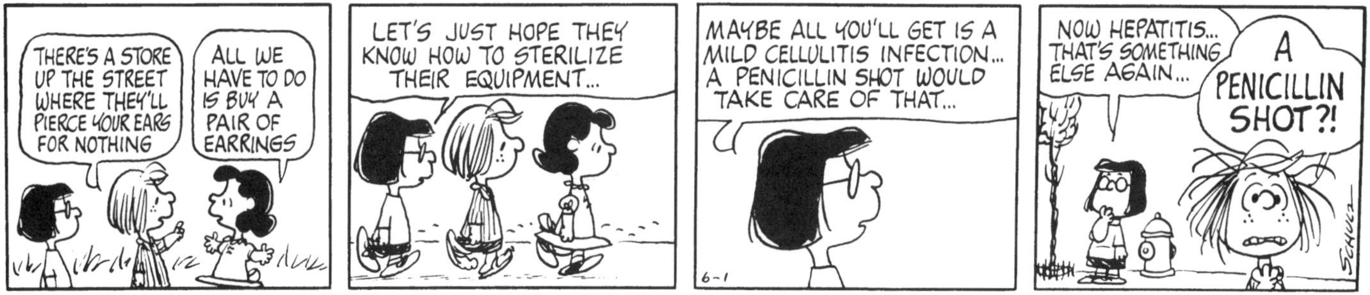
THERE'S A STORE UP THE STREET WHERE THEY'LL PIERCE YOUR EAR FOR NOTHING
ALL WE HAVE TO DO IS BUY A PAIR OF EARRINGS
LET'S JUST HOPE THEY KNOW HOW TO STERILIZE THEIR EQUIPMENT...
MAYBE ALL YOU'LL GET IS A MILD CELLULITIS INFECTION... A PENICILLIN SHOT WOULD TAKE CARE OF THAT...
6-1
NOW HEPATITIS... THAT'S SOMETHING ELSE AGAIN...
A PENICILLIN SHOT?!
SCHULZ

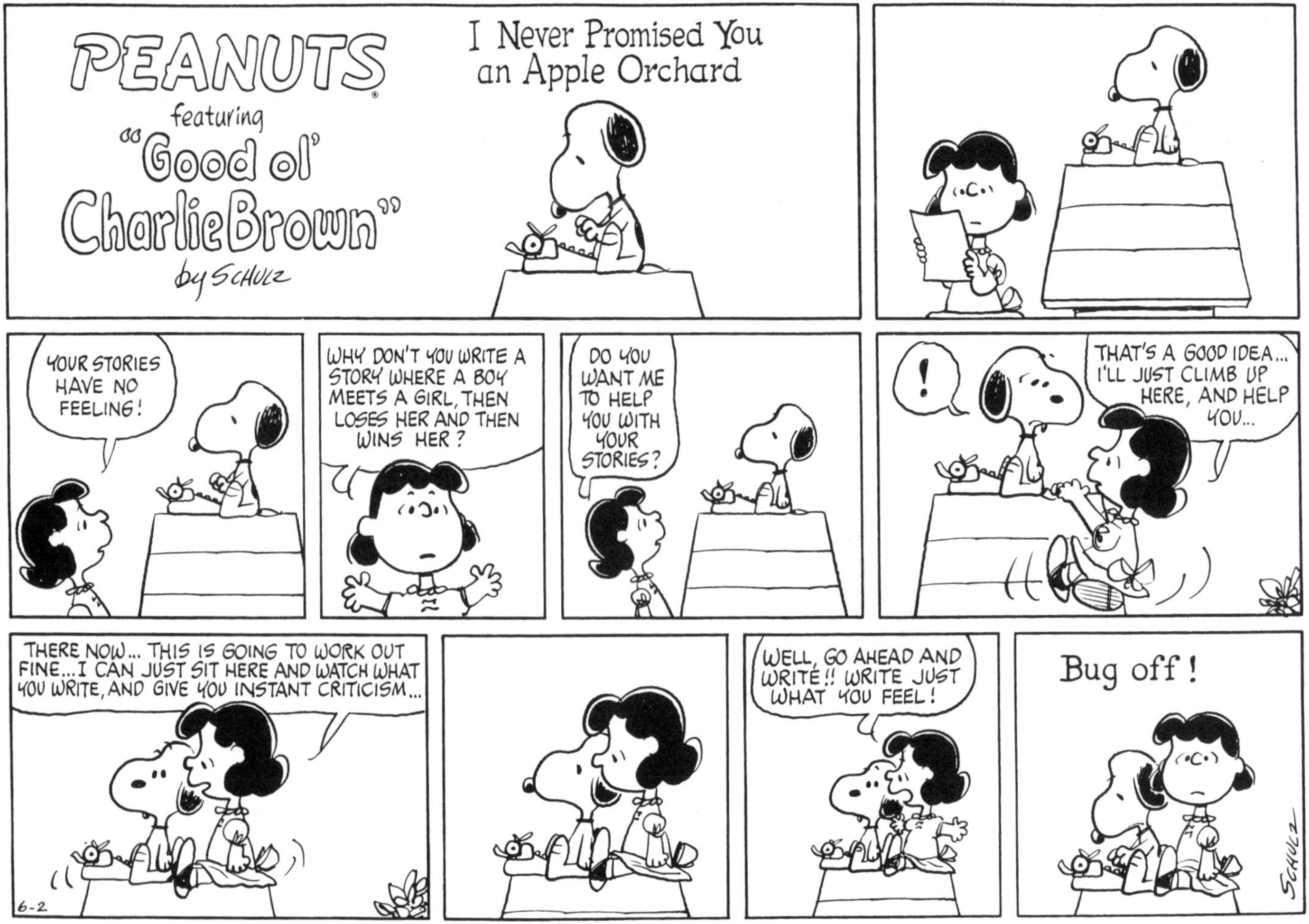
PEANUTS
featuring "Good ol' Charlie Brown"
by SCHULZ
I Never Promised You an Apple Orchard
YOUR STORIES HAVE NO FEELING!
WHY DON'T YOU WRITE A STORY WHERE A BOY MEETS A GIRL, THEN LOSES HER AND THEN WINS HER?
DO YOU WANT ME TO HELP YOU WITH YOUR STORIES?
!
THAT'S A GOOD IDEA... I'LL JUST CLIMB UP HERE, AND HELP YOU...
THERE NOW... THIS IS GOING TO WORK OUT FINE...I CAN JUST SIT HERE AND WATCH WHAT YOU WRITE, AND GIVE YOU INSTANT CRITICISM...
6-2
WELL, GO AHEAD AND WRITE!! WRITE JUST WHAT YOU FEEL!
Bug off!
SCHULZ

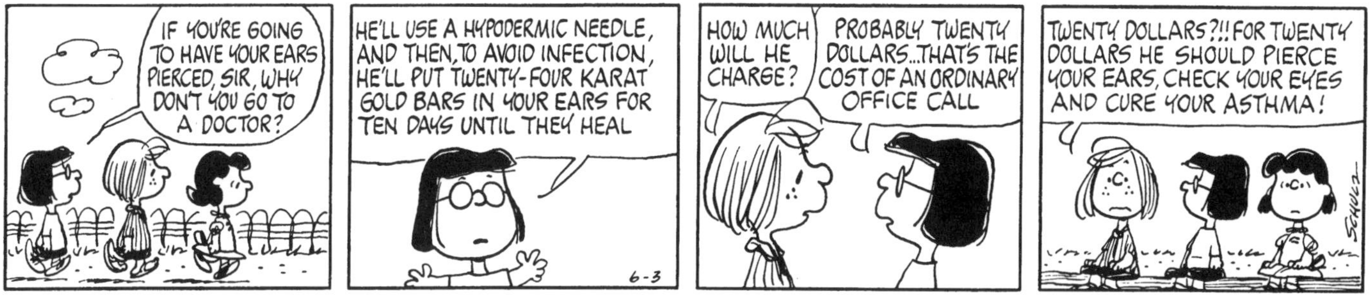
IF YOU'RE GOING TO HAVE YOUR EARS PIERCED, SIR, WHY DON'T YOU GO TO A DOCTOR?
HE'LL USE A HYPODERMIC NEEDLE, AND THEN, TO AVOID INFECTION, HE'LL PUT TWENTY-FOUR KARAT GOLD BARS IN YOUR EARS FOR TEN DAYS UNTIL THEY HEAL
6-3
HOW MUCH WILL HE CHARGE?
PROBABLY TWENTY DOLLARS...THAT'S THE COST OF AN ORDINARY OFFICE CALL
TWENTY DOLLARS?!! FOR TWENTY DOLLARS HE SHOULD PIERCE YOUR EARS, CHECK YOUR EYES AND CURE YOUR ASTHMA!

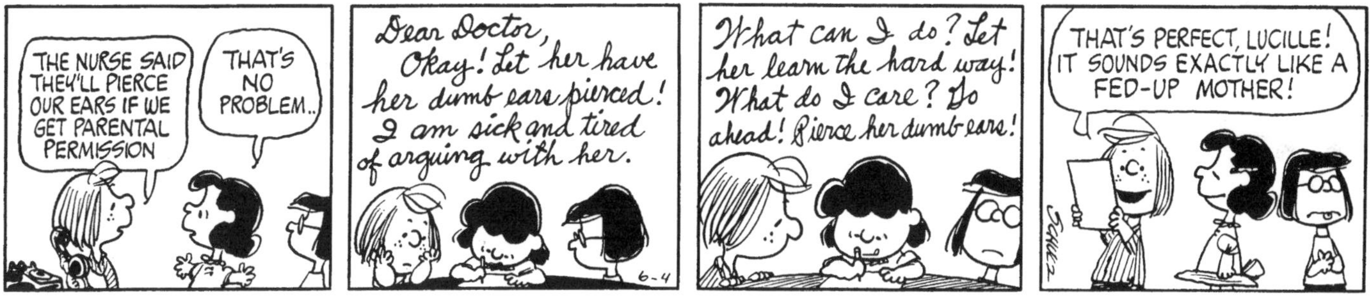
THE NURSE SAID THEY'LL PIERCE OUR EARS IF WE GET PARENTAL PERMISSION
THAT'S NO PROBLEM...
Dear Doctor,
Okay! Let her have her dumb ears pierced! I am sick and tired of arguing with her.
6-4
What can I do? Let her learn the hard way! What do I care? Go ahead! Pierce her dumb ears!
THAT'S PERFECT, LUCILLE! IT SOUNDS EXACTLY LIKE A FED-UP MOTHER!

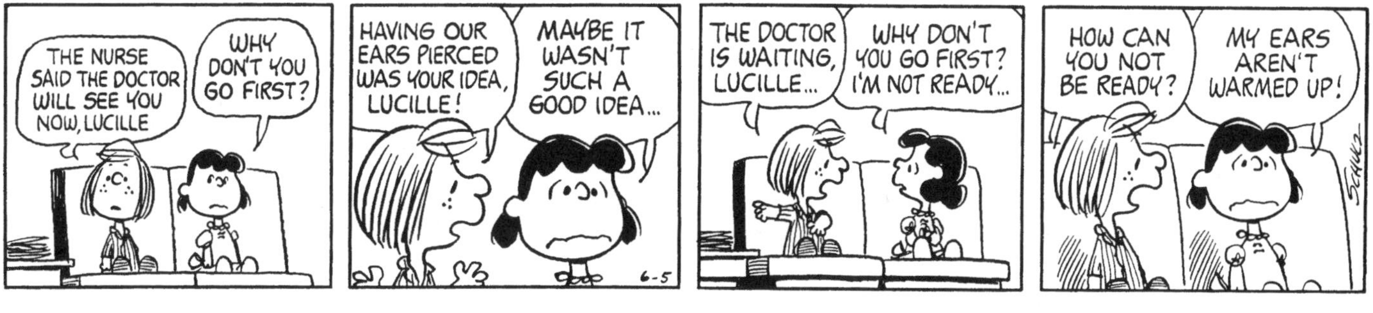
THE NURSE SAID THE DOCTOR WILL SEE YOU NOW, LUCILLE
WHY DON'T YOU GO FIRST?
HAVING OUR EARS PIERCED WAS YOUR IDEA, LUCILLE!
MAYBE IT WASN'T SUCH A GOOD IDEA...
6-5
THE DOCTOR IS WAITING, LUCILLE...
WHY DON'T YOU GO FIRST? I'M NOT READY...
HOW CAN YOU NOT BE READY?
MY EARS AREN'T WARMED UP!

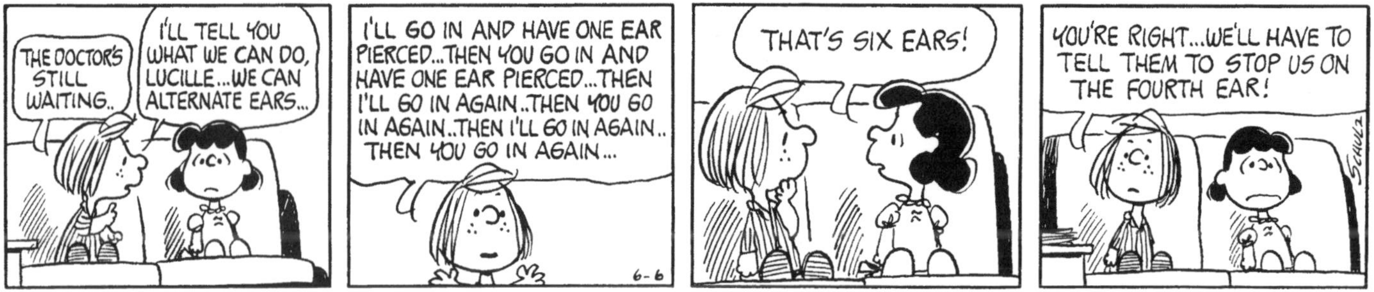
THE DOCTOR'S STILL WAITING..
I'LL TELL YOU WHAT WE CAN DO, LUCILLE...WE CAN ALTERNATE EARS...
I'LL GO IN AND HAVE ONE EAR PIERCED...THEN YOU GO IN AND HAVE ONE EAR PIERCED...THEN I'LL GO IN AGAIN..THEN YOU GO IN AGAIN..THEN I'LL GO IN AGAIN.. THEN YOU GO IN AGAIN...
6-6
THAT'S SIX EARS!
YOU'RE RIGHT...WE'LL HAVE TO TELL THEM TO STOP US ON THE FOURTH EAR!
SCHULZ

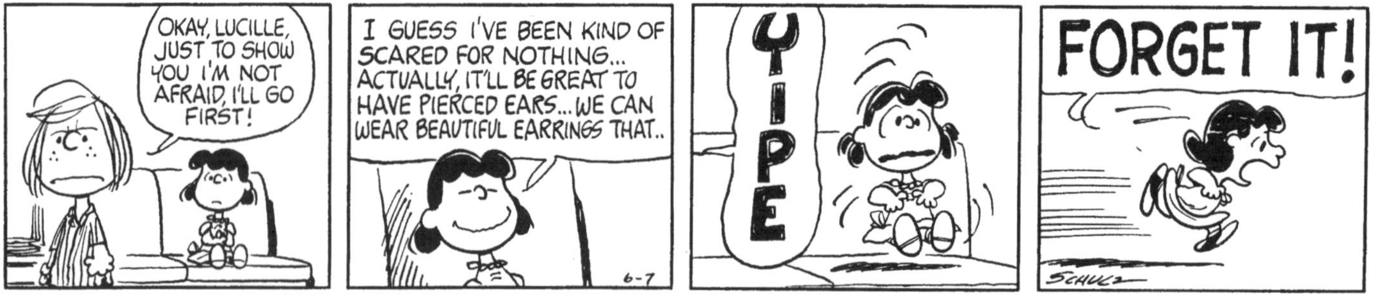
OKAY, LUCILLE, JUST TO SHOW YOU I'M NOT AFRAID, I'LL GO FIRST!
I GUESS I'VE BEEN KIND OF SCARED FOR NOTHING... ACTUALLY, IT'LL BE GREAT TO HAVE PIERCED EARS...WE CAN WEAR BEAUTIFUL EARRINGS THAT..
6-7
YIPE
FORGET IT!
SCHULZ

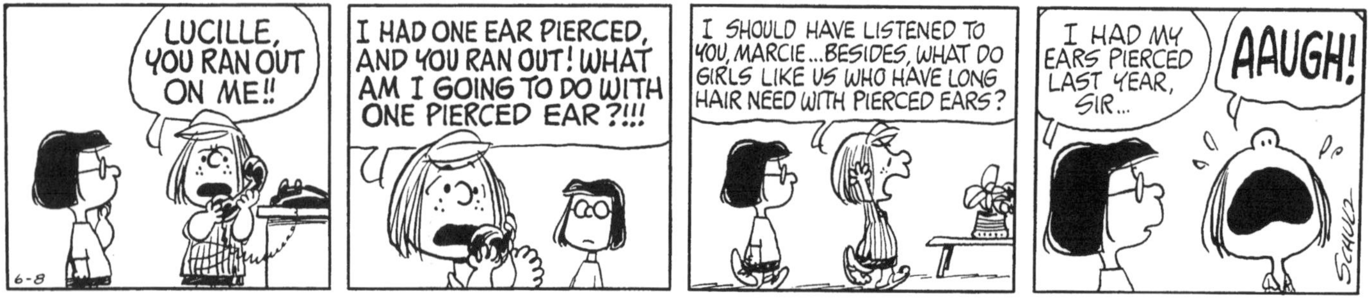
LUCILLE, YOU RAN OUT ON ME!!
6-8
I HAD ONE EAR PIERCED, AND YOU RAN OUT! WHAT AM I GOING TO DO WITH ONE PIERCED EAR?!!!
I SHOULD HAVE LISTENED TO YOU, MARCIE...BESIDES, WHAT DO GIRLS LIKE US WHO HAVE LONG HAIR NEED WITH PIERCED EARS?
I HAD MY EARS PIERCED LAST YEAR, SIR...
AAUGH!
SCHULZ

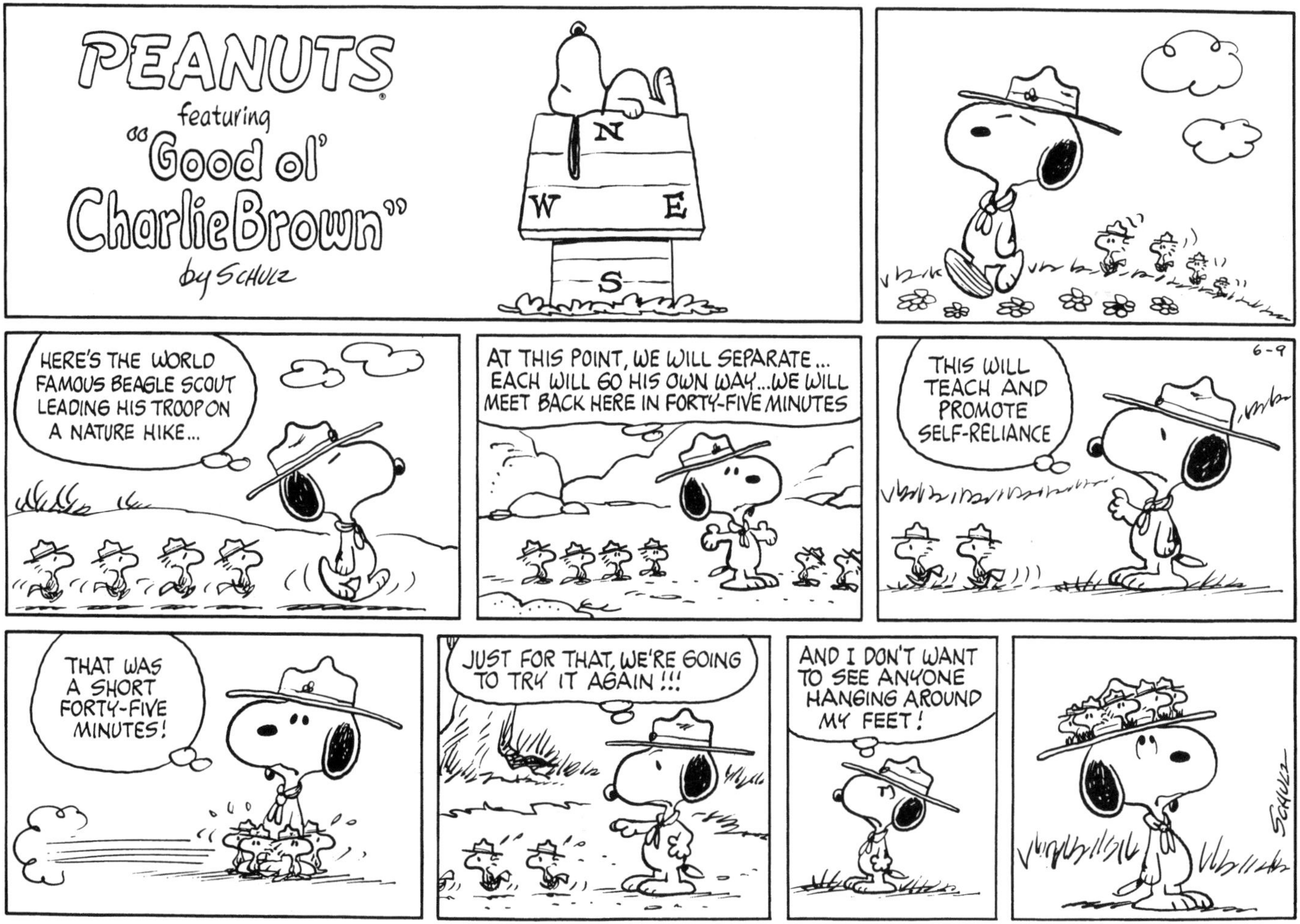
PEANUTS
featuring
"Good ol' Charlie Brown"
by SCHULZ
N
W
E
S
HERE'S THE WORLD FAMOUS BEAGLE SCOUT LEADING HIS TROOP ON A NATURE HIKE...
AT THIS POINT, WE WILL SEPARATE... EACH WILL GO HIS OWN WAY...WE WILL MEET BACK HERE IN FORTY-FIVE MINUTES
6-9
THIS WILL TEACH AND PROMOTE SELF-RELIANCE
THAT WAS A SHORT FORTY-FIVE MINUTES!
JUST FOR THAT, WE'RE GOING TO TRY IT AGAIN!!!
AND I DON'T WANT TO SEE ANYONE HANGING AROUND MY FEET!
SCHULZ

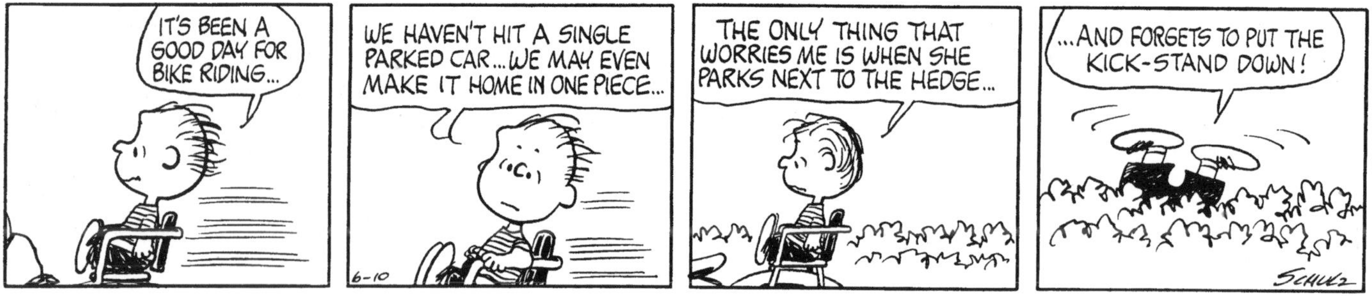
IT'S BEEN A GOOD DAY FOR BIKE RIDING...
WE HAVEN'T HIT A SINGLE PARKED CAR...WE MAY EVEN MAKE IT HOME IN ONE PIECE...
6-10
THE ONLY THING THAT WORRIES ME IS WHEN SHE PARKS NEXT TO THE HEDGE...
...AND FORGETS TO PUT THE KICK-STAND DOWN!
SCHULZ

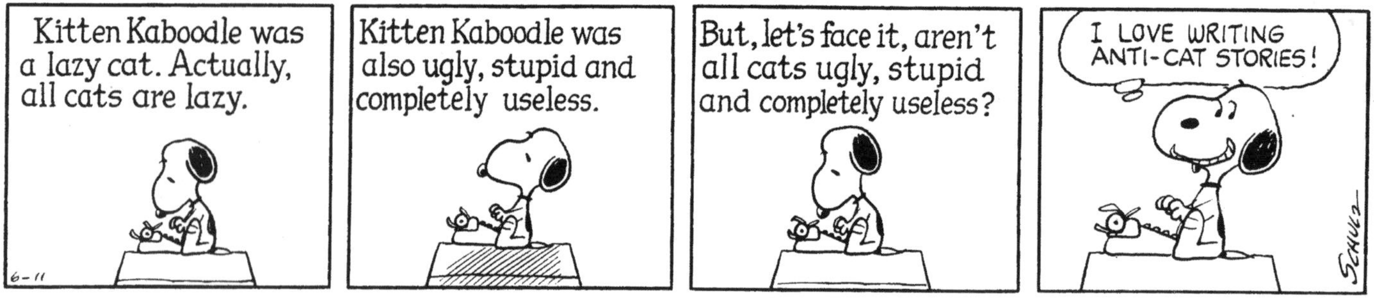
Kitten Kaboodle was a lazy cat. Actually, all cats are lazy.
6-11
Kitten Kaboodle was also ugly, stupid and completely useless.
But, let's face it, aren't all cats ugly, stupid and completely useless?
I LOVE WRITING ANTI-CAT STORIES!
SCHULZ

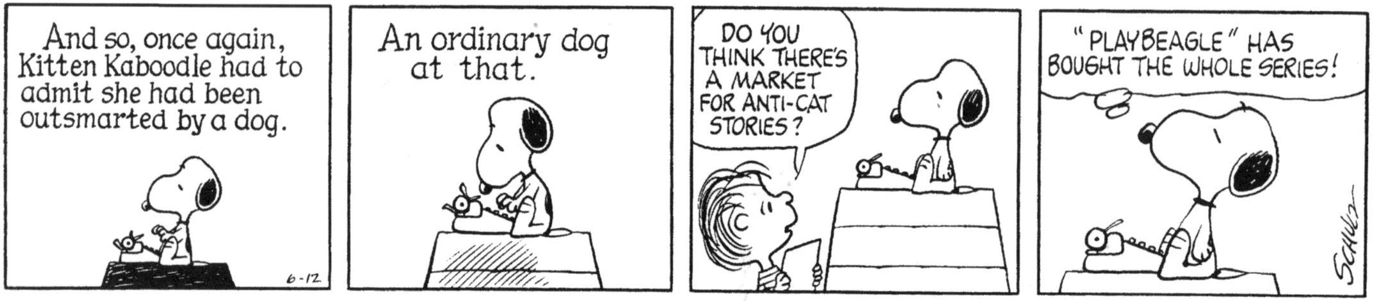
And so, once again, Kitten Kaboodle had to admit she had been outsmarted by a dog.
6-12
An ordinary dog at that.
DO YOU THINK THERE'S A MARKET FOR ANTI-CAT STORIES?
"PLAYBEAGLE" HAS BOUGHT THE WHOLE SERIES!
SCHULZ

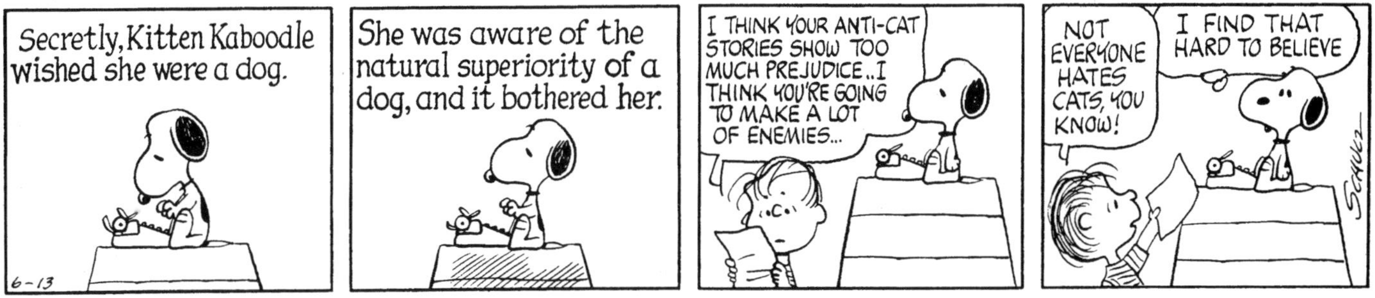
Secretly, Kitten Kaboodle wished she were a dog.
She was aware of the natural superiority of a dog, and it bothered her.
I THINK YOUR ANTI-CAT STORIES SHOW TOO MUCH PREJUDICE..I THINK YOU'RE GOING TO MAKE A LOT OF ENEMIES...
NOT EVERYONE HATES CATS, YOU KNOW!
I FIND THAT HARD TO BELIEVE
SCHULZ
6-13

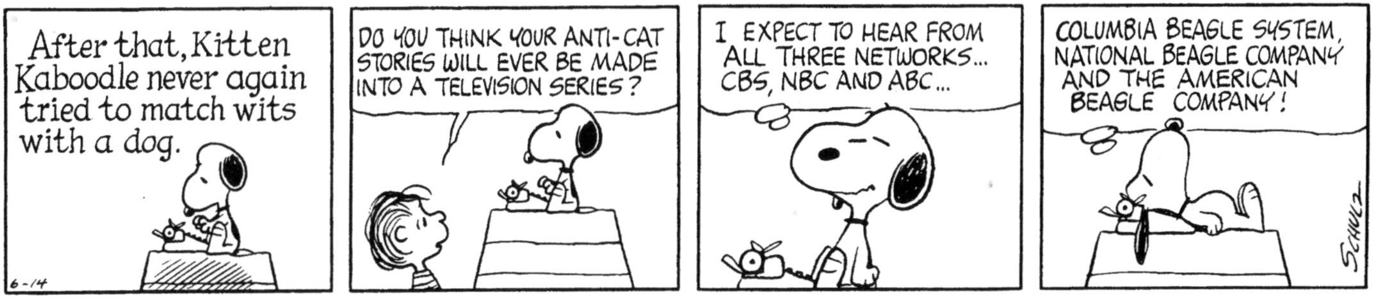
After that, Kitten Kaboodle never again tried to match wits with a dog.
DO YOU THINK YOUR ANTI-CAT STORIES WILL EVER BE MADE INTO A TELEVISION SERIES?
I EXPECT TO HEAR FROM ALL THREE NETWORKS... CBS, NBC AND ABC...
COLUMBIA BEAGLE SYSTEM, NATIONAL BEAGLE COMPANY AND THE AMERICAN BEAGLE COMPANY!
SCHULZ
6-14

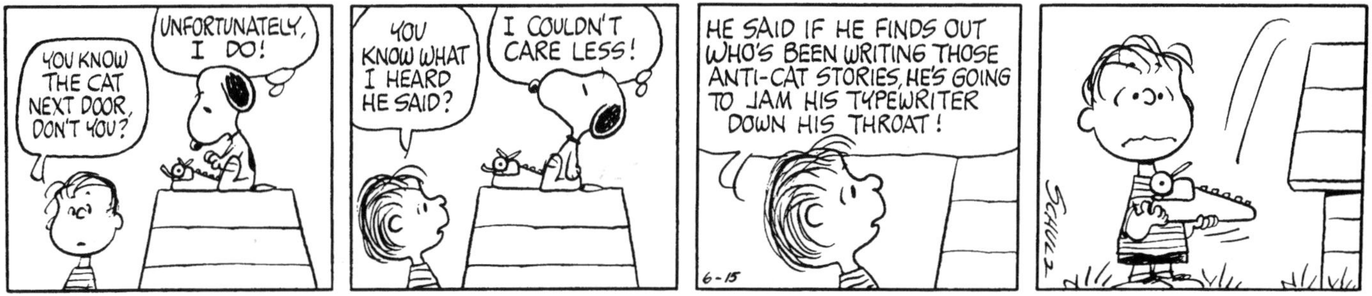
YOU KNOW THE CAT NEXT DOOR, DON'T YOU?
UNFORTUNATELY, I DO!
YOU KNOW WHAT I HEARD HE SAID?
I COULDN'T CARE LESS!
HE SAID IF HE FINDS OUT WHO'S BEEN WRITING THOSE ANTI-CAT STORIES, HE'S GOING TO JAM HIS TYPEWRITER DOWN HIS THROAT!
SCHULZ
6-15

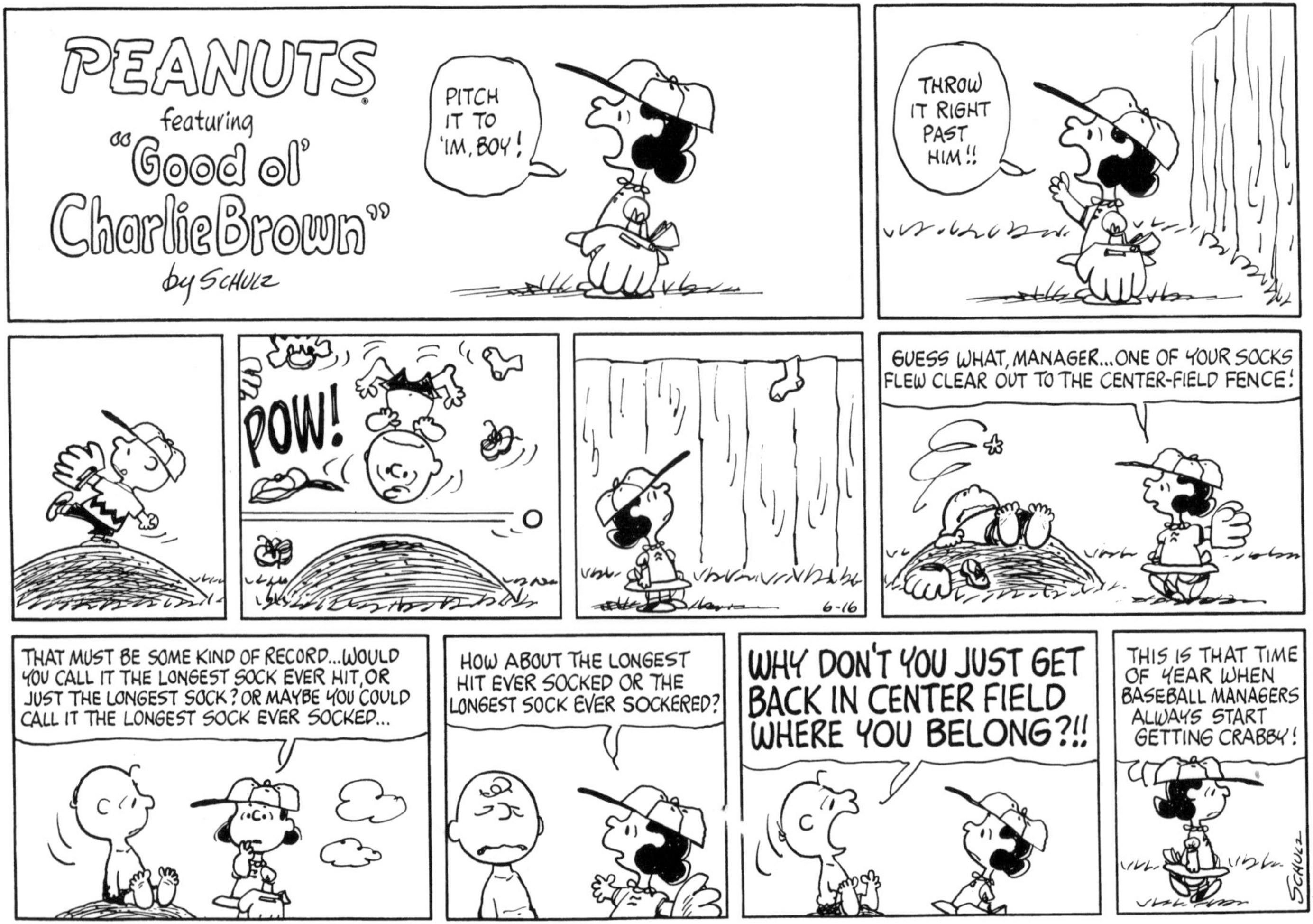
PEANUTS
featuring "Good ol' CharlieBrown"
by SCHULZ
PITCH IT TO 'IM, BOY!
THROW IT RIGHT PAST HIM!!
POW!
6-16
GUESS WHAT, MANAGER...ONE OF YOUR SOCKS FLEW CLEAR OUT TO THE CENTER-FIELD FENCE!
THAT MUST BE SOME KIND OF RECORD...WOULD YOU CALL IT THE LONGEST SOCK EVER HIT, OR JUST THE LONGEST SOCK? OR MAYBE YOU COULD CALL IT THE LONGEST SOCK EVER SOCKED...
HOW ABOUT THE LONGEST HIT EVER SOCKED OR THE LONGEST SOCK EVER SOCKERED?
WHY DON'T YOU JUST GET BACK IN CENTER FIELD WHERE YOU BELONG?!!
THIS IS THAT TIME OF YEAR WHEN BASEBALL MANAGERS ALWAYS START GETTING CRABBY!
SCHULZ

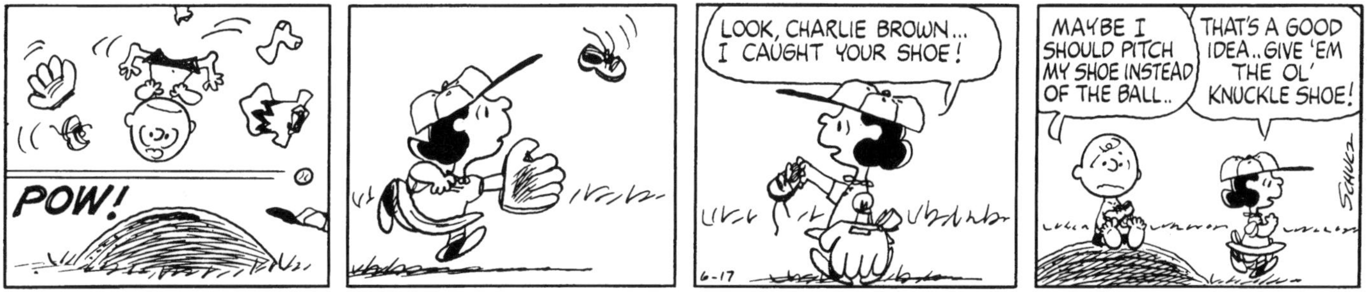
POW!
LOOK, CHARLIE BROWN... I CAUGHT YOUR SHOE!
6-17
MAYBE I SHOULD PITCH MY SHOE INSTEAD OF THE BALL..
THAT'S A GOOD IDEA..GIVE 'EM THE OL' KNUCKLE SHOE!
SCHULZ

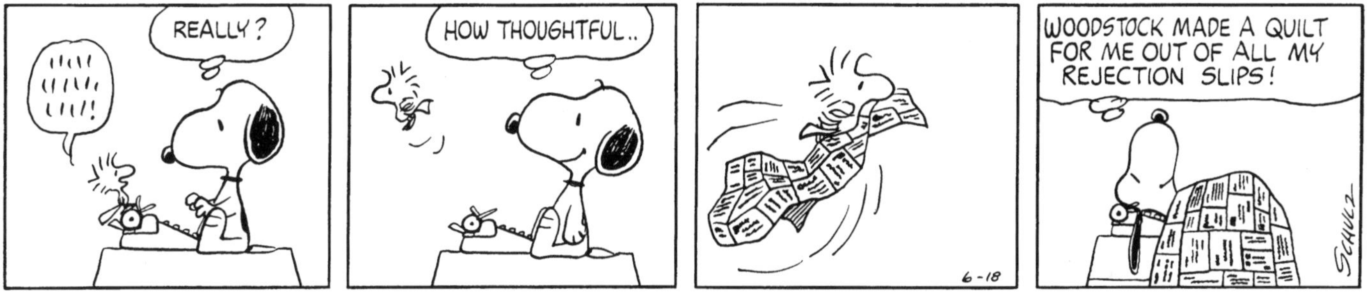
REALLY?
HOW THOUGHTFUL..
6-18
WOODSTOCK MADE A QUILT FOR ME OUT OF ALL MY REJECTION SLIPS!
SCHULZ

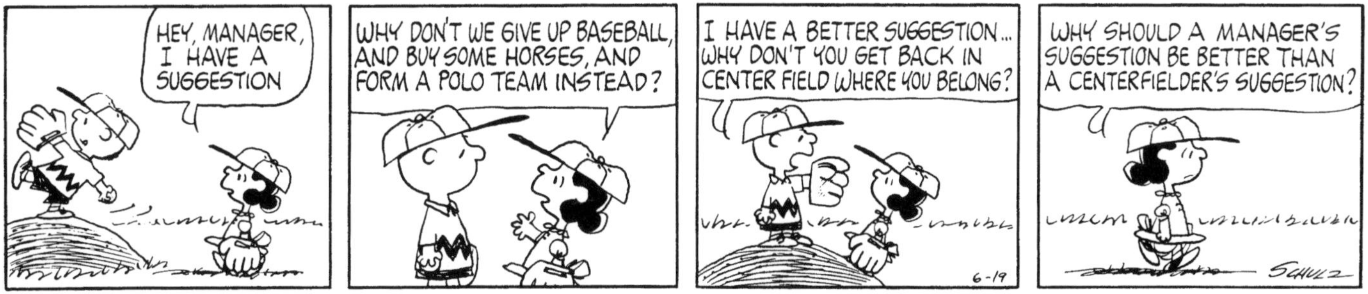
HEY, MANAGER, I HAVE A SUGGESTION
WHY DON'T WE GIVE UP BASEBALL, AND BUY SOME HORSES, AND FORM A POLO TEAM INSTEAD?
I HAVE A BETTER SUGGESTION... WHY DON'T YOU GET BACK IN CENTER FIELD WHERE YOU BELONG?
6-19
WHY SHOULD A MANAGER'S SUGGESTION BE BETTER THAN A CENTERFIELDER'S SUGGESTION?
SCHULZ

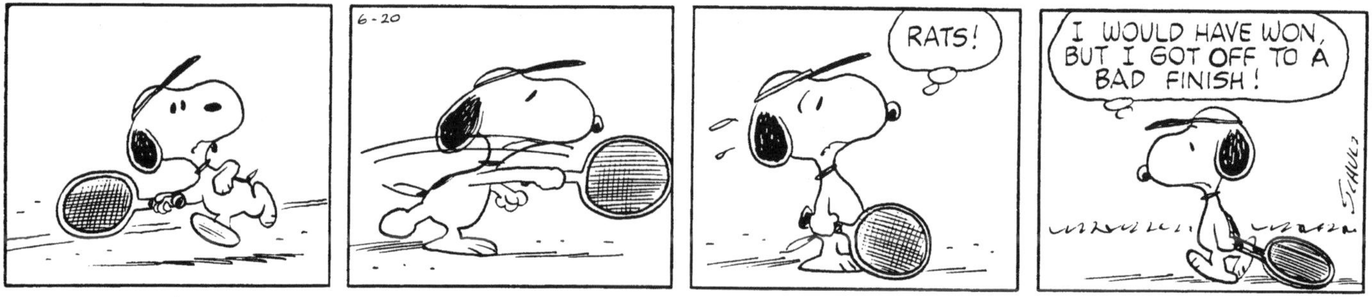
6-20
RATS!
I WOULD HAVE WON, BUT I GOT OFF TO A BAD FINISH!
SCHULZ

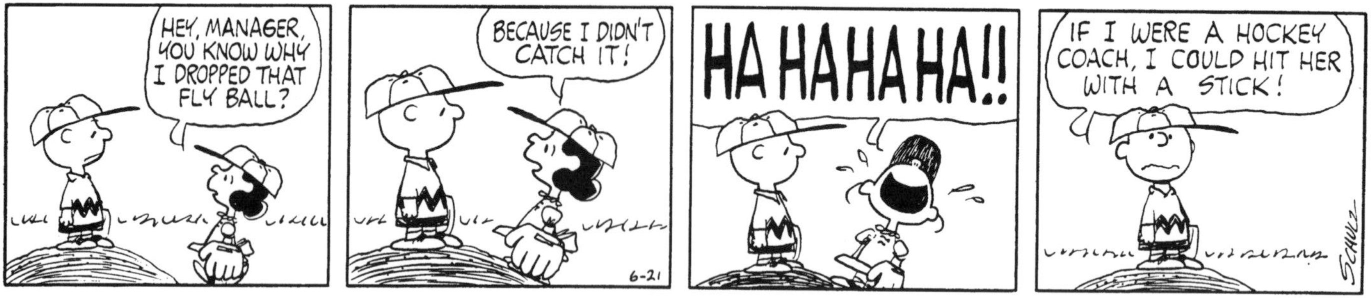
HEY, MANAGER, YOU KNOW WHY I DROPPED THAT FLY BALL?
BECAUSE I DIDN'T CATCH IT!
6-21
HA HA HA HA!!
IF I WERE A HOCKEY COACH, I COULD HIT HER WITH A STICK!
SCHULZ

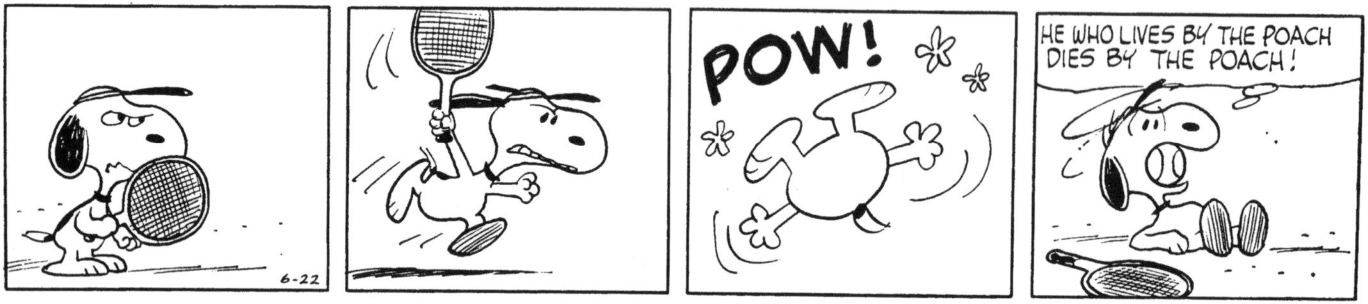
6-22
POW!
HE WHO LIVES BY THE POACH DIES BY THE POACH!

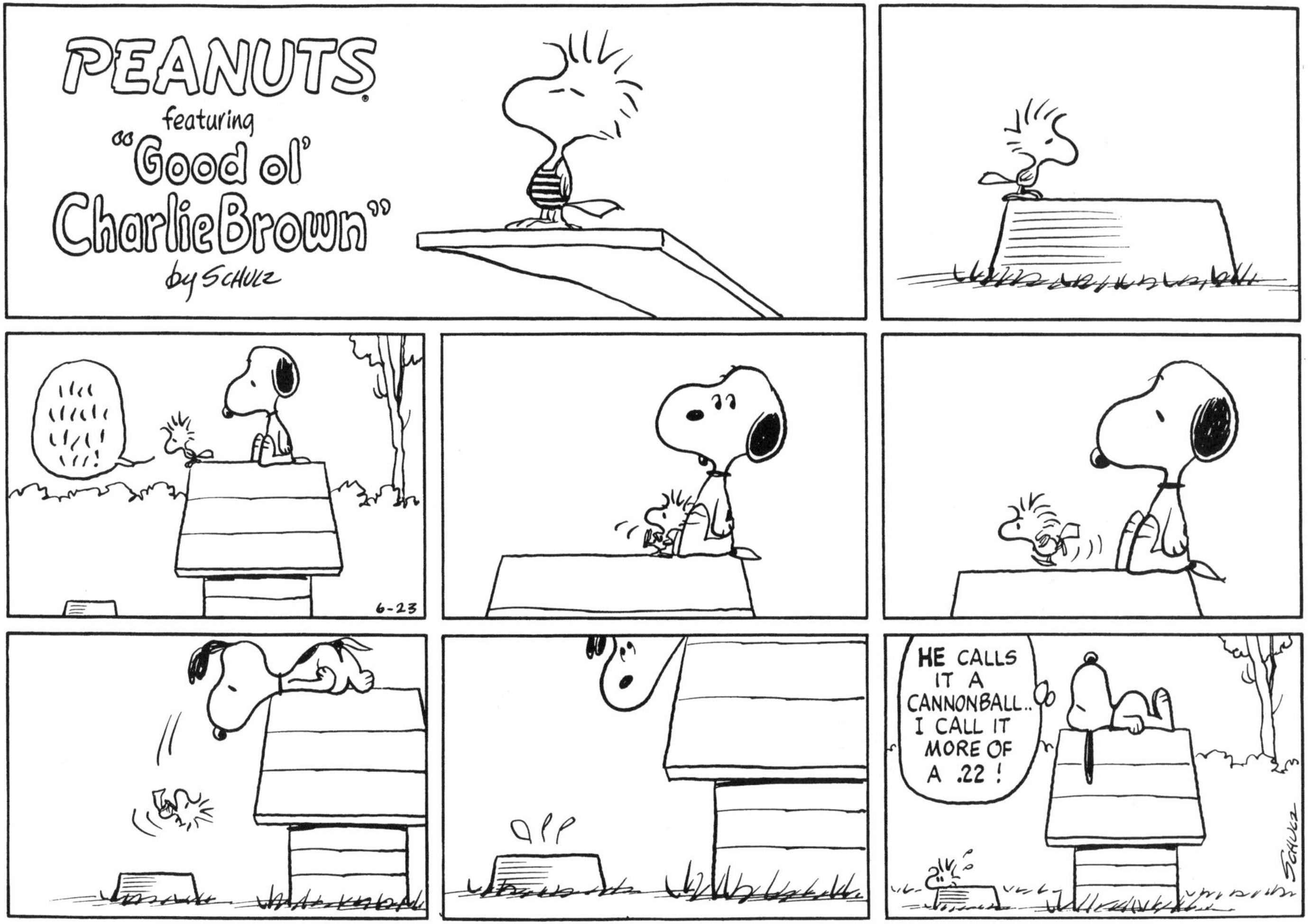
PEANUTS
featuring
"Good ol' Charlie Brown"
by SCHULZ
6-23
HE CALLS IT A CANNONBALL.. I CALL IT MORE OF A .22 !
SCHULZ

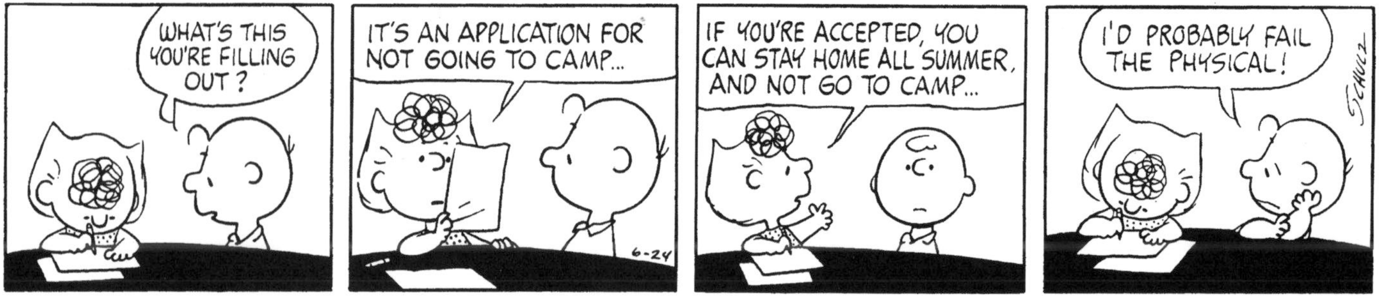
WHAT'S THIS YOU'RE FILLING OUT ?
IT'S AN APPLICATION FOR NOT GOING TO CAMP...
6-24
IF YOU'RE ACCEPTED, YOU CAN STAY HOME ALL SUMMER, AND NOT GO TO CAMP...
I'D PROBABLY FAIL THE PHYSICAL!
SCHULZ

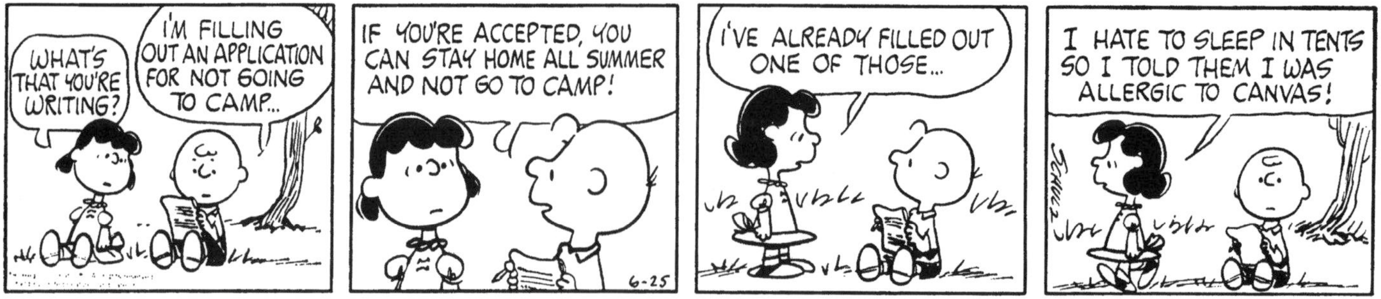
WHAT'S THAT YOU'RE WRITING?
I'M FILLING OUT AN APPLICATION FOR NOT GOING TO CAMP...
IF YOU'RE ACCEPTED, YOU CAN STAY HOME ALL SUMMER AND NOT GO TO CAMP!
6-25
I'VE ALREADY FILLED OUT ONE OF THOSE...
I HATE TO SLEEP IN TENTS SO I TOLD THEM I WAS ALLERGIC TO CANVAS!
SCHULZ

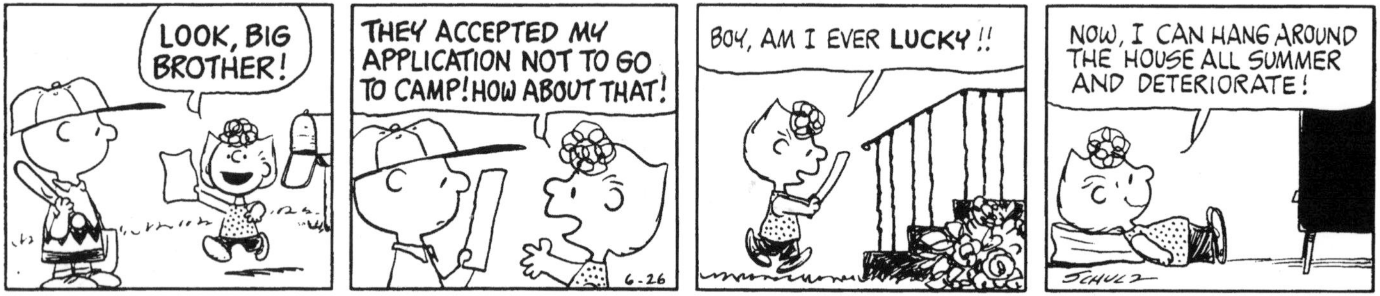
LOOK, BIG BROTHER!
THEY ACCEPTED MY APPLICATION NOT TO GO TO CAMP! HOW ABOUT THAT!
6-26
BOY, AM I EVER **LUCKY**!!
NOW, I CAN HANG AROUND THE HOUSE ALL SUMMER AND DETERIORATE!
SCHULZ

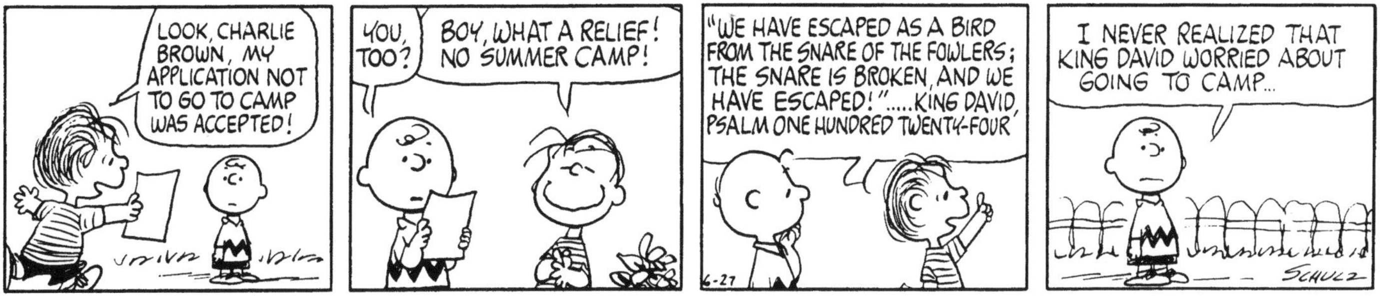
LOOK, CHARLIE BROWN, MY APPLICATION NOT TO GO TO CAMP WAS ACCEPTED!
YOU, TOO?
BOY, WHAT A RELIEF! NO SUMMER CAMP!
"WE HAVE ESCAPED AS A BIRD FROM THE SNARE OF THE FOWLERS; THE SNARE IS BROKEN, AND WE HAVE ESCAPED!".....KING DAVID, PSALM ONE HUNDRED TWENTY-FOUR
I NEVER REALIZED THAT KING DAVID WORRIED ABOUT GOING TO CAMP...

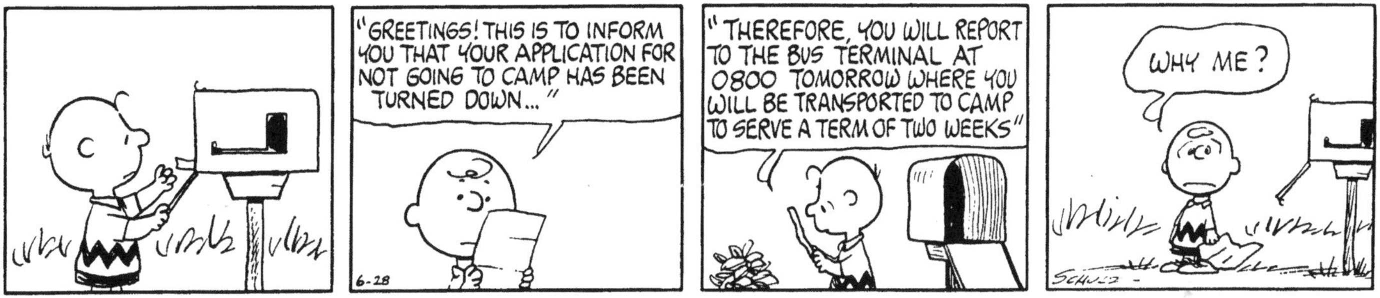
"GREETINGS! THIS IS TO INFORM YOU THAT YOUR APPLICATION FOR NOT GOING TO CAMP HAS BEEN TURNED DOWN..."
"THEREFORE, YOU WILL REPORT TO THE BUS TERMINAL AT 0800 TOMORROW WHERE YOU WILL BE TRANSPORTED TO CAMP TO SERVE A TERM OF TWO WEEKS"
WHY ME?

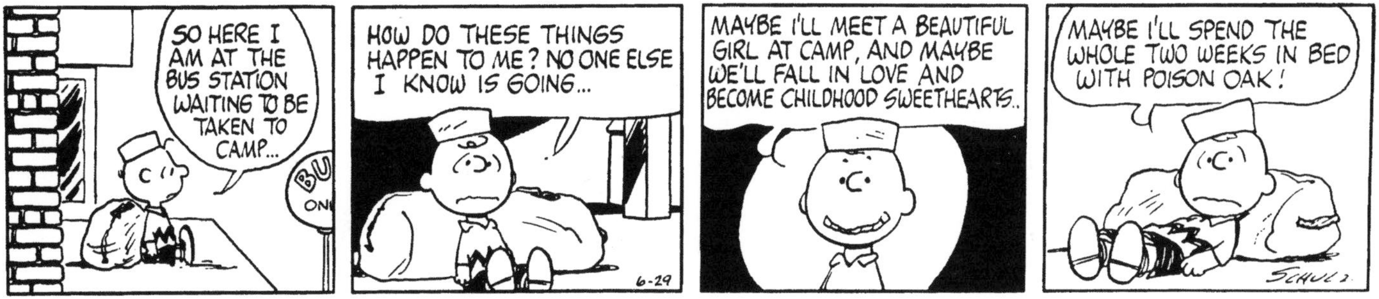
SO HERE I AM AT THE BUS STATION WAITING TO BE TAKEN TO CAMP...
HOW DO THESE THINGS HAPPEN TO ME? NO ONE ELSE I KNOW IS GOING...
MAYBE I'LL MEET A BEAUTIFUL GIRL AT CAMP, AND MAYBE WE'LL FALL IN LOVE AND BECOME CHILDHOOD SWEETHEARTS..
MAYBE I'LL SPEND THE WHOLE TWO WEEKS IN BED WITH POISON OAK!

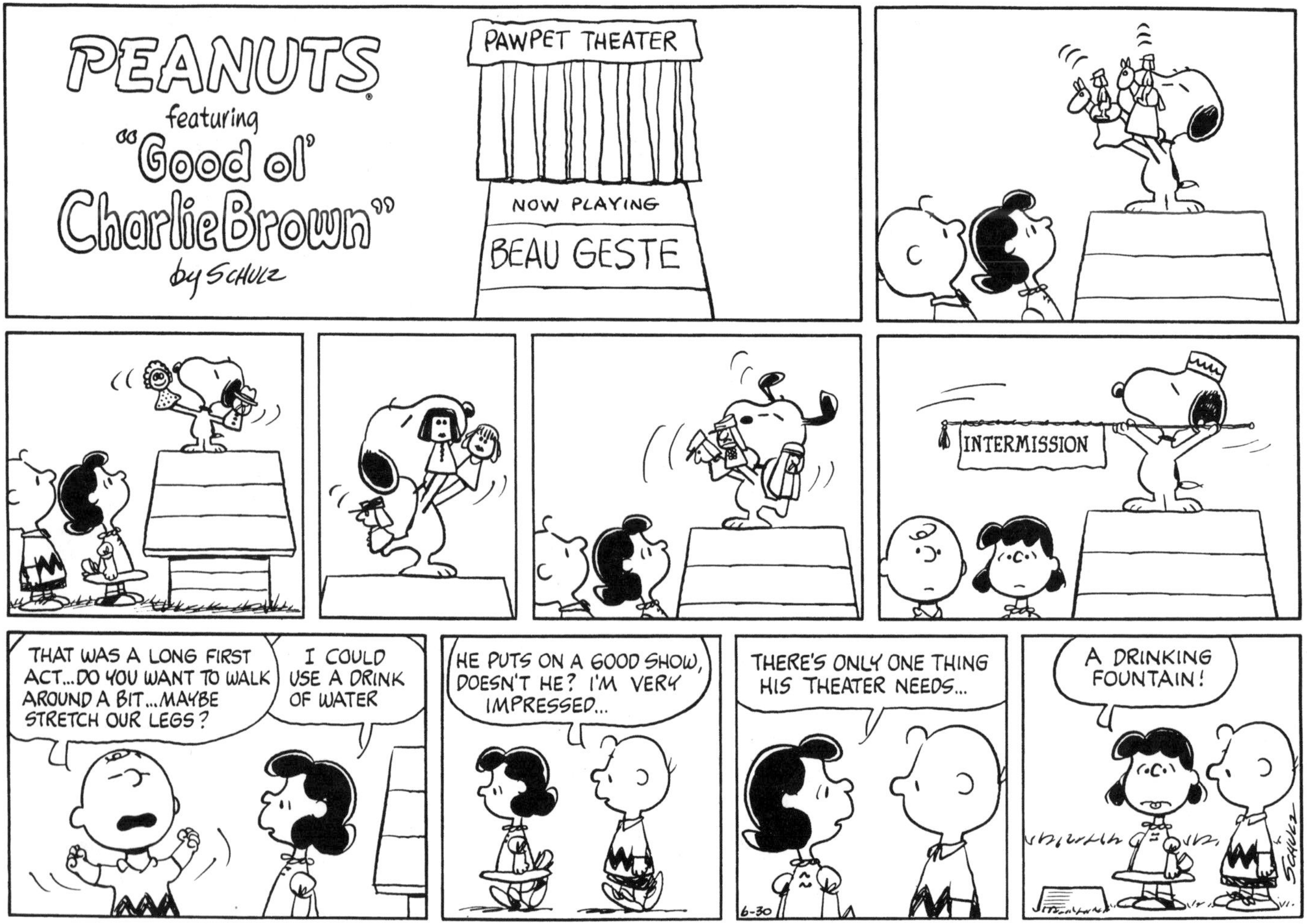
PEANUTS
featuring "Good ol' Charlie Brown"
by SCHULZ
PAWPET THEATER
NOW PLAYING
BEAU GESTE
INTERMISSION
THAT WAS A LONG FIRST ACT...DO YOU WANT TO WALK AROUND A BIT...MAYBE STRETCH OUR LEGS?
I COULD USE A DRINK OF WATER
HE PUTS ON A GOOD SHOW, DOESN'T HE? I'M VERY IMPRESSED...
THERE'S ONLY ONE THING HIS THEATER NEEDS...
A DRINKING FOUNTAIN!
6-30
SCHULZ

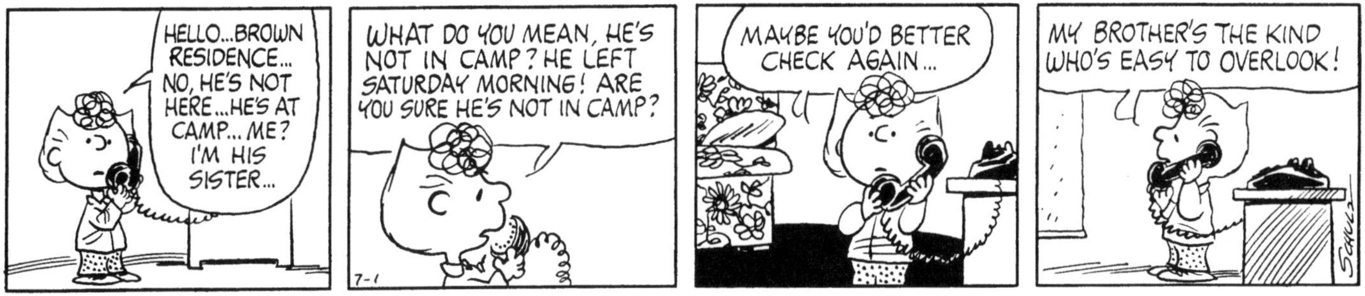
HELLO...BROWN RESIDENCE... NO, HE'S NOT HERE...HE'S AT CAMP... ME? I'M HIS SISTER...
WHAT DO YOU MEAN, HE'S NOT IN CAMP? HE LEFT SATURDAY MORNING! ARE YOU SURE HE'S NOT IN CAMP?
7-1
MAYBE YOU'D BETTER CHECK AGAIN...
MY BROTHER'S THE KIND WHO'S EASY TO OVERLOOK!
SCHULZ

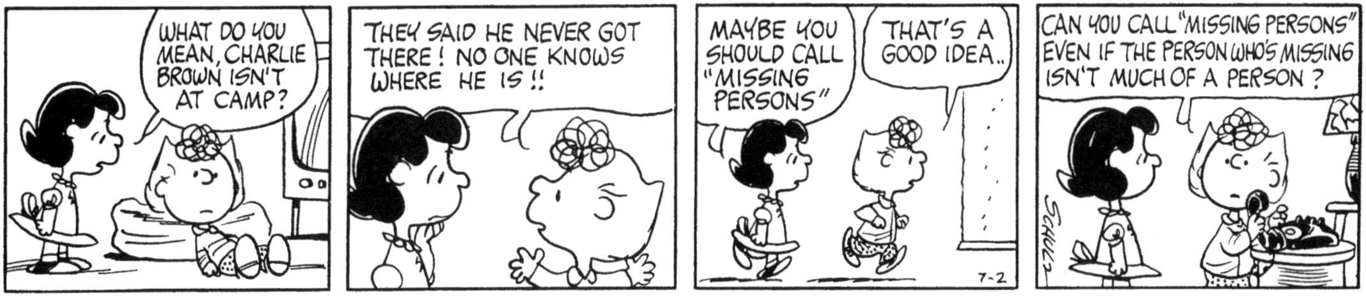
WHAT DO YOU MEAN, CHARLIE BROWN ISN'T AT CAMP?
THEY SAID HE NEVER GOT THERE! NO ONE KNOWS WHERE HE IS!!
MAYBE YOU SHOULD CALL "MISSING PERSONS"
THAT'S A GOOD IDEA..
7-2
CAN YOU CALL "MISSING PERSONS" EVEN IF THE PERSON WHO'S MISSING ISN'T MUCH OF A PERSON?
SCHULZ

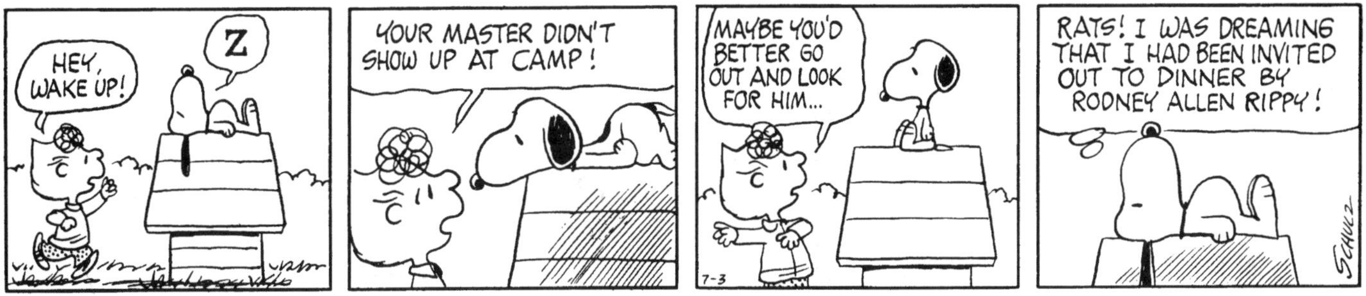
HEY, WAKE UP!
Z
YOUR MASTER DIDN'T SHOW UP AT CAMP!
MAYBE YOU'D BETTER GO OUT AND LOOK FOR HIM...
7-3
RATS! I WAS DREAMING THAT I HAD BEEN INVITED OUT TO DINNER BY RODNEY ALLEN RIPPY!
SCHULZ

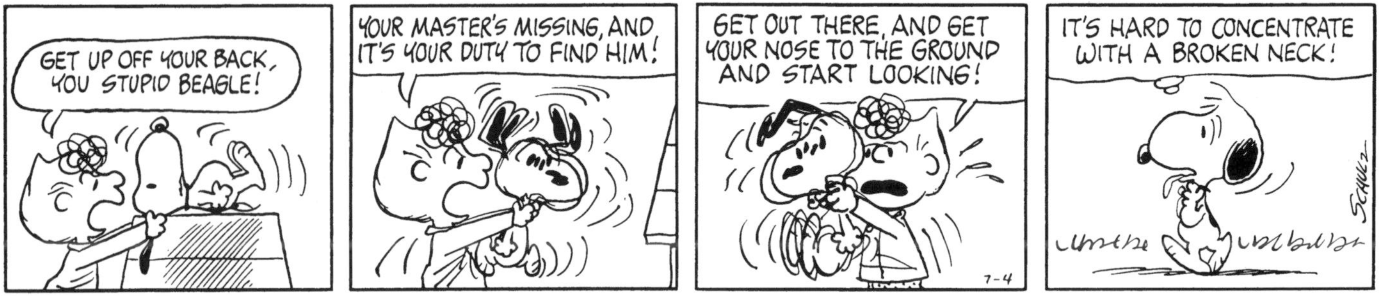
GET UP OFF YOUR BACK, YOU STUPID BEAGLE!
YOUR MASTER'S MISSING, AND IT'S YOUR DUTY TO FIND HIM!
GET OUT THERE, AND GET YOUR NOSE TO THE GROUND AND START LOOKING!
7-4
IT'S HARD TO CONCENTRATE WITH A BROKEN NECK!
SCHULZ

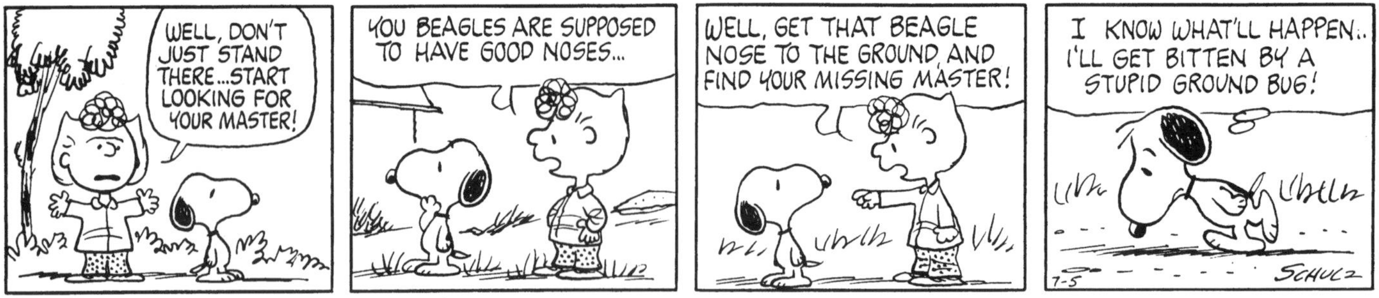
WELL, DON'T JUST STAND THERE...START LOOKING FOR YOUR MASTER!
YOU BEAGLES ARE SUPPOSED TO HAVE GOOD NOSES...
WELL, GET THAT BEAGLE NOSE TO THE GROUND, AND FIND YOUR MISSING MASTER!
I KNOW WHAT'LL HAPPEN.. I'LL GET BITTEN BY A STUPID GROUND BUG!
7-5
SCHULZ

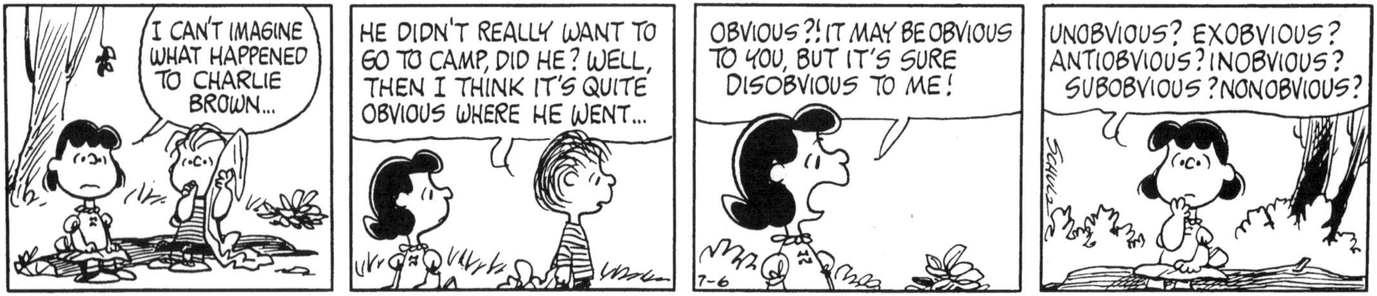
I CAN'T IMAGINE WHAT HAPPENED TO CHARLIE BROWN...
HE DIDN'T REALLY WANT TO GO TO CAMP, DID HE? WELL, THEN I THINK IT'S QUITE OBVIOUS WHERE HE WENT...
OBVIOUS?! IT MAY BE OBVIOUS TO YOU, BUT IT'S SURE DISOBVIOUS TO ME!
7-6
UNOBVIOUS? EXOBVIOUS? ANTIOBVIOUS? INOBVIOUS? SUBOBVIOUS? NONOBVIOUS?
SCHULZ

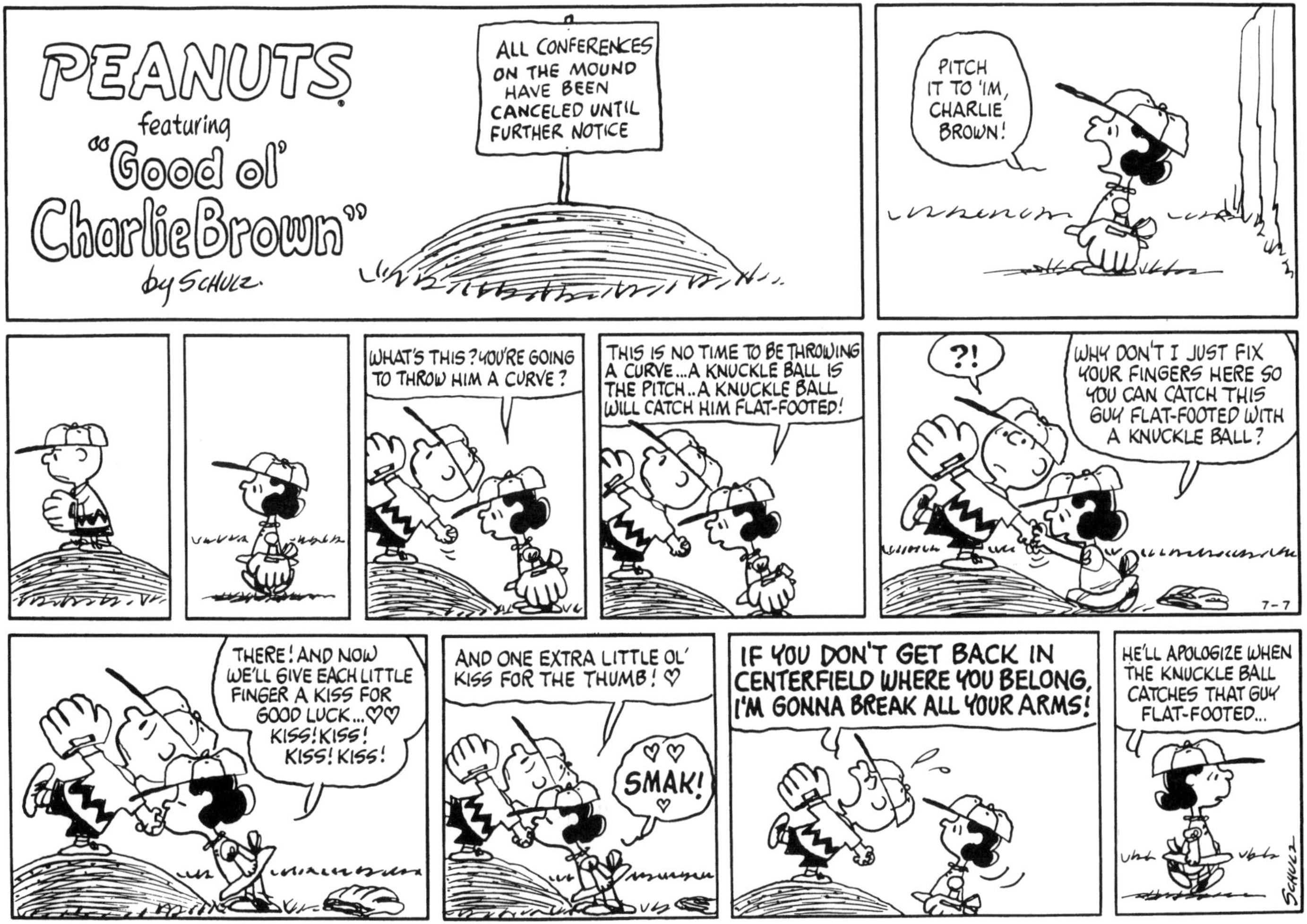
PEANUTS
featuring
"Good ol' Charlie Brown"
by SCHULZ
ALL CONFERENCES ON THE MOUND HAVE BEEN CANCELED UNTIL FURTHER NOTICE
PITCH IT TO 'IM, CHARLIE BROWN!
WHAT'S THIS? YOU'RE GOING TO THROW HIM A CURVE?
THIS IS NO TIME TO BE THROWING A CURVE...A KNUCKLE BALL IS THE PITCH..A KNUCKLE BALL WILL CATCH HIM FLAT-FOOTED!
?!
WHY DON'T I JUST FIX YOUR FINGERS HERE SO YOU CAN CATCH THIS GUY FLAT-FOOTED WITH A KNUCKLE BALL?
7-7
THERE! AND NOW WE'LL GIVE EACH LITTLE FINGER A KISS FOR GOOD LUCK...♡♡ KISS! KISS! KISS! KISS!
AND ONE EXTRA LITTLE OL' KISS FOR THE THUMB! ♡
SMAK!
IF YOU DON'T GET BACK IN CENTERFIELD WHERE YOU BELONG, I'M GONNA BREAK ALL YOUR ARMS!
HE'LL APOLOGIZE WHEN THE KNUCKLE BALL CATCHES THAT GUY FLAT-FOOTED...
SCHULZ

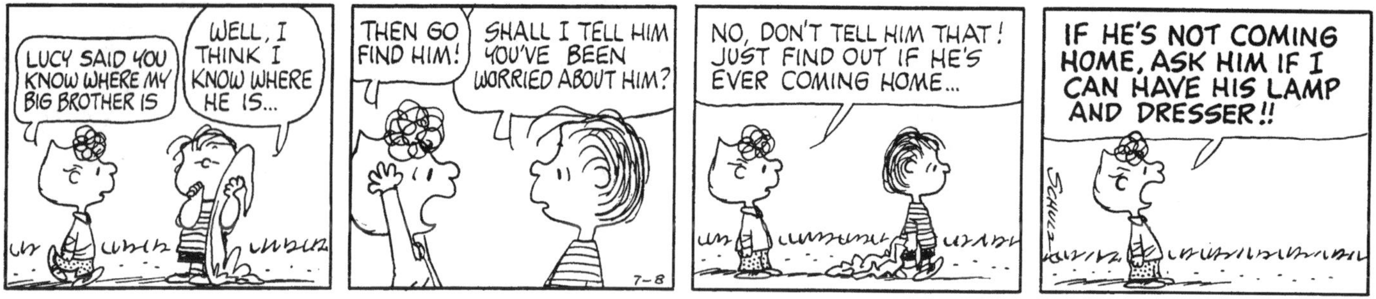
LUCY SAID YOU KNOW WHERE MY BIG BROTHER IS
WELL, I THINK I KNOW WHERE HE IS...
THEN GO FIND HIM!
SHALL I TELL HIM YOU'VE BEEN WORRIED ABOUT HIM?
NO, DON'T TELL HIM THAT! JUST FIND OUT IF HE'S EVER COMING HOME...
IF HE'S NOT COMING HOME, ASK HIM IF I CAN HAVE HIS LAMP AND DRESSER!!

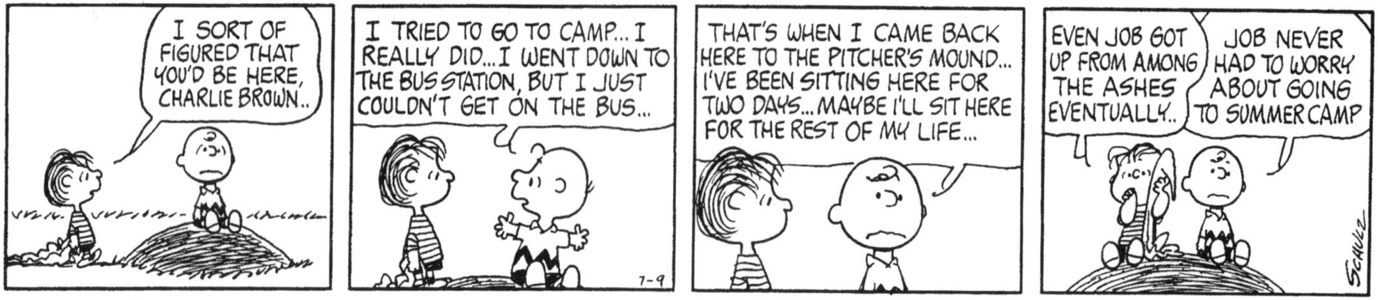
I SORT OF FIGURED THAT YOU'D BE HERE, CHARLIE BROWN..
I TRIED TO GO TO CAMP... I REALLY DID... I WENT DOWN TO THE BUS STATION, BUT I JUST COULDN'T GET ON THE BUS...
THAT'S WHEN I CAME BACK HERE TO THE PITCHER'S MOUND... I'VE BEEN SITTING HERE FOR TWO DAYS... MAYBE I'LL SIT HERE FOR THE REST OF MY LIFE...
EVEN JOB GOT UP FROM AMONG THE ASHES EVENTUALLY..
JOB NEVER HAD TO WORRY ABOUT GOING TO SUMMER CAMP

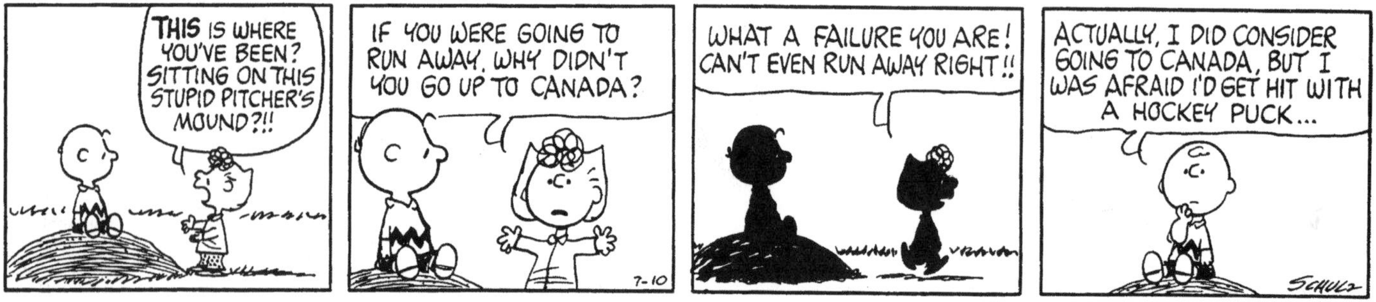
THIS IS WHERE YOU'VE BEEN? SITTING ON THIS STUPID PITCHER'S MOUND?!!
IF YOU WERE GOING TO RUN AWAY, WHY DIDN'T YOU GO UP TO CANADA?
WHAT A FAILURE YOU ARE! CAN'T EVEN RUN AWAY RIGHT!!
ACTUALLY, I DID CONSIDER GOING TO CANADA, BUT I WAS AFRAID I'D GET HIT WITH A HOCKEY PUCK...

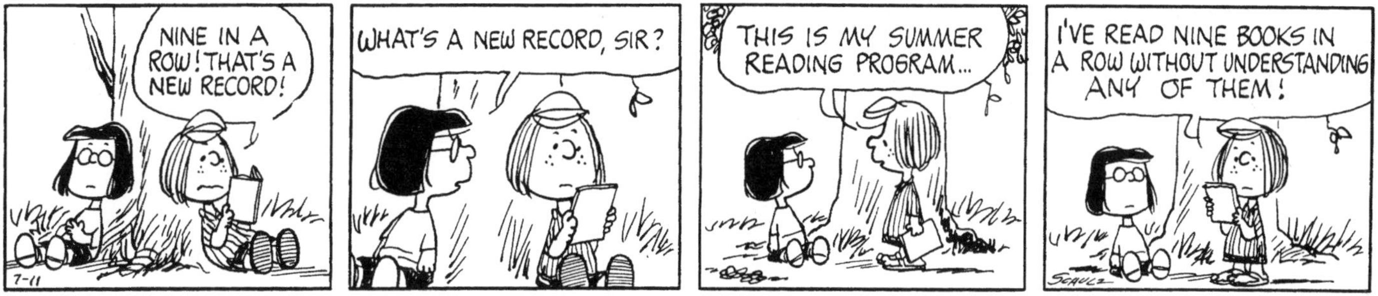
NINE IN A ROW! THAT'S A NEW RECORD!
7-11
WHAT'S A NEW RECORD, SIR?
THIS IS MY SUMMER READING PROGRAM...
I'VE READ NINE BOOKS IN A ROW WITHOUT UNDERSTANDING ANY OF THEM!

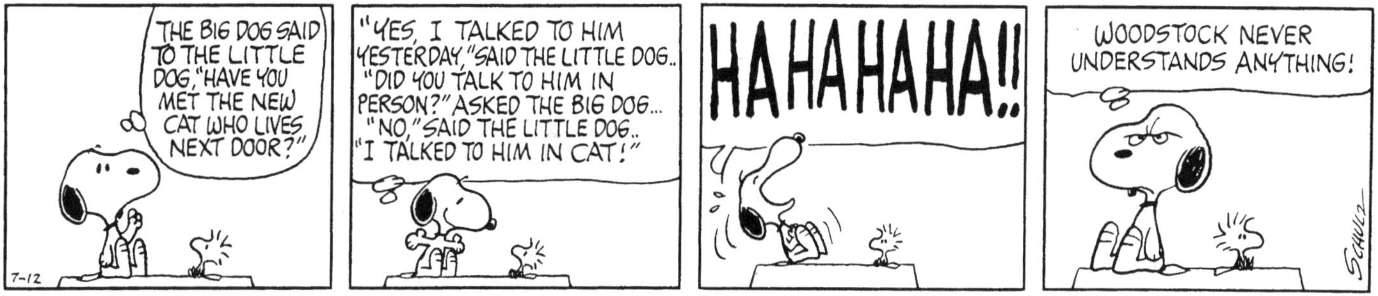
THE BIG DOG SAID TO THE LITTLE DOG, "HAVE YOU MET THE NEW CAT WHO LIVES NEXT DOOR?"
7-12
"YES, I TALKED TO HIM YESTERDAY," SAID THE LITTLE DOG.. "DID YOU TALK TO HIM IN PERSON?" ASKED THE BIG DOG... "NO," SAID THE LITTLE DOG.. "I TALKED TO HIM IN CAT!"
HAHAHAHA!!
WOODSTOCK NEVER UNDERSTANDS ANYTHING!

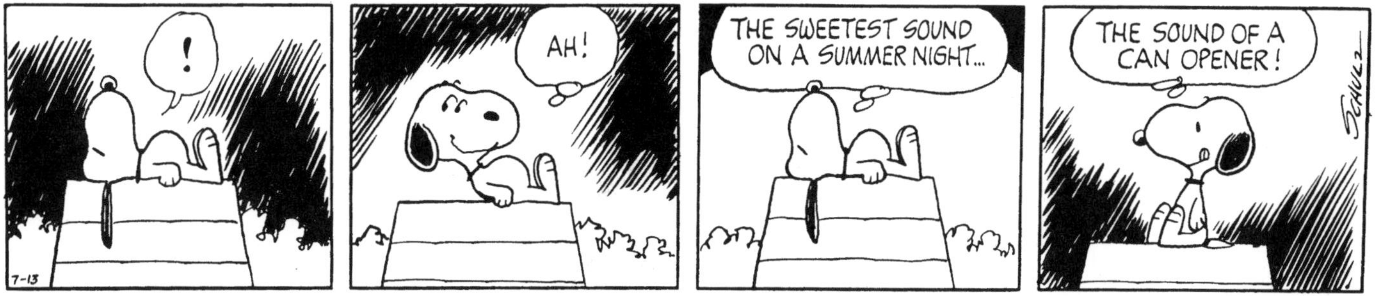
!
7-13
AH!
THE SWEETEST SOUND ON A SUMMER NIGHT...
THE SOUND OF A CAN OPENER!

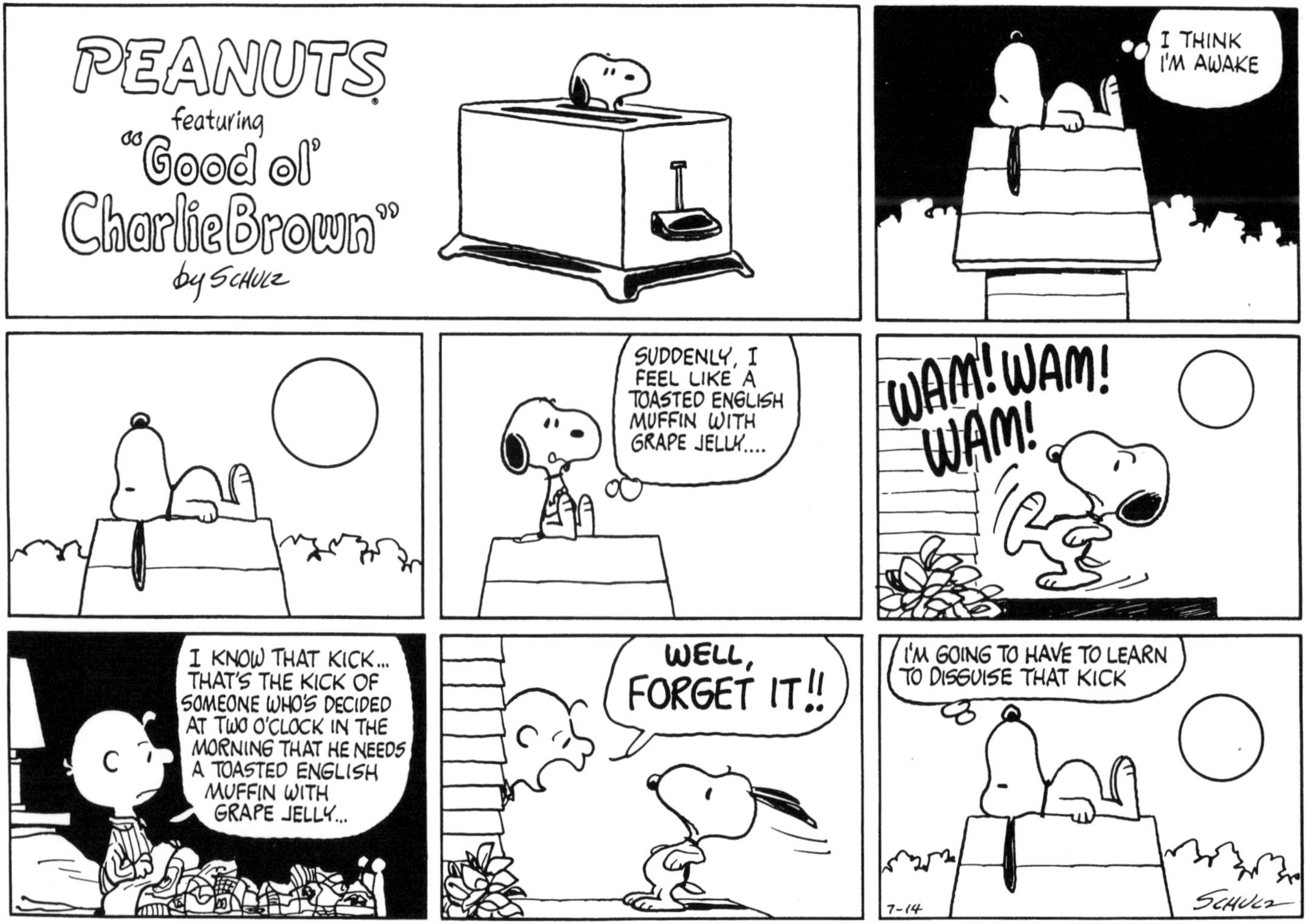
PEANUTS
featuring
"Good ol' Charlie Brown"
by SCHULZ
I THINK I'M AWAKE
SUDDENLY, I FEEL LIKE A TOASTED ENGLISH MUFFIN WITH GRAPE JELLY....
WAM! WAM! WAM!
I KNOW THAT KICK... THAT'S THE KICK OF SOMEONE WHO'S DECIDED AT TWO O'CLOCK IN THE MORNING THAT HE NEEDS A TOASTED ENGLISH MUFFIN WITH GRAPE JELLY...
WELL, FORGET IT!!
I'M GOING TO HAVE TO LEARN TO DISGUISE THAT KICK
7-14
SCHULZ

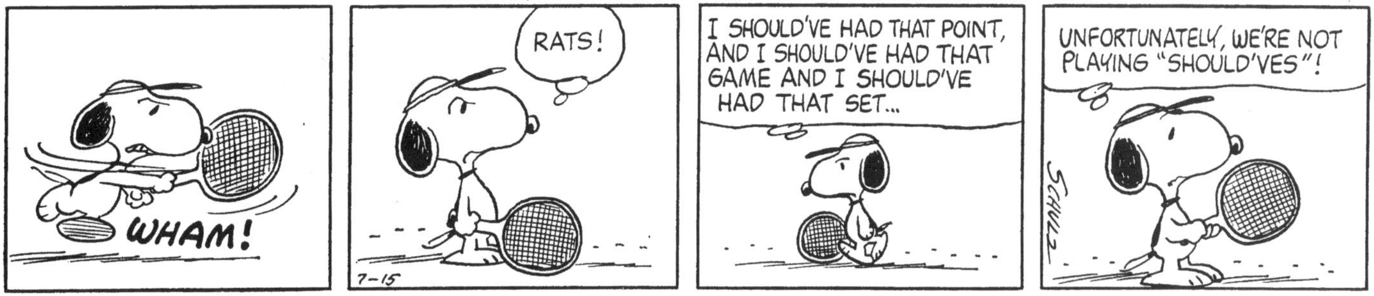
WHAM!
RATS!
7-15
I SHOULD'VE HAD THAT POINT, AND I SHOULD'VE HAD THAT GAME AND I SHOULD'VE HAD THAT SET...
UNFORTUNATELY, WE'RE NOT PLAYING "SHOULD'VES"!
SCHULZ

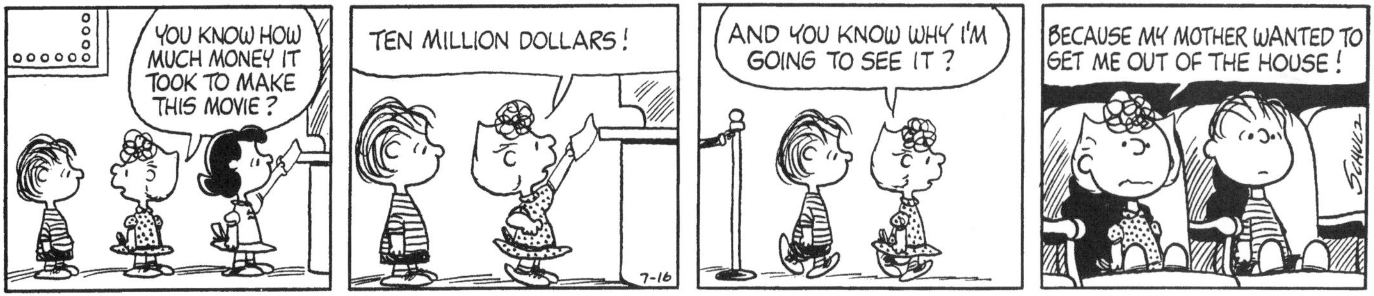
YOU KNOW HOW MUCH MONEY IT TOOK TO MAKE THIS MOVIE?
TEN MILLION DOLLARS!
7-16
AND YOU KNOW WHY I'M GOING TO SEE IT?
BECAUSE MY MOTHER WANTED TO GET ME OUT OF THE HOUSE!
SCHULZ

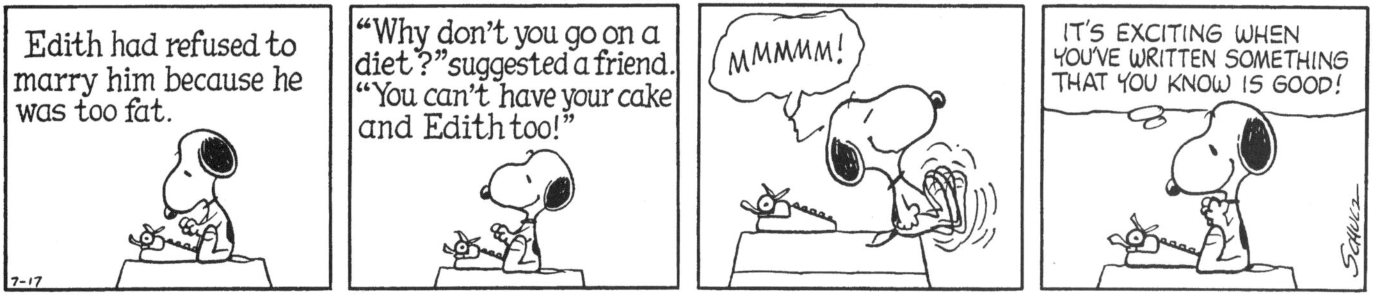
Edith had refused to marry him because he was too fat.
7-17
"Why don't you go on a diet?" suggested a friend. "You can't have your cake and Edith too!"
MMMMM!
IT'S EXCITING WHEN YOU'VE WRITTEN SOMETHING THAT YOU KNOW IS GOOD!
SCHULZ

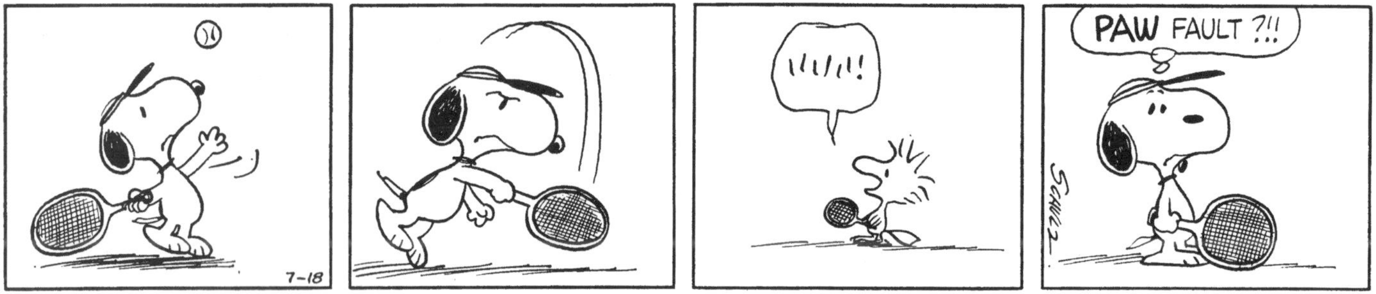
7-18
PAW FAULT ?!!
SCHULZ

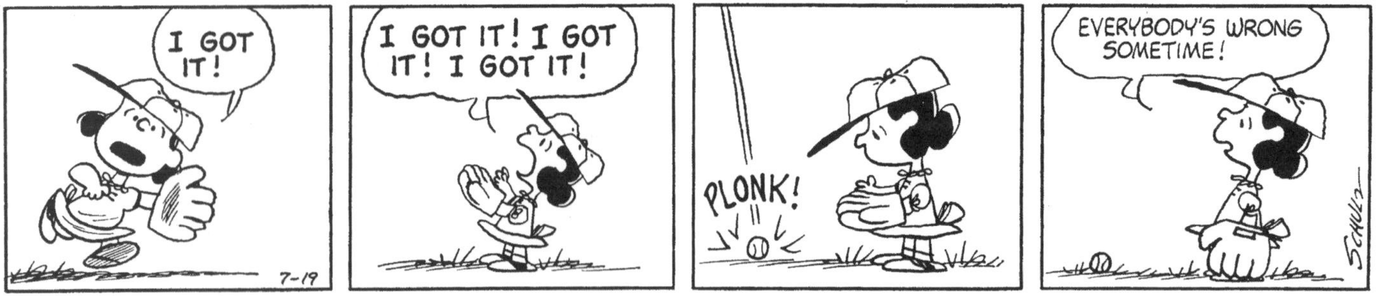
I GOT IT!
7-19
I GOT IT! I GOT IT! I GOT IT!
PLONK!
EVERYBODY'S WRONG SOMETIME!
SCHULZ

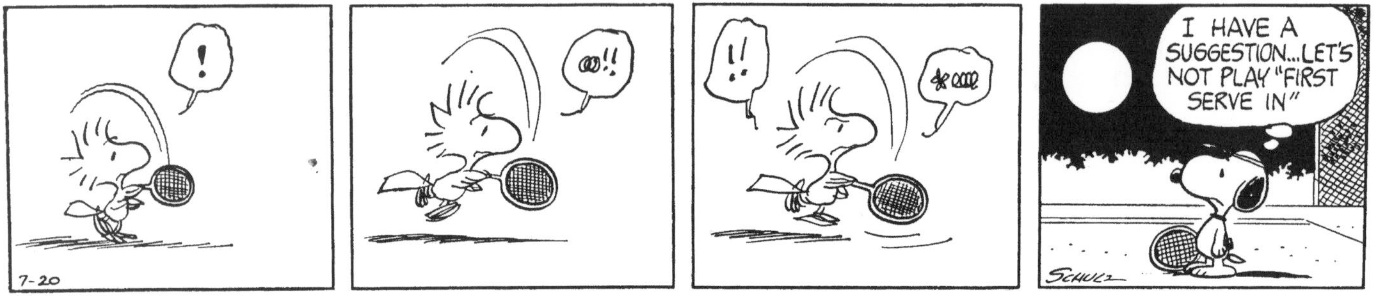
!
7-20
!!
I HAVE A SUGGESTION...LET'S NOT PLAY "FIRST SERVE IN"
SCHULZ

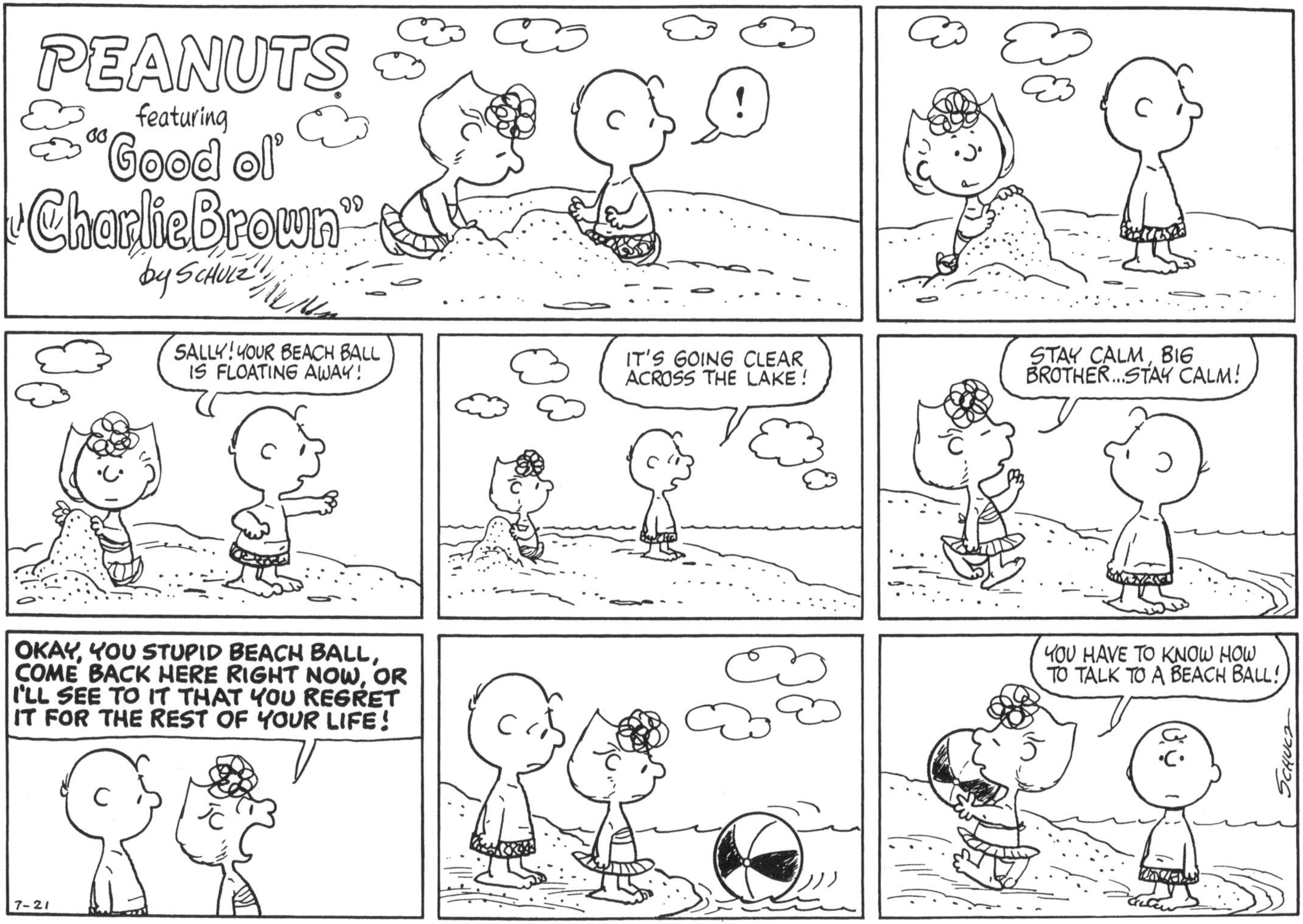
PEANUTS
featuring "Good ol' Charlie Brown"
by SCHULZ
!
SALLY! YOUR BEACH BALL IS FLOATING AWAY!
IT'S GOING CLEAR ACROSS THE LAKE!
STAY CALM, BIG BROTHER...STAY CALM!
OKAY, YOU STUPID BEACH BALL, COME BACK HERE RIGHT NOW, OR I'LL SEE TO IT THAT YOU REGRET IT FOR THE REST OF YOUR LIFE!
7-21
YOU HAVE TO KNOW HOW TO TALK TO A BEACH BALL!
SCHULZ

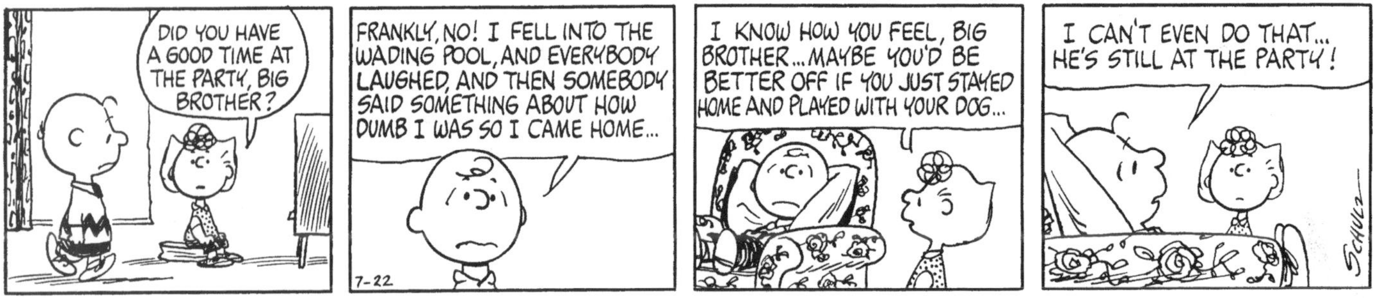
DID YOU HAVE A GOOD TIME AT THE PARTY, BIG BROTHER?
FRANKLY, NO! I FELL INTO THE WADING POOL, AND EVERYBODY LAUGHED, AND THEN SOMEBODY SAID SOMETHING ABOUT HOW DUMB I WAS SO I CAME HOME...
7-22
I KNOW HOW YOU FEEL, BIG BROTHER...MAYBE YOU'D BE BETTER OFF IF YOU JUST STAYED HOME AND PLAYED WITH YOUR DOG...
I CAN'T EVEN DO THAT... HE'S STILL AT THE PARTY!
SCHULZ

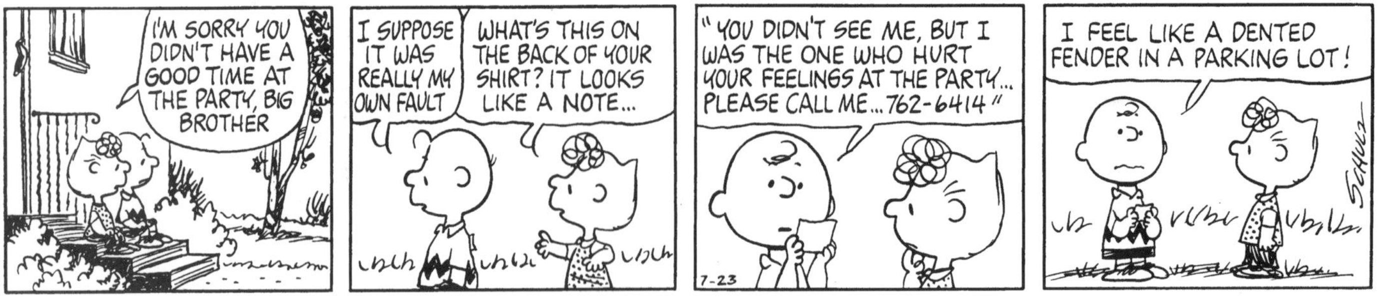
I'M SORRY YOU DIDN'T HAVE A GOOD TIME AT THE PARTY, BIG BROTHER
I SUPPOSE IT WAS REALLY MY OWN FAULT
WHAT'S THIS ON THE BACK OF YOUR SHIRT? IT LOOKS LIKE A NOTE...
"YOU DIDN'T SEE ME, BUT I WAS THE ONE WHO HURT YOUR FEELINGS AT THE PARTY... PLEASE CALL ME...762-6414"
7-23
I FEEL LIKE A DENTED FENDER IN A PARKING LOT!
SCHULZ

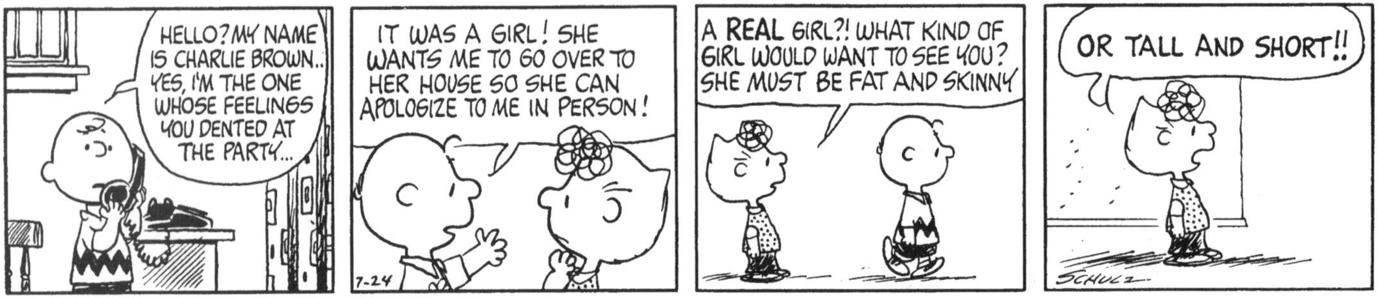
HELLO? MY NAME IS CHARLIE BROWN.. YES, I'M THE ONE WHOSE FEELINGS YOU DENTED AT THE PARTY...
IT WAS A GIRL! SHE WANTS ME TO GO OVER TO HER HOUSE SO SHE CAN APOLOGIZE TO ME IN PERSON!
7-24
A REAL GIRL?! WHAT KIND OF GIRL WOULD WANT TO SEE YOU? SHE MUST BE FAT AND SKINNY
OR TALL AND SHORT!!
SCHULZ

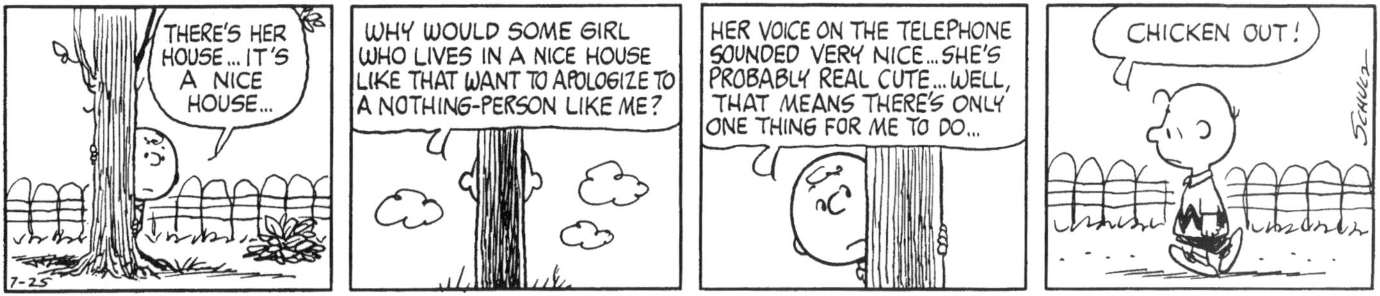
7-25
THERE'S HER HOUSE... IT'S A NICE HOUSE...
WHY WOULD SOME GIRL WHO LIVES IN A NICE HOUSE LIKE THAT WANT TO APOLOGIZE TO A NOTHING-PERSON LIKE ME?
HER VOICE ON THE TELEPHONE SOUNDED VERY NICE... SHE'S PROBABLY REAL CUTE... WELL, THAT MEANS THERE'S ONLY ONE THING FOR ME TO DO...
CHICKEN OUT!
SCHULZ

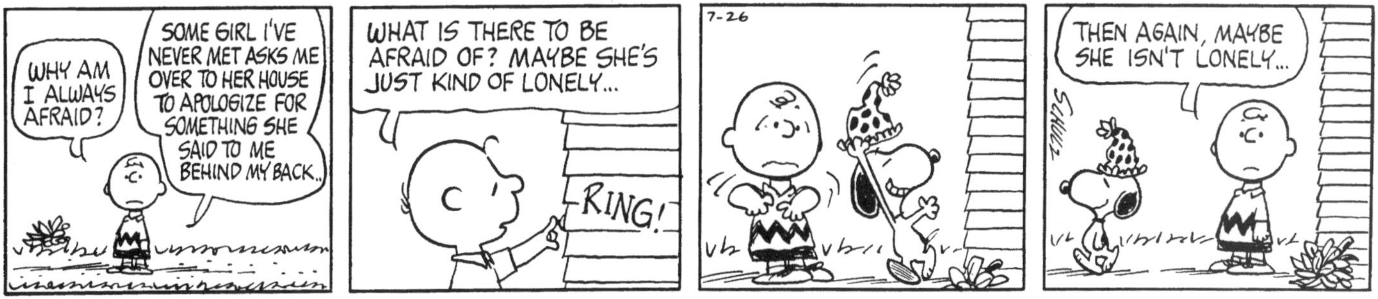
WHY AM I ALWAYS AFRAID?
SOME GIRL I'VE NEVER MET ASKS ME OVER TO HER HOUSE TO APOLOGIZE FOR SOMETHING SHE SAID TO ME BEHIND MY BACK..
WHAT IS THERE TO BE AFRAID OF? MAYBE SHE'S JUST KIND OF LONELY...
RING!
7-26
THEN AGAIN, MAYBE SHE ISN'T LONELY...
SCHULZ

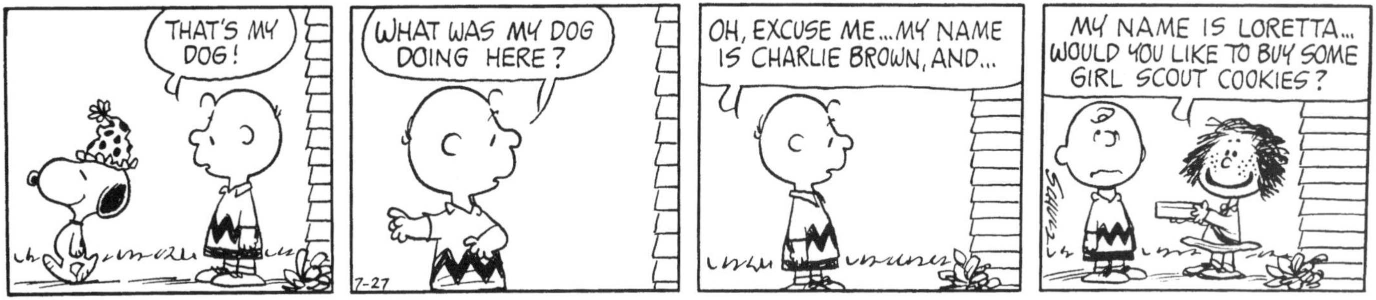
THAT'S MY DOG!
WHAT WAS MY DOG DOING HERE?
7-27
OH, EXCUSE ME... MY NAME IS CHARLIE BROWN, AND...
MY NAME IS LORETTA... WOULD YOU LIKE TO BUY SOME GIRL SCOUT COOKIES?
SCHULZ

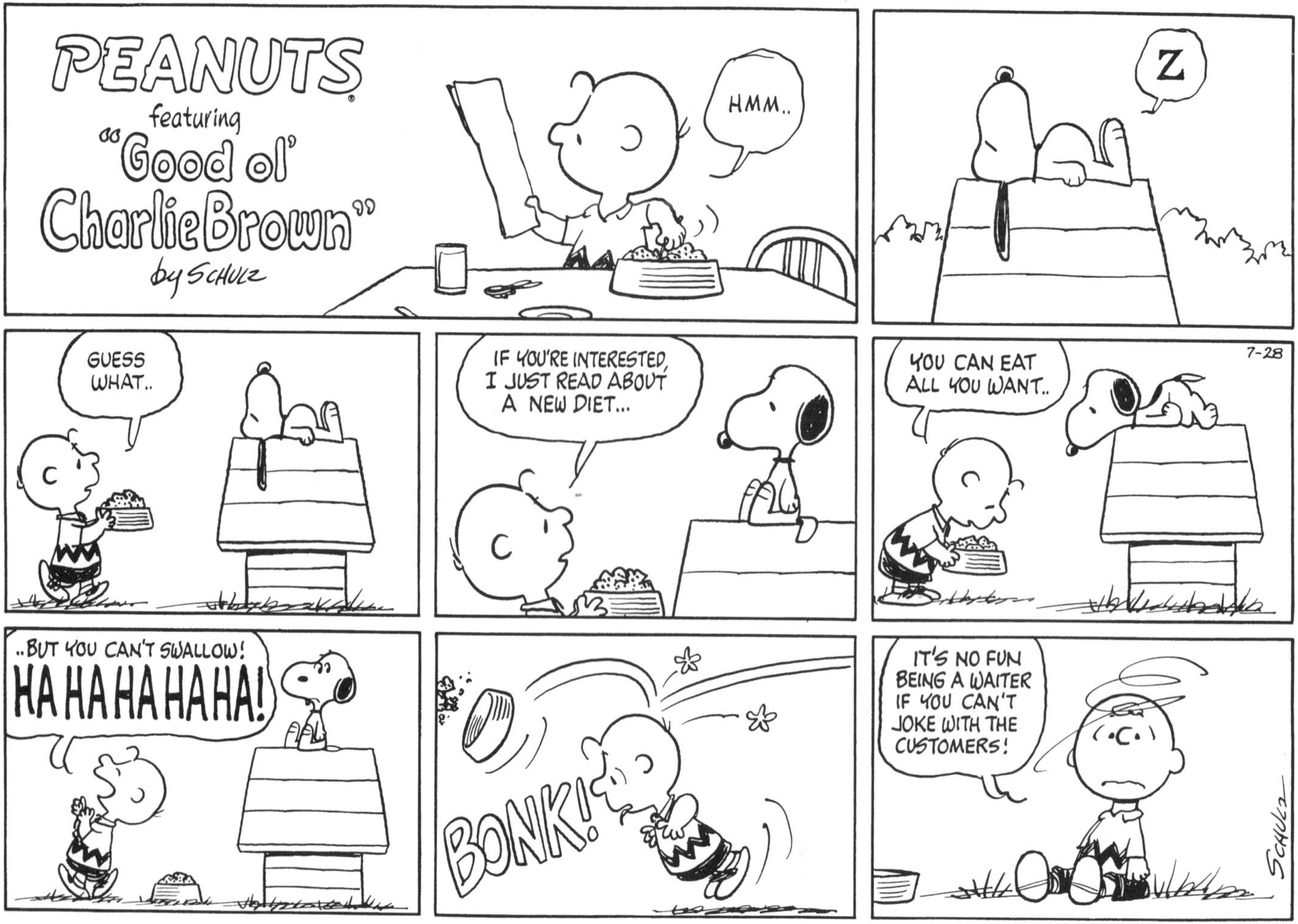
PEANUTS
featuring "Good ol' Charlie Brown"
by SCHULZ
HMM..
Z
GUESS WHAT..
IF YOU'RE INTERESTED, I JUST READ ABOUT A NEW DIET...
7-28
YOU CAN EAT ALL YOU WANT..
..BUT YOU CAN'T SWALLOW! HA HA HA HA HA HA!
BONK!
IT'S NO FUN BEING A WAITER IF YOU CAN'T JOKE WITH THE CUSTOMERS!
SCHULZ

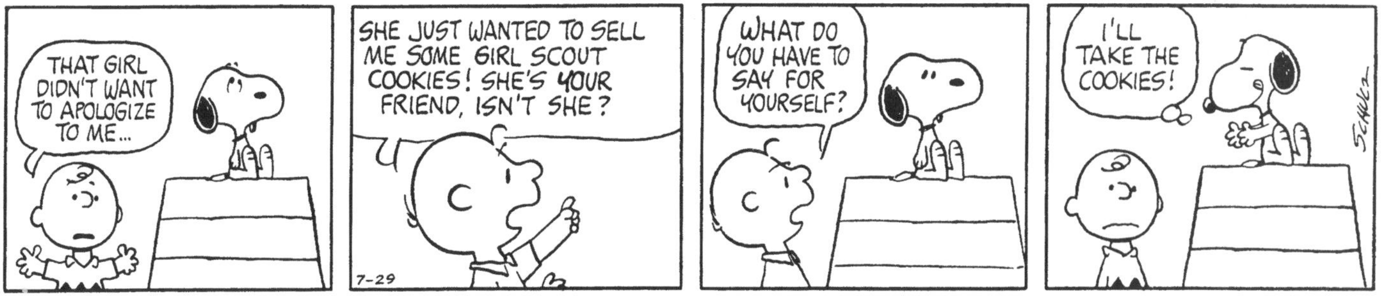
THAT GIRL DIDN'T WANT TO APOLOGIZE TO ME...
SHE JUST WANTED TO SELL ME SOME GIRL SCOUT COOKIES! SHE'S YOUR FRIEND, ISN'T SHE?
WHAT DO YOU HAVE TO SAY FOR YOURSELF?
I'LL TAKE THE COOKIES!

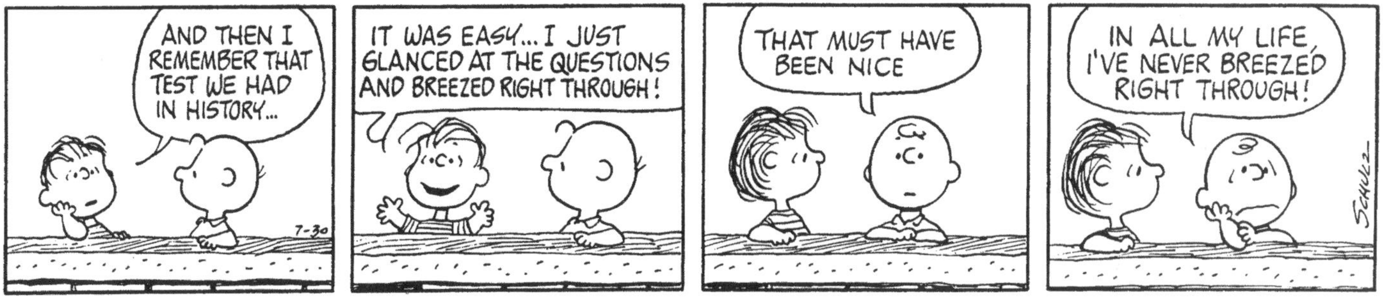
AND THEN I REMEMBER THAT TEST WE HAD IN HISTORY...
IT WAS EASY... I JUST GLANCED AT THE QUESTIONS AND BREEZED RIGHT THROUGH!
THAT MUST HAVE BEEN NICE
IN ALL MY LIFE, I'VE NEVER BREEZED RIGHT THROUGH!

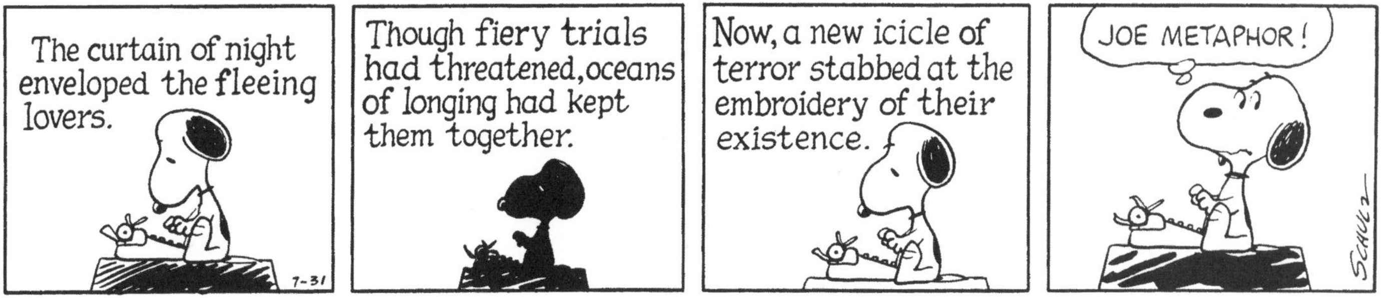
The curtain of night enveloped the fleeing lovers.
Though fiery trials had threatened, oceans of longing had kept them together.
Now, a new icicle of terror stabbed at the embroidery of their existence.
JOE METAPHOR!

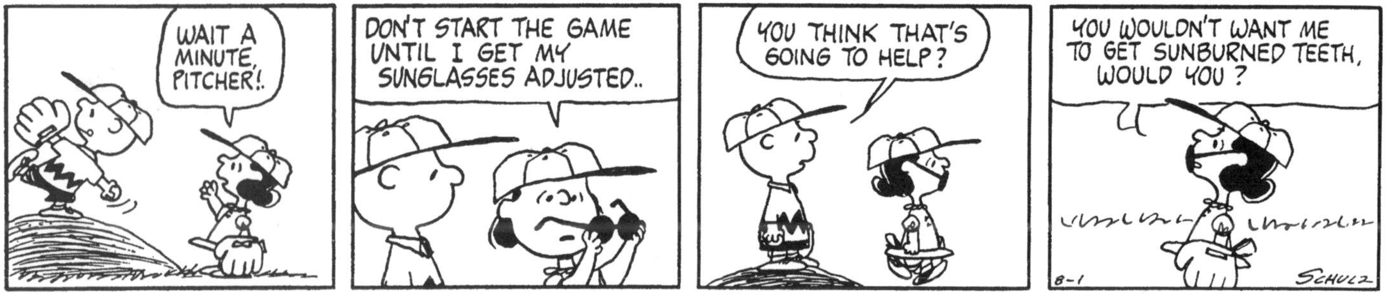
WAIT A MINUTE, PITCHER!.
DON'T START THE GAME UNTIL I GET MY SUNGLASSES ADJUSTED..
YOU THINK THAT'S GOING TO HELP?
YOU WOULDN'T WANT ME TO GET SUNBURNED TEETH, WOULD YOU?
8-1
SCHULZ

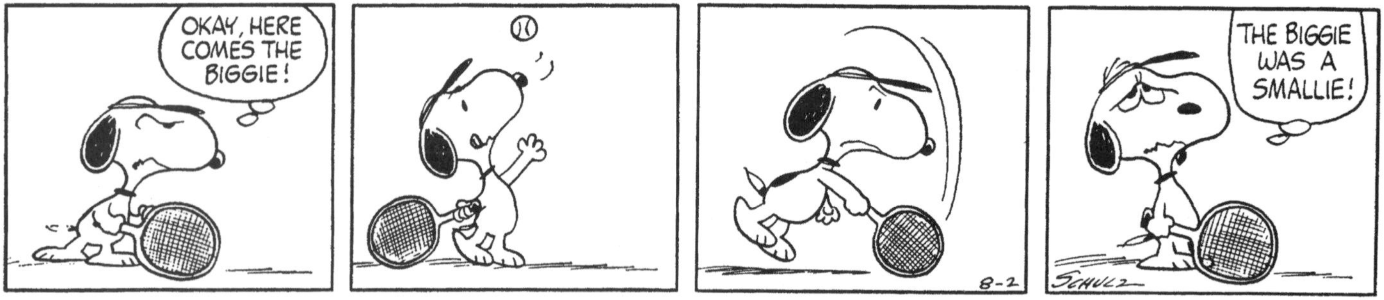
OKAY, HERE COMES THE BIGGIE!
8-2
THE BIGGIE WAS A SMALLIE!
SCHULZ

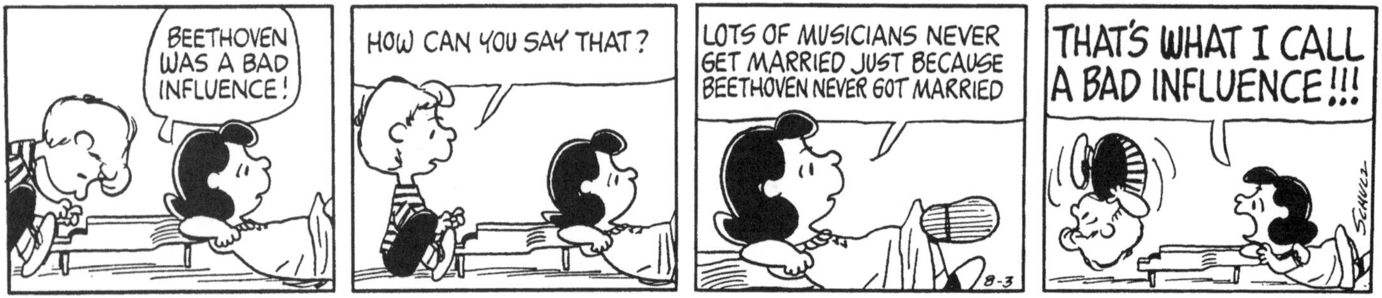
BEETHOVEN WAS A BAD INFLUENCE!
HOW CAN YOU SAY THAT?
LOTS OF MUSICIANS NEVER GET MARRIED JUST BECAUSE BEETHOVEN NEVER GOT MARRIED
8-3
THAT'S WHAT I CALL A BAD INFLUENCE!!!
SCHULZ

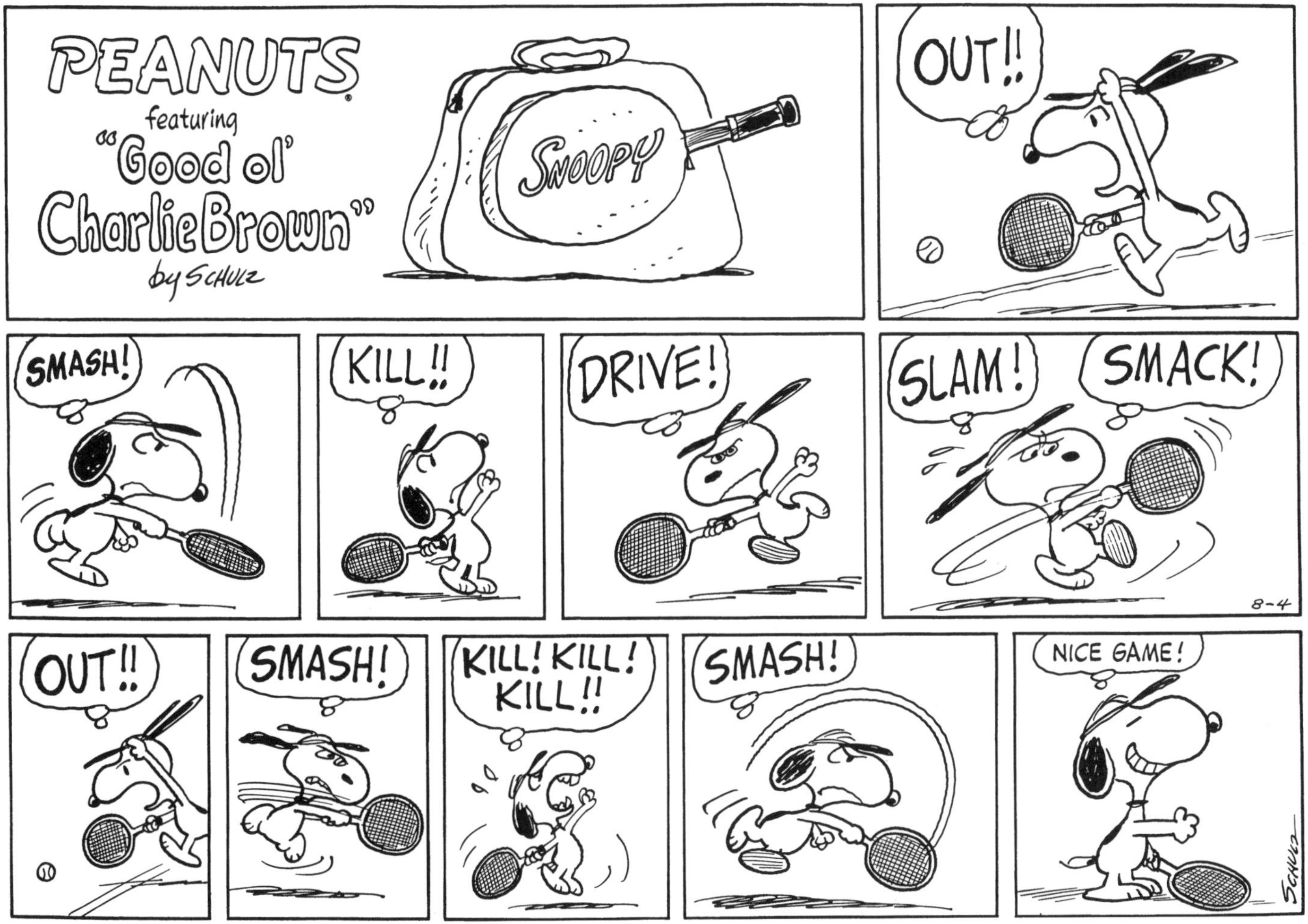
PEANUTS
featuring
"Good ol' Charlie Brown"
by SCHULZ
SNOOPY
OUT!!
SMASH!
KILL!!
DRIVE!
SLAM!
SMACK!
8-4
OUT!!
SMASH!
KILL! KILL! KILL!!
SMASH!
NICE GAME!
SCHULZ

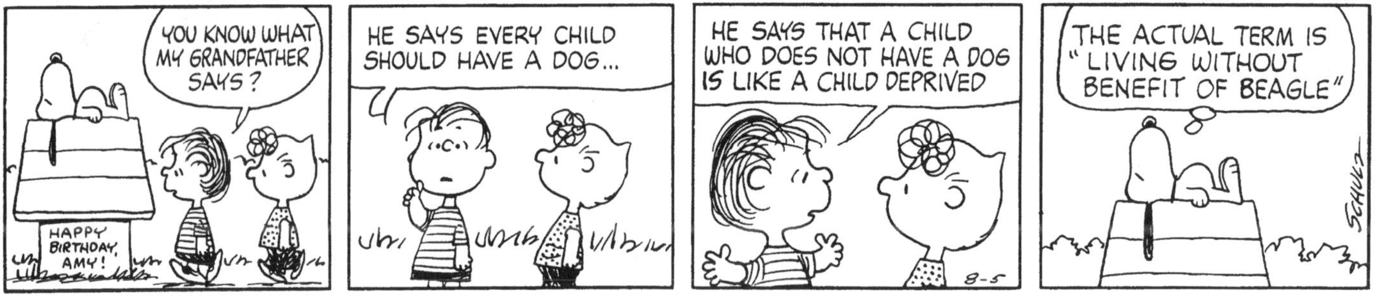

YOU KNOW WHAT MY GRANDFATHER SAYS?
HAPPY BIRTHDAY, AMY!
HE SAYS EVERY CHILD SHOULD HAVE A DOG...
HE SAYS THAT A CHILD WHO DOES NOT HAVE A DOG IS LIKE A CHILD DEPRIVED
8-5
THE ACTUAL TERM IS "LIVING WITHOUT BENEFIT OF BEAGLE"
SCHULZ

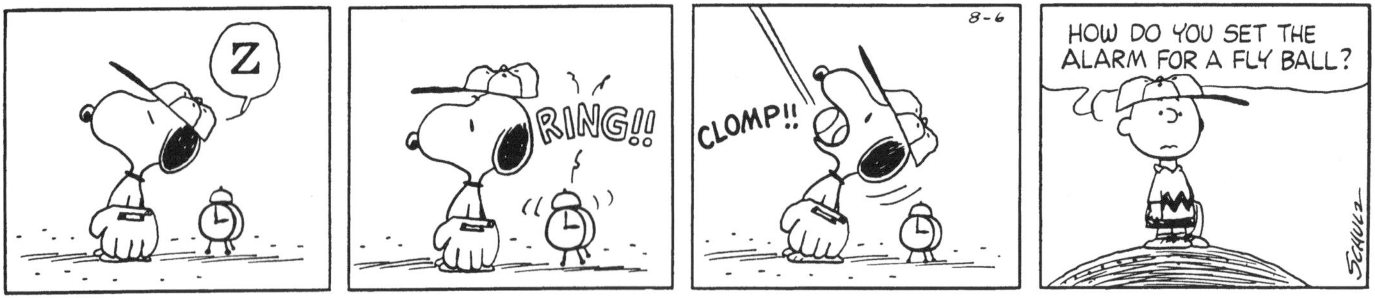

Z
RING!!
8-6
CLOMP!!
HOW DO YOU SET THE ALARM FOR A FLY BALL?
SCHULZ

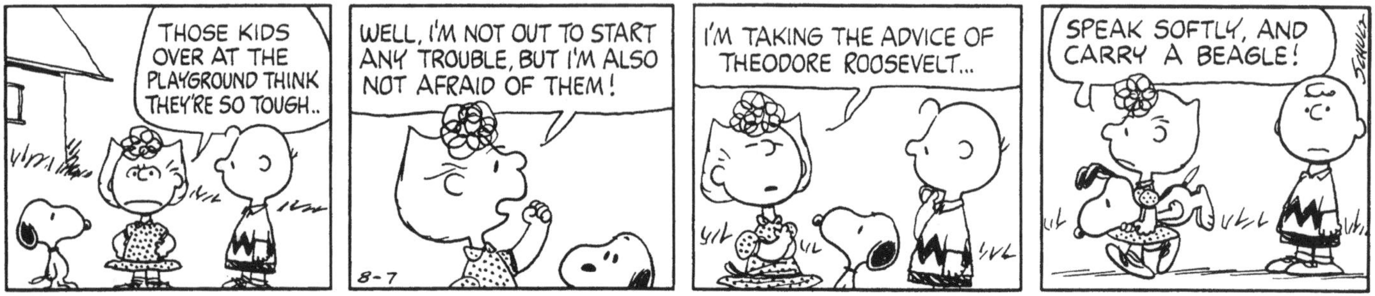

THOSE KIDS OVER AT THE PLAYGROUND THINK THEY'RE SO TOUGH..
WELL, I'M NOT OUT TO START ANY TROUBLE, BUT I'M ALSO NOT AFRAID OF THEM!
8-7
I'M TAKING THE ADVICE OF THEODORE ROOSEVELT...
SPEAK SOFTLY, AND CARRY A BEAGLE!
SCHULZ

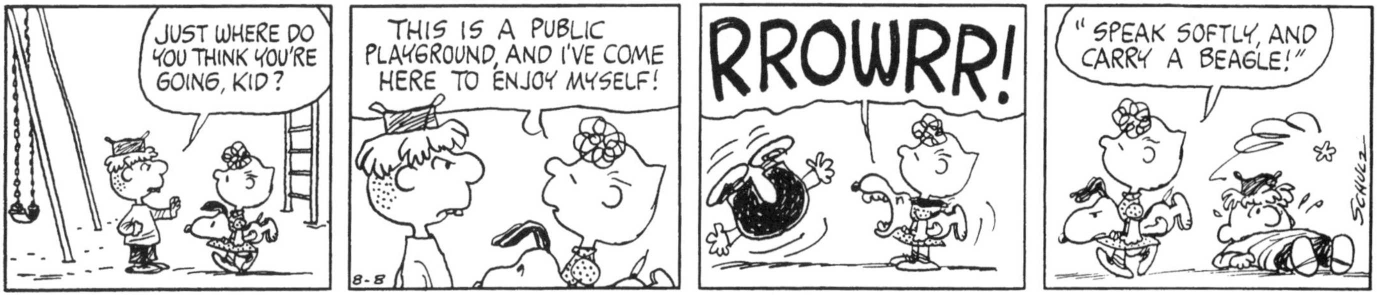
JUST WHERE DO YOU THINK YOU'RE GOING, KID?
THIS IS A PUBLIC PLAYGROUND, AND I'VE COME HERE TO ENJOY MYSELF!
8-8
RROWRR!
"SPEAK SOFTLY, AND CARRY A BEAGLE!"
SCHULZ

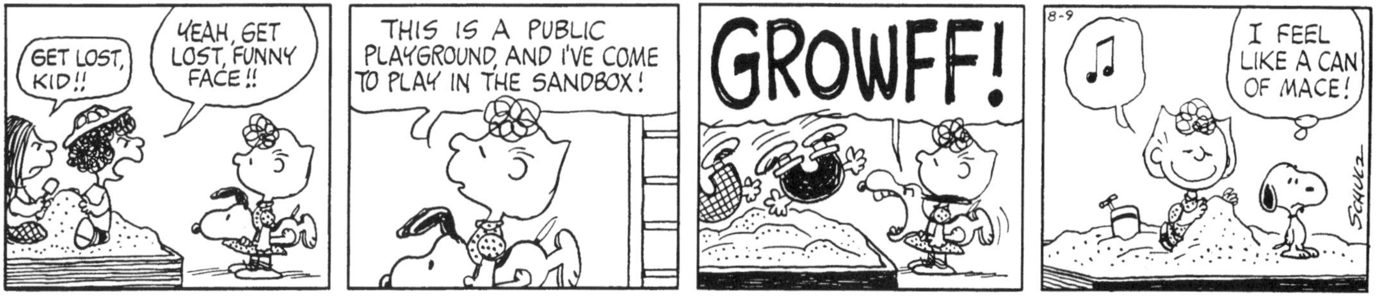
GET LOST, KID!!
YEAH, GET LOST, FUNNY FACE!!
THIS IS A PUBLIC PLAYGROUND, AND I'VE COME TO PLAY IN THE SANDBOX!
GROWFF!
8-9
I FEEL LIKE A CAN OF MACE!
SCHULZ

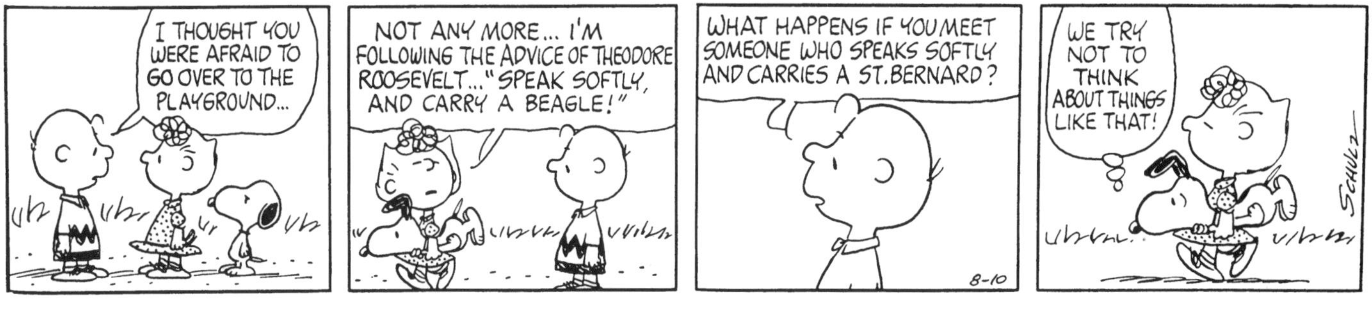
I THOUGHT YOU WERE AFRAID TO GO OVER TO THE PLAYGROUND...
NOT ANY MORE... I'M FOLLOWING THE ADVICE OF THEODORE ROOSEVELT..."SPEAK SOFTLY, AND CARRY A BEAGLE!"
WHAT HAPPENS IF YOU MEET SOMEONE WHO SPEAKS SOFTLY AND CARRIES A ST. BERNARD?
8-10
WE TRY NOT TO THINK ABOUT THINGS LIKE THAT!
SCHULZ

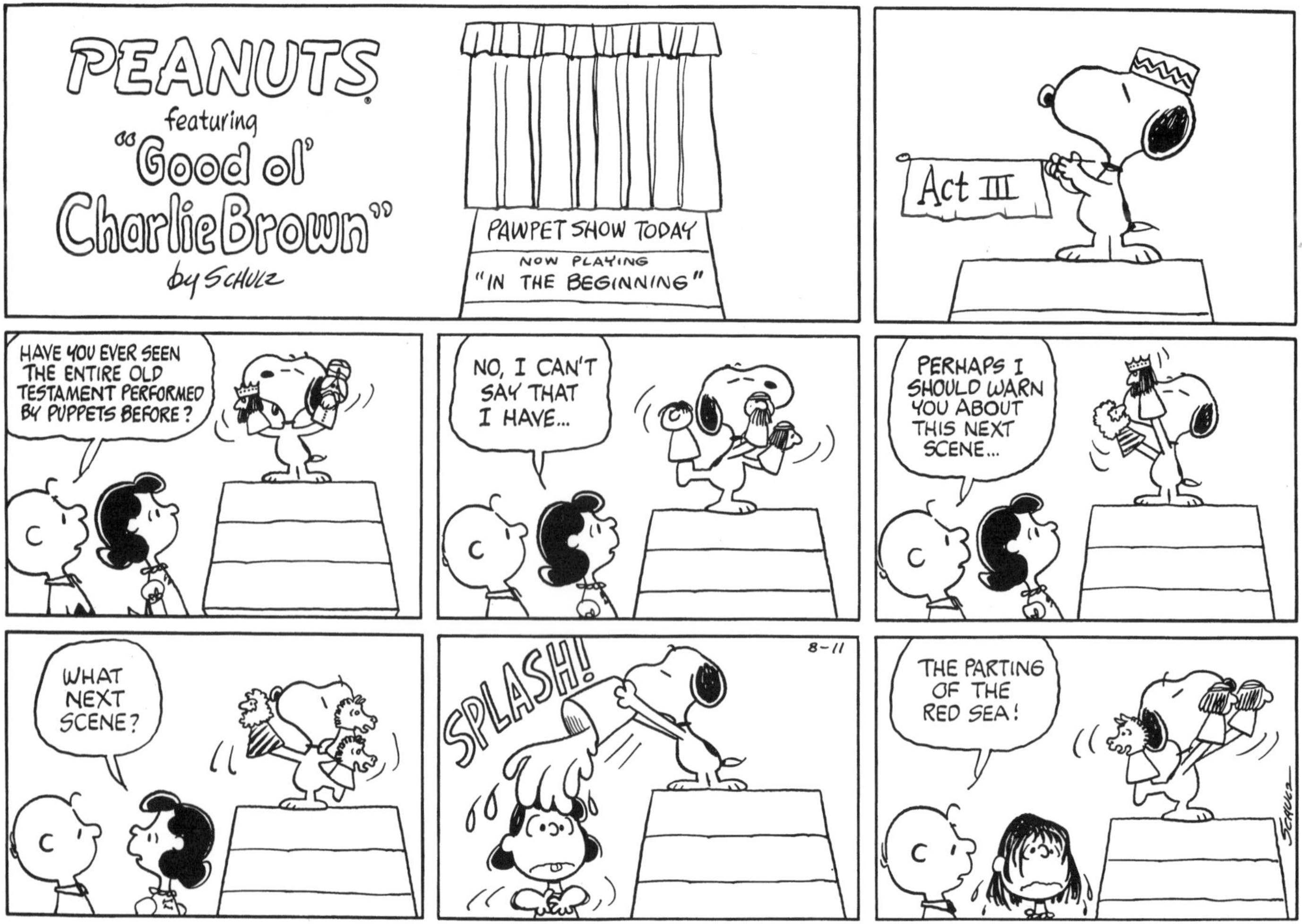
PEANUTS
featuring
"Good ol' CharlieBrown"
by SCHULZ
PAWPET SHOW TODAY
NOW PLAYING
"IN THE BEGINNING"
Act III
HAVE YOU EVER SEEN THE ENTIRE OLD TESTAMENT PERFORMED BY PUPPETS BEFORE?
NO, I CAN'T SAY THAT I HAVE...
PERHAPS I SHOULD WARN YOU ABOUT THIS NEXT SCENE...
WHAT NEXT SCENE?
SPLASH!
8-11
THE PARTING OF THE RED SEA!
SCHULZ

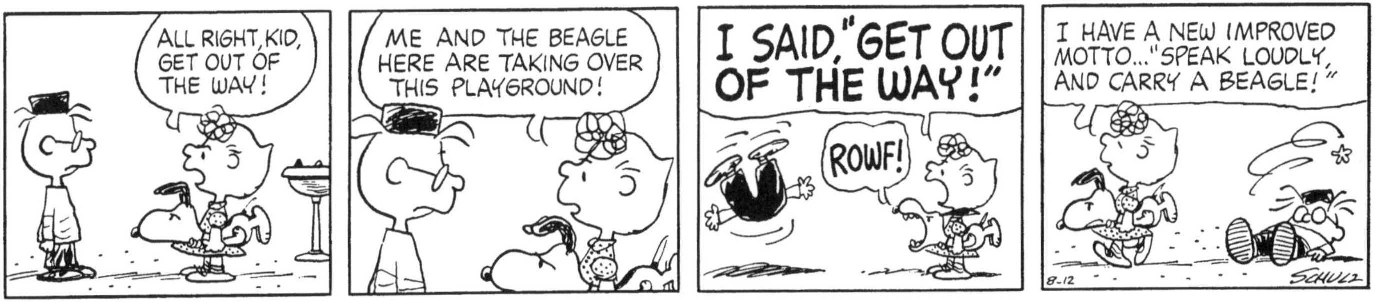
ALL RIGHT, KID, GET OUT OF THE WAY!
ME AND THE BEAGLE HERE ARE TAKING OVER THIS PLAYGROUND!
I SAID, "GET OUT OF THE WAY!"
ROWF!
I HAVE A NEW IMPROVED MOTTO..."SPEAK LOUDLY, AND CARRY A BEAGLE!"
8-12
SCHULZ

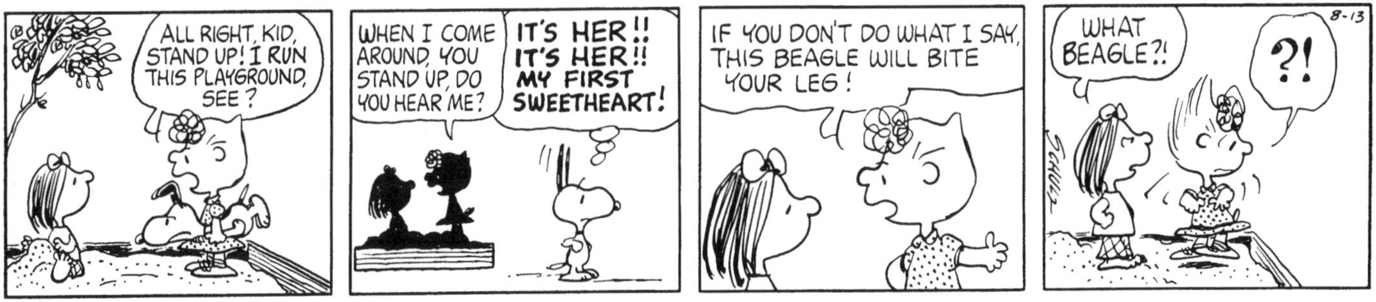
ALL RIGHT, KID, STAND UP! I RUN THIS PLAYGROUND, SEE?
WHEN I COME AROUND, YOU STAND UP, DO YOU HEAR ME?
IT'S HER!! IT'S HER!! MY FIRST SWEETHEART!
IF YOU DON'T DO WHAT I SAY, THIS BEAGLE WILL BITE YOUR LEG!
WHAT BEAGLE?!
?!
8-13
SCHULZ

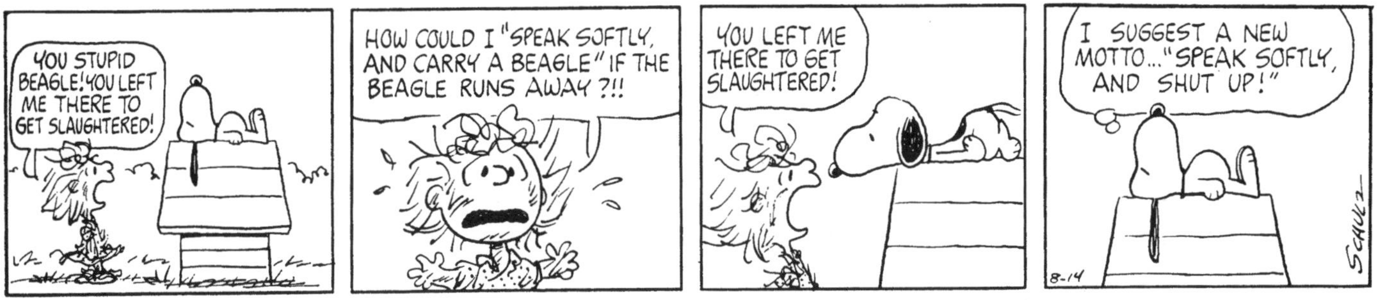
YOU STUPID BEAGLE! YOU LEFT ME THERE TO GET SLAUGHTERED!
HOW COULD I "SPEAK SOFTLY, AND CARRY A BEAGLE" IF THE BEAGLE RUNS AWAY?!!
YOU LEFT ME THERE TO GET SLAUGHTERED!
I SUGGEST A NEW MOTTO..."SPEAK SOFTLY, AND SHUT UP!"
8-14
SCHULZ

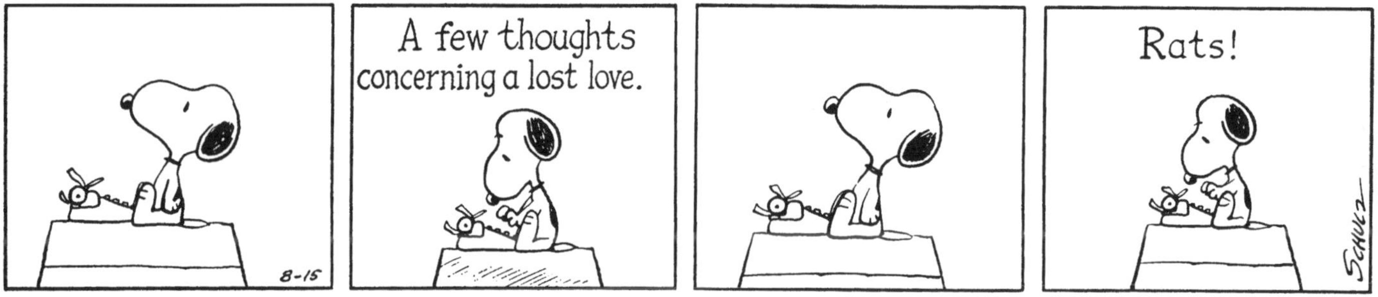
8-15
A few thoughts concerning a lost love.
Rats!
SCHULZ

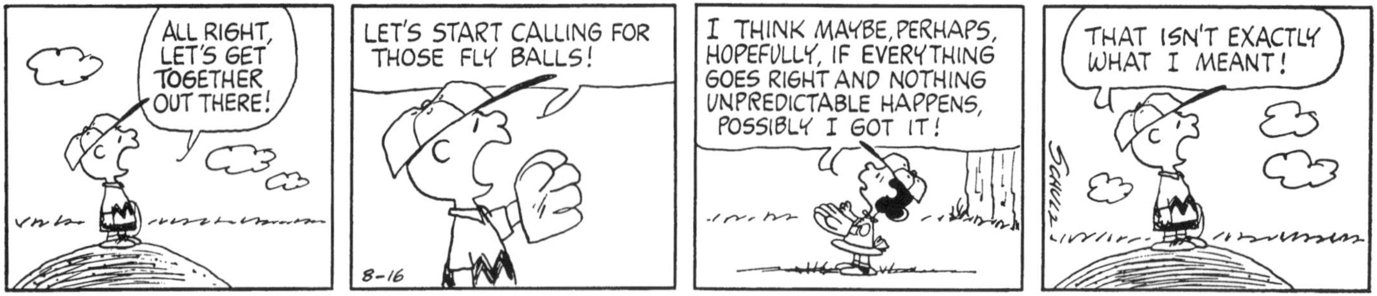
ALL RIGHT, LET'S GET TOGETHER OUT THERE!
LET'S START CALLING FOR THOSE FLY BALLS!
8-16
I THINK MAYBE, PERHAPS, HOPEFULLY, IF EVERYTHING GOES RIGHT AND NOTHING UNPREDICTABLE HAPPENS, POSSIBLY I GOT IT!
SCHULZ
THAT ISN'T EXACTLY WHAT I MEANT!

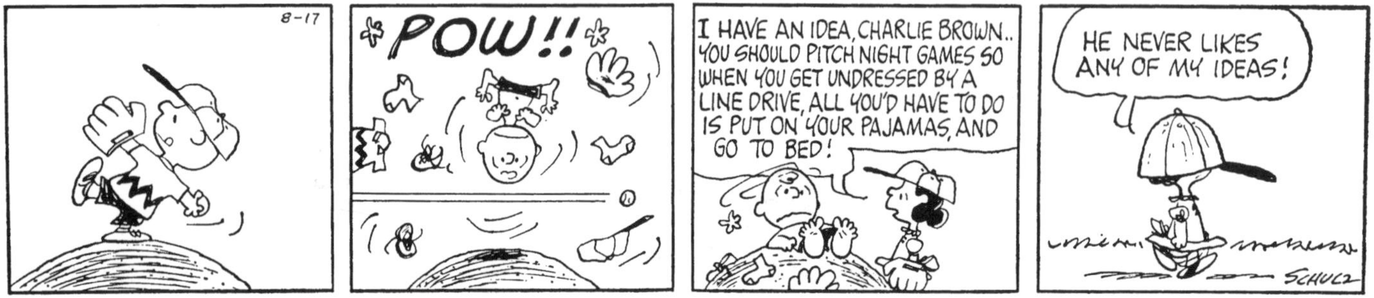
8-17
POW!!
I HAVE AN IDEA, CHARLIE BROWN.. YOU SHOULD PITCH NIGHT GAMES SO WHEN YOU GET UNDRESSED BY A LINE DRIVE, ALL YOU'D HAVE TO DO IS PUT ON YOUR PAJAMAS AND GO TO BED!
HE NEVER LIKES ANY OF MY IDEAS!
SCHULZ

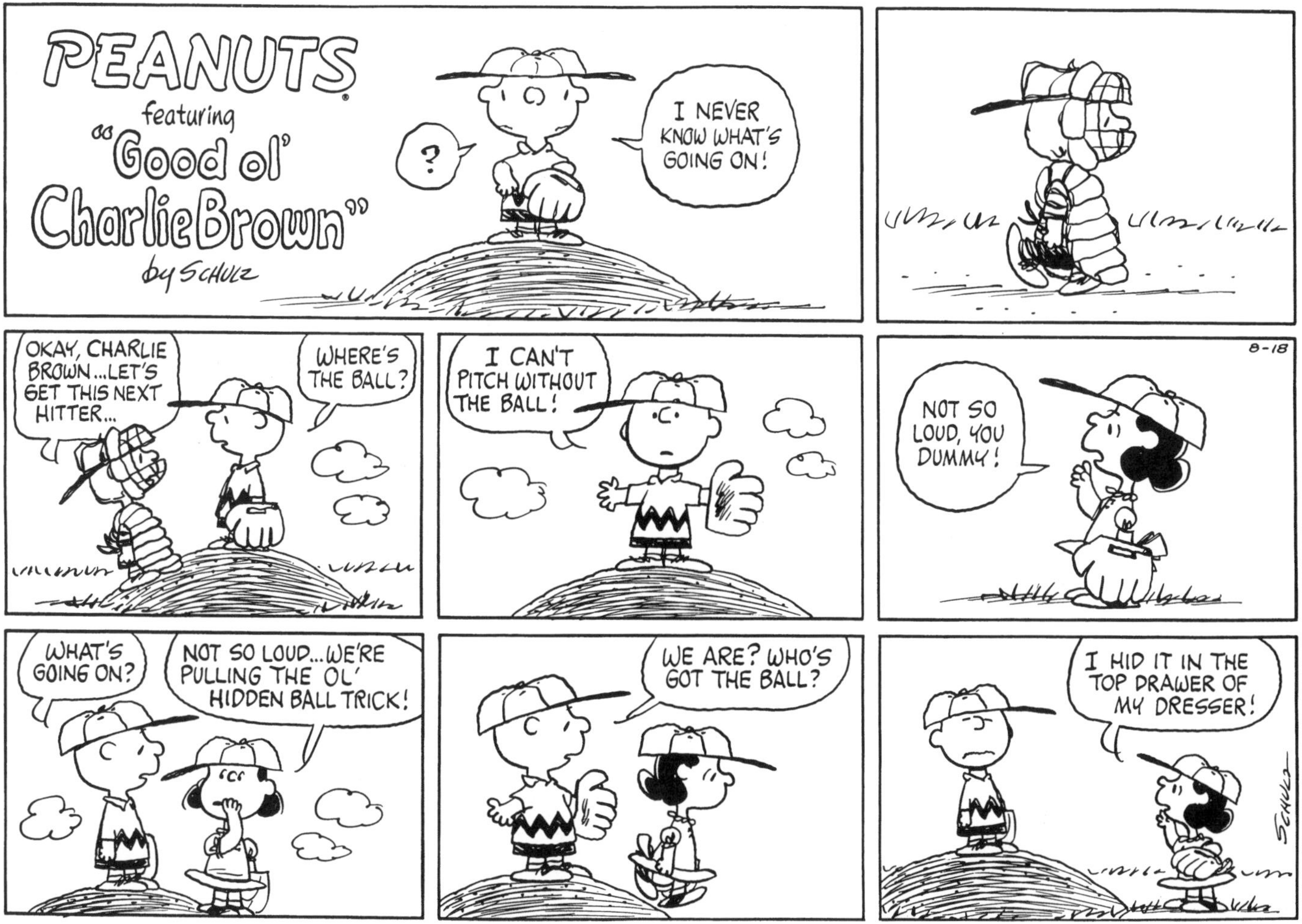
PEANUTS
featuring "Good ol' Charlie Brown"
by SCHULZ
?
I NEVER KNOW WHAT'S GOING ON!
OKAY, CHARLIE BROWN...LET'S GET THIS NEXT HITTER...
WHERE'S THE BALL?
I CAN'T PITCH WITHOUT THE BALL!
8-18
NOT SO LOUD, YOU DUMMY!
WHAT'S GOING ON?
NOT SO LOUD...WE'RE PULLING THE OL' HIDDEN BALL TRICK!
WE ARE? WHO'S GOT THE BALL?
I HID IT IN THE TOP DRAWER OF MY DRESSER!
SCHULZ

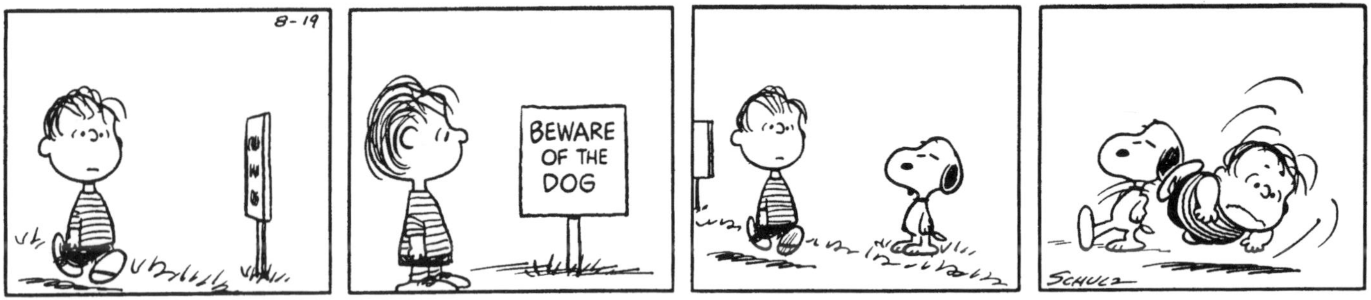
8-19
BEWARE OF THE DOG
SCHULZ

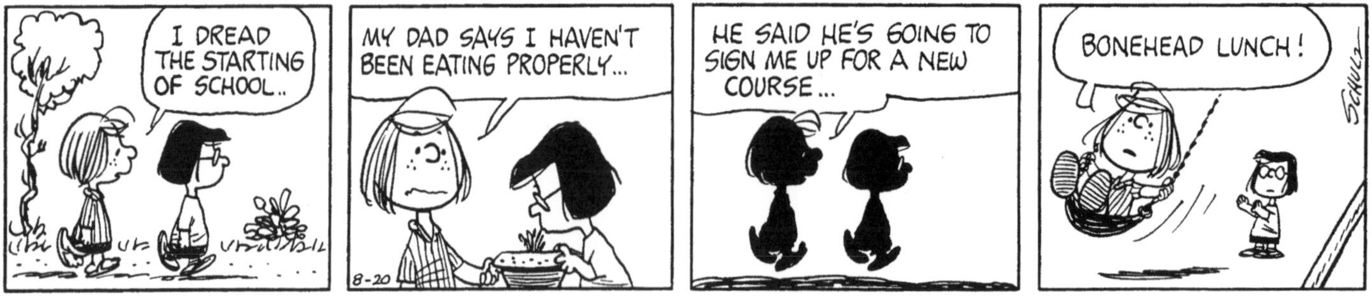
I DREAD THE STARTING OF SCHOOL..
MY DAD SAYS I HAVEN'T BEEN EATING PROPERLY...
8-20
HE SAID HE'S GOING TO SIGN ME UP FOR A NEW COURSE...
BONEHEAD LUNCH!
SCHULZ

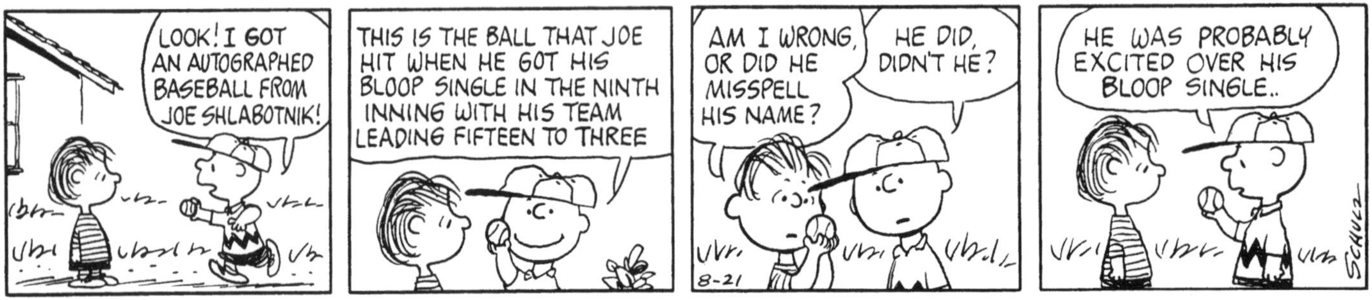
LOOK! I GOT AN AUTOGRAPHED BASEBALL FROM JOE SHLABOTNIK!
THIS IS THE BALL THAT JOE HIT WHEN HE GOT HIS BLOOP SINGLE IN THE NINTH INNING WITH HIS TEAM LEADING FIFTEEN TO THREE
AM I WRONG, OR DID HE MISSPELL HIS NAME?
HE DID, DIDN'T HE?
8-21
HE WAS PROBABLY EXCITED OVER HIS BLOOP SINGLE..
SCHULZ

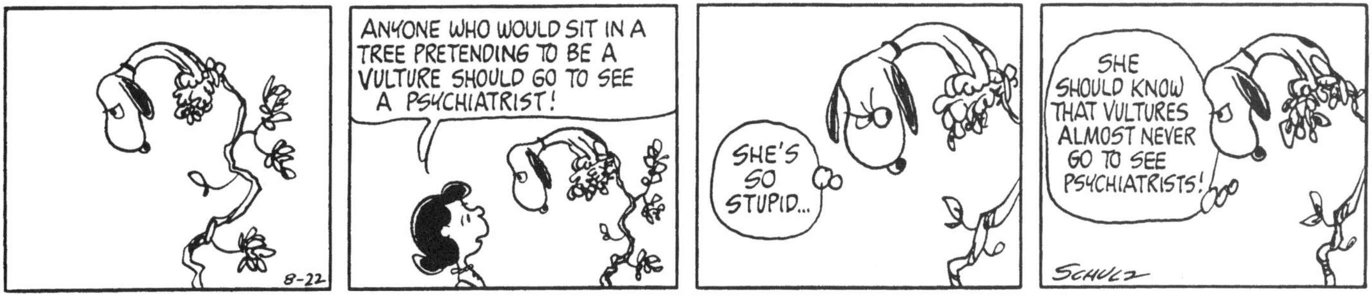
8-22
ANYONE WHO WOULD SIT IN A TREE PRETENDING TO BE A VULTURE SHOULD GO TO SEE A PSYCHIATRIST!
SHE'S SO STUPID...
SHE SHOULD KNOW THAT VULTURES ALMOST NEVER GO TO SEE PSYCHIATRISTS!
SCHULZ

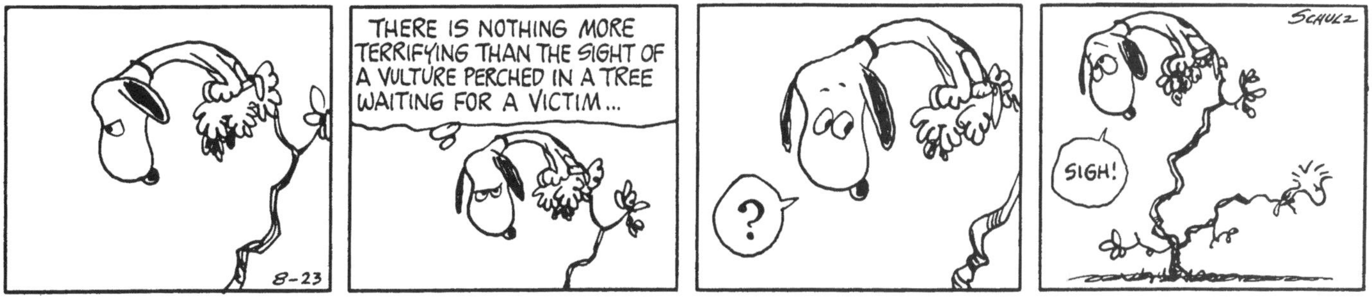
8-23
THERE IS NOTHING MORE TERRIFYING THAN THE SIGHT OF A VULTURE PERCHED IN A TREE WAITING FOR A VICTIM...
?
SCHULZ
SIGH!

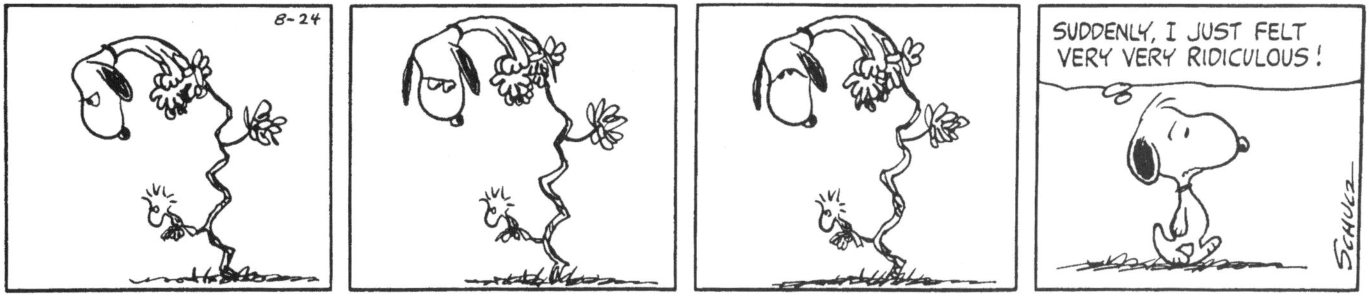
8-24
SUDDENLY, I JUST FELT VERY VERY RIDICULOUS!
SCHULZ

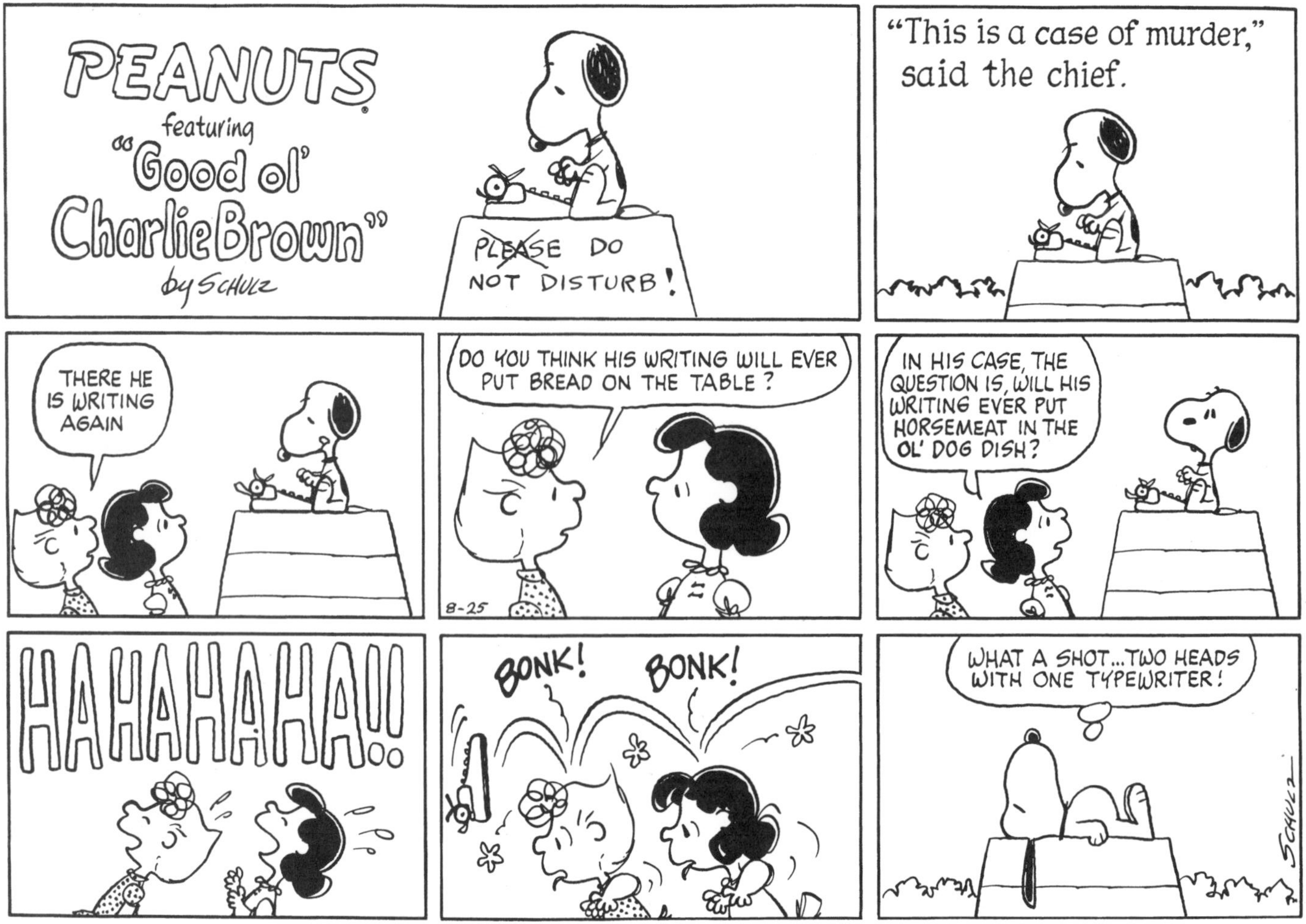
PEANUTS
featuring
"Good ol' Charlie Brown"
by SCHULZ
PLEASE DO NOT DISTURB!
"This is a case of murder," said the chief.
THERE HE IS WRITING AGAIN
DO YOU THINK HIS WRITING WILL EVER PUT BREAD ON THE TABLE?
8-25
IN HIS CASE, THE QUESTION IS, WILL HIS WRITING EVER PUT HORSEMEAT IN THE OL' DOG DISH?
HAHAHAHA!!
BONK!
BONK!
WHAT A SHOT...TWO HEADS WITH ONE TYPEWRITER!
SCHULZ

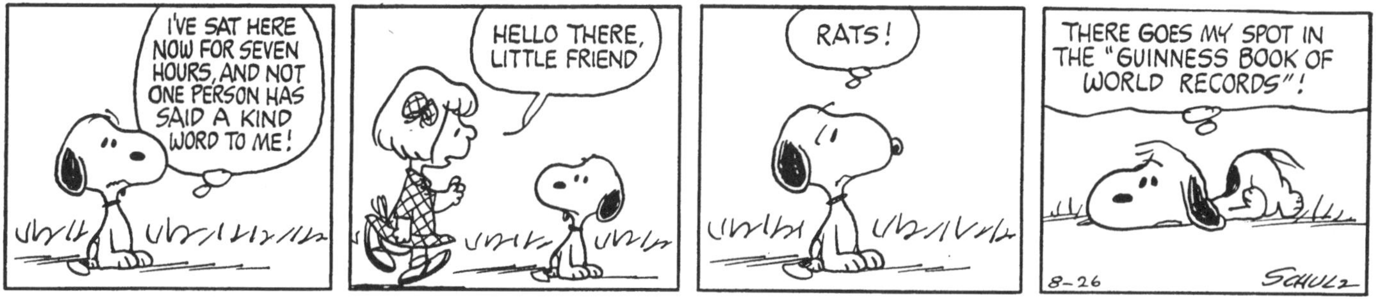
I'VE SAT HERE NOW FOR SEVEN HOURS, AND NOT ONE PERSON HAS SAID A KIND WORD TO ME!
HELLO THERE, LITTLE FRIEND
RATS!
THERE GOES MY SPOT IN THE "GUINNESS BOOK OF WORLD RECORDS"!
8-26
SCHULZ

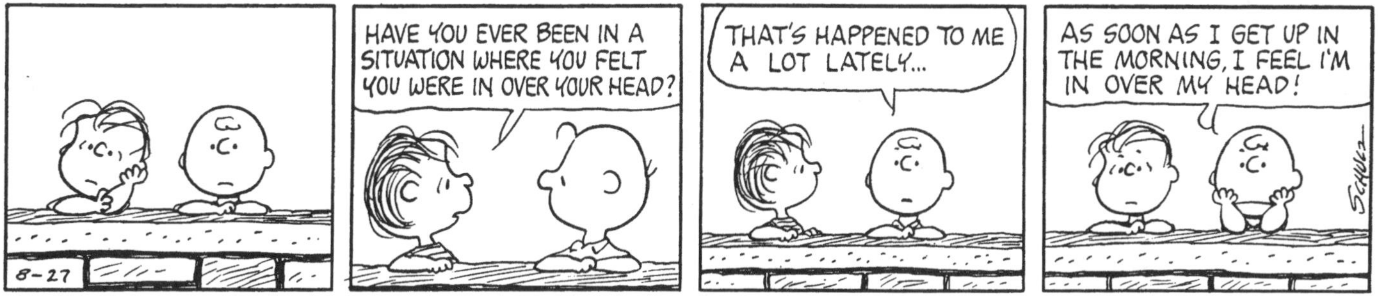
8-27
HAVE YOU EVER BEEN IN A SITUATION WHERE YOU FELT YOU WERE IN OVER YOUR HEAD?
THAT'S HAPPENED TO ME A LOT LATELY...
AS SOON AS I GET UP IN THE MORNING, I FEEL I'M IN OVER MY HEAD!
SCHULZ

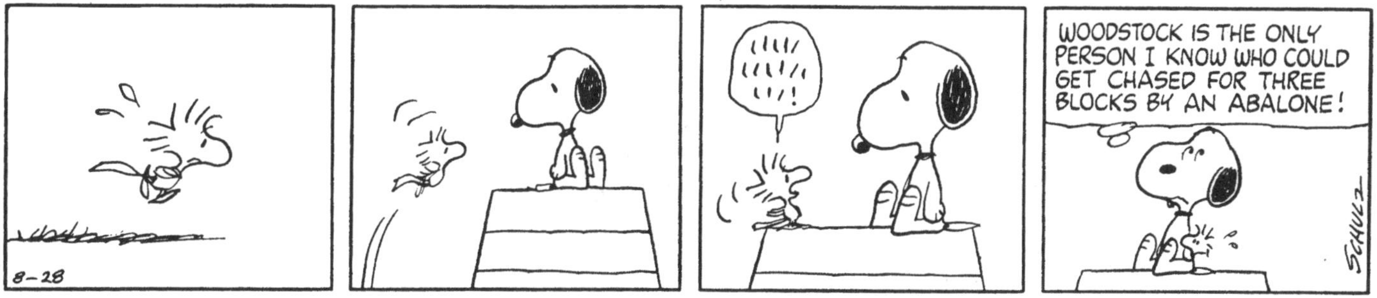
8-28
WOODSTOCK IS THE ONLY PERSON I KNOW WHO COULD GET CHASED FOR THREE BLOCKS BY AN ABALONE!
SCHULZ

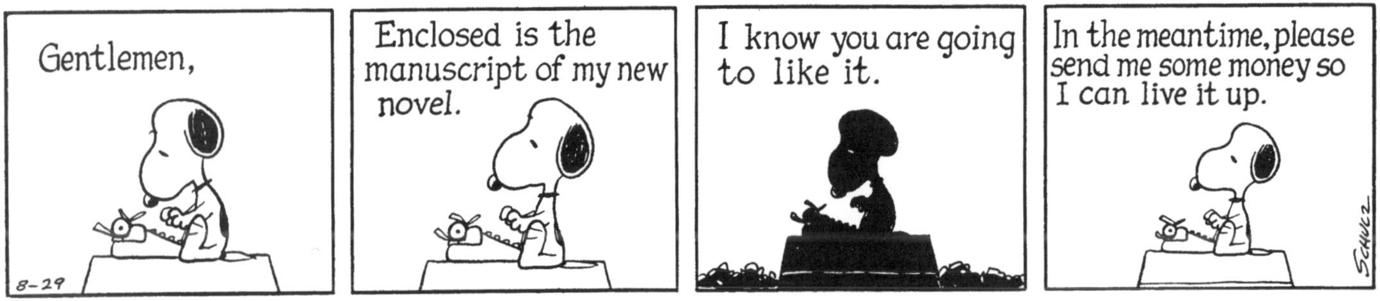
Gentlemen,
Enclosed is the manuscript of my new novel.
I know you are going to like it.
In the meantime, please send me some money so I can live it up.
8-29
SCHULZ

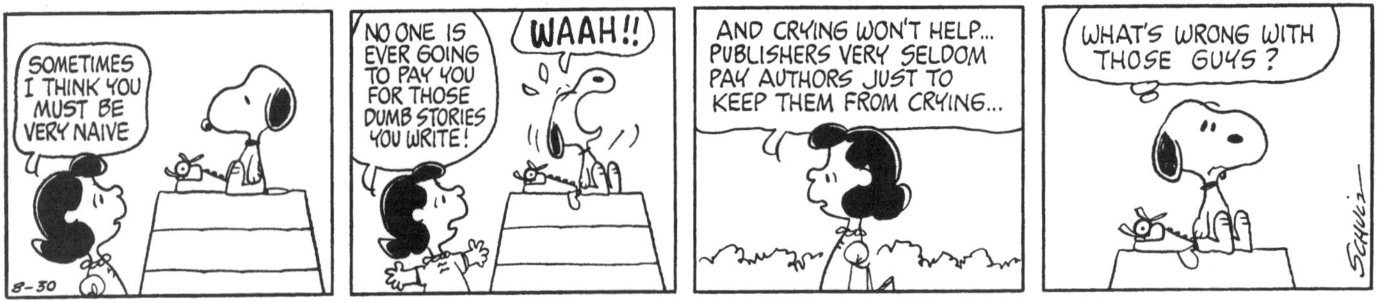
SOMETIMES I THINK YOU MUST BE VERY NAIVE
NO ONE IS EVER GOING TO PAY YOU FOR THOSE DUMB STORIES YOU WRITE!
WAAH!!
AND CRYING WON'T HELP... PUBLISHERS VERY SELDOM PAY AUTHORS JUST TO KEEP THEM FROM CRYING...
WHAT'S WRONG WITH THOSE GUYS?
8-30
SCHULZ

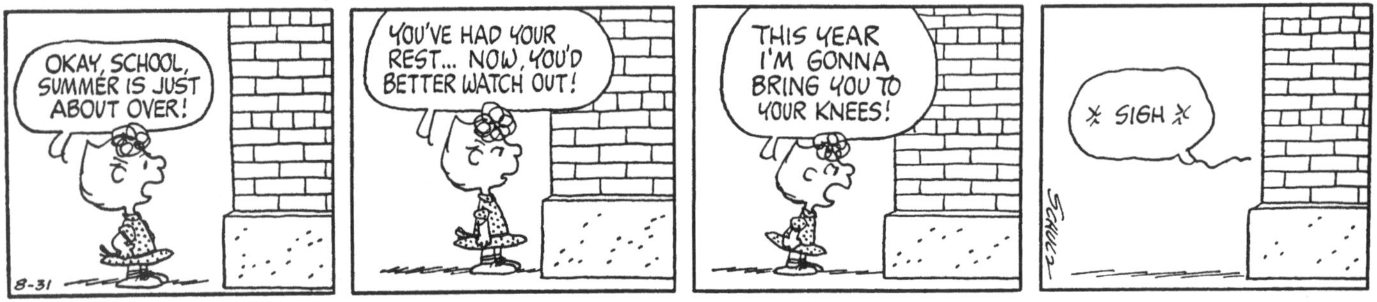
OKAY, SCHOOL, SUMMER IS JUST ABOUT OVER!
YOU'VE HAD YOUR REST... NOW, YOU'D BETTER WATCH OUT!
THIS YEAR I'M GONNA BRING YOU TO YOUR KNEES!
* SIGH *
8-31
SCHULZ

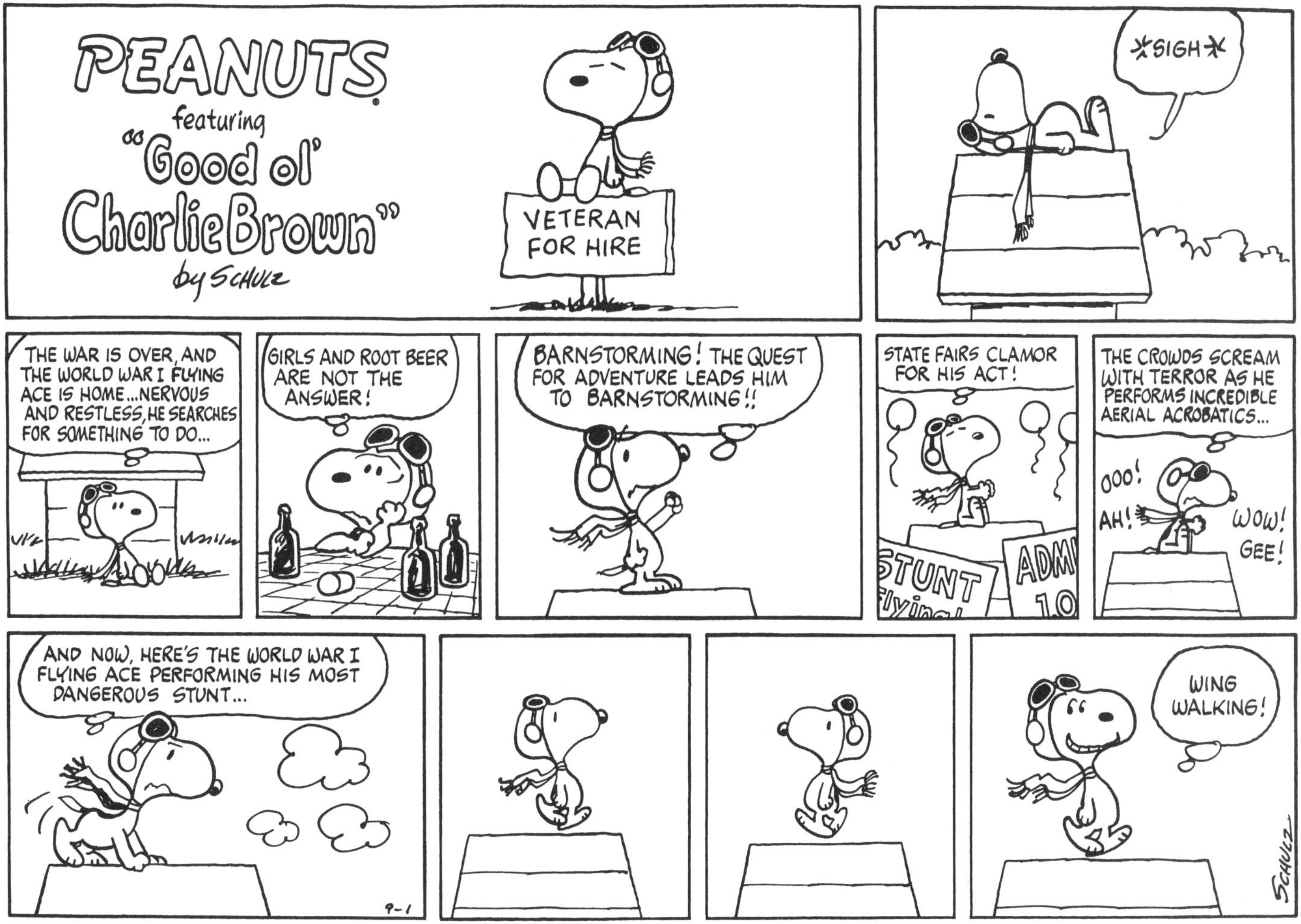
PEANUTS
featuring "Good ol' Charlie Brown"
by SCHULZ
VETERAN FOR HIRE
SIGH
THE WAR IS OVER, AND THE WORLD WAR I FLYING ACE IS HOME...NERVOUS AND RESTLESS, HE SEARCHES FOR SOMETHING TO DO...
GIRLS AND ROOT BEER ARE NOT THE ANSWER!
BARNSTORMING! THE QUEST FOR ADVENTURE LEADS HIM TO BARNSTORMING!!
STATE FAIRS CLAMOR FOR HIS ACT!
STUNT
ADM
THE CROWDS SCREAM WITH TERROR AS HE PERFORMS INCREDIBLE AERIAL ACROBATICS...
OOO!
AH!
WOW!
GEE!
AND NOW, HERE'S THE WORLD WAR I FLYING ACE PERFORMING HIS MOST DANGEROUS STUNT...
9-1
WING WALKING!
SCHULZ

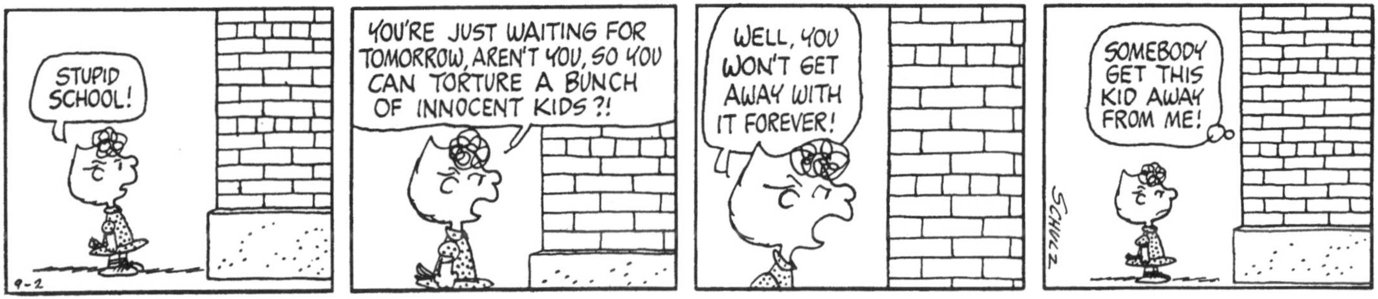
STUPID SCHOOL!
YOU'RE JUST WAITING FOR TOMORROW, AREN'T YOU, SO YOU CAN TORTURE A BUNCH OF INNOCENT KIDS ?!
WELL, YOU WON'T GET AWAY WITH IT FOREVER!
SOMEBODY GET THIS KID AWAY FROM ME!
SCHULZ
9-2

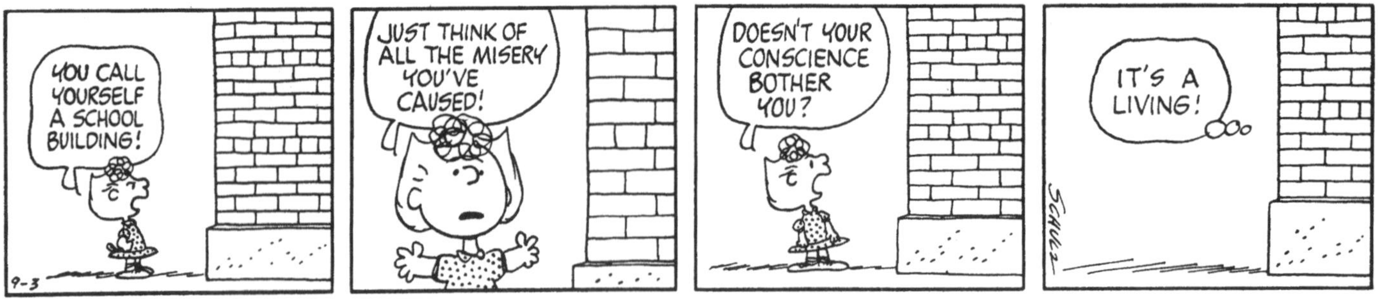
YOU CALL YOURSELF A SCHOOL BUILDING!
JUST THINK OF ALL THE MISERY YOU'VE CAUSED!
DOESN'T YOUR CONSCIENCE BOTHER YOU?
IT'S A LIVING!
SCHULZ
9-3

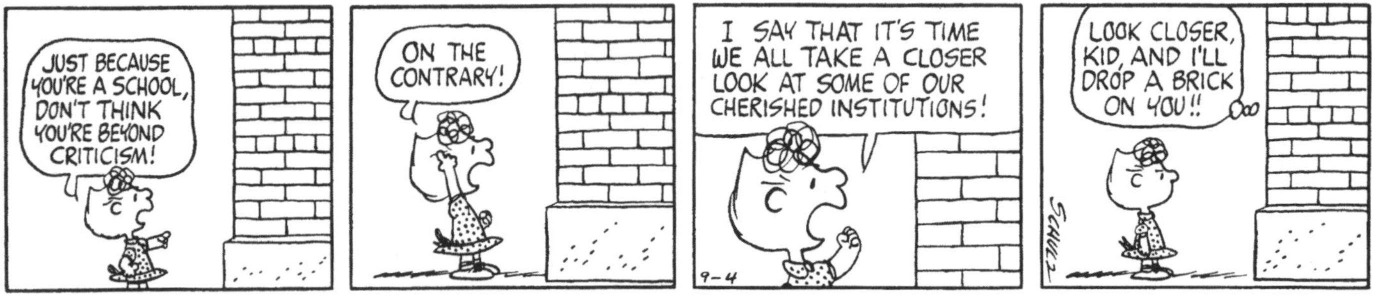
JUST BECAUSE YOU'RE A SCHOOL, DON'T THINK YOU'RE BEYOND CRITICISM!
ON THE CONTRARY!
I SAY THAT IT'S TIME WE ALL TAKE A CLOSER LOOK AT SOME OF OUR CHERISHED INSTITUTIONS!
LOOK CLOSER, KID, AND I'LL DROP A BRICK ON YOU!!
SCHULZ
9-4

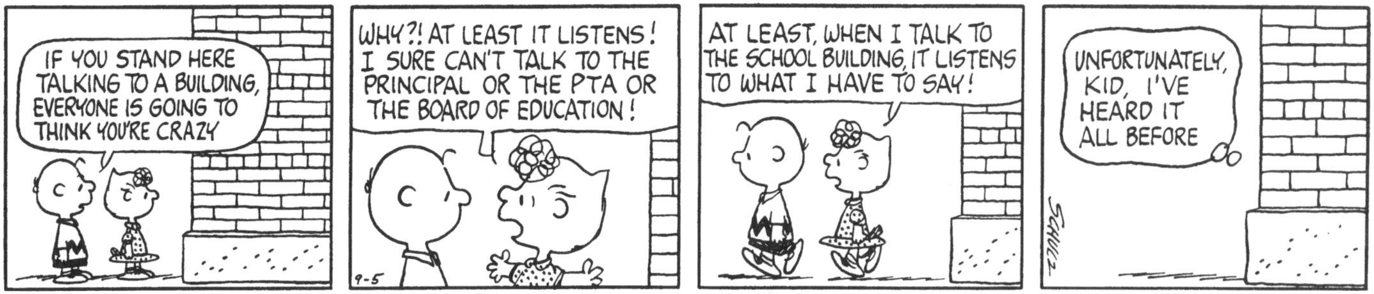
IF YOU STAND HERE TALKING TO A BUILDING, EVERYONE IS GOING TO THINK YOU'RE CRAZY
WHY?! AT LEAST IT LISTENS! I SURE CAN'T TALK TO THE PRINCIPAL OR THE PTA OR THE BOARD OF EDUCATION!
AT LEAST, WHEN I TALK TO THE SCHOOL BUILDING, IT LISTENS TO WHAT I HAVE TO SAY!
UNFORTUNATELY, KID, I'VE HEARD IT ALL BEFORE

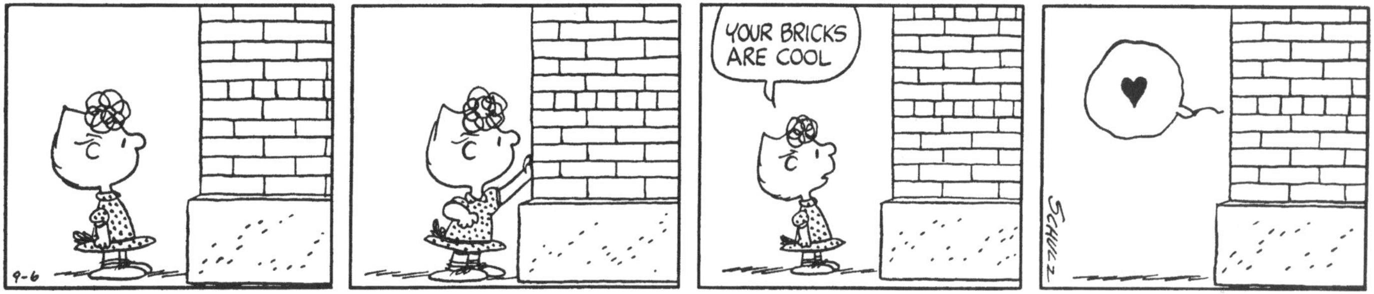
YOUR BRICKS ARE COOL

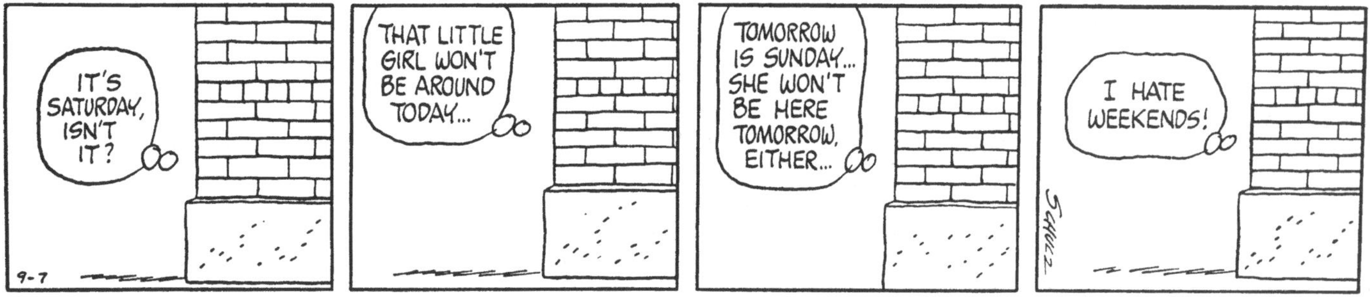
IT'S SATURDAY, ISN'T IT?
THAT LITTLE GIRL WON'T BE AROUND TODAY...
TOMORROW IS SUNDAY... SHE WON'T BE HERE TOMORROW, EITHER...
I HATE WEEKENDS!

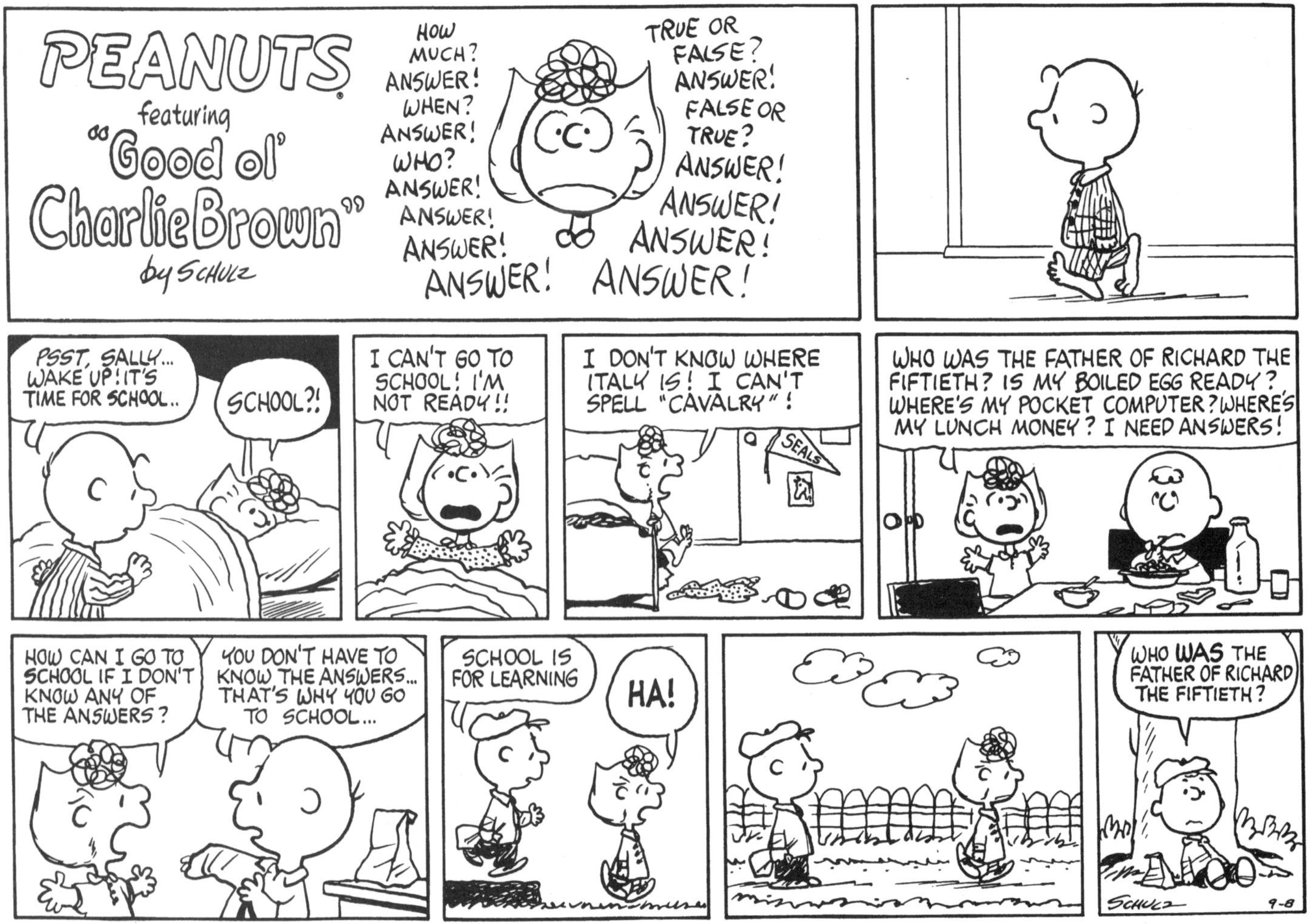
PEANUTS
featuring "Good ol' Charlie Brown"
by SCHULZ
HOW MUCH? ANSWER! WHEN? ANSWER! WHO? ANSWER! ANSWER! ANSWER! ANSWER!
TRUE OR FALSE? ANSWER! FALSE OR TRUE? ANSWER! ANSWER! ANSWER! ANSWER!
PSST, SALLY... WAKE UP! IT'S TIME FOR SCHOOL..
SCHOOL?!
I CAN'T GO TO SCHOOL! I'M NOT READY!!
I DON'T KNOW WHERE ITALY IS! I CAN'T SPELL "CAVALRY"!
SEALS
WHO WAS THE FATHER OF RICHARD THE FIFTIETH? IS MY BOILED EGG READY? WHERE'S MY POCKET COMPUTER? WHERE'S MY LUNCH MONEY? I NEED ANSWERS!
HOW CAN I GO TO SCHOOL IF I DON'T KNOW ANY OF THE ANSWERS?
YOU DON'T HAVE TO KNOW THE ANSWERS... THAT'S WHY YOU GO TO SCHOOL...
SCHOOL IS FOR LEARNING
HA!
WHO **WAS** THE FATHER OF RICHARD THE FIFTIETH?
SCHULZ
9-8

September

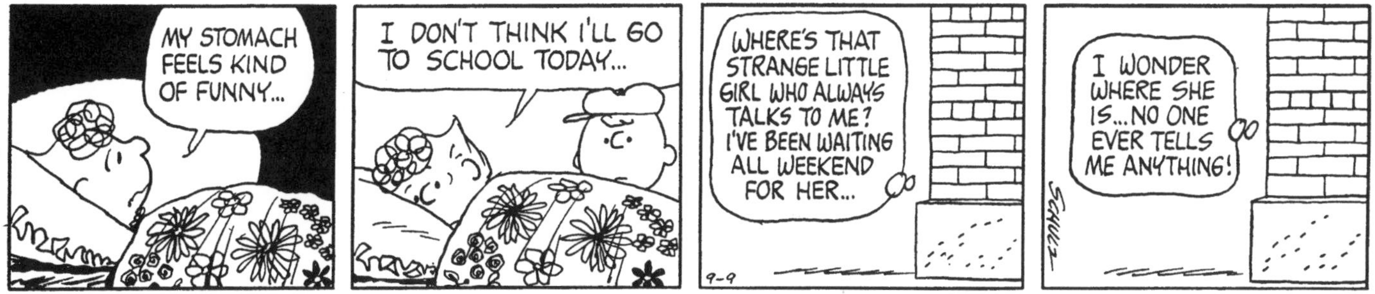
MY STOMACH FEELS KIND OF FUNNY...
I DON'T THINK I'LL GO TO SCHOOL TODAY...
WHERE'S THAT STRANGE LITTLE GIRL WHO ALWAYS TALKS TO ME? I'VE BEEN WAITING ALL WEEKEND FOR HER...
I WONDER WHERE SHE IS...NO ONE EVER TELLS ME ANYTHING!
9-9
SCHULZ

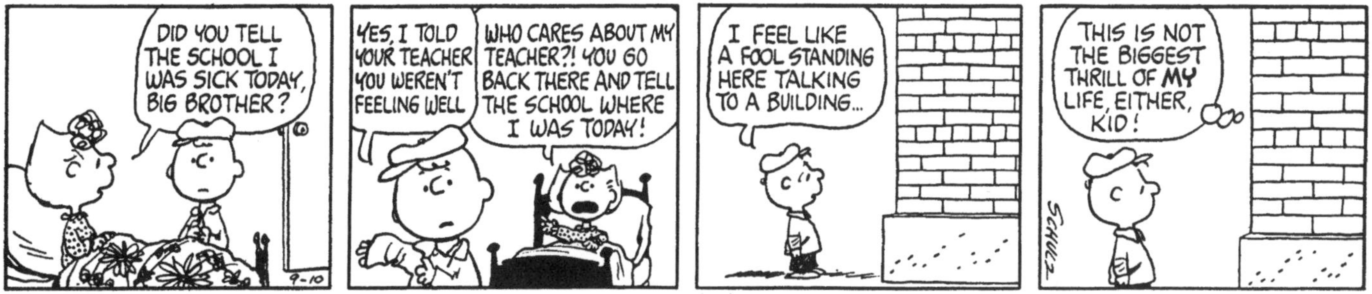
DID YOU TELL THE SCHOOL I WAS SICK TODAY, BIG BROTHER?
9-10
YES, I TOLD YOUR TEACHER YOU WEREN'T FEELING WELL
WHO CARES ABOUT MY TEACHER?! YOU GO BACK THERE AND TELL THE SCHOOL WHERE I WAS TODAY!
I FEEL LIKE A FOOL STANDING HERE TALKING TO A BUILDING...
THIS IS NOT THE BIGGEST THRILL OF **MY** LIFE, EITHER, KID!
SCHULZ

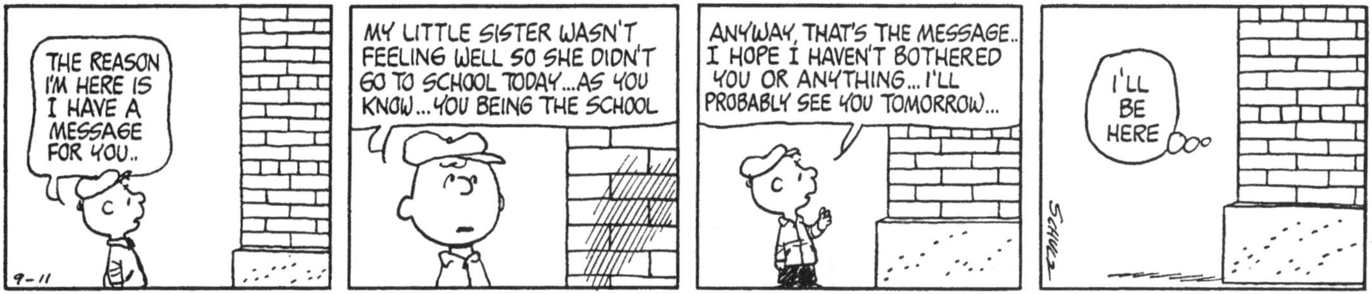
THE REASON I'M HERE IS I HAVE A MESSAGE FOR YOU..
9-11
MY LITTLE SISTER WASN'T FEELING WELL SO SHE DIDN'T GO TO SCHOOL TODAY...AS YOU KNOW...YOU BEING THE SCHOOL
ANYWAY, THAT'S THE MESSAGE.. I HOPE I HAVEN'T BOTHERED YOU OR ANYTHING... I'LL PROBABLY SEE YOU TOMORROW...
I'LL BE HERE
SCHULZ

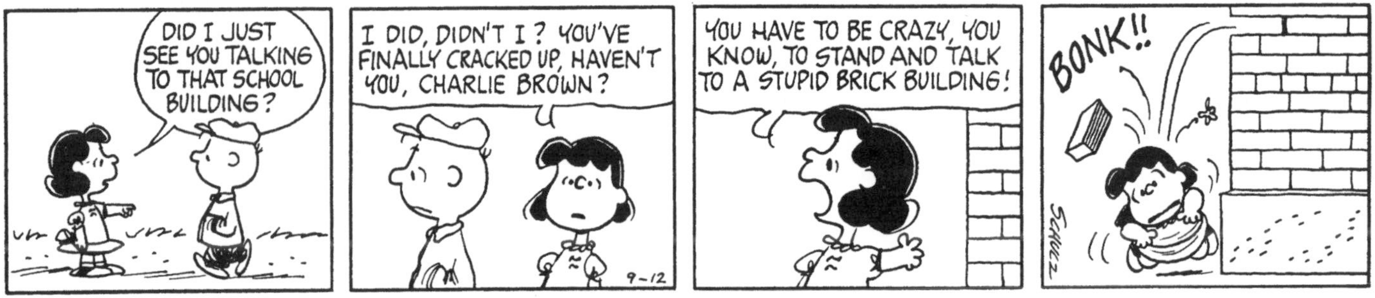
DID I JUST SEE YOU TALKING TO THAT SCHOOL BUILDING?
I DID, DIDN'T I? YOU'VE FINALLY CRACKED UP, HAVEN'T YOU, CHARLIE BROWN?
9-12
YOU HAVE TO BE CRAZY, YOU KNOW, TO STAND AND TALK TO A STUPID BRICK BUILDING!
BONK!!
SCHULZ

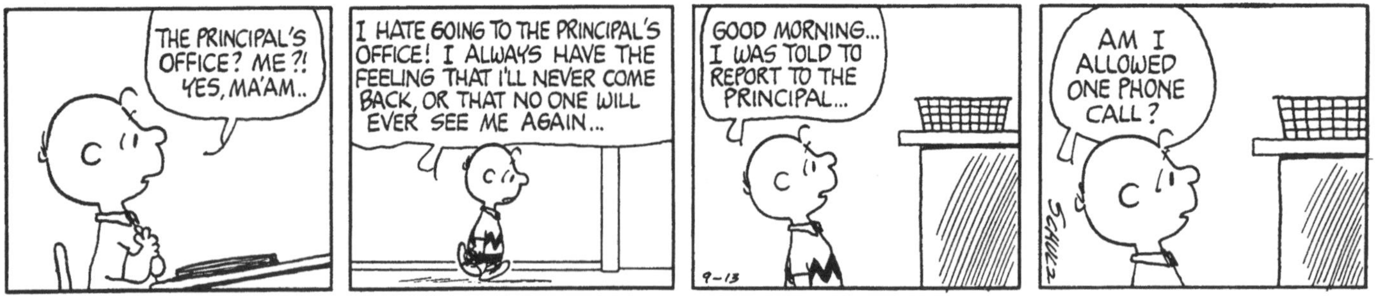
THE PRINCIPAL'S OFFICE? ME?! YES, MA'AM..
I HATE GOING TO THE PRINCIPAL'S OFFICE! I ALWAYS HAVE THE FEELING THAT I'LL NEVER COME BACK, OR THAT NO ONE WILL EVER SEE ME AGAIN...
GOOD MORNING... I WAS TOLD TO REPORT TO THE PRINCIPAL...
9-13
AM I ALLOWED ONE PHONE CALL?
SCHULZ

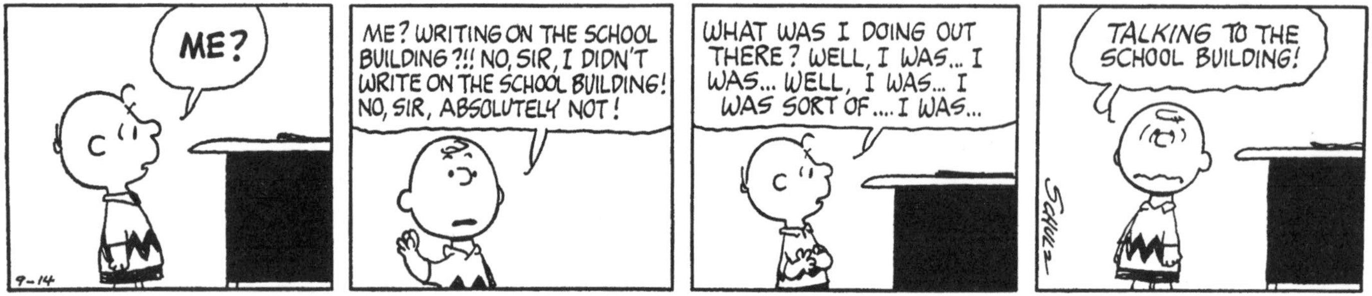
ME?
9-14
ME? WRITING ON THE SCHOOL BUILDING?!! NO, SIR, I DIDN'T WRITE ON THE SCHOOL BUILDING! NO, SIR, ABSOLUTELY NOT!
WHAT WAS I DOING OUT THERE? WELL, I WAS... I WAS... WELL, I WAS... I WAS SORT OF.... I WAS...
TALKING TO THE SCHOOL BUILDING!
SCHULZ

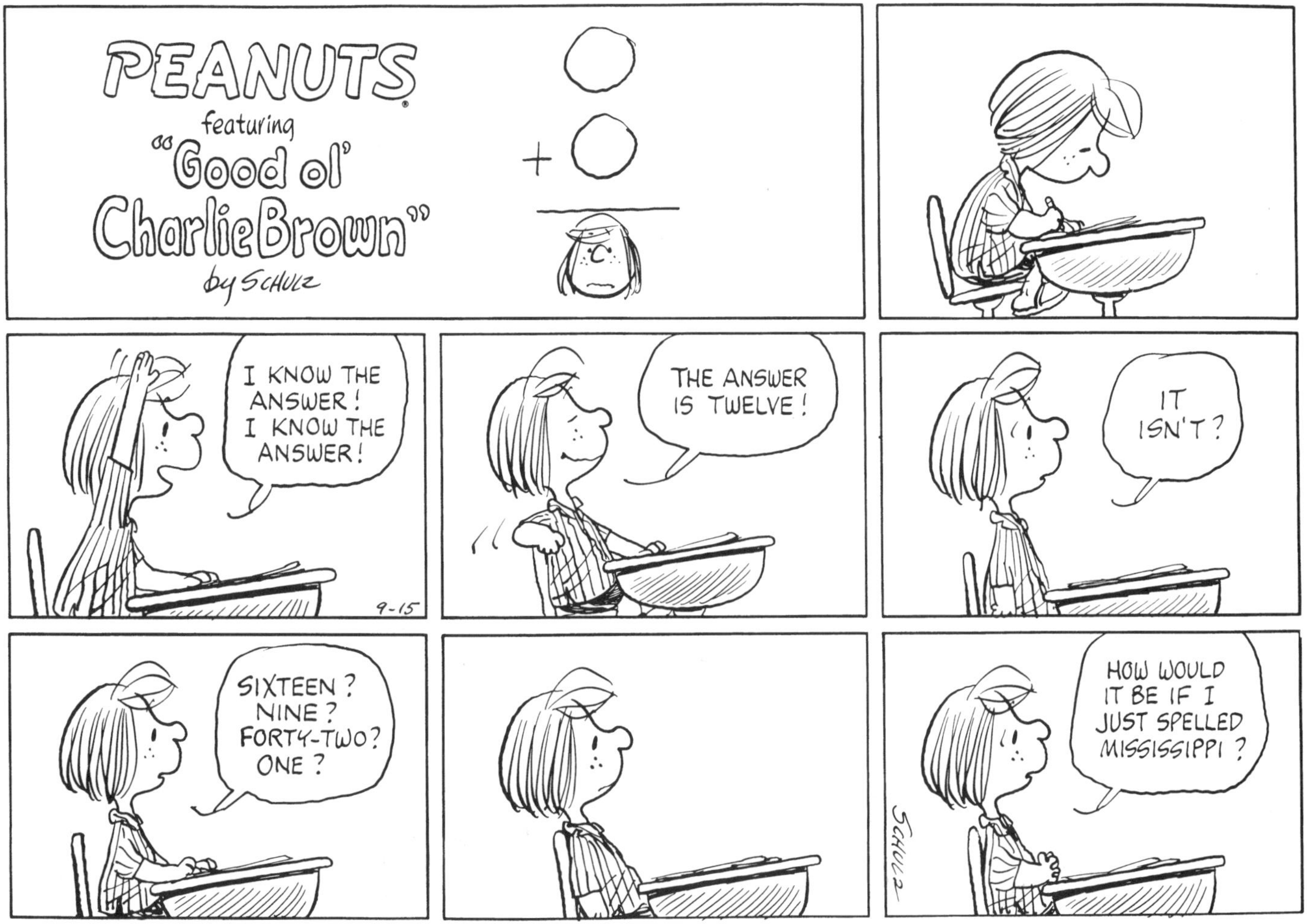
PEANUTS
featuring
"Good ol' CharlieBrown"
by SCHULZ
I KNOW THE ANSWER! I KNOW THE ANSWER!
9-15
THE ANSWER IS TWELVE!
IT ISN'T?
SIXTEEN? NINE? FORTY-TWO? ONE?
SCHULZ
HOW WOULD IT BE IF I JUST SPELLED MISSISSIPPI?

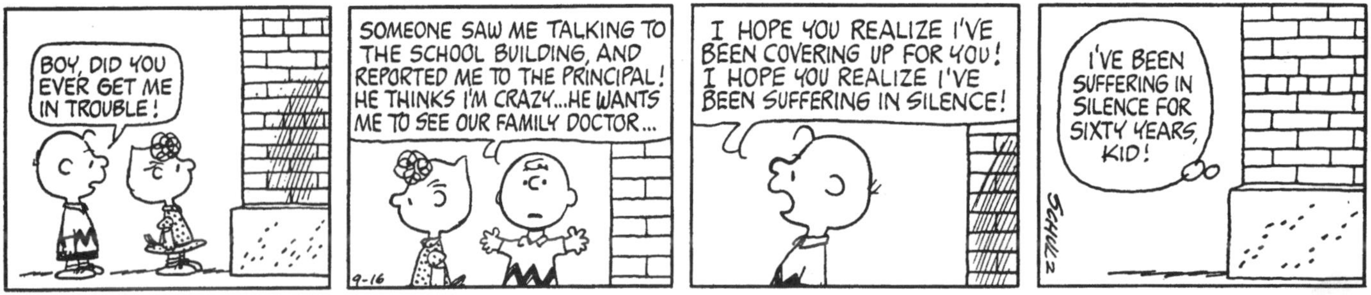
BOY, DID YOU EVER GET ME IN TROUBLE!
SOMEONE SAW ME TALKING TO THE SCHOOL BUILDING, AND REPORTED ME TO THE PRINCIPAL! HE THINKS I'M CRAZY...HE WANTS ME TO SEE OUR FAMILY DOCTOR...
9-16
I HOPE YOU REALIZE I'VE BEEN COVERING UP FOR YOU! I HOPE YOU REALIZE I'VE BEEN SUFFERING IN SILENCE!
I'VE BEEN SUFFERING IN SILENCE FOR SIXTY YEARS, KID!
SCHULZ

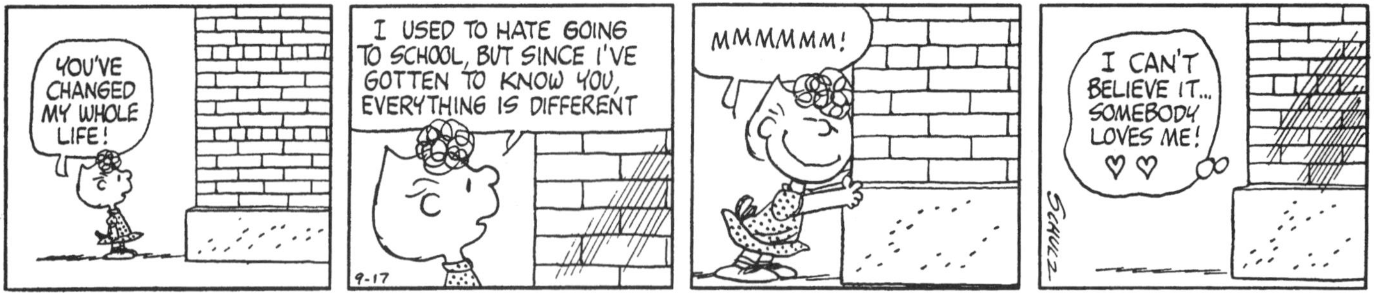
YOU'VE CHANGED MY WHOLE LIFE!
I USED TO HATE GOING TO SCHOOL, BUT SINCE I'VE GOTTEN TO KNOW YOU, EVERYTHING IS DIFFERENT
9-17
MMMMMM!
I CAN'T BELIEVE IT... SOMEBODY LOVES ME!
SCHULZ

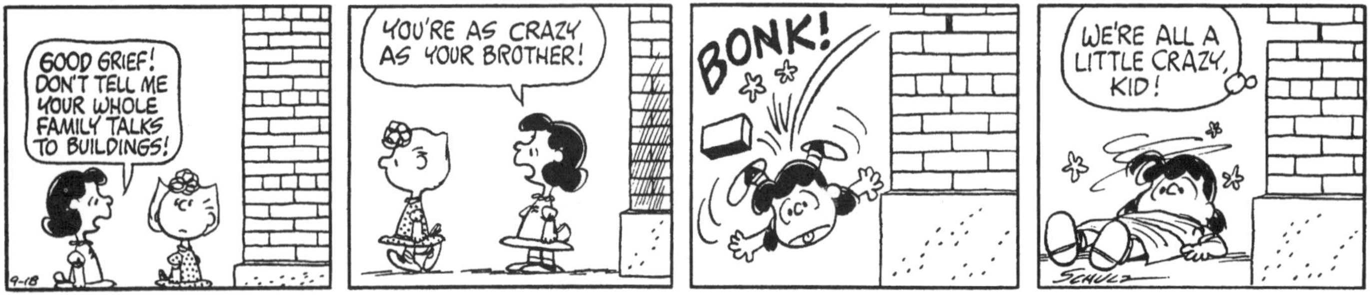
GOOD GRIEF! DON'T TELL ME YOUR WHOLE FAMILY TALKS TO BUILDINGS!
9-18
YOU'RE AS CRAZY AS YOUR BROTHER!
BONK!
WE'RE ALL A LITTLE CRAZY, KID!
SCHULZ

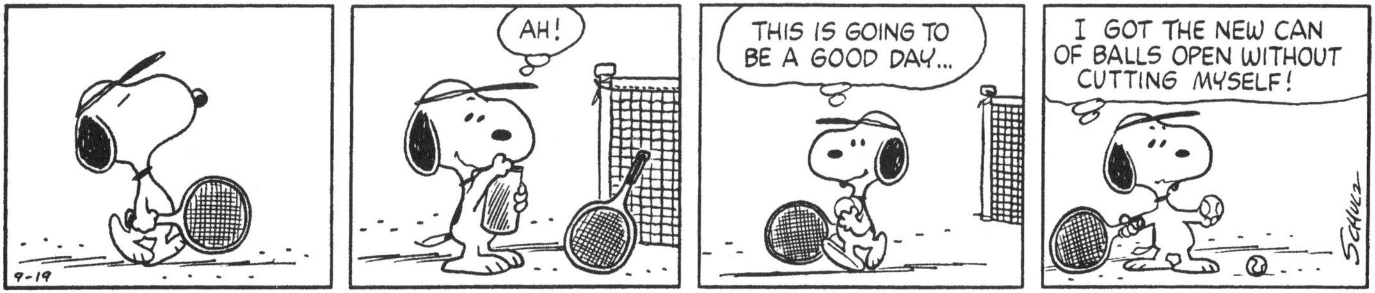
9-19
AH!
THIS IS GOING TO BE A GOOD DAY...
I GOT THE NEW CAN OF BALLS OPEN WITHOUT CUTTING MYSELF!
SCHULZ

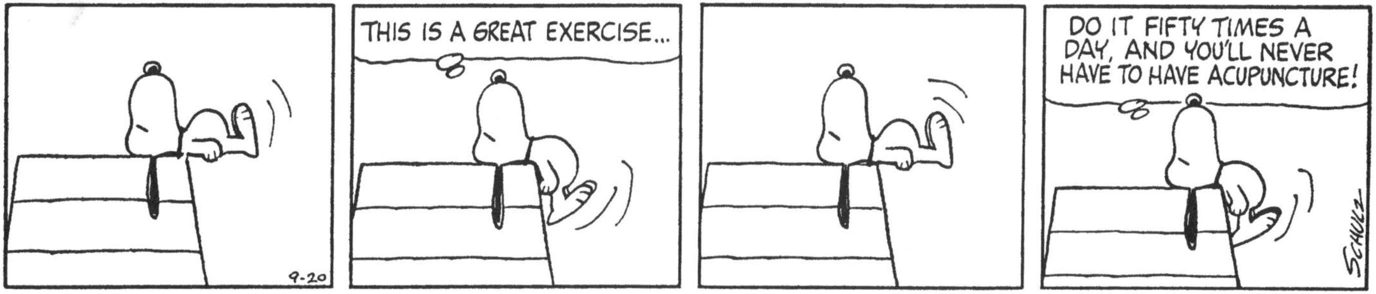
9-20
THIS IS A GREAT EXERCISE...
DO IT FIFTY TIMES A DAY, AND YOU'LL NEVER HAVE TO HAVE ACUPUNCTURE!
SCHULZ

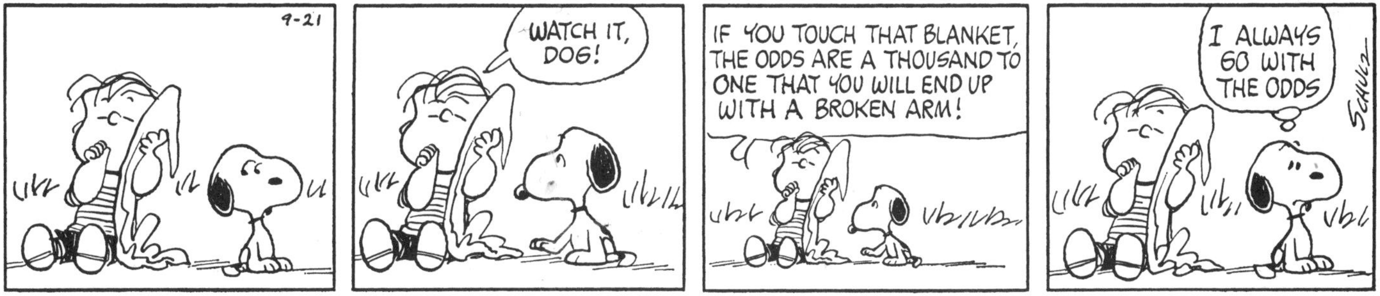
9-21
WATCH IT, DOG!
IF YOU TOUCH THAT BLANKET, THE ODDS ARE A THOUSAND TO ONE THAT YOU WILL END UP WITH A BROKEN ARM!
I ALWAYS GO WITH THE ODDS
SCHULZ

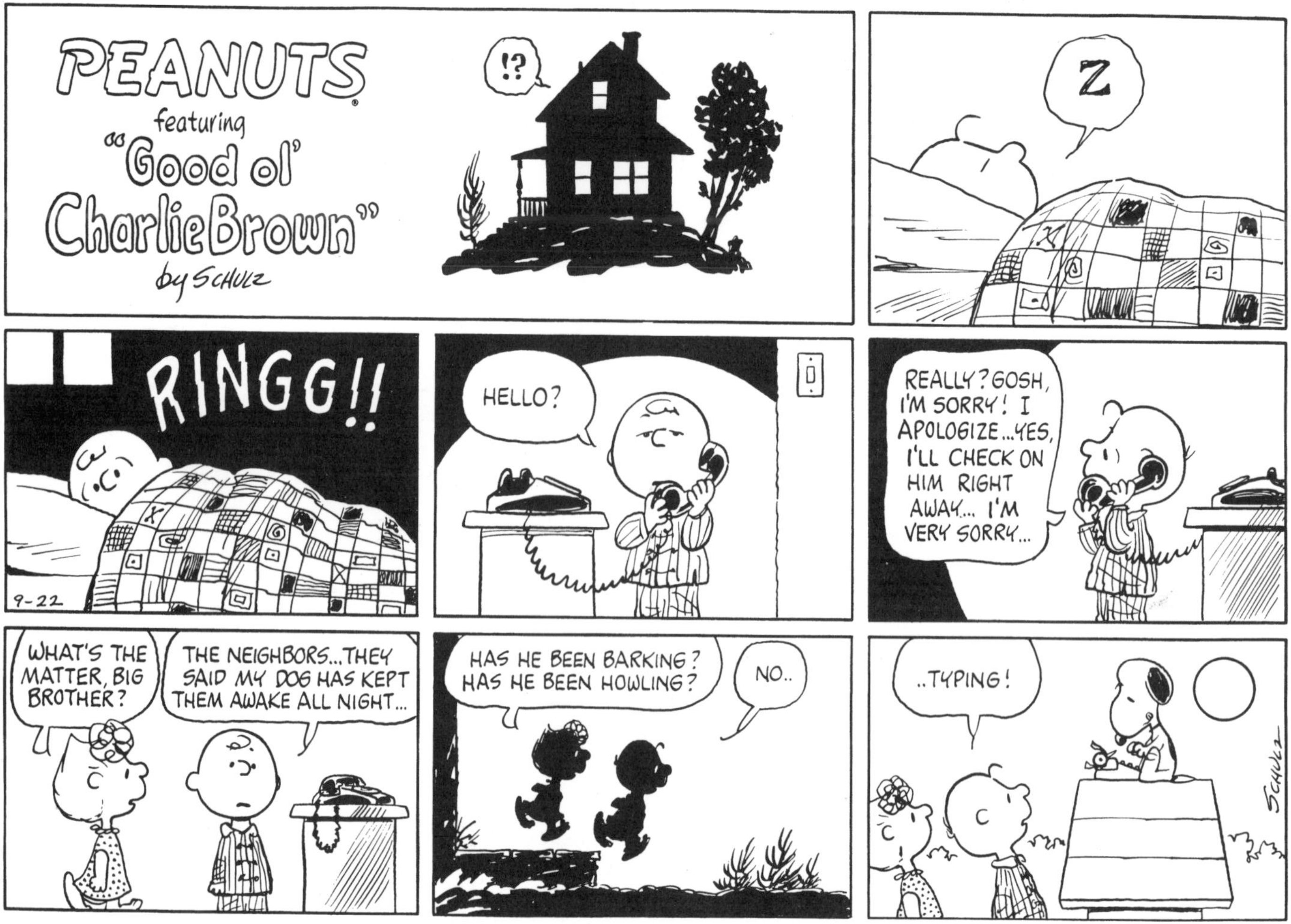
PEANUTS
featuring
"Good ol' Charlie Brown"
by SCHULZ
!?
Z
RINGG!!
9-22
HELLO?
REALLY? GOSH, I'M SORRY! I APOLOGIZE...YES, I'LL CHECK ON HIM RIGHT AWAY... I'M VERY SORRY...
WHAT'S THE MATTER, BIG BROTHER?
THE NEIGHBORS...THEY SAID MY DOG HAS KEPT THEM AWAKE ALL NIGHT...
HAS HE BEEN BARKING? HAS HE BEEN HOWLING?
NO..
..TYPING!
SCHULZ

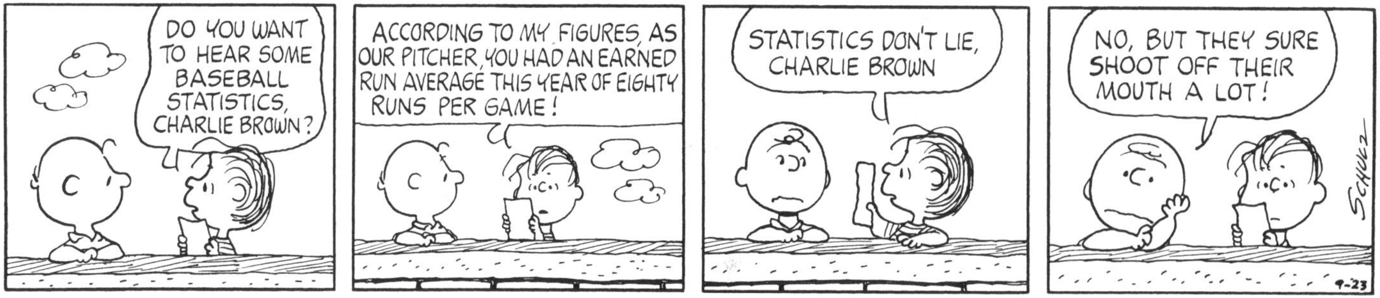
DO YOU WANT TO HEAR SOME BASEBALL STATISTICS, CHARLIE BROWN?
ACCORDING TO MY FIGURES, AS OUR PITCHER, YOU HAD AN EARNED RUN AVERAGE THIS YEAR OF EIGHTY RUNS PER GAME!
STATISTICS DON'T LIE, CHARLIE BROWN
NO, BUT THEY SURE SHOOT OFF THEIR MOUTH A LOT!
SCHULZ
9-23

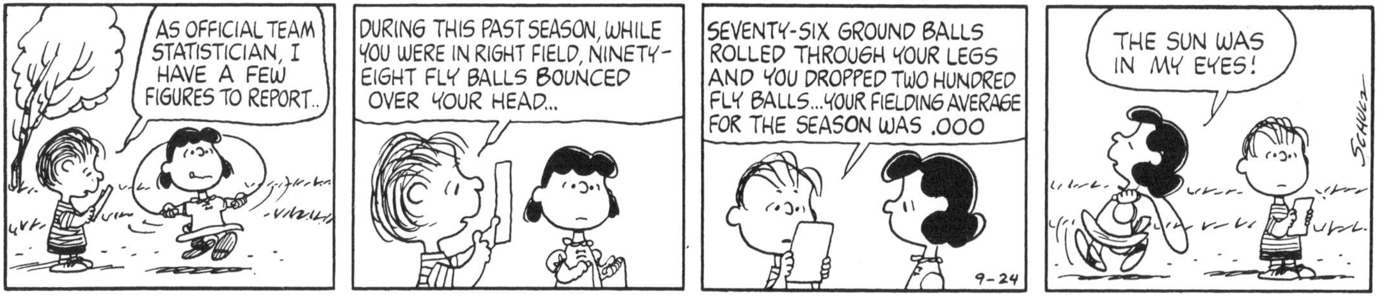
AS OFFICIAL TEAM STATISTICIAN, I HAVE A FEW FIGURES TO REPORT..
DURING THIS PAST SEASON, WHILE YOU WERE IN RIGHT FIELD, NINETY-EIGHT FLY BALLS BOUNCED OVER YOUR HEAD...
SEVENTY-SIX GROUND BALLS ROLLED THROUGH YOUR LEGS AND YOU DROPPED TWO HUNDRED FLY BALLS...YOUR FIELDING AVERAGE FOR THE SEASON WAS .000
9-24
THE SUN WAS IN MY EYES!
SCHULZ

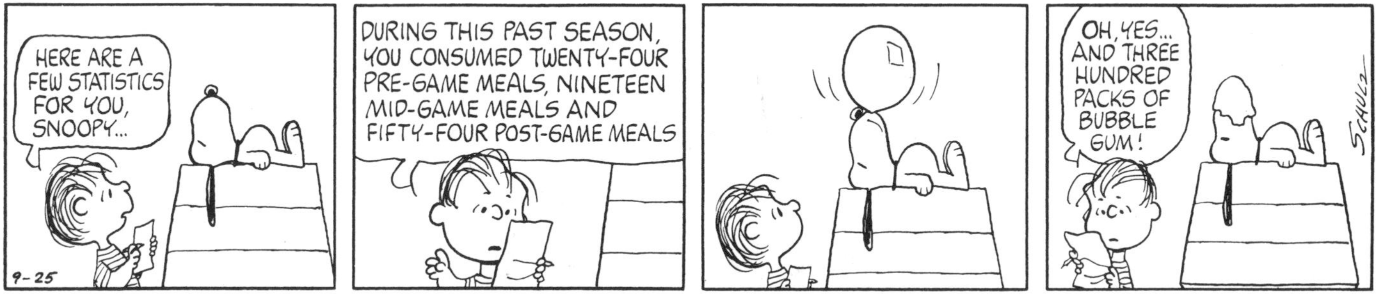
HERE ARE A FEW STATISTICS FOR YOU, SNOOPY...
9-25
DURING THIS PAST SEASON, YOU CONSUMED TWENTY-FOUR PRE-GAME MEALS, NINETEEN MID-GAME MEALS AND FIFTY-FOUR POST-GAME MEALS
OH, YES... AND THREE HUNDRED PACKS OF BUBBLE GUM!
SCHULZ

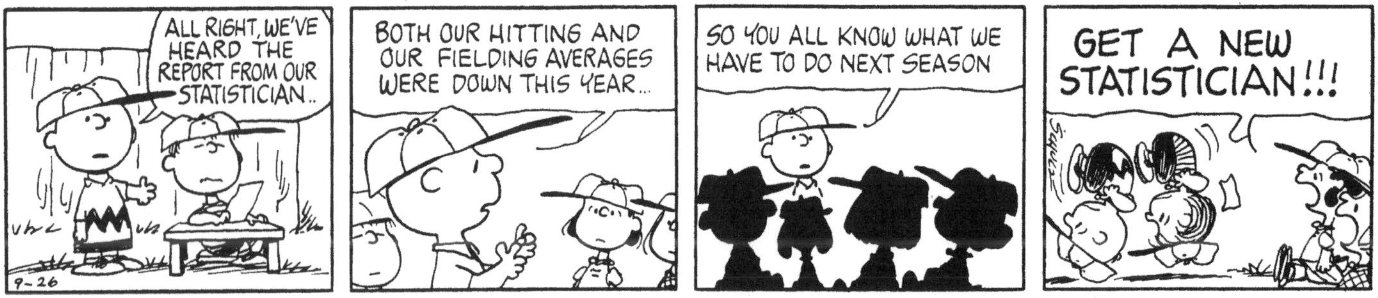
ALL RIGHT, WE'VE HEARD THE REPORT FROM OUR STATISTICIAN..
BOTH OUR HITTING AND OUR FIELDING AVERAGES WERE DOWN THIS YEAR...
SO YOU ALL KNOW WHAT WE HAVE TO DO NEXT SEASON
GET A NEW STATISTICIAN!!!

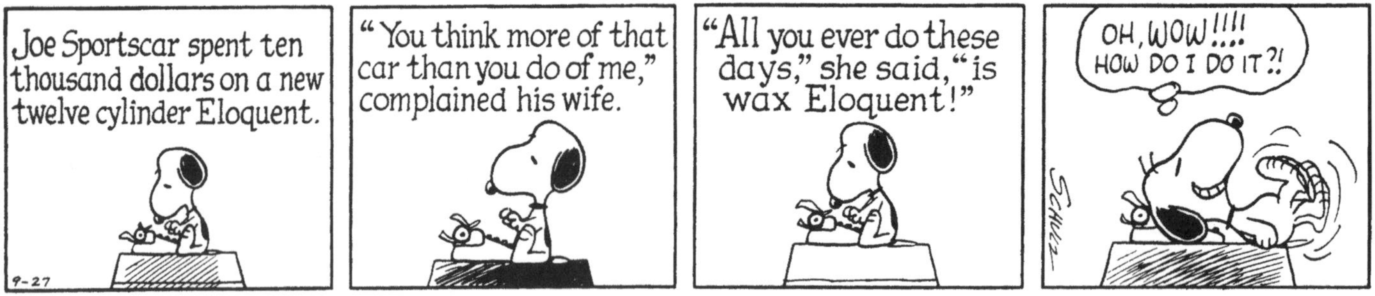
Joe Sportscar spent ten thousand dollars on a new twelve cylinder Eloquent.
"You think more of that car than you do of me," complained his wife.
"All you ever do these days," she said, "is wax Eloquent!"
OH, WOW!!!!.... HOW DO I DO IT?!

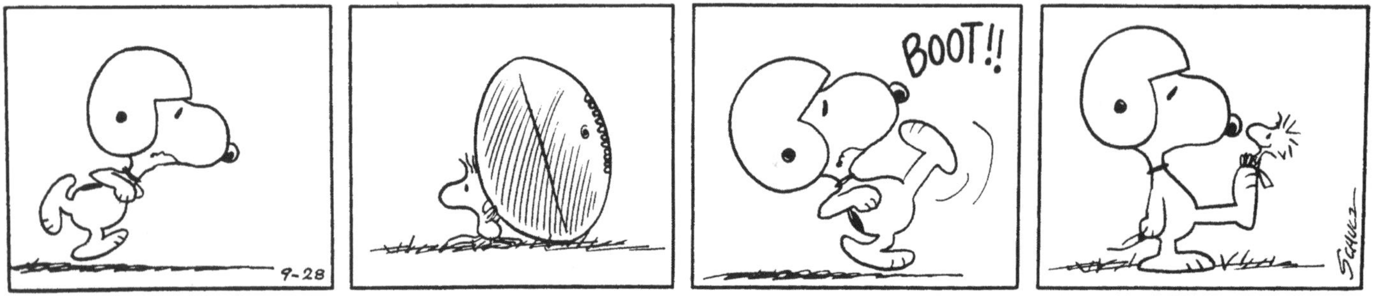
BOOT!!

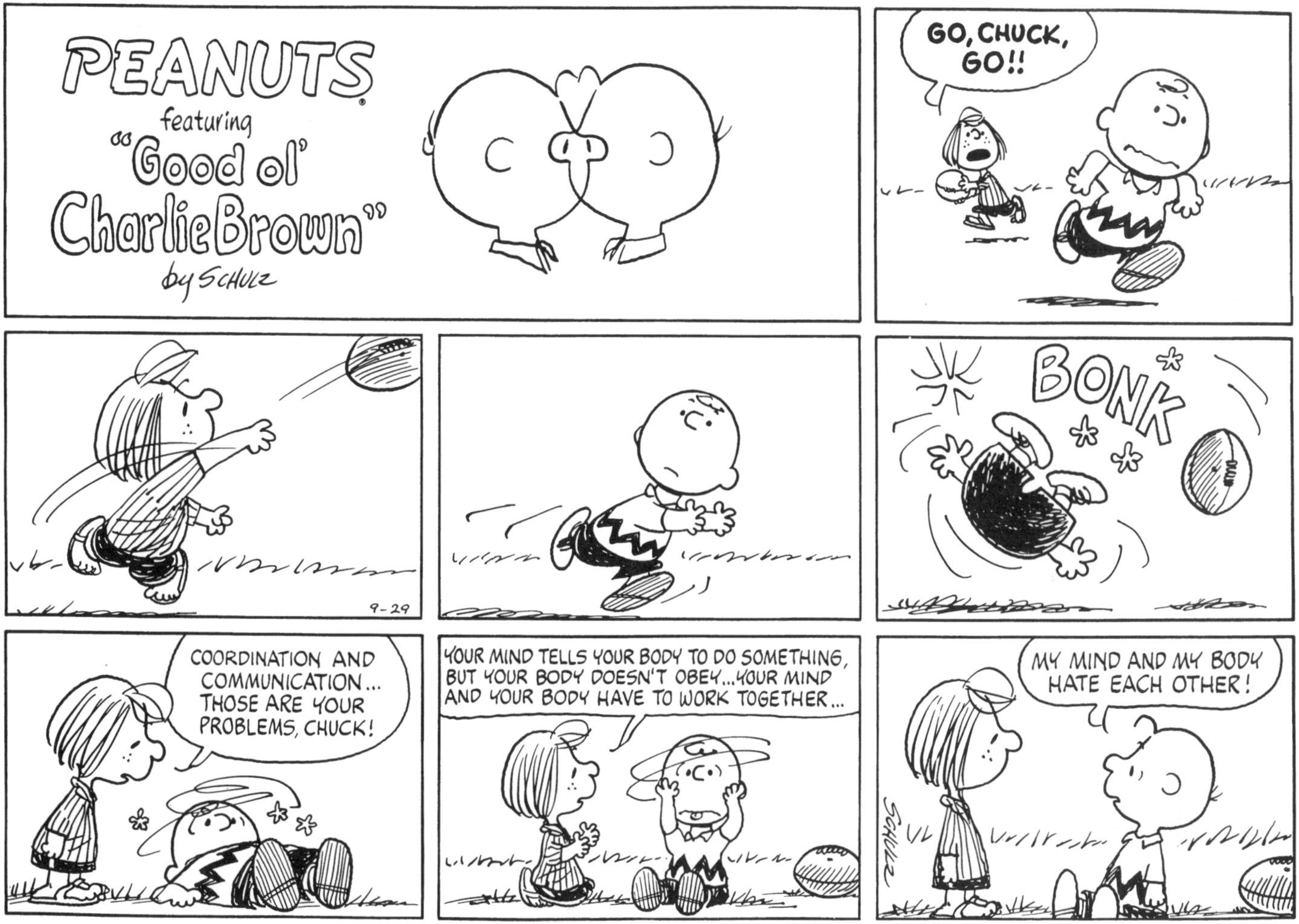
PEANUTS
featuring
"Good ol' Charlie Brown"
by SCHULZ
GO, CHUCK, GO!!
9-29
BONK
COORDINATION AND COMMUNICATION... THOSE ARE YOUR PROBLEMS, CHUCK!
YOUR MIND TELLS YOUR BODY TO DO SOMETHING, BUT YOUR BODY DOESN'T OBEY...YOUR MIND AND YOUR BODY HAVE TO WORK TOGETHER...
MY MIND AND MY BODY HATE EACH OTHER!
SCHULZ

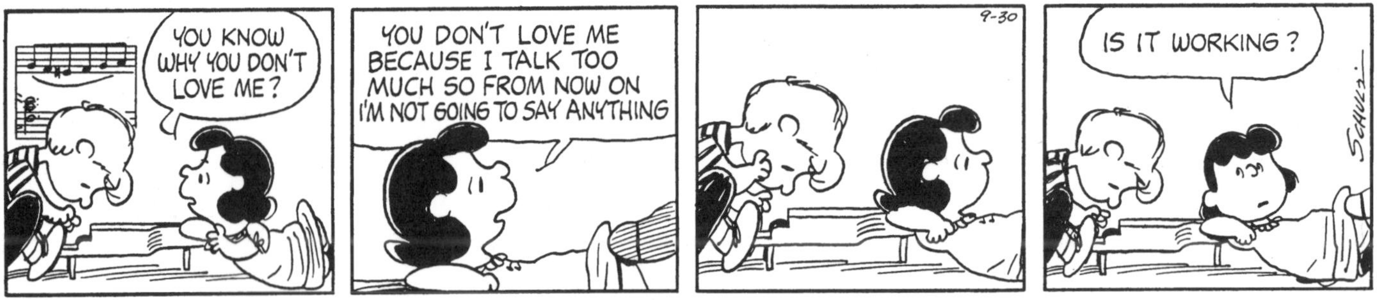
YOU KNOW WHY YOU DON'T LOVE ME?
YOU DON'T LOVE ME BECAUSE I TALK TOO MUCH SO FROM NOW ON I'M NOT GOING TO SAY ANYTHING
9-30
IS IT WORKING?
SCHULZ

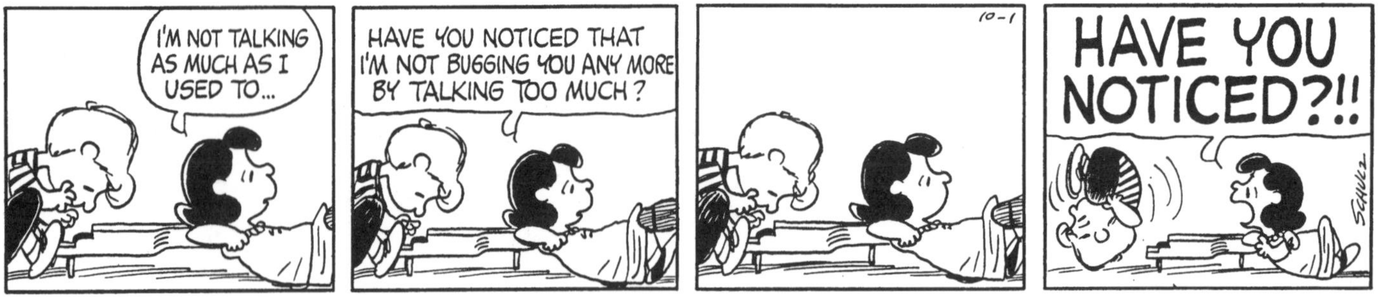
I'M NOT TALKING AS MUCH AS I USED TO...
HAVE YOU NOTICED THAT I'M NOT BUGGING YOU ANY MORE BY TALKING TOO MUCH?
10-1
HAVE YOU NOTICED?!!
SCHULZ

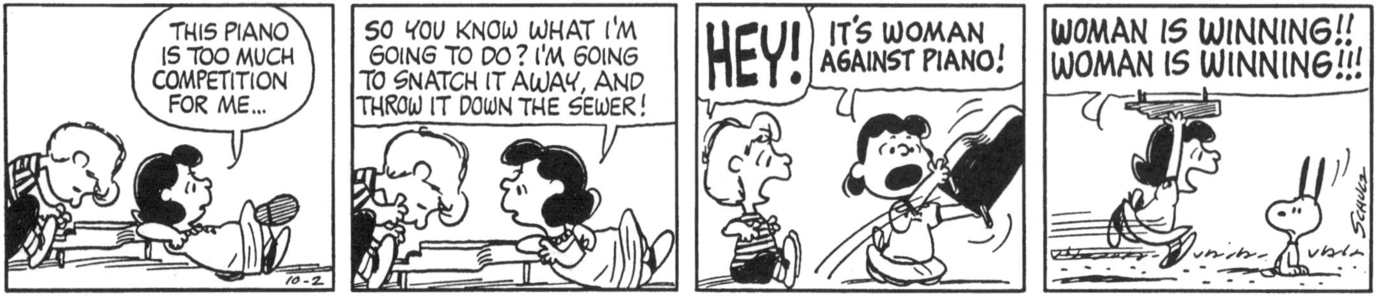
THIS PIANO IS TOO MUCH COMPETITION FOR ME...
10-2
SO YOU KNOW WHAT I'M GOING TO DO? I'M GOING TO SNATCH IT AWAY, AND THROW IT DOWN THE SEWER!
HEY!
IT'S WOMAN AGAINST PIANO!
WOMAN IS WINNING!! WOMAN IS WINNING!!!
SCHULZ

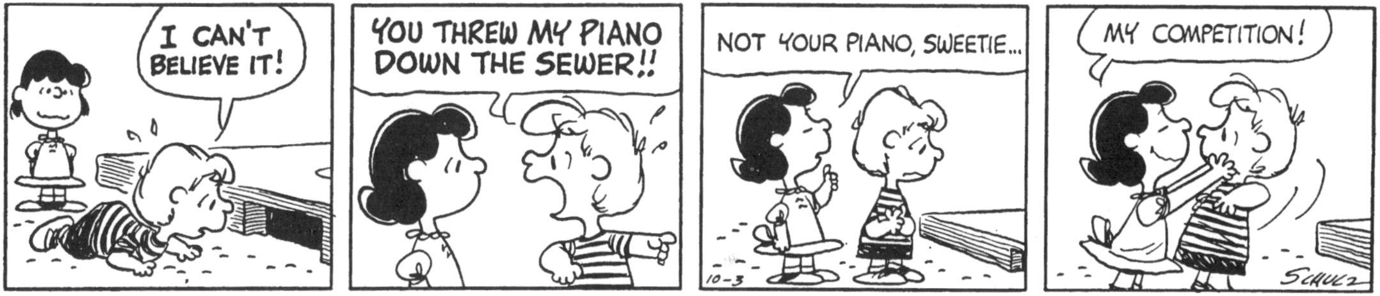
I CAN'T BELIEVE IT!
YOU THREW MY PIANO DOWN THE SEWER!!
NOT YOUR PIANO, SWEETIE...
10-3
MY COMPETITION!
SCHULZ

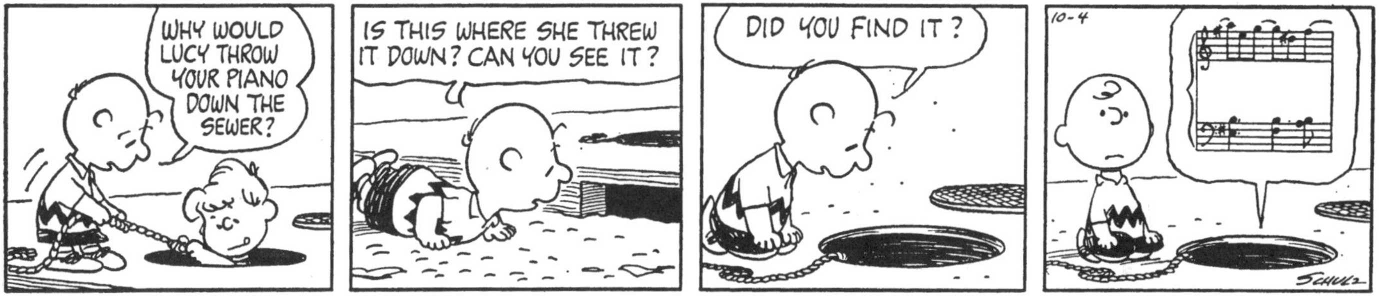
WHY WOULD LUCY THROW YOUR PIANO DOWN THE SEWER?
IS THIS WHERE SHE THREW IT DOWN? CAN YOU SEE IT?
DID YOU FIND IT?
10-4
SCHULZ

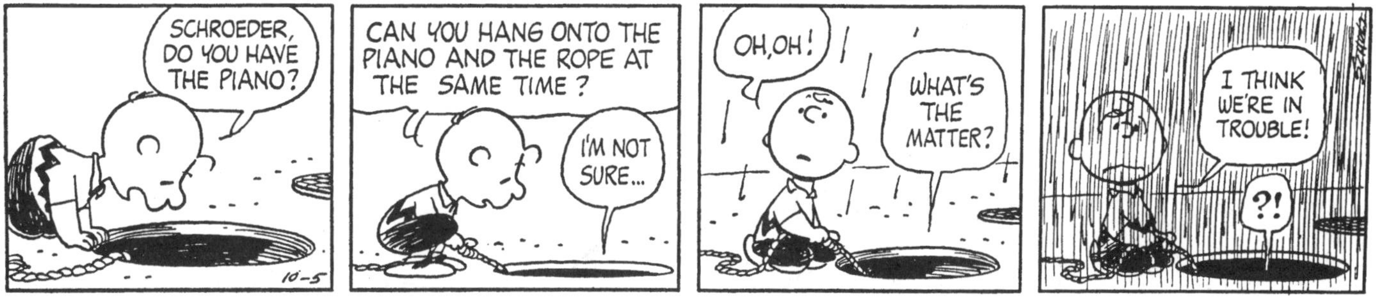
SCHROEDER, DO YOU HAVE THE PIANO?
10-5
CAN YOU HANG ONTO THE PIANO AND THE ROPE AT THE SAME TIME?
I'M NOT SURE...
OH, OH!
WHAT'S THE MATTER?
I THINK WE'RE IN TROUBLE!
?!

PEANUTS
featuring
"Good ol' Charlie Brown"
by SCHULZ
THIS IS THE GREAT NEW EXERCISE I'VE DEVELOPED...
YOU HAVE TO DO THIS FIFTY TIMES A DAY...
10-6
IT'S GOOD FOR YOUR NECK...
AND YOUR BACK...
AND YOUR LEGS...
WUMP!
BUT IT RUINS YOUR BODY...
SCHULZ

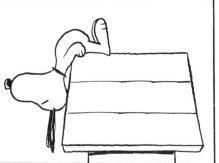

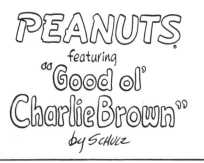

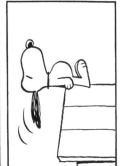

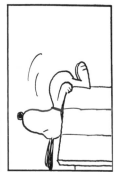

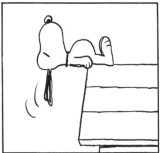

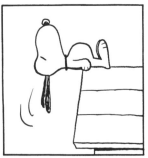

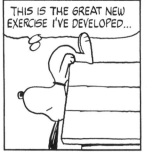

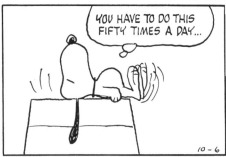

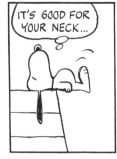

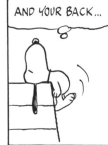

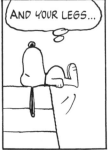

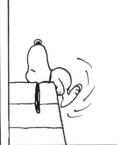

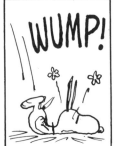

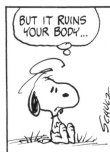

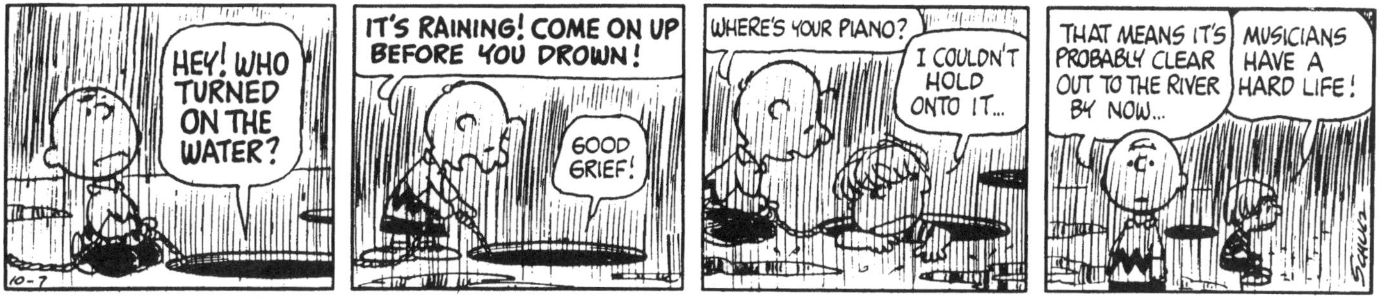
HEY! WHO TURNED ON THE WATER?
10-7
IT'S RAINING! COME ON UP BEFORE YOU DROWN!
GOOD GRIEF!
WHERE'S YOUR PIANO?
I COULDN'T HOLD ONTO IT...
THAT MEANS IT'S PROBABLY CLEAR OUT TO THE RIVER BY NOW...
MUSICIANS HAVE A HARD LIFE!
SCHULZ

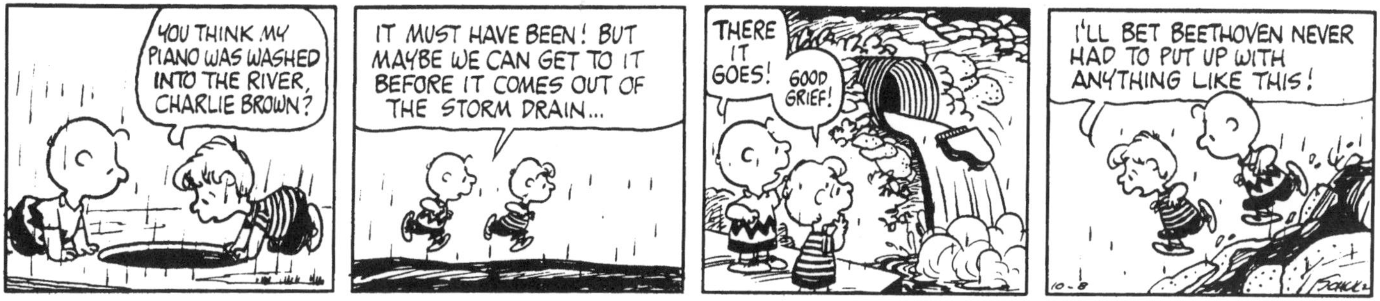
YOU THINK MY PIANO WAS WASHED INTO THE RIVER, CHARLIE BROWN?
IT MUST HAVE BEEN! BUT MAYBE WE CAN GET TO IT BEFORE IT COMES OUT OF THE STORM DRAIN...
THERE IT GOES!
GOOD GRIEF!
I'LL BET BEETHOVEN NEVER HAD TO PUT UP WITH ANYTHING LIKE THIS!
10-8
SCHULZ

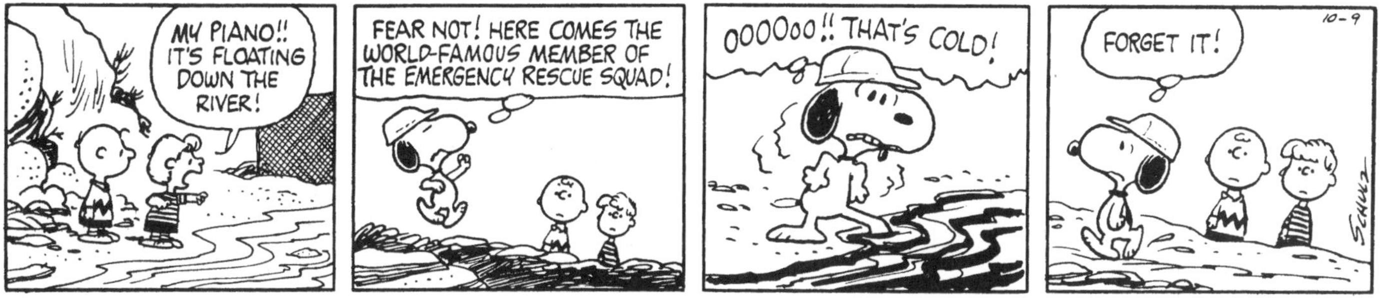
MY PIANO!! IT'S FLOATING DOWN THE RIVER!
FEAR NOT! HERE COMES THE WORLD-FAMOUS MEMBER OF THE EMERGENCY RESCUE SQUAD!
OOOOOO!! THAT'S COLD!
10-9
FORGET IT!
SCHULZ

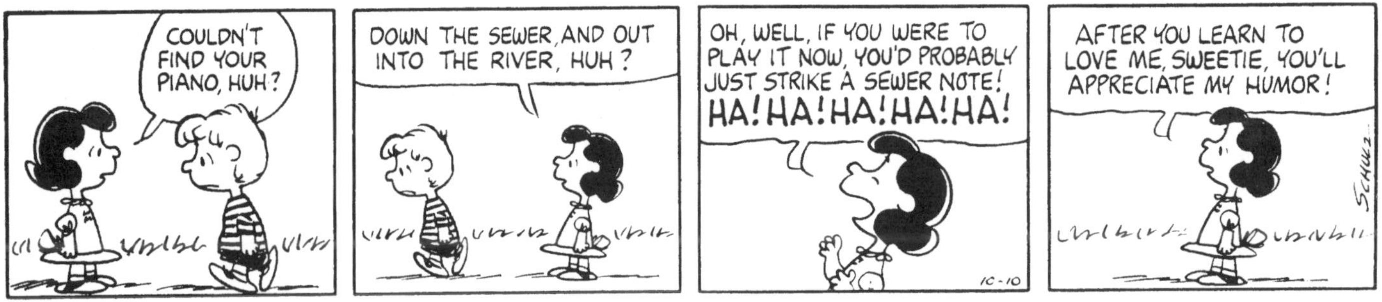
COULDN'T FIND YOUR PIANO, HUH?
DOWN THE SEWER, AND OUT INTO THE RIVER, HUH?
OH, WELL, IF YOU WERE TO PLAY IT NOW, YOU'D PROBABLY JUST STRIKE A SEWER NOTE! HA! HA! HA! HA! HA!
10-10
AFTER YOU LEARN TO LOVE ME, SWEETIE, YOU'LL APPRECIATE MY HUMOR!

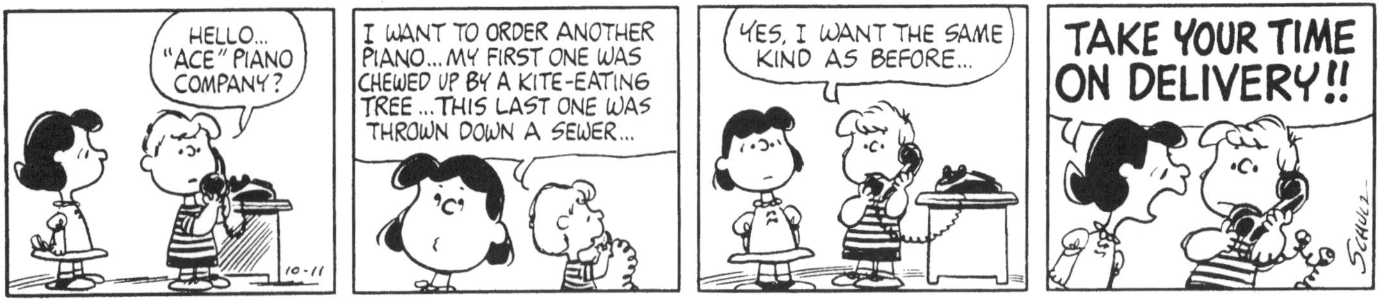
HELLO... "ACE" PIANO COMPANY?
10-11
I WANT TO ORDER ANOTHER PIANO... MY FIRST ONE WAS CHEWED UP BY A KITE-EATING TREE... THIS LAST ONE WAS THROWN DOWN A SEWER...
YES, I WANT THE SAME KIND AS BEFORE...
TAKE YOUR TIME ON DELIVERY!!

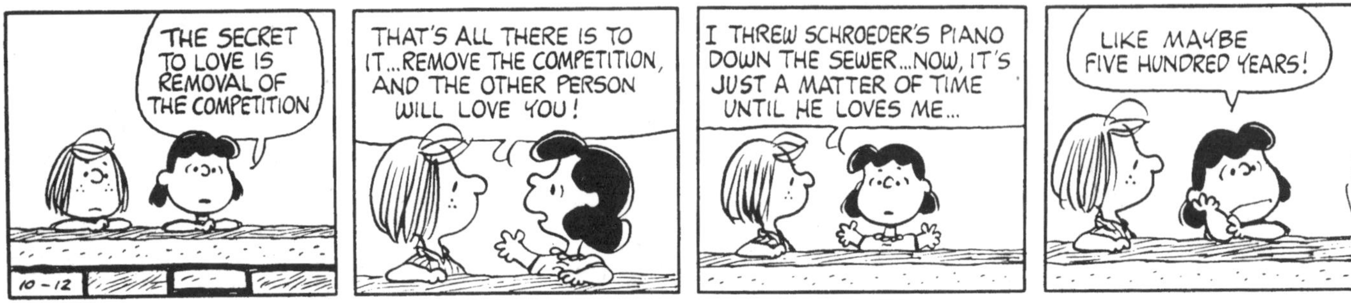
THE SECRET TO LOVE IS REMOVAL OF THE COMPETITION
10-12
THAT'S ALL THERE IS TO IT... REMOVE THE COMPETITION, AND THE OTHER PERSON WILL LOVE YOU!
I THREW SCHROEDER'S PIANO DOWN THE SEWER... NOW, IT'S JUST A MATTER OF TIME UNTIL HE LOVES ME...
LIKE MAYBE FIVE HUNDRED YEARS!

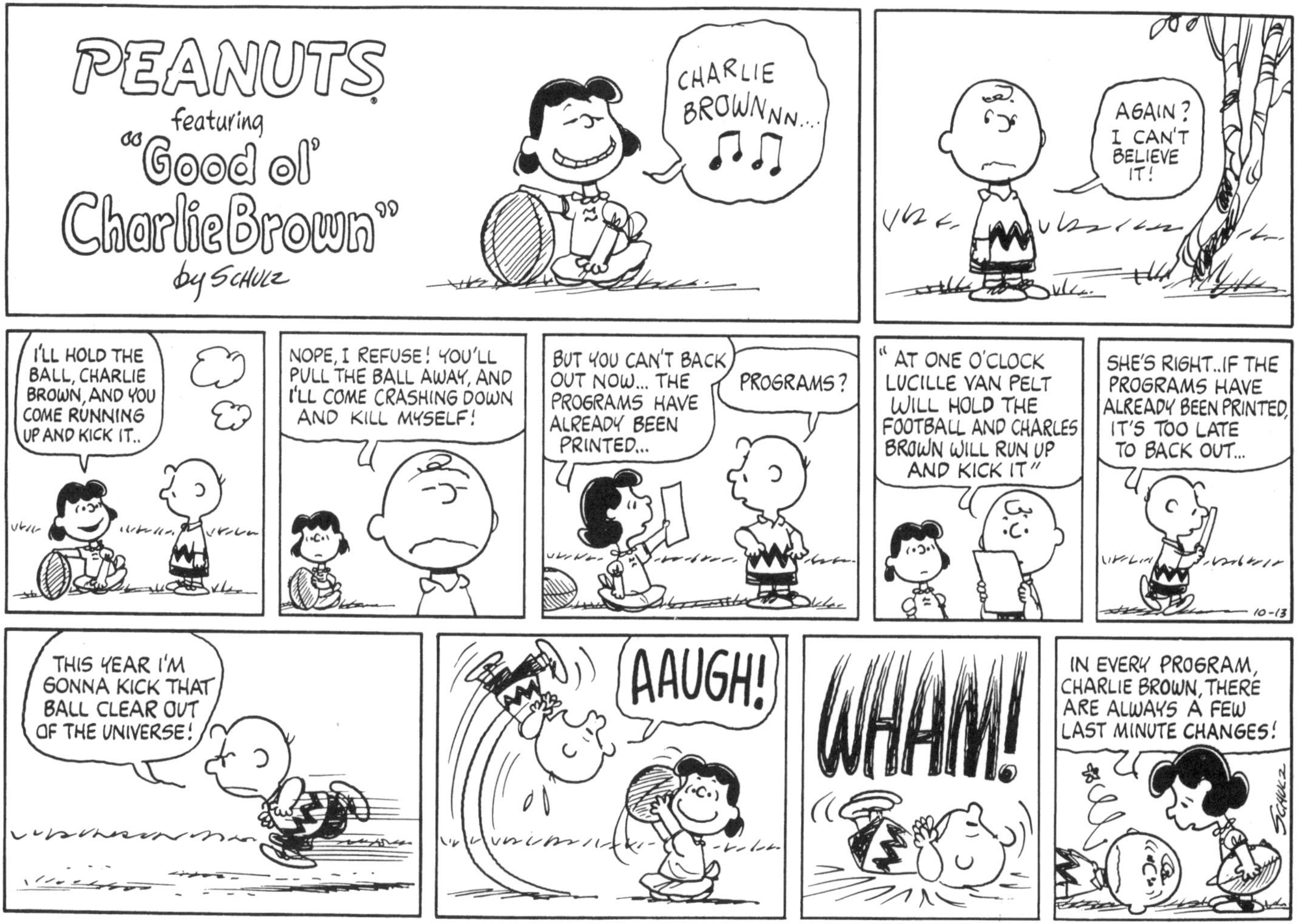
PEANUTS
featuring
"Good ol' Charlie Brown"
by SCHULZ
CHARLIE BROWNNN...
AGAIN? I CAN'T BELIEVE IT!
I'LL HOLD THE BALL, CHARLIE BROWN, AND YOU COME RUNNING UP AND KICK IT..
NOPE, I REFUSE! YOU'LL PULL THE BALL AWAY, AND I'LL COME CRASHING DOWN AND KILL MYSELF!
BUT YOU CAN'T BACK OUT NOW... THE PROGRAMS HAVE ALREADY BEEN PRINTED...
PROGRAMS?
"AT ONE O'CLOCK LUCILLE VAN PELT WILL HOLD THE FOOTBALL AND CHARLES BROWN WILL RUN UP AND KICK IT"
SHE'S RIGHT..IF THE PROGRAMS HAVE ALREADY BEEN PRINTED, IT'S TOO LATE TO BACK OUT...
10-13
THIS YEAR I'M GONNA KICK THAT BALL CLEAR OUT OF THE UNIVERSE!
AAUGH!
WHAM!
IN EVERY PROGRAM, CHARLIE BROWN, THERE ARE ALWAYS A FEW LAST MINUTE CHANGES!
SCHULZ

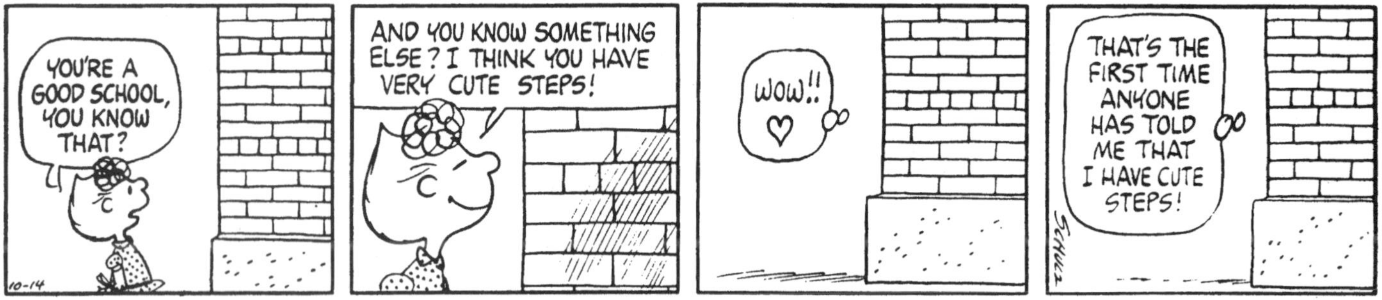
YOU'RE A GOOD SCHOOL, YOU KNOW THAT?
AND YOU KNOW SOMETHING ELSE? I THINK YOU HAVE VERY CUTE STEPS!
WOW!! ♡
THAT'S THE FIRST TIME ANYONE HAS TOLD ME THAT I HAVE CUTE STEPS!

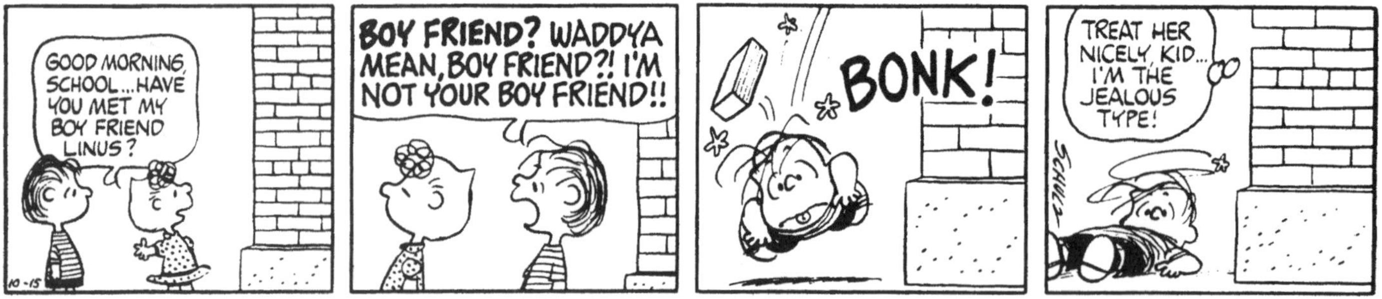
GOOD MORNING, SCHOOL...HAVE YOU MET MY BOY FRIEND LINUS?
BOY FRIEND? WADDYA MEAN, BOY FRIEND?! I'M NOT YOUR BOY FRIEND!!
BONK!
TREAT HER NICELY, KID... I'M THE JEALOUS TYPE!

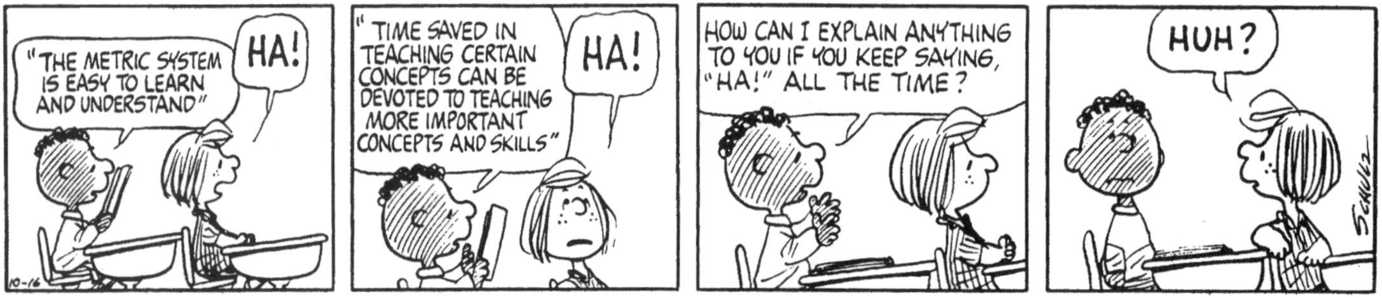
"THE METRIC SYSTEM IS EASY TO LEARN AND UNDERSTAND"
HA!
"TIME SAVED IN TEACHING CERTAIN CONCEPTS CAN BE DEVOTED TO TEACHING MORE IMPORTANT CONCEPTS AND SKILLS"
HA!
HOW CAN I EXPLAIN ANYTHING TO YOU IF YOU KEEP SAYING, "HA!" ALL THE TIME?
HUH?

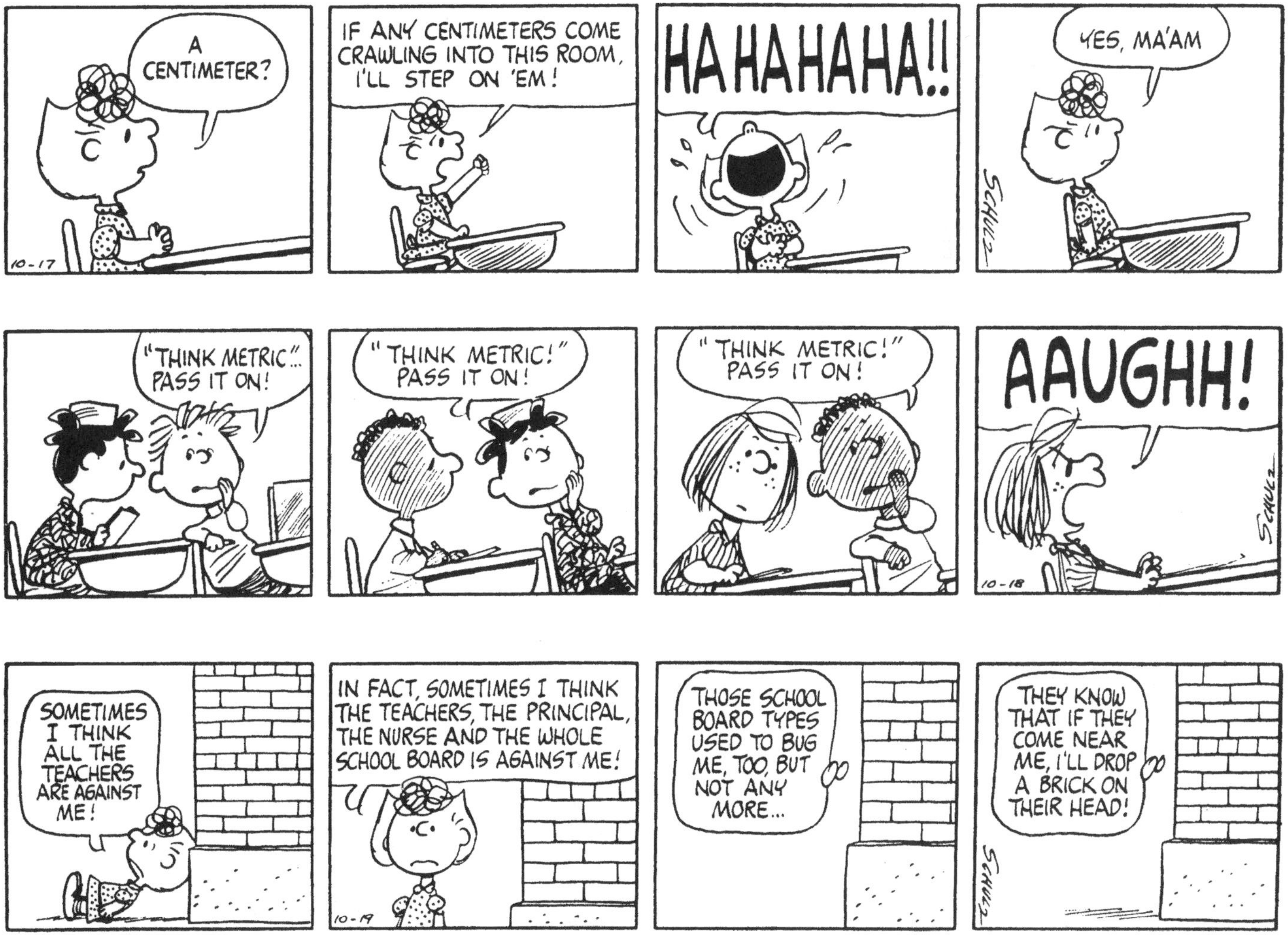
A CENTIMETER?
IF ANY CENTIMETERS COME CRAWLING INTO THIS ROOM, I'LL STEP ON 'EM!
HAHAHAHA!!
YES, MA'AM
"THINK METRIC"... PASS IT ON!
"THINK METRIC!" PASS IT ON!
"THINK METRIC!" PASS IT ON!
AAUGHH!
SOMETIMES I THINK ALL THE TEACHERS ARE AGAINST ME!
IN FACT, SOMETIMES I THINK THE TEACHERS, THE PRINCIPAL, THE NURSE AND THE WHOLE SCHOOL BOARD IS AGAINST ME!
THOSE SCHOOL BOARD TYPES USED TO BUG ME, TOO, BUT NOT ANY MORE...
THEY KNOW THAT IF THEY COME NEAR ME, I'LL DROP A BRICK ON THEIR HEAD!

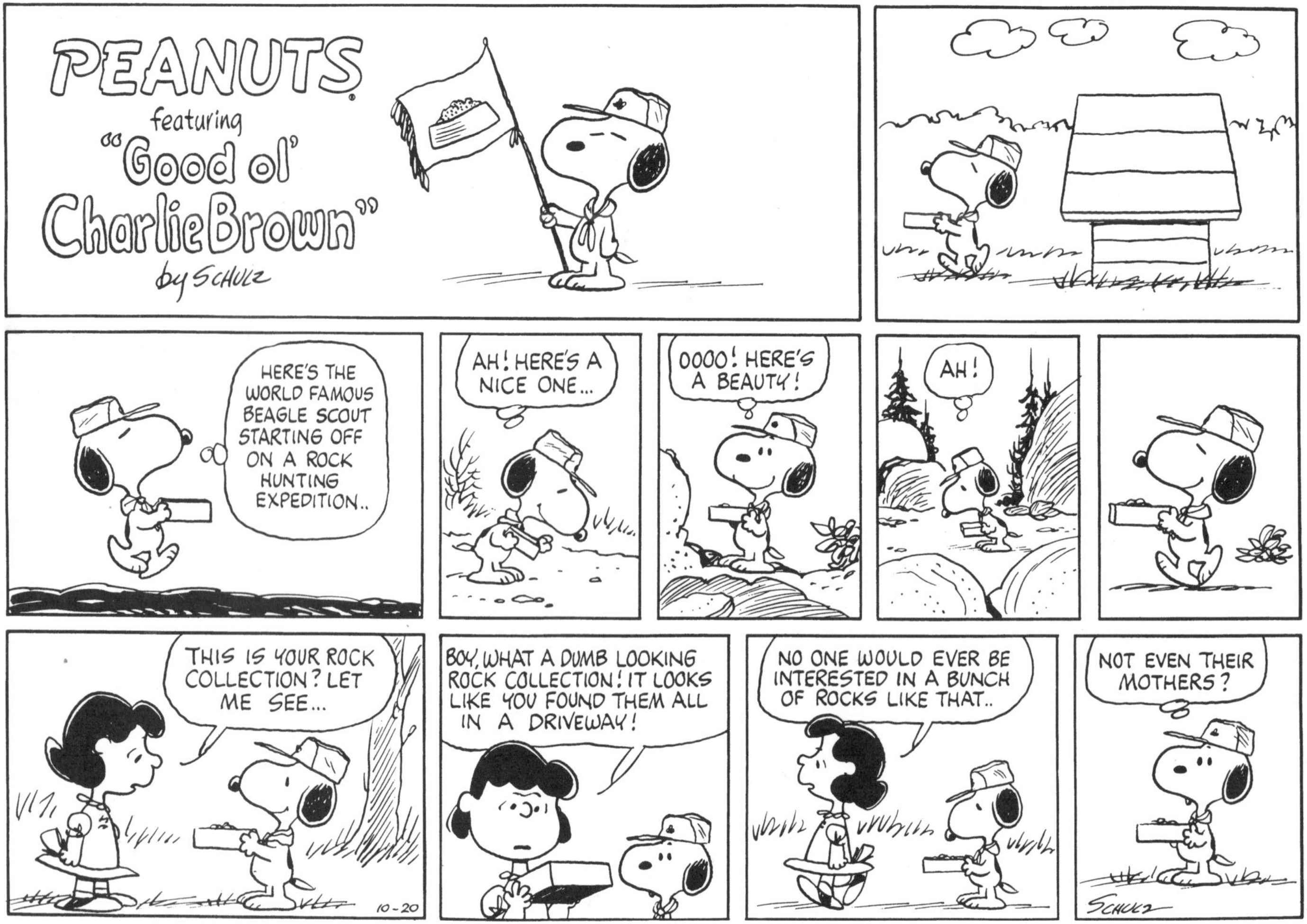
PEANUTS
featuring
"Good ol' CharlieBrown"
by SCHULZ
HERE'S THE WORLD FAMOUS BEAGLE SCOUT STARTING OFF ON A ROCK HUNTING EXPEDITION..
AH! HERE'S A NICE ONE...
OOOO! HERE'S A BEAUTY!
AH!
THIS IS YOUR ROCK COLLECTION? LET ME SEE...
10-20
BOY, WHAT A DUMB LOOKING ROCK COLLECTION! IT LOOKS LIKE YOU FOUND THEM ALL IN A DRIVEWAY!
NO ONE WOULD EVER BE INTERESTED IN A BUNCH OF ROCKS LIKE THAT..
NOT EVEN THEIR MOTHERS?
SCHULZ

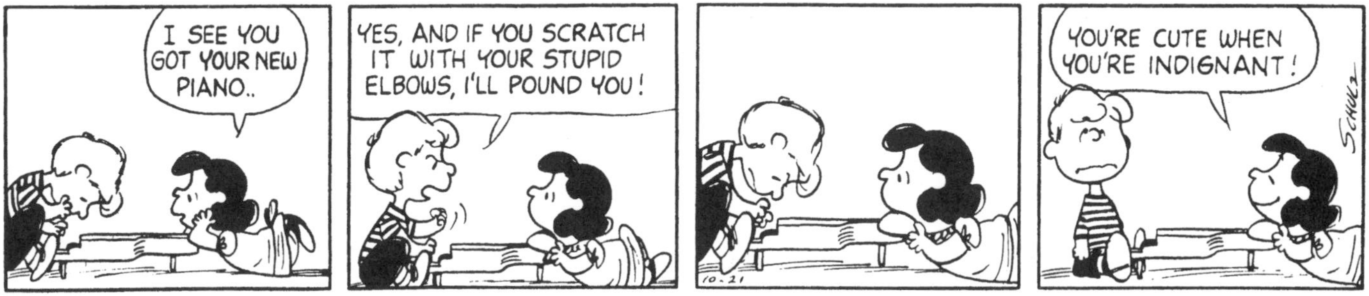
I SEE YOU GOT YOUR NEW PIANO..
YES, AND IF YOU SCRATCH IT WITH YOUR STUPID ELBOWS, I'LL POUND YOU!
YOU'RE CUTE WHEN YOU'RE INDIGNANT!
SCHULZ

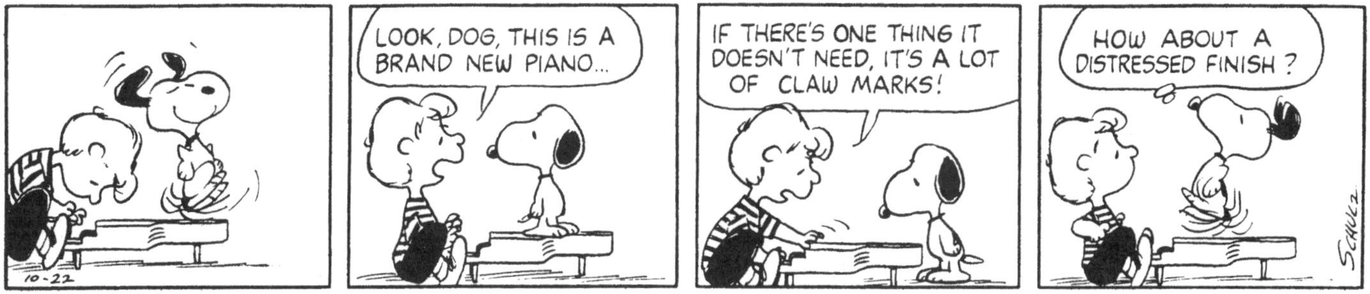
LOOK, DOG, THIS IS A BRAND NEW PIANO...
IF THERE'S ONE THING IT DOESN'T NEED, IT'S A LOT OF CLAW MARKS!
HOW ABOUT A DISTRESSED FINISH?
SCHULZ

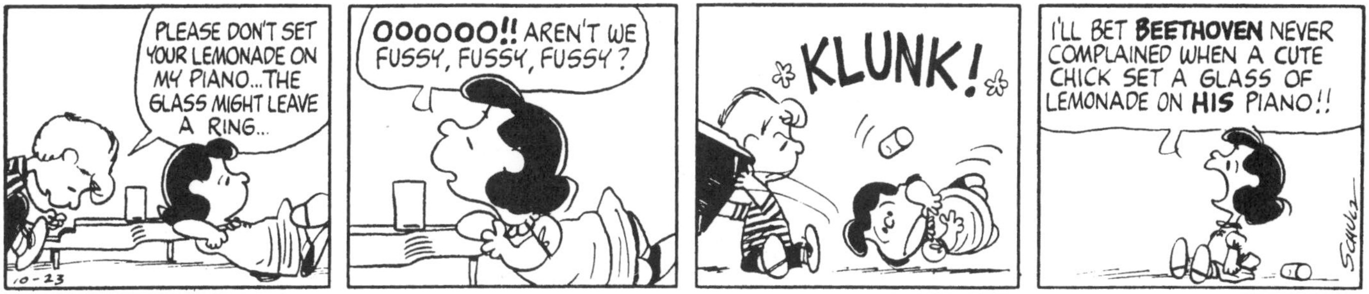
PLEASE DON'T SET YOUR LEMONADE ON MY PIANO...THE GLASS MIGHT LEAVE A RING...
OOOOOO!! AREN'T WE FUSSY, FUSSY, FUSSY?
KLUNK!
I'LL BET BEETHOVEN NEVER COMPLAINED WHEN A CUTE CHICK SET A GLASS OF LEMONADE ON HIS PIANO!!
SCHULZ

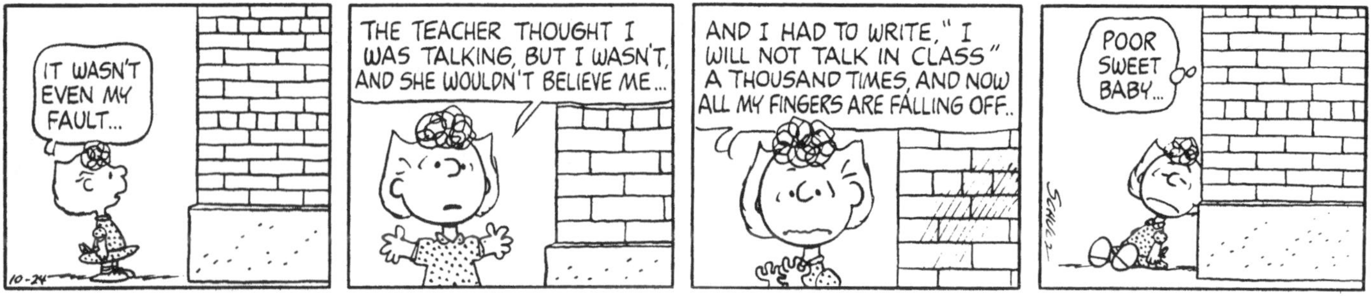
IT WASN'T EVEN MY FAULT...
THE TEACHER THOUGHT I WAS TALKING, BUT I WASN'T, AND SHE WOULDN'T BELIEVE ME...
AND I HAD TO WRITE, " I WILL NOT TALK IN CLASS " A THOUSAND TIMES, AND NOW ALL MY FINGERS ARE FALLING OFF..
POOR SWEET BABY...
10-24
SCHULZ

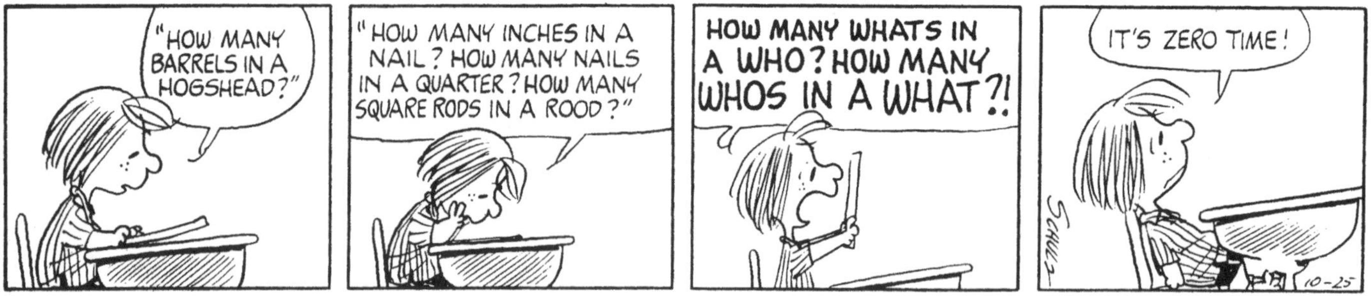
"HOW MANY BARRELS IN A HOGSHEAD?"
"HOW MANY INCHES IN A NAIL? HOW MANY NAILS IN A QUARTER? HOW MANY SQUARE RODS IN A ROOD?"
HOW MANY WHATS IN A WHO? HOW MANY WHOS IN A WHAT?!
IT'S ZERO TIME!
SCHULZ
10-25

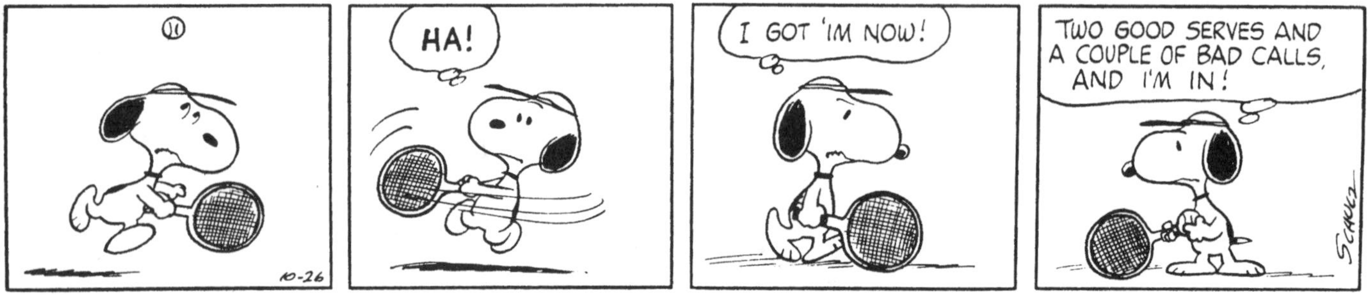
10-26
HA!
I GOT 'IM NOW!
TWO GOOD SERVES AND A COUPLE OF BAD CALLS, AND I'M IN!
SCHULZ

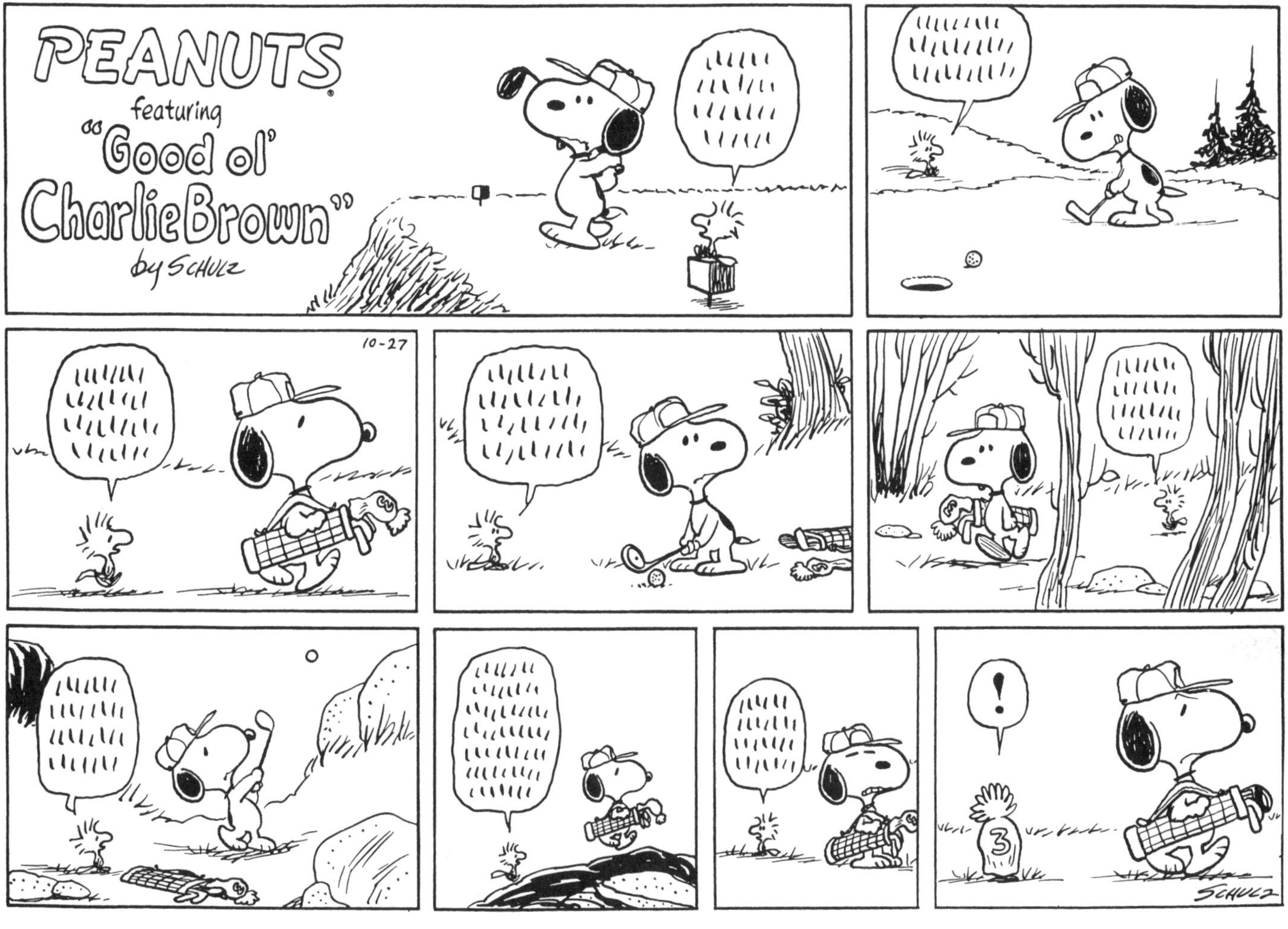
PEANUTS
featuring
"Good ol' CharlieBrown"
by SCHULZ
10-27
!
3
SCHULZ

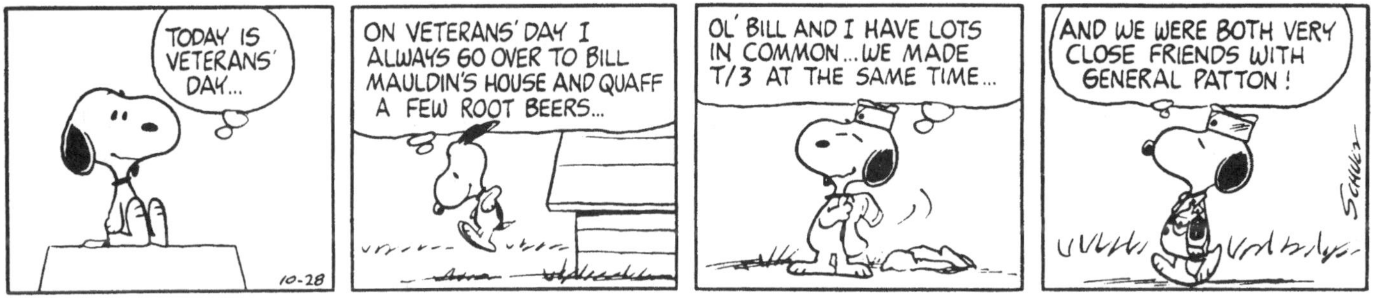
TODAY IS VETERANS' DAY...
10-28
ON VETERANS' DAY I ALWAYS GO OVER TO BILL MAULDIN'S HOUSE AND QUAFF A FEW ROOT BEERS...
OL' BILL AND I HAVE LOTS IN COMMON...WE MADE T/3 AT THE SAME TIME...
AND WE WERE BOTH VERY CLOSE FRIENDS WITH GENERAL PATTON!
SCHULZ

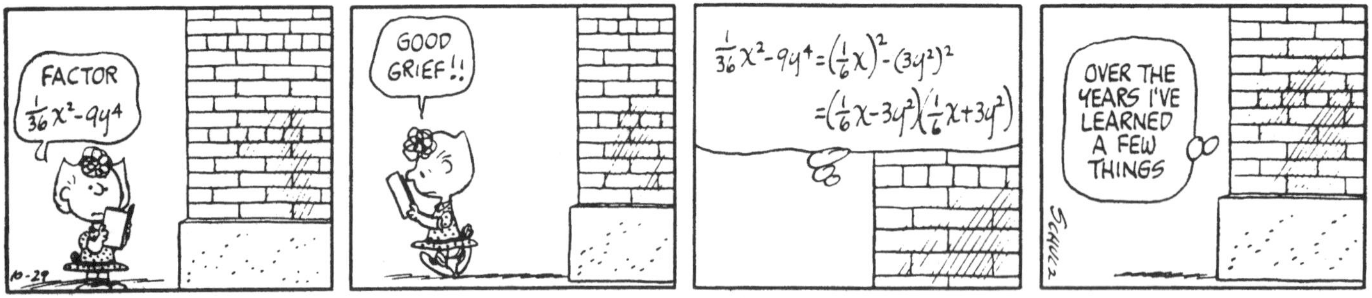
FACTOR $\frac{1}{36}x^2-9y^4$
10-29
GOOD GRIEF!!
$\frac{1}{36}x^2-9y^4=\left(\frac{1}{6}x\right)^2-(3y^2)^2$
$=\left(\frac{1}{6}x-3y^2\right)\left(\frac{1}{6}x+3y^2\right)$
OVER THE YEARS I'VE LEARNED A FEW THINGS
SCHULZ

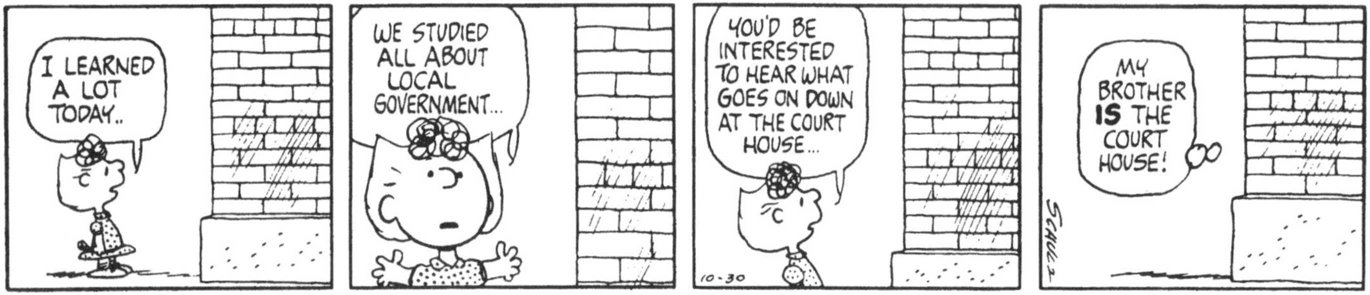
I LEARNED A LOT TODAY..
WE STUDIED ALL ABOUT LOCAL GOVERNMENT...
YOU'D BE INTERESTED TO HEAR WHAT GOES ON DOWN AT THE COURT HOUSE...
10-30
MY BROTHER **IS** THE COURT HOUSE!
SCHULZ

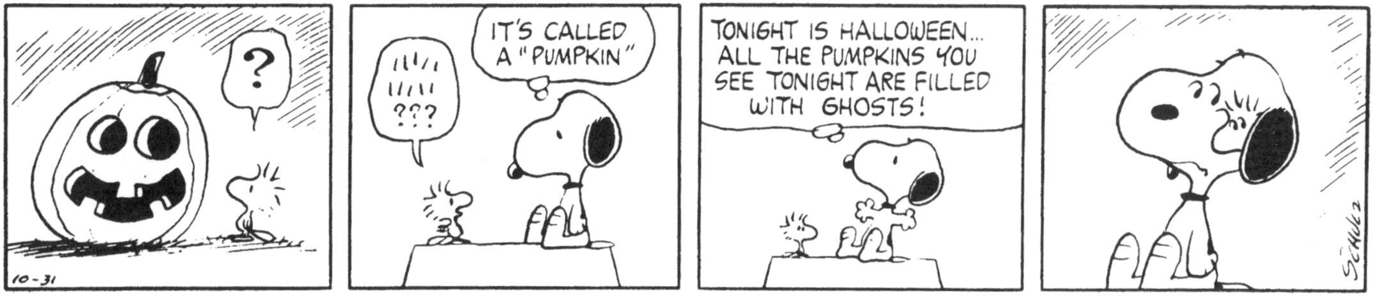
?
!!!!!
!!!!!
???
IT'S CALLED A "PUMPKIN"
TONIGHT IS HALLOWEEN... ALL THE PUMPKINS YOU SEE TONIGHT ARE FILLED WITH GHOSTS!

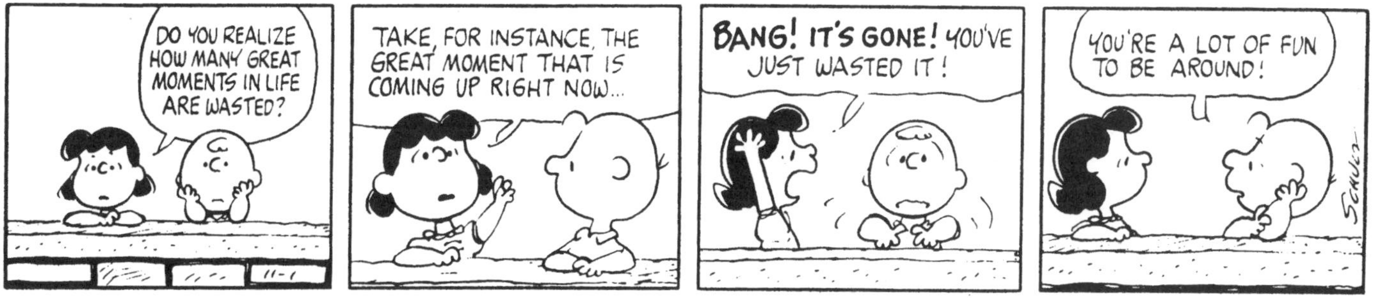
DO YOU REALIZE HOW MANY GREAT MOMENTS IN LIFE ARE WASTED?
TAKE, FOR INSTANCE, THE GREAT MOMENT THAT IS COMING UP RIGHT NOW...
BANG! IT'S GONE! YOU'VE JUST WASTED IT!
YOU'RE A LOT OF FUN TO BE AROUND!

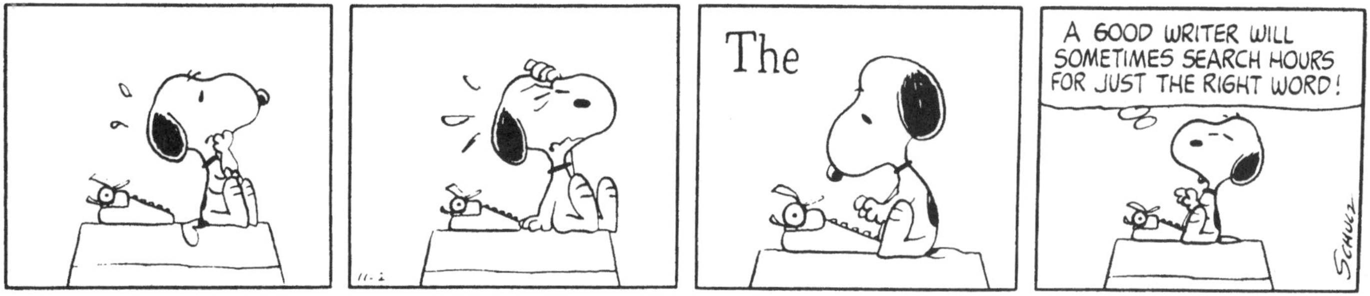
The
A GOOD WRITER WILL SOMETIMES SEARCH HOURS FOR JUST THE RIGHT WORD!

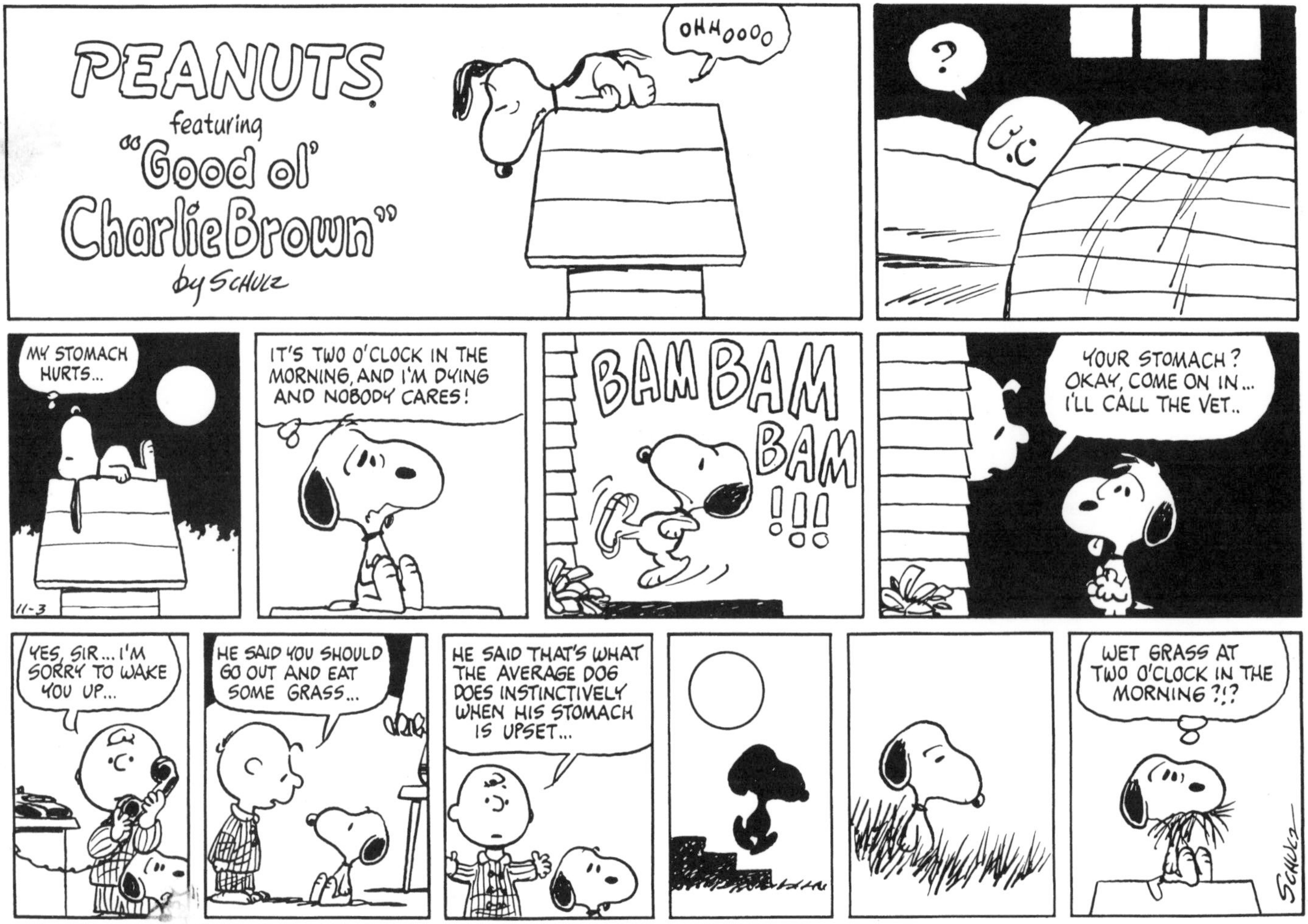
PEANUTS
featuring
"Good ol' Charlie Brown"
by SCHULZ
OHHOOOO
?
MY STOMACH HURTS...
11-3
IT'S TWO O'CLOCK IN THE MORNING, AND I'M DYING AND NOBODY CARES!
BAM BAM BAM !!!
YOUR STOMACH? OKAY, COME ON IN... I'LL CALL THE VET..
YES, SIR... I'M SORRY TO WAKE YOU UP...
HE SAID YOU SHOULD GO OUT AND EAT SOME GRASS...
HE SAID THAT'S WHAT THE AVERAGE DOG DOES INSTINCTIVELY WHEN HIS STOMACH IS UPSET...
WET GRASS AT TWO O'CLOCK IN THE MORNING?!?
SCHULZ

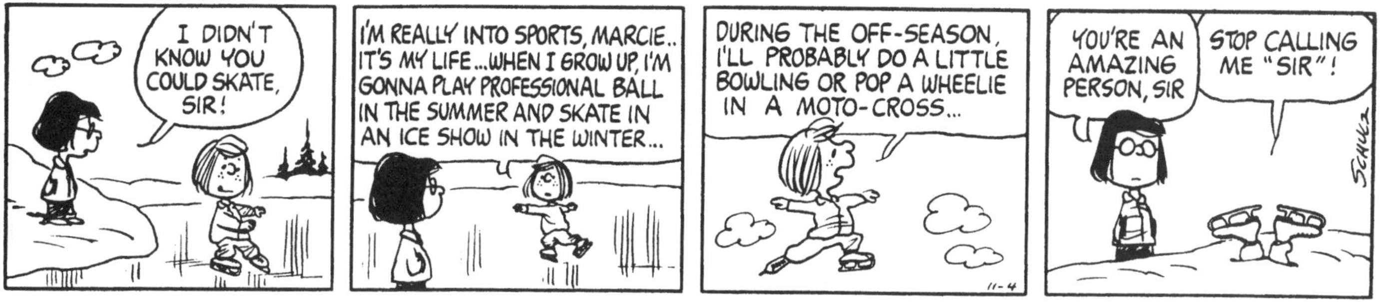
I DIDN'T KNOW YOU COULD SKATE, SIR!
I'M REALLY INTO SPORTS, MARCIE.. IT'S MY LIFE...WHEN I GROW UP, I'M GONNA PLAY PROFESSIONAL BALL IN THE SUMMER AND SKATE IN AN ICE SHOW IN THE WINTER...
DURING THE OFF-SEASON, I'LL PROBABLY DO A LITTLE BOWLING OR POP A WHEELIE IN A MOTO-CROSS...
11-4
YOU'RE AN AMAZING PERSON, SIR
STOP CALLING ME "SIR"!
SCHULZ

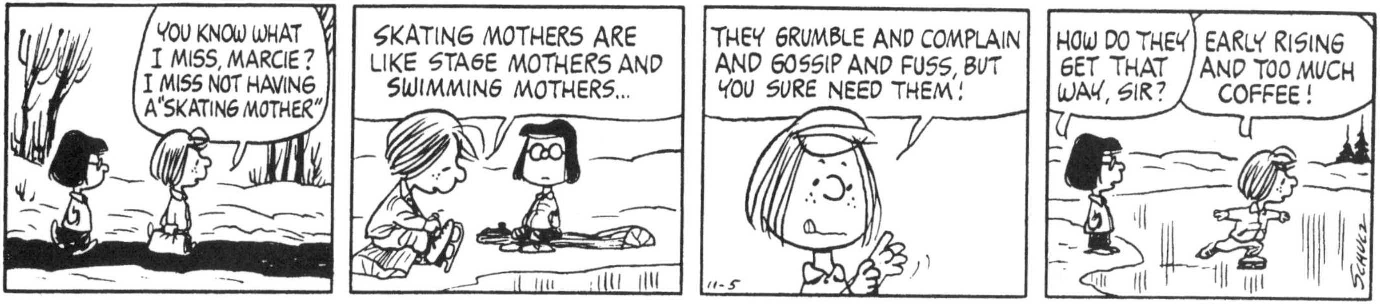
YOU KNOW WHAT I MISS, MARCIE? I MISS NOT HAVING A "SKATING MOTHER"
SKATING MOTHERS ARE LIKE STAGE MOTHERS AND SWIMMING MOTHERS...
THEY GRUMBLE AND COMPLAIN AND GOSSIP AND FUSS, BUT YOU SURE NEED THEM!
11-5
HOW DO THEY GET THAT WAY, SIR?
EARLY RISING AND TOO MUCH COFFEE!
SCHULZ

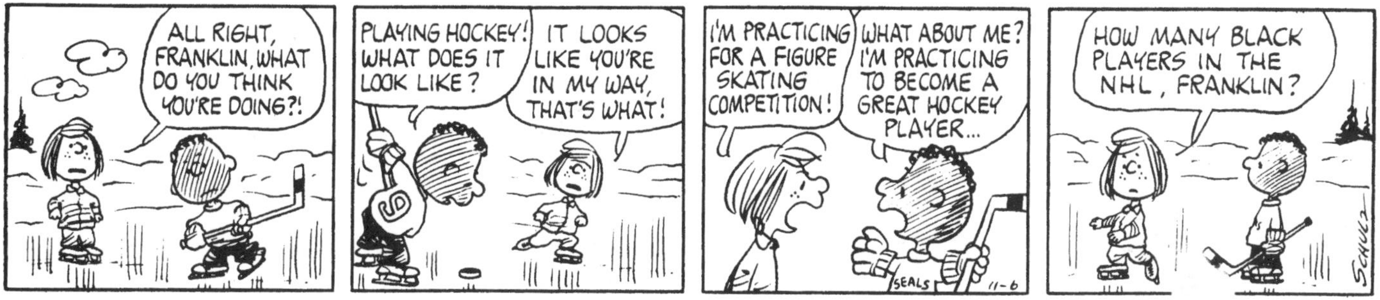
ALL RIGHT, FRANKLIN, WHAT DO YOU THINK YOU'RE DOING?!
PLAYING HOCKEY! WHAT DOES IT LOOK LIKE?
IT LOOKS LIKE YOU'RE IN MY WAY, THAT'S WHAT!
I'M PRACTICING FOR A FIGURE SKATING COMPETITION!
WHAT ABOUT ME? I'M PRACTICING TO BECOME A GREAT HOCKEY PLAYER...
SEALS
11-6
HOW MANY BLACK PLAYERS IN THE NHL, FRANKLIN?
SCHULZ

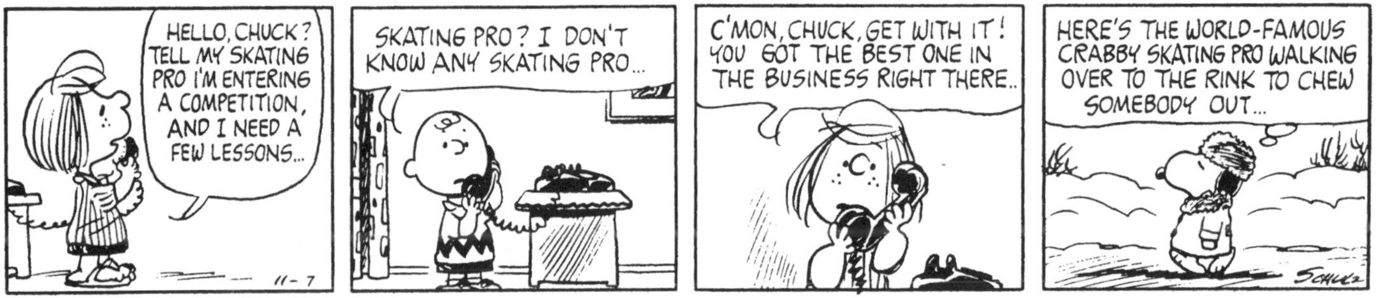
HELLO, CHUCK? TELL MY SKATING PRO I'M ENTERING A COMPETITION, AND I NEED A FEW LESSONS...
11-7
SKATING PRO? I DON'T KNOW ANY SKATING PRO...
C'MON, CHUCK, GET WITH IT! YOU GOT THE BEST ONE IN THE BUSINESS RIGHT THERE..
HERE'S THE WORLD-FAMOUS CRABBY SKATING PRO WALKING OVER TO THE RINK TO CHEW SOMEBODY OUT...

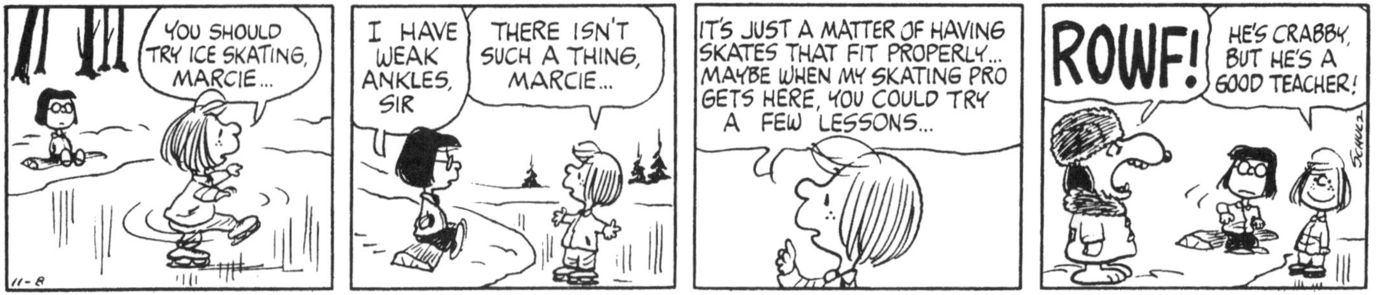
YOU SHOULD TRY ICE SKATING, MARCIE...
11-8
I HAVE WEAK ANKLES, SIR
THERE ISN'T SUCH A THING, MARCIE...
IT'S JUST A MATTER OF HAVING SKATES THAT FIT PROPERLY... MAYBE WHEN MY SKATING PRO GETS HERE, YOU COULD TRY A FEW LESSONS...
ROWF!
HE'S CRABBY, BUT HE'S A GOOD TEACHER!

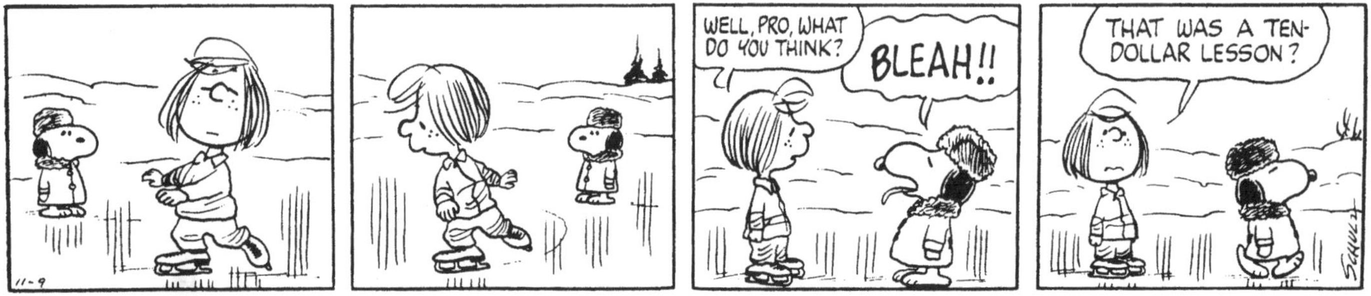
11-9
WELL, PRO, WHAT DO YOU THINK?
BLEAH!!
THAT WAS A TEN-DOLLAR LESSON?

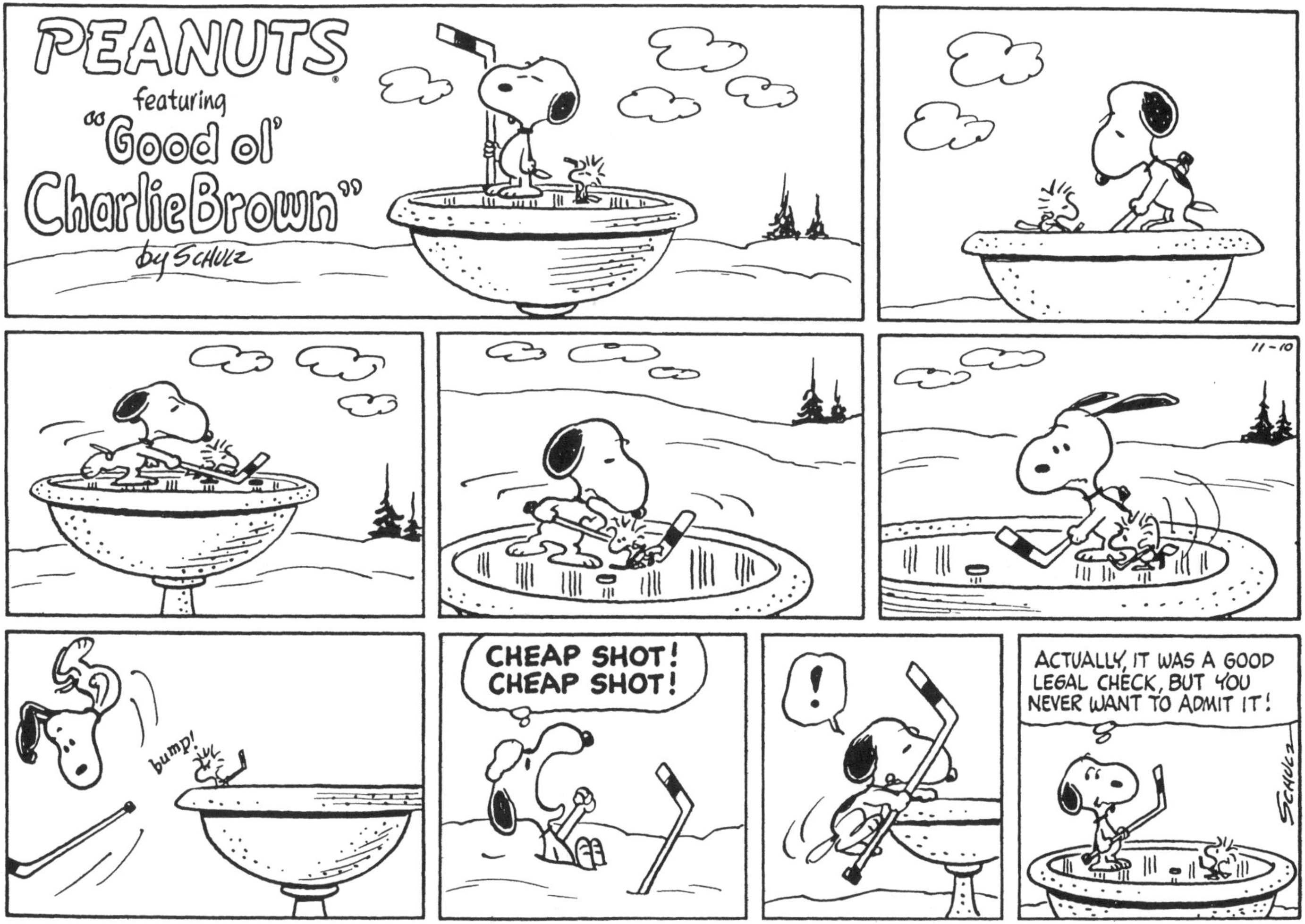
PEANUTS
featuring
"Good ol' Charlie Brown"
by SCHULZ
11-10
bump!
CHEAP SHOT! CHEAP SHOT!
!
ACTUALLY, IT WAS A GOOD LEGAL CHECK, BUT YOU NEVER WANT TO ADMIT IT!
SCHULZ

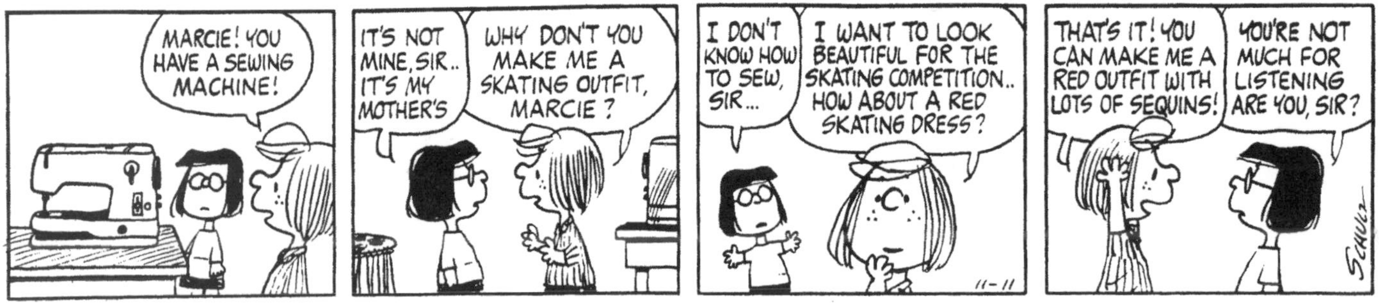
MARCIE! YOU HAVE A SEWING MACHINE!
IT'S NOT MINE, SIR.. IT'S MY MOTHER'S
WHY DON'T YOU MAKE ME A SKATING OUTFIT, MARCIE ?
I DON'T KNOW HOW TO SEW, SIR...
I WANT TO LOOK BEAUTIFUL FOR THE SKATING COMPETITION.. HOW ABOUT A RED SKATING DRESS ?
11-11
THAT'S IT! YOU CAN MAKE ME A RED OUTFIT WITH LOTS OF SEQUINS!
YOU'RE NOT MUCH FOR LISTENING ARE YOU, SIR ?
SCHULZ

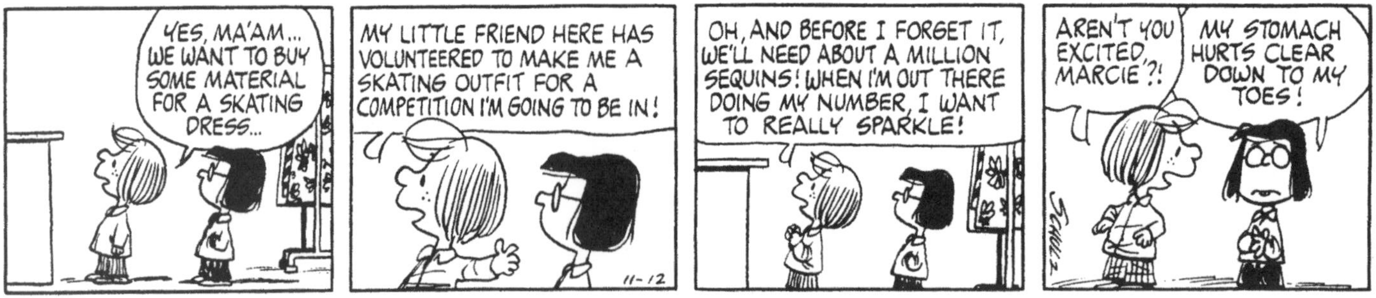
YES, MA'AM... WE WANT TO BUY SOME MATERIAL FOR A SKATING DRESS...
MY LITTLE FRIEND HERE HAS VOLUNTEERED TO MAKE ME A SKATING OUTFIT FOR A COMPETITION I'M GOING TO BE IN!
11-12
OH, AND BEFORE I FORGET IT, WE'LL NEED ABOUT A MILLION SEQUINS! WHEN I'M OUT THERE DOING MY NUMBER, I WANT TO REALLY SPARKLE!
ARE'NT YOU EXCITED, MARCIE ?!
MY STOMACH HURTS CLEAR DOWN TO MY TOES!
SCHULZ

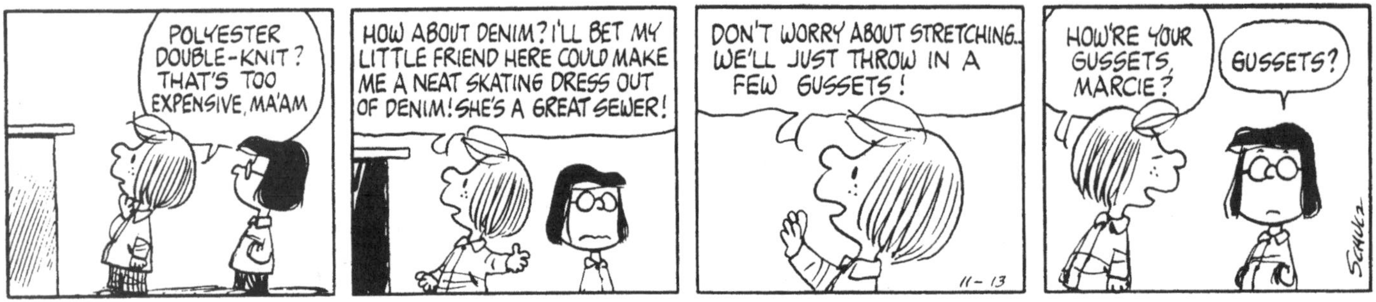
POLYESTER DOUBLE-KNIT ? THAT'S TOO EXPENSIVE, MA'AM
HOW ABOUT DENIM? I'LL BET MY LITTLE FRIEND HERE COULD MAKE ME A NEAT SKATING DRESS OUT OF DENIM! SHE'S A GREAT SEWER!
DON'T WORRY ABOUT STRETCHING.. WE'LL JUST THROW IN A FEW GUSSETS!
11-13
HOW'RE YOUR GUSSETS, MARCIE ?
GUSSETS ?
SCHULZ

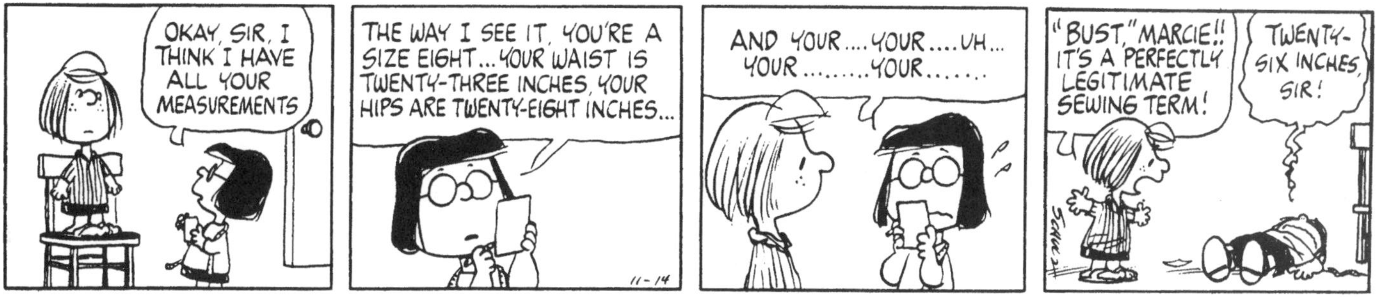
OKAY, SIR, I THINK I HAVE ALL YOUR MEASUREMENTS
THE WAY I SEE IT, YOU'RE A SIZE EIGHT... YOUR WAIST IS TWENTY-THREE INCHES, YOUR HIPS ARE TWENTY-EIGHT INCHES...
11-14
AND YOUR.... YOUR.... UH... YOUR........ YOUR......
"BUST," MARCIE!! IT'S A PERFECTLY LEGITIMATE SEWING TERM!
TWENTY-SIX INCHES, SIR!
SCHULZ

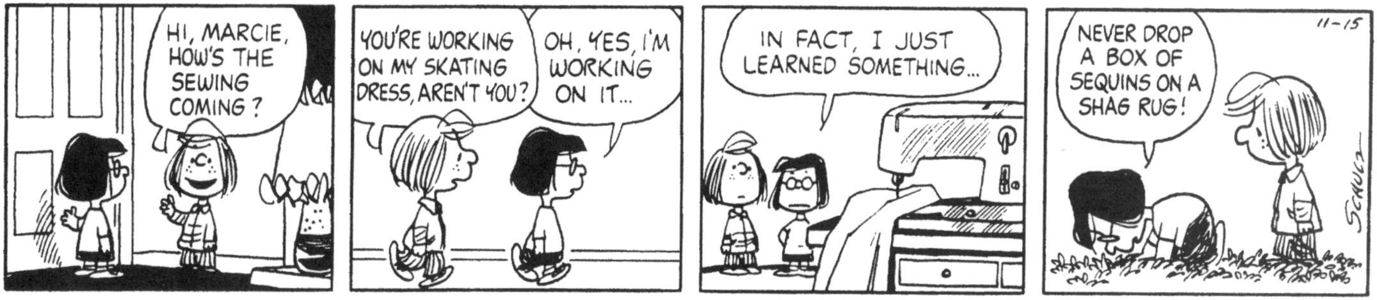
HI, MARCIE, HOW'S THE SEWING COMING?
YOU'RE WORKING ON MY SKATING DRESS, AREN'T YOU?
OH, YES, I'M WORKING ON IT...
IN FACT, I JUST LEARNED SOMETHING...
11-15
NEVER DROP A BOX OF SEQUINS ON A SHAG RUG!
SCHULZ

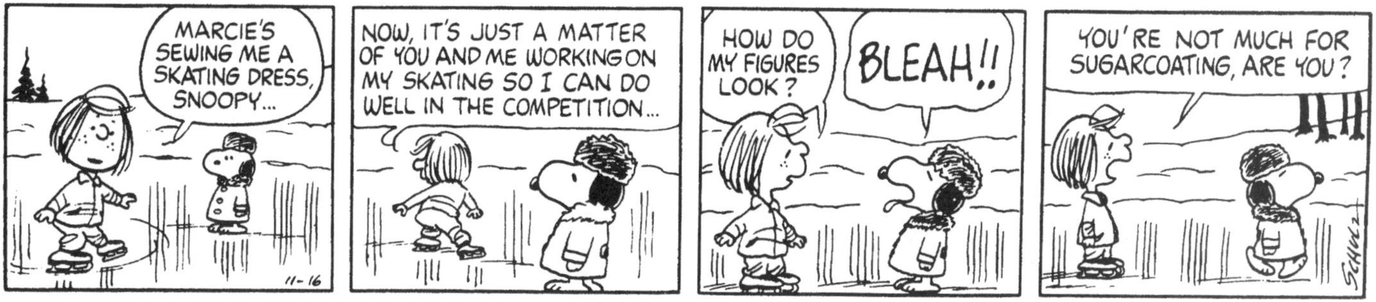
MARCIE'S SEWING ME A SKATING DRESS, SNOOPY...
11-16
NOW, IT'S JUST A MATTER OF YOU AND ME WORKING ON MY SKATING SO I CAN DO WELL IN THE COMPETITION...
HOW DO MY FIGURES LOOK?
BLEAH!!
YOU'RE NOT MUCH FOR SUGARCOATING, ARE YOU?
SCHULZ

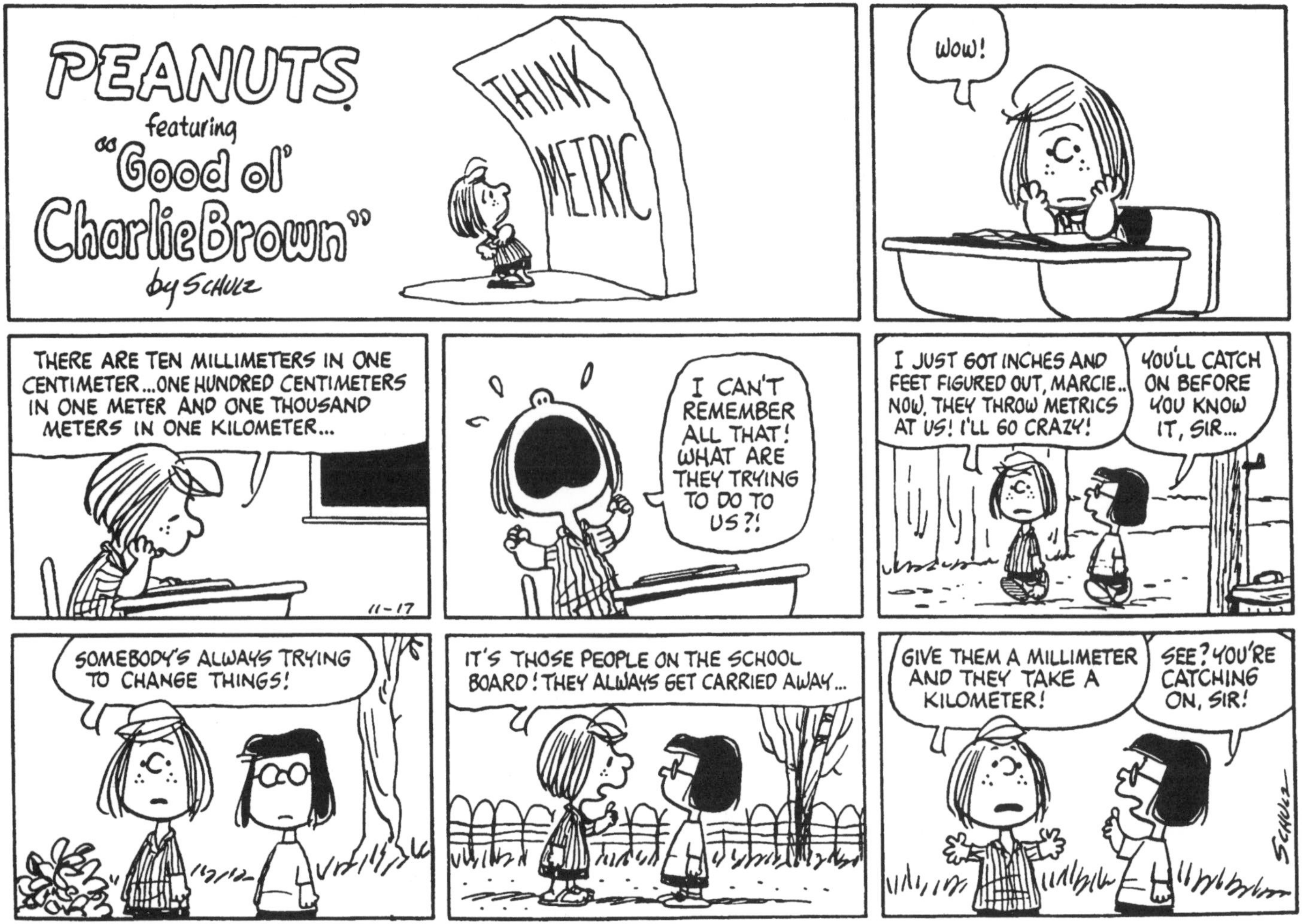
PEANUTS
featuring
"Good ol' CharlieBrown"
by SCHULZ
THINK METRIC
WOW!
THERE ARE TEN MILLIMETERS IN ONE CENTIMETER...ONE HUNDRED CENTIMETERS IN ONE METER AND ONE THOUSAND METERS IN ONE KILOMETER...
11-17
I CAN'T REMEMBER ALL THAT! WHAT ARE THEY TRYING TO DO TO US?!
I JUST GOT INCHES AND FEET FIGURED OUT, MARCIE.. NOW, THEY THROW METRICS AT US! I'LL GO CRAZY!
YOU'LL CATCH ON BEFORE YOU KNOW IT, SIR...
SOMEBODY'S ALWAYS TRYING TO CHANGE THINGS!
IT'S THOSE PEOPLE ON THE SCHOOL BOARD! THEY ALWAYS GET CARRIED AWAY...
GIVE THEM A MILLIMETER AND THEY TAKE A KILOMETER!
SEE? YOU'RE CATCHING ON, SIR!
SCHULZ

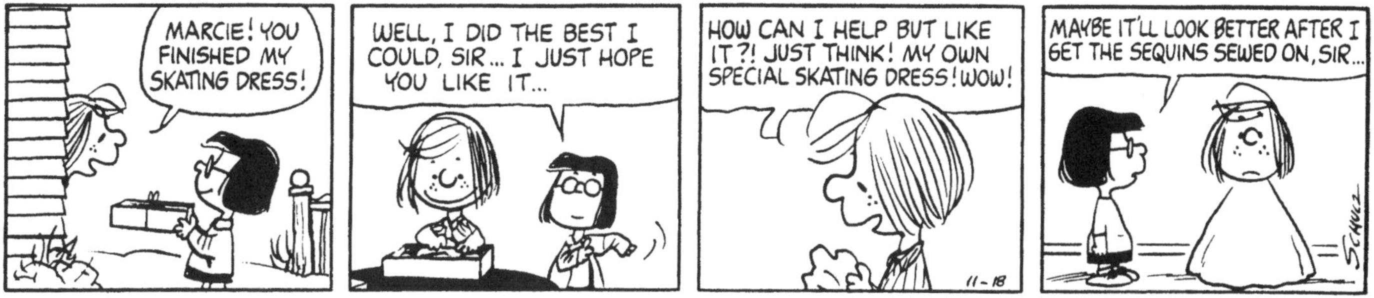
MARCIE! YOU FINISHED MY SKATING DRESS!
WELL, I DID THE BEST I COULD, SIR... I JUST HOPE YOU LIKE IT...
HOW CAN I HELP BUT LIKE IT?! JUST THINK! MY OWN SPECIAL SKATING DRESS! WOW!
11-18
MAYBE IT'LL LOOK BETTER AFTER I GET THE SEQUINS SEWED ON, SIR...
SCHULZ

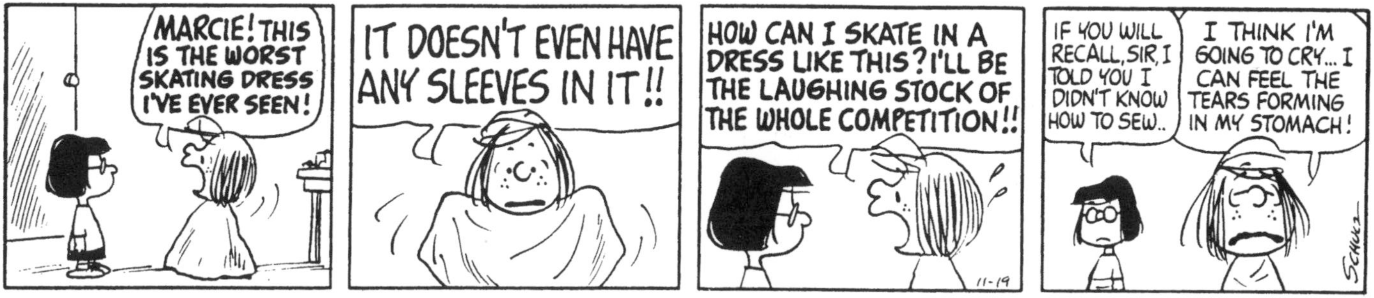
MARCIE! THIS IS THE WORST SKATING DRESS I'VE EVER SEEN!
IT DOESN'T EVEN HAVE ANY SLEEVES IN IT!!
HOW CAN I SKATE IN A DRESS LIKE THIS? I'LL BE THE LAUGHING STOCK OF THE WHOLE COMPETITION!!
11-19
IF YOU WILL RECALL, SIR, I TOLD YOU I DIDN'T KNOW HOW TO SEW..
I THINK I'M GOING TO CRY... I CAN FEEL THE TEARS FORMING IN MY STOMACH!
SCHULZ

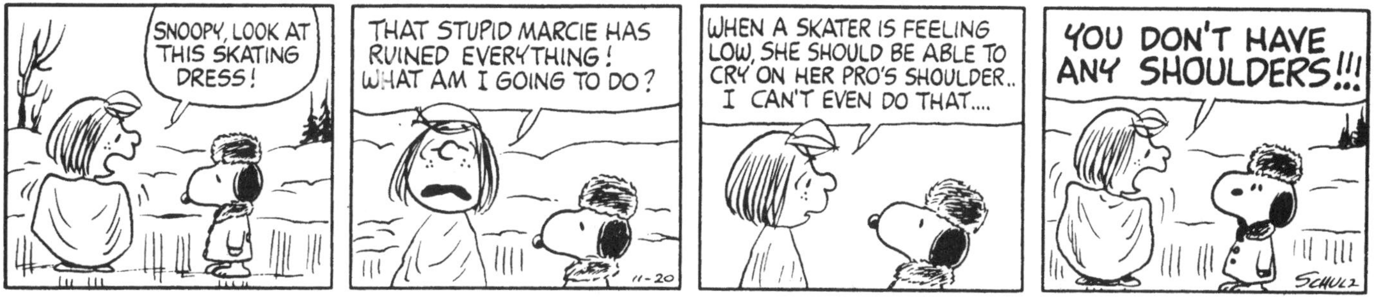
SNOOPY, LOOK AT THIS SKATING DRESS!
THAT STUPID MARCIE HAS RUINED EVERYTHING! WHAT AM I GOING TO DO?
11-20
WHEN A SKATER IS FEELING LOW, SHE SHOULD BE ABLE TO CRY ON HER PRO'S SHOULDER.. I CAN'T EVEN DO THAT....
YOU DON'T HAVE ANY SHOULDERS!!!
SCHULZ

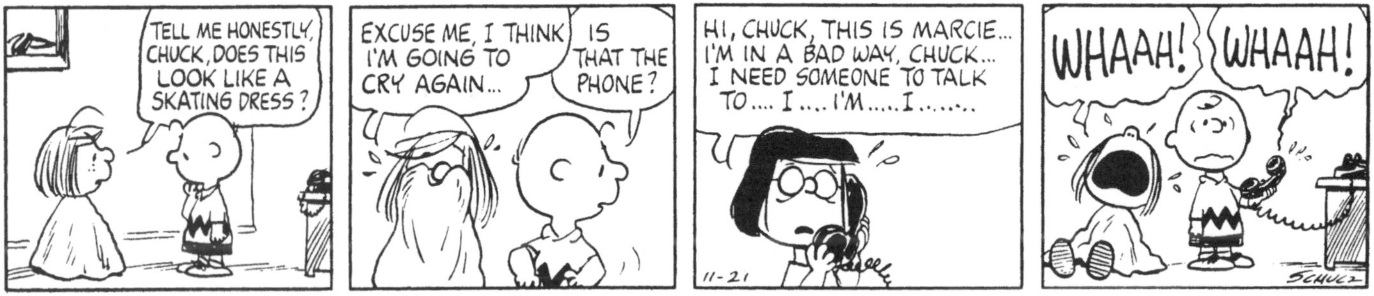
TELL ME HONESTLY, CHUCK, DOES THIS LOOK LIKE A SKATING DRESS?
EXCUSE ME, I THINK I'M GOING TO CRY AGAIN...
IS THAT THE PHONE?
HI, CHUCK, THIS IS MARCIE... I'M IN A BAD WAY, CHUCK... I NEED SOMEONE TO TALK TO.... I.... I'M..... I.......
11-21
WHAAH!
WHAAH!
SCHULZ

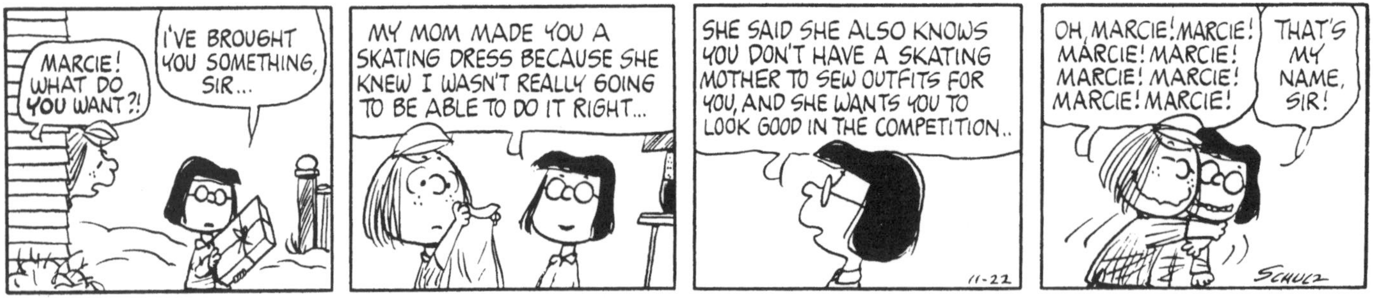
MARCIE! WHAT DO **YOU** WANT?!
I'VE BROUGHT YOU SOMETHING, SIR...
MY MOM MADE YOU A SKATING DRESS BECAUSE SHE KNEW I WASN'T REALLY GOING TO BE ABLE TO DO IT RIGHT...
SHE SAID SHE ALSO KNOWS YOU DON'T HAVE A SKATING MOTHER TO SEW OUTFITS FOR YOU, AND SHE WANTS YOU TO LOOK GOOD IN THE COMPETITION..
11-22
OH, MARCIE! MARCIE! MARCIE! MARCIE! MARCIE! MARCIE! MARCIE! MARCIE!
THAT'S MY NAME, SIR!
SCHULZ

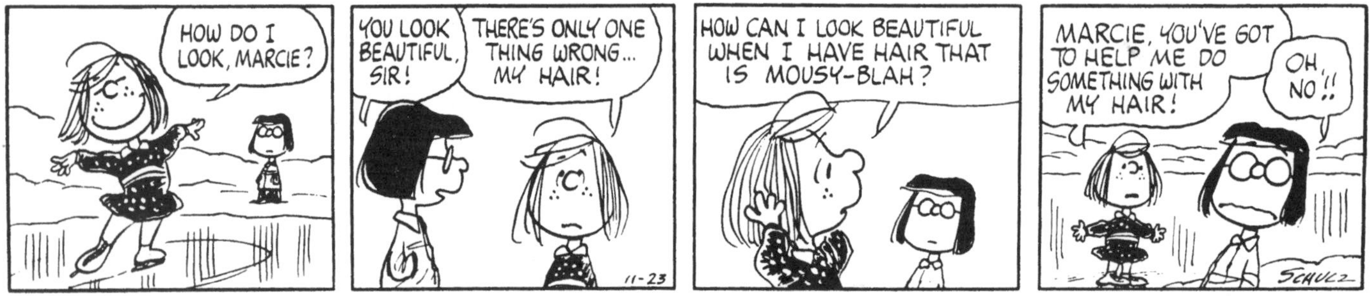
HOW DO I LOOK, MARCIE?
YOU LOOK BEAUTIFUL, SIR!
THERE'S ONLY ONE THING WRONG... MY HAIR!
11-23
HOW CAN I LOOK BEAUTIFUL WHEN I HAVE HAIR THAT IS MOUSY-BLAH?
MARCIE, YOU'VE GOT TO HELP ME DO SOMETHING WITH MY HAIR!
OH NO!!
SCHULZ

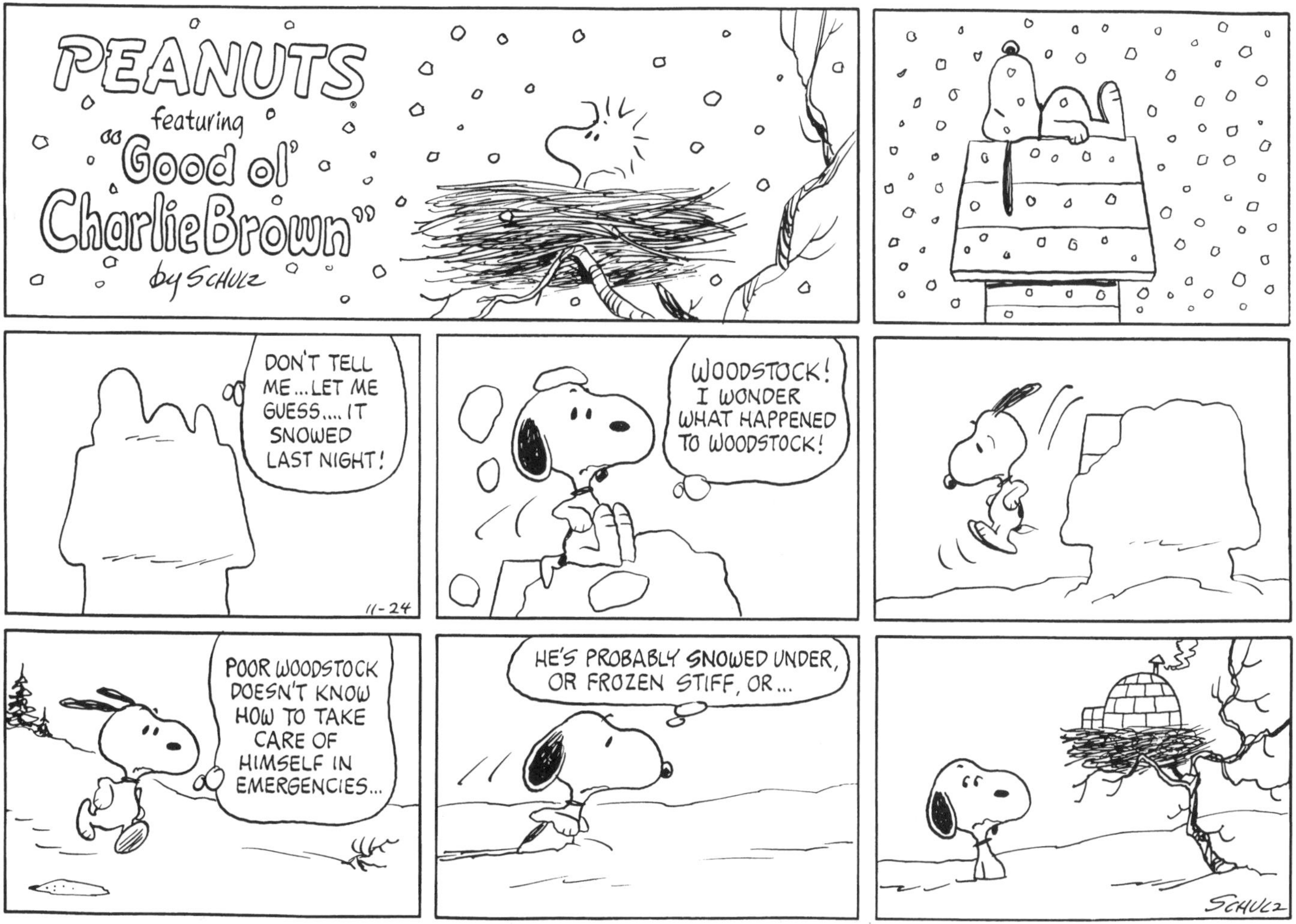

PEANUTS
featuring "Good ol' Charlie Brown"
by SCHULZ
DON'T TELL ME...LET ME GUESS....IT SNOWED LAST NIGHT!
11-24
WOODSTOCK! I WONDER WHAT HAPPENED TO WOODSTOCK!
POOR WOODSTOCK DOESN'T KNOW HOW TO TAKE CARE OF HIMSELF IN EMERGENCIES...
HE'S PROBABLY SNOWED UNDER, OR FROZEN STIFF, OR...
SCHULZ

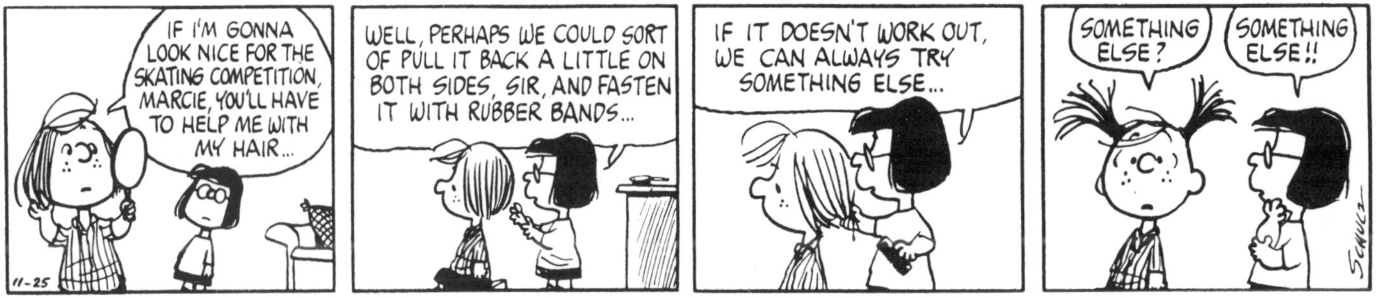
IF I'M GONNA LOOK NICE FOR THE SKATING COMPETITION, MARCIE, YOU'LL HAVE TO HELP ME WITH MY HAIR...
11-25
WELL, PERHAPS WE COULD SORT OF PULL IT BACK A LITTLE ON BOTH SIDES, SIR, AND FASTEN IT WITH RUBBER BANDS...
IF IT DOESN'T WORK OUT, WE CAN ALWAYS TRY SOMETHING ELSE...
SOMETHING ELSE?
SOMETHING ELSE!!
SCHULZ

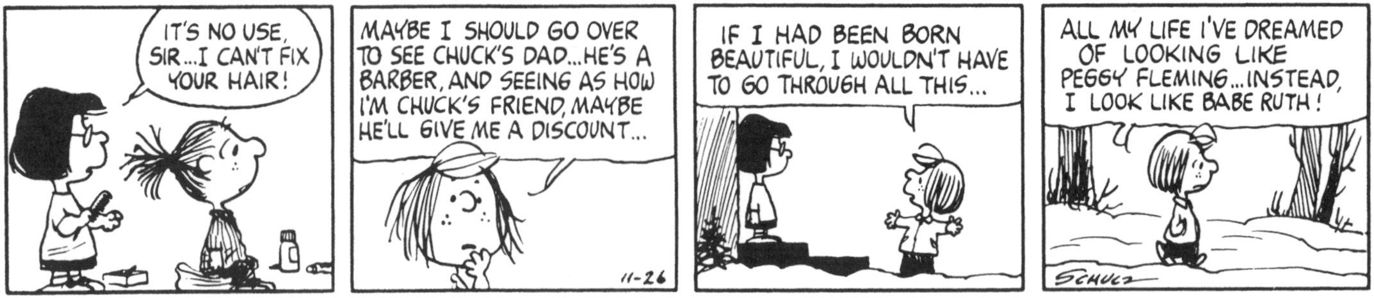
IT'S NO USE, SIR...I CAN'T FIX YOUR HAIR!
MAYBE I SHOULD GO OVER TO SEE CHUCK'S DAD...HE'S A BARBER, AND SEEING AS HOW I'M CHUCK'S FRIEND, MAYBE HE'LL GIVE ME A DISCOUNT...
11-26
IF I HAD BEEN BORN BEAUTIFUL, I WOULDN'T HAVE TO GO THROUGH ALL THIS...
ALL MY LIFE I'VE DREAMED OF LOOKING LIKE PEGGY FLEMING...INSTEAD, I LOOK LIKE BABE RUTH!
SCHULZ

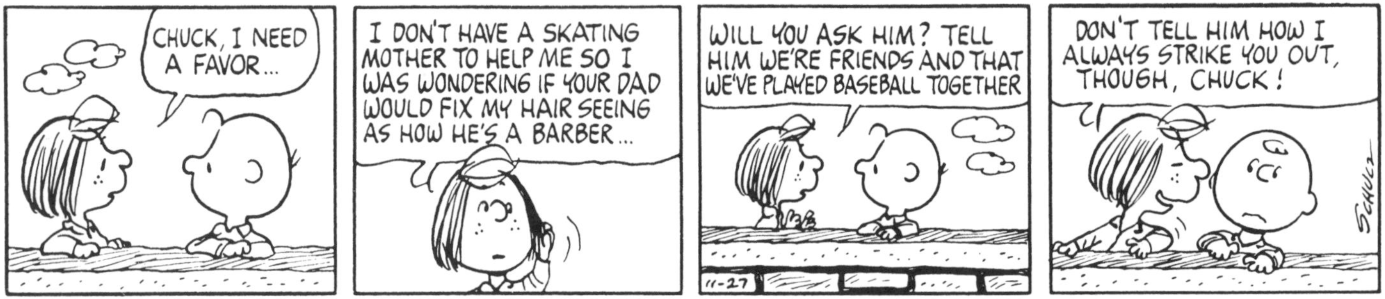
CHUCK, I NEED A FAVOR...
I DON'T HAVE A SKATING MOTHER TO HELP ME SO I WAS WONDERING IF YOUR DAD WOULD FIX MY HAIR SEEING AS HOW HE'S A BARBER...
WILL YOU ASK HIM? TELL HIM WE'RE FRIENDS AND THAT WE'VE PLAYED BASEBALL TOGETHER
11-27
DON'T TELL HIM HOW I ALWAYS STRIKE YOU OUT, THOUGH, CHUCK!
SCHULZ

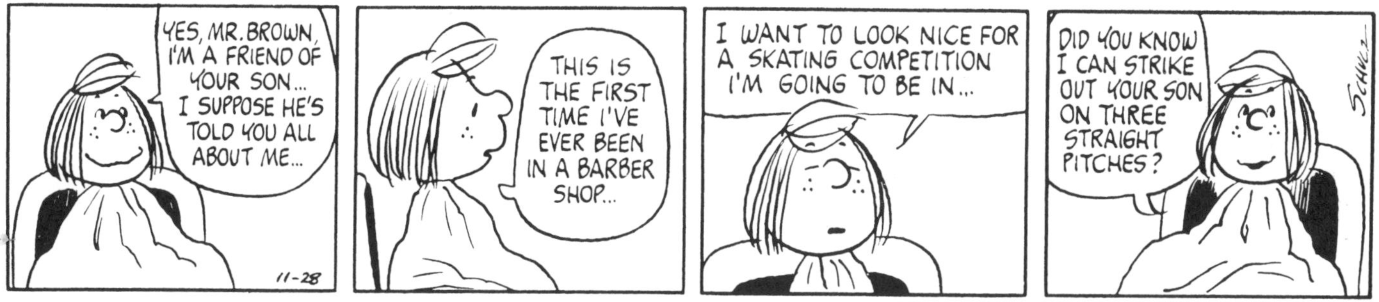
YES, MR. BROWN, I'M A FRIEND OF YOUR SON... I SUPPOSE HE'S TOLD YOU ALL ABOUT ME...
11-28
THIS IS THE FIRST TIME I'VE EVER BEEN IN A BARBER SHOP...
I WANT TO LOOK NICE FOR A SKATING COMPETITION I'M GOING TO BE IN...
DID YOU KNOW I CAN STRIKE OUT YOUR SON ON THREE STRAIGHT PITCHES?
SCHULZ

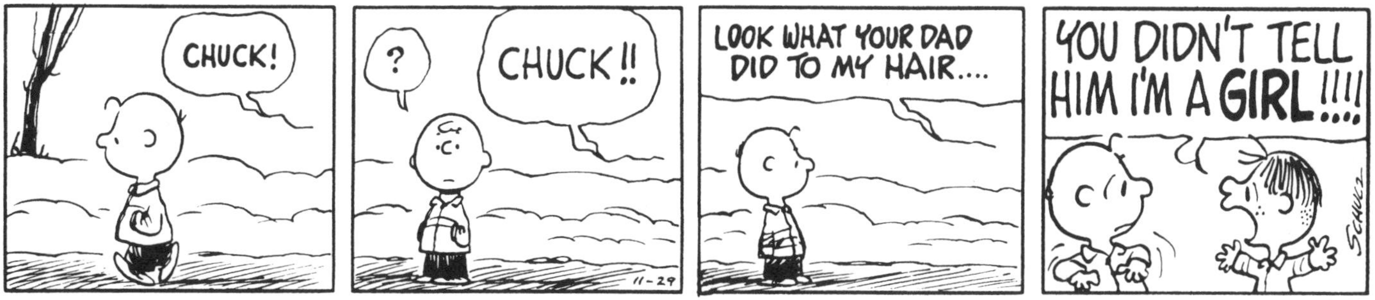
CHUCK!
?
CHUCK!!
11-29
LOOK WHAT YOUR DAD DID TO MY HAIR....
YOU DIDN'T TELL HIM I'M A GIRL!!!!
SCHULZ

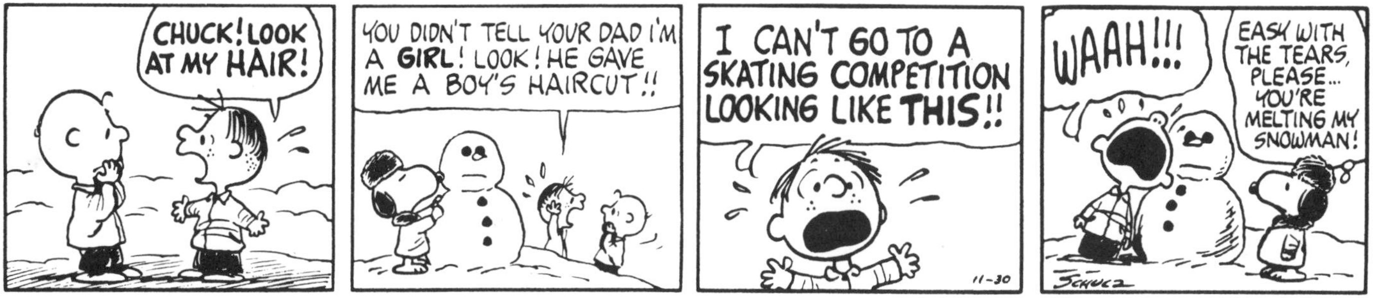
CHUCK! LOOK AT MY HAIR!
YOU DIDN'T TELL YOUR DAD I'M A GIRL! LOOK! HE GAVE ME A BOY'S HAIRCUT!!
I CAN'T GO TO A SKATING COMPETITION LOOKING LIKE THIS!!
11-30
WAAH!!!
EASY WITH THE TEARS, PLEASE... YOU'RE MELTING MY SNOWMAN!
SCHULZ

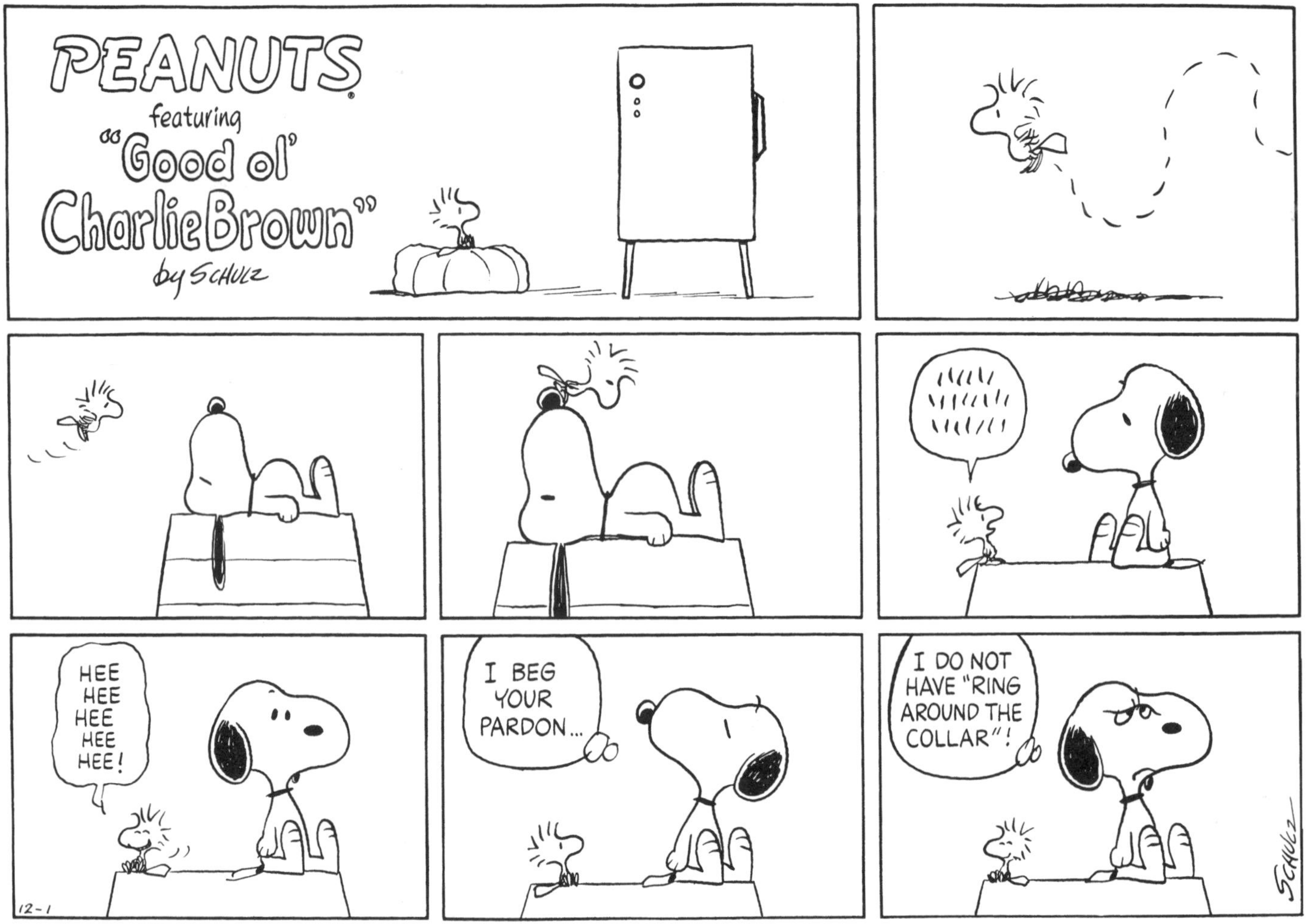
PEANUTS
featuring
"Good ol' Charlie Brown"
by SCHULZ
HEE
HEE
HEE
HEE
HEE!
I BEG YOUR PARDON...
I DO NOT HAVE "RING AROUND THE COLLAR"!
12-1
SCHULZ

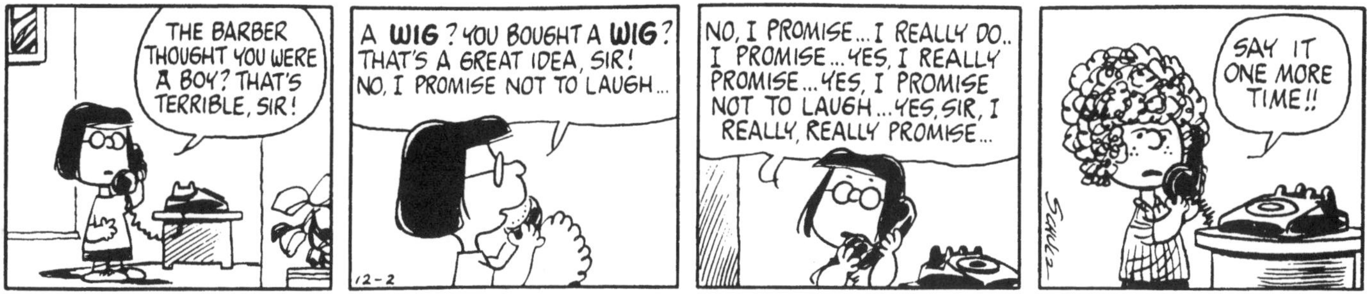
THE BARBER THOUGHT YOU WERE A BOY? THAT'S TERRIBLE, SIR!
A WIG? YOU BOUGHT A WIG? THAT'S A GREAT IDEA, SIR! NO, I PROMISE NOT TO LAUGH...
12-2
NO, I PROMISE... I REALLY DO.. I PROMISE... YES, I REALLY PROMISE... YES, I PROMISE NOT TO LAUGH... YES, SIR, I REALLY, REALLY PROMISE...
SAY IT ONE MORE TIME!!
SCHULZ

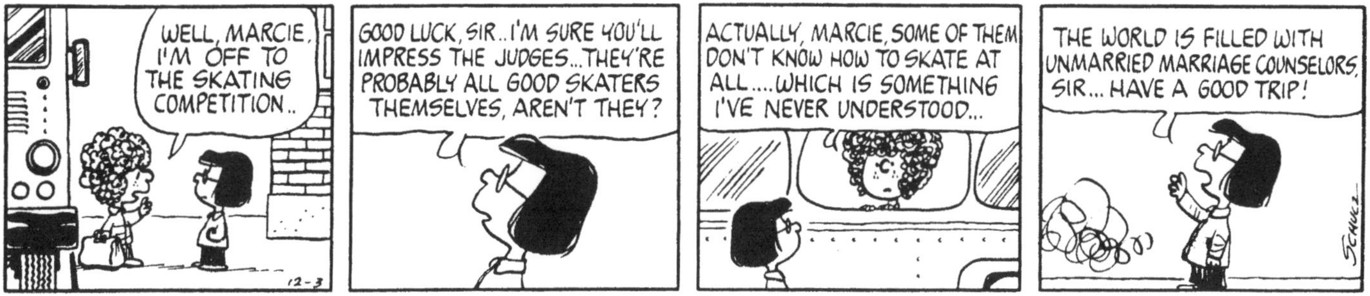
WELL, MARCIE, I'M OFF TO THE SKATING COMPETITION..
12-3
GOOD LUCK, SIR.. I'M SURE YOU'LL IMPRESS THE JUDGES... THEY'RE PROBABLY ALL GOOD SKATERS THEMSELVES, AREN'T THEY?
ACTUALLY, MARCIE, SOME OF THEM DON'T KNOW HOW TO SKATE AT ALL.... WHICH IS SOMETHING I'VE NEVER UNDERSTOOD...
THE WORLD IS FILLED WITH UNMARRIED MARRIAGE COUNSELORS, SIR... HAVE A GOOD TRIP!
SCHULZ

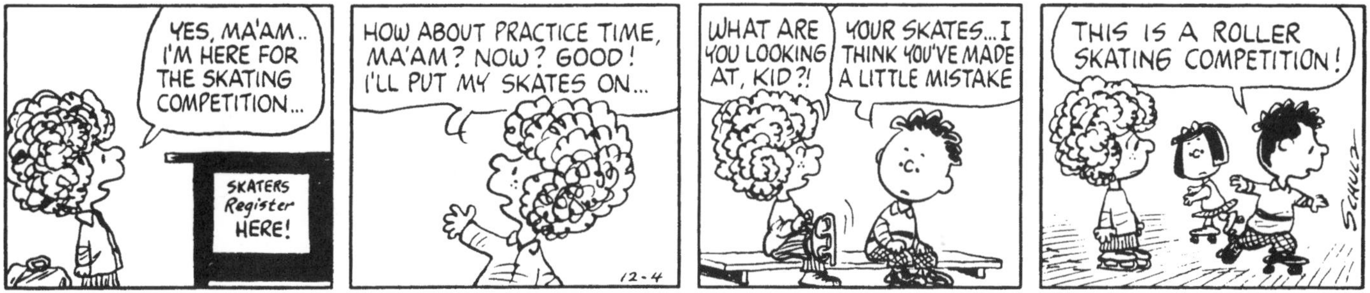
YES, MA'AM.. I'M HERE FOR THE SKATING COMPETITION...
SKATERS Register HERE!
HOW ABOUT PRACTICE TIME, MA'AM? NOW? GOOD! I'LL PUT MY SKATES ON...
12-4
WHAT ARE YOU LOOKING AT, KID?!
YOUR SKATES... I THINK YOU'VE MADE A LITTLE MISTAKE
THIS IS A ROLLER SKATING COMPETITION!
SCHULZ

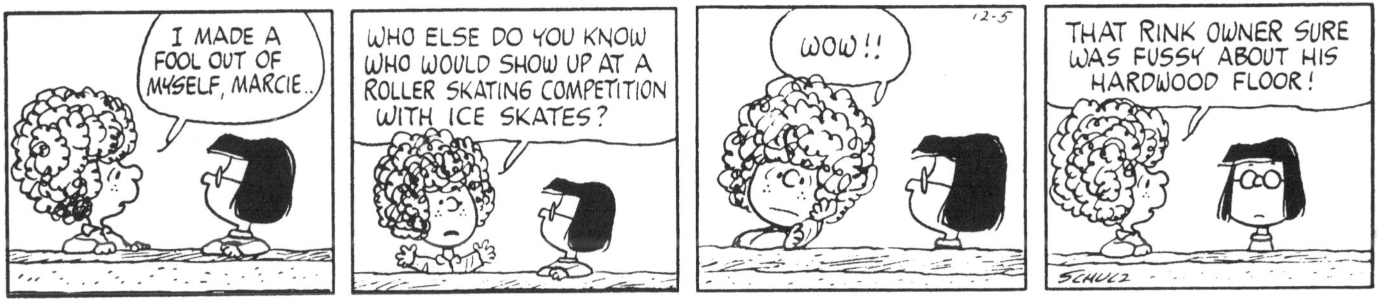
I MADE A FOOL OUT OF MYSELF, MARCIE..
WHO ELSE DO YOU KNOW WHO WOULD SHOW UP AT A ROLLER SKATING COMPETITION WITH ICE SKATES?
12-5
WOW!!
THAT RINK OWNER SURE WAS FUSSY ABOUT HIS HARDWOOD FLOOR!

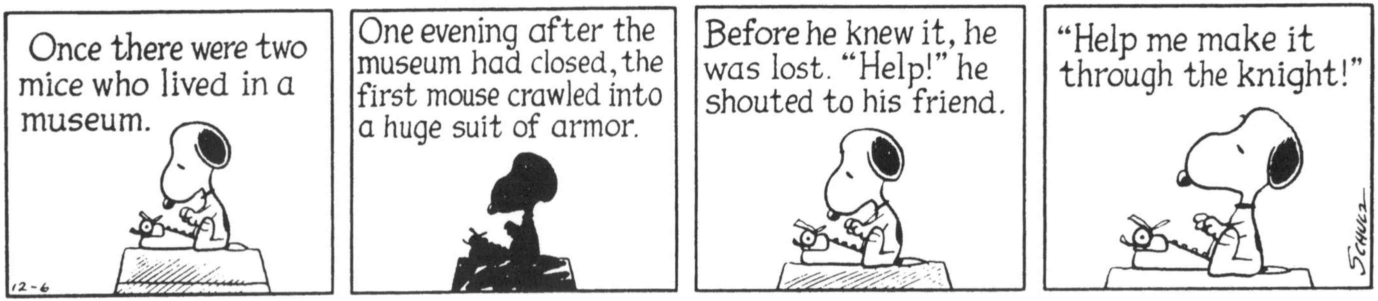
Once there were two mice who lived in a museum.
12-6
One evening after the museum had closed, the first mouse crawled into a huge suit of armor.
Before he knew it, he was lost. "Help!" he shouted to his friend.
"Help me make it through the knight!"

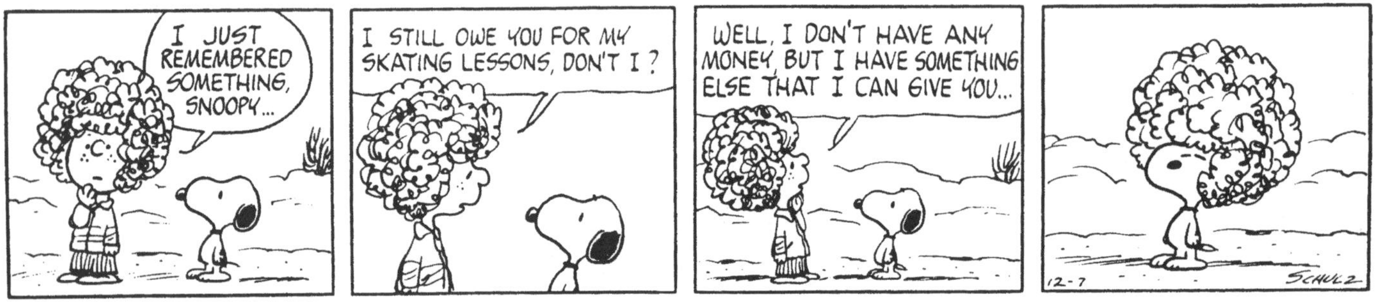
I JUST REMEMBERED SOMETHING, SNOOPY...
I STILL OWE YOU FOR MY SKATING LESSONS, DON'T I ?
WELL, I DON'T HAVE ANY MONEY, BUT I HAVE SOMETHING ELSE THAT I CAN GIVE YOU...
12-7

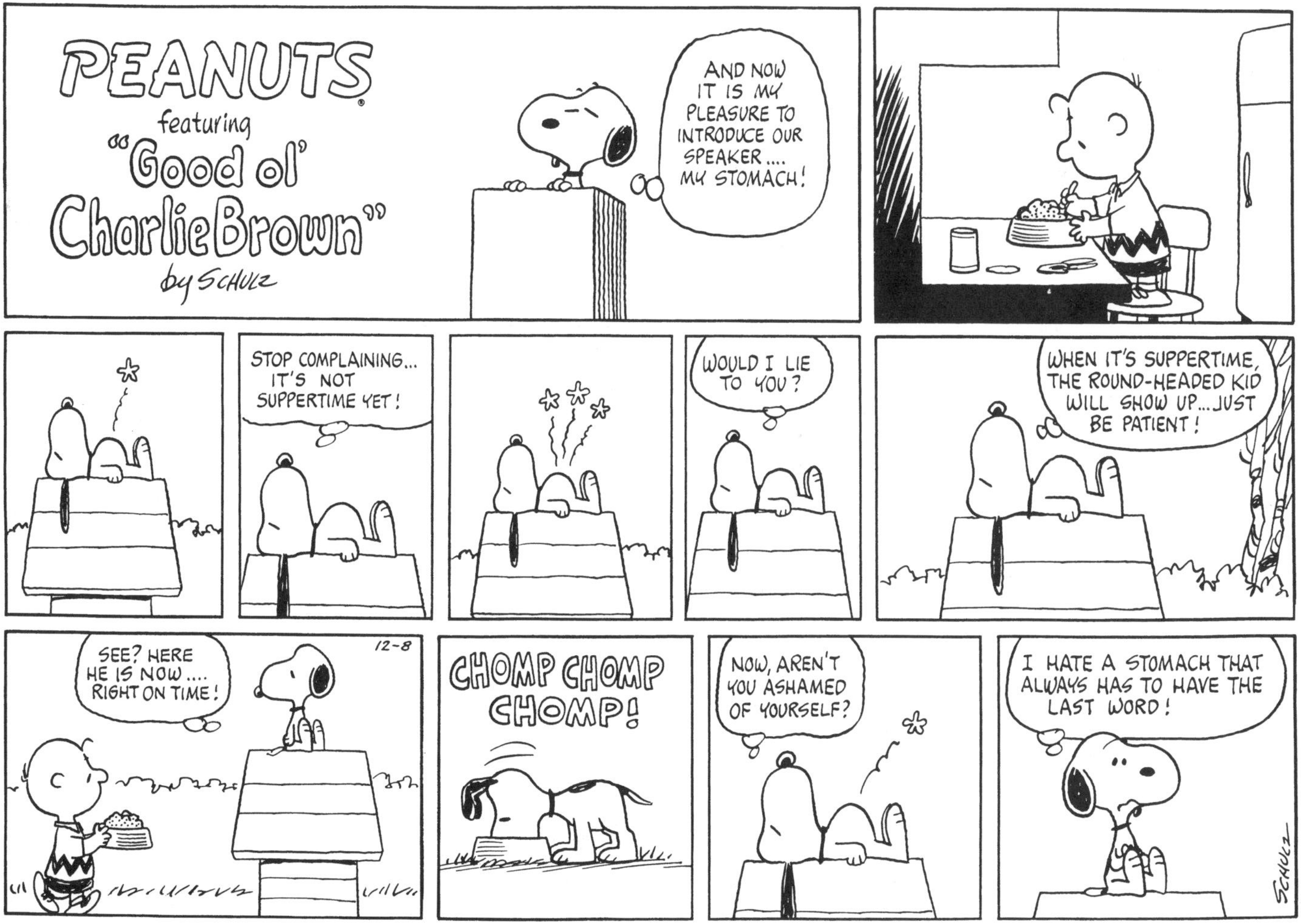
PEANUTS
featuring
"Good ol' CharlieBrown"
by SCHULZ
AND NOW IT IS MY PLEASURE TO INTRODUCE OUR SPEAKER.... MY STOMACH!
STOP COMPLAINING... IT'S NOT SUPPERTIME YET!
WOULD I LIE TO YOU?
WHEN IT'S SUPPERTIME, THE ROUND-HEADED KID WILL SHOW UP...JUST BE PATIENT!
SEE? HERE HE IS NOW.... RIGHT ON TIME!
12-8
CHOMP CHOMP CHOMP!
NOW, AREN'T YOU ASHAMED OF YOURSELF?
I HATE A STOMACH THAT ALWAYS HAS TO HAVE THE LAST WORD!
SCHULZ

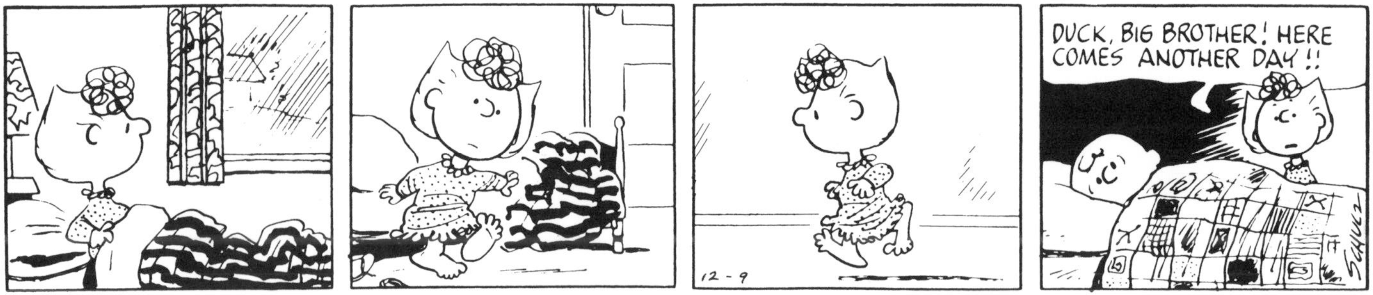
DUCK, BIG BROTHER! HERE COMES ANOTHER DAY!!

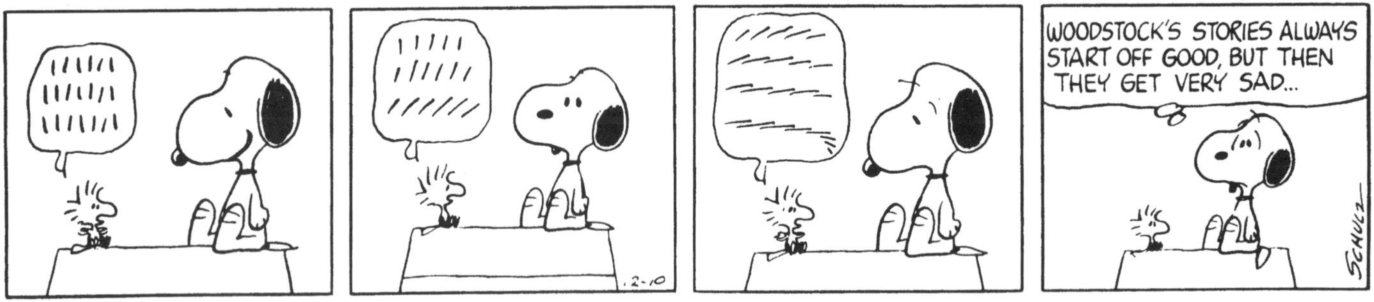
WOODSTOCK'S STORIES ALWAYS START OFF GOOD, BUT THEN THEY GET VERY SAD...

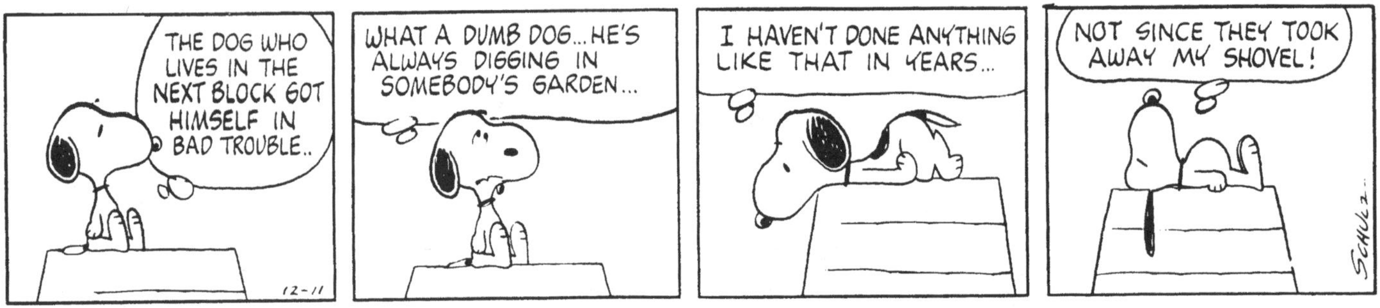
THE DOG WHO LIVES IN THE NEXT BLOCK GOT HIMSELF IN BAD TROUBLE..
WHAT A DUMB DOG...HE'S ALWAYS DIGGING IN SOMEBODY'S GARDEN...
I HAVEN'T DONE ANYTHING LIKE THAT IN YEARS...
NOT SINCE THEY TOOK AWAY MY SHOVEL!

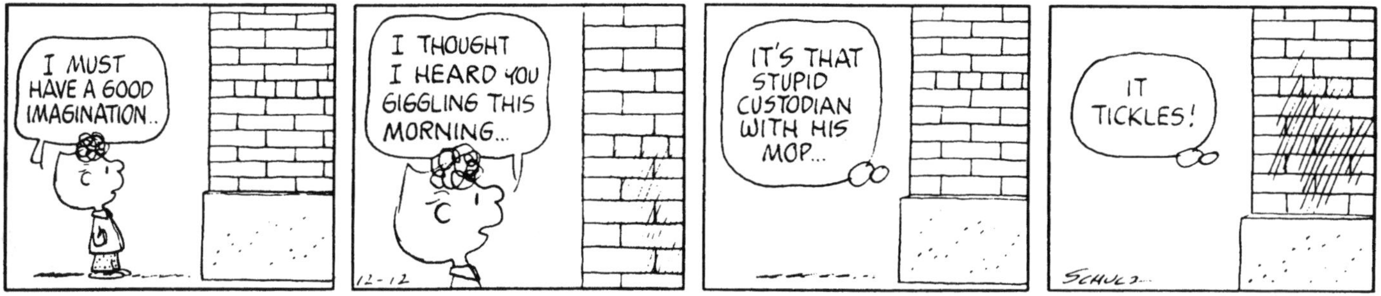
I MUST HAVE A GOOD IMAGINATION..
I THOUGHT I HEARD YOU GIGGLING THIS MORNING...
IT'S THAT STUPID CUSTODIAN WITH HIS MOP...
IT TICKLES!

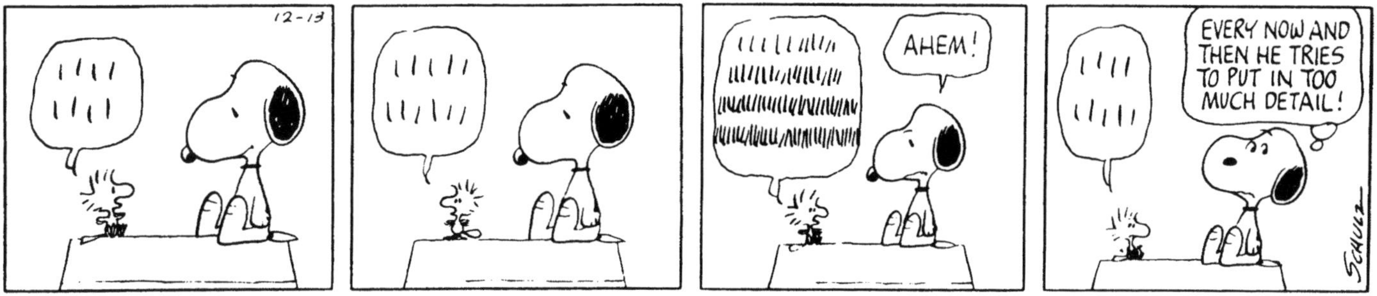
AHEM!
EVERY NOW AND THEN HE TRIES TO PUT IN TOO MUCH DETAIL!

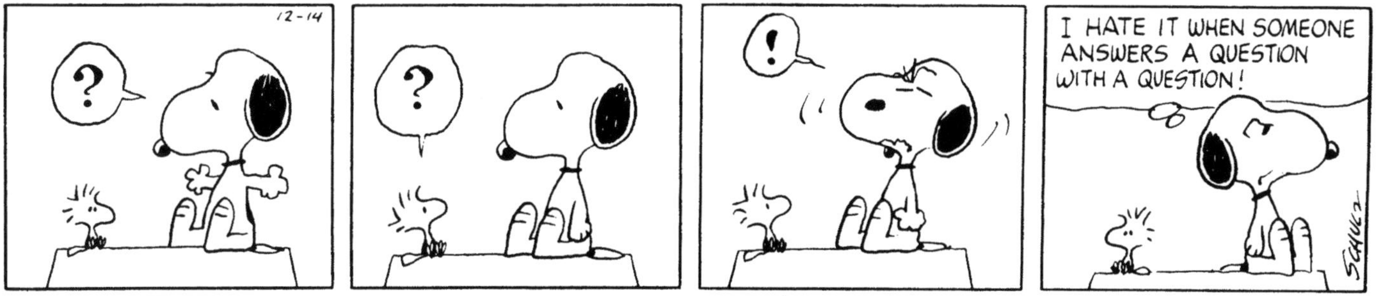
?
?
!
I HATE IT WHEN SOMEONE ANSWERS A QUESTION WITH A QUESTION!

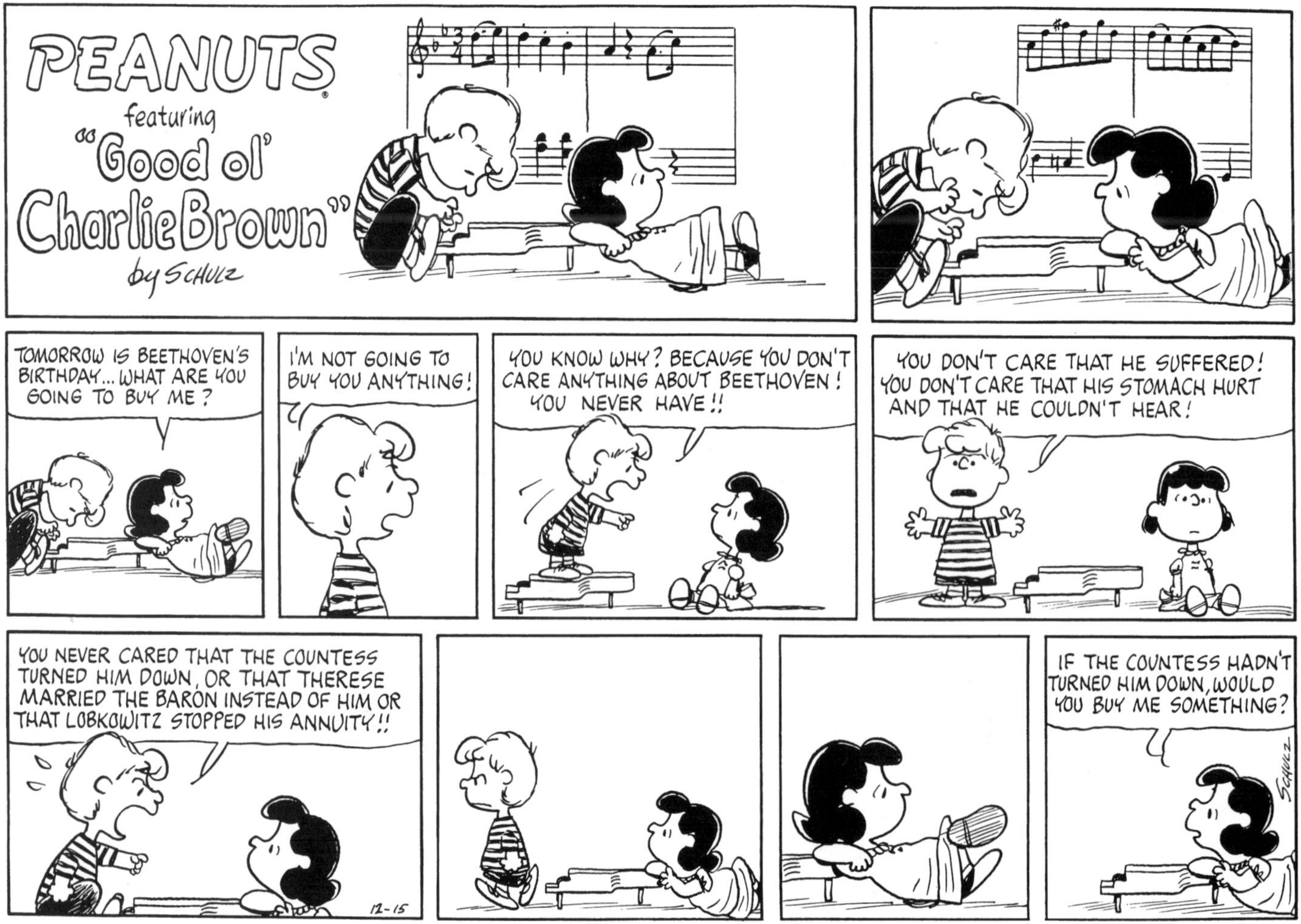
PEANUTS
featuring "Good ol' Charlie Brown"
by SCHULZ
TOMORROW IS BEETHOVEN'S BIRTHDAY... WHAT ARE YOU GOING TO BUY ME?
I'M NOT GOING TO BUY YOU ANYTHING!
YOU KNOW WHY? BECAUSE YOU DON'T CARE ANYTHING ABOUT BEETHOVEN! YOU NEVER HAVE!!
YOU DON'T CARE THAT HE SUFFERED! YOU DON'T CARE THAT HIS STOMACH HURT AND THAT HE COULDN'T HEAR!
YOU NEVER CARED THAT THE COUNTESS TURNED HIM DOWN, OR THAT THERESE MARRIED THE BARON INSTEAD OF HIM OR THAT LOBKOWITZ STOPPED HIS ANNUITY!!
12-15
IF THE COUNTESS HADN'T TURNED HIM DOWN, WOULD YOU BUY ME SOMETHING?
SCHULZ

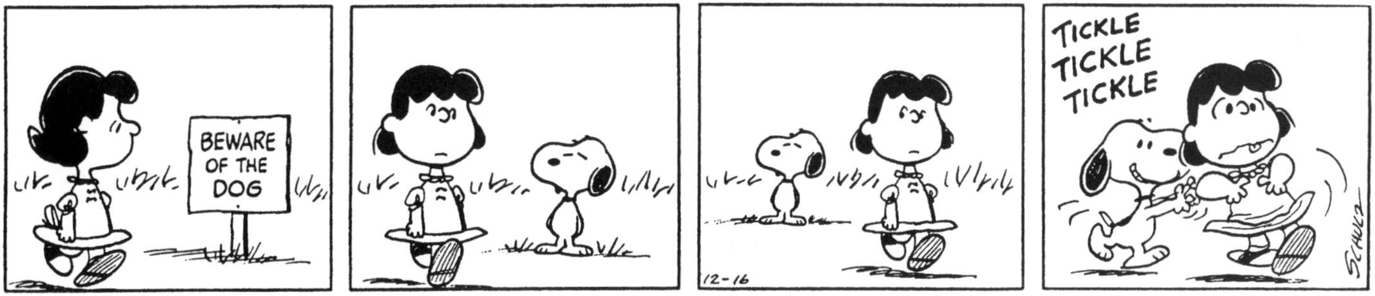
BEWARE OF THE DOG
12-16
TICKLE TICKLE TICKLE

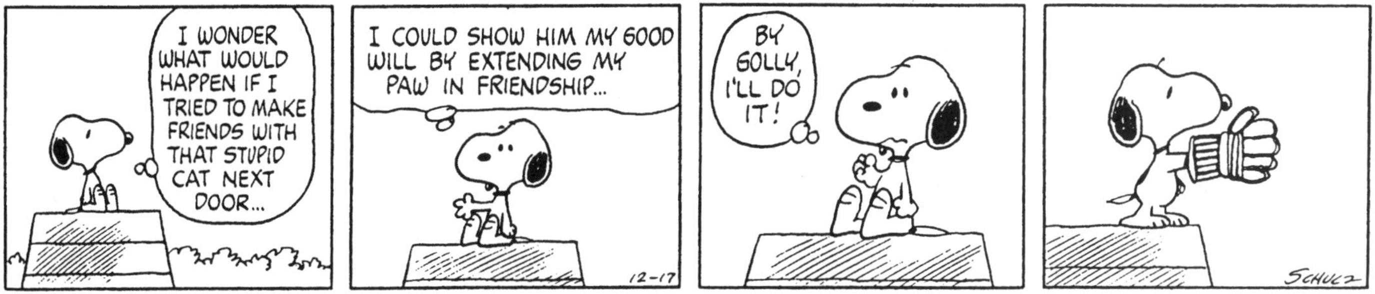
I WONDER WHAT WOULD HAPPEN IF I TRIED TO MAKE FRIENDS WITH THAT STUPID CAT NEXT DOOR...
I COULD SHOW HIM MY GOOD WILL BY EXTENDING MY PAW IN FRIENDSHIP...
12-17
BY GOLLY, I'LL DO IT!

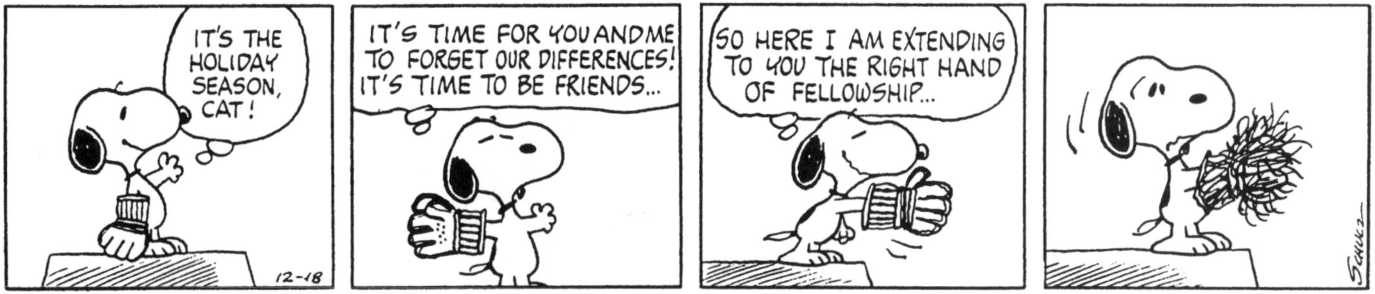
IT'S THE HOLIDAY SEASON, CAT!
12-18
IT'S TIME FOR YOU AND ME TO FORGET OUR DIFFERENCES! IT'S TIME TO BE FRIENDS...
SO HERE I AM EXTENDING TO YOU THE RIGHT HAND OF FELLOWSHIP...

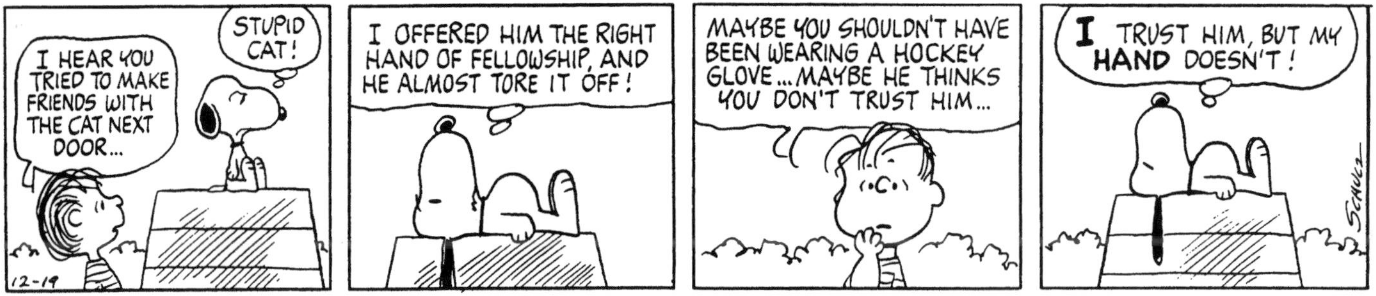
I HEAR YOU TRIED TO MAKE FRIENDS WITH THE CAT NEXT DOOR...
STUPID CAT!
12-19
I OFFERED HIM THE RIGHT HAND OF FELLOWSHIP, AND HE ALMOST TORE IT OFF!
MAYBE YOU SHOULDN'T HAVE BEEN WEARING A HOCKEY GLOVE...MAYBE HE THINKS YOU DON'T TRUST HIM...
I TRUST HIM, BUT MY HAND DOESN'T!
SCHULZ

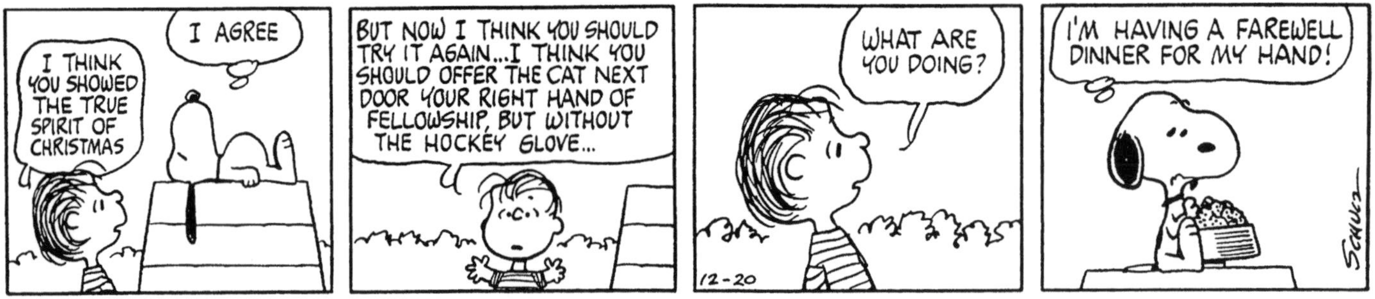
I THINK YOU SHOWED THE TRUE SPIRIT OF CHRISTMAS
I AGREE
BUT NOW I THINK YOU SHOULD TRY IT AGAIN...I THINK YOU SHOULD OFFER THE CAT NEXT DOOR YOUR RIGHT HAND OF FELLOWSHIP, BUT WITHOUT THE HOCKEY GLOVE...
WHAT ARE YOU DOING?
12-20
I'M HAVING A FAREWELL DINNER FOR MY HAND!
SCHULZ

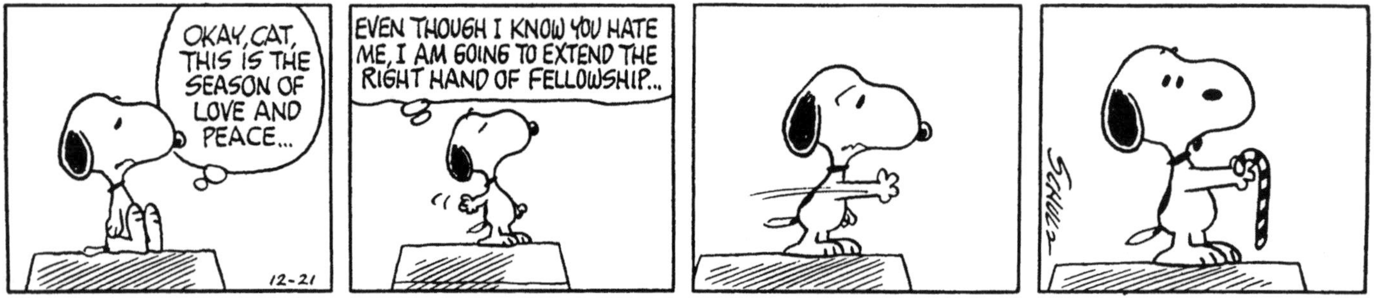
OKAY, CAT, THIS IS THE SEASON OF LOVE AND PEACE...
12-21
EVEN THOUGH I KNOW YOU HATE ME, I AM GOING TO EXTEND THE RIGHT HAND OF FELLOWSHIP...
SCHULZ

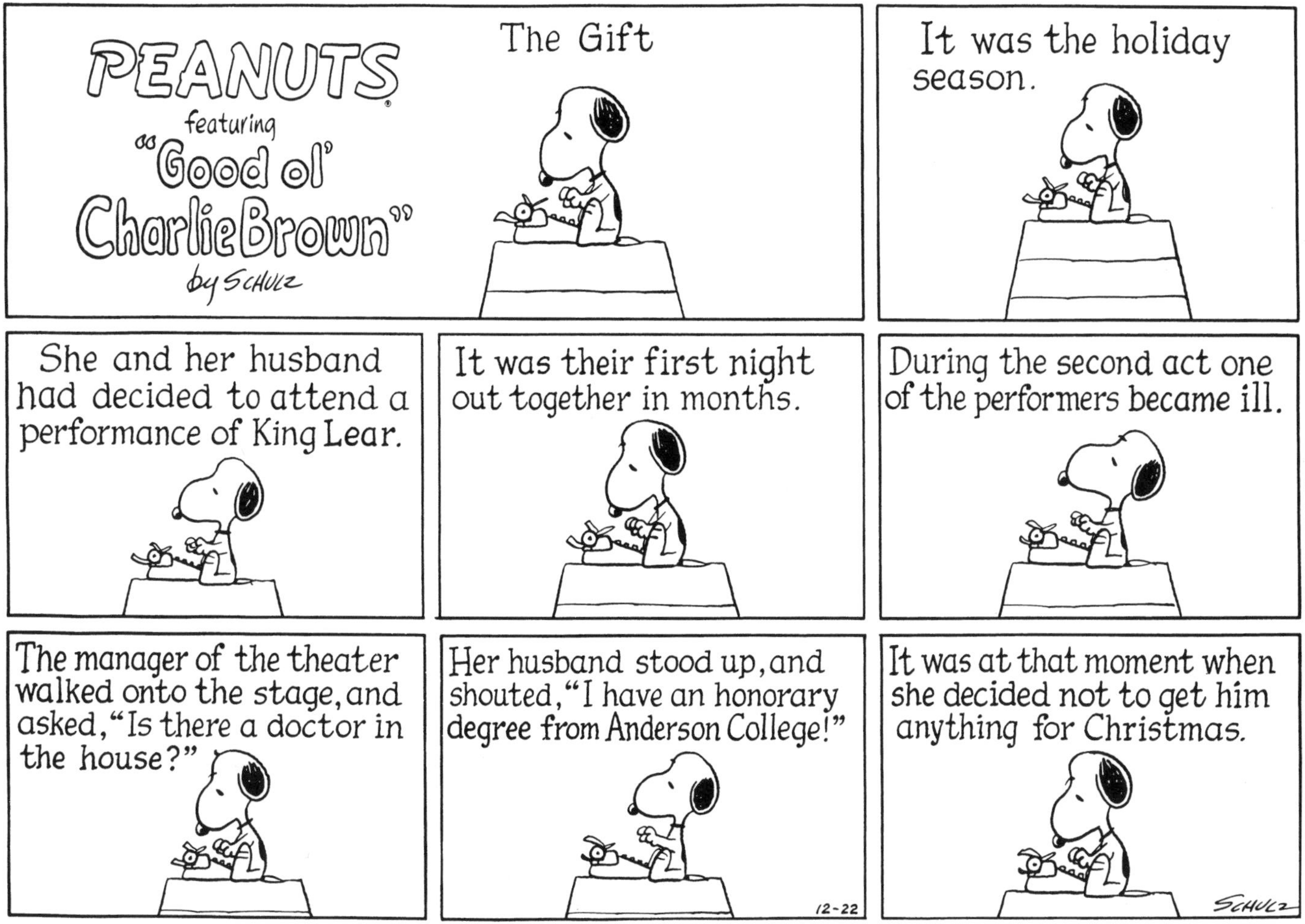
PEANUTS
featuring
"Good ol' Charlie Brown"
by SCHULZ
The Gift
It was the holiday season.
She and her husband had decided to attend a performance of King Lear.
It was their first night out together in months.
During the second act one of the performers became ill.
The manager of the theater walked onto the stage, and asked, "Is there a doctor in the house?"
Her husband stood up, and shouted, "I have an honorary degree from Anderson College!"
12-22
It was at that moment when she decided not to get him anything for Christmas.
SCHULZ

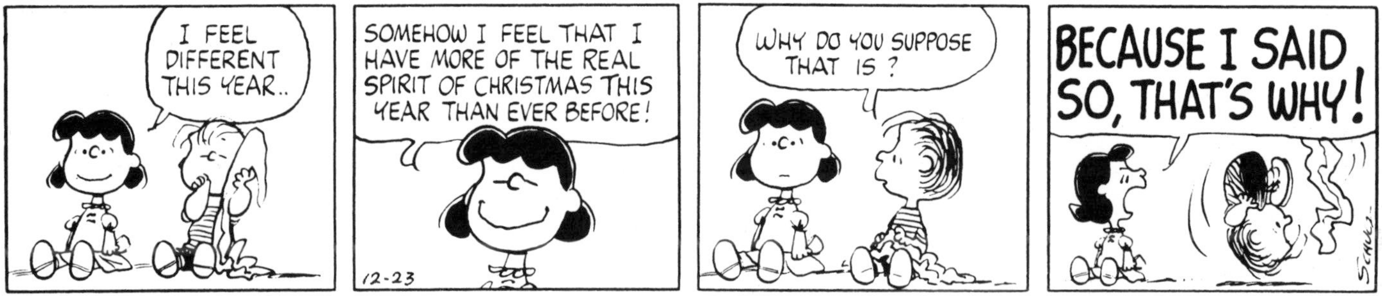
I FEEL DIFFERENT THIS YEAR..
SOMEHOW I FEEL THAT I HAVE MORE OF THE REAL SPIRIT OF CHRISTMAS THIS YEAR THAN EVER BEFORE!
12-23
WHY DO YOU SUPPOSE THAT IS ?
BECAUSE I SAID SO, THAT'S WHY!

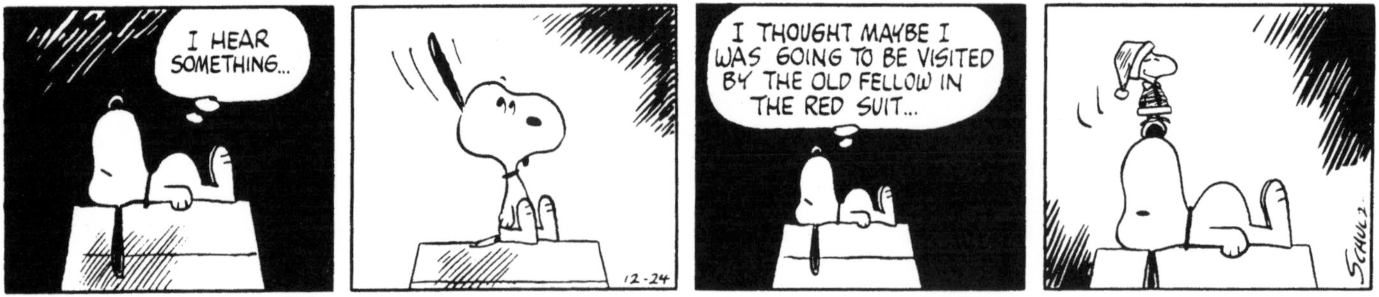
I HEAR SOMETHING...
12-24
I THOUGHT MAYBE I WAS GOING TO BE VISITED BY THE OLD FELLOW IN THE RED SUIT...

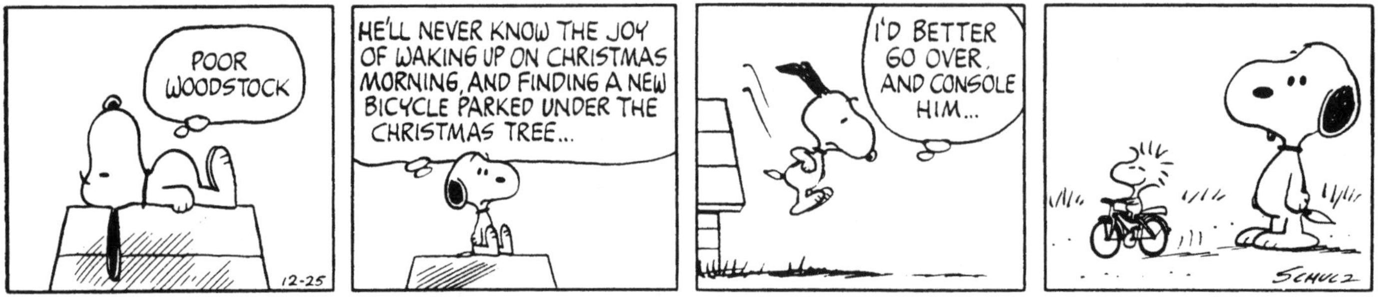
POOR WOODSTOCK
12-25
HE'LL NEVER KNOW THE JOY OF WAKING UP ON CHRISTMAS MORNING, AND FINDING A NEW BICYCLE PARKED UNDER THE CHRISTMAS TREE...
I'D BETTER GO OVER AND CONSOLE HIM...

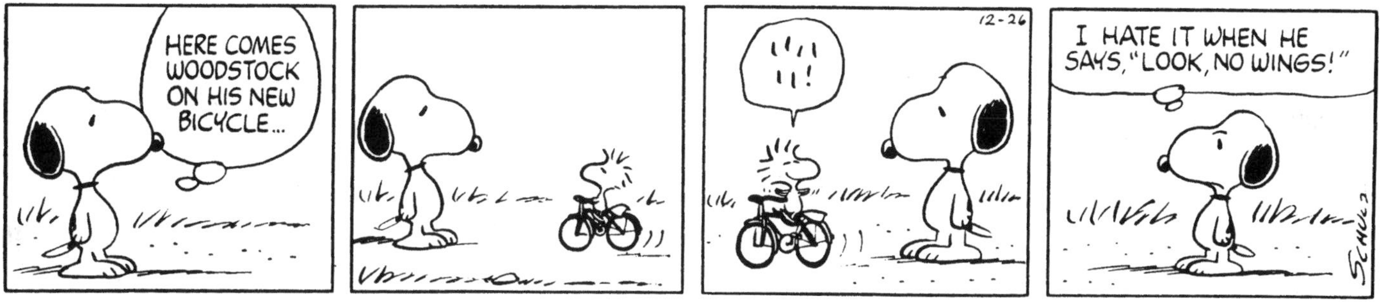
HERE COMES WOODSTOCK ON HIS NEW BICYCLE...
12-26
!!!!!
I HATE IT WHEN HE SAYS, "LOOK, NO WINGS!"
SCHULZ

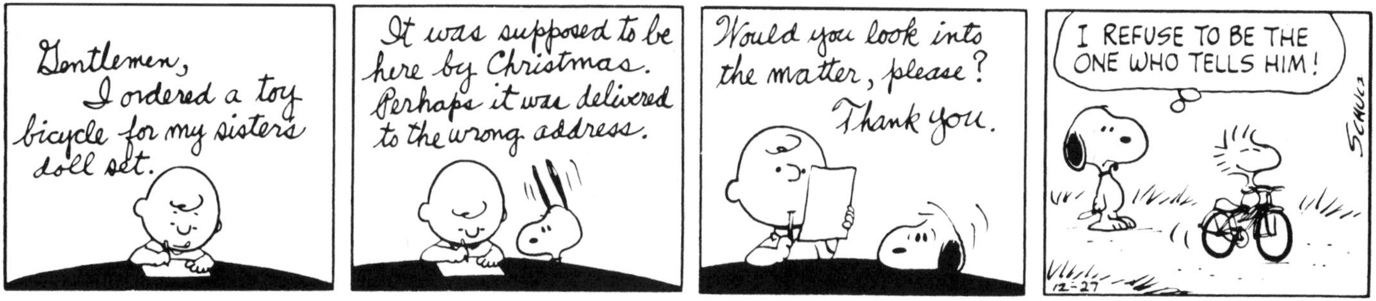
Gentlemen,
I ordered a toy bicycle for my sister's doll set.
It was supposed to be here by Christmas. Perhaps it was delivered to the wrong address.
Would you look into the matter, please?
Thank you.
I REFUSE TO BE THE ONE WHO TELLS HIM!
SCHULZ
12-27

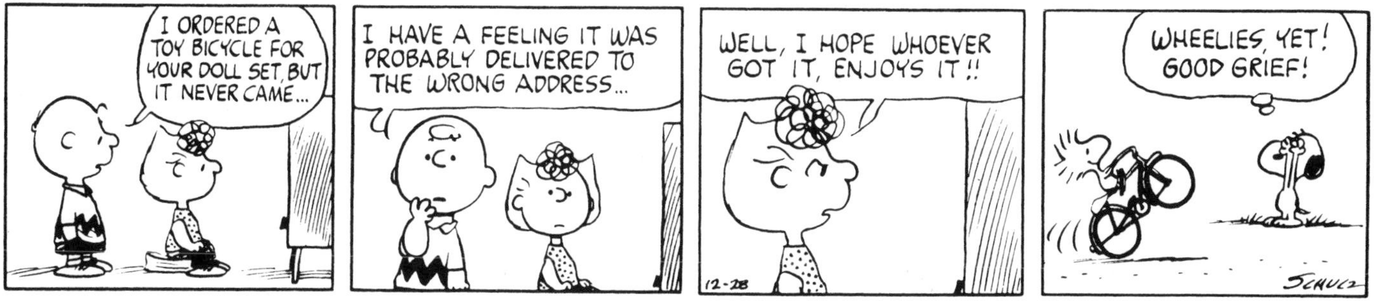
I ORDERED A TOY BICYCLE FOR YOUR DOLL SET, BUT IT NEVER CAME...
I HAVE A FEELING IT WAS PROBABLY DELIVERED TO THE WRONG ADDRESS...
WELL, I HOPE WHOEVER GOT IT, ENJOYS IT!!
12-28
WHEELIES, YET! GOOD GRIEF!
SCHULZ

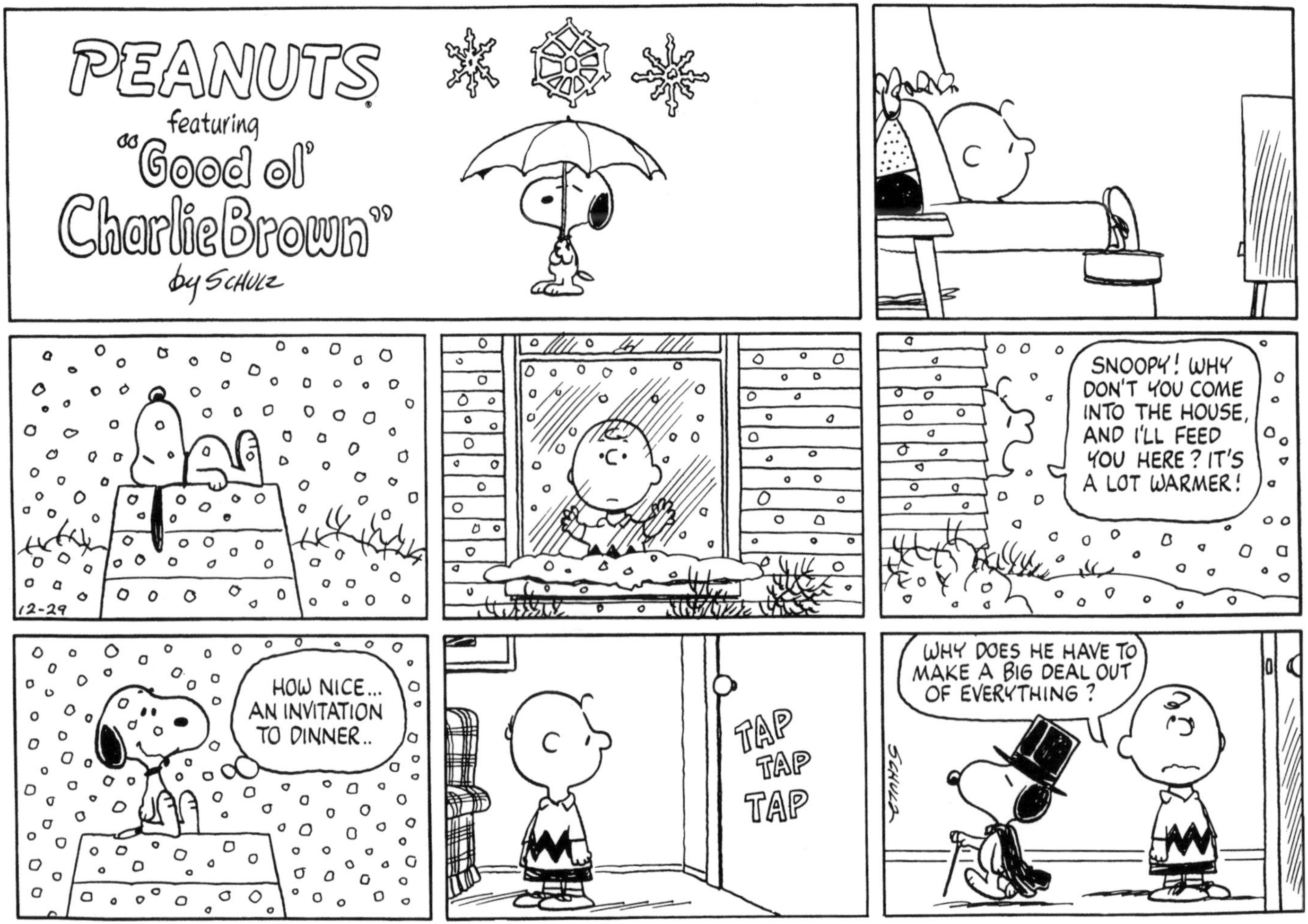
PEANUTS
featuring
"Good ol' Charlie Brown"
by SCHULZ
12-29
SNOOPY! WHY DON'T YOU COME INTO THE HOUSE, AND I'LL FEED YOU HERE? IT'S A LOT WARMER!
HOW NICE... AN INVITATION TO DINNER..
TAP
TAP
TAP
SCHULZ
WHY DOES HE HAVE TO MAKE A BIG DEAL OUT OF EVERYTHING?

I HEAR THE PARENTS CLUB HAD A PARTY HERE LAST NIGHT..

12-30

YEAH, THEY KEPT ME AWAKE ALL NIGHT!

I HATE THOSE PARTIES... I'M TOO OLD FOR THAT SORT OF THING...

THEY MAKE MY HALLS ACHE!

SCHULZ

HAPPY NEW YEAR!

(!!!)

12-31

HAPPY NEW YEAR TO ALL!

(!!!)

(!!!)

Z

½ SIGH ½

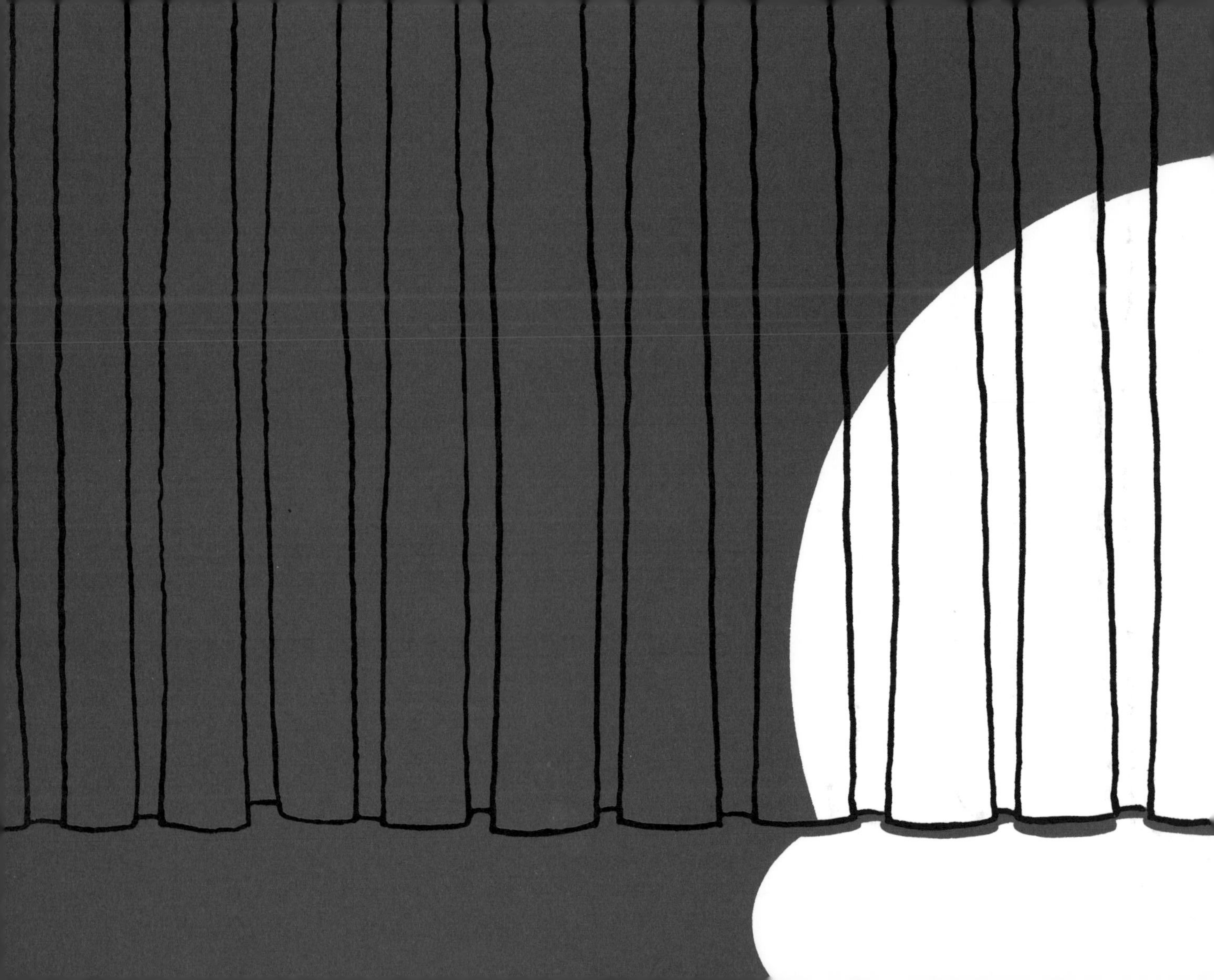

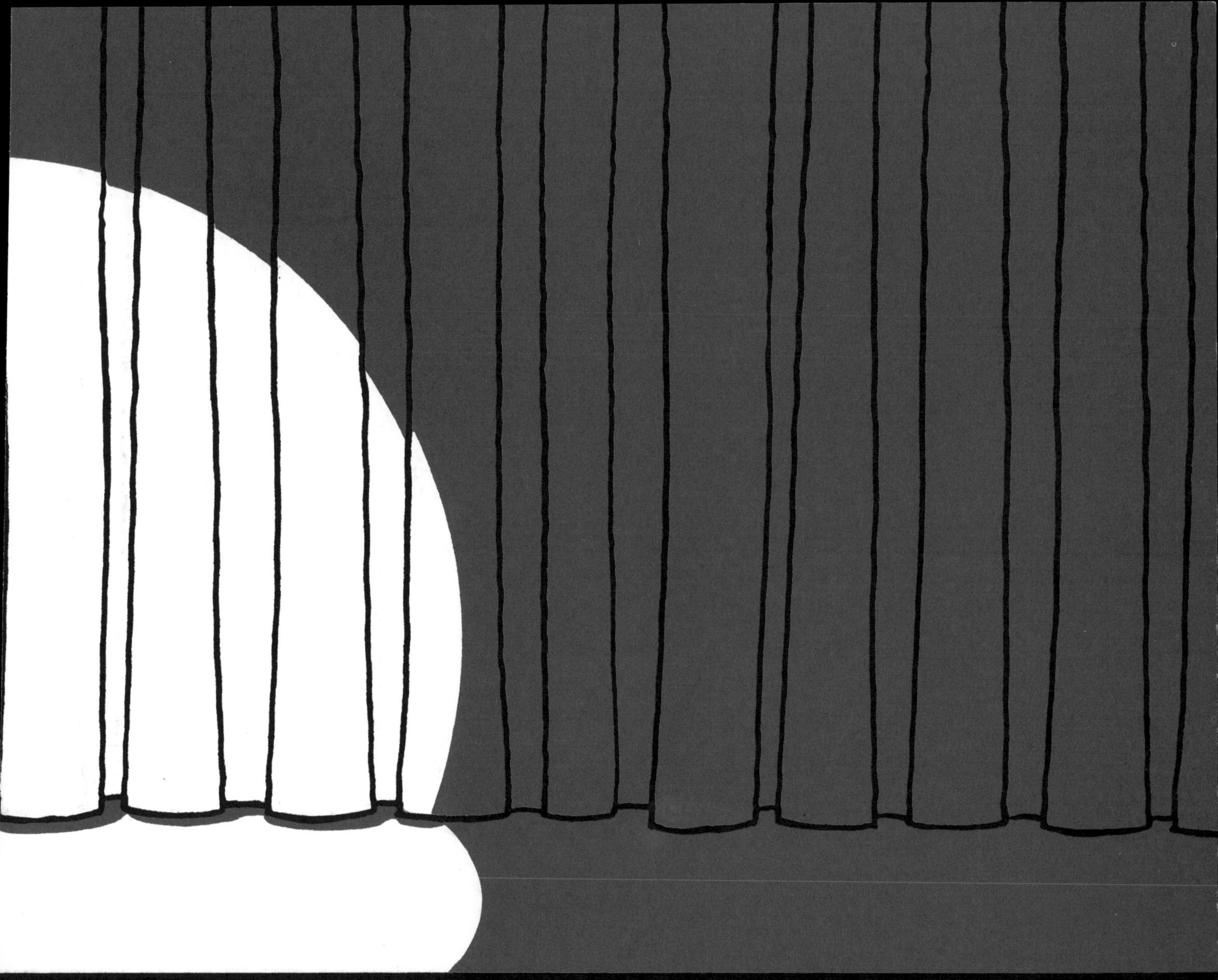

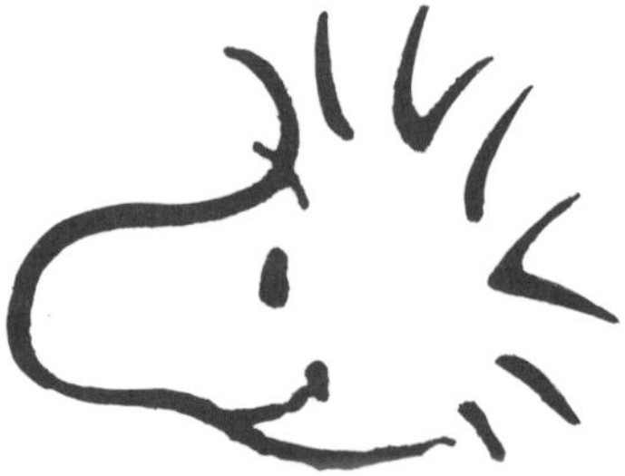

INDEX

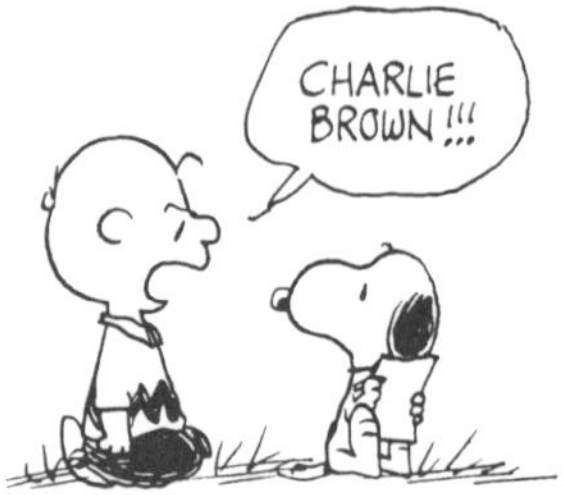

CHARLIE BROWN !!!

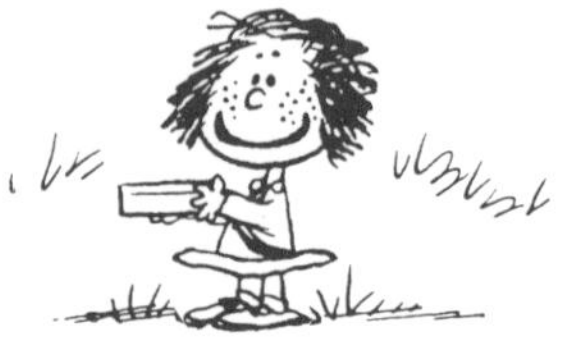

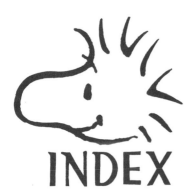

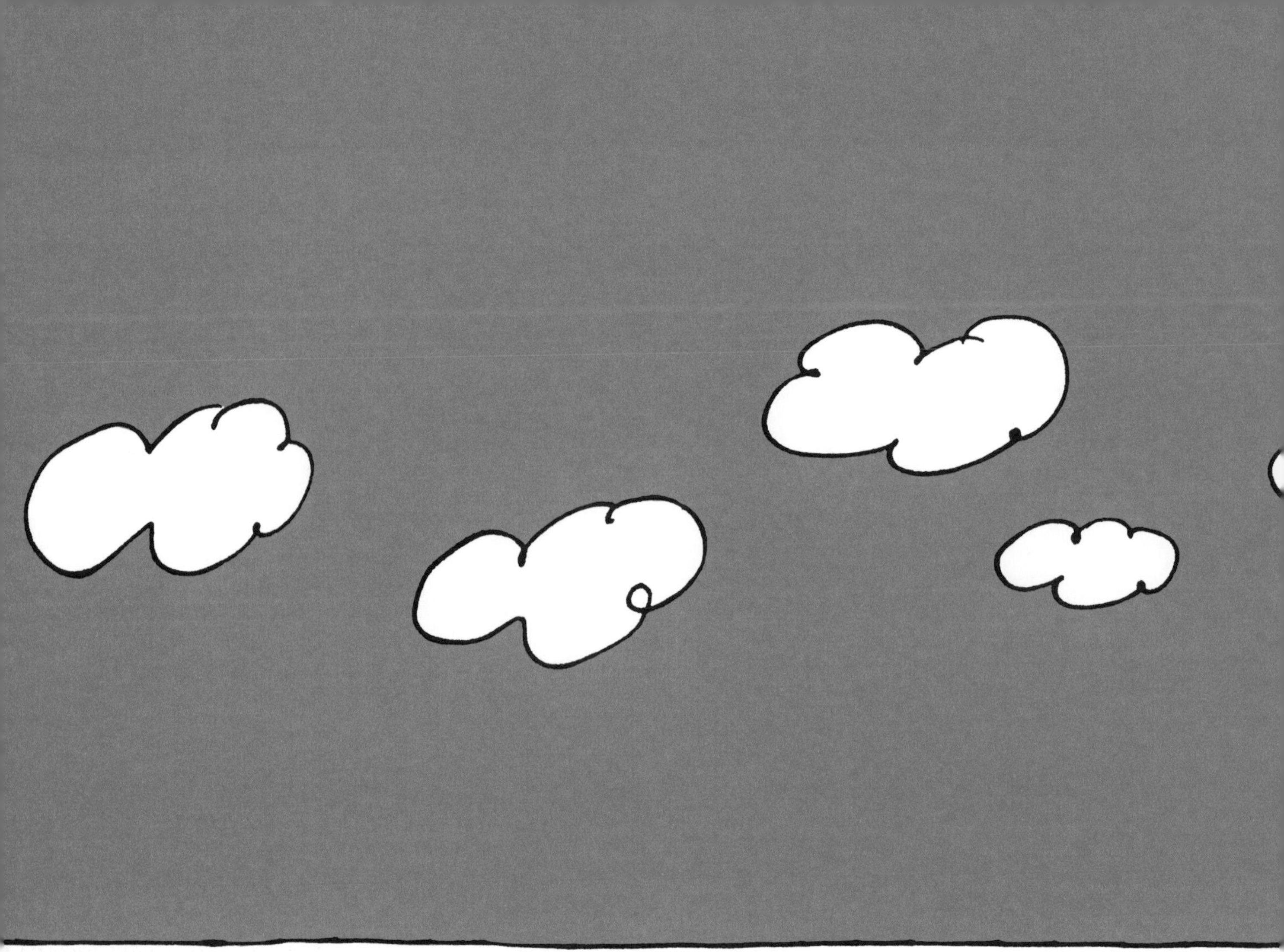

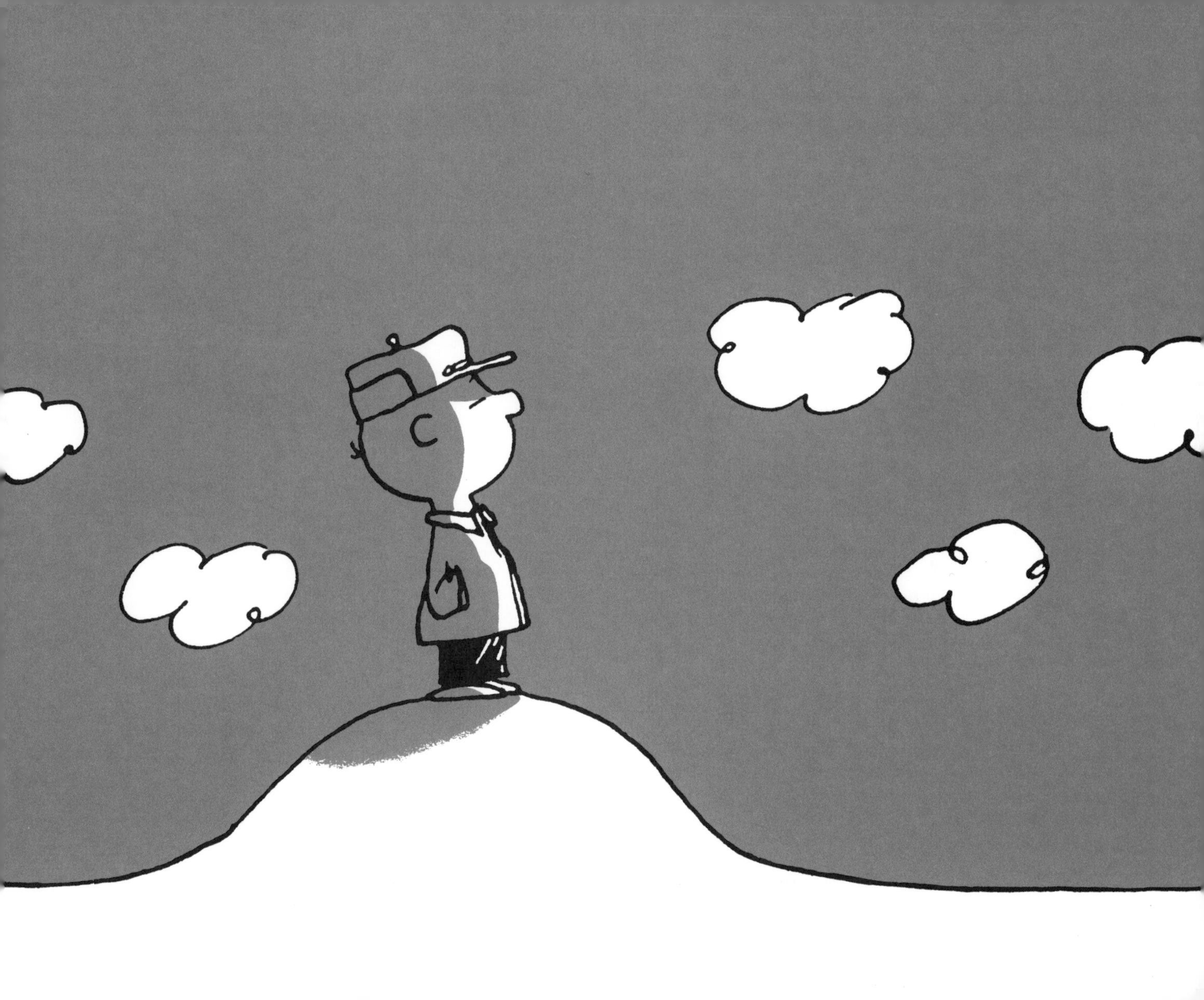

CHARLES M. SCHULZ · 1922 To 2000

Charles M. Schulz was born November 25, 1922 in Minneapolis. His destiny was foreshadowed when an uncle gave him, at the age of two days, the nickname Sparky (after the racehorse Spark Plug in the newspaper strip *Barney Google*).

Schulz grew up in St. Paul. By all accounts, he led an unremarkable, albeit sheltered, childhood. He was an only child, close to both parents, his eventual career path nurtured by his father, who bought four Sunday papers every week — just for the comics.

An outstanding student, he skipped two grades early on, but began to flounder in high school — perhaps not so coincidentally at the same time kids are going through their cruelest, most status-conscious period of socialization. The pain, bitterness, insecurity, and failures chronicled in *Peanuts* appear to have originated from this period of Schulz's life.

Although Schulz enjoyed sports, he also found refuge in solitary activities: reading, drawing, and watching movies. He bought comic books and Big Little Books, pored over the newspaper strips, and copied his favorites — *Buck Rogers*, the Walt Disney characters, *Popeye*, *Tim Tyler's Luck*. He quickly became a connoisseur; his heroes were Milton Caniff, Roy Crane, Hal Foster, and Alex Raymond.

In his senior year in high school, his mother noticed an ad in a local newspaper for a correspondence school, Federal Schools (later called Art

Instruction Schools). Schulz passed the talent test, completed the course and began trying, unsuccessfully, to sell gag cartoons to magazines. (His first published drawing was of his dog, Spike, and appeared in a 1937 *Ripley's Believe It Or Not!* installment.)

After World War II had ended and Schulz was discharged from the army, he started submitting gag cartoons to the various magazines of the time; his first breakthrough, however, came when an editor at *Timeless Topix* hired him to letter adventure comics. Soon after that, he was hired by his alma mater, Art Instruction, to correct student lessons returned by mail.

Between 1948 and 1950, he succeeded in selling 17 cartoons to the *Saturday Evening Post* — as well as, to the local *St. Paul Pioneer Press*, a weekly comic feature called *Li'l Folks*. It was run in the women's section and paid $10 a week. After writing and drawing the feature for two years, Schulz asked for a better location in the paper or for daily exposure, as well as a raise. When he was turned down on all three counts, he quit.

He started submitting strips to the newspaper syndicates. In the Spring of 1950, he received a letter from the United Feature Syndicate, announcing their interest in his submission, *Li'l Folks*. Schulz boarded a train in June for New York City; more interested in doing a strip than a panel, he also brought along the first installments of what would become *Peanuts* — and that was what sold. (The title, which Schulz loathed to his dying day, was imposed by the syndicate). The first *Peanuts* daily appeared October 2, 1950; the first Sunday, January 6, 1952.

Prior to *Peanuts*, the province of the comics page had been that of gags, social and political observation, domestic comedy, soap opera, and various adventure genres. Although *Peanuts* changed, or evolved, during the 50 years Schulz wrote and drew it, it remained, as it began, an anomaly on the comics page — a comic strip about the interior crises of the cartoonist himself. After a painful divorce in 1973 from which he had not yet recovered, Schulz told a reporter, "Strangely, I've drawn better cartoons in the last six months — or as good as I've ever drawn. I don't know how the human mind works." Surely, it was this kind of humility in the face of profoundly irreducible human question that makes *Peanuts* as universally moving as it is.

Diagnosed with cancer, Schulz retired from *Peanuts* at the end of 1999. He died on February 12th 2000, the day before his last strip was published (and two days before Valentine's Day) — having completed 17,897 daily and Sunday strips, each and every one fully written, drawn, and lettered entirely by his own hand — an unmatched achievement in comics.

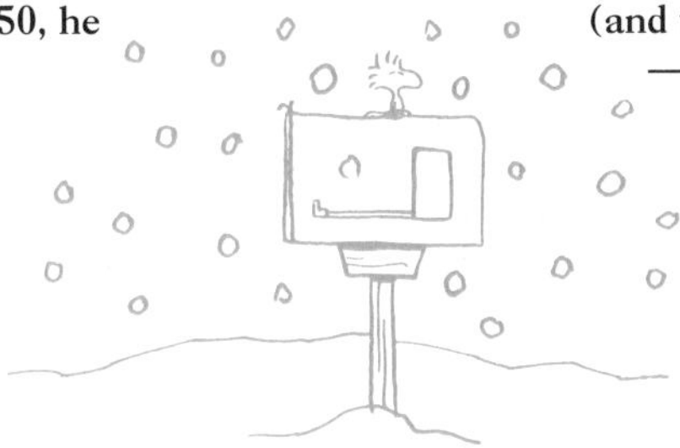

—*Gary Groth*

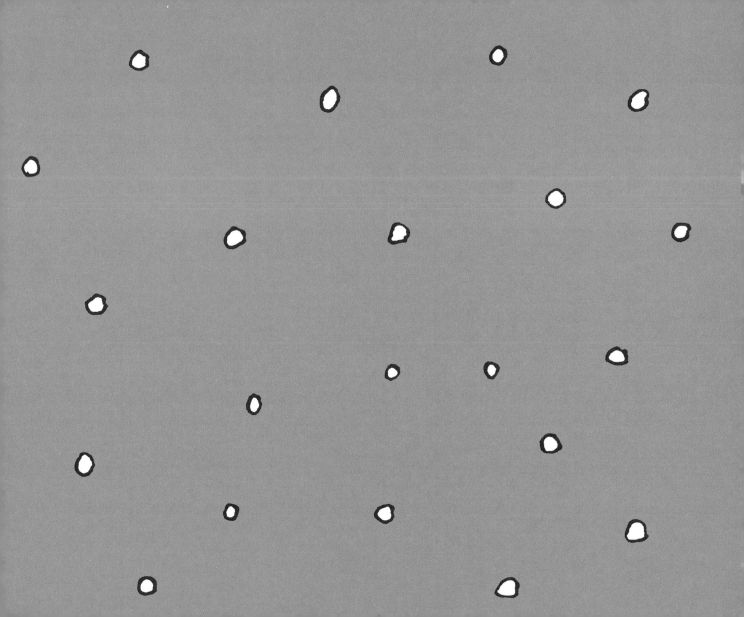

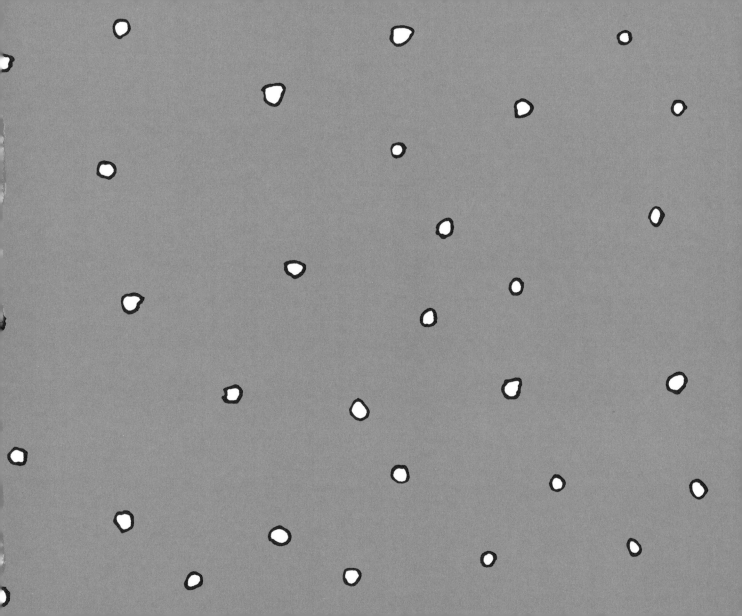

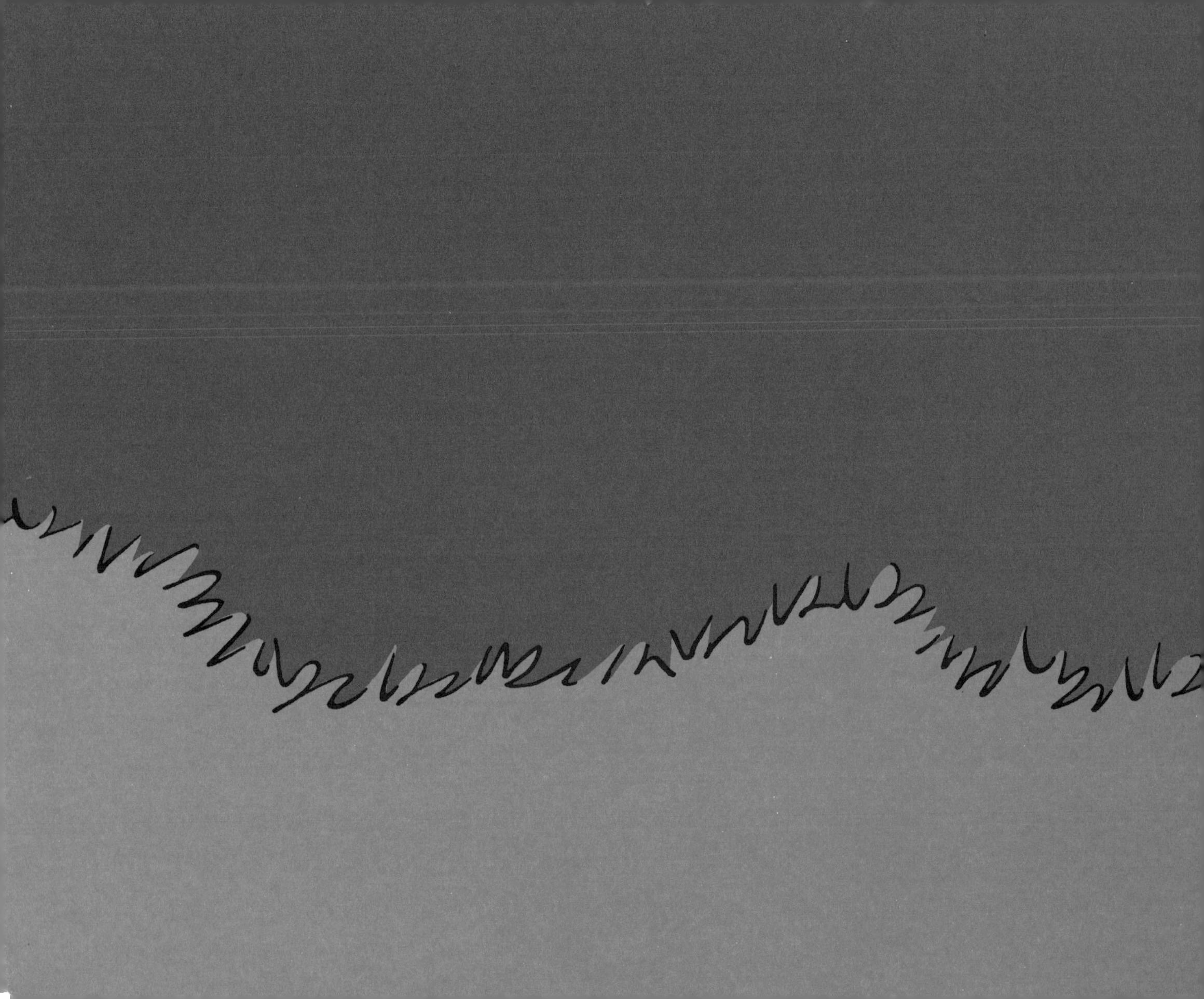

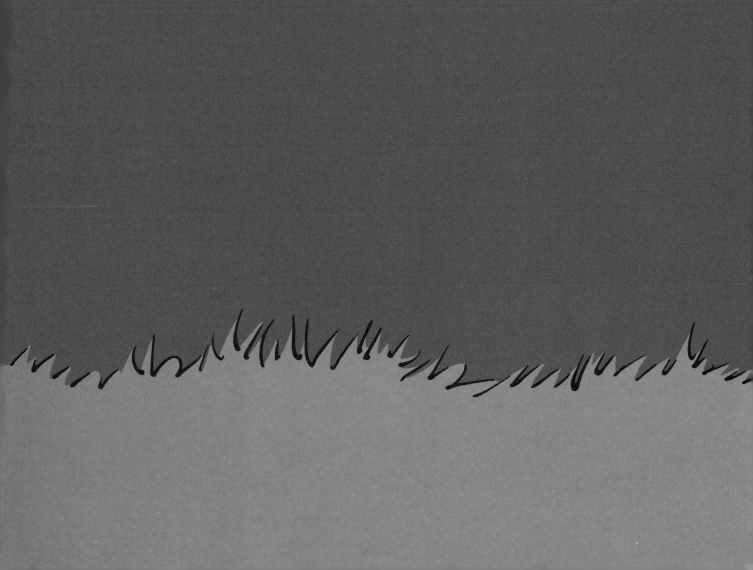

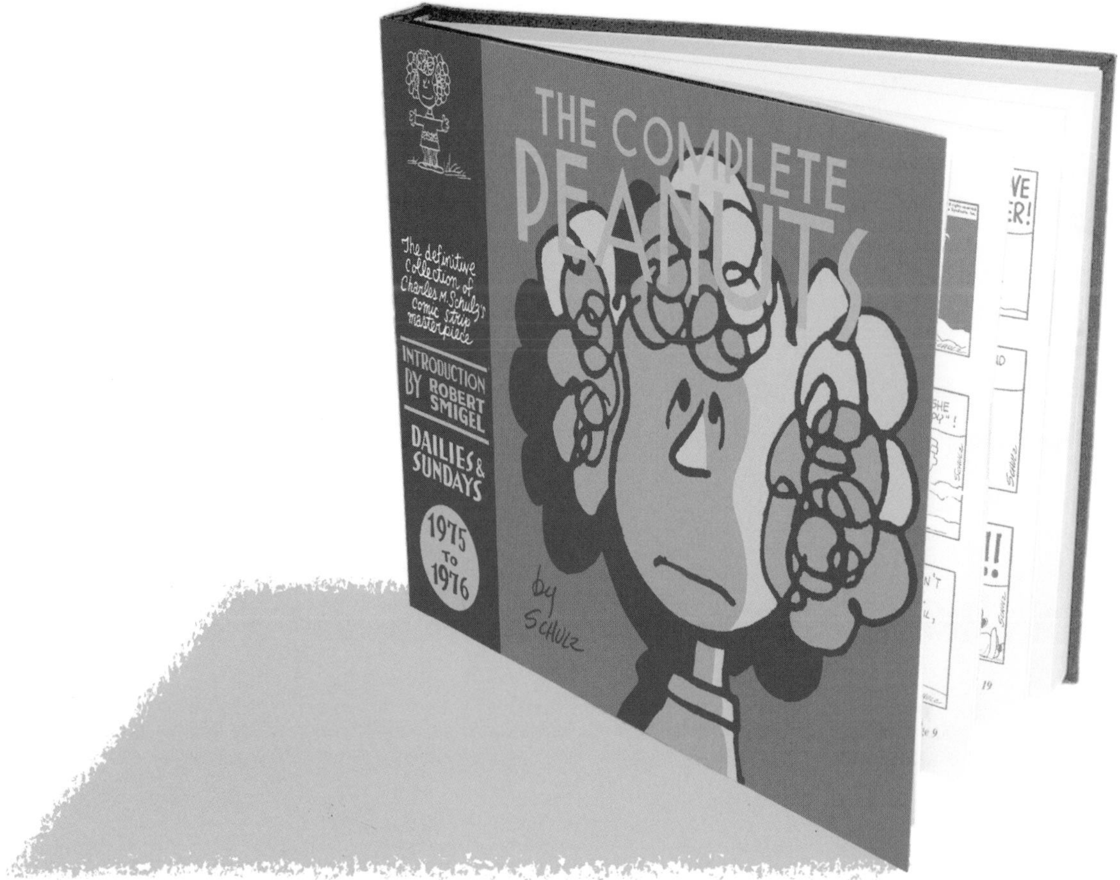
THE COMPLETE PEANUTS
The definitive collection of Charles M. Schulz's comic strip masterpiece
INTRODUCTION BY ROBERT SMIGEL
DAILIES & SUNDAYS
1975 TO 1976
by SCHULZ

COMING IN *THE COMPLETE PEANUTS: 1975-1976*

Snoopy breaks his foot... A burglary at Peppermint Patty's house is exacerbated by waterbed problems... Linus and Snoopy battle over a girl named Truffles... Woodstock gets the "vapors"... Marcie acquires an unwanted suitor... The talking school building collapses... "Beanbag camp"... Charlie Brown meets Joe Shlabotnik... and three, count 'em three, new Snoopy relatives!

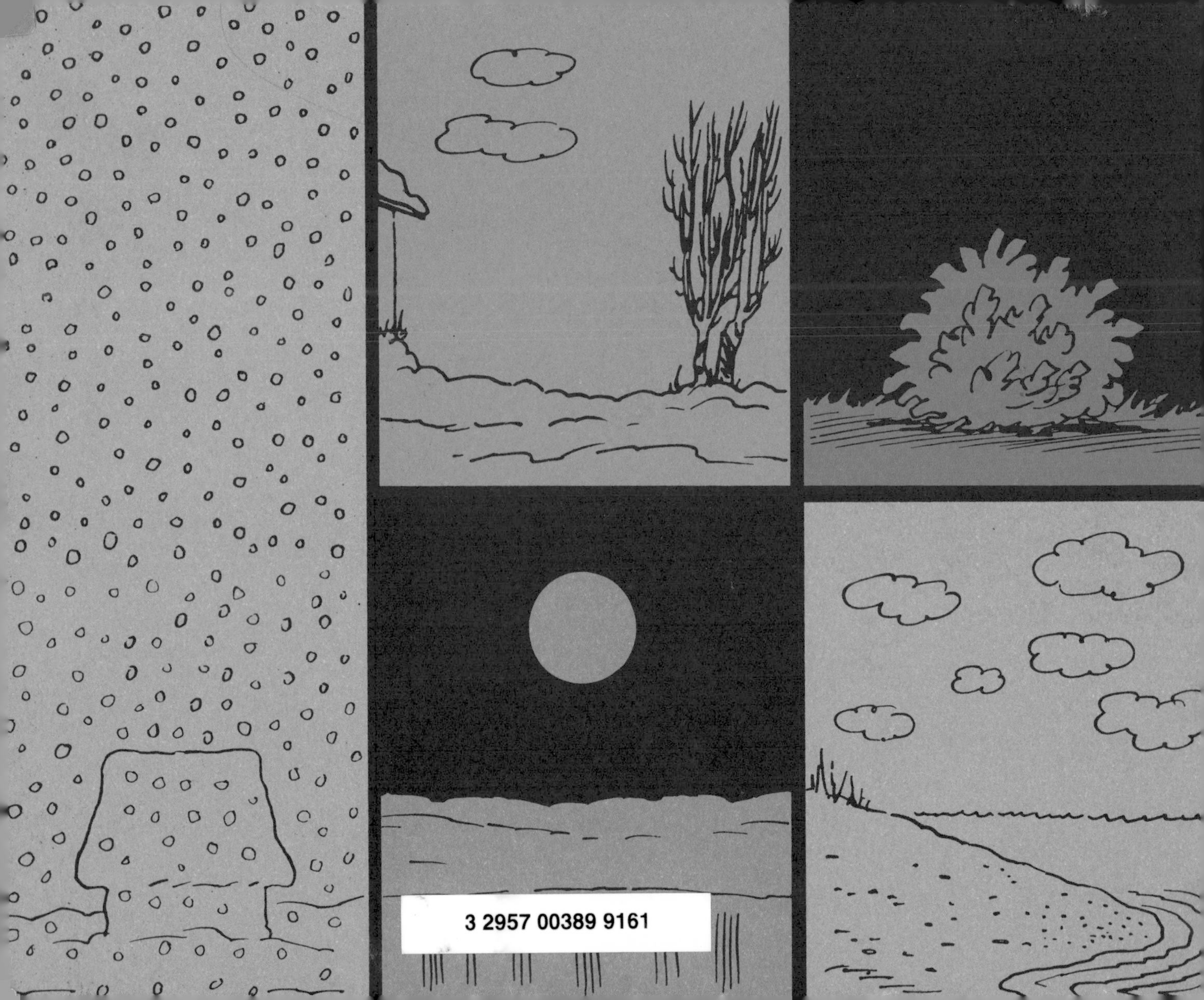